Why on Earth should we pray?

A discovery tour of the Bible

Ray Case

MORLING PRESS

Published by Morling Press,
Macquarie Park,
Sydney Australia 2113
www.morlingcollege.com/morlingpress

Ray Case ©2022

The publication is copyright. Other than for the purpose of study and subject to the conditions of the Copyright Act, no part of it in any form or by any means (electronic, mechanical, micro-copying, photocopying or otherwise) may be reproduced, stored in a retrieval system or transmitted without the permission of the publisher.

Cover and internal design by Impressum
www.impressum.com

ISBN: 978-0-6454927-0-5

CONTENTS

FOREWORD

PRELIMINARY WORD: The Prayer Phenomenon 11
    Public Anguish 11
    Request for Help 12
    Universal Phenomenon 13
    A Heartfelt Plea 14
    Personal Curiosity 15
    Perspective of the Bible 16
    Jesus The Intercessor 18

CHAPTER 1: THE CONVERSATION 20
    The Written Witness 21
    God's Grace Agenda 23
    A Significant Activity 24
    A Discovery Tour 25

CHAPTER 2: BACK TO THE BEGINNING 27
    Books of the Law 29
    The Creator King 30
    God's Rescue Operation 33
    God's Favoured Family 37
    Abraham the Intercessor 40
    Isaac the Petitioner 49
    Jacob the Pleader 50

Joseph The Dream Interpreter 54

CHAPTER 3: THE DIVINE SAGA 57

    A Kingdom of Priests 58

    A Holy Nation 72

    A Rebellious Army 74

    A Renewed Covenant Community 84

        First Address, 1:1-4:43 86

        Second Address, 4:44-28:68 87

        Third Address, 29-34 88

CHAPTER 4: RISE & DEMISE OF THE KINGDOM 92

    Covenant Inheritance 93

        Explanation: God's "Holy War" 100

    Covenant Kingship 109

    Rise of the Monarchy 112

    God's Covenant With David 116

    Demise of the Monarchy 120

    Solomon's Reign (1 Kings 1-11) 121

    Divided Kingdom (1 Kings 12-16) 124

    Enter Elijah The Prophet (1 Kings 17-22) 125

    Elisha The Prophet Until Israel's Downfall (2 Kings 1-17) 125

    Sole Kingdom of Judah (2 Kings 18-25) 126

CHAPTER 5: THE PROPHETIC OUTCRY 129

    The Last Days of Israel 131

    The Last Days of Judah 135

    The Exile 138

    After The Exile 141

CHAPTER 6: GOD'S COVENANT WISDOM 145

    The Book of Psalms 146

The Book of Proverbs 149

The Book of Job 150

The Book of Daniel 153

The Five Scrolls 157

    Ruth (Pentecost) *158*

    Song of Songs (Passover) *159*

    Ecclesiastes (Tabernacles) *160*

    Lamentations (Fall of Jerusalem) *160*

    Esther (Purim) *162*

Ezra-Nehemiah 165

1 & 2 Chronicles 167

CHAPTER 7: THE SON'S INHERITANCE 173

A Covenant Context for Prayer 173

Rebellious Nations on Earth, v 1-3. 174

The Enthroned LORD in Heaven, v 4-6. 178

The Divine Decree, v 7-9. 182

Warning to the Nations, v 10-12. 185

CHAPTER 8: ENTREATING THE FATHER 187

Prayer in the New Testament 187

Significance of Jesus 188

God's Identity 189

Written Witness 191

Prayer 191

New Testament 192

CHAPTER 9: "SAVIOUR OF THE WORLD" 193

Prayer in Luke's Gospel and Acts 193

Luke's Gospel/Acts 194

Influences 195

The Remarkable "Journey" 197
Prayer in Luke's Gospel 197
The Ministry of Jesus: *His Activities in Galilee (4:14-9:50)* 201
The Teachings of Jesus: *Moving towards Jerusalem (9:51-19:27)* 209
Opposition to Jesus: *Experiences in Jerusalem (Chap. 19:28-21:38)* .. 220
The Triumph of Jesus: *Suffering and Resurrection (22:1-24:53)* 223
Prayer in Acts 228
   Chapters 1-2 The Good News Explosion 228
   Chapters 3-5 The Good News in Jerusalem 231
   Chapters 6:1-9:31 The Good News Scatters Through Judea & Samaria 232
   Chapters 9:32-12:25 The Good News Spreads to Syria 236
   Chapters 12:25-16:5 The Good News in Asia Minor 239
   Chapters 16:6-19:20 The Good News Crosses to Europe 241
   Chapters 19:21-23:35 The Good News Faces Antagonists 242
   Acts 24-28 The Good News Reaches Rome 243

CHAPTER 10: "THE SON ON EARTH" 246
Prayer in Mark's Gospel 246
Messiah With A Mission 247
Dependent Petitioner 248
The Father's Fellowship 250
Prayer Was The Source Of Jesus' Authority 252
Prayer Was Crucial For Jesus' Mission 253
Prayer Gave Jesus Power Over Darkness 257
Prayer Was A Kingdom Priority For Jesus 263
Prayer Had Essential Requirements For Jesus 264
Prayer Is The Epitome Of True Devotion 267
Prayer Keeps Watch For The Son Of Man 269
Prayer Pleads For The Father's Will 272
Jesus' Triumph 276

CHAPTER 11: "THE FATHER IN HEAVEN" 282
- Prayer in Matthew's Gospel 282
- Jesus' Teaching about Prayer 287
- Jesus' Call for Prayer 292
- Jesus' Personal Practice of Prayer 293
- God's Right Hand Man 297

CHAPTER 12: "IN MY NAME" 299
- Prayer in John's Gospel 299
- 1:1-18 The Declaration: The Word Became Flesh 302
- 1:19-51 Forerunner and Followers 306
- Chapters 2-12 Public Ministry of "Signs" 307
- Chapters 13-17 Private Discourses 310
- Chapters 18-20 Passion Narrative 311
- Chapter 21 Restoration 312
- Regarding Prayer 312
- Jesus' Farewell Prayer (Chapter 17) 314
  - *Jesus Prays Concerning Himself (v 1-5)* *315*
  - *Jesus Prays Concerning His Disciples (v 6-19)* *315*
  - *Jesus Prays Concerning Future Believers (v 20-26)* *317*

CHAPTER 13: "IN ACCORD WITH GOD'S WILL" 319
- Prayer in Paul's Letters 319
- Letters Written to Troubled Churches 320
- Letters Written from Prison 343
- Letters Written to Associates 363

CHAPTER 14: "DRAW NEAR TO GOD" 370
- Prayer in Other New Testament Books 370
- HEBREWS: Jesus Is Our Kingly High Priest 370

JAMES: True Religion 374

1 & 2 PETER: A Living Hope 377

1, 2, 3 JOHN: Walking in the Truth 379

JUDE: Contending for the Faith 382

CHAPTER 15: "FIRE ON THE EARTH" 384

AFTERWORD: TWENTY - TWENTY VISION 392

Twenty-Twenty Insight 393

Twenty-Twenty Hindsight 394

Twenty-Twenty Outlook 395

Twenty-Twenty Upward Look 396

Index

FOREWORD

This book on prayer is big-picture thinking. It is refreshingly different, providing a new angle on the idea of prayer in the Scriptures. Too often we see verses on prayer picked out and elaborated. This does the opposite. It gives the broad sweep of Scripture and finds prayer embedded within God's revelation in history. It summarises the whole of Scripture drawing attention particularly to the call of God on people's lives. It is well researched, clearly expressed and comprehensively covered. Ray Case comes to the task after a lifetime of expounding God's Word as a pastor and teacher. Starting at Genesis he skillfully outlines the content of each book in both Old and New Testaments, bringing out the place prayer occupies in each one. Thus prayer is set in context within the whole theological and historical framework of Scripture. Implications are mostly for the reader to draw out for him or herself. This has been a mammoth but rewarding task and well worth the time for the reader to put into reading and considering its contents.

Case writes with a fluent style, easy to read and absorb. He avoids discussion of literary, historical or interpretive interest, but his understanding of scholarly matters underlies all that is presented. Many of his statements are followed by brief explanations to clarify the point for his readers. I found it easier to read in smaller portions, thus giving time to ponder the deep truths contained. At times I would have appreciated further exploration of insights raised, but that is not the purpose of this book. This is not a 'how to' book, or one which gives short answers to problems or curly questions on prayer. It goes to the heart of the theology of prayer, as a two-way communication between the sovereign, creator God and his people in both old and new covenant agreements with him, and links it with his kingly purpose for the world.

After dealing with prayer in the Pentateuch, historical books, prophets and writings, Case paints a picture which skilfully links Old and New Testaments themes. This is an enlightening, helpful discussion before moving into better known New Testament writings and Jesus, Paul and the church community's understanding of prayer. Here more attention is given to comments on prayer. *"Prayer is an act of submission to God's sovereign authority." "Prayer is a crucial ingredient. It is the means of communion with God, actual, vital, meaningful fellowship with him, who is the essential source of the community's life."*

Finally in his concluding chapter Case brings his thinking into our present world with this challenge. *"Our discovery tour through the Bible has revealed why we on earth should pray. God is the living gracious Creator King who has accomplished his plan to redeem the world from its rebellious and chaotic state, and to restore his loving rule over his creation. Jesus is the redeemer of the world, and the Lord over all creation. Integral to God's plan is prayer. By prayer we partner with God in saving the world."*

I pray that the God presented in this extensive summary of Scripture will inspire the hearts of readers to listen to his communication and respond in faithful, heart-warming prayer.

Dr Sylvia Collinson
(former lecturer Morling College, Sydney
February 2022)

PRELIMINARY WORD

THE PRAYER PHENOMENON

Prayer is a peculiar phenomenon. Prayer is the instinctive habit of the human heart. It is a universal human practice. Prompted by outward circumstances of life, or by inward spiritual compulsion, people pray. Deep down in the heart our innermost soul craves to relate to God. So we pray. Not every one is convinced that God exists. Yet even then most people will resort to some form of prayer at a crucial time. Through prayer we hope to find a fuller measure of life.

Public Anguish

Saturday 7 February 2009 was a black day for the state of Victoria, and for Australia. Devastating bushfires consumed mountain forest landscapes, destroyed hundreds of homes and whole townships, and claimed more than two hundred human lives. The inferno struck like a cyclone of fire, fuelled by record level temperatures in the mid 40's degrees Celsius, hurricane force winds, and accumulated dry combustible undergrowth. It was a major national disaster, and the whole nation watched news coverage with horror and anguish. An outpouring of community support for victims of the holocaust saw more than three hundred million dollars donated to the Red Cross Appeal. Fire, police, and medical services, together with a variety of other government and community agencies, and countless volunteers, converged on the situation to deal with the crisis. Emergency conditions in numerous places prevailed for several weeks. The whole event was a terrifying ordeal. Stories emerged of heroic actions by many, miraculous escapes by some, surreal experiences, despicable acts of arson, inexplicable and uncontrollable passage by the firestorm, horrendous loss. Perhaps the most frequently used term to describe the occasion, whether referring to the conditions, the firestorm, its impact and consequences, peoples' reactions, or community response, was "unprecedented". Nothing like this had been known in the civil history of Australia beforehand.

A conspicuous and widespread response to this disaster was spontaneous prayer. From the Prime Minister onwards all kinds of people publicly expressed their assurances of prayer for the situation, for those in harm's way, and for those who suffered as a result of the tragedy. It was as if prayer was the highest gesture of compassion and support for the helpless, and the most meaningful resort in seeking protection against the irresistible ferocity of such an aggressive enemy. It was very heart-warming to hear so many people offer to pray, and to appeal for the public to pray.

However, there was a puzzling aspect to this public display of prayer. No one actually indicated that prayer was being made to God. And afterwards no one mentioned that prayer was answered, or not answered. Yet there were significant and inspiring moments throughout the traumatic period which are worth pondering. Following that first cataclysmic weekend, why did the weather suddenly and unexpectedly alter favourably? Why were some homes unaccountably spared in the midst of the annihilation all around? Why did some people miraculously survive? What bonded the local community in a spirit of solidarity? Why amongst the heartache and sorrow of heart wrenching bereavement were there occasionally tears of joy when missing loved ones suddenly appeared just as hope was fading? What generated the nationwide movement of generosity and compassion? Was prayer effective, or were these random chance happenings?

Judging from public commentary, the positive outcomes resulted from the "strength of mankind". It seemed that many people were willing to applaud the strength of the human spirit, but few gave any acknowledgement of God. In fact there was a strong impression that prayer was generally viewed as a release of some form of higher energy to combat the forces of the elements. The combined efforts of many people praying unleashed a human spiritual power. Apparently it was the act of prayer which was efficacious, not Someone or Something moved by prayer.

Often when tragedy occurs it has become commonplace for a public figure to express sympathy for those affected, and to state something like, "Our thoughts and prayers are with you". Is this just a platitude? Is it a hangover from a previous more religious era? Do we actually pray as we say we will? What do we actually mean by it? If we do pray, do we expect anything will happen? Or do we just hope so?

The question we need to ask is, Why on earth should we pray?

Request for Help

Roy was a well-respected man. He was married with an adult family, and was the foreman of the dispatch department in a large industrial factory. He related well with everyone and worked conscientiously. He led his workers competently, and ran an efficient department. He was decent, reliable, and pleasant. One day at the end of a week as his team was preparing to knock off work, he commented that he was intending to go to church on the following Sunday. Since he was not a regular churchgoer, the men were surprised and asked what the special occasion was. "To pray for rain", he said. Roy owned a small hobby farm which was his interest outside of work hours, and at this time there was a prolonged dry spell which was causing him anxiety for his crops and few cattle. Although he was not normally religious, he believed in God as a higher power, and was respectful in his attitude towards God and those who were serious about Christian beliefs. He considered that God had authority over the weather, and was good and trustworthy. Therefore he would be approachable for a reasonable request for help.

Lots of people whose outlook has been influenced by Christian views think similarly. So in times of special need they turn in prayer to God. They believe that God is real. They believe that he is the Creator and supreme Ruler of all that exists, that he has unlimited power, and may be willing to take care of them. When crises occur and life's circumstances get beyond personal control, they can appeal to him for help. Often he does seem to answer, and either provides a solution or enables them to cope. Though not always. Views about the efficacy of prayer to God cover a wide spectrum. Non churchgoers resort to prayer in an attitude of speculative hope, without clear certainty. On the other hand churchgoers display a range of attitudes.

Most churchgoers consider that prayer is important and effective. They believe that God hears and answers prayer. Often that belief is confirmed by apparent "answers". Various explanations are given for lack of answers: the prayer was not according to God's will; the pray-er lacked faith; the prayed-for lacked faith; God said "no"; or, "wait"; the prayer was too general; sin not dealt with in the life of the pray-er or prayed-for was an obstacle; and other reasons. Basically churchgoers expect prayer to make a difference.

Many churchgoers see prayer as a religious duty and aim to maintain a regular habit of disciplined devotions. Many would like to be more consistent with their prayers of devotion, but struggle because of other interests, distractions, and responsibilities. There are those who see prayer as a measure of spirituality. Others as a means of power for service. Or a privilege for enjoying fellowship with God. Some value private prayer. Others collective prayer. Or both. Some prefer written prayers. Others extempore. Some people prefer a contemplative approach, while more active people like to be brief and direct and practical in their requests. Prayer lists of people and needy situations have become a widespread practice. Prayer is a prominent and important feature of Christian faith.

But why? Why on earth should we pray?

Universal Phenomenon

Other religions also practice some form of prayer. After moving into a new community with my young family many years ago, I went to get a haircut at a local barber's shop. There were no other customers when I arrived, and the barber was taking the opportunity to pray.

He was kneeling with his forehead to the floor in a rear alcove off the main room. He was a Muslim and was taking his prayer obligations seriously. One of the pillars of Islam is the obligation to pray five times each day. Assembling together for communal prayer on Friday evening is an imperative not to be neglected. Prayer for a Muslim is a religious duty to express reverence to Allah and to cultivate a constant mindset of submission to him. It takes the form of recitation of standard prayers performed in a solemn attitude.

Original Buddhism was not a religious system and did not include a place for God or for such interests as worship, prayer, evil and judgement, redemption and forgiveness, or life after death. It was primarily concerned with the problem of pain and suffering, and proposed a way of deliverance by the elimination of desire through ethical discipline. Yet ironically Buddhism has become one of the major religions of the world. It has been influenced by various historical developments, and acquired conspicuous religious features in its practice. Especially prayer! Although Buddha made no claims about possessing divine status, his followers declared that he displayed special powers, and revered him as an object of faith. Images of Buddha are erected in shrines and temples, and offerings and prayers are made to him. There seems to be a natural compulsion within human beings to engage in prayer.

Jews, Hindus, Shintoists, Animists also engage in prayer as a means for coping with life's affairs. People who attend AA groups or similar groups for narcotic, gambling, or other addictions, acknowledge a Power greater than them, and pray regularly for help in managing their afflictions. Business people and elite sports athletes manage their stressful pressures by practicing forms of prayer and meditation. Some religions use prayer beads, or flags, or wheels, or chants, or written messages as aids for their prayer exercises. Around the world, in all cultures, people pray.

I have even known of atheists, on rare occasions, to pray!

A Heartfelt Plea

A renowned author demonstrated this. Her response was so strange it was striking. It seemed contradictory. Although she professed to be an atheist, she admitted that at times she prayed.

Geraldine Doogue, Presenter of the ABC television program "Compass", was interviewing Geraldine Brooks, an Australian novelist and Pulitzer Prize winner. Throughout the session Brooks showed herself to be a woman who is compassionate, intelligent, thoughtful, and articulate. Her life's journey began with a Roman Catholic upbringing, both at home and at school. As a young university student, she became a social activist and an atheist. Then she married an American Jew and converted to Judaism. Her conversion was not religious, since she remained atheistic in her views. It was cultural, as she fully embraced the customs of her husband's racial heritage. She is a person who is wholehearted in her commitments.

Towards the conclusion of the interview, Doogue hesitatingly asked Brooks if she ever prayed. She asked the question even though she indicated that, given Brooks' atheistic outlook, she wouldn't expect her to. Surprisingly, Brooks said that sometimes she did. When she was confronted with an overwhelmingly distressing situation such as the devastation caused by a tsunami, or the oppressive abuse of a child, her sense of despair and compassion for helpless victims caused her to appeal to "Transcendence" for respite.

She was not acknowledging the existence of a transcendent Person or particular entity. It was more a way of referring to the overall cosmos. Neither did she expect an answer to her prayer. She was simply expressing the anguish and futility of her human hopelessness in the face of harsh impassive natural forces. Apparently prayer was a cry of the heart to vent her painful feelings which rose from her thwarted inner desire to see compassion and justice triumph.

I was both impressed and intrigued by her statement. She articulated a view of prayer which I thought was filled with helpful insight, and yet described an experience which was hollow and hopeless. Her actions illustrate the instinctive response of the human heart to the great dilemma which confronts the human race. Where do we find ultimate satisfying reality? How or where do we find true justice, unrestricted compassion, pure goodness, benevolent power, meaning and purpose, a higher "source" which can calm and comfort our troubled finite spirits? A common instinct amongst human beings, and an instinct which is unique to humans amongst all earthly living things, is a consciousness of rational, ethical, relational dimensions to human living and spiritual yearnings for higher meaning, reality, and fulfilment. Prayer, in one form or another, is the typical human response to, and symptom of, this human quandary. People cry out (whether passionately, or only listlessly, depending on their convictions and sense of desperation) to be heard from "above". Brooks has no faith that an ultimate reality exists, and so projects her wishful desire for a transcendent order into her expression of prayer.

Why? Why do people pray? Does it make any difference?

Personal Curiosity

As a young boy I often used to lie in bed at night and, before dropping off to sleep, think a child's thoughts about God. My parents taught me about God and to say my prayers. In my imagination I visualized the starry heavens and pondered where God was up there, and what he was like. I had no doubt that he was there, but I had no clue about how to think of him. My childish contemplation was prompted by childish curiosity. There was nothing more to it than that. Yet from my earliest memories I learned the habit of speaking to an unseen vague Someone and asking him to "bless" those near and dear to me.

However, prayer for me has been a persistent curiosity. At the core of my being I have always wanted to understand and experience prayer meaningfully. This desire has taken me on a journey of exploration.

I have wrestled in my mind with deep questions about the reality, purpose, relevance, and value of prayer. Does prayer really matter? Is it merely a religious activity and nothing more than a ritual habit? If so, what is its purpose and value? Or is prayer simply an instinctive human response to overwhelming difficulties, a venting of mortal limitation? Are the prayers of all people, regardless of their religious convictions or personal attitudes, efficacious? If prayer is actually engaging with God in some way, what does it accomplish? Do our prayers inform God, or change his mind, or cause him to take action in some way? If God is all supreme, all powerful, all knowing, and is carrying out his plan for the universe, do our prayers have any bearing on what he does? If so, what? What are we actually doing when we pray? How should we go about it? Or is prayer really only a therapeutic activity which at best merely benefits our own mental well-being? Is prayer worthwhile? Different people answer these questions in different ways. Opinions about prayer are numerous.

I have also pondered the apparent universal human instinct for prayer, and at the same time the apparent universal half-heartedness about prayer. Prayer is a curious phenomenon.

Personal experiences of prayer have led me to many insights. I have learned that praying can be quite simple and easy, and yet consistency in prayer is a struggle. At times occasions of prayer have been inspirational, edifying, or strengthening. Sometimes there have been astonishing outcomes from prayer. Yet there have also been periods when prayer has not seemed to have made any difference.

Prayer has been a prominent interest for me as I have travelled through my life's personal experiences, through deep and intimate experiences in other peoples' lives in my role as a pastor, and through the influence of writers, speakers, and practitioners of prayer, mainly Christian, but not only so. My personal exploration has been a life-long interest.

Above all I have explored the Bible for its instructions and insights about prayer, and this has led to profound discoveries about knowing God and living in relation to him, and that prayer is crucial to everything. My motivation in writing this book is pastoral, and my intention is to write in narrative style. I want to tell the story of prayer in the Bible.

Perspective of the Bible

Prayer in the Bible is distinctive. It is a conscious and meaningful communication with the living God who is the maker and ruler of the universe. It is not a religious formality, and is far more than mere mental or vocal projection of inner thoughts and feelings. Prayer in the Bible is effective, not as a power in itself, but because God is responsive, and acts with transcendent power.

The Bible is not a single book, but a collection of many books, written by many authors about many topics over the course of many centuries. Nevertheless, the books constitute a whole, because together they bear witness to a unique phenomenon in history. They reveal the presence of the living God, who looms large in the affairs of human history. He is engaged in accomplishing a sublime plan for the human race. That plan is for God to make himself known, and to make it possible for people to enter a life-fulfilling relationship with him. The books of the Bible trace an unfolding story of God's progressive actions and disclosures in his interaction with the nation of Israel, which he chose for his purposes, until the arrival of Jesus who culminated the plan. The story bears witness to the plight of humanity. It illustrates human experience both in its most heroic and laudable accomplishments, and when it behaves in appallingly debased ugliness. It reveals that the human race possesses a majestic dignity because God created mankind in his own image. Yet mankind has alienated itself from God by defying God's sovereign authority and become enslaved to the tyranny of evil. The story also bears witness to the love of God who undertook extraordinary measures to redeem mankind from its bondage and to reconcile it with himself. Throughout the various books of the Bible, as they relate the successive stages of the story and present their respective subjects, a significant feature appears. Throughout successive generations people called out to God in prayer.

Prayer in the Bible has an important place. On the one hand, it represents the response of the heart to the human quandary of needing help and deliverance by a supreme source. On the other hand, it expresses human heart to divine heart companionship and worship.

Mentions of prayer in the Bible form intriguing patterns. Sometimes prayer is prominent in a book; sometimes it only appears occasionally; at other times it is completely absent. These patterns have significant bearing on both what is being related in the broader context, and the subject of prayer itself. It is not always obvious that the patterns were composed consciously and intentionally by the hands of the human authors, or whether they simply emerged coincidently. Do they reflect a "higher hand" at work?

The Bible's most important perspective concerning prayer is a simple yet profound truth. The key to meaningful prayer is knowledge of God. It is not prayer which must be our focus, but God. Prayer is merely our response to God. Becoming aware of God, or of our need of God, evokes our movement towards him. Prayer is the language of conversing with God. It is a cry of the heart which calls out to the transcendent Maker of heaven and earth. He is the Living One, the eternal God, the ultimate Reality who transcends the cosmos and all of life, which derive their very existence from him. He is the sublime Original Person who has revealed his presence and identity, and who enters into intimate mutual relationship with created human beings. Prayer is communicating with God.

Prayer is the language for speaking with God. It is a language with many intonations and accents. Its format and terminology cover every contingency of life and thought. It can express the most sophisticated and profound notions, as well as the simplest child-like comment. It is the language for making conversation with the King of Heaven and for enjoying the interaction of his companionship. It is the language for offering him praise, and for making petition and intercession. Prayer addresses the divine Creator and Ruler of the universe and communicates whatever is on the heart. It does not always need to use words.

Prayer is the language of the heart. It gives utterance to the deepest thoughts and longings of our soul. It is a communication from our soul, laying bare our human finiteness, deepest hurts, and highest hopes, addressed to the Holy One on high.

Relationship with God is possible, and meaningful. But it is lopsided. It is a relationship between One who is absolute, transcendent, and completely self-sufficient and one who is a dependent creature. Humans are marvellous and superb beings with amazing powers of intellect, spirit, and character, yet finite creatures nevertheless. To be granted fellowship with their eternal Creator is the ultimate privilege. Because of the inequality of the relationship, human beings are the dependent partners. Companionship with God is intimate and vital, yet on the human side is one of humble respect and dependence. For this reason prayer has the nature of entreaty. Conversation with God is a matter of requesting: his help, his will to be done, his name to be honoured. This is not a matter of coming before God with a "shopping list". It is engaging with God in a two-way dialogue, where God reveals his glory and plans, and we respond with requests of humble and adoring agreement. Prayer involves petitions (regarding events and things), intercessions (regarding people), and requests for praises and thanks (regarding God) to be received. In prayer we submit to God in trusting love and obedience, and express our heart desire for God's purposes to succeed.

Peoples' prayers have a special role in God's plans, and the way he answers those prayers illuminates his purposes. There is also a place in God's plans for the cumulative prayers of many. This larger picture is important for understanding apparent inconsistencies and disappointments in our individual experiences of prayer. When the events of Victoria's horrific firestorm are viewed from a biblical perspective, we can find comfort not only in the strength of human solidarity, but more profoundly in the sublime presence of God who acts with transcendent love.

God also acts according to his own purposes. He is personal, with his own higher view of things. He does not simply act like a supernatural genie who grants every wish. He is supreme sovereign over all affairs and has his own objectives through all that happens.

Jesus The Intercessor

When it comes to prayer the most outstanding authority is Jesus. It could be said that he is himself the "prayer phenomenon". He personally prayed. He prayed often. He prayed for long periods of time. He prayed before making critical decisions and before facing critical events.

He prayed privately, and publicly. His praying accomplished astonishing, even miraculous, outcomes. He taught about prayer. He inspired his followers to pray. He urged them to pray.

Jesus' praying was unlike the formal religious practices of contemporary Jewish rabbis, and unlike either the fervent unintelligent prattle or the sober contemplation of pagan gurus. His praying was a meaningful, deeply intimate fellowship with his Father in heaven. All of his life was governed by, and flowed out of, his prayer relationship with God. Prayer was not merely a religious feature of his life, not even a major feature. It was the essence of his life. Praying was as essential as breathing.

This is depicted emphatically by the writer of the Book of Hebrews in the New Testament in a summary statement of Jesus' earthly life. His whole life and ministry are condensed into a picture of intense prayerfulness which vividly recalls Jesus' hour of anguish and agony in Gethsemane, which was the pinnacle of his life before his crucifixion.

> *"During the days of Jesus' life on earth, he offered up prayers and petitions with loud cries and tears to the one who could save him from death, and he was heard because of his reverent submission"* (5:7).

Probably recollection of Gethsemane is intended, although the statement describes the whole course of Jesus' life as one of fervent intercession. The writer also declares that Jesus continues to perform a role of intercession in his present state of resurrection life.

> *"Therefore he is able to save completely those who come to God through him, because he always lives to intercede for them"* (7:25).

Jesus' intercessory role defines his identity as the redeemer of mankind. He is the mediator between mankind and God, who offered up both prayers, and himself as a sin-offering, for mankind's salvation. His example also highlights intercession as the central purpose of prayer for his followers. Jesus ensures a radical new relationship for his followers with God, and prayer is the characteristic expression of that relationship. Through Jesus they have a privileged new identity, and they enjoy a privileged intimate fellowship where prayer is the language of the sons of the Father, of the friends of Jesus, of the partners of the Spirit, of the citizens of the Kingdom. In particular, they represent Jesus on earth as he intercedes in heaven, and that is why they, on earth, pray!

CHAPTER 1

THE CONVERSATION

There are two ways of viewing a painting in an art gallery. You can stand up close and examine the various details which make up the overall picture, identifying the images and features which make up the whole, and admiring the artist's brushstrokes and techniques. Then you can also step back and take in the broad scene depicted on the canvass. To fully appreciate the painting, you need to do both.

The Bible presents a magnificent picture. To appreciate the significance of the Bible, and the revelation it presents, we need both to study its parts closely and to step back and discern the full mosaic of their cumulative effect. The Bible is not a single book. It is a collection of books, a virtual library. Some books cluster together in sequence. Others stand alone. Up close it is not always easy to see how all the books relate to one another. The variations of authors, themes, and literary styles and features provide fascinating reading and insights, and each book contains a wealth of enlightenment. But taken together and viewed from a discerning position an overall inspiring impression presents itself. It is possible to see the big picture of the Bible as a "conversation" between the sovereign living God and human beings.

The Bible reveals an astonishing reality. It reveals – assumes – asserts - that God is there. He is a transcendent personality who is sovereign over the universe. He is real, absolute, and personal. He is supernatural, and acts supernaturally in history to achieve his plan for the world. This revelation possesses innate authority, and cuts through the confusion of multiple religious notions, and secular scepticism and indifference in our modern world. The Bible tells us that there is a living God, and affirms his transcendent nature and the historical character of his actions. Because he is personal, he can be known, and can be approached in prayer.

We human beings tend to have an intuitive awareness of God, a "sixth sense" that he is there. Yet our opinions of what he is like vary. He is an unseen presence, and is unknowable by our normal senses. Our finite limitations restrict us, our changing moods and changing circumstances blur our perspectives, and the disposition of our inner spirit distorts our views. The only way God can be known is through his self-revelation. He cannot be discovered by human effort. He is above the reach of our observation, scientific investigation, rational enquiry, and any activity by which we might try to find out whether he even exists, let alone anything about him. We can only respond to what he chooses to disclose. The Bible bears witness that God has made himself known. He has "spoken". He intruded into human affairs and acted in special ways to communicate with us. He "conversed" with people, revealing his existence, his identity, and his purposes. The Bible is a record of that "conversation".

The people who "heard" God and responded to his revelation entered into meaningful relationship with him. Their way of life became shaped by their engagement with him as they "replied" to what he was saying. Their story is their side of the "conversation". The "conversation" is a dialogue in which God reveals and Man replies. On Man's part, the core feature of his conversation with God is prayer.

The Written Witness

Michelangelo, the renowned Italian artist of the sixteenth century, decorated the Sistine Chapel in the Vatican Museum with paintings of biblical figures and scenes across the ceiling and around the walls. The central painting, in the middle of the ceiling, depicts God, in human form, with outstretched arm reaching down towards Man who is reaching up, so that their fingers almost touch. A rushed sweeping glance around the room might easily gain the impression of only a motley array of colourful medieval paintings. However, on closer inspection, and even considered contemplation, an observer makes profound discoveries. Not only does he appreciate the talented genius of the artwork. He also recognises the rich biblical insight which has inspired it. To portray God in human form captures the anthropomorphic (human imagery) language of the Bible used to present God as a living person. The choice of supporting biblical scenes, together with their order and presentation, discerningly identifies the essential testimony of the Bible's revelation.

The Bible is a written witness to the actions and intentions of God in his relationship with the human race. By his actions God shows us what he is like. His purpose, or "grace agenda", is to restore mankind to a state of harmony, joy, and intimate fellowship with himself under his kingly rule, a relationship of mutual love and loyal commitment.

The Bible consists of two parts, the Old and New Testaments. The Old Testament is a collection of various forms of literature, written by numerous authors at various periods of history over the course of many centuries. It is primarily concerned with God's relationship with the nation of Israel, and his purpose for the nation, in terms of its unique "covenant". It does not set out to record the general progress of world history and human affairs. It is "sacred revelation", concerning God and his agenda for the world. So, we must read what it says carefully, discerning its message, not drawing unintended conclusions on inappropriate matters.

The New Testament bears witness to an even greater historical phenomenon. It concerns the person and actions of Jesus Christ, proclaiming him as the Messiah, the Son of God, who was crucified and raised back to life from the dead. The New Testament is also a collection of various forms of literature, written by a number of different authors in various situations over a period of decades during the second half of the first century of our modern calendar. The common interest of these writings is the "gospel" about Jesus and his significance for God's purposes for the world. The gospel declares that Jesus is restoring God's Kingdom in the world, and has fulfilled God's covenant with Israel by means of a "new covenant", which applies not only to Israel, but to all nations of the world. The gospel is the proclamation that God's favour has been bestowed on the world through the person of Jesus, God's Messiah. Every person who humbly receives Jesus as their Saviour and King enters into the blessing of an intimate and eternal relationship with God as Father. We can only really understand the significance of Jesus by comprehending the Old Testament background to his advent. He is the flowering fulfilment of its extraordinary exploits and promises. Throughout its story prayer has an important and meaningful role. That role has deep relevance for why Jesus gave high prominence to prayer in both his personal practice and his teaching.

How we read the Bible is important. We must read its various books as they were originally intended to be understood. We must not impose on them modern perspectives. Each book had its own author, its own purpose, its own literary style, and its own context. When we look closely at the various texts, we come across a wide array of terms, ideas, imagery, and details. Often, we meet literary expressions and methods which are unfamiliar to us, and we can easily misinterpret. We have to discern between prose and poetry, apocalyptic imagery, eschatological (end-time) features, anthropomorphic (human attributes for God) language, and ancient colloquialisms. Numbers can be problematic, because the ancient world was not always precise with numerical figures, which were often used to express ideas rather than measurement. The way in which history was written was very different from our modern approach. In addition, the Bible reports supernatural activity which is unfamiliar to normal experience, and it does so by a variety of means (metaphor, analogy, figurative language, poetic imagery, angels, visions, uncanny weather, and even utterances by God, both on earth and in heaven). In fact, the more carefully we examine the "canvass" of the Bible, the greater our surprise (and sometimes discomfort) at what we learn about the literary "brushstrokes".

Over the centuries the Bible has been subjected to intense scholarly scrutiny. Experts in literary forms, history, archaeology, and various other fields of study have shone new light on numerous aspects of its narratives. It is important to learn from these endeavours because they give us clearer and fuller understanding of the Bible's message. Theories of interpretation generated by such studies may be helpful, or harmful, depending on personal biases and the extent of objective discernment. However, there is a subjective dimension to the Bible which goes beyond theories about it to a knowledge of God himself. Reading the Bible affects not only the mind and understanding, but the heart and conscience as well. The Bible is not a text book about history, or religion, or culture, even though such features are prominent. It is primarily revelation of the knowledge of God and his purposes. Readers of the Bible can easily be distracted by the details of its contents. These need to be examined closely in order to grasp the message they present. Yet they can cause confusion because they do not meet our standards of approval. They are products of a different period of history and different outlook. Modern readers may ridicule their "primitive" nature, or rush to defend their "authenticity" in their zeal to uphold the Bible's truthfulness. The appropriate response is to accept what is written, without prejudice and without presupposition, because it displays the "brushstrokes" which paint the picture to be discerned. It portrays the living God and his activity in the world. Actually, the literature of the Bible was skilfully written, and profound, holding its own in any era. Many books show masterly creativity in format and style, and simply from a literary point of view are outstanding. Even in its own day, its views and values stood apart from its surrounding milieu. In particular, it presented a unique take on God. He was real. He was the living God, who acted and spoke, and could be known. He was holy. He was absolutely sublime, majestic above all creation, and perfectly righteous in his character and conduct. He was the only God. In a world which believed in a multiplicity of gods, God was considered to be the only true God, the creator and ruler of all that existed. He was full of love and grace. Because of his faithfulness and mercy, he came to the rescue, he forgave, and he established binding relationships with individuals, communities, and nations. The great truth revealed by the Bible is the truth about God. This is why the Bible must not be confused as a text book about history, science, religion, or some other subject. It is the word of God!

God's Grace Agenda

The Bible opens with the description of an extraordinary phenomenon. The first five books tell the dramatic saga of the divine Creator King taking action within human history, causing great upheaval, to establish within the world a startling new wonder. He acted majestically, powerfully, and spectacularly by intruding into world affairs to overrule nature and human political and military opposition in order to give birth to a new, free, and autonomous nation, Israel, with which he established a personal and covenant relationship. The Old Testament is a body of literature which bears witness to this astonishing phenomenon and to subsequent developments resulting from God's interactions with his covenant people.

The pivotal events were Israel's exodus from slavery in Egypt and God's formation of a covenant with the liberated nation at Mount Sinai. These amazing events are related in the Bible's second and third books, Exodus and Leviticus. The first book, Genesis, is a prologue which gave rise to these events. The book of Numbers continues the saga by tracking the new covenant nation on its desert journey from Sinai to the plains of Moab where it prepared to cross the river Jordan to possess its Promised Land. Deuteronomy describes a covenant renewal ceremony with the nation's second generation before it proceeded any further. These five books are known as the "Books of the Law", because they depict Israel entering into its covenant relationship with the divine Creator King in submission to his Law. The rest of the Old Testament, consisting of two general collections of literature known as the "Books of the Prophets" and "The Writings", traces the outworking of God's covenant with Israel over the course of more than a millennium.

God's covenant set Israel as distinctive among the nations. God was creating a unique nation within the world and binding himself to it by means of a special treaty. This was central to his strategy for human history to accomplish his purposes in the world in accord with his original intention at creation. God's agenda is revealed in his remarkable promise and covenant with Abraham and his descendants, described in Genesis. His strategy is not explained at the outset, but emerges as time passes. In reality, Israel was not a large and powerful nation. Yet strategically, it was located geographically in the centre of the region occupied by the powerful kingdoms around the Mesopotamian, Mediterranean, and Nile areas. Providential!

Jesus was the culmination of God's plan. Everything which unfolded through the Old Testament reached the pinnacle in him. Four books, called "Gospels", narrate the "message" concerning him, from different perspectives in accord with their authors and readers. These are not biographies about Jesus, but presentations which show his significance, as fulfilment of Old Testament anticipation, and as astonishing provision of grace for the world. They proclaim Jesus to be the true, God-appointed King of the world, who gave himself as a sacrifice to redeem the world from sin and death, and by resurrection from the dead to usher in a transcendent, eternal world order. Other writings in the New Testament reveal the impact and implications of the "message" about Jesus for life in the present world.

A Significant Activity

A distinctive description recurs throughout the Bible which captures a central theme of its unfolding story. As the story traces out the progress of God's agenda and strategy of grace, there emerges a stream of people who "call upon the name of the LORD". Although a variety of human authors contribute to the "library" which makes up the Old Testament, this description acts as a binding thread to the written tapestry which they collectively weave. Sometimes the description applies to a particular action at a particular time, such as calling out to God for help in time of trouble. At others it can express a general continuous attitude, such as relying on God as a basic outlook of life. It means consciously acknowledging and depending on God because he is the Creator and Ruler of the world, and the Saviour and

Covenant Father of his people. The "name of the LORD" refers to God's revealed identity. Those who "call" on that name are those who turn to him in dependence and devotion. To "call" on God indicates a basic posture of life, an attitude of relating to him and relying on him. It includes a wide range of actions, such as acknowledging him, invoking, worshiping, petitioning, entreating, interceding, supplicating, shouting or crying out, and appealing for help. It is essentially an attitude of prayerful dependence, often manifested in the actual activity of prayer.

In the New Testament, calling on the name of the Lord takes on a sharper focus. It especially expresses calling on the name of "Jesus", in order to be saved spiritually and eternally. In an interesting twist, those who do so are said to be "called" by God. These descriptions paint a vivid picture of the core nature of the "conversation" between God and his people. They "call" to one another!

This description highlights the prominence and strategic importance of prayer in the Bible. It provides a framework for understanding purposeful prayer. It shapes the Old Testament's concept of prayer, which then blossoms into a rich and purposeful practice in the New Testament. The description serves to identify the attitude and activity of people who respond and relate to God. They are said to "call upon the name of the LORD". To explore the Bible in regard to calling on the name of the LORD, and in particular to prayer, leads to the discovery of illuminating insights.

A Discovery Tour

Before setting out as readers on a journey of discovery you need to be aware of a few travel procedures. In the first place you need to know what path we will be following. We will be taking a discovery tour through the Bible. There are two aspects to our journey. On the one hand, I want to provide an overview of the Bible's presentation. This involves discerning the magnificent picture which the books collectively display. It is a stunning, vibrant picture of the living God accomplishing a gracious plan to bestow lavish blessing on the world. On the other hand, I want to identify references to prayer mentioned in the Bible, to show the role of prayer in the scheme of God's plan. We will examine what the references reveal about the purpose and practice of prayer. After all, our quest is to discover why on earth we should pray! So, we will follow a path which highlights what the Bible reveals about prayer. We will explore the locations of references to prayer to see how their settings contribute to their significance, and to see what prayer contributes to the settings. In other words, we need to examine the **content** and the **context** of any given passage. When you read any part of a book, you need to see it in the broader context of the whole book, which in turn you need to see in the context of all the books. Our task then is twofold. It involves getting a pretty good understanding of the books of the Bible, as well as then learning how prayer fits in. That is quite an enterprising challenge.

You also need to be aware of the nature of our journey. It will be a discovery tour not a research expedition. By that I mean you will not have to do the basic hard slog of investigation and research, the painstaking activity of examining all the details of the text and context, and considering the opinions of other researchers. That is a mammoth task beyond the scope of this book. It is a necessary task, but here in this book I am simply presenting personal conclusions. I am conducting a guided tour along the road I have already travelled. I want to present a readable, popular-style composition, without the trappings of heavy-duty academic details. So there are no footnotes or references to other literary sources. You might be relieved at that. Or you might be disappointed. Please do not be discouraged if you find yourself travelling through unfamiliar territory. It is not feasible to provide a full explanation of every setting, only enough to provide the context for understanding the purpose of prayer. However, you might want to keep note of unfamiliar settings in order to follow them up later. If I can keep your attention, and point out the interesting landmarks as we undertake our tour, you will be satisfied with the enlightening discovery you make. Enjoy the journey!

CHAPTER 2

BACK TO THE BEGINNING

Stars seen from the bottom of a deep well blaze with magnified brilliance.

Catastrophic events can sometimes precipitate new beginnings.

Spring follows winter. New growth emerges after devastating bushfires. Survivors of deep tragedy may press on with fortified spirit, strengthened courage and stamina, and enriched confidence and character. Setbacks may stimulate renewed vision, determination, and creative enterprise.

Failure may not be the end, but an opportunity for a fresh start.

In the year 597 BCE Nebuchadnezzar king of Babylon captured the city of Jerusalem. He raided the temple and removed all its treasures, and took king Jehoiachin, his officials, and all the aristocracy prisoners. He appointed twenty-one years old Zedekiah as his puppet king in Jerusalem. Nine years later Zedekiah rebelled. Nebuchadnezzar returned with his army and laid siege to the city. After two years, in 586 BCE, the city fell, and the Babylonians destroyed and ransacked Jerusalem. They were brutal. Zedekiah's sons were executed before his eyes, which were then gouged out, and he was taken away in shackles to Babylon. The temple was burnt down, and the leading priests executed, as also other civic leaders. Captives were taken into exile to Babylon.

Exile was a place of misery. The Jews were displaced from their homeland, exposed to humiliation and torment from their Babylonian captors, and filled with despair and disillusionment. What would become of them?

Yet their situation was not totally hopeless. This was not the end, but a metamorphosis, generating new and brighter prospects beyond the cocoon of captivity. It was an opportunity to reflect, rethink, and re-evaluate. Among the exiles were priests, prophets, and "wise men", who became voices of hope. During the decades of captivity their experiences, insights, and faith awakened convictions of identity and purpose, which gave rise to grand expectations. An extraordinary literary enterprise flowed from the pens of scholarly, creative composers. Some works collated documents and records from past eras, added ingenious touches, and shaped them into a comprehensive whole. Others projected an optimistic picture for the future. This literary material laid a foundation for faith, and inspiration for perseverance. The exile was pivotal for producing the body of literature which became the basis of the Bible.

The exile was also pivotal as an experience because it became a paradigm for God's ways with the world. Human behaviour eventually leads to calamity, but God accommodates that calamity to produce new beginnings. Throughout the Bible, this pattern recurs over and over again.

The literature which appeared at this time varied in style and format. The first five books of the Bible, Genesis to Deuteronomy, became known as the "Books of the Law", because they described the process which established God's covenant with Israel, and prescribed the Law which set out the relationship and requirements of that covenant. These books are also known as the "Books of Moses", and probably the bulk of their contents was written by him, incorporated within the final compositions completed during the exile. Deuteronomy (28:61, 29:21, 31:24-26) refers to a "Book of the Law" which Moses wrote, containing the laws of the covenant. Because this title became applied to the first five books of the Old Testament, traditionally Moses has been held responsible for them. However, the books were not finally completed until well after Moses, since his own death was recorded in Deuteronomy (chapter 34), and there is internal evidence that their final composition was after the establishment of Israel's kingship (Genesis 36:31).

The series of books containing Joshua, Judges, 1 & 2 Samuel, 1 & 2 Kings traces the story of Israel's covenant relationship until the capture of Jerusalem and the exile. The last chapter (2 Kings 25) shows the end date for the series, which was towards the end of the exile. The contents of these books may have been contributed by different authors along the way, but the final product was not until the exile.

The pivotal book in this whole collection of books was Deuteronomy. The book of Deuteronomy concluded the sequence of the "Books of the Law" (Genesis to Deuteronomy), and provided the perspective which shaped the series which followed, a "Deuteronomic History" (Joshua to 2 Kings). It was the link between the two series. The final composer(s) of the books is unknown, but it is apparent that the books were prepared for the benefit of the exiled Israelites in Babylon.

Jeremiah was a prophet in Jerusalem at the time of its destruction. He warned in advance that God's judgement was coming on the city, and he witnessed it come to pass. He continued to preach after the exiles were taken away. His messages contained in his book show in his language and thoughts his association with the "Books of the Law", and especially the book of Deuteronomy.

Ezekiel was an exiled priest who became a prophet, and his book demonstrates the fervour of serious scrutiny which took place in the exile community, the emergence of a visionary future, and the creativity of literary publications.

Another significant literary work was the book of Isaiah, which is lengthy and complex. The first section of the book (chapters 1-35) reflects the historical period in which Isaiah lived, which was prior to 700 BCE. A middle section (chapters 36-39) is a slightly modified version of an extract from the Book of Kings (2 Kings 18:13-20:19), which was not composed until after 600 BCE. Inclusion of the extract implies that the book of Isaiah was also compiled later, incorporating preserved materials from Isaiah and other contributions by editors in the exile responsible for the finished work. The final section (chapters 40-66) contains material which relates to the period of the exile, and anticipates the return of the Jews to their homeland and thrilling prospects for their future. The book is another example of the flurry of literary productivity precipitated by the exile. Out of devastation sprang a concerted new faith vision, set out in a body of inter-connected writings to explain, inspire, and guide.

The composers of the "Books of the Law" and the "Deuteronomic History" had a purpose in mind. They were taking their readers back to the beginning, in order for them to understand their covenant faith, and why they had come to such a disastrous catastrophe. In particular, they looked back to the days of Moses, the exodus, and the formation of God's covenant with Israel as the golden moment which defined their identity and destiny. It is important that we understand that they were not composing the history of those early events. The history was assumed, and they creatively composed inspirational versions about those events in order to enlighten and excite readers in their own day. Similarly, prophecies about future expectations and responsibilities were also often expressed in language and images from Israel's legendary origins. The writers wanted to show their dispirited readers how to rise from their ashes, and move forward to embrace their ordained destiny. When we join those readers, we find a message for ourselves, a heart-captivating revelation. It shines an illuminating light on the value and purpose of prayer.

Books of the Law

The first five books of the Bible are stunning pieces of literature. They bear witness to astonishing actions of God in regard to the nation of Israel, and they present their message by ingenious techniques. We need to recognise their literary nature in order to grasp their inspiring revelation. The primary interest was the spectacular phenomenon of Israel's emergence on the world's stage. The nation's exodus from slavery in Egypt, formation of a covenant with the living God at Mount Sinai, and journey through the desert towards their Promised Land were extraordinary events.

The presence of God throughout these events was pretty dramatic. He burst into the world, confronting powerful political and military forces, evoking awe and terror, performing supernatural signs and wonders, and establishing an astonishing new nation unlike any other heard of before or since. It all happened within a matter of months. From being an oppressed and powerless sub-cultural group in a small area of the land of the mighty pharaohs, the tribes of Israel were liberated by a display of supernatural power which humbled Egyptian forces. They were then constituted as a unique social, political, and military confederation, with a privileged covenant relationship with the living God as their King, who established his presence in conspicuous glory in the centre of their camp. The story is mind-blowing.

In fact, it seems too amazing to be true. Many historians and archaeologists have serious difficulties accepting the historicity of these events, and they point out numerous discrepancies and fallacies in the Bible's version of them. We must not dismiss their views, because they help us to look more closely at what the Bible actually says, and how. If we simply assume that the Bible is reporting history, as is usually done, we can become confused. Yet the Bible was not tracing human history. It was bearing witness to actions of God within history, and it used creative literary techniques to do so. The three books Exodus-Leviticus-Numbers are a trilogy which presents a continuous narrative, and they are written like an "epic drama". Genesis has its own literary style, and acts as an overture to the drama, and Deuteronomy, which has a different style again, is the finale. We will point out some of their features as we go.

The Creator King

Have a look at the overall format of Genesis. The book was written in a carefully designed format, and its successive stages were clearly marked. There is an opening proclamation, followed by ten "*accounts*".

> Opening Proclamation (1:1-2:3)
> Account of the Heavens and the Earth (2:4-4:26)
> Account of Adam's Line (5:1-6:8)
> Account of Noah (6:9-9:29)
> Account of Shem, Ham, and Japheth (10:1-11:9)
> Account of Shem (11:10-26)
> Account of Terah (11:27-25:11)
> Account of Abraham's Son Ishmael (25:12-18)
> Account of Abraham's Son Isaac (25:19-35:29)
> Account of Esau (36:1-37:1)
> Account of Jacob (37:2-50:26)

Five "*accounts*" precede the entrance of Abraham, and five concern Abraham and his family. Abraham is a pivotal figure. Genesis is not intended to be a history of the ancient world, as often assumed. It is a presentation of God's strategic plan for the world, in which Abraham was a key participant.

Let us set out on our tour, and look more closely at the story of Genesis.

The opening proclamation is a magnificent word picture (1:1-2:3). It commences with a sublime declaration.

"In the beginning God created the heavens and the earth. Now the earth was formless and empty, darkness was over the surface of the deep, and the Spirit of God was hovering over the waters" (v 1-2).

The poetic imagery of the *"Spirit of God hovering"* is a graphic picture of God's personal, powerful, supernatural activity gently overruling the process of creation. Like the atmosphere of air which floats over the ocean, God's Spirit is the presence of his essential being, his life-giving "Breath", as it were, intimately, directly, bringing creation into existence. The universe did not come into existence by mere natural forces, or by the efforts of mythical gods, but by God's personal operation.

The rest of the proclamation is an ingenious word portrait of God as the Creator and majestic Ruler of heaven and earth. What was *"formless and empty"* (a rhythmic expression which sets out a blueprint) is replaced by forms and fullness from a dynamic series of divine commands (v 3-31). God's work was done simply by issuing commands (*"Let there be light!"*, etc), his word, reflecting the fact that he is a living "Person", and the great King over all which exists. The portrait of God is discerned more clearly if you sketch the series of scenes.

FORMS	*FULNESS*
LIGHT (Day 1)	**LIGHTS** (Day 4)
SEA/SKY (Day 2)	**FISH/BIRDS** (Day 5)
LAND/VEGETATION (Day 3)	**ANIMALS/MAN** (Day 6)

Everything depicted includes everything which now exists. It is not a record of the order in which these entities were created, but a display of the completed creation. Across the sketch inscribe the word **G O D**. In the thirty-four verses of Genesis 1:1-2:3 the term *"God"* occurs thirty-five times! **He is the primary feature of the picture.**

This opening proclamation is **not** about the process of creation. It is a word "sketch" of the **Producer** and his finished product. Most readers tend to interpret the passage as a description of creation, **how** God made the universe. But it is actually about **who** created the universe. Against the backdrop of a brief "sketch" of what now exists, God is portrayed as the active, commanding, overseeing Producer of it all. This literary "sketch" is a magnificent work of art. It is a picture of God in action as the sublime Creator King accomplishing his will by his word! Pause your reading for a moment to contemplate the grandeur of the described scene.

But who is God? He is not named in this portrait. Instead he is **depicted** masterfully as the God of seven days! The seven days of creation do not refer to how long God took to do his work. They form a literary pattern for presenting the finished product of his work, and to identify who the Creator is. The God of seven days is the God of Israel, known as the "LORD"! Israel's later covenant relationship with God was distinguished by a seven-day cycle of community life expressly to identify the Creator as the God who liberated the nation from Egypt. The reason Israel was required to keep a weekly cycle of six days of work and a seventh day of rest was to bear witness to both the state of "Sabbath rest" when God completed his creation (Exodus 20:8-11), and the nation's freedom when God liberated them from slavery in Egypt (Deuteronomy 5:12-15).

The repeated term "God", and the pattern of seven days to depict his completed creation, powerfully identify the divine Creator as the covenant God of Israel! This opening proclamation was a powerful assertion, to a depressed and disillusioned people in exile, that the LORD, the God of Israel, their God (!), was the Creator Ruler of all the earth.

The proclamation contains many secondary features which are relevant for the inspiring narrative which follows. We cannot be side-tracked from our tour to explore them. However, we should especially note that God "*blessed*" both the humans he had made (1:22, 28) and the Sabbath when he had completed his work (2:3). This means that originally they were endowed with favour and well-being, and shows that God was the kingly Benefactor of his newly created dominion. This primary presentation of the reality of God, as Creator and Ruler of the universe, and covenant LORD of Israel, was intended to offer fresh hope for the disillusioned Jewish exiles in Babylon. It is a revelation which is relevant to people of the whole world in every generation, including our modern times. To recognise and accept that reality is the starting point as to why, on earth, we should pray.

God's Rescue Operation

At the dawn of human history, the unspoilt pristine world suffered a tragic spiritual downfall. Human beings rebelled against their Creator King, and the invasion of sin into human hearts shattered earth's original harmony and delight. The first "*account*" of Genesis (2:4-4:26) begins with the disclosure of this grim reality. We must consider the language being used. Vivid pictorial imagery portrays primordial events meaningfully and realistically. The "account" is describing human origins **in relation to God**. Three pictures depict the LORD God as the source of life.

He is a **"sculptor"** who forms Man from the dust of the ground and intimately imparts to him the breath of life (2:4-8). Man became a living person.

The LORD God is also a **"gardener"** who plants a garden (of "trees") where he locates the Man (2:9-17). In ancient times a garden was the royal estates of a king, so God's "garden" was his kingdom. Man was appointed to enjoy the "garden" and manage it. The "trees" in the garden are figurative, reflecting the various dimensions of human life, and these enrich and sustain the experience of life. Two "trees" are central to life in the "garden" (kingdom), the "tree of life" and the "tree of the knowledge of good and evil". I take the "tree of life" to refer figuratively to the source of life at the heart of the realm of creation, intending to mean either God himself or harmonious fellowship with God. God forbade Man to eat from the second "tree", the "tree of the knowledge of good and evil", at the consequence of death. This "tree" probably refers figuratively to the human privilege of freedom and choice, to choose a course of life in obedience or disobedience to God, to resolve to serve and depend on God, or to rebel against his sovereignty and strike out in independence. How Man chose would determine his knowledge of good and evil, whether he would know good unsullied by evil, or good in conflict with evil. Whether he would retain the dignity of his humanity, or become tarnished by depravity. Whether he would remain in fellowship with God, or become severed from the source of life, and "die".

The LORD God is also a **"builder"** (the language is from the imagery of manufacturing) who makes a woman to be the Man's partner (2:18-25). She is not a radically new creation made "from the ground", nor one of the animals who are ruled ("named") by the Man. She is made from a "rib", or "part", taken from the Man's side so that they naturally and compatibly complement one another in companionship and in their unique role as human beings. Originally there was no embarrassment or disharmony between them, as signified by their lack of embarrassment in the face of their nakedness. The sexual language reflects their mandate to populate the world, but probably includes all expressions of openness and intimacy in harmonious communal relationships. The picture of the woman being taken from the man does not imply his priority or dominance, but that as a single entity Man was inadequate. So Man was divided into two diverse yet complementary parts, and finds fulfilment as a couple in unity, enjoying compatible companionship and being bonded in partnership.

Life derived from God, and originally nothing marred life's exhilarating fullness, which was found in knowing God and reverencing his sovereignty in loving obedience.

However, **a devastating change** occurred when the man and the woman severed their relationship with God by wilful disobedience (chapter 3). The event is described in highly colourful imagery. God, humans, and animals (represented by a talking serpent) interact on a common level. Physical, sensual language depicts profound spiritual experience. The man and woman succumbed to the lure of tasting "forbidden fruit", thereby defying God's authority, disregarding his warnings, and destroying their fellowship with him. They then faced the uncomfortable consequence of being confronted by God, having their disobedience exposed, and learning about the calamitous effects of their actions on their relationships, roles, and responsibilities.

Notice verse 9. "*But the LORD God **called** to the man and said to him, 'Where are you?'*". This is the first occurrence of the term "*call*", and represents God's initiative in reaching out to mankind. God was not ignorant of the man's whereabouts. He was exposing the man's sudden new predicament, hiding from God, rather than walking with him. The language is figurative, and vividly depicts the broken fellowship between God and the man, the reality of death. Yet God's "*call*" indicates his immediate response of seeking to draw the Man back.

Harmony between humans and the rest of creation which they were to govern became marred by hostility. Relationship between the man and the woman became a troubled affair of female craving and male dominance, and their privileged task of increasing the human population afflicted by suffering. Their work and well-being became a burdensome matter of hardship. Notably, a curse was pronounced upon the serpent, which was the source of Man's temptation, and upon the ground, which was the sphere of his work.

Rebellious disobedience brought about alienation from God, resulting in death. God banished the man and woman from the Garden of Eden, so that they were cut off from the original state of harmony in God's presence and kingdom. The way back to the Garden, and to the tree of life, was barricaded by guarding cherubs with flashing swords of flame. God's action in the Garden showed that the Creator King judges those who rebel against his beneficent rule, yet he still desires their fellowship.

Great calamity has fallen upon the world, and shattered the joy and hope of the human race. Disobedience has alienated mankind from the beneficent Creator and King of the universe, and death has invaded the realm of life. The literary picture is simple, but the reality depicted is profound. This is the fundamental and universal reality which plagues the human race. It is the origin of the paradigm that human behaviour leads to calamity.

At the same time, there was a flashing glimmer of hope. The LORD's condemnation of the serpent foretold on-going enmity between the serpent's offspring and the woman's offspring (3:14-15). In vivid imagery typical of each protagonist, he depicted the woman's offspring crushing the serpent's head as it struck the heel of its human opponent. This was a suggestive picture that in the long run Man would destroy the enemy which caused his downfall. It does not say how, or when. But the prospect of hope is there. The subsequent unfolding story of the Bible traces the progress of this conflict, and the outworking of this hope. God has an agenda of grace, and this is the unifying factor of the Bible.

The vivid figurative language and imagery used to depict truth about God and his activity in these opening scenes is a clue for understanding descriptions of God's conduct later in the story. How can we discuss God meaningfully and realistically without resorting to suitable human-like expression? What we say is not meant to be taken in its bare literalness. We humanise our language in familiar terms to refer to matters which are above ordinary experience and description. Pictorial language is ideal for discussing matters of a higher spiritual order or abstract nature. Descriptions of God and his activity are portrayed in metaphorical imagery and anthropomorphic language, to be understood realistically, not literally.

Human life continued outside the Garden, but under a dark shadow of separation from the source of life. There was also an additional grim reality, a sinister presence, like a beast of prey. As the Lord says to Cain, "... *sin is crouching at your door*" (4:7).

The presence of sin is shown in the tragic incident involving Cain and Abel, and moral deterioration in subsequent generations. Ugly attitudes of callous indifference, violence, and arrogance corrupted personalities and relationships. Moral and social deterioration polluted cultural progress. Spiritually, society was rapidly spiralling downward into depravity. Genesis was not relating human history, but depicting the reality of human fallenness.

Yet God had not abandoned his purpose for humanity, despite its sinful rebellion. God "*granted*" (a pun on the name of Seth) another son to Adam and Eve to replace murdered Abel. God was initiating a new opportunity for the human family. In turn Seth had a son Enosh. And then people **"began to call on the name of the LORD"** (4:26).

Coming as it does at the end of the first "*account*" shows that this activity was significant. Original fellowship with God had been shattered by human disobedience, but in response to God's favourable initiative (giving us a glimpse of his grace agenda) there is recognition of a new opportunity of associating with God. It was now the people's turn to call to God. The context implies that calling on the name of the Lord signified at least four self-evident attitudes. People were acknowledging God, the Creator King. They were seeking a restored relationship with him. They were appealing to him, making petition to him. They were acknowledging their dependence on him.

The readers in exile for whom the book was written were quite familiar with the expression "calling on the name of the LORD". It was a typical description of their attitudes and actions of devotion towards the LORD. Invoking God's name was meant to be the disposition of their nation's heart. They would read these words at the end of this first "*account*" with discerning comprehension.

Here at the beginning of the Bible we gain our first insight into the significance of prayer. Essentially prayer is the act of turning to God the Creator King in humble submission to make dependent petition. It is a response to the living God who has not abandoned rebellious humanity, but who has graciously taken the initiative to woo mankind back into harmonious relationship with himself.

The next series of "*accounts*", the second to the fifth, which are clearly indicated, traces the period from **Adam to Abraham**. It is presented by means of an unusual literary format. The whole period was spanned by a chain of genealogical tables, except for the story of Noah and the Great Flood. Without delving into the details, we will simply follow the overall linking scheme.

The second "*account*", called the "written account of Adam's line" (5:1-6:8), catalogues a list of ten men who lived extraordinarily long lives, followed by a commentary about the appalling godless conditions of their period. It is the line through Seth, who was born to replace godly Abel. Despite their long lives, they all died (except Enoch because God intervened), showing that death overshadowed the human race.

The third "account", called the "account of Noah" (6:9-9:29), describes the Great Flood, and is lengthy and prominent. The Flood was widespread in extent, and legendary in the ancient world. Descriptions of the event in the records of other regional nations confirm its historical factualness, though the embellished mythical and grotesque features of their accounts stand in sharp contrast to the plain version in Genesis. The apparent absolute language of the biblical account about the Flood was not meant to be literal, anymore than about the famine in Joseph's day (41:57), but it indicated that the event was extreme and highly important. Information about what actually happened is skimpy, with the account emphasising details about the event's significance. Construction of the ark was described by a vivid picture of God instructing Noah what to do (6:11-21), followed by a brief statement that "*Noah did everything just as God commanded him*" (6:22). It was all about what God said (as divine Ruler of the world) and what Noah did (as God's obedient servant).

The fourth "*account*", called "*the account of Shem, Ham, and Japheth*" (10:1-11:9), followed a similar pattern to the second. It catalogued the descendants of the sons of Noah and their spread across the earth, and concluded with a commentary about how God thwarted the building of the tower of Babel. These two "*accounts*" were like bookends to the extended story of the Great Flood which came in between. The fifth "*account*", called "*the account of Shem*" (11:10-26), was simply a register of the line of Shem's descendants until Terah, the father of Abraham, and, like the second "*account*", contained ten generations. The whole period was covered by the sequence of tables, with only the two commentaries and the Flood episode to vary the style.

The narrative was not relating history, but presenting its message by means of unusual features. It was a very creative literary tactic. What was the message? God was responding to the movement of men calling on the name of the LORD. The series of "*accounts*" traced a chosen line from Adam to Abraham, and the story of the Great Flood demonstrated God's gracious intention to deal with his wayward world. The chosen line was God's rescue operation. It was the means by which God was intruding into his world in order to restore his relationship with it. God had not abandoned his world because of human rebellion. He was still pursuing his original kingly purpose to bless it. According to his plan, calling on the name of the LORD was not in vain but powerfully effective.

God's Favoured Family

When we get to Terah, the sweeping panorama of the first "*accounts*" zooms in on a special family in the final "*accounts*". This family was the roots of Israel. The pace of the narrative slows down to present the experiences of four men from successive generations. The sixth "account" is called the "account of Terah" (11:26-25:11), but Abraham is its primary focus. The seventh "account" (25:12-18) concerns Abraham's son Ishmael, and briefly lists Ishmael's sons' names. The eighth "account" is called the "account of Abraham's son Isaac" (25:19-35:29), but mainly includes the affairs of Jacob. The ninth "account" is called the "account of Esau" (36:1-37:1), and is a summary list of his descendants. The final tenth "account" is called the "account of Jacob" (37:2-50:26), but mainly relates the experiences of Joseph. Genesis is not relating history, but presenting the story of God's dealings with four men from his chosen family which was the origin of his covenant nation Israel.

The story is extraordinary. The first three men, Abraham, Isaac, and Jacob, experience unique encounters with God, who befriends them and forms a special bond with them. The men themselves are just ordinary people, without any particular talents or virtue to commend them. In fact quite the opposite, since each of them displays unattractive and unworthy traits of character and behaviour. Yet God calls them into a covenant relationship with himself as part of his agenda of grace for the world. God's interactions with the men are surprising in many respects. They form a progressive process which reveals what he is like. The fourth man, Joseph, on the other hand, is squeaky clean by nature, and only experiences God indirectly, providentially, through adversity and prosperity. The whole story is fascinating and enlightening.

Take a look at the four men. Abraham was called by God to leave his homeland in Mesopotamia and migrate to the land of Canaan, with the promise that he would be blessed and the source of blessing for all nations. At the age of 75 he was assured that in the future he would become the father of a special son, and that through him his descendants would inherit the land of Canaan. Abraham believed God's promise, and was granted a visionary experience in which God bound himself to Abraham in a permanent covenant. Many incidents transpired before the promise was fulfilled, and there were occasions when Abraham's faith was tested, and when his own actions threatened to jeopardise God's purposes. Abraham showed himself to be inclined to cowardice and self-serving attitudes, but through his relationship with the LORD grew in faith and loyalty. Eventually, when he was 100, his son Isaac was born. The climax of Abraham's odyssey was a supreme test to his trust in God and loyalty to the covenant when he was asked to offer up Isaac in sacrifice. Abraham showed his willingness to obey God absolutely, in complete confidence in God's trustworthiness. At the last moment, God intervened and provided a lamb as a substitute. Despite Abraham's fluctuating tendencies, God became known as the "God of Abraham".

Isaac turned out to be a self-centred and self-indulgent man, a big disappointment after all the suspense of waiting for the promised son. His personal exploits were quite unimpressive. Although Isaac lived longer than his father Abraham and any of his descendants, his life's story is glossed over with hardly a mention. Focus centred instead on the family squabbles between his twin sons Esau and Jacob, which depicted Isaac in very poor light. All the more striking then was the fact that God chose to bless Isaac in terms of his covenant promise to Abraham. God became known as the "God of Abraham and Isaac".

Jacob was an ambitious scoundrel. The younger of the twins, he was inwardly driven by the desire to usurp the privileges of birth-right of his brother Esau. This ambition cultivated a character trait of contentious disposition which affected his relationships with others, including members of his family, work associates, and even with God. His deceptive inclinations were detected at birth and noted in his unattractive name "Jacob", which literally means "he grasps the heel", and figuratively "he deceives". After stealing his father's blessing intended for his brother, he became a fugitive from his brother's fury and went to live with his uncle Laban in Aram (Syria). There he received a taste of his own medicine when his uncle deceived him on his wedding night by giving him his bride's older sister Leah instead of the promised Rachel. He married Rachel a week later, and then faced twenty years of jealous rivalry as the two sisters vied for his attentions to father their children. The two wives even resorted to offering him their maidservants in their attempts to outdo one another in the number of children they acquired. Meanwhile their father Laban cheated him with regard to wages for his labour. Despite his personal behaviour, contentious home life, and unfair treatment, God enabled Jacob to prosper, and accommodated his hassles and failings in accomplishing his own plans. Jacob's life was marked by an undeserved and uncanny prosperity. God later renamed him "Israel" after a night long struggle with a mysterious man. The reason given for that name is that he *"struggled with God and men"* and overcame. It is uncertain whether the name Israel means *"he struggles with God"*, or (more likely) *"God struggles"*. Mirrored in the man's personal ambitious strivings was a contrasting reflection of God's own persistent efforts to accomplish his divine ambitions. The strange experience and name change marked a profound moment in Jacob's personal relationship with God. Later the name change was confirmed, and linked with confirmation of his inclusion in the covenant promise to Abraham. The name "Israel" eventually became the family name of Jacob's descendants, and of the nation they became, a perpetual reminder of God's "struggle" to re-establish his kingship over mankind. God became known as the "God of Abraham, Isaac, and Jacob".

The fourth man, Joseph, was the son of Jacob's favourite wife Rachel, and was himself favoured by his father. He was betrayed by his jealous brothers and sold into slavery in Egypt. Despite his adverse circumstances and unjust experiences, he remained honourable, and prospered uncannily. He ended up becoming Chief Administrator of all Egypt, second only to Pharaoh, and the saviour of that nation during a period of extreme drought. Joseph stands out in all the pages of Genesis as a man of great integrity and kindly nature, who possessed God-given discernment and godly wisdom. He accepted his experiences of life through adversity and prosperity as providential to the greater scheme of God's intentions for the world. Though not a foundational father of the developing nation Israel, he was instrumental in his father Jacob and family moving to Egypt.

The narrative is not recounting history, but relating selected incidents in anecdotal style. There is much important historical information missing, so it is not possible to date precisely when these men lived. For example, both Abraham and Joseph had dealings with Pharaohs of Egypt, yet no Pharaohs are named. In fact, it is anachronistic to refer to the rulers of Egypt then by the title Pharaoh, since that practice did not begin until after 1200 BCE when Israel was already settled in the Promised Land. There are other curious historical omissions, anachronisms, and unverifiable details which are somewhat tantalising. At the same time, many cultural and geographical features confirm the authenticity of the historical background. What we must recognise is that the purpose of the narrative is to provide a prelude to the extraordinary events of Israel's exodus, covenant formation, and conquest of the Promised Land. Genesis reveals the origins of God's plan of redemption, not general human history. Therefore, what is included in the story is important for that purpose. Primarily Genesis is concerned to reveal God's dealings with the chosen men. In doing so, it progressively reveals truths about God himself, clarifying his identity. It also gives a clear impression of what the men were like, showing their characters and attitudes. In particular it is Abraham, Isaac, and Jacob who are the foundational figures, since it is Jacob's family which became the nation Israel. Yet a prominent feature which marks each of these three men is their activity of prayer. In fact, both Abraham and Isaac are said to have "called on the name of the LORD". Repeated use of this expression highlights its significance for Genesis' message, and for God's rescue agenda.

With this broad picture as our context, let us draw closer to observe the occasions of prayer experienced by these four men.

Abraham the Intercessor

God chose Abraham to be the starting point for his rescue plan for his alienated world. He would become an intimate friend of God, and the father of a favoured people who would enjoy a unique relationship with God. He and his family would become the means by which God would restore the nations of the world to harmonious fellowship with himself. Central to his relationship with God, and responsibility for God, was his privileged role as intercessor.

The pivotal passage which described the inauguration of Abraham's role was 12:1-3 where God simply declared his intentions to Abraham and ordered him to migrate to a new land which he would show him. God's will expressed by his word.

> *"The LORD had said to Abram, 'Leave your country, your people and your father's household and go to the land I will show you. I will make you into a great nation and I will bless you; I will make your name great, and you will be a blessing. I will bless those who bless you, and whoever curses you I will curse; and all peoples on earth will be blessed because of you"*.

This promise set the agenda for the rest of the Bible. It revealed God's intended plan of grace. God declared that he would bless Abraham, make his *"name"* great, and through him bless all nations. The promise was a renewal of God's original intention at creation to bless his world, and a reminder that true human greatness was granted by God, not achieved by human endeavour. Later there was the promise of a land which God would give him (12:7, 13:14-17), and a son through whom the nation would emerge (15:4-6). All God required of Abraham was trusting obedience.

At this point of time Abram (his original name), at the age of 75, had no children. Yet he responded obediently to God's word, and completed the journey to Canaan. He travelled to Shechem, where the LORD appeared to him, and promised him the land for his children. Abram responded to the announcement by building an altar. He then travelled on to a place between Bethel and Ai, where he built another altar and there *"called on the name of the LORD"* (12:8). These words naturally recall the days of Enosh (4:26). They indicated that Abram was making a similar response to God's new initiatives as people had in those earlier times. Readers in the exile were intended to be stirred in their hearts.

An episode then followed in which Abram's actions contradicted his initial worthy response, and threatened to bring God's enterprise undone (12:10-13:4). Acting fearfully out of concern for his own security, he took refuge in Egypt during a severe famine and allowed his wife Sarai to be taken into the Pharaoh's harem. Abram not only failed to trust God, but jeopardised God's plans for his future family line. However, God resolved the problem, and Abram returned from Egypt to the land, and to the LORD. After settling back in the Negev, he returned to his altar between Bethel and Ai, where he again *"called on the name of the LORD"*.

Friction between the herdsmen of Lot and Abram was resolved by a peaceable separation, with Lot choosing to relocate to the fertile Jordan Valley (13:5-18). This separation completed the requirement that Abram leave his father's household. God urged Abram to fix his eyes on the Promised Land, with the assurance that he would give it to him and to his descendants, who would be numerous. Abram relocated to Hebron, where he built another altar to the LORD. Does this imply that he again *"called on the name of the LORD"*?

Soon after this period war broke out in the Jordan Valley, and when Lot was taken captive, Abram mounted a successful rescue campaign (14:1-24). On his return home he passed through Jerusalem just north of Hebron, and was met by Melchizedek the king, who was also a priest of God. Since virtually no details are given about him, because of this incident he acquired a somewhat mysterious aura. What is highlighted is that God is called *"God Most High"* (Hebrew, *"El Elyon"*). This is a title indicating God's exalted status. The title is rare in the Old Testament, yet occurs four times at this point. It indicated that God was supreme above all gods, a significant revelation concerning God's identity, and an important perspective for the original demoralised readers in exile. He was also identified as the *"LORD"* and *"Creator* (or, *Possessor) of heaven and earth"*. Melchizedek gave hospitality to Abram and blessed him, crediting God with the victory. Abram responded by presenting him with a tenth of the recaptured spoil, representing a king's portion. He was giving tribute to God's kingly/priestly representative in Jerusalem. The reason for including this story in the narrative was not to recount history for its own sake. It was to provide revelation about God and his agenda for rescuing the world. The more clearly we understand what God is like, and his purpose, the more readily we respond to him, and are stimulated to pray.

Sometime later God confirmed his relationship with Abram, and his promise of blessing to him, in a spectacular manner (15:1-21). By means of a vision he communicated with Abram in dialogue. God urged Abram not to be afraid (an apparent tendency of his). He assured him that he was his *shield* (protection) and *very great reward* (rather than material prosperity). Yet Abram faced a dilemma. He was aware of God's plan to make him into a great nation, but he was childless, and currently his servant was his heir. He asked what God could give him, since he had not given him a child. This was a bold request, in keeping with God's own revealed intention, and showed both respect for God's sovereignty and his own confidence. Although this was not described as prayer, it was a vivid picture of prayer. Abram was asking God, in dependent confidence, to do what was necessary to accomplish his revealed purpose.

In response, God revealed further information about his proposed rescue plan for the world. *The word of the LORD came to him*, informing him that a son and heir would come from Abram's own body (v 4). Taking him outside to survey the stars of the heavens, he declared that Abram's offspring would be as numerous. And Abram believed him! This was a daring act of faith, and the observation was made that God *credited it to him as righteousness* (v 6). Just to make this observation showed that it was crucial. God and his selected servant were in a right relationship, characterised by God's promise to Abram, and Abram's accepting trust. This relationship of being in right standing with God by faith became a foundational principle of the gospel in the New Testament (Romans 4:23. Galatians 3:6, James 2:23).

As the vision continued, God also confirmed his own identity, and his purpose for Abram (v 7). The LORD had brought Abram from Ur in order to possess this land. His language was in the form of an ancient covenant between a king and his dependent servant. Abram asked for some indication by which he could know that he would indeed gain possession, and was granted a special display of sacrificial ritual as a symbolic act of covenant making. God guaranteed Abram in a covenant commitment that his descendants would return to the land and take possession of it after a period of 400 years slavery in another country. One reason for the long delay was that the current occupants of the land, the Amorites, had not yet reached their full measure of sin. This implied that the LORD was king over all nations, and that dispossession of the land from the Amorites by Abram's descendants would be an act of judgement. Yet God was patient in enacting his judgement, and Abram's descendants would be both the instrument of judgement and the beneficiaries of the land. These events would demonstrate the LORD's kingship over his world.

Ten years after the promise was made, when Abram was 86 years old, and still there was no son, Sarai arranged for Abram to father a child by means of her slave Hagar (16:1-16). When Hagar successfully fell pregnant, jealousy and tension sparked between Sarai and her slave, prompting Hagar to flee into the desert. Through an "angel" (a heavenly messenger), God encouraged her to return, with assurance that she too would have a son and many descendants. Hagar was deeply affected by this news, and responded by giving her own name for God, *"You are the God who sees me"*. She was conscious of God's powerful, living, attentive, and overruling presence in her circumstances, accommodating her misfortune in the bigger scheme of his will.

Another thirteen years passed by in silence (17:1-27). Then when Abram was 99, the LORD appeared to him again. He firstly identified himself by a new title, "*God Almighty*" (Hebrew, "*El Shaddai*"), then stated Abram's covenant responsibility, "*walk before me and be blameless*", and finally declared his intention to confirm his covenant with Abram.

The new title for God, "*El Shaddai*", was given at a crucial stage in the development of God's plan for Abram, and was a special title revealed to the successive fathers, Abram, Isaac, and Jacob. "*El*" is a special term for God which emphasised his power and might. "*Shaddai*" is a unique term, but has a close likeness, and connection, to the Hebrew term for "breasts" ("*shadayim*"). This was a bold and stunning expression. In a narrative which was strongly pictorial, the name "*El Shaddai*" brought to mind images and experiences pertaining to breasts, such as nursing, nurturing, nourishment, intimacy, satisfaction, abundance. At the same time, the unusual word indicated something radically different. It deliberately avoided being precisely likened to the breast. In the ancient world there were gods and goddesses of fertility, and images of goddesses were prominently characterised by their breasts. Religious practices associated with fertility gods were sensuous, crude, and often involved sexual perversions. "*El Shaddai*" stands in sharp contrast. It seems to express abstract ideas rather than a visual representation. The name revealed deeper understanding about God's identity and capacity. Because Abram would become the father of many nations, God changed his name to Abraham in anticipation. He said he would make Abraham "very fruitful" (v 6), and the name "*El Shaddai*" expresses the idea of fruitfulness. It indicates that God is a God of fertility, but not in the distorted sense prevalent among idolatrous nations. The title was relevant to God's original intention to bless mankind, and for his mandate to newly created men and women to be fruitful and increase in number (1:28). It would be very encouraging and assuring to the ears of Abram (and to the ears of discouraged readers in exile).

Abram spontaneously fell face down before God in reverent submission. God announced his own covenant commitments (v 4-8). He said, "*As for me, my covenant is with you*". He called it "*my covenant*", a phrase repeated 9 times. It was God's covenant, which he initiated, and which only he could fulfil. It depended on God, not Abram. It was not a conditional covenant, but a solid commitment by God to do what he promised.

At the heart of God's covenant was his promise that Abram would be the father of many nations. To underscore that promise, his name from now on would be "*Abraham*" (which means "Father of many"), and it was an accomplished fact ("*for I have made you a father of many nations*"), even though the guaranteed heir had still not been born. God insisted that he would establish his covenant with Abram and his descendants as an "*everlasting covenant*" (v 7), and that the whole land of Canaan would be an "*everlasting possession*" to them (v 8). He guaranteed his commitment with a strong affirmation that he would be their God.

God set out Abram's responsibility in return (v 9-14). He said, "*As for you, you must keep my covenant, you and your descendants after you for the generations to come*". Yet all Abraham had to do was to ensure that he and all males in his household were circumcised. Abraham did not contribute anything to the covenant, other than actively acknowledge his acceptance of his privileged partnership. The covenant was one-sided, in which God was the provider, and Abraham the receiver. Circumcision was not an unknown practice in the ancient world. But for Abraham it now took on special meaning as a sign of the covenant. Perhaps it was an appropriate reminder that procreation was a matter of God's will, not man's. For Abraham to obey and carry out this requirement, he would be consciously expressing his faith that God would even yet produce the promised son who was still not born.

Not only was Abraham's name changed, but so too was his wife's, from "Sarai" to "Sarah" (v 15-16). There was no change of meaning in the name, but the alternative spelling marked the occasion when, for the first time, she was announced as the mother of the son to be born, and of future nations and kings. God was only progressively disclosing details relating to his promise as it suited his timing.

Abraham's immediate response to these new revelations was mixed (v 17-18). Once more he fell prostrate before God in humble reverence. But he also laughed inwardly to himself in delighted amazement at the prospect of him and Sarah producing a son at their age. At the same time, he expressed the desire that Ishmael might be included in God's purpose of blessing. This was an understandable and natural desire, yet it showed that Abraham was still inclined to see things from his own human perspective. He was not governed solely by God's purpose and promise.

God's reply emphasised his determined purpose (v 19-22). He affirmed that Sarah would indeed bear a son, whose name would be Isaac (meaning "Laughter", reflecting Abraham's delighted response). He declared his intention of establishing his covenant through Isaac, and that it would be an everlasting covenant for the sake of Isaac's descendants. At the same time, he acknowledged Abraham's desire for Ishmael, and agreed to bless him and make him into a great nation. This generous response was very revealing, showing God's compassionate nature, his considerate attitude towards his covenant servant, and his willingness to accommodate human mistakes as he advanced his own purposes in human affairs. Yet he repeated his insistence that his covenant was with Isaac, whom he now announced would be born in a year's time. This was the first time that a date for the child's birth was given, and the prediction at this time would confirm the divine enabling of the birth when it occurred.

Abraham's obedience was prompt and total (v 23-27). On the same day as God had commanded him to keep the covenant by being circumcised, he did so. All the males in the household, including Abraham himself, his son Ishmael, and all his servants whether born in his company or bought by his money, were circumcised immediately.

Another significant experience occurred at this time which confirmed and strengthened the LORD's covenant relationship with Abraham (chapters 18-19). Abraham received three guests at the entrance to his tent and provided them hospitality (18:1-8). One of the guests was an appearance of the LORD, and the other two were angels. The occasion of fellowship illustrated the friendly relationship Abraham enjoyed with the LORD, who took the opportunity to disclose two vital pieces of information. He firstly confirmed that he would enable Sarah to give birth to a son in a year's time (v 9-15), and, secondly, indicated that he intended to investigate and take action against Sodom because of its terrible sin (v 16-21).

The LORD's announcement to Abraham of his intentions concerning the cities of Sodom and Gomorrah was profoundly significant. In the first place, the fact that the LORD confided in Abraham demonstrated his intimate privileged relationship as the LORD's friend (v 17). Secondly, the LORD indicated that Abraham needed to be informed because of the role the LORD had chosen for him (v 18-19). Abraham was destined to become a powerful nation which would be a source of blessing for all other nations on earth, because he would ensure that his household would keep the way of the LORD. For this reason, the LORD informed him of his intentions (v 20-21). Because there was an outcry against the two cities whose sin was so grievous, the LORD intended to investigate to learn for himself. His comment did not imply his ignorance, but was figurative description to emphasise his personal, direct involvement.

The outcry was mentioned twice, for emphasis. Actually, two different terms were used, but meant basically the same, a cry of distress for help. The scene was reminiscent of the days of Enosh (4:26), although different language was used, and there was no explicit mention of "calling on the name of the LORD". It was also reminiscent of a later period which Israelite readers would immediately recognise, where the same terms are used (Exodus 2:23). An emerging pattern can be discerned, where the build-up of oppressive evil producing an outcry of distress prompted a response from the LORD.

The announcement moved Abraham to intercede for the condemned city (v 22-33). This was a notable action, and provided insight into both Abraham's covenant role, and into the purpose of prayer. Although terms for "prayer" do not appear, the description of the experience helpfully illustrated important aspects involved in the activity of intercession.

The passage comments that *"Abraham remained standing before the LORD"* (v 22). He was very conscious of being in the presence of God.

"Then Abraham approached him" (v 23). In bold confidence and intimacy, he drew closer. He was not being arrogant, nor intimidated, but definite and forthright. His relationship with God was natural and open, and familiar.

There was consternation in his question about whether God would sweep away the righteous with the wicked (v 23-25). He was concerned about the injustice of such an action, and its incompatibility with his conviction that the Judge of all the earth would do right. He appealed for God to spare the city if fifty righteous people could be found in it. God responded to his plea, and agreed to spare the city for the sake of fifty righteous people (v 26).

That began a bargaining process as Abraham humbly yet persistently prevailed upon God to spare the city for the sake of ever reducing numbers of righteous people being present, until he reached only ten (v 27-32). Even then God agreed to his request. God then ended the conversation and left (v 33).

Bargaining was a common practice in the ancient world, as people haggled in trade and social agreements. Abraham's bargaining was typical in style, but different in motivation and principle. He was not seeking his own interests, but God's. He was interceding, in line with God's character and God's purpose. We should note that Abraham does not mention his nephew Lot. He was concerned about God's justice and the security of the righteous, not simply the rescue of his relatives.

As it turned out, God did not spare the city, presumably because there were not ten righteous citizens residing there. Yet he did provide opportunity for Lot and his family to be spared (chapter 19). Only Lot and his two daughters benefited from the opportunity by obeying instructions, while his wife and sons-in-law perished because they disobeyed.

The whole episode highlights two important matters. Firstly, God chose Abraham to be his covenant partner, with the promise to bless him, and through him to bless the world. There was nothing Abraham could do to accomplish that promise, other than to trust and obey God. Secondly, Abraham's privileged relationship with God provided him the opportunity to intercede before God, the divine Judge, concerning his rule over human affairs. He could appeal to God's justice and mercy, because of God's revealed character.

It is surprising that explicit mention of the term "prayer" in Genesis was rare. It only occurs twice in all of the book, and even then two separate terms are used. Yet these references were very instructive. The first occurrence (20:7, 17) used a term which means "intercede" and described a role which Abraham performed in his capacity as a "prophet". The second occurrence used a term which meant "entreat", and appeared later in connection with Isaac (25:21).

Motivated by self-preservation, Abraham was responsible for causing a dangerous situation to arise (20:1-18). He was repeating his failure of a previous occasion (12:10-20), as we noted earlier. He exposed his wife Sarah to moral risk, and a local king of Gerar, Abimelech, to the risk of divine judgement. Although Abraham was the cause of the problem, and Abimelech had acted in good faith and with a clear conscience, God instructed Abimelech to seek Abraham's help in prayer to resolve it.

> *"Now return the man's wife, for he is a prophet, and he will pray for you and you will live. But if you do not return her, you may be sure that you and all yours will die"* (v 7)

The incident was significant, because Abraham had placed God's own cause in jeopardy. It is apparent (v 18) that the incident involved a substantial period of time. God used circumstances and special intervention (v 3) to prevent Abimelech from unwittingly compromising Sarah, and warned him of the dire consequences if he continued with his intentions to take Sarah for himself. Once he had become aware of Abraham's role, and Sarah's true relationship to Abraham, he would be guilty of opposing God's chosen servant. His immediate and extravagant God-fearing response disproved Abraham's misplaced fear (v 11), and his honourable compensation exposed Abraham's craven self-protectiveness. It is obvious that Abraham behaved poorly. Yet it was God's purpose which was at stake, and this did not depend on Abraham's character, but his appointed role. His intercessory prayer, which he previously showed was a feature of "calling on the name of the LORD" (13:4), was pivotal in resolving the problem. His intercession was effective because it was in accord with God's purposes and his own privileged role as partner with God in regard to those purposes.

"Then Abraham prayed to God, and God healed Abimelech, his wife and his slave girls so they could have children again, …" (v 17)

This was the first mention of anyone as a prophet, and implied that Abraham had a special relationship with God. He was able to act as a mediator between God and other people, speaking to people for God, and speaking to God for people. These early experiences in Abraham's life illustrated the privileged relationship he enjoyed with God which shaped his role in terms of God's purposes. On the one hand he received revelation from God, and in response he pleaded for God's revealed will to be accomplished. He was a prophet and pray-er. Fundamental to the nature of prayer was to call on the name of the LORD. This was an orientation of life devoted to worship God as the Creator King and to appeal for him to fulfil his intentions of restoring the world to a state of blessing. It especially involved intercession within the framework of God's own covenant purpose.

Abraham's intercession for Sodom and Gomorrah, and for Abimelech of Gerar, followed the visit of the LORD with his two angels at Mamre (which was at Hebron), during the one year period immediately prior to the birth of Isaac. This highlighted Abraham's appointed role. God's own role was to accomplish his purpose of grace and fulfil his promise. Sarah became pregnant and bore a son (21:1-21). It was at the very time God promised, and he was called Isaac as stipulated. Abraham was a hundred years old, and he circumcised the boy on the eighth day. All the promised and agreed details were fulfilled exactly, and laughter filled Sarah's life. However, her pleasure was overshadowed by the presence and attitude of Hagar's son. She was opposed to him having any share in Isaac's inheritance, and she pressed Abraham to send him away. Although Abraham was distressed to lose his son, God persuaded him to comply, because God's own purpose was to be through Isaac's line. At the same time, God assured Abraham that Ishmael would also develop into a great nation because he too was Abraham's son. Hagar and her son were sent off into the desert, where God took special care of them, and was with the lad as he matured into manhood.

There was a third occasion when it was said that Abraham *"called upon the name of the LORD"* (21:33). The previous two occasions were while he was at Bethel. This time it was while Abraham was living at a place which he named Beersheba (21:22-34). The impression given in the story was that this was Abraham's continuous practice, not just a once off incident. The reference occurred after records of the birth of Isaac, separation from Ishmael, and formation of a treaty with Philistine neighbours to secure his settlement in the area. The name Beersheba (which means "well of oath", or "well of seven") was given to a well to mark the treaty oath and/or Abraham's gift of seven lambs to the Philistine king Abimelech. It was a lengthy period of time during which God's covenant promise to Abraham was being fulfilled and protected from all threats. As an old man Abraham had learnt that God was faithful to his promise, but patient in bringing it to fruition. God's covenant with him was *"everlasting"*

(17:7, 13, 19), and this was because, he realised, God was the *"Everlasting God"* (21:33) upon whose name he called. This was the second occasion the term "El" was used for God, emphasising his power as well as his eternal existence. He was the "Everlasting Mighty God".

This third reference to Abraham calling on the name of the LORD was a description of the nature of his lifestyle. He was conspicuous for his worshipful, prayerful devotion to God focussed on God's covenant purpose for his life.

In due course his trust in God and loyalty to the covenant were put to supreme test when he was asked to offer up Isaac in sacrifice (22:1-19). He passed the test with flying colours because he had matured as a man who called upon the name of the LORD! Without raising a single question, and the abhorrent request would prompt many, he set off to obey. He revealed his confidence in God by declaring to his servants, *"We will come back to you"* (v 5), and to his son, *"God himself will provide the lamb for the burnt offering, my son"* (v 8). Abraham was saying much more than he realised, and unwittingly was providing a prophetic glimpse of the end of the story which he was beginning. A substitute lamb would figure prominently in the rescue of Israel from bondage in Egypt (Exodus 12). The New Testament presents Jesus as the *"Lamb of God who takes away the sin of the world"* (John 1:29).

While Abraham was living at Beersheba, Sarah, apparently living at Kiriath Arba (Hebron), died at the age of a hundred and twenty seven. Abraham purchased the cave of Machpelah as a burial site for her. It was the only territory in the land of Canaan which Abraham ever owned, and where in turn he, and Isaac, and Jacob would also be buried.

After the death and burial of Sarah, Abraham commissioned his chief servant by solemn oath to return to his home country and family to obtain a wife for Isaac (24:1-66). Apart from the story of Abraham's intercession for Sodom and Gomorrah (chapters 18-19), it is the longest story in Genesis, indicating its importance. The servant was faithful to his task, and relied prayerfully on the God of Abraham to give success to his mission. Mention of his prayer twice in the story (v 10-15, 42-45) highlights it as the prominent and significant feature. Actually the term "prayer" does not occur (contrary to English translations), although it is obvious that the idea of prayer was intended when it said that the servant spoke to God in his heart (v 45).

What the story depicted was "entreaty". The servant appealed to the God of his master Abraham, and entreated him in accord with God's own purpose to provide success for his mission and to show kindness to his master. And God did. The servant was led directly to Rebekah, who willingly agreed to become Isaac's wife. The story is a clear picture of the nature of true prayer. It also explained the motivation for Isaac's persistent prayer of entreaty for that same Rebekah because she was barren (25:21). Her situation was a threat to God's promise of descendants. The description of the servant's prayer illustrated the nature of Isaac's later entreaty.

"*The Account of Terah*", which traced the events of God's dealings with Abraham, concluded with Abraham's death and burial (25:1-11). Mention was made of Abraham's second wife, Keturah, and her six sons which she bore to him. It is not clear whether this was while Sarah was still living or after her death. Various people groups descended from these sons. As offspring of Abraham, they were part of the fulfilment of God's promise of a large progeny to Abraham (13:16). Abraham gave these sons gifts and sent them on their way, but inheritance of all his possessions was left to Isaac. He died at the age of a hundred and seventy five years, and was buried by Isaac and Ishmael in the cave of Machpelah (at Hebron) beside Sarah. The narrative ended with the observation that after Abraham's death "*God blessed his son Isaac*".

Isaac the Petitioner

The second occurrence of "prayed" in Genesis uses a term which means "entreat" to describe Isaac's prayer for his barren wife Rebekah (25:19-26). The term expressed what was demonstrated by Abraham's servant when he was led to Rebekah. Isaac's prayer was effective, and Rebekah became pregnant.

> "*Isaac prayed to the LORD on behalf of his wife, because she was barren. The LORD answered his prayer, and his wife Rebekah became pregnant.*"

Since God's purposes required Isaac to have offspring, it is clear that this mention of prayer indicated its importance in the scheme of things. This was all the more so when we see that little else is told about Isaac, and that what is mentioned shows him to be rather pathetic and self-indulgent. Neither must we overlook the stated details that Isaac was forty years old when he married Rebekah, and sixty when she gave birth to her twin sons (25:20, 26). Isaac had been entreating God for his wife, in accord with God's own desires, for nearly twenty years! Prayer is effective, but not necessarily instantaneous. It is a vital feature in God's plan, which also includes other factors in his complex scheme.

The two explicit references to prayer, by Abraham (20:7, 17) and Isaac (25:21), show that prayer is not incidental to the progress of God's purpose, but crucial. They also came in the context of a broader narrative which vividly depicted the vitality of prayer, not by explicit terms, but by graphic activity.

Rebekah eventually became pregnant with twins who jostled one another in her womb. Puzzled and anxious by what was happening to her, Rebekah went to enquire about it of the LORD (25:22). She learned that her two sons would be fathers of two separate, opposing nations, and the older would serve the younger. Her pregnancy troubles, after all the years of prayerful entreaty, were not a threat to God's promise of offspring, but related to the outworking of God's purpose through them. There is no explanation about how she enquired, or how she was answered, only the revelation given to her. Yet her experience demonstrated the importance and effectiveness of prayerful dependence on God with regard to cooperating with God in accomplishing his will.

A famine in the land was the reason for Isaac's move to Gerar. Like his father before him, it seems that he intended to travel on to Egypt (contrary to God's will). God personally appeared to him and forbade him to enter Egypt, yet he stayed in Gerar. There he repeated the mistake of his father (chapter 20), by intimating that his wife Rebekah was his sister in order to protect himself. When his deceit was exposed, king Abimelech ordered that he not be molested, and he settled down in the land. He prospered greatly, but had to keep moving to new locations because the local Philistines were jealous and hostile. At last he went up to Beersheba where God appeared to him *"that night"*. He confirmed for him the covenant promise made to Abraham. While he was out of the land he was out of God's will. But now he was where God wanted him to be. In response, Isaac built an altar and *"called on the name of the LORD"* (26:25). Abraham had previously done the same in that same location.

Not only did Isaac realise that God intended to bless him, in accord with his purpose disclosed to Abraham, but the Philistines also recognised God's hand upon him. Abimelech, with his advisor and military commander, came from Gerar to make a peace treaty with Isaac, that he might not do them any harm. Just as Abraham before him had done with an earlier Abimelech (probably his title rather than name, meaning "my father is king"), Isaac agreed to the treaty, and confirmed it by naming a new well "Beersheba".

Jacob the Pleader

When the twin boys were born, they were given names which reflected conspicuous characteristics which they displayed. The firstborn was red and hairy, and received the name Esau. Perhaps Esau means hairy, since he was also known as Edom which means red. His brother was grasping Esau's heel when they were born, an action which figuratively implied deceptive behaviour, so he was named Jacob which carried that connotation.

The twin boys grew up to be very different from one another. Esau was a skilled hunter and preferred the outdoors. Jacob was quiet and stayed around the tents. They were a cause for polarising their parents, with Isaac loving Esau, because Isaac was fond of wild game (!), and Rebekah preferring Jacob. The simple detail about Isaac's food tastes was an eloquent illumination of his self-indulgent sensuous nature. Esau was like his father in that regard. A revealing incident became the occasion for opportunistic Jacob to take advantage of Esau's basic craving for food and acquire his birthright. Esau's preference for an immediate meal and disregard for his birthright prompted the damning conclusion, "*So Esau despised his birthright*" (25:34).

Jacob's first encounter with God was while he was journeying towards his mother's family in Haran in search of a wife. In contrast to the prayerful enterprise undertaken by Abraham's servant in successfully finding Rebekah for Isaac, their son was travelling alone, a virtual fugitive, fleeing from the domestic distress of his brother's fury and parent's anguish which his devious actions had caused. He had tricked his elderly father into bestowing the blessing intended for Esau upon himself. Guided by Rebekah his mother, Jacob deceived Isaac by fooling him on the level of his natural senses. He brought him a meal to taste, took advantage of his blindness, relied on his touch and smell of hairy skins worn to give the impression that he was Esau, to avoid being identified by the sound of his voice. Isaac's pronounced blessing assured Jacob of status, privilege, and prosperity. When Esau learned what Jacob had done, he was furious. His anger smouldered for a long time, and he harboured plans to kill Jacob once his father died. Rebekah urged Jacob to flee to her brother's home, and persuaded Isaac to send him in search of a wife who was not from among the local Hittites. Notably, Isaac expressed the prayerful wish that "*El Shaddai*" (the "Mighty God of Nurturing") would bless him and make him fruitful (28:3).

Jacob's experience of God was by means of a dream, consisting of a stairway (probably a ziggurat) reaching from earth to heaven on which angels were ascending and descending, and above which stood the LORD. The dream vividly suggested there was a distance between the realm where humans lived and the realm where God was, but not beyond being bridged so that communication could occur between them. In fact, in the dream God spoke directly to Jacob, identifying himself as the God of Abraham and Isaac, and declaring that the covenant promises made to Abraham and Isaac were to be continued with him and his descendants. He assured him of his constant personal presence and protection until all was accomplished.

The dream was so awe-inspiring it convinced Jacob that he was actually in the presence of God, and he called the place "*Bethel*", which meant "House of God". He marked the site, and the event, by setting up as a pillar the stone which had served as his pillow during the night. He made a vow to acknowledge the LORD as his God and to dedicate to him a tenth of all that he acquired as God prospered him. Jacob was vowing to serve God as the Creator King of heaven and earth, in response to God's kingly promise to fulfil his intentions of blessing the peoples of the world through him.

The place where this occurred was in the vicinity of the location where God had previously appeared to Abraham and inspired him to erect an altar and call upon the name of the LORD (12:8, 13:3-4). Although different aspects were described, Jacob's response to God's appearance to him, and choice of him to be his human partner in his divine enterprise to restore the world to the blessing of his kingship, was essentially the same as that of Abraham.

Despite his experience and vows Jacob still had a long way to go before his disposition matched his declarations. Though he had outwardly acknowledged God and his purposes, inwardly he remained self-determined and unsubdued. Over the next twenty years his life was marked by hassles and hostility, frustration and disappointment, yet extraordinary prosperity. He was cheated by his father-in-law Laban, and distressed by the sibling rivalry between his two wives Leah and Rachel. He experienced for himself what he had once expressed towards others. He resorted to superstitious tactics when it came to breeding his flocks, and succeeded anyway. He was fruitful both with his own offspring and with flocks. Whatever he touched prospered. Through these experiences God was patiently cultivating his inner spirit.

Although there is no explicit mention of Jacob engaging in prayer during these years of growing prosperity, we gain a brief glimpse of a background of prayer behind the birth of Jacob's children. The litany of their births is provided in Genesis 29:31-30:24, and was depicted in terms of intense jealous rivalry between Jacob's wives Leah and Rachel, as the two sisters vied for their husband's affections. At the same time the births were attributed to the LORD's overriding enabling. It was even indicated at one stage that "*God listened to Leah*" (30:17), clearly implying her prayerful request for God to assist her to become pregnant, similar to Isaac's prayer for his wife Rebekah (25:21).

When Jacob desired to return home (30:25), he was persuaded to stay longer by Laban who realised that God was blessing Jacob, and he wanted to profit from it. Instead, Laban experienced loss through Jacob's gain, causing his attitude to turn against Jacob. Then God himself advised Jacob to return home, with the assurance that he would be with him, reminding him of his earlier vow at Bethel (31:3, 10-13). Jacob recognised God's touch on his life, yet still relied on his own resourcefulness, and resorted to his old tricks by trying to steal away deceptively. Laban however learned of his flight and pursued him. God intervened to ensure Jacob's safety from Laban, and eventually the two men parted on amicable terms based on a formal covenant established between them in the name of God (31:51-55). As Jacob resumed his journey with his family and flocks he was met by the angels of God, yet another reminder of his experience at Bethel, and an assurance that alongside his own camp was the *"camp of God"*. So he called the place *"Mahanaim"* ("Two Camps", 32:1-2).

Jacob then had to face his brother Esau whom he had wronged, and whom he feared. Again he acted out of his own sufficiency. He adopted elaborate measures to ameliorate Esau when he anticipated meeting him. He sent messengers ahead to prepare Esau for his coming. He divided his company into his own two *"camps"* with the idea that at least one group might avoid Esau's assault. He entreated God for protection on the basis of God's former relationship with Abraham and Isaac, and his commitment to prosper Jacob and his descendants. (The "account", 32:9, is translated *"Jacob prayed"*, but is literally *"Jacob said"*, and the content of what he said was an entreaty). He also sent herds of sheep, goats, camels, cattle, and donkeys ahead as extravagant gifts for Esau. Finally, he sent his family and possessions ahead, while he remained alone. This became another occasion, like at Bethel earlier, when God intruded into his state of solitude. Jacob spent an eventful night wrestling with God (32:22-32), and when it was over, and Esau arrived, all his anxiety and efforts were unnecessary. Esau accepted him generously, and without any hostility.

Jacob's wrestle with an opponent in the night was pivotal. All his life Jacob had been contending with those around him in order to prevail over them. Now before returning home he met God who contended with him. An unidentified man wrestled with "Jacob" near the river "Jabbok" (a play on words). The physical struggle gave tangible expression to the inner struggle of his spirit which asserted its independence, resistance, and self-determination. Their struggle lasted until daybreak because Jacob refused to yield, so the man finally disabled him to subdue him, and then sought to leave. But Jacob clung on refusing to let him go until the man blessed him. No longer struggling and resisting, Jacob was now tenaciously pleading for his mysterious assailant's goodwill. The man asked Jacob his name, and then declared that from now on it would be "Israel" ("God struggles"). The night of wrestling and the name change reflected the struggles which characterised Jacob's life, and the forcible manner in which God subdued him. Now Jacob requested the man to tell him his name, but in reply was asked why he asked. This probably meant that it should have been obvious to Jacob who his opponent was. There and then the man blessed him, and Jacob acknowledged that he had seen God *"face to face"*. He called the place *"Peniel"* (*"Face of God"*) just as he had given the name *"Bethel"* to the place of his original encounter with God.

This dramatic incident demonstrated the crucial need for an inner disposition of submission to God's prevailing supremacy, power, and purpose. Such a disposition is what is needed by those who will live their lives humbly and prayerfully calling upon the name of the LORD. The three founding fathers of God's specially chosen people, responding to God's gracious intrusions into their lives, matured in their faith and devotion, orientating their lives around consciousness of him and his purposes.

Following his momentous experience with his divine opponent in the night, and subsequent peaceful encounter with Esau, Jacob then had a set-back. He returned to Canaan and camped near the city of Shechem, on a plot of land which he purchased, where he also erected an altar which he called "*El is the God of Israel*". He was apparently acting in response to his recent experience, conscious of God's mighty power (calling him "El") and his own new name ("Israel"). However, disastrous circumstances struck Jacob and his family through association with the citizens of Shechem (chapter 34). Both the local citizens, under the leadership of Shechem (who seems to have been named after the city), and the sons of Jacob, behaved in appalling ways. Shechem sexually assaulted Dinah, Jacob's only daughter. Her brothers retaliated by massacring the men of the city, under the guise of welcoming them into their covenant family by requiring their circumcision. Jacob was passive in reaction to the violation of his daughter, and concerned only for his own reputation and safety as a consequence of his sons' slaughter and pillage of the citizens of Shechem. God told Jacob to go to Bethel, and build an altar there (in order to *"call on the name of the LORD"*?).

Jacob appealed to his household to dispose of their foreign gods, and to join him in his move to Bethel. They buried their gods and charms under the prominent oak tree at Shechem, and travelled to Bethel, protected from the surrounding population by the *"terror of God"*. This divinely imposed fear which restrained the Canaanites from harming Jacob's family was undeserved. Jacob erected an altar at Bethel, and called the place *"El Bethel"* ("Mighty *God of Bethel"*). Deborah, the aged nurse of his mother, Rebekah, died and was buried there. God again appeared to him and renewed his change of name to "Israel". He identified himself as *"El Shaddai"* (the "Mighty God of Nurturing"), and confirmed his guarantee of Jacob's fruitfulness. Even though Jacob was already father of a large family, his fruitfulness was now assured in terms of his future posterity. The language used echoes God's original creation mandate (1:28), showing that he was still pursuing his original purpose. He also confirmed his promise made to Abraham and Isaac by guaranteeing the gift of the land to Jacob, and to his descendants. Jacob responded by erecting a pillar there, pouring a drink offering and oil upon it, and again calling the place Bethel. His life had gone full circle.

Yet life was marked by sorrows. While travelling on from Bethel, Jacob's wife, Rachel, died in childbirth when giving birth to her second son, Benjamin. Rachel was buried on the way to Ephrath, an early name for Bethlehem. Soon afterwards, the eldest son Reuben slept with his father's concubine, who was Rachel's maidservant, Bilhah. This was a premature, and brazen, claim of his rights as the firstborn. The only comment made was the ominous *"Israel* (Jacob's new name) *heard of it"*. His conduct was not forgotten (49:3-4). His rightful role as leader was ineffective (37:21-22), and eventually displaced by Judah. At last Jacob reached the home of his father Isaac at Mamre, near Hebron. In due course Isaac died, at the age of 180, and his sons Esau and Jacob buried him.

Joseph The Dream Interpreter

The story of Joseph was the final stage of the Genesis narrative. A fascinating change comes over this final *"account"* in Genesis. God disappears! Well, that is not strictly so, but certainly his overt activity is conspicuously reduced. For example, nowhere throughout this *"account"* does God directly speak to anyone or engage with anyone as he did in earlier stages of the story. Similarly, the name of God, the *"LORD"*, occurs much less frequently, only appearing in several clusters (38: 7, 10; 39:2, 3, 5; 21, 23; 49:18). Instead, he is simply indicated by the term *"God"* (*"Elohim"*). Even then, that term only crops up 36 times, in 13 chapters! Compare that with the beginning of Genesis, where the term *"God"* occurred 35 times in only 34 verses (1:1-2:3). It is obvious that the drama has changed its setting. On the other hand, God was still the lead actor, except that he remained hidden. His presence and activity were manifest by uncanny providential circumstances. The different clusters of references to the "*LORD*" highlight that. The deaths of Er and Onan in the grubby affair of Judah's treatment of Tamar, threatening Judah's lineage, were attributed to the LORD's doing (38:6-10). Similarly, Joseph's success in the home of Potiphar (39:2-5) and in prison (39:20-23) was attributed to the LORD. Joseph also interpreted Pharaoh's dream as an indirect revelation from God, needing to be discerned (41:16, 25, 28, 32, 38). The whole experience of Joseph in Egypt, and the eventual outcome which saw all Jacob's family relocate to Egypt, give the impression of an overriding providential influence. God's divine orchestration of events was not stated, but implied.

When we look at this part of the story for helpful insights concerning prayer, we find no references to such activity, except for an appeal for deliverance by Jacob in the course of his pronouncements about the future of his sons (49:18). Actually, this was quite a significant prayer. It was the only situation when God was directly addressed. He was called "LORD", which was the final occasion in Genesis where that name appeared. It came between Jacob's pronouncements concerning his sons Dan and Gad, both of whom he said would be violent, snapping at the heels of their opponents (49:17, 19). This imagery recalls God's verdict in the Garden on the serpent which would attack the heels of the woman's offspring. It also recalls his own name, Jacob, which meant "grasping the heel". This prayer for deliverance was prompted by awareness of his own tendencies and those of his sons and the surrounding world. It was reminiscent of the days of Enosh when men called on the name of the LORD.

We have already noticed that there were not any appearances of God to Joseph as there were with Abraham, Isaac, and Jacob. Theirs were out of the ordinary experiences because they were chosen for special roles in God's kingdom purposes. Nevertheless, Joseph also had a special role, as the one by which the family of Jacob and his sons, migrated to Egypt. In the early stages of God's covenant purposes with his chosen founding fathers, Abraham, Isaac, and Jacob, God discouraged them from leaving Canaan the land of promise. Now, however, a new phase in God's purposes was reached, and through Joseph the whole expanded family was led into Egypt. Although there were no reported direct interactions between God and Joseph, there were two conspicuous features relating to Joseph's experience of God.

Firstly, God governs the affairs of life and the world. Joseph's personal prosperity was attributed to God, and Joseph himself testified that all his circumstances of life, both adverse and prosperous, were intended by God for a larger purpose, to save lives and to preserve his special family (God's rescue plan). Having such a confident view of God enabled Joseph to endure injustice and hardship, to remain upright in character and loyal in devotion, and to help his brothers face up to the responsibility of their guilty treatment of him, while graciously forgiving them.

Secondly, God reveals insights to guide his people. He does this with Joseph through dreams. Joseph had personal dreams about his own future destiny (37:1-11) which probably sustained his hopes during the years of rejection and harsh ordeals. He certainly recalled them when they came to fruition (42:9). His fellow prison inmates had dreams which God enabled Joseph to interpret (40:1-23), giving him a reputation which eventually brought him to the attention of the Pharaoh. Similarly, he was able to interpret dreams of Pharaoh (41:1-40), catapulting him into a position of high authority in Egypt where he was able to serve God's purposes.

While nothing is said about Joseph praying, these two perspectives, concerning God's rule over the world and his guiding revelation, are fundamental for living as someone who calls upon the name of God, which essentially includes the activity of prayer.

There are two more references to God as "El Shaddai". Both are on the lips of Jacob. One was when Joseph brought his sons Ephraim and Manasseh to meet him (48:3). Jacob told Joseph that "El Shaddai" had appeared to him at Luz (Bethel) and blessed him, with the promise of becoming fruitful with increased descendants. This was a clear indication of the meaning of "Shaddai" in terms of nourishing offspring. He then informed Joseph that Ephraim and Manasseh would be numbered among his children, and he blessed them, prophetically reversing their order of prominence in regard to their ages.

The second occasion was when Jacob was making prophetic pronouncements about his sons, and was speaking about Joseph (49:25). He was telling about Joseph being a fruitful vine. He talked figuratively about bitter archers shooting at him with hostility, but Joseph holding his own bow steady because God was with him. Specifically, he said,

"... because of the hand of the Mighty One of Jacob, because of the Shepherd, the Rock of Israel, because of your father's God who helps you, because of the "Almighty" ("Shaddai"), who blesses you with blessings of the heavens above, blessings of the deep that lies below, blessings of the breasts ("shadayim") and womb."

These final references to "El Shaddai" in Genesis colourfully draw out the imagery of God being the source and sustainer of bountiful blessings, and the guarantee of fruitful posterity. As *"El Shaddai"* he had promised Abram a son and many descendants, and changed his name to Abraham in anticipation. Now he was Jacob's hope of such satisfying blessings continuing.

The end of Genesis is not the end of the story. We are left in suspense, aware of God the Creator King pursuing his promise to bless the nations, and his divinely-favoured extended family relocated to a foreign land. The next phase of God's plan is stunning.

CHAPTER 3

THE DIVINE SAGA

The story of Israel's dramatic liberation from slavery in Egypt, extraordinary experiences at Mount Sinai and in the wilderness, and eventual conquest of Canaan and settlement in the Promised Land, is told in spectacular fashion. It is not history to inform, but saga to inspire.

These events were pivotal for God's strategy for human history. The Creator King was intruding into world affairs to establish Israel as a unique nation in a special covenant relationship with himself to be his holy kingdom. God's presence and actions were pretty dramatic. He burst into the world, confronting rulers and armies, evoking awe and terror, performing supernatural signs and wonders, and establishing an astonishing political kingdom unlike anything heard of before or since. It all happened with remarkable speed. From being an oppressed and powerless sub-cultural group in a small area of the land of the mighty pharaohs, the tribes of Israel were liberated by a display of supernatural power which humbled Egyptian forces. They were then constituted as a nation under the living God as their king. For forty years God camped amongst his people in the wilderness, and then led them into the Promised Land, overpowering their enemies and allocating territorial heritages to every family. The story is mind-blowing. Although the person of Moses looms large across the scenes of that period, and his successor Joshua proves to be a formidable leader, the more dominant character is God himself. He is the regal presence who commands attention, and his authority, power, and holiness are awesome.

The literary presentation of this remarkable episode is primarily about God, and the historic events are backdrop. The presentation includes a series of various books composed in creative formats and styles. The books were not presenting history, but historical "saga" in the form of an epic drama, building on the legend of Israel's sensational beginnings. The literary format portrays the actual events in a grandiose manner in order to unveil the higher realities involved. The underlying bulk of Exodus-Leviticus-Numbers, and Deuteronomy, was probably the written work of Moses. However, an overriding editorial hand from a much later era is evident in the completed books. The book of Joshua bears a similar dramatic style. The books present the legend of Israel's redemption from bondage in Egypt, covenant formation at Sinai, forty years experience in the desert, and taking possession of the Promised Land in an aggrandised manner to highlight the full significance of God's role in it. From a general point of view, there may have been little to notice about a small company of fugitives taking occupancy in the land of Canaan. But in reality, something stupendous was taking place in history. The books were written in a manner to magnify that reality. They reveal a divine hand at work, which is awe-inspiring. The story has been embellished by a variety of literary techniques. The presentation of events is skilfully designed in its overall outline to make maximum impact. The books contain different styles and emphases, and the narrative includes innuendo, hyperbole, suspense, sensational events, pathos, verbatim conversations, divine activity, and powerful emotional scenes. The presentation is a block-buster! Ideal for Hollywood! Take a closer look at each book, to recognise its saga style, and to learn what it reveals about the place of prayer.

A Kingdom of Priests

The book of Exodus tells the dramatic story of how God liberated Israel from bondage in Egypt and led the people across the desert to Mount Sinai where he established his covenant with them, and then gave instructions for the erection of a tabernacle in which he himself lived at the centre of the new nation's camp. God's covenant with Israel set them apart from all other nations as his *"treasured possession"* (19:5). Although the whole earth belonged to God, Israel would be for him a *"kingdom of priests and a holy nation"* (19:6).

Exodus contains many curiosities and some very creative script writing. Let me highlight some important features, and draw your attention to incidents of prayer.

Why was there reference to the arrival of a new king of Egypt (1:8), and to his daughter (2:5), who both were highly influential in the events which unfolded, yet neither was named? These omissions are more curious when we consider that the names of the midwives were given (1:15)! The king is usually called Pharaoh, which is a title rather than a name. It means "Great house", and originally applied to Egypt's national realm. It was not until after about 1200 BCE, when Israel was already settled in the Promised Land, that this title was applied to the nation's ruler. Exodus was using the term anachronistically. Arguments can be made for identifying the king as either Rameses II (1290-1225 BCE) or Amenhotep II (1447-1421 BCE) whose daughter Hatshepsut later became a formidable ruling queen (1501-1479 BCE). Yet such proposals are only speculation, because there is insufficient information to go on. The fact is, Exodus has intentionally avoided being locked into a specific time setting. The events were deliberately lifted out of their historical period to give them a sense of timelessness. This was because the narrative was presenting God, not history, and so that every generation of Israel was included by way of solidarity with the original liberated nation as beneficiaries of the divine saga. Instructions for the festival of Passover (12:14-28) provide the key for recognising this concept.

We could ask why there is no inscriptional or archaeological evidence of Israel's presence in Egypt, or escape from Egypt, when there is a rich abundance of information about ancient Egypt's military, trade, and political activities? There are tantalising references to migration groups, military skirmishes, and construction projects which validate the general historicity of Israel's story, but just no mention of Moses or Israel. Exodus does not enlighten us about that, but it does bear witness to Israel's origins in Egypt, and presents its exodus as a sensational achievement by the "*hand*" of God (7:4-5). Exodus is primarily about God, so his impressive exploits are magnified to indicate their divine significance, not to report their historical spectacle.

Why were there only two midwives for such a large population (1:15), unless the original community was not actually as numerous as the impression given? The company which fled from Egypt was said to have numbered 600,000 men, plus women and children, as well as many others who joined them, together with large droves of livestock (12:37). They would be a company of more than two million. That would be a very large community, too large to be realistic, and they left no confirming archaeological footprint. Biblical numbers are notoriously difficult, because they are not always used for precision, but for conveying ideas. 600,000 could mean 600 military units, or include later generations to indicate national solidarity. Probably both.

After the opening section of Exodus, which depicted the plight of the Israelites, and introduced Moses who had to flee for his life from Egypt to escape from Pharaoh, an interesting statement was made.

> "*The Israelites groaned in their slavery and cried out, and their cry for help because of their slavery went up to God. God heard their groaning and he remembered his covenant with Abraham, with Isaac and with Jacob. So God looked on the Israelites and was concerned about them.*" (2:23-24).

How could anyone know what God heard and remembered, and what his outlook was like? The language is anthropomorphic, using human expressions with regard to God, and the composer was using literary freedom to express a point of view about God. This is a clue about the nature of Exodus. It is divine saga. The more closely we look, the more it becomes evident that the book has a striking literary character. There is an underlying layer of historical facts, but the finished composition has been skilfully embellished. This is because Exodus was not presenting history, but revelation about God in historical events.

There was a special intention in this comment about God's awareness of the oppressed Israelites. It was deliberately claiming that the Israelites' cries were a contributing factor to what God subsequently did. The narrative presented a poignant picture of a helpless, enslaved and suffering people who were seen and heard by God who had a long-standing vested interest in them. At this stage the Israelites could not be called a nation, nor did they currently have a close relationship with God. Yet God had them both in his plans and in his sight.

The Israelites crying out for help take our minds back to Enosh and his generation who called on the name of the LORD (Genesis 4:26). Mention of God's covenant with Abraham, Isaac, and Jacob also recalls that these men similarly *"called on the name of the LORD"* (Genesis 12:8, 13:4, 26:25). The wording in Exodus is different, but the action was the same. Israel's cries are also reminiscent of the outcry against Sodom and Gomorrah (Genesis 18:20). At the outset of the saga, it was the Israelites' groaning in their slavery which acted as the human catalyst which launched God's assault on Egypt and his deliverance of Israel. The Israelites' experience in Egypt was a formational background for a people destined to become a *"kingdom of priests"*. There is a connection between God's kingship and agenda of grace on the one side, and prayerful dependence on the human side.

Evidence of God's presence throughout Exodus was frequently manifested conspicuously. Moses' intriguing encounter with God in the desert while he was leading his flock in the vicinity of Mount Horeb was quite dramatic (chapters 3-4). He experienced an awesome confrontation with God at a bush which was burning without being consumed. The *"angel of the LORD"* appeared to him in *"flames of fire"* from within the bush. The *"angel of the LORD"* was the representative of God's personal presence. *"Flames of fire"* signified God's purifying and consuming nature. This is the language of saga, metaphorical imagery to describe the ineffable. From this encounter Moses received revelation about God's name and a mission to deliver Israel from its bondage. God cautioned him to revere the holy ground of his presence, and identified himself as the God of the patriarchs. God made a speech in which he indicated his awareness of his peoples' afflictions, that he intended to rescue his people, and that he was sending Moses to be the deliverer. Moses was reluctant and raised five objections to excuse himself from the task. He lacked self-confidence. He did not know what name to give for God. He was anxious about Israel's scepticism. He lacked eloquence. He was reluctant to go. God handled each excuse with seriousness, and a divine solution.

To dispel Moses' ignorance about God's name, God revealed himself by several ambiguous expressions. He said he was *"I am who I am"*; *"I am"*; and *"The LORD the God of your fathers - the God of Abraham, the God of Isaac, and the God of Jacob"* (3:14-15). God's name represented his identity. The term *"LORD"* is a fabricated name for an unpronounceable Hebrew term *"YHWH"* (often also rendered in English as "Yahweh"). To have a name implies that God is personal. The name YHWH is derived from the verb "to be", as also the expressions *"I am who I am"* and *"I am"*. They mean that God is self-existent, the living

God. They also mean that God was not to be known by his static existence, his being, but by his dynamic presence and versatile activity, his doing, which revealed what he was like. He was self-revealing. Furthermore, they imply that he will be whatever he chooses to be. He was self-determining. "LORD" is an appropriate term to represent the untranslatable Hebrew expression, YHWH, because it identifies God as the unique and absolute Lord of the universe. The revelation of his name identified him as the Creator King who made the heavens and the earth, and who was continuing to pursue his original plan of blessing for the world through his kingly covenant with his specially chosen servants Abraham, Isaac, and Jacob. It gave deeper meaning and stronger motivation to those who were moved by their circumstances to *"call on the name of the LORD"*.

God diffused Moses' third excuse, that the Israelites would not believe him, by God granting three signs for him to perform to convince them. His staff turned into a snake, and then became a staff again. His hand became leprous, and was then restored. Water from the Nile became blood when poured out. Each sign was relevant. In particular, a snake symbolised opponents to God. Egypt represented the seed of the serpent which raged against the seed of the woman as foretold by the Genesis prologue to Exodus (Genesis 3:15). The Nile in Egypt snaked its way through desert terrain like a serpent; crocodiles infested the Nile; pharaohs displayed a cobra on their headdress as their symbol of sovereignty; poets and prophets called Egypt by the names of mythical serpents and sea monsters (Rahab, Leviathan). At the very beginning, Genesis stated categorically that God created the great creatures of the sea (Genesis 1:21). Likewise, sinister powers opposed to God's purposes, likened figuratively to such huge creatures, were to be viewed as no more than created monsters. Exodus dramatically demonstrates God's crushing victory over such malevolent adversaries. The other two signs were also indicative. Leprosy and skin diseases disqualified people as ceremonially unclean from worship of God. Poured out blood represented the spilling of life, and anticipated the first plague which struck Egypt.

The first confrontation with the Egyptians (chapter 5) met with failure, resulting in an increased workload for the Israelites, and disillusionment for Moses. The LORD gave no explanation for the setback, but assured Moses that his mighty hand would force Pharaoh to let them go. Then, in a speech (6:2-8) which began and ended by declaring his identity, *"I am the LORD (YHWH)"*, and repeated twice more during his message, God explained that Israel's release was a significantly new development in his purposes. What he said shows that his name "LORD" is associated with this new development. He said that he had appeared to Abraham, Isaac, and Jacob by the title, *"El Shaddai"*, the Mighty God who was nurturing their fruitful increase, but not by the name *"YHWH"*. They were familiar with the title which indicated his capacity, but they did not know him in terms of his name. This is a little puzzling, since Genesis has already shown that God actually revealed himself to Abraham and Jacob as the "LORD" (Genesis 15:7, 18:27, 28:13), and that name appears all the way throughout that book. It is not clear what the patriarchs understood by the name, but its complete meaning had not been revealed to them. It was not the term "LORD" which was unknown, but what it represented, and that was yet to be unveiled. "God Almighty" ("El Shaddai") was the title given to the successive fathers of his future covenant people, and indicated his incomparable power and nurturing sufficiency to accomplish his purposes. God adds that he also established his covenant with the fathers to give them the land of Canaan, and now that he heard the Israelites groaning in their slavery he remembered his covenant. Therefore, Moses must tell the Israelites that God is the "LORD" and what he will do for them. God lists a series of actions which he will perform to convince them that he is *"the LORD your God who brought you out from under the yoke of the Egyptians"*. *"I will free you from being slaves ... redeem you ... take you as my own people and be your God ... bring you to the land ... give it to you as a possession."*

This whole statement reveals the meaning of Israel's liberation, and of God's name "YHWH". Israel's liberation was the nation's redemption, and the fulfilment of God's covenant promise to the fathers. The name "YHWH" identified God as Israel's redeemer and covenant keeper. This was the message for later generations, who were familiar with the name "YHWH", and their national association with him, but who needed to understand the full meaning of his name, and be inspired by him, and actually know him!

The showdown between the LORD and Pharaoh was a battle of wills (chapters 7-12). The divine Creator Ruler of the world launched an assault against the earthly ruler of the world's most powerful, idolatrous nation. How conspicuous the conflict was to the general population of Egypt, or even how much the significance of what was occurring was understood by the authorities, is difficult to discern. No records of what happened were left by the Egyptians, who usually made note of strange events or phenomena. A good case can be made to explain them as natural consequences of an extraordinarily high flooding of the Upper Nile. Their significance was their prior announcement, timing, and controlled impact, clearly demonstrating the God of Israel as the Lord of nature, and their threatening effect upon Egypt, showing God's antagonism towards the oppressors of his people. Exodus describes what happened in an artificial pattern, portraying the confrontation as a war of words. The battle was conducted on the LORD's terms. He commanded, and Pharaoh responded. There were no clashes of arms, and no political, legal, or physical reprisals by Pharaoh. Moses was respected as the LORD's representative. God attacked Pharaoh in the realm of nature and Egypt's occultic religion. The outward nature of the war could easily be dismissed as the result of "natural causes", and therefore would not rate a mention in inscriptional records. The Bible explains them as "acts of God"!

Nine plagues afflicted Egypt to convince Pharaoh that God had sent Moses to liberate Israel, and to exhibit God's mighty power. They occurred in three cyclic patterns of 3 plagues each. In each cycle Moses firstly presented himself before Pharaoh in the morning beside the

Nile and warned him of what was coming (7:15, 8:20, 9:13). He then went to the palace to announce the next plague (8, 9, 10). The third plague came without warning (8:16, 9:8, 10:21). Each initial plague indicated the purpose of each cycle. The first series (blood, frogs, lice) proved the superiority of God and his representatives over the Egyptian magicians (7:12). The second series (flies, livestock, boils) distinguished between the Israelites and the Egyptians, revealing God's presence and control. The third series (hail, locusts, darkness) emphasised the intensity of the plagues, and therefore God's awesome power. The description of the plagues follows a formulaic pattern, and there is a climactic build-up of tension. The hardening of Pharaoh's heart at the relief from each plague intensifies from self-hardening (7:22, 8:15, 19, 32, 9:7, 35) to being hardened by the LORD (9:12, 10:20, 27, 11:10). The plagues are variously called "wonders", "signs", "plagues", "diseases", "strokes", "blows". They are exceptional phenomena, destructive, and designed to catch Pharaoh's attention.

A strategic activity was performed by Moses. In his confrontation with Pharaoh, whenever God's afflictions persuade Pharaoh to relent (Exodus 8:8, 29, 30; 9:28; 10:17, 18), Moses "*prays*" (It is the same term "*entreats*" occurring previously in Genesis). On one occasion this took the form of "crying out to the LORD" (8:12); on another, the gesture of spreading out his hands towards the LORD (9:33). The LORD always granted his request. The "saga" makes it abundantly clear that Moses' prayer was a vital contribution to the battle.

The final "stroke" of God was far more crushing than all the other nine, and finally forced Pharaoh's hand. Every firstborn son in Egypt, from the son of Pharaoh to the son of the lowliest female slave, had to die. In stark contrast, no one in Israel experienced any harm, not even the threat of a barking dog. This was a life and death struggle, and Pharaoh's firstborn had to die to rescue God's "firstborn" from a living death. Every firstborn in Israel had to be redeemed with a lamb as a sign that the LORD brought them out of Egypt, the land of slavery, with his mighty hand (13:13-16). It is crucially important to appreciate this. The Israelites were not merely rescued, but "redeemed". This was the reason for the elaborate procedure of selecting and sacrificing a substitute lamb. The lamb was especially chosen, just as Israel was chosen. There was no moral basis for the choice. God chose Israel on the basis of his own purpose of grace, not any merit of the nation. Neither was there any suggestion of atonement associated with the sacrifice, since at this stage there was no law. The lamb was simply a substitute, the price of redemption. In principle it was similar to the lamb which was a substitute for Isaac on Mount Moriah (Genesis 22:1-19).

The events of the final "strike" were the first major climax in the "saga". Yet little is actually said about the horrendous experience of death which struck every Egyptian home at midnight on a single night. Instead, emphasis was placed on instructions given to Israel concerning special preparations to be undertaken for the crucial night (12:1-13), and for future observance of the Passover and Feast of Unleavened Bread which were to be a perpetual memorial celebration of Israel's liberation (12:14-20). Every family was to make preparations for the fourteenth day of the month, by daubing the doorframes of their houses with blood from a chosen year-old sheep or goat, which was to be roasted and eaten that night, and by being ready to leave. This night was to be the "LORD's Passover", when he struck down Egypt's firstborns, but passed over Israel. It was a night of judgement on all the gods of Egypt (12:12). So important was this night, that in the future it was to be celebrated by a week-long festival. It was to be known as the Feast of Unleavened Bread, a celebration of when the LORD brought Israel's "divisions" (a military term) out of Egypt.

God did not lead his people by the shorter and more direct route, the way of the land of Philistia, but along the desert road towards the "Sea of Reeds" (13:17-22). He led by means of pillars of cloud and fire, symbols of his presence. Cloud is suggestive of a covering of God's indescribable wonder. Fire indicates God's consuming and purifying essence. The pillars are associated with the "angel of God" (14:19), who is God's personal representative. Under God's sovereign watchfulness Pharaoh pursued the Israelites to the "Sea of Reeds", where God provided a dramatic escape for his people through the sea, which became a place of judgement for the Egyptians (14:1-31). Afterwards Miriam led a song and dance of praise to celebrate crossing the Sea (15:1-21).

When the Israelites found themselves trapped between the advancing Egyptians and the sea, they were terrified and *"cried out to the LORD"* (14:10). Here again is the crucial response from God's helpless people, precipitated by God's own strategy. The people reproached Moses for bringing them into the desert to die. However Moses urged them not to fear, but to expect the LORD to deliver them. The LORD instructed Moses to move forward, and to stretch his upraised staff over the sea, repeating his intentions to harden Pharaoh's heart and gain glory through him. The angel of God and the pillar of cloud moved from before the Israelites (called an *"army"*) to a position between the two armies of Egypt and Israel. This was war, and God was personally engaged. What happened was a strange upheaval of weather conditions. An east wind blew through the night, and dried a pathway across the sea, leaving a wall of water on either side. We should not imagine a mountainous wall of Hollywood proportions! Just a shallow stretch of water on either side to protect the fugitives from chariot attacks on their flanks. The Israelite *"army"* surged forward along the dried path, and then the pursuing Egyptians plunged in behind. During the last watch of the night, the LORD took direct action and threw the Egyptian army into confusion. "Saga" language is used, so the specific action is vague. The chariots lost their wheels, and the Egyptians their lives, in the returning waters when Moses followed the LORD's instructions to again stretch out his hand over the sea. It was a stunning victory. None of the Egyptians survived. All Israel was saved. At daybreak, the Israelites saw the bodies of Egyptians on the shore, the evidence of God's great power, and they feared the LORD, trusting both him and Moses his servant.

The climax of the "battle" scene was a victory song (15:1-21). It was a jubilant celebration of triumph and adoration, accompanied by women playing tambourines and dancing.

The song is about the LORD, extolling his victory over Pharaoh's military forces (v 1-12), and exclaiming his future conquest of the land of Canaan (v 13-18). The heart of the song proclaims the LORD's absolute supremacy (v 11):

"Who among the gods is like you, O LORD? Who is like you – majestic in holiness, awesome in glory, working wonders?"

The carefully composed song expressed, and revealed, the purpose of the "saga", to extol the LORD.

For several months they followed a route through the desert, experiencing some critical faith-challenging incidents along the way. Israel learnt important lessons about God's provision (healing, food, and water, 15:22-17:7), protection (through intercession, 17:8-16), and priorities (justice and leadership, 18:1-27). At Marah, where the water was bitter, Moses *"cried out to the LORD"*, who sweetened the water, and revealed that he was *"the LORD who heals you"* (15:22-26). In the Desert of Sin, the LORD provided meat and bread each day, and established the unique innovation of Israel's Sabbath (chapter 16). At Rephidim, because there was no water to drink, Moses once more *"cried out to the LORD"* (17:4). At God's instruction, he struck a rock with his staff, and water gushed out of it. While still at Rephidim, the Amalekites battled against them, but Moses ensured victory by lifting up his hands *"to the throne of the LORD"* (17:8-16), a conspicuous gesture of entreaty. These dramatic gestures, actions and cries provide glimpses which illustrate the effectiveness and importance of prayerful entreaty.

The epic drama reached its culmination when the liberated fugitives arrived at Sinai. The LORD appeared on the mountain in an awesome manifestation of fire and smoke, and, through Moses' mediation, established his covenant with the nation. The sights and sounds of this theophany engulfed the Israelite spectators with terror. They stayed their distance, and only Moses ascended the mountain to converse with God directly.

Recognise the literary layout of the book. From this point on, everything happens at Sinai, and most of it is instruction by word from God to Moses, to be passed on to the people. There is a narrative framework which provides background activity. This pattern continues in Leviticus, and as far as Numbers 10. A series of major developments occurred to shape Israel as God's covenant people. The LORD's spectacular revelation at Sinai was the climax of the magnificent drama which installed redeemed Israel as God's *"kingdom of priests"*. Among all the nations of the world, Israel was to be a *"holy"* nation, God's *"treasured possession"*.

The literary format was dramatically designed to galvanise readers' heart devotion. It was not simply recording historic events from the past. The verbatim reporting of God's words allowed readers to listen to God directly. The descriptions of Moses' interactions with God allowed readers to visualise God's rapturous presence. The literary presentation aimed to present the LORD as interactively as possible.

Formation of the covenant came first. A lively dramatic performance unfolded over seven days, as Moses ascended and descended the mountain, acting as a mediator between God and the people. God appeared on the mountain cloaked in dense cloud, and negotiated a covenant with the people who stayed at the foot of the mountain at a distance. Moses acted as go-between, setting out God's requirements, and reporting the people's response. On the first day God reminded them of what he had already done in Egypt, and how he had carried them on *"eagles' wings"* to himself. He declared that on the condition of their obedience to his covenant, he would set them apart from all other nations as his *"treasured possession"*. Although the whole earth belonged to him, they would be for him a *"kingdom of priests and a holy nation"*. The people agreed to the terms of the covenant, and were then told to undergo strict consecration procedures during the rest of the day and the next in readiness to meet with God. On the third morning, the mountain was shrouded in thunder, lightning, and dense cloud, and emitted a very loud trumpet blast. The LORD descended upon the mountain in blazing fire and billowing smoke, causing the mountain to tremble violently and the trumpet sound to grow louder. The description gives the impression of an erupting volcano in the midst of a turbulent storm, to portray the spectacular theophany. The people and the priests were told to remain at a distance and not draw near to the LORD, although Moses was sent to bring Aaron up with him.

The vivid scene is awesome. The LORD is terrifyingly magnificent. Readers were intended to be overwhelmed by a mixed sense of trepidation and elation. How much the description was actual or metaphorical is difficult to tell, but the presentation depicted God's transcendent nature and very real intrusion into historical affairs. The physical imagery represented spiritual reality.

Moses descended the mountain and reported what God had said. God's words were reported verbatim (20:2-17), and were later called the "Ten Commandments" (34:28). Their format follows the pattern of contemporary royal covenants, or treaties. The people trembled with fear before the display of frightening phenomena which manifested God's presence, and kept their distance from him. Moses encouraged them not to be afraid of the LORD, because he was only wanting them to respect him in order to keep them from sinning. Only Moses approached the thick darkness where God was. God then gave Moses instructions for the people about how they were to worship him (20:22-26), and a series of laws for Israel's community life, which were a radical innovation to society for their respect for life and property, and humanitarian quality (21:1-23:19). Notice that God himself spoke the *words* of the Ten commandments directly (20:1), whereas his additional *laws* were mediated through Moses (21:1). There was a distinction. The Ten Commandments were absolute (and therefore universal in nature), known as apodictic laws, which demonstrated God's ideal rule. The additional laws were relative, applicable to life in Israel at that time. These are called casuistic laws, or case examples of covenant law in realistic situations, dealing with life's recognised unideal realities.

We should especially note the third of the Ten Commandments which forbade the misuse of the LORD's name (Exodus 20:7, Deuteronomy 5:11). This was not a command against merely speaking God's name inappropriately, as Israel misunderstood and so never uttered the name, and substituted other terms instead. It also means more than forbidding false statements when taking oaths in God's name. This command forbids falsely claiming covenant loyalty to God. The expression *"misuse the name of the LORD your God"* literally means *"lift up the name of YHWH your God falsely"*, referring to the swearing of allegiance to God as the great covenant King. For Israel to be God's covenant nation meant they were the "people who called on the name of the LORD", following in the tradition of the generation of Enosh, and especially the covenant tradition of Abraham, Isaac, and Jacob!

God concluded his instructions with some reassuring promises, and then the final action of confirming the covenant arrived (chapter 24). The people agreed to keep God's *words* and *laws*, and Moses wrote them all down. The next morning he built an altar at the foot of the mountain and set up twelve stone pillars to represent the twelve tribes of Israel. Young men offered burnt offerings and sacrificed bulls for fellowship offerings. Moses collected half the blood in a bowl, and sprinkled the other half on the altar. He read the "Book of the Covenant" (as the written *words* and *laws* were now called) to the people, who agreed to obey, and sprinkled them with the blood of the covenant.

Moses, Aaron and his sons, and the elders then ascended the mountain where they saw the "God of Israel". God was now known in terms of his covenant relationship with Israel. To say that they "saw" God meant not so much "sight", as "insight". The appearance of what they "saw" was described in anthropomorphic language, mentioning only his feet and hands. Under his feet was a sky-blue sapphire pavement, and he did not raise his hands against the leaders. The lack of explicit description implied that God was indescribable. Yet there was an impression of an enthroned, sublime Person who was welcoming, rather than hostile. At the "burning bush" Moses had hidden his face in God's presence, but these leaders "saw" God, and feasted in his presence. It is reasonable to take the pavement of sapphire as a metaphor, perhaps suggested by the dome of the sky, and possibly the blue precious stone lapis lazuli which was used for royal ornamentation in Egypt and Mesopotamia. It is the only visual feature indicated, and implies that God's splendour was beyond the most regal element, in earth and sky, known to man.

Moses was called to ascend higher and stay with God until he received the tablets of stone containing God's written laws and commands. Accompanied by Joshua, his righthand man, and future successor, Moses went up on the mountain of God. It was called the "mountain of God" because God's presence was located on its summit. The cloud which symbolised God's presence covered the mountain, and the glory of the LORD "settled" on Mount Sinai. The term "settled" gave rise to the formal term "shekinah" which indicated the outward manifestation of God's presence. The Israelites' experience of seeing his presence on the mountain was depicted in vivid physical imagery, covering cloud and inner glory like a "consuming fire". Again, physical imagery depicted deeper reality. A "consuming fire" metaphorically indicated destruction and purging. It implied God's purity, and the absence of anything contaminating in his character, as well as his eradication impact on evil. Altogether the cloud covered the mountain for six days, and on the seventh God called Moses to enter his presence, confirming the seven day pattern as a sign for Israel. Moses then remained on the mountain forty days and nights.

With all the movement taking place on the mountain, as Moses ascended and descended between the people and God, a deliberate pattern became obvious. The people remained at a distance from God, at the base of the mountain. Aaron, his sons, and the elders were able to draw closer to God, but only Moses and Joshua could enter his presence. The vertical height of the mountain symbolised God's higher status, and the pattern for Israel's relationship to him. This pattern was the blueprint for the Tabernacle.

Construction of the Tabernacle was the second major development at Sinai, and takes up the rest, and largest part, of the book of Exodus (chapters 25-40).

While Moses was still on the mountain waiting to receive the stone tablets on which God's laws and commands were inscribed, he also received verbal instructions for making the sanctuary where God would dwell among his people, and its furnishings, priestly robes and consecration of the priests, and various other related features (chapters 25-31). Then there is a brief report of an idolatrous rebellion in the camp which almost proved catastrophic, except for the intercession of Moses, who obtained assurance from God that his divine presence would always be with them, and a renewal of commitment to the covenant from the people (chapters 32-34). Finally, there is a description of the Tabernacle's construction in language which is quite repetitious of the earlier instruction, concluding with a brief statement about the glory of the LORD filling the erected Tabernacle (chapters 35-40). At the heart of the covenant relationship between the LORD and Israel there was to be a conspicuous and God-given procedure for worship. A worshiping relationship with God was the outcome and culmination of their experience of redemption from bondage and covenant commitment. The materials for the Tabernacle and its furnishings were to be provided by voluntary contribution (25:1-7). The facilities expressed the new situation that God, whose awesome glory had been terrifyingly manifested on the mountain, was now going to live among them (25:8). The construction and practices were to be carried out in strict obedience to God's master plan (25:9). The Tabernacle on earth would symbolically represent in tangible form God's immaterial Palace in heaven.

The structure was based on a pattern given to Moses on the mountain (25:40). Its layout was a horizontal version of the vertical plan of the mountain. A two-roomed tent was surrounded by a fenced courtyard. Worshippers entered the courtyard and participated in sacrifices, but remained outside the tent, just as the people had remained at the foot of Mount Sinai. Priests entered the first room of the tent, the "Holy Place", and performed ritual duties, similar to Aaron and the elders who ascended part way up the mountain. However, no one was permitted to enter the inner sanctuary, the "Most Holy Place", or "Holy of Holies", where God's enthroned presence was symbolically represented, but veiled from view, just as God's presence on top of the mountain had been excluded for all except Moses. Not only was the Tabernacle central to the camp; it was also conspicuously, extravagantly, brilliant. Its white courtyard curtains, brightly coloured tabernacle curtains, gold and silver furnishings, altars, and support posts, along with white-robed priests, would be dazzling. The presence of the cloud and glory of the LORD hovering over the Tabernacle would ensure a magnificent spectacle. The activities associated with the Tabernacle would highlight the near proximity of God, the privilege of access to him, and the priority of worship. The Great King had set up camp in the midst of his chosen people, near and approachable for whoever wished to call on his name!

Details about the construction, materials, and furnishings were full of rich symbolism and meaning. The Sabbath was also significantly associated with the construction of the Tabernacle. It was on the seventh day when God called Moses to enter his presence on the mountain to receive instructions concerning the Tabernacle (24:15). Those instructions were concluded with advice about the Sabbath (31:12-17), and that advice repeated immediately prior to construction commencing (35:1-3). The Sabbath was a sign of the covenant, and a reminder of Israel's relationship to the LORD whom they would worship. Because they were holy, the Sabbath was to be holy, observed as a day of rest from work, and identifying them with the God of creation. Sabbath and Tabernacle both highlighted the reality and priority of the LORD's central place in the life of the nation.

God concluded his instructions by handing over the two tablets of the Testimony, inscribed by his "finger" (unseen divine power) to Moses.

Between instructions about the Tabernacle (chapters 25-31) and its actual construction (chapters 35-40), a catastrophe occurred. The people below became impatient and restless because of Moses' lengthy absence, and they persuaded Aaron to make them a god in the shape of a calf (chapters 32-34). The people blatantly engaged in idolatry and an orgy of debauchery. As the LORD handed over the stone tablets to Moses, he informed him about the people's rebellion, and angrily threatened to destroy them. The LORD's attitudes were described in vivid human-like language. He offered to replace them with a new nation derived from Moses. This was a revealing proposal. It indicated that God's covenant was not bound to the institutional nation, but to those within the nation whose hearts were responsive, a faithful inner nation. However, the proposal was abandoned in response to Moses' intercession. He appealed to the LORD's established relationship with Israel and his rescue of the nation from Egypt, to the integrity of his reputation amongst the Egyptians, and to his covenant promise with Abraham, Isaac, and Israel (32:11-14). It was not so much that Moses persuaded God to remain true to his purpose, but that Moses remained true to his role in the face of serious testing. He was the mediator of God's covenant with Israel, and he remained loyal to God and to God's intention. What we should recognise is that Moses' intercession was governed by God's agenda and strategy of grace, and was influential in persuading God's response. The dialogue between God and Moses demonstrated their close inter-personal relationship.

When Moses approached the camp and saw for himself the blasphemous revelling, he furiously hurled the tablets to the ground, smashing them. His action dramatically and symbolically showed that the covenant was already in ruins. He destroyed the calf idol that had been made in his absence, ground it to dust which he scattered on the water, and forced the people to drink. After enquiring how the situation had come about, he appealed for those who were loyal to the LORD to join him, and then sent them to slaughter the rebels by sword. It was a case of the inner loyal "nation" cleansing itself. Three thousand were slain by these zealous Levites whose savage executions of fellow Israelites were interpreted as religious gestures of their consecration to the LORD (32:27-29). As ghastly as this scene strikes us, we must understand the crucial significance of their actions. They were the LORD's "ordained warriors" executing justice upon rebels who had blatantly rejected the covenant will of the King who had called them to share in his holy kingdom. They were a demonstration of Israel's role in the broad world. The significance of God's violent retribution against these rebels would not be lost on exiled survivors who had witnessed the Babylonian savage destruction of Jerusalem.

The LORD is a King of righteousness engaged in a campaign of overthrowing human rebellion and re-establishing his rightful rule over the earth. Just as disobedience in the Garden of Eden resulted in death, so disobedience in this place of privileged opportunity to participate in the LORD's astonishing strategy for restoring his loving rule in the world had the same consequences. The manner of punishment was in the familiar form meted out by ancient kingdoms at that time. Moses sought to atone for the people's sin by pleading for their forgiveness, and even requested that he be removed from God's book of life in their place. This was an astonishing gesture of grace. Was he motivated by his close familiarity with God and with God's motives of grace? His plea was rejected, and God declared that the guilty would bear their own punishment. He then sent a plague to punish the rebels who had broken the covenant.

This disastrous incident demonstrated several momentous issues. In the first place it highlighted the supreme importance of the covenant which the LORD was establishing with Israel. The Creator King was inaugurating an astounding enterprise within his estranged world. By forming a new nation, to be his priestly kingdom within the world, in accord with prior promises and preparations, he was launching a subversive strategy intended eventually to restore blessing to all nations.

Secondly, we see in this incident the intensity of God's zeal to succeed in his plan.

In the third place we see how perilous it is to be contemptuous of God and blatantly disobedient to his privileged call to become his *"treasured possession"* (19:5). To reject the Creator of all things, the Giver of life, the Divine Ruler and Covenant Maker, is to invoke certain destruction.

Fourthly, we see the significance of the role of intercession demonstrated by Moses' mediation. Commitment to the covenant is expressed by prayerful loyalty to God's honour and purpose.

Other consequences followed this incident. The LORD informed Moses that his personal presence would not accompany the nation to the land he had promised them, but that he would send an angel with them instead (33:1-3). He wanted to spare them further destruction which their stubborn sinfulness in his immediate presence was likely to incite. As a sign of their mourning at this distressing news the people removed all their ornaments, apparently permanently (v 4-6). Moses responded in one of his *"face to face"* tent meetings with God by directly appealing for God's presence to go with them (v 12-16). He appealed on the basis of his close personal relationship with the LORD, arguing that only the LORD's presence would distinguish him and the people from all other nations. The LORD agreed to the request because he was pleased with Moses and knew his *"name"* (v 17). That is, he knew intimately what Moses was like by nature, and responded positively to his prayerful appeal.

This prompted Moses to make a bold request. He asked the LORD to show him his glory (v 18). He wanted to know what God was like. The LORD agreed to display his goodness and to proclaim his name, and even allow Moses to see where his glory had passed by. But he refused to manifest his direct glory, his *"face"*, because it was not possible to see God and live (v 19-23). To see God's glory after it had passed meant to discern the radiance of his character and majesty in his past actions. Moses was granted the experience the next day on Mount Sinai, where he took two new stone tablets to replace the broken ones. The LORD joined him, cloaked in cloud, and proclaimed his name (34:1-7). The proclamation declared what God was like by nature, in words which became a recurring description throughout the Old Testament.

> *"The LORD, the LORD, the compassionate and gracious God, slow to anger, abounding in love and faithfulness, maintaining love to thousands and forgiving wickedness, rebellion and sin. Yet he does not leave the guilty unpunished; he punishes the children and their children for the sin of the fathers to the third and fourth generation"*. (v 6-7)

This proclamation made explicit what had been implicit in all his past activities. As Creator and King, as Covenant-Maker with Abraham, Isaac, and Jacob, and as Israel's Redeemer and Covenant King, all his actions and motives had expressed, and revealed, his identity as the loving and merciful God.

Against the background of the recent rebellion and God's fierce reaction to it, God's self-identification as abundant loyal loving kindness shone starkly.

Moses responded spontaneously in worship, and with a plea that the LORD would forgive the people and take them as his inheritance. The LORD assured him that he was committing himself to a covenant relationship with them, and required their exclusive devotion and loyalty. He declared that by name he was a *"jealous God"* (34:14), not meaning in a selfish envious sense, but indicating the ardour of his love and his exclusive devotion to them. When Moses returned from the mountain, after another forty days and nights, carrying the replacement tablets, called "tablets of the Testimony", his face shone with a radiant aura reflecting his interaction with the LORD. Consequently, because sight of this radiance frightened the people, in public Moses veiled his face, but removed the veil when he entered the presence of the LORD. This experience gave Moses an intimate and exclusive insight into the depths of God's nature. Knowledge of what God was like deepened his reverent adoration and emboldened his prayerfulness.

In obedience to God's instructions, the Tabernacle was completed, using donated materials from the people, divinely chosen craftsmen, and skilled workers (chapters 35-40).

A Holy Nation

As our reading tour takes us into **Leviticus** we come to the third major development at Sinai. It is the central piece of the "divine saga" of Exodus-Leviticus-Numbers. The book consists predominantly of rules and regulations proclaimed directly by the LORD to govern his covenant community, broken only by a brief section of historical episode, which is highly significant. The format stunningly prescribes Israel's special role as a priestly and holy kingdom. The book is not a democratically devised "bill of rights", but a divinely decreed "bill of responsibilities"! Recognise the book's layout.

Chapters 1-7   Instructions Concerning Sacrifices: *Offerings to God dominated Israel's life*
Chapters 8-10   Consecration & Service of Aaron & His Sons: *The priesthood began service*
Chapters 11-15 Ritual Laws of Cleanliness: *Diet, disease, & domestic life required purity*
Chapters 16-17 Day of Atonement & Laws About Eating Blood: *Blood (= life) was sacred*
Chapters 18-27 Priestly & Community Holiness: *Morality & customs from belonging to God*

Leviticus opens with an important statement.

"The LORD called to Moses and spoke to him from the Tent of Meeting".

This was only the fifth, and final, occasion when it was said that the LORD "called" him. The LORD first "called" him at the "burning bush" (Exodus 3:4), then three times on top of Mount Sinai (Exodus 19:3, 20, 24:16), and now here at the recently constructed Tent of Meeting. Through Moses, as mediator, God was calling his covenant people to respond to his instructions. The picture is emerging that the LORD and his redeemed nation have a relationship in which each "calls" to the other.

The significance of God's call to Moses becomes more conspicuous and meaningful when we realise how rare was such an experience for God to call to anyone. The first time he is described as doing so was in the Garden of Eden immediately after the man and woman's original act of disobedience (Genesis 3:9). God's call then confronted them about hiding from him because of their guilty awareness of their nakedness. God condemned the pair, yet personally took steps to clothe them. The only other person to hear God call to them was young Samuel serving in the Tabernacle (1 Samuel 3:4, 6, 8, 10). He was informed that the LORD was about to take drastic action against the priesthood because of their corrupt conduct. The outcome was the capture of the Ark of the Covenant and removal of God's glory from Israel. Yet God also raised up Samuel to be an alternative national leader as a prophet who revealed God's word. In time, Samuel became the means of appointing Israel's kingship.

An important feature of Leviticus, which recurs over and over again, is the statement, *"The Lord spoke to Moses"*, to introduce a new set of instructions. This keeps the dominant presence of the LORD and the context of Sinai in focus, and emphasises the revelatory nature of the content. These were instructions which the LORD gave to Moses while the nation was still at Sinai. God's word was his means of operating. The Divine King, whose presence was conspicuously and dramatically present, was speaking. He was issuing his orders to his chosen covenant servant nation about how they were to conduct themselves as a people living in privileged relationship to him. The first 17 chapters focus almost exclusively on Israel's priestly matters, and the people's approach to the LORD's presence. The closing chapters focus on the demand for national holiness.

The pattern of Leviticus follows the pattern of the Tabernacle, which in turn followed the pattern of the three levels of Mount Sinai. The first 17 chapters of Leviticus concern sacrifices performed in the outer courtyard and matters relating to the priests and people. The instructions in the rest of the book, prescribing holy practices for a priestly nation, might be seen to reflect the layout of the Holy Place. The recurring references to the LORD speaking to Moses were a constant reminder of God's rule from the Most Holy Place. Life based on the analogy of the Tabernacle highlighted God's living presence amongst his people.

Leviticus casts a radical vision for society in Israel under its covenant relationship with God. It contains radical laws for governing a revolutionary new nation in the world. These must be viewed from a threefold perspective. Firstly, they must be seen in contrast to other surrounding, degraded, ruthless, idolatrous nations. Secondly, they are presented by the living and holy Creator King of all that exists. Thirdly, they are laws prescribed for a nation of flawed people like the rest of mankind, as part of a long-term strategy for restoring the world. The laws express the will of the LORD who, as an act of grace, had bound himself in covenant to an unlikely and undeserving people. It is a magnificent step on a long journey which will lead to the world's most amazing act of grace. This law points forward to the coming and triumphant achievement of the Lord Jesus Christ. God's big plan is to produce a Holy People, and these laws reveal wonderful insights into what that means.

Though Leviticus contributes nothing explicitly about prayer, the book nevertheless makes Israel's priestly role as a nation conspicuous. Israel's privileged responsibility was to reveal the LORD's holy kingship amongst all other nations, and to demonstrate the radical and total need of holiness in order to draw near to his presence. Their whole way of life was a way of prayer. Their sacrificial practices, in particular, highlighted the way of access to God, requiring continuous atonement, confession of sin, cleansing, reconciliation, worship, and thanksgiving. The elaborate ritual procedures demonstrated God's majesty, goodness, and reverence.

A Rebellious Army

The opening section of **Numbers** (chapters 1-10:10) presents the fourth major development **at Sinai**. The new nation became God's holy army. The LORD ordered a military census to be taken of all men from the age of 20, each tribe recorded with precision in exactly the same words (chapter 1). Previous instruction about such a census (Exodus 30:11-16) indicated that it signified their redemption from slavery in Egypt (Exodus 13:13, 15). They were the LORD's redeemed army. Israel had undergone a transformation from a motley crowd of loose-knit tribal groups to a coordinated cohort of militia, consisting of 12 troop divisions. The tribes of Israel, identified by their respective divisional standards and tribal banners, were arranged in fixed, orderly patterns, both as a military camp when stationary, and a marching army when on the move (chapter 2). The LORD's sacred royal tent was erected at the heart of the camp, and was carried in the middle of the marching divisions. Israel was the LORD's holy army, with a combat role to perform. As such, they were to be dedicated to his purposes, not an invading force for their own political ambitions.

The tribe of Levi had a special role (chapters 3-4). Moses, as national leader, served as the LORD's spokesman, proclaiming what God (Creator King) commanded. Aaron, as high priest, ensured that the nation remained holy, in honour of, and in harmony with, God's holiness. Aaron's remaining two sons (after two were destroyed by the LORD for offering unauthorised fire, Leviticus 10:1-2) assisted him, as priests, and the rest of the Levites assisted as caretakers of the tabernacle, each with a specifically appointed task. The Levites belonged exclusively to the LORD, representing the firstborn sons of Israel who were consecrated as belonging to the LORD at the time of Passover in Egypt. They were the inner priestly "nation".

Additional miscellaneous commands emphasised the regimental nature of Israel's new way of life (chapter 5). Instructions concerning the Nazirite voluntary vow of separation and dedication (6:1-21) laid down guidelines for ensuring that it was carried out in accord with Israel's unique character of belonging to the LORD. The priestly blessing bestowed by Aaron and his sons (6:22-27) was in accord with the LORD's command, because they acted on his behalf, not their own, and was in keeping with God's promised intention to Abraham (Genesis 12:2-3).

Presentation of offerings for the tabernacle, with all leaders contributing equally and liberally, demonstrated the nation's solidarity and family unity (chapter 7). The LORD was the army's military leader, mediating his commands through Moses (7:89-8:4), indicating when the camp was to set out and stop on its journeys by the movement of the pillar of cloud above the Tabernacle (9:15-23), and sounding military signals by trumpet (10:1-10).

We need to pause for a moment and contemplate the census numbers. As they stand, they constitute a very large army. 603,550 troops, similar to the 600,000 mentioned earlier (Exodus 12:37). Each warrior had a family, which would imply a total population of more than 2 million. Plus, there were large herds accompanying them. That is a massive crowd. The numbers are inflated and unrealistic. The layout of the camp would be enormous. The territory, whether at Sinai, Kadesh, or Moab, would not accommodate them. The length of their marching column would be extreme. If the soldiers were formed up 20 across, spaced at about 1/3 metre behind each other, the column would stretch more than 10 kilometres. And that doesn't allow for the families and herds. Progress would be slow and hampered. Such a large population, camped at Sinai for more than a year, might be expected to leave an archaeological footprint, but nothing has ever been found. Neither is there any evidence of Israel's nearly 40 years nomadic occupation of the desert region around Kadesh. Israel's numbers also greatly exceed the populations of settled inhabitants in the territories encountered along the way. Various explanations are suggested for the large numbers, confirming that they are a problem. Yet the numbers were carefully recorded, and are arithmetically complex and consistent. They were meant to be read as they appear. In keeping with "saga" imagery, probably to incorporate later Israel within the original liberated company of refugees, the "picture" projected by the census statistics is that of Israel as God's large holy army!

Numbers was not meant to be a record of Israel's travels, but a portrayal of important features of the LORD's experiences with his covenant people during those travels. It was written with later readers in mind. Although the journey from Mount Sinai to the plains of Moab took 40 years, only a relatively few events are mentioned in the book. The "saga" is a story of Israel's rebellious tendencies and the LORD's commitment to his covenant purposes.

Tough disciplinary measures prepared his "invasion army" ready to enter and possess the Promised Land.

The "army" set out from Sinai after being stationed there for a year, and **marched to Kadesh** (chapters 10:11-12:16). The journey was marred by three incidents of grumbling and dissension, rousing *the LORD's anger* each time, using vivid human language. The people complained about their hardships (11:1-3). So the camp was struck by *fire from the LORD* (lightning?), prompting cries of dismay to Moses, who averted the judgement by his intercession to the LORD. This was reminiscent of Israel's previous experiences in Egypt of God responding to their cries (Exodus 2:23-25, 14:10). Their stopover place became known as *"Taberah"* ("Place of Burning"). Then rabble rousers spread dissatisfaction throughout the camp over their food supply (11:4-35). They hankered for the variety of foods and meat they had in Egypt, and resented the constant diet of manna. Moses complained about the burden of having to take care of all the people alone, and of having to provide them with meat. He would be better off dead! The problems were resolved by the appointment of 70 Spirit anointed elders, and the remarkable provision of quail for meat. Details of Moses' dialogue with God (v 21-23), and his response to the conduct of Eldad and Medad (v 26-30,) reveal much about the need for faith and humility in service for God. The troublemakers, however, were eliminated by means of a plague, and, as a sober reminder, the place was given the name *"Kibroth Hattaavah"*, which meant "graves of craving". From there they travelled on to Hazeroth, a location now unknown on the way to the Desert of Paran. The third problem came from Moses' older brother and sister, Aaron and Miriam, who objected to Moses' marriage to a Cushite woman (12:1-16). Nothing is known about Moses' Cushite wife, but she was only the occasion which sparked Miriam and Aaron's resentment, because they were primarily offended at Moses' exclusive role as God's messenger. In contrast to their attitudes of pride and jealousy, Moses was described as the most humble man living (v 3). The LORD summoned the three siblings to the Tent of Meeting and rebuked Aaron and Miriam by defending Moses' unique role as a true and faithful servant. He received direct verbal communication from the LORD, which was clear and unambiguous, unlike dreams and visions which were typical of other prophets. When the LORD departed, leaving Miriam with leprosy, Aaron pleaded with Moses not to hold their sin against them. Moses interceded for Miriam's healing, but before granting it the LORD required her to undergo a period of public shame because of her public offense.

While Israel was camped in the Desert of Paran **at Kadesh**, a rebellious decision not to advance and take possession of the Promised Land disqualified that whole generation from ever entering (chapters 13-14). Though God forgave them, he nevertheless condemned them to a life of wandering in the wilderness. This was a disastrous beginning for God's holy army.

Kadesh was close to the southern border of the Promised Land, located where the Deserts of Paran and Zin merged. Scouts were sent to explore the country, and they brought back a huge cluster of grapes which took two men to carry, and a report that the land was good and fertile. However, ten leaders warned against invading because the people were powerful and their cities fortified. Only Caleb and Joshua expressed confidence about taking possession. "*All*" the people listened to the 10, and rebelled, grumbling against Moses and Aaron, wanting to choose a new leader and return to Egypt. The LORD appeared in his glory, and spoke to Moses, proposing to replace Israel with a new people developed from him, since he was "faithful in all my house" (12:7). This was the second time God had suggested this proposal, and Moses responded here in much the same way as previously at Sinai. His plea was for the sake of God's honour, and appealed to God's revealed character. He thus showed his faithfulness to God's covenant, resisting personal temptation, and his prayer was in accord with that covenant. God agreed to forgive yet again, but condemned them to wander in the desert for 40 years. The punishment was limited to the men counted in the military census, and did not apply to the children and Levites (14:29). This had been a military mutiny. When the scouts who brought back the bad report were struck down dead, and the people learned about their own judgement, they mourned bitterly, admitted their sin, and tried to rectify their position by attempting an invasion of the land. But this was only further rebellion, and they were routed. Israel had acted presumptuously, and was not accompanied by Moses and the LORD (represented by the Ark of the Covenant).

Little was recorded of Israel's experiences during its dark period in the Desert of Paran, apart from a few significant events and ritual matters which were relevant primarily for future generations (chapter 15). One matter involved a man who gathered wood on the Sabbath and was stoned to death by the assembly outside the camp (v 32-36). This illustrated that it was a period of rebellion.

A major attempt to overthrow the leadership of Moses and Aaron left a long-lasting memory and impact (chapter 16). The great revolt which erupted involved an alliance between Korah, from the tribe of Levi, who apparently wanted to usurp Aaron's position, and two brothers, Dathan and Abiram, together with On, from the leading tribe of Reuben (Jacob's firstborn son), who presumably wanted to usurp Moses' position. They were jealous and resentful of Moses' and Aaron's prominence over the nation, claiming that they had *gone too far* in their self-appointment, and that all the people were equally "holy". Moses responded firstly by telling Korah and the Levites that it would be the LORD who would choose who would draw near to him (as high priest), and that they were the ones who had *gone too far*. He rebuked them for not being satisfied with their present privileged role, and for wanting to be priests as well. Then Moses tried to summon Dathan and Abiram in order to deal with their complaint, but they refused to come. They criticised Moses for having taken them away from the luxury of Egypt but failing to lead them to the luxury of Canaan, for wanting to make himself their "lord" (a military term for a superior), and for blinding the outlook of the men.

Although there were two factions vying for two separate positions, the double revolt was actually a united rebellion against the LORD who had made the appointments of Moses and Aaron. The account makes that clear, by oscillating between the two offending parties, and by the manner in which the leaders were destroyed together by the same sinkhole which opened up beneath them. Their 250 supporters also died by unnatural fire from the LORD, who gave instructions for their censors to be hammered into sheets of overlay for the altar as a reminder to the Israelites that only Aaron was to burn incense before the LORD. Even so, the assembled Israelites remained mutinous, and blamed Moses and Aaron for the deaths of the rebel leaders. Throughout the whole sordid affair, only God's restraint in response to the mediation of Moses and Aaron prevented the complete nation from being destroyed (v 4, 22, 46-50). Prayer was a powerful function.

Although Aaron's high priesthood had already been confirmed as the LORD's appointment several times, the LORD took special action to provide a permanent *sign* to end the grumblings of the rebellious community (chapter 17). Overnight in the tabernacle Aaron's staff sprouted, budded, blossomed, and produced almonds. For the benefit of future generations, this staff was placed in the tabernacle in front of the ark of the Testimony. To further clarify matters in the wake of the attempted revolt, the LORD addressed Aaron directly (a rare event, only occurring elsewhere at Leviticus 10:8, because God usually spoke through Moses) to explain the high responsibility of his priestly office, and the relationship between the priests and the Levites (chapter 18). Regulations for ritual cleansing highlighted the requirement for the LORD's troops to keep themselves undefiled (chapter 19).

The single sentence record of Miriam's death at Kadesh in the first month of Israel's 40th year in the desert (20:1) poignantly demonstrated the tragic reality that the shadow of death in the desert hovered over that whole generation. That reality provided a revealing perspective for the people's next quarrel with Moses and Aaron (20:2-13). They were preoccupied with dying, and they blamed Moses and Aaron for their predicament. Despite their complaining arrogance, God's responsive attitude, and his supernatural provision of water, displayed sheer grace and holiness. On the other hand, Moses and Aaron were not so patient. They took the rebellious hostility personally, and reacted out of exasperation and unbridled anger. They failed to trust and honour God. Consequently, they too were sentenced to share the same condemnation as the people in not being able to enter the Promised Land, since they had also rebelled (20:24). The severity of God's punishment for rebellion was stunning. Yet his purpose for the nation continued. Although Israel's rebellion disqualified that generation, the next generation had the opportunity to achieve what they had failed.

The next stage of Numbers tracks Israel marching from **Kadesh to Moab**, noting significant experiences along the way which trained them to become God's invasion forces ready to take the Land (20:14-22:1). After the failure to enter the Promised Land from the south on the western side of the Dead Sea, God gave the nation a fresh start with her second generation.

When the time came to move on, they intended to travel along the eastern side of the Dead Sea through the territories of Edom and Moab (who were racially related to Israel), in order to enter the Land further north from the east across the River Jordan (20:14-21). Negotiations with Edom, however, were unsuccessful, so Israel had to take a longer roundabout route. It needed to travel south to the Gulf of Aqaba, then further east along Edom's southern border, then turn north along Edom's and Moab's eastern borders. In addition to this setback, several incidents occurred early in the piece before they left that desert region, which were significant experiences for the next generation.

Before we look at those, however, we must give our attention to a couple of crucial features. Notice firstly the beginning of Moses' message to the king of Edom (v 14-16). He appealed to the king's knowledge of Israel's experiences of hardship at the hands of Egypt and the LORD's deliverance. In particular, he mentioned how Israel had *"cried out"* to the LORD, who in response had sent an angel to bring them out of Egypt. He was succinctly highlighting the significant elements of the exodus event, Israel's appeal to the LORD, and the LORD's response of divine intervention to liberate them. His focus demonstrated the importance and efficacy of prayer.

Moses' message to the king requested permission to travel through Edom's territory along the king's highway (v 17-21). The king refused to grant Israel passage, and Edom prepared to prevent them with military force. *"Edom came out against them with a large and powerful army"*. Because Israel respected their brotherly relationship (v 14), and was seeking a peaceful negotiation (v 17, 19), it avoided hostility by turning aside.

The incident was revealing. Why was Edom so aggressive and inhospitable towards its brother nation? Why was Edom not affected by its knowledge of the LORD's involvement in Israel's deliverance? What the opposition demonstrated was Israel's isolation, oppressed and shunned by all other peoples. Israel's calling was unique, and its mission for God was resisted.

Some significant events occurred at the start of the journey away from Kadesh. The first incident was the death of Aaron at Mount Hor (20:22-29). His death took place at a time and place decided by the LORD. This was an indication to the next generation that their lives were in God's hands, and a warning reminder of Aaron's (and his generation's) previous rebellion. On top of the mountain, in the presence of only the LORD and his servant Moses, an exchange of Aaron's clothes to his son Eleazar marked a handover ritual of the high priesthood. When Eleazar returned from the mountain without his father, a new era for the nation had begun.

Then the Canaanite king of Arad attacked them as they began to make their way south (21:1-3). This was the new generation's first battle, which, in response to their cries for help, the LORD enabled them to win. This experience was an encouragement in two respects. They would know that the LORD responded to their cries just as he had listened to the cries of their fathers when they were in bondage in Egypt, and had remembered his covenant with

Abraham (Exodus 2:24-25). Yet they would also remember that their fathers had suffered a defeat at the hands of the Canaanites in this very same region because of their disobedience at their first opportunity to enter the Promised Land (Numbers 14:45). So they would recognise that their covenant with the LORD remained, and they would be confirmed concerning their new advance towards the Land.

The third incident revealed important insights about both what the people were like and what God was like (21:4-9). The people showed that they were just like their fathers, complaining for the same reasons about their living conditions as they travelled through the harsh desert, and rebelling against God. On the other hand, God showed the same covenant character towards them as he had towards their fathers, punishing wickedness, yet also graciously forgiving those who repented. On this occasion the people recognised that the infestation of venomous snakes (remember Genesis 3:15!) was punishment for their sin, and they turned to Moses to intercede for them. The unusual remedy of elevating a bronze snake on a pole for bitten victims to look at in order to live, was meaningful and memorable. The raised replica snake represented the source of their punishment being lifted up before the throne of God as a public gesture of looking to the LORD for rescue (Exodus 17:8-16). In effect, they were calling on the LORD for his rescue and healing.

The trek north, skirting around Edom and Moab on their eastern borders, traces Israel's various campsites along the way. Most of these sites can no longer be identified. Important experiences of the journey are highlighted by references taken from the Book of the Wars, a book only known now because of this record (v 14). The quoted references seem to be highlighting important conquests (v 14-15) and the provision of water from a well at Beer (v 16-18). The point being shown is that the LORD is with the new generation, giving them victory and caring for them, just as he was with their fathers.

The defeat of kings Sihon and Og, and the Amorites (21:21-35) is significant for a couple of reasons. In the first place, the Amorites (who were **not** racially related to Israel) were a powerful people and formidable opposition. This is highlighted by a poem which gloats over Israel's victory against Sihon, who had recently conquered the northern region of Moab (v 27-30). The LORD had enabled his "army" to conquer the forces of successful warriors. Secondly, The victory over the Amorites implied that their sin had now reached its full measure as predicted to Abraham (Genesis 15:16). The territory of the Amorites, which Israel now occupied, was the first possession of what was to become their allocated inheritance.

At last the Israelites arrived **at the plains of Moab** and camped along the banks of the Jordan River, waiting for the signal to cross over and wage war against the Canaanites (chapters 22-32). A non-military strike was made against them. The enemy turned to occult practices and sexual immorality as tactics to separate the Israelites from God and his protection. The episode gives insight into the deeper nature of God's campaign to establish Israel as his kingdom in the Promised Land.

The story of Balaam is prominent in Numbers because it tells about a significant threat, which was not military, but spiritual and moral. The threat was very serious, even though Balaam had no direct dealings with Israel. The Moabites were afraid rather than pleased when they saw Israel defeat the Amorites, who had previously conquered their territory. The Moabites assumed Israel's vast numbers would swallow up their pasture lands. Yet Israel had no designs on Moab, because of their racial connection, and because their objective was the land of Canaan on the other side of the Jordan River. Again, Israel found itself isolated, and opposed even by related nations. Balak's alliance with the seminomadic Midianites, and his intention to use divination tactics against Israel instead of a military strategy, represent a major spiritual confrontation. His attempt to employ Balaam, a prophet who came from the River (Euphrates), to curse Israel, put him in direct conflict with God's original covenant promise to Abraham (Genesis 12:1-3), who also came from that same region, and became a prophet. The second generation was facing a threat from the idolatrous region of Mesopotamia similar to the first generation's conflict with idolatrous Egypt. This was especially relevant to exiled Israelite readers now in captivity there, and is the reason the story is given so much attention.

God told Balaam plainly not to get involved in Balak's plan, because Israel was blessed. Yet when a second and more impressive delegation came, with a more lucrative offer, Balaam could not resist looking for other options. God agreed that he could go, but insisted on strict obedience, yet he was angry when he did go, because he knew Balaam's true motives. God exposed his spiritual blindness (though he was a diviner) when he was unable to see the angel of the LORD, which his donkey could. The strange experience of the donkey seeing and speaking is not a fairy-tale myth, but an experience associated with the realm of divination.

Balaam's oracles were pronouncements based on what he "saw" concerning Israel as he looked down upon the nation from various elevated vantage points. Balak wanted him to curse Israel, but God overruled and gave him vision of only blessing. There were seven oracles, which confirmed Israel's covenant status. This event was a supernatural war, prior to entering the Promised Land, which God won by the supremacy of his word. It is a similar victory to Moses' defeat of the magic occult arts of the Egyptians, prior to Israel's exodus from the land of bondage. Israel was not privy to the great spiritual drama, yet while it was happening it had become embroiled in moral tragedy. Balaam (31:16) incited Moabite women to seduce Israelite men to participate in sexual immorality associated with the worship of their god, the Baal of Peor (chapter 25).

As Israel prepared to cross over the Jordan into the land of Canaan, Moses had several crucial matters to finalise. Firstly, he conducted another census of the nation, since the first generation had now almost all passed away (chapter 26). As with the first census, the count was based on men of military age. However, the purpose of the census also had in mind the allocation of tribal territories with regard to their share of the LORD's inheritance in the Land.

The case of Zelophehad (26:33, 27:1-11) highlighted some important covenant principles. Zelophehad was a first generation Israelite who died in the desert for failing to enter the Land to possess the inheritance. Yet he, and his family, were entitled to a share in the promised inheritance, since he had not been cut off from the nation, like Korah and his followers. Respect for his name (Exodus 20:12), provision for his family, and national solidarity were fundamental covenant requirements. He had died, however, without leaving a son and heir. So his daughters' request for recognition was commendable, and led to guarantees being established to safeguard family inheritances.

Moses humbly submitted to God's will when told he would see the Land, but not enter it because of his earlier disobedience (27:12-23). He showed no concern for himself, but for his people. He accepted God's authority over the allotment of human life (v 15), and prayed that God would appoint a replacement for himself so that the people would not be "like sheep without a shepherd". The LORD responded by nominating Joshua, and instructing Moses to publicly commission him. Moses handed over his leadership authority to Joshua, so that the people would follow him obediently. But he did not pass on his privilege of intimacy with God for receiving direct guidance, which was to be learned instead by means of enquiry through Eleazar the high priest, using the sacred lots of the Urim and Thummim.

Changing leadership and circumstances would also mean changes to community life. Israel would soon change from a nomadic camp formation, where the LORD's presence was conspicuously visible and central, to settlement scattered across the Land with the LORD's presence no longer in sight. The instructions concerning sacrifices and festivals (chapters 28-29) were probably given for the benefit of the new generation, to show that community life in the Land would be maintained by its ritual culture of sacrificial worship and fellowship in reverence to the LORD. The offerings had to be made "by fire" (purified), and be pleasing to the LORD (28:2). Though not visible, he would still be present and central. There was probably a similar significance with regard to the instructions about vows made to the LORD (chapter 30). They must be kept! Both the LORD and personal integrity must be taken seriously. The principle was laid down with regard to a man either making a vow (promise to do something) or taking an oath of obligation (pledge of self-denial or discipline) (v2). Application was illustrated with regard to vows taken by unmarried and married women, who were under the authority of their father or husband respectively, unless widowed or divorced. These guidelines reveal important insights into family life. Women were respected and had personal autonomy, yet were accountable to God, and, unless living alone, to the head of their family.

One of Moses' final responsibilities was to take vengeance on the Midianites because of their seduction of Israel (chapter 31). God did not strike them down with a plague or natural disaster (an "act of God"), but ordered his army to make war on them. The destruction was thorough and severe. Israel did not engage in its own wild killing spree, but represented God in carrying out his commands to execute his enemies. The soldiers and plunder were ritually purified. All this would show the Israelites that they were God's holy army, involved in a holy war, and warn them about the dangers of seductive idolatry. All Israel also benefitted from the death of the Midianites. The plunder belonged to the LORD, but was divided, and distributed to both the army and the community. To recognise that they were sharing in the LORD's spoils, tribute was set aside by all for him, handed over to the Levites who cared for the tabernacle. This episode was a foreshadowing of the policy that would be followed when Israel conquered the Canaanites. Balaam was among those killed, not dying the death of the righteous as he once desired (23:10). That is because he was the person who advised the Midianites to entice the Israelites away from the LORD (v 16).

When a delegation from the Reubenites and Gadites came to Moses with the request that they be allowed to settle where they were, and not cross over the Jordan River into the Land, he was understandably upset. They were sinning just like their fathers who had failed to enter the Land from Kadesh almost 40 years previously. However, when they offered for their men to go with the rest of the nation and participate in the war of invasion, leaving their families and flocks behind in secure enclosures until they returned, Moses was agreeable. They indicated that they would not return until the rest of Israel had obtained their inheritance in the Land, and that they would not take an inheritance there, because theirs would be on the east side of the Jordan. This agreement was confirmed by command, and Moses allocated the territories of the former Amorite kingdoms of Sihon and Og to the tribes of Reuben and Gad, and to half the tribe of Manasseh which joined the other two.

The final chapters of the Book of Numbers highlighted the nearness of Israel crossing over into the Promised Land. They look back over the way the nation has come, and look forward to what was ahead. When the book ends, everything is ready for Israel to move into his inheritance.

The recorded stages of Israel's travels from Rameses in Egypt to the plains of Moab contained 40 place names (chapter 33). Not every site where Israel camped was listed, and not every site that was listed had been mentioned previously. So, in addition to indicating the route followed, the record subtly drew attention to the 40 years that the journey took. Various comments were included also as reminders of significant events during the whole period. These were Passover, exodus, and the LORD's victory over Egypt's gods (v 3-4), crossing the sea, Marah, and Elim (v 8-9), Rephidim (v 14), Aaron's death and the king of Arad (v 38-40). Yet other major events, such as the formation of the covenant and receiving the Law at Sinai, the failure to enter and take the Land, the great revolt under Korah, and the seduction instigated by Balaam were not mentioned. This was because the focus was simply on the journey. The record showed that life for Israel since leaving Egypt had been a long journey through the desert, a nomadic existence of living in tents. Yet it was not a meaningless existence of wandering around in circles. The journey took them from Egypt to the plains of Moab.

Now everything was about to change. They had not quite reached their final destination, but they were now at the point of crossing over into their inheritance. As God's army, they were commanded to destroy and dispossess the current Canaanite occupants. As God's firstborn "son", they were to claim their inheritance, distributed fairly to each family by lot (God's will). The boundaries clearly prescribed the territory of their inheritance, and each tribe was represented to ensure that land distribution was appropriately assigned to all (chapter 34). The switch from the record of their past travels to a focus on their future inheritance makes a vivid impact. In contrast to the nomadic journey in the desert, life was about to become a permanent settlement in their own Land, and on their own family properties.

Throughout the tribal territories, cities were set aside for the Levites (chapter 35). Because the LORD himself was their inheritance, their presence and role amongst the people served as a vivid reminder of the unseen presence of the LORD, that Israel's inheritance was actually sharing the LORD's inheritance, and that their unity as a nation was centred on him. The six cities of refuge impressed upon all the sanctity of human life, based on reverence for the LORD who lived among them (35:33-34).

The final note in the "saga", concerning the family inheritance of Zelophehad, emphasised the requirement that the permanence and security of every inheritance must be guaranteed (chapter 36). God's redeemed covenant people had arrived at the point of possessing their promised inheritance.

Conspicuous throughout the nation's troubled experiences in its relation to God was Moses' role as mediator. He enjoyed intimate access to God and received direct communication from God. He acted as God's spokesman to the people, and at critical times he prayed to God on behalf of the nation. His intercession more than once averted God's anger from destroying the people (Numbers 11:2, 14:20, 16:47-48, 21:7). He powerfully demonstrated the fundamental role of prayer in response to God's astonishing historic covenant. The "saga" style presentation of God's majestic greatness and magnificent covenant, penetrating a world of oppression and hostility, and overcoming rebellious obstinacy, stirringly promotes his gracious plan of redemption. A crucial feature in the real-life drama of responding to God's interventions to restore harmonious relationships with his world is prayer.

A Renewed Covenant Community

Deuteronomy marks a grand event for the young nation Israel assembled on the plains of Moab adjacent to the Jordan River. The event took place a short time before Israel embarked on its conquest of Canaan. The book essentially represents a proclamation of God's Covenant with his chosen people. It contains three addresses by Moses made to the second generation of Israel. In them Moses reminds the people of their history, what God had done for them to this moment, and expounds the laws of their covenant obligations. He calls on his listeners to ratify their commitment to the covenant.

The book of Deuteronomy is complete within itself, and can stand alone. It is a strategic document within the Bible. It acts as a transition link between the "exodus saga", the books of Exodus-Leviticus-Numbers, and the "conquest saga", the book of Joshua. If Deuteronomy is removed, Joshua picks up where Numbers ends, and adds its own "saga". Although the first five books Genesis to Deuteronomy are usually linked together, and have been called the Pentateuch ("Five Books"), Deuteronomy has its own style, which is different from the "saga" genre, and relates to a single occasion. Yet it confirms the events of Exodus to Numbers, and expounds the covenant which was established at Sinai. Deuteronomy is foundational to all which issues subsequently throughout both the Old and New Testaments. In particular, its perspective is the shaping influence on the prophetic story told in the books of Joshua, Judges, 1&2 Samuel, and 1&2 Kings which traces the rise and collapse of Israel's kingship until the time of the exile. That same perspective also informed the views of the prophets who successively proclaimed God's word to the nation across its history until New Testament times, and whose messages are contained within their respective books. The book of Deuteronomy contains the essence of God's unique covenant with Israel, which was his extraordinary and exciting strategy for accomplishing his agenda of grace for the world. What is striking is the structure of the book, which bears distinct features similar to contemporary covenant treaties of that period.

"Deuteronomy" means "second law" or "repetition of the law", and suits as a title to the book which calls the next generation of Israelites to be committed to God's covenant which was first established with their parents at Mount Sinai. The first generation failed to keep the covenant, so Deuteronomy calls for it to be renewed by the second generation. The Hebrew title for the book is its first phrase, "These are the words". When we read through Leviticus we "listen" to the voice of God instructing Moses about covenant requirements. Here in Deuteronomy we again mainly "listen", but this time it is to the voice of Moses, speaking to Israel's second generation. He is worth listening to.

However, an in-depth discussion of Deuteronomy is not our intention here. It is certainly a worthwhile and enriching activity, but for our purpose at the moment we will focus on the overall picture and its stimulus for prayer. Let us briefly review the book. Its format is itself very interesting, since it follows the basic structure of an ancient suzerain/vassal covenant, with its own added unique features. Moses acts as mediator of the covenant by way of proclamation, presenting a series of addresses to the gathered nation, probably preached on the same day.

The outline of Deuteronomy shows its carefully composed literary format.

1:1-4:43	Moses' First Address	
1:1-5	Introduction	
1:6-4:40	Message: *God's past actions reviewed; appeal for the present*	
4:41-43	Appointment of Cities of Refuge	

1:44-28:68	Moses' Second address	
4:44-49	Introduction	
5:1-26:19	Message: *General Covenant Requirement & Detailed Stipulations*	
27:1-28:68	Covenant Ratification and Consequences	

29:1-30:20	Moses' Third Address	
29:1	Introduction	
29:2-30:20	Message: *Covenant Review & Appeal*	
31:1-34:12	Moses' Final Activities & Death	

An editorial framework around the speeches includes important details of the occasion and setting (1:1-5, 4:44-49, 29:1), legal arrangements concerning cities of refuge (4:41-43), ceremonial guidelines for ratifying the covenant (27-28), farewell provisions by Moses in the forms of endorsement of Joshua as future leader of the nation, a song of testimony about the nation's relationship with the LORD, and pronouncement of blessing upon the nation (31-33). The book concludes with an account of Moses' death (34).

First Address, 1:1-4:43

An Introduction (1:1-5), beginning with "These are the Words", provides a brief description of the location and occasion of the first speech. It was in the desert east of the Jordan in the territory of Moab on the first day of the eleventh month of the fortieth year. Moses began with a concise Historical Retrospect (1:6-3:29). He summarised what the LORD had done for Israel during her journey from Mount Horeb (Sinai) to their present location. Firstly, he recounted his appointment of additional leaders to assist him in carrying out judicial matters for the people. Then he reminded them of their reluctance to enter the Promised Land because of the adverse report of the scouts, which resulted in the LORD's verdict for them to be forever barred from the Land. They rebelled against this command and tried to go anyway, but were routed by the Amorite inhabitants. Consequently, they were condemned to wander around the hill country of Seir for forty years until the whole generation had died out. Then the next generation travelled to Moab, defeating Sihon king of Heshbon and Og king of Bashan along the way. The lands of these Amorite kings were divided among the Reubenites,

Gadites, and the half tribe of Manasseh. Moses concluded by saying that he had urged Joshua to have confidence of victory when he crossed over into Canaan, since he himself had been refused the privilege of entering the Land. Moses concluded his first speech with Practical Exhortation, making an appeal for Israel's future obedience to covenant decrees, forbidding idolatry, and urging allegiance to the LORD (4:1-40). An editorial Appendix completes the section, identifying three Cities of Refuge on the east side of Jordan (4:41-43).

Second Address, 4:44-28:68

Moses' second speech was the major segment of the book. It also had an Introduction, which began with the words, "This is the Law", giving a brief description of its content and location (4:44-49). Then followed an extensive Covenant Exposition, in which Moses proclaimed Israel's covenant obligations (5:1-26:19). Firstly he recalled the covenant given at Mount Horeb (Sinai), consisting of the Ten Commandments (5:1-6:3). Then he charged them to keep the covenant, emphasising its heart obligation (6:4-11:32). His charge included

(i) Demand for Allegiance (6:4-11)
(ii) Policy of Conquest (6:4-25)
(iii) Past Lessons (8-10:11)
(iv) Call to Commitment (10:12-11:32)

By way of practical obligation, he set out a number of Specific Duties, 12-26

(i) Worship (12-16:17)
(ii) Leaders (16:18-18)
(iii) Legal Procedures (19)
(iv) War (20)
(v) Miscellaneous Laws (21-25)
(vi) Two Rituals (26:1-15)
(viii) Conclusion (26:16-19)

The section was completed with a second Appendix, requiring Ratification of the Covenant after Israel crossed the Jordan (27), and declaring the Consequences of Obedience and Disobedience (28)

Third Address, 29-34

Moses' final speech commenced with another Introduction, which began, "These are the Words", and contained a brief description of its content and occasion. It was a Summons to Covenant Commitment (29-30). The closing Appendix concerned Moses:

- Final Arrangements & Song, 31-32:47
- Final Blessings & Death, 32:48-34

Significant themes which appear in Deuteronomy include inheritance of the Land in accord with God's promise to Abraham, the LORD's "holy war" against the nations which are to be driven from the land, the land as an Eden-like place of rest and worship, the covenant relationship as a bond of commitment love expressed in obedience to the Law, community life of personal and social well-being under God's blessing, and responsibility of covenant choices.

The Book of Deuteronomy provides a historical record of words and events on a significant day on the Plain of Moab. It is essentially rhetorical in style with an editorial framework. Its literary structure is striking, marked by prominent features. It has been called a "Covenant Treaty" because it conforms to the pattern of a suzerain treaty, with unique variations. It has been described as a "Theological History" to serve as an introduction to the series Joshua – 2 Kings. Its rhetorical style, however, differs from the "reporting" style of the history series, and the "saga" style of Joshua differs from both Deuteronomy and the subsequent series. Yet the theological perspective of the history series is certainly taken from Deuteronomy. This is highlighted by the discovery of the "Book of the Law" in the temple during the days of Josiah (2 Kings 22:8) which was likely some form of Deuteronomy. The rhetorical nature of the book has been compared to farewell speeches of other prominent biblical figures, such as Joshua and Samuel, and the contents provide an exposition of the covenant by Moses, preserved by the next generation (29:15), and subsequently edited by the prophetic movement. Although it is different in style, Deuteronomy complements the series of books Genesis to Numbers. It is a "finale" which culminates the process of God's purposes from creation through the covenants with Abraham and Israel. Its style is not "saga"-like as with Exodus-Leviticus-Numbers and with Joshua, but its occasion and format, rhetorical nature, and momentous contents give it an aura of its own. It makes its own dramatic impact. Because it has its own style, and represents a call to Israel's second generation for the covenant to be renewed, Deuteronomy subsequently serves as the measure of the nation's progress in the messages and historical writings of the prophets. It leaves Israel poised on the banks of the Jordan about to enter the Promised Land, and poised on the verge of an exciting future.

A primary requirement for Israel's covenant relationship with God when they settled in their new land was a central place of worship. The LORD's living presence was to be conspicuously the heart of national life. After appealing to his second generation audience for inner commitment to the covenant (Deuteronomy 5-11), Moses goes on to detail outward ordinances and institutions which must be established (12-26). This order is crucial. The covenant called Israel to a heart relationship with the LORD. Without inner commitment, the outward ordinances only produced a religious veneer. That is why the primary requirement of the covenant was succinctly expressed in Moses' appeal in 6:4-9:

"Hear, O Israel: the LORD our God, the LORD is one. Love the LORD your God with all your heart and with all your soul and with all your strength. These commandments which I give you today are to be upon your hearts. Impress them upon your children. Talk about them when you sit at home and when you walk along the road, when you lie down and when you get up. Tie them for a sign on your hands and bind them on your foreheads. Write them on the doorframes of your houses and on your gates."

Jews recite these words as part of a daily creed, and literally attach them in written form to their hands, foreheads and houses. The intent of the appeal, however, was not for outward ritual observance, but rather for heartfelt commitment applied to all spheres and relationships in life. It was a way of life expressing heart devotion, not a way of religion. The outward expression of a heart to heart relationship, not a ritualistic form of living. The LORD was to be loved whole heartedly, both personally and communally. Prescribed outward ordinances were intended to express that nationally. Later prophets frequently confronted Israel for practicing a ritualistic veneer, but failing miserably to maintain a genuine heart devotion to the LORD. The message of Deuteronomy was their inspiration.

The first outward national responsibility mentioned was the task of destroying all places and practices of idolatry throughout the land, and appointing a national centre of worship at a place chosen by the LORD (chapter 12). Just as the tabernacle was located central to the camp in Israel's nomadic life in the wilderness, so a central place of worship for the nation would be established in the land they were about to enter and possess. In particular Moses says,

"You are to seek the place the LORD your God will choose from among all your tribes **to put his name there** *for his dwelling"* (12:5).

God himself would determine where the national place of worship would be located, and for God to "put his name there" meant that his identity would be associated with it. The worship practices at the heart of Israel's community life expressed the intimate covenant relationship between God and his people, between God whose identity was the LORD and his people whose identity was the nation who "called upon the name of the LORD".

The covenant with the LORD gave Israel a distinctive identity amongst the nations. That distinction was not because of the nation's wealth or military might. Moses declares that the nation's distinctiveness would be the peoples' *"wisdom and understanding"* resulting from their obedience to the Law (4:6). Their greatness would be found in the nearness of their God whenever they prayed to him, and the righteousness of his law (4:7-8).

> *"What other nation is so great as to have their gods near them the way the LORD our God is near us whenever we pray to him? And what other nation is so great as to have such righteous decrees and laws as this body of laws I am setting before you today"*

The term "pray" here is actually the term "call"! In other words, Israel's greatness was the intimate covenant relationship between them and the LORD, marked by them hearing and obeying God's law, and God listening to their prayers. Prayer was intended to be meaningful and effective, not merely a pious performance. Israelites would have a privileged and real relationship with the living God, and could approach him in prayer with an expectation of being heard and answered. They would become renowned as the people who called on the name of the LORD. As a conspicuous feature of God's strategy for restoring his relationship with his wayward world, God had opened the door to prayer.

Moses' role as mediator between the LORD and Israel is revealing. He was God's covenant messenger to the people, and intercessor for the people. In recounting the nation's past rebellious ways, he reminds his listeners how he had interceded on their behalf to prevent their destruction at God's hand (9:7-29).

> *"I lay prostrate before the LORD those forty days and forty nights because the LORD had said he would destroy you. I prayed to the LORD and said, 'O Sovereign LORD, do not destroy your people, your own inheritance that you redeemed by your great power and brought out of Egypt with a mighty hand. Remember your servants Abraham, Isaac and Jacob. Overlook the stubbornness of this people, their wickedness and their sin. Otherwise, the country from which you brought us will say, 'Because the LORD was not able to take them into the land he had promised them, and because he hated them, he brought them out to put them to death in the desert'. But they are your people, your inheritance that you brought out by your great power and your outstretched arm'"* (v 25-29).

His intercession was deeply personal and intense, protracted, and appealed to God in terms of his covenant commitment. Although he pleaded on behalf of the people, he was also simultaneously representing the LORD. It was not a matter of the man Moses pacifying the LORD's anger, but the LORD's covenant messenger moderating the LORD's anger in accord with the LORD's own covenant intention. Moses' intercession revealed the merciful and compassionate nature of the covenant, and the importance of intercession within the framework of the covenant. It highlighted the central role of prayer in God's covenant which called his people to call on him. Deuteronomy's exposition of the LORD's covenant with Israel showed that the whole orientation of the nation was meant to revolve around the LORD as King in humble, worshipful dependence and obedience. The covenant set Israel apart as distinctive among the nations. At its heart was prayer, which demonstrated the LORD's approachability. It demonstrated why we, on earth, should pray!

CHAPTER 4

RISE & DEMISE OF THE KINGDOM

Our guided tour now reaches a new stage in its journey through the Bible's "sacred history". Following the death of Moses, and the first generation of Israelites, a new era for God's chosen covenant nation began. God's intention to restore his kingdom and to bless all mankind remained firm, but his campaign followed a long and eventful course. The books of the Old Testament are the literary legacy of that campaign, and bear witness to God's commitment to his covenant and to his self-revelation. The first five books, Genesis to Deuteronomy, which we have reviewed, are called the "Books of the Law". The rest are divided into two general groupings referred to as the "Books of the Prophets", which we will turn to now, and "The Writings", which we will get to in due course.

The "Books of the Prophets" consist of a series of apparent historical accounts (Joshua through to 2 Kings, excluding Ruth which belongs to "The Writings") often referred to as the "Former Prophets", and a collection of records of the messages and actions of various individual prophets (Isaiah to Malachi, excluding Lamentations and Daniel which also belong to "The Writings") known as the "Latter Prophets". These two bodies of literature provide a special perspective on the progressive state of Israel's covenant relationship with God. We must recognize, however, that the focus of the books is primarily on God, not Israel. The historical accounts reveal God's actions, and the prophecies express his words. The books are also very creatively composed, so it is necessary for us to discern the various literary features which are included.

The popular picture of the Hebrew prophets in many peoples' minds is of outspoken, wild-eyed, woolly haired, unkempt men who suddenly turned up out of the blue and unceremoniously predicted doom and gloom for all and sundry. But they were not really like that, although they were certainly messengers with a serious message.

Prophets in Israel were people chosen by God to have a close and privileged relationship with him. They were granted access to his kingly presence and "council" where he declared his will to them, and they became his messengers in making it known. Abraham was the first person to be called a prophet (Genesis 20:7), and he was not only told of God's intentions but participated in God's determinations by way of intercession (Genesis 18:16-33).

Moses also fulfilled the role of prophet, both as messenger and intercessor. Just prior to his departure he announced that God would continue to raise up successive prophets like him to guide the nation in accord with their covenant relationship (Deuteronomy 18:14-22). When eventually the monarchy was established in Israel, a movement of prophets became a prominent feature, consisting of both independent individuals and companies of prophets living in particular localities.

The books of the "Former Prophets" (Joshua – 2 Kings) present an interpretive history of God's dealings with his covenant people Israel, from the time of Moses' death until the Babylonian captivity. Various sources were used in compiling this history, but the final composition was obviously produced by an editorial prophet or group of prophets sometime during the exile. The interpretative style reflects a prophetic perspective in accord with the terms of God's covenant, especially as expressed in Deuteronomy. Along with creative literary elements, this perspective greatly affects the finished product. It is the message about God which is important, not the details which make up the composition. The series of historical accounts traces successive phases of Israel's history, including significant national developments such as conquest and settlement of the Promised Land, and establishment of the monarchy and the temple, as well as the general degeneration of covenant faithfulness, division of the kingdom, and eventual demise of the monarchy.

To get a proper perspective, we need to recognize the overall pattern of the series of books, and how each book fits in. Joshua presents the conquest and settlement of the Promised Land, a period of one generation. Judges provides an overview of Israel's conditions in the Land during the first couple of centuries. 1&2 Samuel describes the rise of the monarchy in Israel, and the reign of David. 1&2 Kings traces the fortunes of kingship in Israel for nearly 400 years until its disappearance. Obviously the books are not similar in the chronological periods they cover, nor their subjects. Neither are they similar in their formats, styles and messages. The series is not simply a chronological history of events. It is a theological interpretation of history, using creative literary methods to highlight important truths. The books provide a helpful overview of Israel's historical progress, but their primary aim is to reveal crucial insights.

Covenant Inheritance

Joshua is the first book in the series, and records Israel's conquest and settlement of the land of Canaan under the leadership of Joshua, who succeeded Moses as God's appointed national leader. The purpose of the book was to demonstrate God's fulfilment of his promise to Abraham of a land and an inheritance for the nation of Israel.

Joshua is famously remembered for his military exploits, and especially for his dramatic capture of Jericho where the city walls fell down after Israel marched around it each day for seven days, and for the extraordinary tale of the sun standing still. Such sensational events have either captivated people's imaginations or repulsed people's credulity. Either reaction can distract from the book's message, which is an invaluable contribution to the unfolding revelation in the Bible's sacred story. It is imperative that we recognise the literary nature of the book. What Joshua shows is that with regard to God's agenda of grace, God keeps his promises, and has an inheritance for his people! It also highlights the role and value of prayer.

Before we take up the book, however, we need to consider a couple of matters. It has long been recognised that Joshua's sweeping victorious conquest of Canaan is somewhat at odds with the view of the book of Judges which follows. In contrast to the lightning military overthrow of Canaan's kings in Joshua, Judges depicts a long gradual process of conflict before Israel fully gained the upper hand. The two versions are not incompatible. The book of Joshua conflates everything into a swift overall conquest, while the book of Judges reflects the reality that not all Canaanites were immediately eliminated. The initial events included in concept the subsequent outworking process. Israel's occupation of the land was more like wheat and weeds growing together in the same field, than a new crop planted in freshly cleared and cultivated soil. The editorial team of the complete series Joshua-2 Kings would be fully cognisant of the apparent inconsistency, and intend the two versions to complement one another in order to provide the whole picture.

A less recognised inconsistency is between the version of Joshua and that of archaeology. The general archaeological opinion is that excavations have failed to substantiate the biblical story, leading to the conclusion that the book of Joshua was nationalist propaganda of much later kings of Judah. Some scholars have gone so far as to say that Joshua was merely fiction. This could be a disturbing threat to our confidence in the book, yet it actually prods us to a sharper appreciation of its literary nature. Before we turn to Joshua, however, we must firstly recognise that the full archaeological picture itself is not clear. On the one hand, archaeological discoveries have confirmed the authenticity of many aspects of the biblical background, such as social customs, cultic practices, architecture, agriculture, warfare, and cultural features. They have also advanced our knowledge of historical periods and personalities, numerous biblical sites, and ancient literary practices. All these have contributed greatly to our understanding of the Bible. On the other hand, not all biblical sites have been established beyond doubt. Many sites have not been completely excavated, and the exact chronology of layers of occupation can be uncertain. We need not take archaeology's views about Joshua as conclusive. For a start, we are not able to pinpoint from the Bible exactly when Joshua lived, so archaeology's chronology is difficult to compare. We have to suspend our judgement concerning the historical world of both Joshua and archaeology. At the same time, some aspects of the conquest campaign are in agreement with archaeological discoveries. For example, archaeology confirms the sudden destruction and burning of Jericho (6:24) and Hazor (11:11, 13) and other cities of ancient Canaan, as the book of Joshua describes, but it is their dating which is problematic. Joshua's version seems to be another case of conflation of events. Such a thought might be unsettling. However, we have to be careful how we apply modern standards of history and literature to ancient attitudes. The book of Joshua had its own purpose and style which we must respect. Let me repeat, it is imperative that we recognise the literary nature of the book!

The book was not intended to be a historical account of Israel's conquest of Canaan. Rather, it was a reframed version of the legend of the conquest, in order to reveal God's role in it. He was the primary player. A careful review of the book reveals that there is not a lot of historical information in it. The book consists mainly of summary matters together with several lively anecdotal segments. In it God was shown to be personally and dramatically involved in the action, while Joshua and Israel were secondary players. In the book of Joshua, we are presented with the "conquest saga". The narrative relies on vivid and sensational features, depicted with embellishments and anecdotal descriptions. The "conquest saga" and "exodus saga" have similar literary styles, although marked differences. Symbols for God found in Exodus-Leviticus-Numbers, such as the pillars of fire and cloud, don't appear in Joshua. Instead, God is represented by the ark of the covenant, and his actions detected in uncanny natural phenomena. Neither are Israel's troop numbers in Joshua anywhere near those which marched out of Egypt and through the desert to Moab under Moses' leadership. If events have been conflated, it represents its "saga" style.

The historical details have been glossed over to depict God's active presence. The narrative of Joshua is both historical and theological, and we need to read it with that understanding in order to grasp its message. The historical and theological features are merged as one, and they require careful discernment to distinguish them. We must not ignore the theological perspective, and consider the historical account to be confused or fantasised. Nor should we ignore the history as irrelevant, and merely concentrate on the theology. God's revelation was disclosed in historical actions, and its meaning was presented in the style of the narrative. This was a very creative and inspiring literary technique. Furthermore, the book was composed with a carefully laid out plan in mind.

Entrance to the Land: *Preparation for Invasion* (1:1-2:24), *Crossing the Jordan* (3:1-4:24), *Circumcision & Passover at Gilgal* (5:1-12)
Conquest of the Land: *Victory over Jericho & Ai; Covenant Renewal in the Land* (5:13-8:35), *Victory in the South* (9:1-10:43), *Victory in the North* (11:1-23), *Summary of Defeated Kings in Canaan* (12:1-24)
Settlement of the Land: *Unconquered Regions (v1-7) & Allocated Regions East of Jordan* (13:1-33), *Allocated Regions to Tribes & to Joshua in the Land* (14:1-19:51)
Cities of Refuge (ch 20) **& Cities for Levites** (ch 21)

Covenant Commitment: *Altar of Witness East of Jordan* (22:1-34), *Joshua's Farewell to Israel's Leaders* (23:1-16), *Covenant Renewal at Shechem* (24:1-28), *Deaths of Joshua & Eleazar* (24:29-33)

The first half of the book (chapters 1-12) describes the conquest, using a three campaigns strategy. The first campaign invaded the central region of the land and thus divided the country. Then the second campaign took the south, and the third campaign the north. The presentation of these campaigns was embellished by the inclusion of gripping anecdotal descriptions. In the second half of the book (chapters 13-24) the victorious Creator King allocated the land as an inheritance to his covenant nation, and strategically appointed cities of refuge both for ready access and to bind the tribes in unity. Two and a half tribes received territory on the east side of the Jordan as previously agreed with Moses. Nine and a half tribes settled on the west of Jordan. Distribution of land was determined by lot, thus relying on divine direction. The tribe of Levi received no territory, apart from towns and pasture lands, because it had been chosen for a special priestly role to the whole nation. Instead, the tribe of Joseph was allotted a double portion through allocations to the tribes of Joseph's sons, Ephraim and Manasseh. The major division of the land was between Judah in the south and Joseph (Ephraim and Manasseh) in the central region. The remaining tribes received their allotments in relation to these two divisions. Caleb and Joshua each received a personal allocation. The book concluded with Joshua confirming the nation's commitment to the covenant in the settled land at the end of his days.

It is not possible to explore everything mentioned in Joshua. We will focus on the main themes which shape the flow of the book. That allows the primary message of the book to be understood. The book of Joshua presents a very positive outlook, and shows that the LORD is a God who keeps his promises!!

Although Joshua was the prominent leader who decisively led Israel in its successful conquest of the land and its allocation of territories for each tribe's covenant inheritance, behind every action was the living LORD. He spoke and acted and overruled. The book begins by indicating what "*the LORD said to Joshua*" after the death of Moses (1:1-9). He told Joshua to prepare to cross the Jordan River with the Israelites to enter the land which he would give them. He assured him that he would give him all the territory that he promised Moses, and that he would be with him as he was with Moses. He urged Joshua to be "*strong and courageous*" and obedient to the law given by Moses without deviating from it, and to meditate in the "Book of the Law" constantly. This was a relevant emphasis for Israel's new era. Joshua was Moses' successor, having a similar relationship with the LORD and a similar role with Israel, but a different responsibility. His task was to lead Israel into the Promised Land and to take possession of it. The instruction was also relevant at the start of the next book in this series of books presenting the eventful origins of Israel, which were written for the benefit of their exiled readers. The message of the book was that God accomplished it all, through Joshua his obedient servant, a message which was relevant for its later readers.

Joshua sent two scouts on a fact-finding mission concerning the land about to be invaded, and especially the city of Jericho (chapter 2). As commander about to lead his forces into military combat, Joshua was taking wise preliminary investigation. Perhaps he recalled his own experience as one of the twelve scouts who had spied out the land a generation earlier (Numbers 13). As it happens, the story of their reconnaissance makes no mention of any relevant military intelligence gathered. Neither, as events will reveal, was it necessary, since Jericho would be taken by non-military methods. Instead, the story reiterates, through Rahab's confession (2:9) and the scouts' oath to her (2:14) and report to Joshua (2:24), the earlier truth that God will "give" the land to Israel.

The major focus of the story was Rahab, who was a prostitute living in a house on the city wall. As a place frequented by men, it was a good cover for the scouts to lodge there. Rahab hid them from the king of Jericho, and helped them to escape. The key points in the story were Rahab's confession (2:9-11), and her contract with the scouts (2:12-14). In her confession, Rahab showed knowledge and fear of the LORD because of his exploits on behalf of Israel, recognising him as the God of heaven and earth. She mentioned particular events at the beginning and end of Israel's journey from Egypt to their present position. She confessed her conviction that the LORD had already given the land to them. In making a deal with the scouts, she used the language of God's covenant with Israel. She had shown *"kindness"* (*"covenant faithfulness"*) to them, and she wanted them to take an oath in the name of the LORD to show her and her family the same *"kindness"*. She was wanting her family to be treated as if they were Israelites! The scouts agreed, on conditions that the arrangement was kept secret and was strictly obeyed. All family members had to gather within Rahab's home, and a red rope, by which the scouts escaped, had to be fixed in the window. This was perhaps reminiscent of the Passover blood daubed on Israelite houses back in Egypt. What the scouts' reported to Joshua was all that was needed.

Israel's crossing the Jordan river to enter the Promised Land was a dramatic, miraculous event (chapters 3-5). The story was told with skill, surprise, and suspense. The main focus was the ark of the covenant, which led the way, and took up position in the middle of the river until all Israel crossed over. Little is said about Israel's experience, but the main interest was the erection of memorial stones to mark the event, and some unexpected activities in the new Land.

After receiving the spies' encouraging report, Joshua rose early next morning and moved camp closer to the river, ready to cross when the order came. The river at that time was in flood. The people were told to take their cue from the movement of the ark of the covenant, which symbolised God's presence among them.

The expression, "*The LORD said to Joshua*", occurs frequently throughout the narrative, indicating that he was living, personal, and directing affairs, but without explaining how he was speaking. God's word was the means for achieving his will. The ark represented the unseen presence of the LORD. Joshua demonstrated that to the Israelites when he gave instructions about how they were to cross the Jordan. He told them,

> "*This is how you will know that the **living God** is among you and that he will certainly drive out before you the Canaanites, Hittites, Hivites, Perizzites, Girgashites, Amorites and Jebusites. See, the ark of the covenant of the Lord of all the earth will go into the Jordan ahead of you. Now then, choose twelve men from the tribes of Israel, one from each tribe. And as soon as the priests who carry the ark of the LORD – the Lord of all the earth – set foot in the Jordan, its waters flowing downstream will be cut off and stand up in a heap.*" (3:10-13)

It happened as Joshua said. As the priests who were carrying the ark stepped into the river the waters dried up. The river bank upstream had caved in and dammed off the water flow. The cause was natural, and the miracle was in the timing. The incident was a dramatic reminder of the crossing of the Sea of Reeds by the original Israelites led by Moses, and a promise that the same living God would be with them as they followed Joshua.

The ark dominated the whole event of the crossing, which was told with dramatic flair. Leading the way, conspicuous to all nearly a kilometre ahead of the consecrated nation which followed in military formation, the ark entered the river. As foretold, the swollen waters ceased to flow at that moment, because of a damming of the river far upstream. The ark was carried to the middle of the Jordan, where it waited until all Israel had crossed over. As with the earlier preparation (chapter 1), there was emphasis upon the whole of Israel.

The telling of the story of Israel's crossing the Jordan retraced its steps to focus on the erection of memorial stones. Twelve men, each chosen on behalf of his tribe so that the whole of Israel was represented, were appointed to collect stones from the river. They erected two monuments, one on land at their new campsite (4:8), and one in the middle of the river where the ark of the covenant had been stationed (4:9). The role of the ark was significant. Once the nation had crossed over in military formation ready for war (a point highlighted), the priests carrying the ark of the covenant were commanded to leave the river, which immediately began to flow again. Joshua explained that the memorial stones were set up for the benefit of future generations, as a reminder that God had enabled Israel to cross over on dry ground, just as it had crossed the Red Sea previously. From this day on, Joshua was revered in the same way as Moses had been.

The drying up of the Jordan (5:1) had the same effect on local inhabitants as God's previous exploits (2:9-11). Their hearts melted from fear. Israel, however, now in the Land by God's gracious faithfulness to his promise, had some neglected matters to attend to before taking possession of it. The LORD ordered Joshua to perform a mass circumcision of all who had not received the rite, and to celebrate the Passover. These covenant obligations linked the new generation with the original exodus from Egypt. Circumcision was a physical rite with a spiritual meaning (Deuteronomy 10:16), and was a sign of Israel's covenant relationship with the LORD (Genesis 17:11). It was a condition for participating in the Passover (Exodus 12:48), which commemorated the passing over Israelite homes by the angel of death which slew the firstborn sons of Egypt (Exodus 12:13, 23, 27). On the day following the Passover in the Promised Land, Israel ate produce from the Land for the first time, and provision of manna stopped. Israel had begun a new era! When Joshua encountered a mysterious man holding a drawn sword (5:13), ready for battle, he asked whose side he was on. He replied that he had not come to take sides, but to take over! He was commander of the LORD's army, a theophany of the LORD himself. Joshua worshipped him, and obeyed his instruction to remove his sandals because he stood on holy ground. His experience was identical with that of Moses at the "burning bush" (Exodus 3:5).

The story of the conquest focused on selected features to illustrate important matters to be noted (chapters 6-12). So, with the conquest of Jericho, attention was given to the prominent role of the Ark of the Covenant to show that victory resulted from the presence of the LORD (6:8-14). There is also a sharp contrast drawn between Rahab the Canaanite prostitute (6:25) and Achan the Israelite (7:24-26). She was shown grace, and spared like an Israelite because of her recognition of the LORD and allegiance to his invading nation. He was shown justice, and destroyed like the Canaanites because he was disloyal and disobedient to the LORD.

Notice how the battle of Jericho was described. The key features were the central place of the ark of the LORD, which represented his invisible presence; the circling of the city in multiples of seven times, which highlighted God's sign of seven days in regard to his covenant with Israel; the blowing of trumpets, which was a reminder of God's presence (Exodus 19:16-19) and the signal for attack; and the loud shout by the people, which was their battle cry. Description of these is extensive and vivid. Yet nothing is said about the city itself, and the story is virtually silent about details of the battle. All that is simply stated is that the wall collapsed, and Israel was able to enter and capture the city. The city was devoted to the LORD, with every living thing within it completely destroyed, the whole of it burnt, and its treasures placed in the treasury of the house of the LORD. This description was theological in nature, and historical facts were ignored. It was not intended to be a historical account. Neither was it political propaganda. Neither was it fiction. It was the presentation of a theological perspective of a past historical episode in dramatic "saga" style. The book of Joshua was a prophetic interpretation of Israel's occupation of the former land of Canaan, which came about by the LORD's conquest of the country. The land was not taken by Israel. It was taken by the LORD, and "given" to Israel!

Two features were highlighted by the presentation. In accord with God's policy, everything in the city was devoted to the LORD, and was destroyed. In accord with the special covenant made by the spies with Rahab, she and all in her house were spared. Jericho was the first city in the Promised Land to fall, and was therefore a symbol of what would happen to the rest of the Land.

While Rahab the Canaanite behaved, and was treated, like an Israelite, Achan behaved, and was treated, like a Canaanite. The Achan affair was given prominent, lengthy, artfully composed, and vivid anecdotal coverage. Buoyed by success at Jericho, Joshua confidently set out on his campaign to subdue the rest of the Land, unaware that Israel, through the transgression of Achan, had breached the covenant, and that God's anger blazed against them. Obedience to the covenant was essential for success (1:6-9, Exodus 23:22). Yet Achan had disobeyed the specific command to destroy what God had banned. The painful experience of humiliating defeat at Ai filled Joshua with overwhelming grief. Probably recalling previous experiences (Exodus 32:11-13, Numbers 14:15-16), he discerned that Israel (*"this people"*, 7:7) must have been at fault somehow, so he prostrated himself before God (*"Sovereign LORD"*) in prayer. As the new leader of God's people, Joshua's reaction was meant to be seen as an example. He expressed his regret that God had brought them into the Land, and his fear that news of their defeat would rally the rest of the country to surround them and wipe them out. What then would become of God's great name? This was his primary concern. The LORD stood Joshua up, informed him of the sin which had occurred, and ordered him to track down and deal with the culprit. The next day Joshua investigated the whole nation, and identified Achan, who confessed his sin, and was condemned to death. He and his family (presumably complicit in the crime) were stoned to death in the Valley of Achor, and burned with all their possessions. A covering rock pile became a second memorial in the Land, and God's anger abated.

What message would Achan's experience have for the intended readers languishing in exile?!!

Explanation: God's "Holy War"

The degree of brutal violence and "ethnic cleansing" at God's command evokes horror and calls for explanation. The policy to exterminate the Canaanites highlights the fact that the conquest was an act of God.

This was because God was at war! He was reclaiming his world from godless usurpers. This was the context for understanding the military invasion of the land of Canaan. It was God's first step towards repossessing his world, in a journey which eventually led to the crucifixion of his anointed Saviour. His redeemed covenant people, Israel, was his army, and the campaign against Jericho was the first operation. But with this first attack against Jericho, God showed dramatically that he was the assailant! He won an astonishing victory. However, there was a spoiler in the ranks of his forces, who had to be eradicated. In both his victory and his judgement, God revealed who was the divine foe.

On the one hand this was a "holy war" by which the LORD, the true and living God, overthrew and destroyed the idolatrous and debauched occupants of the land. He was judging them, just as he had previously punished Sodom and Gomorrah in Abraham's day, and Egypt in Moses' day. God's personal presence meant total destruction for his rebellious enemies. His presence was manifested in Israel, his covenant people among whom he lived, and who, under Joshua, were his "holy army", an instrument of judgement.

This was not merely an invading nation brutally displacing and eradicating the rightful owners of their land. The land, as did the whole world, belonged to God, who was the Creator King. At this time he was repossessing this portion of the earth from its corrupt human occupants who controlled it by relying on their false gods and military powers. God defeated them on their own terms, by overthrowing them through military action and a policy of total extermination. God was supreme commander throughout the campaign, and Joshua simply implemented his orders.

Israel was the LORD's covenant servant, his "army", carrying out his commands in order to reclaim what was rightfully his. Therefore the nation had to be ceremonially clean, strictly obedient to orders, and scrupulously observant of the "ban" on all Canaanite plunder, because it was not acting as a free agent, but as a dedicated instrument. Israel's mission was specific and limited. It was not authorised to take up arms to conquer all lands or to establish an empire of its own volition. The requirements of total destruction of the people and the "ban" on all spoil emphasised their dedication to the LORD.

The conquest of Canaan was a witness to the nations that the LORD was the living God, the rightful ruler of the world, that he was just, and that Israel was his "army", appointed to fulfil a righteous mission. It demonstrated the reality and power of God's kingdom, which was reasserting its authority over a rebellious world. It also graphically demonstrated that the whole world was already under the judgement of death because of its rebellion against the Creator King. This was one step in God's outworking plan to overthrow all evil, and restore his kingdom on earth.

On the other hand, the conquest of Canaan was also a witness to Israel. Its success was only achieved according to the LORD's orders and power. It also highlighted the need for moral and cultural purity. The drastic eradication of all things Canaanite protected Israel from the contamination of idolatry and depravity. As God's kingly priesthood and holy nation, it was imperative for Israel to be righteous in all its ways, and untainted by the world's pollution.

***

Joshua marked the progress of invasion into the Promised Land by erecting stone piles: in the middle of the Jordan river; at Gilgal; and over the body of Achan. The story comments that they *"remain to this day"*, a phrase which draws attention to the permanent significance of the stone piles, and shows that the account was being written at a much later date. In the next campaign the conquest of Ai was also marked by stone piles and the accompanying phrase. Then the phrase was used in connection with a peace treaty made with the city of Gibeon, implying that it too was a virtual monument to the invasion. These "monuments" represented highly important features of Israel's progress.

Contrary to the earlier advice of scouts (7:3), God told Joshua to take the *"whole army"* in his attack against Ai. This was over the top for such a relatively small city. That is because it was not a normal military operation, but an act of God. As with Jericho (6:2), Joshua was assured that Ai was *"delivered"* into his hands, yet unlike at Jericho (6:18-19), God's ban was less strict, and Israel was allowed to take plunder and livestock. Whereas at Jericho the ark of the covenant, representing the presence of God, prominently led the assault, at Ai Joshua led. Yet he followed God's strategy and commands. God was the real commander-in-chief! The story elaborately described the ambush as the major feature of the battle, an ingenious strategy which was especially effective because of Israel's earlier defeat (7:6, 8:6). God turned failure into victory. The story was skilfully told, adding information and vague details as events proceeded, giving surprise and suspense. It was disclosed that the close neighbouring city of Bethel was also involved (8:9, 12, 17).

The eventual capture of Ai, though achieved by clever tactics, was dramatically seen to be the result of strict obedience to the LORD's instruction (8:18, 26). Joshua sent 30,000 warriors ahead by night, with orders to set up an ambush between Ai and Bethel, while he stayed at the main camp. Early the next day Joshua led the rest of his force to the north of Ai and made camp across a valley from the city. The ambush contingent was now said to be 5,000, which is at odds with the original number. This means that 25,000 were unaccounted for. Neither was there any mention about what happened to Bethel. Joshua directed operations by raising his javelin, like Moses of old (8:18). The story's main interest was Ai, which included Israel's earlier failure there (chapter 7). The point is that both Achan and Ai were completely destroyed!! The whole population was exterminated, the city looted and burned, and its king slain and hung. As with Achan, the city was left as a heap of stones, and the king's corpse covered with another stone pile, making three permanent monuments of God's judgement. What the story shows is that God sent his army as an instrument of judgement to wipe out the wicked, as he reclaimed his own Land which they had polluted. Bethel is only mentioned in passing, although it seems also to have been captured (perhaps by the 25,000), but not destroyed (12:9, 16).

The erection of an altar on Mount Ebal and the holding of a national ceremony there, in the glow of these initial victories over Jericho and Ai, made a significant statement. This was a renewal of the covenant in the Promised Land as commanded by Moses (Deuteronomy 27:2-4). The sacrifices were the same as those offered at Mount Sinai when the law was first given to Israel (Exodus 20:24). Stones were inscribed with a copy of the law, and Joshua read out the law to the whole assembly. God had now re-established his presence and rule in the Land, his Land! The episode has a prominent theological significance.

The next story is a surprise. In reaction to what happened at Jericho and Ai, a coalition of independent kings from all over the country united to war against Joshua and Israel (9:1-2). This was not a particular event, but a summary introduction to the sequence of events which followed. It presents a picture of united opposition to God and his people. Another coalition of cities (9:17), however, governed by elders, not kings (9:11), adopted a strategy to seek peace. Pretending to come from a distant country, and not admitting that they knew about Jericho and Ai, they used the same explanation for their motives as Rahab (9:9-10, 2:10). They deceived Joshua and Israel's leaders into making a treaty. These leaders disregarded God's explicit policy (Deuteronomy 7:1-2), and failed to consult the LORD (9:14). When the deception was discovered, Israel was bound by oath not to kill them, even though they were Hivites under God's condemnation. The people of Israel murmured their disapproval against their leaders, though God remained silent. Without approving their actions, there is a sense that God was accomplishing his own purpose. The leaders rebuke the Gibeonite envoys, and put them under a "*curse*" (9:23) to be woodcutters and water carriers for the house of God. They were to be slaves performing menial tasks. Yet from the Gibeonites' perspective, they were "*saved*" from extermination (9:26), they showed a submissive attitude (9:25), and actually gained a privileged role in God's service. Their role became a permanent "monument" of Israel's invasion (9:27). In time, Gibeon, became the location for the tabernacle (2 Chronicles 1:3). The "*curse*" had turned out to be blessing!

The legendary occasion when the "sun stood still" was reported to illustrate conquest of the south. Joshua and Israel defeated a coalition of five kings by the timely intervention of a devastating hail storm which demonstrated the LORD's alliance with Israel. The story was important for several reasons. It was the first time that Canaanites initiated hostility, and was an example of the banding together of independent royal cities to resist Israel's invasion, as previously mentioned at 9:1-2. It was a challenge to Israel's loyalty to its treaty with Gibeon. Israel won a decisive victory because of God's miraculous intervention. It was the last battle in the campaign for the middle region of the Land.

The five Amorite kings came from the hill country and lowlands in the south. They were alarmed because Gibeon had made a peace treaty with Israel. Gibeon was different from the royal cities, being a republic not a monarchy. Located in the centre of the country, and allied with other nearby cities in its treaty with Israel, it had become a strategic threat to the whole Land. When the attack came, Gibeon, a city in the high country, appealed for help to its treaty overlord, Israel, camped about 35 kilometres away. Joshua responded immediately, and, assured of victory by God, marched all night with his whole army to the rescue. He took the besieging troops by surprise and defeated them in a great victory. The description of the battle and the subsequent chase as the enemy fled alternates between Israel's actions and God's, and moves back and forth in time. Although God's actions were mentioned secondly, they actually preceded Israel's, and were the explanation for Israel's success. In particular, God's personal involvement was described in highly vivid, animated, anthropomorphic language. The LORD "*threw them into confusion*", and "*hurled large hailstones down on them from the sky*". The enemy's flight via Beth Horon was westwards, down a steep incline to the coastal plain, and then south towards Azekah and Makkedah. This made them vulnerable to Israel's forces coming from behind and above them. So Israel was able to "*cut them down*". Yet then it is explained that it was God's deluge of hail which killed more of them than Israelite swords. Israel itself was untouched by the hail. This miracle of divine intervention was explained as an answer to prayer offered beforehand by Joshua in the presence of Israel (10:12). Judging from the quotation derived from the Book of Jashar, it seems to have been early in the morning as the sun rose in the east above Gibeon and the moon could still be observed in the west above Aijalon. Therefore, before the battle began.

The purpose of the account was not to report the sun literally standing still. Such an impression gained from a superficial reading of the story has excited both extravagant claims of astronomical proof in support, and scornful mockery. The language is figurative. Joshua addressed the sun and moon in the language of natural observation, similar to speaking about the rising and setting of the sun. It was not meant to be taken literally, nor did the sun literally stop in the middle of the day. From the point of view of normal observation it stopped because the abnormal hailstorm blotted it out. The extraordinary weather conditions, which caused such devastating impact on the enemy and enabled Joshua's spectacular victory, were a direct answer to prayer, and evidence of God's supernatural intervention.

The point of the story was to highlight Joshua's bold public prayer, and "*a day when the LORD listened to a man. Surely the LORD was fighting for Israel*" (10:12-14). The term "prayer" was not mentioned, but the act of prayer was conspicuous, and God's response was memorable. In the whole of the book of Joshua this incident relating to prayer stands out. It therefore gives added prominence to the role and effectiveness of prayer offered to the living God, in accord with his own purposes and in confident dependence. Joshua again serves as an example of intercessory prayer, as Moses had before him.

Although the narrative indicates that after the victory Joshua returned to Gilgal (10:15), it then returns to describe in a somewhat lengthy account what happened to the five kings (and further events, until 10:43). On the one hand, it rounds out the story which began with an ominous picture of the threat posed by the alliance of the five kings, who were identified twice (10:3, 5), by concluding with a gruesome account of their humiliation and death. The kings were incarcerated in a cave where they took refuge, and then brought out and forced to submit to Israel's army commanders placing their feet on their necks before Joshua executed them. On the other hand, the end of the story tells how all the forces of the five kings, except for a few who managed to reach safety, were destroyed, and the bodies of the five kings were hung on trees until evening, before being thrown back into their cave which was sealed with large rocks. These rocks were yet another "monument" (10:27) of God's judgement upon the inhabitants of the Land of Canaan.

After the defeat of the five kings, Joshua pressed on to overthrow the cities from which they came, and then to penetrate further into the south to conquer other strategic cities. As with previous conquests, he completely exterminated everyone. Israel then had control of all the middle and southern regions of the country.

Alarmed by these events, Jabin, king of Hazor, which was a large and powerful city, formed an extensive coalition in the north to resist the invasion (11:1-5). Events followed a similar pattern, though less dramatic, to those of the five kings led by Adoni-Zedek of Jerusalem. Encouraged by the LORD not to be afraid, Joshua surprised the coalition forces at the Waters of Merom, defeated them, and pursued those who fled until all were killed. Then he executed Jabin, totally destroyed Hazor, and burnt it. As commanded by the LORD, he had all the enemy's horses hamstrung and chariots burnt, thus removing opportunity for the Canaanites to rally their forces, and temptation for Israelites to rely on military strength rather than trust the LORD. He went on to take all the royal cities in the north, until eventually Israel possessed the entire Land. In particular Joshua wiped out the dreaded Anakim who had been a reason for the previous generation of Israel failing to enter the Promised Land under Moses (Numbers 13:22, 28).

The land of Canaan was the Land of God's promised inheritance for his people. God promised it to Abraham, to be received by his descendants when the sin of the Amorites had reached full measure (Genesis 15:16-20). When Joshua and Israel invaded the Land, eliminated the Amorites, and took possession of the country, the Land was allocated to Israel in tribal divisions as their inheritance. The conquest of Canaan is summarised by describing, in relation to the Jordan River, the geographical territory possessed, and by listing the kings who were defeated (chapter 12). On the eastern side of the Jordan, the Land stretched from the Arnon Gorge, which was about the midway point of the Dead Sea, up to Mount Hermon, and was formerly the kingdoms of the Amorite rulers Sihon and Og who were defeated by Moses. On the western side of the Jordan, the Land stretched from Baal Gad in the Lebanon Valley, near the foot of Mount Hermon, down to Mount Halak near the southern end of the Dead Sea, formerly occupied by numerous royal cities which Joshua defeated. Moses allocated territories in the east as inheritances for the tribes of Reuben and Gad, and half the tribe of Manasseh. Eleazar the priest, Joshua, and the tribal heads allocated territories in the west, under divine guidance determined by lot, to the remaining nine and a half tribes. The tribe of Levi was allocated cities to live in throughout the country, but no tribal territory of its own, because their inheritance was their priestly service to the LORD himself. The conquest summary demonstrated the victory of God's kingship over Canaan's kings, and his repossession of his Land. Distribution of the Land to Israel as an inheritance demonstrated that Israel was God's firstborn son and heir (Exodus 4:22). Even so, there was still unfinished business. Amorites still lived amongst the Israelites in the east after Moses was gone (13:13), and there were still unconquered Canaanite territories in the west when Joshua was old (13:1-7). The inheritance was allocated to Israel, but the LORD was still intending to drive out the remaining former inhabitants before them (13:6).

God keeps his promises!! The Land promised to Abraham, and confirmed to Moses and Israel's first generation liberated from Egypt, was successfully conquered and occupied by the nation. God now allocated to each tribe its own precisely defined territory. This whole segment is primarily geographical in nature, but demonstrated God's faithfulness to his word. However, several significant anecdotes and comments highlighted some important matters to note.

The purpose of this lengthy section concerning the distribution of the Land to the tribes of Israel was to demonstrate God's fulfilment of his promise to their forefathers (see 21:43-45). The full scale of the achievement was highlighted by the descriptions of tribal boundaries and extensive lists of towns settled throughout the country. The lists might make tedious reading, but for those living in the Land they presented a vivid tour of familiar places and a fully occupied territory. It was tangible evidence of God keeping his word! Significantly, the first allocation of territory was made to the tribe of Judah, which was located in the south. This anticipated the leading role which Judah would have in the future affairs of the nation. The allocation to the house of Joseph was second, and was distributed between two tribes which descended from Joseph's two sons, Ephraim and Manasseh. There were two reasons for this. Together they made the most populous segment of the nation, and the tribe of Levi received no tribal territory. It was dispersed throughout all the tribal territories in allocated towns because of its priestly role within the nation. So the house of Joseph made up for it. It was located in the north of the country, and would also have a dominant role in future days. Allocations to the other tribes were carefully made by lot before God, so that effectively the whole settlement of the nation was divinely determined. Nevertheless, the tribes themselves had a part to play. They must drive out the previous occupants from their respective territories. A sombre refrain throughout the record is that this was not always fully done. On the other hand, Caleb's example in this regard was exceptional, and was mentioned a second time (14:6-15, 15:13-19).

When God settled Israel in the Promised Land, he followed a deliberate plan for tribal allocations. He also strategically located "cities of refuge" and cities for the tribe of Levi among them. "Cities of refuge" had a legal and social function, while the Levitical cities provided priestly services for the spiritual well-being of the nation. These served the whole nation, and gave shape to a unique national character which honoured God and his covenant rule. God had promised that Israel would be a great nation.

Cities of refuge ensured that justice and protection, not vengeance, prevailed throughout the nation. Retribution for murder was carried out by the *"avenger of blood"*, a person (the closest male relative or an officially recognised citizen) who was obligated to execute the guilty manslayer. The avenger, however, did not distinguish between intentional and unintentional killing. Therefore cities of refuge allowed opportunity for distinction between murder and manslaughter. Someone who killed unintentionally could find asylum in a city of refuge until a trial was held, and, if not guilty of murder, remain there safely for the duration of the high priest's life. Cities of refuge were located strategically throughout the Land, three in the east and three in the west, in the north, centre, and south. They represented the administration of God's rule of justice, peace, and security over his people, and his respect for life.

Israel was God's priestly kingdom among the nations. Its own national life in relation to God was conspicuously maintained by the priestly tribe of Levi, which was dispersed in cities across the whole country. In particular, specific priestly duties at the national sanctuary were carried out by descendants of Aaron. These were settled in the centre of the country, within the tribes of Judah and Benjamin. Providentially, this anticipated the location of the temple which would be built at a later date.

A brief summary paragraph acknowledged the achievement and faithfulness of the LORD (21:43-45). The LORD *"gave"* all the Land to Israel, fulfilling his *"sworn"* promise (v 43), summing up chapters 13-21. The LORD gave *"rest"* to Israel from its enemies, as he had *"sworn"*, referring to chapters 1-12 (v 44). Not one of the LORD's promises failed (v 45).

God's covenant with Israel was a lopsided affair. God had the lion share of responsibility. He chose Israel to be his covenant people on the basis of grace. He chose to be their God and to be as a "father" to them. He promised to love them, protect them, and provide for them. He promised to give them a land and life. In return they were obliged to be his "son", to love and honour him, and be faithful to him. God kept his promise and gave them the Land. But to enjoy life in the Land they had to stay true.

With the conquest of Canaan accomplished, and God having given Israel its promised *"rest"*, Joshua dismissed the two and a half tribes from the east side of the Jordan (chapter 22). He commended them for keeping Moses' and his own commands to share with the rest of the nation in the task of conquest, and urged them to keep obeying God's covenant commands to love him and walk in his ways. The major concern now was to maintain the unity of the nation, which was divided by a river. The unauthorised erection of a replica of the national altar by the eastern tribes sent shock waves through Israel which saw the action as a breach of covenant. It was as serious as the worship of Baal of Peor (in the east, Numbers 25:1-9) and the sin of Achan (at Jericho in the west, Joshua 7), both of which had devastating consequences for the nation. Israel rallied for war, ready to stamp out the offenders immediately. However, an investigation by Phinehas, son of the high priest, clarified the matter before action was taken. The eastern tribes affirmed their loyalty, and explained the purpose of the new altar to be not an alternative place of sacrifice, but a witness of their unity with the rest of Israel to worship at the LORD's sanctuary.

Joshua's address to Israel's leaders when he was an old man was especially concerned for their relationship with the nations (chapter 23). They were called *"enemies"* (v 1). Joshua declared God's faithfulness in driving them out, both in the past and in the future, and called Israel to be faithful by separating themselves from them and their practices. These concepts are repeated three times over for emphasis (v 1-8, 9-13, 14-16). Israel must hold fast to the LORD, and love him. God will be true to keeping his promises, but Israel's sharing in their benefits required faithfulness.

Joshua assembled the leaders of Israel at Shechem (chapter 24), the place where God first promised the Land to Abraham, where Jacob purchased a plot of ground, and where both men built altars (Genesis 12:6-7, 33:18-20). Jacob disposed of his foreign gods beneath the tree at this site (Genesis 35:4). At this sacred location Joshua led them through a covenant-making ceremony, following the usual pattern. This included a history recital of the actions of God, who was the superior party in the covenant, followed by an appeal to Israel, the secondary party, to dispose of their foreign gods and be loyal to God and the covenant, and Israel's pledge of allegiance in response. This was a second renewal in the Land, of the original covenant made under Moses. Joshua documented a record of the occasion, and a stone monument was set up beneath the oak tree there as a permanent witness.

The death and burial of Joshua, who led Israel to gain the Promised Land, comes at the end of the book, similar to the death and burial of Moses at the end of the book of Deuteronomy. There are many other parallels between Joshua and Moses throughout the book, not all noted here. The mention of the burial of Joseph was significant. At the time of his death, he had looked forward in faith to the future fulfilment of God's promise (Genesis 50:24-26), and his burial site was at Shechem on the tract of land purchased by Jacob. Eleazar had played a part in the distribution of the Promised Land to the tribes. Burial of these three men within the Promised Land, relatively close to one another, to close the book, has the purpose of showing that the task of gaining the Promised Land was complete. God had kept his promise!!

Covenant Kingship

The book of **Judges** begins the prophetic series of books which trace the progress of God's covenant nation from the conquest and possession of the Promised Land until the destruction of Jerusalem and the exile. As the first stage of the series, it spans the period of Israel's history from Joshua to Samuel, approximately 200 years or more. The book's aim was not to provide an account of Israel's history, but to present a picture of the nation in the Land under the covenant kingship of the LORD. Conditions were quite fragile and unstable. Israel was a loose confederation of tribes, unified only by their common covenant with the LORD, but without political or social cohesion. The book demonstrates the vulnerability of God's covenant kingship over Israel due to Israel's continual faithlessness. It describes the exploits of significant leaders who emerged at times of crises of oppression from neighbouring idolatrous ethnic groups.

Like the other books of the "Former Prophets", Judges was related from the perspective of Israel's covenant, especially reflecting Deuteronomy. Its theme was concerned about leadership in Israel after the passing of Joshua. God had not appointed anyone to be his successor. This was because the LORD was King, who governed by means of his covenant law. They did not need a human leader, if they faithfully trusted God and obeyed his law. However, the story of Judges reveals that Israel was prone to disobedience and disorder. Despite their rebellious ways, though, God remained true, and ruled over them graciously by raising up "judges" to lead them. What is surprising is that, apart from Othniel, God chose such sorry characters to be his judges. They reflected the sad state of affairs which prevailed at their time, and at the same time revealed an important truth about God. He was willing and able to work through the most unlikely people. They splendidly demonstrated God's grace agenda.

The narrative depicts the nation repeatedly passing through cyclic phases. Israel deserted God for idols; God caused them to suffer oppression by giving them into the hands of enemy nations; Israel "*cries out*" to God for help; God sends a deliverer; all is well under that judge, but after his or her death the old pattern of disloyalty recurs. This reveals Israel's failure to complete the mandate for conquest laid down by Moses and Joshua, and the natural tendency towards tribal disintegration and covenant disobedience. The purpose of the book shows God's covenant kingship under threat because of the nation's spiritual dysfunction, yet his kingly loyalty and love in his readiness both to respond to their need and to use the most unpromising people as his deliverers. God was shown to be in sovereign control both when punishing his rebellious people (acting justly) and when rescuing them (showing grace).

There is a clear pattern to the book, with a two part introduction and a two part conclusion around an extensive main body.

Prologue: Incomplete Conquest (1:1-3:6)
    1:1-2:5   *Israel's Failure to Drive Out the Canaanites*
    2:6-3:6   *Israel's Pattern of Rebellion, Raiders, & Rescue*

Major & Minor Judges (3:7-16:31)
    3:7-11   *Othniel*
    3:12-31   *Ehud (12-30); Shamgar (31)*
    4:1-5:31   *Deborah*
    6:1-9:57   *Gideon (ch 6-8) [Abimelech (ch 9)]*
    10:1-12:15   *Tola, Jair (10:1-5), Jephthah (10:6-12:7), Ibzan, Elon, Abdon (12:8-15)*
    13:1-16:31   *Samson*

Epilogue: Moral & Religious Degeneration (17:1-21:25)
    17:1-18:31   *A Levite's Corrupt Religion, & the Tribe of Dan's Violent Ways*
    19:1-21:25   *Immoral & Violent Disorder in the Tribe of Benjamin*

The main body describes the exploits of 12 judges, who probably represent all tribes (although not actually from every tribe), thus emphasising God's rule over the whole nation. Anecdotal accounts were given for six judges, while the other six were mentioned with minimum remarks. **Othniel**, brother and also son-in-law of the renowned Caleb, was the first judge, and was a good model for the role. Empowered by the Spirit of God he defeated the king of Aram (Syria). **Ehud** came next, and by brazen deception assassinated Eglon king of Moab. Being left-handed may imply that he had a deformity which would exclude him from entering the tabernacle. **Shamgar**, a minor judge and able warrior from Naphtali in the north, rescued Israel from the Philistines. Barak, also from Naphtali, was appointed commander of the army by **Deborah** the prophetess who was based between Ramah and Bethel in the hill country of Ephraim in the centre of the land. However, he was reluctant to lead unless Deborah accompanied him. Consequently, honour for victory over Sisera, who commanded the forces of the Canaanite king Jabin, went to a woman, Jael, who was a non-Israelite. Jael betrayed friendship, hospitality, and guaranteed refuge by cold-bloodedly hammering a tent peg through Sisera's head while he slept. The central story concerned **Gideon**, who was insignificant in his family and community, and needed supernatural demonstrations to reassure him, even though he was empowered by the Spirit of the LORD (6:34). But he then won a spectacular victory over the Midianites by clever tactics and divine help with an army of only 300 men. He declined to be appointed king by the people, acknowledging that the LORD was Israel's king. However, he adopted the ways of a king, especially customary practices of the kings of surrounding nations which were specifically forbidden by God's law. When he died, his son Abimelech (which means "My Father is King") brutally seized kingship at Shechem, but his vicious reign was short-lived. **Tola** from Issachar was a minor judge, who lived and judged in the hill country of Ephraim. **Jair** was a minor judge in Gilead on the eastern side of the Jordan. **Jephthah**, from Gilead, rescued Israel from the Ammonites who came from the east. He had been rejected by his family because of the circumstances of his birth, and had become a renowned warrior with an army of mercenaries behind him. His own family appealed to him to rescue them, with the promise that he would become their head. He defeated the enemy, but a rash vow bound him to offer his own daughter as a human sacrifice, and his harsh attitude led to the brutal slaughter of fellow Israelites from Ephraim.

Minor judge **Ibzan** was renowned for his thirty sons and thirty daughters whom he married off outside his own clan. **Elon** lived, judged, and died in Zebulun in the central north of the country. **Abdon** lived and died in Ephraim, and was remembered for his large family of forty sons and thirty grandsons.

Samson was the last of God's judges, and was different in several respects. On this occasion God was not responding to the cries of the people. They had failed to cry out to him, even though again they had done evil in the eyes of the LORD and he had consequently delivered them into the hands of the Philistines (13:1). This time God was taking the initiative, and he provided Samson. He acted sovereignly to enable Samson's birth to a sterile, childless mother (13:2-5, 24). He appointed Samson to be a Nazirite (13:5), a person dedicated to live by particular vows and set apart to the service of God. His task was to begin the deliverance of Israel from the hands of the Philistines (13:5). God's Spirit empowered Samson to perform astonishing feats of strength (13:25, 14:6, 19, 15:14). Tragically, however, Samson betrayed his Nazirite calling by yielding to lust for Philistine women (14:1-3, 16:1, 4), allowing himself to become ritually unclean by contact with dead carcasses (14:8-9, 15:15), and allowing his hair to be cut contrary to his lifelong vow (16:19). He was captured by the Philistines, who gouged out his eyes and forced him into hard labour. In the end, he gained victory over his enemies, but at the cost of his own life. The Philistines held a huge celebration in honour of Dagon their god, gloating about Dagon's triumph over Samson. Samson *"cried out"* to the LORD for the return of his strength in order to get his revenge. His prayer was answered, and with his renewed strength he pulled the building down on all who were assembled, killing himself in the process.

The book of Judges showed its disapproval of human kingship, even though surrounding nations had had established kings for several centuries. This was because the LORD himself was the true King of Israel, and the one who was alone maintaining the unity of the nation. At the same time its story traces the evolving process which eventually led to the appointment of an earthly monarch. It was not the concept of kingship which was resisted, since God himself had already approvingly anticipated the appointment of an earthly king through Moses (Deuteronomy

17:14-20). It was the nature of human kingship "like the nations" which was unwelcome, since it was a political institution, determined by human decision, and acted according to human practices. Appointment and practices of kingship in Israel were to be according to God's standards. Judges raised up by God prefigured Israel's eventual establishment of a king. In his special task, the last judge Samson anticipated King David who eventually completed Israel's deliverance from the Philistines. The final episodes in the book, however, present a disgusting picture of Israel's religious and moral depravity.

Israel's "crying out" to the LORD in times of oppression was reminiscent of the days of slavery in Egypt. Although the language was different, it reflected the attitude of "calling on the name of the LORD". Even when Israel behaved appallingly, and God's sent judges were embarrassments, the LORD nevertheless remained loyal to his chosen people. He ruled over them, both in judgement and salvation, through providential circumstances and unusual intervention, and he responded to their pathetic calls for help.

Gideon, who was central in the format of the book, and primary to its purposes, conversed with God, and was graciously granted what he requested to reassure his lack of confidence and doubting fears (chapter 6). But the big surprise was Samson. He was the only one who was actually reported as praying, twice, and the term used is "call" (15:18, translated "cried out", and 16:28, translated "prayed"). In his divinely provided birth, dedication, and endowed power, Samson illustrated the nation of Israel. By his failures he also illustrated Israel's failures to God's covenant. This is why his calling on God in his distress was so significant, because in this he was again like Israel. The nation was now represented by its leader as he called on the LORD for help. This would become a significant role for Israel's future kings.

The period of the judges was a picture of lopsided covenant loyalties, where prayer, or calling on the name of the LORD, in its most basic rawness, was depicted as effective. What stands out conspicuously against the sordid background of this period is God's persistent grace agenda.

Rise of the Monarchy

You are probably shaking your head in wonder as you turn from the appalling stories in Judges. What can God do with his "priestly kingdom" which keeps getting it all wrong? What will **1 & 2 Samuel** disclose?

The two books of Samuel were originally part of a single work, including also 1 & 2 Kings, called "Books of the Kingdom". They continued the story begun in Joshua and Judges. The narrative incorporates a variety of sources (including prose, poetry, traditions, and chronicled records) within a skilfully composed literary framework, shaped by a covenant perspective.

1 & 2 Samuel present a major turning point in the historical development of God's purpose: the emergence of Israel's monarchy, a national event second only to the exodus.

RISE & DEMISE OF THE KINGDOM

The story revolved around three successive figures, Samuel, Saul, and David. The books are named after Samuel, because he was the first prominent figure and was Israel's "kingmaker", being the one who anointed both Saul and David as the nation's first two successive kings. In particular they traced the response of Israel to the LORD's kingship, in terms of obedience to God's covenant, and especially worship before the Ark of the Covenant at the national shrine. 1 Samuel begins at the national shrine at Shiloh, and 2 Samuel concludes with King David purchasing a site at Jerusalem for the future temple. These features indicate the advance of God's purpose to restore a right attitude amongst his covenant people towards his kingship.

Samuel the Prophet (1 Samuel 1-7): *Birth and Call of Samuel, Rejection of the House of Eli* (1-3). *Capture and Return of the Ark of the Covenant, Samuel the Judge* (4-7).

Saul the King (1 Samuel 8-15): *Samuel chooses and establishes Saul as King* (8-12). *Saul Fails as King* (13-15).

Rise of David & Decline of Saul (1 Samuel 16-31): *David is anointed, serves under Saul, and then flees from Saul* (16-26). *David flees to the Philistines; Saul and sons are killed in battle* (27-31).

David the King (2 Samuel 1-24): *David becomes King* (1-5:5   ). *David's Accomplishments* (5:6-9:12). *David's Failures & Troubles* (10-20). *Reflections on David's Reign* (21-24).

When we turn the page from the gruesome events at the end of the Book of Judges to open the next book in the series, **1 Samuel**, we find ourselves still at Shiloh. But soon we are listening in on a heart-broken woman's private prayer. Barren Hannah *"entreats"* the LORD at the Tabernacle for a son. Her request was granted, and she gave birth to Samuel. After Samuel was weaned, Hannah presented him before the LORD at the Tabernacle, and, to fulfil an earlier vow, left him there to be brought up in its service. Her dedicatory prayer at the time is recorded. Although there are marked differences, Samuel's birth was reminiscent of Samson's birth.

The role of prayer in connection with Samuel's birth was highlighted, both by repetition of the term (1 Samuel 1:10, 12, 26, 27, 2:1) and by the explanation given for his name (1:20). Hannah *"named him Samuel, saying, "Because I asked the LORD for him"*. There was a subtle pun in Hannah's explanation when she said, *"I asked"*, because the name "Saul" is derived from this Hebrew word. The story was linking Samuel with Saul right from his birth, highlighting the significance of his role as the one appointed to anoint the first king of Israel.

What was especially striking about this event was the fact that this was the first mention of the term for prayer in this series of books so far. The activity of prayer was depicted previously, but the actual term for prayer was not used. Now it appeared repeatedly in the opening incident of 1 Samuel. Prayer will again be associated with Samuel at a critical time in his later ministry relating to the period of Saul's anointing (1 Samuel 7:5, 8:6, 12:19, 23). These are the only mentions of prayer ("*entreaty*"), except for one significant occasion (2 Samuel 7:18-29, "*intercede*"), in the whole of 1 and 2 Samuel. So, in the sequence of books about God's covenant people Israel, from the time that Joshua assumed the leadership after Moses until near the end of the reign of King David, the prophetic author applied the term for prayer ("*entreaty*") only with Samuel, and then with regard to the appointment of Israel's first monarch. From the prophetic writer's point of view, with the birth of Samuel a major development in God's long-term strategy for restoring his kingdom in the world was "birthed" in the womb of prayer!

Samuel was a prophet (1 Samuel 3:20-21). In many ways he emerged as a leader not unlike one of the judges, but on a nation-wide scale. He was also based at the Tabernacle at Shiloh, associated with the priests who served there. But he especially rose as a messenger of God's revealed word to the whole land. His role was like a second Moses. As we have already noticed, it is only said of Moses and Samuel that the LORD "called" to them (Exodus 3:4, 19:3, 20, 24:16, Leviticus 1:1; 1 Samuel 3:4, 6, 8, 10).

During his youthful years, spiritual and moral conditions within the covenant community reached a low state, particularly conspicuous in the corrupt behaviour of the sons of Eli the chief priest at Shiloh. Matters came to a head when Israel lost a battle to the Philistines, and both the Ark of the Covenant was captured and Eli's sons were killed. The news of this disaster brought about elderly Eli's death. The excursion of the Ark amongst the Philistines had dire consequences for their population, prompting their rulers to return the Ark to Israel. During this dark period while the Ark was in the hands of the Philistines, Samuel was conspicuous for his absence from the narrative. Disrespectful actions towards the Ark by some of the Israelites after its return brought devastating judgement upon them, so the Ark was committed to the care of the people of Kiriath-Jearim. It was not restored to the Tabernacle, and remained in obscurity for several generations. Without the Ark and without a priesthood, the nation mourned the apparent absence of the LORD, and looked to Samuel for leadership. He persuaded them to discard their idols and serve the LORD; he offered sacrifices and "*cried out*" to the LORD on their behalf; and in response to his entreaty God enabled them to subdue a force of invading Philistines, who were still the major threat to the nation. Samuel was their prophet, priest, and judge (1 Samuel 7).

When he became old, and it was obvious that his sons were not walking in his footsteps but acting corruptly, the elders asked Samuel to appoint them a king to lead them like other nations (1 Samuel 8). Samuel was not pleased with this request so he prayed to ("*entreated*") the LORD (8:6). In reply the LORD indicated that it was not Samuel they were rejecting, but his own kingship, and that Samuel should inform the people of the consequences of appointing a human king to rule over them. When the people still persisted with their request, Samuel reported it to God, who told him to give them a king. This was a momentous decision for the covenant relationship between the LORD and Israel. Yet despite the failure of the people to trust God as their king, and their insistent desire to be led by a human monarch, God acceded to their request and accommodated it to begin a new phase in his "struggle" to reinstate his kingship and reconcile the world to himself.

First of all **Saul** was selected to be the initial king of Israel. Samuel had the leading role in identifying him, anointing him as the king-designate, and eventually proclaiming him as king before the gathered representatives of the nation (1 Samuel 9-12). Saul began well, and by a display of charismatic leadership demonstrated actions which showed that he enjoyed God's approval.

On the day of Saul's confirmation as king, Samuel led the celebrations and made a passionate speech to the nation (1 Samuel 12). He pointed out how God had provided adequate leadership for them in the past, especially when they had *"cried out to the LORD"*. Yet now when there was a threat, they were ignoring the fact that the LORD was their King and they were requesting an earthly king to reign over them. Samuel declared that the LORD was the one who had appointed their new king and warned that they and their king must obey and serve the LORD. If they did not, they would find that the LORD was opposed to them. To drive home his warning, he announced that he would confront them with evidence of God's *"righteous acts"* (actions in keeping with his covenant faithfulness). He said that he would *"call upon the LORD to send thunder and rain"*, even though it was out of season, in order to expose their evil in requesting a king (12:17). The narrative reports,

"Then Samuel called upon the LORD, and that same day the LORD sent thunder and rain. So all the people stood in awe of the LORD and Samuel" (12:18).

The demonstration was convincing, and the terrified guilty people responded by turning to Samuel and pleading for him to *"pray"* (*"entreat"*) for them (12:19). Samuel reassured them, urging them to serve the LORD loyally, declaring that the LORD *"for the sake of his great name"* would not reject them, asserting that he himself would not *"sin against the LORD by failing to pray for you"*, yet warning that if they persisted in doing evil God would sweep away both them and their king (12:20-25).

This was obviously a day to be remembered, and, judging from the description, a day which was reminiscent of the formation of the covenant at Sinai. The awe-inspiring display of thunder and rain, indicating God's majestic power, had a similar impact on the people as did the spectacle of fire and thunder on Mount Sinai. Although the LORD was granting the appointment of an earthly king, it was a new development in keeping with the established covenant, reinforcing the covenant relationship, not changing anything.

The language about "calling upon the LORD" and "praying" links this event with previous occurrences of these expressions, highlighting a developing pattern which draws attention to God's unfolding strategy, and further illuminating the identity of God's covenant people and the nature of their covenant relationship. It was becoming more and more evident that dependent prayer was a critical and privileged aspect of that relationship, and was at the heart of what it meant to be a people who "call upon the name of the LORD". It was also becoming apparent that prayer was important in regard to God's kingship over his people.

However, Saul overstepped his authority and performed a sacrifice before going into battle in direct disobedience to Samuel's orders, so his kingship was aborted. He continued to reign as long as he lived, but he was denied an on-going dynasty, and God commissioned Samuel to seek his replacement. **David** was the new choice, and after his anointing the rest of 1 Samuel traced his heroic rise to fame and favour in contrast to the tragic decline of King Saul. It tells of the breakdown of the relationship between Saul and David, who was forced to become a fugitive and live in the Judean badlands to avoid Saul's jealous hostility. Their story is told with considerable detail, and in gripping, heart-stirring style. The skilfully composed narrative illuminates many subtle and significant features affecting the development of the LORD's purpose for his covenant people, which are worthy of attention. However, our tour follows a different path. 1 Samuel concludes with Saul's death on the battle field.

2 Samuel relates the story of the reign of David. David was very careful to avoid giving any impression of taking advantage of Saul's death out of personal ambition to be appointed king, even though he had been anointed by Samuel to be Saul's successor. His reaction to the news of Saul's death showed his respect for the man and the monarchy, and he only returned to his home region after firstly seeking the LORD's approval. In Hebron he was made king over Judah (2:4), where he reigned for two years until he became king also over Israel (5:1-3), after the rival house of Saul completely collapsed. During those two years, relationships between the court of David and the court of Ishbosheth (Saul's surviving son) were hostile and violent. Afterwards David ruled over both Judah and Israel for five and a half years from Hebron, until he conquered Jerusalem and set up there his personal capital from which he ruled over the whole united nation for the next thirty three years. All up, David was king for about forty years.

God's Covenant With David

After David was established in Jerusalem, the narrative takes up two matters of critical importance, the Ark of God, which was God's throne (chapter 6), and the throne of David (chapter 7). These relate to divine and dynastic kingship respectively, and occur in the proper order.

With much fanfare and celebration David transferred the neglected Ark of the Covenant from Kiriath-Jearim to Jerusalem, publicly showing his veneration of God and that he was establishing his kingdom on the traditions and foundation of the Sinai covenant and covenant law (chapter 6). A shocking incident in the process, in which one of the attendants to the Ark was struck down dead for failing to show appropriate respect for it, taught David a profound lesson about the need for reverence for God. He then unabashedly displayed his devotion for God by personally dancing in uninhibited self-humiliation amongst the revellers who accompanied the procession of the Ark, to the disgust of his spectator wife who mocked him. She was Michal the daughter of Saul, given to him in marriage when he had defeated the giant Goliath. Her attitude of proud indifference towards God was a typical reflection of her father, and was punished by her inability to have children. This meant that as David's first wife she produced no heir to the throne, who would also have been a descendant of Saul.

Jerusalem was now both the religious and political capital of the nation. At this time a momentous incident quietly occurred, which had profound ramifications for future generations and for the cause of God's kingship (chapter 7). It was highlighted by the record of a dialogue between God, the divine King, and David, the earthly king of Israel. The incident arose when David expressed his desire to construct a palace for the Ark (i.e. for God). God responded and informed David through Nathan the prophet that David would not be the person to build a house for God. Instead he, God, would build a "house" (dynasty) for David. He promised that he would make David's name great, that Israel would have a settled home, and there would be rest from enemies (7:9-11), an echo of God's promise to Abraham (Genesis 12:1-3). He also declared that David's kingdom would continue through his offspring, and that it would be a son of his who would be the one to build a "house" for God's name, and who would have a special covenant relationship with himself (7:11-17).

God was here entering into a new covenant partnership, within the framework of his covenant relationship with Israel, to advance his plan of restoring his kingship within the world. Israel's earthly king was not to become an alternative king replacing the LORD, but the LORD's representative serving as his dependent partner and accomplishing his will. He would be a second Adam, God's earthly vice-regent. God's promise of perpetual kingship for David's line became the foundation for Israel's messianic hope.

It is in this context that the only mention of prayer in the whole of 2 Samuel occurs. David responded to God's declaration through Nathan in a prayer ("*intercession*", v 27) which was recorded (2 Samuel 7:18-29). The fact that the full content of the prayer was recorded makes it conspicuous. It underscores the immense importance of this incident for the foundation of David's dynastic kingdom, and demonstrates the intimate nature of the king's relationship with God. We also need to appreciate that the ramifications of the incident for the role and purpose of prayer are more significant than the narrative indicates here. We will discover at a later point (in Chapter Seven) that in terms of the covenant partnership between the LORD and his earthly king, prayer was the king's strategic contribution!

In response to God's revelation through the prophet Nathan, David went and sat before the LORD and spoke to him (v 18). Acknowledging the LORD's sovereignty (repeatedly),

David humbly expressed his wonder at God's dealings with him and his family, both in the past and as he intended to do in the future.

"Who am I, O Sovereign LORD, and what is my family, that you have brought me this far? And as if this were not enough in your sight, O Sovereign LORD, you have also spoken about the future of the house of your servant. Is this your usual way of dealing with man, O Sovereign LORD?" (v 18-19)

He recognised that God's proposed actions were in accord with his *"word"* [of covenant commitment to his people] and with his *"will"* [for restoring the world to his blessing].

"What more can David say to you? For you know your servant, O Sovereign LORD. For the sake of your word and according to your will, you have done this great thing and made it known to your servant" (v 20-21).

This prompted him to acclaim God's greatness for having redeemed Israel from Egypt, and thereby making a name for himself, and for having established them as his people.

"How great you are, O Sovereign LORD! There is no one like you, and there is no God but you as we have heard with our own ears. And who is like your people Israel – the one nation on earth that God went out to redeem as a people for himself, and to make a name for himself, and to perform great and awesome wonders by driving out nations and their gods before your people, whom you redeemed from Egypt? You have established your people Israel as your very own forever, and you, O LORD, have become their God (v 22-24). "

He prayed that God would carry out his promise so that his name would be great forever.

"And now, LORD God, keep forever the promise you have made concerning your servant and his house. Do as you promised, so that your name will be great forever. Then men will say, 'The LORD Almighty is God over Israel!' And the house of your servant David will be established before you" (v 25-26).

He indicated that because God had revealed his intentions to him to build his house (dynasty), and was trustworthy, therefore he had courage to pray (*"intercede"*) that God would do what he proposed and bless his house.

"LORD Almighty, God of Israel, you have revealed this to your servant, saying, 'I will build a house for you.' So your servant has found courage to offer you this prayer. O Sovereign

LORD, you are God! Your words are trustworthy, and you have promised these good things to your servant. Now be pleased to bless the house of your servant, that it may continue forever in your sight; for you, O Sovereign LORD, have spoken, and with your blessing the house of your servant will be blessed forever" (vs 27-29).

The amount of space in the narrative given to this incident, involving only Nathan and David, highlights its importance. Psalm 89, especially verses 26-29, throws further understanding on its significance.

"He will call out to me, 'You are my Father, my God, the Rock my Savior.' And I will appoint him to be my firstborn, the most exalted of the kings of the earth. I will maintain my love to him forever, and my covenant with him will never fail. I will establish his line forever, his throne as long as the heavens endure."

God's promise to David was a *"covenant"*, an unconditional royal decree of the divine King to his loyal servant, who, as *"firstborn son"* would call God *"Father"*. This was because he would be the kingly representative of the nation, which was God's royal "firstborn son" (Exodus 4:22). As king, David was the "Son of God", which was a title for his earthly role, not implying divine status. The promise was both a generous privilege bestowed on David, and a perpetual reminder of the LORD's higher sovereignty. It was also for Israel's benefit in keeping with God's covenant with the nation, reminding them also that the LORD was their true King, and their earthly monarch was his servant. David's response in prayer vividly depicted his intimate relationship with God, and forms the framework for meaningful, purposeful prayer for restoring God's kingship in the world.

Although this incident contained the only actual mention of prayer in 2 Samuel, King David of course was renowned for his written prayers and songs which formed a large portion of the Book of Psalms. He was a man of prayer, and 2 Samuel actually depicts that on occasions by other terms (12:16, 15:31). His recorded response here is inevitably reinforced by his reputation. That too is made more compelling by the inclusion, in full, and with little variation, of Psalm 18, an exuberant song of praise for God's deliverance of him from his enemies (2 Samuel 22). The song is an acclamation of God's faithful protection of David and his kingship, and appears in the concluding, carefully arranged appendix of the book (chapters 21-24).

The main narrative of the book, after the description of David's responsive covenant prayer (7), is an account of David's reign. It included reports of his victories in war, *"granted by the LORD"* (chapters 8-10), and of his survival of his tragic adulterous affair with Bathsheba and subsequent family turmoil and national rebellions (chapters 11-20). It is a selective history of David's reign, and the events reveal David's human weaknesses to show that his kingdom's success was due to God's higher rule, not his own accomplishments.

The appendix (chapters 21-24) was thoughtfully designed so as to demonstrate God's sovereign protection of his anointed king.

> 21:1-14   Correcting an offence made by Saul
>   21:15-22   Heroic exploits against the Philistines
>   22:1-51   David's Song of Praise
>   23:1-7   David's Last Words
>   23:8-39   Heroic exploits against the Philistines
> 24:1-25   Correcting an offence made by David

David's "song of praise" (22:1-51), together with a second, shorter song identified as the "last words of David" (23:1-7), form the central feature of the appendix. These songs were flanked on either side by accounts of heroic exploits against the Philistines (21:15-22; 23:8-39), demonstrating how God brought victory to enable David to complete the task begun with Samson (Judges 13:5), and framed on the outer structure of the appendix by two offences made by Saul (21:1-14) and David (24:1-25) respectively, which needed to be set right. Both songs commended David's "*righteousness*" with regard to his covenant kingship, meaning his right relationship with God in terms of devoted dedication to God's sovereignty and trusting dependence on God's salvation, not claiming any sense of personal sufficiency or sinlessness.

Significantly, David testified in his song, "*I call to the LORD, who is worthy of praise, and I am saved from my enemies*" (22:4)

"*In my distress I called to the LORD; I called out to my God*" (22:7)

His language echoes the familiar supplication of those who "call upon the name of the LORD", and portrays the king's role within his covenant relationship with God as that of prayerful dependence.

Demise of the Monarchy

The two Books of Kings are a sequel to the Books of Samuel. They trace the line of Israel's kingship, not from a political or social or economic perspective, but in the light of God's covenant. This is obvious when it is seen that some politically successful kings (like Omri who appears in archaeological records as an influential monarch) are dismissed in a few verses, while less successful kings (like Ahab, Omri's son) are treated at length because of their notable obedience or disobedience to the covenant. Notice the layout of the two books.

Solomon the King (1 Kings 1-11): *Accession to the Throne, Reign, and Wisdom* (1-4), *Building Programme* (5-9:9), *Reign, Splendour, & Folly* (9:10-11:43).
Divided Kingdom: Israel & Judah (1 Kings 12-16): *Succession of Rehoboam, Rebellion of Jeroboam* (12), *King Jeroboam of Israel, King Rehoboam of Judah* (13-14), *Successive Kings of Judah and Israel to Asa/Ahab* (15-16).
Elijah the Prophet (1 Kings 17-22)
Elisha the Prophet (2 Kings 1-13)
Divided Kingdom until Assyria's Conquest of Israel (2 Kings 14-17)
Kingdom of Judah until the Babylonian Exile (2 Kings 18-25)

The narrative begins encouragingly with the construction of the Temple in Jerusalem and the establishment of Solomon's grand empire. However, Solomon himself displays disappointing tendencies, and shortly after his death the nation split into two kingdoms. The rebellious northern kingdom, Israel, was marked by violence and instability, ruled by 20 kings who represented 9 different dynasties over a period of a little more than 200 years. The southern kingdom, Judah, was ruled by descendants of David, also 20 kings, for a period of about 350 years. Except for a few reforming kings, who tried to renew the nation in terms of the covenant, Judah's kings were no better than their northern counterparts, and that kingdom only survived longer because of God's covenant with David. In the end both kingdoms collapsed, Israel destroyed by the Assyrians (in 721 BCE), and Judah exiled by the Babylonians through two campaigns (in 597 BCE and 586 BCE respectively).

The extensive record of the ministries of the prophets Elijah and Elisha, especially to confront the enthroned kings of Israel in the north, emphasised the importance and independence of the prophetic role which had now emerged, and demonstrated that covenant sovereignty remained with God. Judging from the theme of the history, the author's purpose seemed to be to describe the decline and fall of Israel's monarchy, including the line of David. This does not mean that God's purposes had failed, or that his kingship had ended. It showed that God's kingdom was not to be identified with Israel's political kingdom. Other prophetic writings promised continuation of God's covenant intentions.

Within the framework of this history of Israel's kings, prayer had a strategic role.

Solomon's Reign (1 Kings 1-11)

Prominent in the history of Israel's kings was David's immediate successor, Solomon. 1 Kings begins with an account of his ascension to the throne and forceful consolidation of his kingly authority (chapters 1-2). The description of his rule highlights his loyalty to God's covenant, his request for wisdom for exercising his judicial responsibilities, his administrative developments, and prosperity which fulfilled God's promise to Abraham (chapters 3-4). However, his shortcomings included marriage to foreign wives, political alliances, and worship at high places (3:1-3), practices expressly forbidden in Deuteronomy. The dominant feature of Solomon's reign was his building program (chapters 5-9). Solomon took 7 years to build the Temple, and 13 years to build his own palace. The Temple's importance may be gauged by the amount of space given to its description. At its dedication, the Ark of the Covenant was brought in, and the cloud of God's glory filled the Temple, as it had previously filled the Tabernacle in the desert. Solomon led the dedication, and later God appeared to him with assurances that he would consolidate his kingdom if he remained obedient.

The account concluded by presenting an evaluation of Solomon's reign, depicting both the magnificent splendor of his kingdom, and his tragic failures (chapters 10-11). No other king of Israel reached a higher peak of worldly splendor than Solomon. He set up a trading fleet, engaged in widespread commercial transactions, accumulated chariots and horses, and acquired an international reputation for his wisdom and wealth. Sadly, he also developed an enormous harem, and then followed their influence in the worship of foreign gods. God was angry and declared he would tear the kingdom from him in subsequent generations. In his final years, Solomon faced hostility both from without and within the nation. He had become a king like the nations around him!

What was most significant for Solomon's reign, and for the whole history of Israel's kingship in 1 Kings, was the construction of the temple in Jerusalem. This is obvious from the amount of attention given to it by the account. Yet it was also underscored by the recurring comment that the temple was where the *"Name of the LORD"* resided. 1 Kings was not merely a historical record of the kings of Israel. Its primary concern was God's kingship, and it presents an evaluation of the kings of Israel in terms of their loyalty and respect shown to the LORD. It is important to note that almost all references to the *"Name"* in 1 Kings appear in the account about Solomon's reign, and mainly in his prayer of dedication of the temple where Solomon repeated it on nine occasions (chapter 8).

Solomon's prayer of dedication was presented in a manner so as to conspicuously highlight its importance. In the first place it is only in respect to Solomon's prayer, apart from only one other incident (13:6), that the term *"prayer"* occurs in the whole of 1 Kings, and then it does so numerous (14) times. It is quite an eye-catching feature. But secondly, the literary layout of the prayer in 1 Kings 8 had been carefully constructed in order to give prominence to the prayer. It is obviously meant to be noticed.

The prayer was offered in a setting of high celebration. At a time of special festival the priests carried the Ark of the Covenant, which represented God's presence and kingship, to its place in the inner sanctuary of the temple, while the king led the national gathering in offering innumerable sacrifices (verses 1-13). The ark contained only the two stone tablets placed there by Moses when the LORD's covenant with Israel was established. When the priests withdrew, the cloud of the presence of God's glory filled the temple. Thus the revealed will of God and the veiled presence of God became the focus in the new temple.

At the end of proceedings, the king and the gathered nation continued their sacrifices and celebration (verses 62-66). This literary description of national celebration forms a framework for Solomon's prayer, which becomes the centerpiece in the written account.

That framework is highlighted even more by special actions of Solomon both immediately before and immediately after his prayer when he stood and blessed the assembly (v 14-21, 54-61). His first blessing honoured God for keeping his special promise to David that his son would succeed him to the throne and would complete his desire to construct a temple for the LORD. His second blessing praised the LORD for keeping his covenant promise of providing *"rest"* for the nation. Solomon's blessings focused attention on the LORD's two covenants with the nation Israel and with King David respectively, which the LORD had established for the accomplishment of his divine intention to restore the world to his blessing and *"rest"*.

The prayer itself (v 22-53), at the centre of this carefully constructed account, reveals the importance and purpose of prayer. Solomon basically prayed that the temple would become a house of prayer. He began by acknowledging the LORD's incomparability because he kept his covenant of love with Israel and had kept his promise to his father David. Then he prayed that God would continue to keep that promise always to have a descendant of David seated on the throne of Israel, a promise contingent on the descendant remaining true to the LORD. Solomon realized that God could not be confined to a man-made temple, but he pleaded for God's mercy on the basis that God had said he would locate his **name** in the temple, that God would give attention to his supplication and that of his people when they prayed towards it. Essentially he was asking that the temple would be a place where God in heaven and his people on earth could draw near to one another. And prayer was the form of their meeting.

It is clear from Solomon's language that prayer is not a mere formality. It is a heartfelt cry and supplication. It appeals to God's mercy, on the basis of his covenant relationship. Solomon mentioned a variety of scenarios as examples of those who might seek God in prayer, and they all reflected situations covered by laws of the covenant. And they were all examples of seeking God's forgiveness and restoration for having sinned in disobedience to the law. Solomon's prayer was that the temple would become renowned as a place where God had obviously located his name because of his subsequent evident actions in response to his people's prayers towards it. This was a bold prayer, based on God's own revealed intention for his name to be identified with the temple, important for the nation and kingdom.

When Solomon's building program was completed, the LORD appeared to him and responded to his prayer (9:1-9). He declared that he had consecrated the temple by putting his name there, and would consolidate Solomon's throne forever if he continued in integrity of heart and uprightness. Yet he also warned that disobedience by those on the throne would result in rejection of the nation and the temple.

Divided Kingdom (1 Kings 12-16)

The account of 1 Kings presents a selective version of the fortunes of Israel's kingship after Solomon to highlight important prophetic interests. Firstly, it reports the division of the kingdom into two separate dominions, and then traces their respective experiences.

Jeroboam's Rebellion (12-13): When Solomon died, a former supervisor of the northern tribes' labour force, Jeroboam, rebelled against the new King Rehoboam. Instead of easing the harsh work load imposed by Solomon, Rehoboam intensified it. Jeroboam established the kingdom of Israel with his capital at Shechem, which had traditional associations with the Patriarchs and the early settlement of Israel in the land. Jeroboam had prophetic approval for his actions, but then went beyond his mandate. He set up two rival shrines to Jerusalem, at Bethel and Dan, where he installed golden calves for worship. He was probably wanting to strengthen his authority by having religious links with early traditions, but his actions were virtually a repeat of Israel's spiritual rebellion in the desert (Exodus 32). He received a prophetic rebuke which reaffirmed the House of David in Jerusalem, and rejected his House.

Successive Kings (14-16): The lines of successive kings in both Israel and Judah are reported in alternating sequence. The northern rulers were determined by prophetic word, while the southern rulers descended from David, and were compared with him whose attitude to the covenant represented the ideal. Jeroboam's son **Ahijah** died as a child according to a prophet's prediction, so that another son **Nadab** succeeded his father to the throne of Israel. Rehoboam's rule in Jerusalem was evil in God's eyes, as was that of his son, **Abijah**, who followed him. However his son **Asa** did what was right, like David. In Israel, Nadab was assassinated in a coup by **Baasha** who replaced him on the throne and wiped out all the rest of the family of Jeroboam. However, Baasha's rule was condemned as evil by a prophetic word, and his son **Elah** who succeeded him was assassinated in an attempted coup by one of his high-ranking military officials, **Zimri**. Zimri reigned only for a week, and then suicided because the people appointed **Omri** the commander of the army as their king instead. A rival pretender to the throne, **Tibni**, could not mount a strong enough challenge, so Omri prevailed and established a dynasty which eventually lasted four generations. Omri purchased a city which he called Samaria, and which became his own personal capital, similar to David's Jerusalem. **Ahab** his son succeeded him, and was notorious for his evil, his marriage to Jezebel, and his promotion of Baal worship.

Enter Elijah The Prophet (1 Kings 17-22)

In reaction to Ahab's policy of syncretism of worship of both the LORD and Baal, the prophet Elijah suddenly appeared and confronted the nation with God's word. A spectacular showdown on Mount Carmel (chapter 18) confirmed the LORD as Israel's sovereign God. Intimidating threats from Jezebel drove Elijah to seek personal reassurance at Sinai where Israel's covenant with God began (chapter 19). Standing where Moses once stood, and encountering God, he did not receive any additional revelation, but was challenged about why he was there, and informed that he was not alone in his allegiance to God. This means that the original covenant was adequate, and he needed to be occupied with his prophetic duties. God gave him specific tasks to perform. The mention of 7000 who had not bowed the knee to Baal was the first mention of a faithful remnant. This began a theme which highlighted that God's kingdom was not to be equated with the institutional kingdom, but with those whose hearts were true to God's covenant. Elijah returned from Sinai to continue his prophetic role. He anointed **Elisha** as his successor, and, with other prophets, challenged Ahab in accord with terms of the covenant. Meantime, **Jehoshaphat**, son of Asa, reigned in Jerusalem, following his father's good practices. He fought with Ahab against Syria in a battle in which Ahab was killed as predicted by a prophet. Upon Ahab's death, his son **Ahaziah** followed him to the throne, and in his ways. When he was injured by a fall, he tried to consult Baal-Zebub, the god of Ekron, for help. Instead, he came up against Elijah, who accurately predicted his death. His younger brother **Joram** took over the throne.

The extensive coverage of Elijah's activities in 1 Kings demonstrated the book's prophetic interest in God's kingship rather than merely the political fortunes of the various earthly kings. In particular, Elijah's clash with the prophets of Baal at Mount Carmel represented a confrontational challenge to acknowledge the LORD not only as true God, but as unified Israel's covenant God. This was why Elijah rebuilt the broken altar with twelve stones and prayed to the *"LORD, God of Abraham, Isaac and Israel"* (18:36). Especially significant is Elijah's language when challenging the prophets of Baal. *"Call on the name of your god"*, he urged, and declared that he would *"call on the name of the LORD"* (18:24). This was the language of Israel's covenant relationship with the LORD, which identified their relationship as one of prayerful dependence on the him, the kingly Creator who was their covenant King.

Elisha The Prophet Until Israel's Downfall (2 Kings 1-17)

Elijah was whisked into heaven by a whirlwind, witnessed by Elisha who assumed his mantle. Elisha performed many remarkable feats, demonstrating God's power and care, and carried out his prophetic ministry both in Israel and beyond. It was especially noted that Elisha *"prayed"* (4:33, 6:17, 18), an action made all the more conspicuous by the rare mention of prayer throughout the rest of 2 Kings. The comment was also made that Naaman the Syrian expected Elisha to *"call on the name of the LORD his God"* when he healed him of his leprosy (5:11). Use of these expressions reflects their familiar association with the nature of Israel's covenant relationship with the LORD.

Elisha served during the days of Joram in Israel and Jehoshaphat in Jerusalem, who was then followed by his son **Jehoram**. Jehoram married Ahab's daughter Athaliah (Joram's sister), and followed the ways of the kings of northern Israel. When he died after eight years as king, his son **Ahaziah** succeeded him, and continued to follow the ways of the House of Ahab in Israel. So Elisha arranged for **Jehu,** commander of the army, to be anointed as king over Israel, thus completing the final task given to Elijah at Mount Sinai. After massacring both Joram of Israel and Ahaziah of Judah, and all the descendants of Ahab's family in a blood bath, including Jezebel, Jehu ascended the throne of Israel. He destroyed all Baal worship in Israel, but continued to worship the golden calves originally set up by Jeroboam. At his death, his son **Jehoahaz** succeeded him. In Jerusalem, when Ahaziah was killed, his mother **Athaliah** (Ahab's daughter) took over the throne and destroyed the whole royal family in order to eliminate all rival contenders, except for baby **Joash** who was hidden by his aunt. Six years later Joash was appointed king. His reign was long and basically faithful to the covenant, including repair of the Temple, although he allowed high places and gave sacred temple articles as tribute to the king of Syria to protect the city. He was eventually assassinated by his officials and succeeded by his son **Amaziah**. In Israel, Jehoahaz was followed by his son **Jehoash,** during whose reign Elisha pronounced his last prophecy and died.

Jehoash's son was a second **Jeroboam**, and he turned out to be the final stable king in Israel, although he walked in the disobedient ways of his forerunners. The sequence of kings after him was characterized by violent coups, until the kingdom fell during the rule of **Hoshea** to the Assyrians. Parallel to this period, Jerusalem experienced a lengthy rule of 52 years under **Azariah (Uzziah),** followed by **Jotham** and then **Ahaz**. At the time of the Assyrian invasion **Hezekiah** was on the throne.

Sole Kingdom of Judah (2 Kings 18-25)

Hezekiah introduced reform measures which temporarily delayed the process of spiritual decline in Judah, and averted the threat of Assyria. Hezekiah was conspicuous among the kings of Israel as a man of prayer. When Jerusalem was being besieged by the armies of Assyria he appealed to the prophet Isaiah to pray for deliverance (19:4). Then when he received a blasphemous letter from Sennacherib, the invading Assyrian king, he immediately and personally went into the temple to pray for deliverance, and received assurances from God via Isaiah the prophet that his prayer was heard and that God would save the city, *"for my sake and for the sake of David my servant"* (19:14-34). Deliverance came that night. It is apparent that Hezekiah's effectiveness in prayer depended on God's covenants with Israel and

David. He later prayed for healing from a terminal illness, and was favourably answered on the basis of his covenant loyalty and God's covenant with David (20:1-11). It is significant that Hezekiah is viewed favourably in the prophetic presentation of Israel's kings, and that only he and Solomon among all the kings were mentioned for their acts of prayer.

Sadly Hezekiah's son **Manasseh** reversed his father's policies, filling Jerusalem with idolatry and bloodshed. His son **Amon** continued along the same path, until he was assassinated by his officials. The general population executed the murderers and installed 8 years old **Josiah** on the throne. Josiah's reign was viewed by the prophetic composer of the history of the kings as the model rule. It fulfilled an earlier prophecy (1 Kings 13:1-3), and was marked by significant reforms which especially brought to light the "Book of the Law" discovered while cleaning up the temple. Most likely this book was some kind of version of Deuteronomy. It inspired Josiah to lead the nation into a renewal of the covenant, including the removal of all idols and a celebration of the Passover. But all this was too late for the institutional state. God rejected the kingdom and the temple because of the faithless history of the monarchy. Josiah was killed in a battle against Egypt. His son **Jehoahaz** was only on the throne three months before being taken prisoner to Egypt, and replaced by his brother Eliakim (changed to **Jehoiakim** by the Pharaoh) under Egyptian control. When Babylon overshadowed Egypt, Jehoiakim became a vassal to Nebuchadnezzar, until he revolted after three years and provoked the Babylonian forces to besiege Jerusalem. Jehoiakim died during the siege and was replaced by his son **Jehoiachin**. He was forced to surrender to Nebuchadnezzar, who took him, with his officials, military force, and temple treasures, as captives to Babylon. Nebuchadnezzar appointed Mattaniah, Jehoiachin's uncle as the new king, and changed his name to **Zedekiah**. Nine years later Zedekiah rebelled, and after a two years siege Jerusalem fell to the Babylonians a second time. The temple and city walls were destroyed, and national leaders taken to Babylon and executed. So the nation went into exile. Yet a glimpse of hope was noted by the kind treatment shown to Jehoiachin, who was released from chains and invited to eat at the king's table.

Our discovery tour has been travelling at a fairly fast pace. It is easy to feel overwhelmed by the mass of details and developments covered by the storyline. These are the brushstrokes which need to be appreciated, and they give understanding and meaning to the overall picture. But it is the big picture which is important, and we have been taking notice of the prominent features of that picture as we have been examining the literary canvass before us.

There is a living God who is the Creator King of the universe. Mankind was created to enjoy friendship with God, and to be his earthly partner ruling over the world. But tragically Mankind has become alienated from God because of rebellious disobedience and independence. Disharmony, disorder, degradation, and death have resulted. However, God has revealed his rescue plan, based on his agenda of grace. By means of a series of royal divine covenants with chosen earthly partners, God is restoring his kingship over the world and redeeming the world from its estrangement. His promise to Abraham was that he would bless the world. He established Israel as his priestly kingdom. He installed David as his ruling earthly "Son" over his eternal kingdom. The consistent response to God's plan of grace has been prayer. God's chosen partners, and so many helpless victims of oppression and distress have cried out in their anguish and called upon the name of the LORD. This was the message revealed to the exiles in Babylon, and to all who read the sacred witness inscribed on the Bible's pages. Yet there is more to come.

CHAPTER 5

THE PROPHETIC OUTCRY

Elisha the prophet died at the beginning of the eighth century BCE. It was not until the latter half of the century, when national decay was well entrenched, that a new series of prophetic voices was heard. As messengers of God they raised their voices and spoke out against the covenant breakdown and the evils of their day. Over a period of several centuries successive prophets proclaimed God's displeasure with his people and pronounced inevitable judgement coming upon them. At the same time, they declared God's faithfulness to his covenant commitment and revealed an exciting new prospect for the future. What we have to keep in mind is that prophets were God's spokesmen. What they had to say was really God speaking.

The terrain of our guided tour now changes. We are no longer travelling through prophetic versions of Israel's history. Instead we survey documents containing the written legacies of the messages and experiences of individual prophets. These are compiled as a separate section of the Old Testament, and each book stands alone. We have to figure out from its internal contents where it fits into the larger scheme of the "sacred story".

The large books of Isaiah, Jeremiah, and Ezekiel come first in their arrangement in the Bible, and in chronological order. They mark the critical periods of the fall of Israel (Isaiah, concerned for Jerusalem), the fall of Judah (Jeremiah), and the exile (Ezekiel). The shorter books of Hosea, Joel, Amos, Obadiah, Jonah, Micah, Nahum, Habakkuk, and Zephaniah belong to this same stretch of history, each relating to a particular stage, but they are not arranged according to any particular pattern. Haggai, Zechariah, and Malachi came after the exile, and in chronological sequence complete the series. To understand these books correctly, it is important to take into account their period of history, their literary format, and their original purposes and themes. They must not be misinterpreted by superficially reading them out of their context and from a modern day perspective.

Amos and **Hosea** were the earliest of these later prophets, and arose prior to the fall of Samaria in 721 BCE. They attacked the conditions of Israel in the north, which had rebelliously split from Jerusalem after the death of Solomon, and pronounced God's coming judgement on the nation. **Isaiah** and **Micah** launched their attacks against Judah and Jerusalem in the south, beginning their ministries a little later than the prophets to the north. They pronounced similar dire warnings against the southern kingdom. Each prophet expressed his own style and concerns, but together they presented a formidable prophetic onslaught against the spiritual and moral deterioration of God's chosen covenant people.

Tragically the northern kingdom of Israel failed to heed the prophetic warning and God's judgement fell in 721 BCE. The Assyrian army invaded, conquered the nation, and deported the population from their homeland.

The southern kingdom of Judah responded to the prophetic appeal and reformed its ways, thereby averting judgement. However, the reform measures were only temporary and superficial, and spiritual decline continued. A hundred years later a new wave of prophetic challenge arose, declaring disaster for the nation inevitable. That disaster came in the form of Nebuchadnezzar and the Babylonians, who besieged and destroyed Jerusalem, firstly in 597 BCE, and then again in 586 BCE. The population was taken into exile in Babylon. This wave of prophets included **Nahum**, **Zephaniah**, **Jeremiah**, and **Habakkuk**.

Prophesying amongst the exiles in Babylon, **Ezekiel** pronounced inescapable judgement which would utterly annihilate the temple at Jerusalem and all features of the covenant. He also proclaimed a vision of hope, a return from exile and a bright future. The prophecies of **Joel**, **Obadiah**, and **Jonah** are difficult to date, but present messages which are relevant for this period or a little later. The exile ended in 539 BCE, and an enthusiastic company of emancipated Jews returned to their homeland. Conditions there, however, were not as rosy as they expected.

After the exile, **Haggai** and **Zechariah** successfully roused the despondent returnees in the homeland to rebuild the temple at Jerusalem (520 BCE). At a later period (about 450-400 BCE) **Malachi** confronted the spiritual complacency of the returned nation which showed the same old neglect of covenant obligations which had characterized earlier generations.

The experience of God's covenant nation Israel during the era spanned by these prophets marked a long dark and troubled chapter in the course of their history. Yet in the midst of their gloom a light of hope emerged.

With regard to prayer a new picture emerges from these later prophets linked to their vision of a bright new era beyond the days of judgement, although there is actually little explicit mention of prayer in their writings. In fact, for most of these prophets, prayer is conspicuous by its absence. They report more what God says to his people than what they say to him! We will peruse the prophets briefly to gain a broad appreciation of their messages, and note the significance of their few references to prayer.

The Last Days of Israel

There is no mention of prayer by **Hosea** and **Amos** who declared God's inevitable judgement upon northern Israel during its final decades, nor by **Micah** who was their contemporary who preached to the southern kingdom of Judah. They mainly announced what God's reaction was going to be to the covenant disobedience, idolatry, and social evils of their generation. Yet despite the disaster that was going to overtake the nation, these same prophets foresaw that God's love and compassion for his people would in the end restore their covenant relationship and ensure a revived and unified nation under the righteous kingship of David's line. On the other hand, their other contemporary, **Isaiah**, makes significant comment about prayer. He especially contrasts the emptiness of praying to idols with the reality of calling upon God.

We will take a brief look at each of these prophets, in order to get a sense of the conditions of their period and their respective messages at that time. They help fill out the big picture which is the context for understanding the nature and purpose of prayer.

Amos was the first of these prophets to speak out. He emerged about 40 years after Elisha (around 760 BCE) during the reigns of Uzziah in Judah and Jeroboam II in Israel. This was a period of political stability and prosperity, together with a superficial religious veneer. These masked the tragic reality of an underbelly of greed, injustice, oppression of the poor, and disregard for covenant obligations. Amos, who came from the southern kingdom Judah and preached against the northern kingdom Israel (about as popular as a pork chop in a synagogue!), denounced his listeners in a stinging attack. In his own words,

"*The LORD roars from Zion and thunders from Jerusalem*" (Amos 1:2).

His book begins with a series of prophecies against neighbouring nations. He circles around from one to the other, until finally he hones in on firstly Judah and then Israel at the centre. For Amos, the LORD is a God of justice and righteousness. He accuses Israel of ruthless oppression of the poor, religious corruption, and abusive disregard for God's dedicated servants, and declares that the LORD will crush them with inescapable judgement. The rest of the book consists of a collection of colourful prophetic oracles exposing the nation's unrighteousness and pronouncing inevitable disaster as the consequence. He primarily targets matters of social injustice as the evidence of their covenant disobedience. Of special interest is his condemnation of the nation's enthusiastic celebration of the coming Day of the LORD (5:18-24, 8:9-14). This is the first mention in the Bible of such an event, but reflects an apparent established expectation and the tradition of a regular festival to celebrate its advent in advance. Based on past victories in battle under Moses, Joshua, and David, Israel looked to a future grand victory by the LORD against all his enemies to establish his rule over the world. Israel longed for the Day to arrive because it expected to share with the LORD in the victory. However, Amos warned that the Day for them would be one of "*darkness, not light*". He expressed God's hatred for their feasts, sacrifices, and songs, and eloquently urged them to "*let justice roll on like a river, righteousness like a never-failing stream*". The prospect of the coming Day became a recurring feature in subsequent prophets. Despite Amos' abrasive condemnation and prediction of imminent judgement, he nevertheless holds out hope of a favourable future in a coming day through the restored rule of King David (9:11-15, predicted at a time when David's line had not yet fallen).

Hosea followed the ministry of Amos, and spoke out of the tragedy of his own domestic experience. He showed love to his faithless wife by restoring her from prostitution to her place in the home. His personal experience was a symbol for his message, which condemned Israel for her faithlessness, but declared that God would show her faithful love. For Hosea, the LORD was a God of loyal covenant love.

The most common metaphor in Hosea's messages is that of prostitution (1:2, 2:2-5, 4:12,15,18, 5:3,4, 9:1). A significant word, translated "love" but having the particular meaning "steadfast covenant faithfulness", is a recurring term throughout the book (2:19, 4:1, 6:4,6, 10:12, 12:6). It expresses the permeating atmosphere which inspires the whole prophecy. It highlights a prominent characteristic of God. The purpose of the book seems to be to give a true understanding of God and the national condition, and to evoke a loving, trusting return to covenant relationship.

Micah had an influential and memorable ministry (see Jeremiah 26:16-19), and attacked the abuses of his day in Judah, especially greedy landlords and the love of power, materialism, and idolatry. His renowned statement (6:8) is an effective summary of the emphases of his contemporary prophets:

"He has showed you, O man, what is good. And what does the LORD require of you? To act justly (Amos) and to love mercy (Hosea) and to walk humbly with your God (Isaiah)."

The outline is a three-part structure, each section introduced by the term "Hear" (1:2, 3:1, 6:1) and consisting of juxtaposing statements of punishment and promise. The first and third sections are mainly messages of judgment with a concluding brief oracle of hope. The middle section begins with judgment and then gives extensive presentations of hope.

Isaiah was a powerful figure in Jerusalem during the reigns of Uzziah, Jotham, Ahaz, and Hezekiah, and he prophesied prior to, and at the time of, the downfall of the northern kingdom of Israel. His prophecies are included in a book composed during the exile. Other writings from the period of the exile, in the same vein, are included as well, and the book is known by the name of Isaiah. The message of Isaiah (both the prophet and the book) can be summed up in his name, which means "Yahweh saves". Though he warned of coming judgement, he nevertheless declared God's ultimate and certain salvation for his people. The central focus of the book is "Zion", a term which represents where God's name resides, which is the city of Jerusalem, the temple of God, and the palace of David, and therefore the heart of the covenant community. Historical Jerusalem was decadent and rebellious, and therefore under God's condemnation. But God intended to create a new Jerusalem which would be holy to the LORD and would ensure peace for all nations. Judgement would be followed by restoration. *"Zion will be redeemed with justice"* (1:27) sums up the book's message.

Isaiah's book is lengthy and complex. The first section of the book (chapters 1-35) reflects the historical period in which Isaiah lived, consisting mainly of prophecies by Isaiah, but edited by the final composer. It contains prophecies about both judgement and salvation for Jerusalem, for contemporary nations, and the whole world, together with accounts of personal experiences, and predictions of a revived Davidic kingship (prior to the fall of the Davidic kings). There is a notable prophetic feature. Contemporary historical events are viewed and evaluated in the light of the coming day/s of the end. Eschatological (Endtime) events cast their shadow in advance over historical events, so that the present is understood in light of the future, and the approach of the future is sensed in the current events of the present. The writings are eloquent and informative, and full of challenge, insight, and inspiration.

A middle section (chapters 36-39) is a slightly modified version of an extract from the Book of Kings (2 Kings 18:13-20:19) which was composed during the exile. It concerns Isaiah's role in relation to King Hezekiah, and supplements Isaiah's personal prophecies. Since 2 Kings traces the history of the monarchy in Jerusalem until its collapse, and concludes with the deportation of Jewish captives into exile in Babylon more than a hundred years after the period of Isaiah, the inclusion of an extract from it in the Book of Isaiah implies that the Book of Isaiah was compiled later. Probably editors in exile were responsible for the finished work, incorporating preserved materials from Isaiah and other contributions of their own. Their work with the Book of Isaiah is an example of what most likely occurred with the final composition of other books about God's covenant dealings with Israel prior to the exile, such as those in the series Genesis to 2 Kings.

The Book of Isaiah also contains material which relates to the period of the exile, and anticipates a thrilling restoration under the triumphant victory of God. The "Book of Comfort" (chapters 40-66) speaks to a new era with a new message and style, although much of its language and thought harmonise with the earlier section. This third section proclaims an exhilarating revelation of God and his magnificent salvation. In contrast to lifeless man-made idols, God is revealed as the Lord of History, the Creator, Redeemer, Only God, Destroyer of the wicked, Remover of sin, Holy, Covenant-keeper, Lord of Justice. As in the book's first section, the process of redemption is through judgment and restoration, but there is a strong focus on the vindication of justice, a new creation, and a new exodus. Where in the first section the agent of redemption is the Spirit–anointed offspring of the fallen House of David, the third section attributes the role to a mysterious Spirit-anointed suffering Servant, and other anointed figures of history (like Cyrus, a pagan ruler, who unwittingly participates in the progress of God's agenda). The book is large and complex, but a simple outline of its format clarifies it.

The Book of Judgement (1-35)
 1-12 *re Zion*
 13-23 *re Nations*
 24-27 *re the World*
 28-33 *Book of Woes*
 34-35 *re Zion*

Historical Extract (36-39)
 2 Kings 18:13-20:19: Siege of Jerusalem

The Book of Comfort (40-66)
 40-55 *re The Servant*
 56-66 *re Redeemed Zion*

Throughout this three-stage structure of the book brief glimpses into the practice of prayer show a consistent attitude towards it.

Isaiah mentions the term "prayer" twelve times. Half of these (36:7, 37:4, 15, 21, 38:2, 5) refer to Hezekiah's praying recorded in the inserted historical extract taken from 2 Kings. Three other occurrences refer to the ineffectiveness of praying to lifeless idols, once in the first section (16:12), and twice in the third section (44:17, 45:20). The very first mention of prayer (1:15) is a declaration by God that he refuses to listen to the prayers of his people because of their persistent rebellion. Prayer is seen as a meaningful and effective activity, provided it is exercised in an appropriate attitude, to God who is able to respond. The final mention of prayer (56:7), however, in the third section of the book, presents a gracious prospect for the nations in the time of God's future salvation.

"… my house will be called a house of prayer for all nations."

God's intended salvation would be for all the world, without exclusion because of nationality or social inadequacy. Salvation is depicted as having access to prayerful fellowship with the Sovereign LORD.

Beyond the specific references to prayer, however, Isaiah has more to contribute. He is concerned about "calling" on God. A prophecy in the first section of the book foretells a coming day when the nation will eagerly urge its people to call on the name of the LORD (12:4). Prophecies in the final section either lament that God's people fail to call on him (43:22, 59:4, 64:7) because they have neglected him and his justice, or forecast the coming day when God's people will call on him for salvation and he will answer (55:6, 58:9, 65:24).

The consistent use of the term *"call"* indicates its relevance for God's covenant people, and the sense of its meaning is borne out in one particular exhortation:

"Seek the LORD while he may be found; call on him while he is near. Let the wicked forsake his way and the evil man his thoughts. Let him turn to the LORD, and he will have mercy on him, and to our God, for he will freely pardon" (55:6-7).

This heartfelt appeal takes us back to the beginning with Enosh (Genesis 4:26), and to the essential nature of the LORD's covenant with Israel (Deuteronomy 4:7). It shows that the need for reconciliation with God and restoration to his original purpose still remains beyond the exile, and that calling on the name of the LORD is still the required attitude. This is the framework for true prayer. Isaiah was pointing forward to a future day when God's intended salvation would be a reality, and calling on the name of the LORD would be fully effective.

The Last Days of Judah

Jeremiah also provides meaningful insights concerning prayer. He had a high view of prayer, but painful experiences. He was consistently told by God not to pray for his people (7:16, 11:4, 14:11). The people were too entrenched in their wickedness, and God had determined to condemn them and bring them to judgement.

Jeremiah was spokesman for God at his nation's most crucial moment of history until that time, the fall of the southern kingdom of Judah and of the kingship of the house of David. Much of our knowledge of the events preceding the fall of Jerusalem comes from the book of Jeremiah. His task was primarily to denounce the nation for its covenant failure and for its hypocritical religious practices without reality of devotion in the heart. He predicted the Babylonian invasion of Jerusalem and the exile, and witnessed their fulfilment. His was a lonely ministry, confronting leaders and people, and attacking the nation's most cherished establishments and policies. After watching his people ignore his warnings for decades, and eventually suffer the devastating holocaust which shattered the nation, he was finally kidnapped and taken to Egypt where he died in obscurity.

As a prophet Jeremiah had a role of intercession, like Abraham of old. But God's intention now was to tear down the nation and its kingship, so Jeremiah's prayers for the protection of the people were no longer in accord with God's will. For that reason he was not to pray for them. After Nebuchadnezzar's first siege of Jerusalem and deportation of exiles to Babylon, the new leaders in Jerusalem also disobeyed God's word through Jeremiah, and defied the Babylonian forces. Yet they requested Jeremiah to pray for them (37:3, 42:2, 4, 20). Their view of prayer was superstitious. Jeremiah agreed to pray for them, but gave them honest blunt answers, rather than false, pleasing advice as given by the false court prophets.

Jeremiah also proclaimed a message of hope for the future, beyond the period of judgement and exile. This message expanded knowledge relating to the coming day of the LORD. Jeremiah promised a time of rebuilding after the tearing down (1:10, 12:14-17, 18:7, 24:6, 31:4, 42:10). Because of God's everlasting love for his people, he would restore them to his favour, reunite the divided nation, and establish a new covenant with them (31:31-34). The new reality in the purposes of God was that currently God's people were banished from their land and submerged amongst the nations, but in the future would become the people of a "new covenant", a covenant in the heart. This development in God's relationship with his people called for a new attitude for prayer. Jeremiah wrote a letter to the exiles in Babylon explaining God's plans for their future and urging them in the meantime to settle down in their new environment and to pray for it (29:7). This shows that prayer was crucial to their relationship with God, and needed to express true devotion and dependence. They were to pray submissively in accord with God's current action and intention, and not treat prayer as a mere religious formality or superstitious practice. Jeremiah indicated that God's future plans to prosper them would see them restored once more to their land, and ensure a meaningful and effective prayerful relationship with him.

"Then you will call upon me and come and pray to me, and I will listen to you. You will seek me and find me when you seek me with all your heart" (29:12-13).

Prayerful calling on the name of the LORD was the essence of the covenant relationship. It was consciously relating to God and completely relying on him in every respect.

Knowing God's future intentions prompted Jeremiah to personally take actions of obedient faith by purchasing land for the future, and to pray accordingly, at the very moment that the Babylonians were mounting their siege against the city (chapter 32, see verse 16-25).

Jeremiah's attitude to prayer was clear and confident, reflecting his view of God and the role of prayer according to God's covenant relationship with his chosen people. God was living, active, personal, and communicative. He was the King, over nature, over the nations, over his people. He was the God of covenant relationships, loyal, righteous, and gracious. He was sovereign, unwavering, and creative in advancing his divine purposes, which were centred in his own people, but universal in their embrace. The purpose of prayer was to relate meaningfully, personally, and dependently to him in covenant devotion.

Nahum was a contemporary of Jeremiah who denounced the city of Nineveh which fell in 612 BCE. His whole prophecy revolves around the one thought of the coming downfall of "the bloody city". The Fall of Ninevah was the judgment of the LORD for her oppression, cruelty, idolatry and wickedness, and shows that the God of Israel is truly the God who controls the destinies and actions of all nations. Nahum makes no mention of prayer, but his message was encouragement to his covenant people to look to him for their security.

Zephaniah, another contemporary of Jeremiah, speaks primarily about the coming great Day of the LORD. He says it will be a day of divine judgement which will purify all the nations, leading eventually to the restoration of Jerusalem. As a result, he foresees the day when all nations will share the covenant privilege with Israel of *"calling on the name of the LORD"*.

"Then will I purify the lips of the peoples, that all of them may call on the name of the LORD and serve him shoulder to shoulder" (3:9).

Habakkuk, also a contemporary of Jeremiah, immediately prior to Jerusalem's first capture by Nebuchadnezzar, reveals his personal intercession with God. Prophets pray, and Habakkuk's prophecy tells what he prayed, and what answers he received. His book contains two parts.

Habakkuk's Payer Dialogue (chapters 1-2)
Habakkuk's Prayer of Celebration and faith (chapter 3)

In the first part he was troubled by two moral questions. Firstly, God did not seem to be responding to his call for help because of the violence and injustice around him (1:2-4).

"How long, O LORD, must I call for help, but you do not listen?" (Note the term *"call"*!)

The LORD answers and urges him to look at the nations and be amazed at what he is about to do. He is raising up the ruthless, lawless Babylonians to take action (1:5-11).
But that presents Habakkuk with a greater quandary. How can the everlasting holy God appoint the wicked to execute his judgement – against those who are actually more righteous? (1:12-17). Using the imagery of standing on a watch tower to keep lookout, he indicates that he will look *"to see"* what God will *"say"* (2:1).
The LORD replies with a plain revelation which will not immediately come to pass but will certainly do so at its appointed time (2:2-3). The Babylonian (Nebuchadnezzar) is puffed up and not upright, but arrogant, greedy and oppressive, so the righteous (like Habakkuk) will *"live by his faith"* (2:4-5). This is the outlook which belongs to the tradition of Abraham (Genesis 15:6). The Babylonian's captives will taunt him with a five-fold series of woes which are his destiny (2:6-20), because
"The earth will be filled with the knowledge of the glory of the LORD, as the waters cover the sea" (2:14), and
"The LORD is in his holy temple; let all the earth be silent before him" (2:20).
This double perspective of God's future and present status provides a larger framework for viewing contemporary human affairs, and for prayer.

Habakkuk concludes his short prophecy with a psalm-like prayer (chapter 3). It depicts the coming of the LORD, in the imagery of the exodus, as an awesome divine warrior to deliver his people. The prayer sees the future in terms of God's liberating covenant actions of the past, enabling Habakkuk to wait patiently and confidently despite his perplexity about God's present dealings with his people.

We gain a lot of insight about prayer from Habakkuk. His personal example as a prophet who prays, and the perspectives he shares, sharpen our appreciation and understanding. His prophecy strengthens our view of prayer and its purpose, and confirms what has already been disclosed in the writings we have reviewed earlier.

The Exile

During the exile **Ezekiel** exercised a significant ministry which reshaped the nation's understanding of God's purposes for them, and stimulated faith and hope to lift them out of their despair. He was taken into exile with the first contingent of captives from Jerusalem. In the first part of his book, he predicted Jerusalem's second, and final, fall. Later in his book, he foretold Jerusalem's restoration and future glory. Ezekiel's personal actions seem eccentric and dramatic, his imagery symbolic and unusual, and his book lengthy. The outline of his book is straight forward.

Prophecies of Doom for Israel (1-24)
Prophecies of Doom for the Nations (25-32)
Prophecies of Restoration for Israel (33-39)
Prophecies of a New Jerusalem (40-48)

Ezekiel makes no mention of prayer, even though his focus is the temple, which represents God's kingship over his people and the place where his people call on the name of their LORD. Yet omission of reference to prayer actually suits his message. His emphasis is on God's sovereign action in accomplishing his own purposes, rather than on any participation by his people. Initially Ezekiel exposes the corruption of Jerusalem's priesthood and temple practices, and declares their utter destruction. Then later he brings a message of hope, promising restoration of the temple, God's kingship, and the nation, not in political and ritual terms, but in spiritual reality by his life-giving Spirit. Ezekiel highlights God's initiating action in his agenda of grace.

There are no details which allow **Joel** to be clearly dated, though his themes suit a time in or around the period of the exile. His language and thoughts echo the works of other prophets, but it is uncertain how dependent the authors are on one another.

Invasion of Locusts & Call for Repentance (1-2:17)
Restoration of the Land & Renewal of the People (2:18-32)
Day of the LORD: Judgement of Nations & Blessing to Zion (3)

Joel vividly describes the devastating invasion of an army of locusts which reminds him of the coming Day of the LORD. That Day will be a visitation of the LORD, not, as popularly conceived, an event of victory, but of judgement for Zion. Like Jeremiah, Joel calls for genuine heartfelt repentance. At the core of such repentance is the cry of prayer. This will lead to God's restoration of the nation, and to a visitation of the LORD's presence in an overflow of his Spirit, ensuring salvation for his people. Once God's people have been spiritually restored, the nations will be drawn into a war of judgement, and God will establish his presence amongst his people forever. His graphic description is expressed in apocalyptic type imagery. Joel's message is similar to Ezekiel's.

Joel's language concerning prayer uses the typical terminology of covenant relationship. His call for repentance urges everyone to *"cry out to the* LORD" (1:14). When his eyes gaze at the shrivelled and fire-devoured pastures he utters "*To you, O LORD, I call*" (1:19). In describing the effects of the outpouring of God's Spirit in the age of salvation, he makes (in similar sentiment to that of Isaiah 55:6-7) the reassuring announcement,

"*And everyone who calls on the name of the LORD will be saved*" (2:32).

Joel's prophecy is interpreted by the New Testament as fulfilled by the gospel of Jesus Christ (Acts 2:16-24).

The brief prophecy of **Obadiah** (which probably dates to the early stage of the exile) condemns Edom for arrogantly and smugly standing by while Israel collapsed.

Judgement on Edom (v 1-14)
Day of the LORD (v 15-21)

Like Israel, Edom will also be destroyed, but without recovery. Edom is typical of what the Day of the Lord will mean for all nations, who will also be judged, while Zion will be restored. This very short book contains no mention of prayer.

The book of **Jonah** is a prophetic instruction story. Although Jonah lived in the ninth century BCE (2 Kings 14:25), the book was probably written during the exile in the sixth century BCE, or a little later. The size of the city (3:3, 4:11) points to the period of its grandeur, rather than to its earlier days of less significance. The book's literary shape is very carefully crafted.

Jonah Fails His Mission (1-2)
1: *Jonah flees; storm at sea; cast overboard and swallowed by a great fish*

2: *Jonah's prayer*
Jonah Fulfills His Mission (3-4)
3: *Jonah preaches to Nineveh; Nineveh repents; God shows compassion to Nineveh*
4: *Jonah resents God's compassion; Jonah resents a vine withering, and is rebuked*

The prophet Jonah is likened to Elijah in subtle details. Both Elijah and Jonah flee, face death, fall asleep, sit under a tree wanting to die, and have a forty-day experience. There are also parallels between Jonah and the nation Israel. The book's purpose is to illustrate God's national challenge to Israel in the personal experiences of the prophet. Both Jonah and Israel failed to be messengers of God's word to the nations, were stopped by a terrifying calamity (great fish; Babylon), were preserved within a monstrous sanctuary, and were reluctant to show covenant compassion. The book is creatively composed, and cleverly provocative. It provokes reflection on a number of concerns, such as God's divine freedom and sovereignty, the mission of God's people, the effectiveness of God's word to generate faith (embodied in Jonah in chapter 1, and proclaimed by Jonah in chapter 2), and the priority of covenant grace.

There are several strategic references to prayer which cleverly draw attention to key matters. Firstly, there is much irony in the outburst of the heathen captain who was terrified by the ferocious storm which threatened to sink his ship,

> "*How can you sleep? Get up and call on your god! Maybe he will take notice of us, and we will not* perish (1:6)."

Jonah's role as a prophet included intercession, and the LORD had sent the storm precisely because Jonah was avoiding God and running away from his prophetic responsibilities. Similarly the LORD had sent a storm of judgement to sink the nation Israel because of its covenant failure to truly "call on the name of the LORD".

Jonah prayed from within the fish when his life was in grave danger, in his heart looking towards God's holy temple (2:1, 7), and God graciously saved him. This is what exiled Israel also needed to do, from the depths of its immersion within the monstrous creature Babylon which had swallowed it.

Jonah later prayed again when God showed compassion on repentant Nineveh and relented from destroying the city as he had originally intended (4:2-3). Jonah had been thankful and joyful when God had delivered him from death, but became displeased and angry at God's kind treatment of the Ninevites. He confessed that he had always known that God was a "*gracious and compassionate God, slow to anger and abounding in love*" (echoing Exodus 34:6 and Psalm 103:8 concerning God's revealed character), but in contrast he was hard-hearted and quick to anger, and would rather be dead than show mercy towards the Ninevites. He was disapproving of God and rejecting his prophetic commission. Like him, Israel was also guilty of neglecting their covenant God and calling. The book of Jonah skilfully presents its message by strategically using references to the crucial covenant practice of prayer.

After The Exile

Haggai and **Zechariah** were contemporaries who roused the recently returned exiles in Jerusalem to restore the abandoned temple which lay in ruins. **Malachi** appeared on the scene about a century later to correct covenant abuses which had become entrenched in the restored Jerusalem community.

The Book of **Haggai** concerns a period of three months ministry by the prophet Haggai (in 520 BCE) who stirred up the returned exiles to rebuild their temple.

First Message: First Day, Sixth Month, Second Year of Darius (1:1-15)
    1:1-11: *Haggai calls the exiles to rebuild the temple*
    1:12-15: *Zerubbabel and the people obey*

Second Message: Twenty First Day, Seventh Month (2:1-9)
    2:1-5: *The leaders and people encouraged*
    2:6-9: *Glory and peace promised*

Third Message: Twenty Fourth Day, Ninth Month (2:10-19)
    2:10-14: *The infectious nature of sin indicated*
    2:15-19: *From this day God will replace crop destruction with fruitfulness*

Fourth Message: Twenty Fourth Day, Ninth Month (2:20-23)
    2:20-22: *God will shake the heavens and earth, and overthrow the nations*
    2:23: *Zerubbabel will be God's chosen servant on that day*

Four messages by Haggai are set out in a chronological and logical pattern, dealing with the problem of spiritual lethargy and despondency, as apparent by the neglect of the temple. Haggai stirred the people to action by exposing their neglect and by assuring them of a glorious future in the purposes of God. Haggai makes no mention of prayer, but the role of the temple would presuppose its importance. Indifference concerning the temple would mean indifference concerning prayer.

The Book of **Zechariah** is complex in structure and style, and requires in-depth Israelite historical and cultural understanding to interpret.

Zechariah's composition includes a series of visions depicted in symbolic imagery (chapters 1-6), an account in plain language of a significant incident (chapters 7-8), and two oracles presented in highly figurative expression (chapters 9-14). The style is "apocalyptic" – appealing to imagination and fascination, using colourful, familiar imagery to present a plain message in a veiled way which requires decoding. Like Haggai his contemporary, Zechariah was aiming to stimulate spiritual enthusiasm, which he did by exposing complacency and mere religious formality, and by stimulating messianic expectation.

Zechariah's Visions (1-6)
    1:1-6: *Call to repentance*
    1:7-6:8: *8 symbolic visions*
    6:9-15: *Joshua the High Priest*

Zechariah's Plain message (7-8)
    7: *In reply to enquiry about fasting, Zechariah calls for repentance*
    8: *The LORD promises Jerusalem's restoration*

Zechariah's Apocalyptic Oracles (9-14)
    9-11: *The coming of the Messiah (9-10) and his rejection (11)*
    12-14: *That Day: Jerusalem saved, the nations destroyed (12-13), Messiah reigns (14)*

Chapters 7-8 in the middle of the book describe in plain language an occasion when the people of Bethel "*entreat*" the LORD about whether they should continue mourning and fasting in the fifth month as they had been doing during the exile (7:2). In reply, the LORD prompts Zechariah to accuse them of self-interest in both their fasts and feasts in the past. He reminds them of God's requirements,

"*Administer true justice; show mercy and compassion to one another. Do not oppress the widow or the fatherless, the alien or the poor. In your hearts do not think evil of each other*" (7:9-10).

Because those in the past had stubbornly disobeyed, God had become angry with them, refused to respond to their pleas, and scattered them among the nations.

"*When I called, they did not listen; so when they called, I would not listen*" (7:13).

This is the typical language of the intimate covenant relationship between God and Israel, and shows that prayerful intercourse was at the heart of their commitment. The breakdown of that relationship had brought about the nation's collapse and exile.

But now the exiles have been restored to their land, and God declares his zeal for his covenant people, *"I am very jealous for Zion; I am burning with jealousy for her"* (8:2).

He declares that he will return to Zion and live amongst his people, whom he will save from east and west and restore to Jerusalem. The future will be prosperous, and fasts will become feasts. Other nations will also be included, and together both Jews and non-Jews will come to Jerusalem to *"entreat"* the LORD (8:22).

This incident illustrates the essential nature of Israel's covenant relationship, which has prayerful intimacy and dependency at its heart.

Zechariah's final oracle (chapters 12-14) announces a coming day of deliverance for God's people through the smiting of their kingly shepherd, the *"man who is close to"* the LORD Almighty (13:7), causing the sheep to be scattered. Only a third of the population will survive and even they will undergo a fiery refining. But then the traditional terms of the covenant will effectively operate once more.

"They will call on my name and I will answer them; I will say, 'They are my people,' and they will say, 'The LORD is our God'" (13:9).

This is another reference to the Day of the LORD. Zechariah confirms the identity of God's covenant people as those who *"call on the name of the LORD"*, who relate to their divine King in prayerful dependence, and he foretells the time when that relationship will be restored and effective.

Malachi tackles the problems of religious leaders having become careless about their responsibilities, God's people having lost their enthusiasm for worship and service, faith having been undermined by scepticism, morals having become lax, marriages having become fragile and broken, and vision of God's glory and love having become obliterated.

God's Covenant Love Assured (1:1-5)
Israel's Priests Rebuked for Covenant Failure (1:6-2:9)
    1:6-14: *Blemished sacrifices*
    2:1-9: *Failure to live and teach God's law*

Israel's People Rebuked for Covenant Failure: *Family breakdown* (2:10-16)

Day of Judgement Announced: *Justice for the unjust* (2:17-3:5)

Call to Repentance (3:6-18)
    3:6-12: *Stop robbing God and restore tithes*
    3:13-18: *The arrogant mock God's service; God remembers the reverent*

The Day of the LORD: The arrogant destroyed, the reverent healed (4:1-6)

The book of Malachi is carefully arranged, and in dramatic style the prophet arouses the interest of his readers and presses home his arguments with convincing force. Indignantly he denounces the wrongs of his day, but always with the aim of pointing God's people back to their favoured relationship with God whose loving purposes for them are unfailing. As he appeals to them to return to God he reveals insights about God's plan for the ages which are helpful and relevant to God's people in all generations.

CHAPTER 6

GOD'S COVENANT WISDOM

We have seen enough already to recognise the consistent pattern concerning prayer throughout the Old Testament books which trace the progress of Israel's history as a nation. Prayer is a matter of entreaty and intercession made to the sovereign Creator God who has unique covenant relationships with both the nation of Israel as a whole and with the king who reigns in Jerusalem in particular. It is an expression of the privileged intercourse enjoyed as people who *"called on the name of the LORD"*. Prayer is to converse with God in accord with his covenant prescriptions and purposes.

But we are not done with the Old Testament yet. The Old Testament includes a whole range of other books, which are mainly independent, but compiled together (in the Hebrew Bible) to form a complete collection of their own. The next stage of our tour takes us into a varied field of literature.

The arrangement of these books in the Hebrew Bible is a different order than that found in the English Bible, which follows a chronological pattern, placing each book according to its historical period. This third segment of the Old Testament, after the segments of books of "The Law" and "The Prophets", was known as "The Writings". They consist of a variety of material such as songs, poetry, wisdom statements, inspirational literature, and history. **Psalms** and **Proverbs** are anthologies of worship materials and wisdom material respectively. There are five independent scrolls which are usually lumped together for convenience (although English Bibles have located them according to their links with other settings on the basis of history or topic). Each scroll was associated with a Jewish festival: **Ruth** with Pentecost, **The Song of Solomon** with Passover, **Ecclesiastes** with The Feast of Tabernacles, **Lamentations** with commemoration of The Fall of Jerusalem, and **Esther** with Purim. **Daniel** and **Job** are both unique forms of literature, difficult to compare with anything else either within the Bible or elsewhere. **Ezra-Nehemiah** and **1 & 2 Chronicles** present periods of Israel's history from a post-exilic perspective. Proverbs, Ecclesiastes, Job and several Psalms bear the marks of belonging to the "Wisdom Movement" which was a widespread phenomenon over many centuries. The last books in the Hebrew Bible are

1 & 2 Chronicles, following Ezra-Nehemiah, even though they present a history which precedes them.

"The Writings" have a different purpose than the books of "The Law" and "The Prophets". Their themes are concerned with other issues of personal and national interest rather than the focus on God's salvation history. At the same time they have the same perspective of belief in God as the Creator and the God of Israel as the rest of the Old Testament. When it comes to prayer the same emphasis emerges as we have found already. That is, prayer is at the heart of God's covenant relationship with Israel and his kingly purpose for the world. Not that all the books contained among "The Writings" actually even mention prayer! Those which do, share the same perspective and attitude as the rest of the Old Testament literature. But those which do not, nevertheless generally share the same views concerning God's nature and covenant purposes.

The Book of Psalms

Our discovery tour of the Psalms will have to be no better than a "flypast" because the work to do them justice would be too exhaustive. Nevertheless, for our purposes we can glean enough insight from a brief excursion. The Psalms are actually a series of five books: Book 1 (1-41), Book 2 (42-72), Book 3 (73-89), Book 4 (90-106), Book 5 (107-150).

It would be valid to say that the Book of Psalms is a composite literary expression of "calling on the name of the LORD". The psalms consist of prayers, praises, laments, songs, and a wide range of creative literary expression composed by Israelites across the centuries of their nation's history. Their common perspective is governed by the narrative witness of the books of "The Law" and "The Prophets" to God's covenant purposes and actions with Israel. Each individual Psalm had its own particular origin, but reflected the common framework of covenantal faith. Because of wider appeal each psalm became included in one of the growing collections of psalms which developed through common use or common theme over the course of time. Eventually the various collections were carefully compiled to form a book, which was finally completed sometime after the exile, probably in about the third century BCE, and became the hymn book of the second temple. The Book is actually an album of five books of psalms, perhaps meant to follow the pattern of the five "Books of the Law". It is a book of praise proclaiming that God, as Creator and Redeemer, has given to Israel, through the Law and through the revelation of himself in history, a privileged relationship and the prospect of full true life. It is a magnificent treasury of devotion and celebration for use by the covenant people of God.

Creation, exodus, covenants with Israel and with David, the Law as God's light to his redeemed people, God in various roles (Creator, Ruler, Warrior, Judge, Saviour, Shepherd, Refuge), "Zion" convictions, and messianic expectation all find their place in the compendium of the Psalms. A prominent note is God's universal and eternal kingship, and a variety of psalms are celebrations of his rule over creation, history, life, and the nations. God is adored throughout the psalms for his rich personal characteristics and attributes. He is holy and majestic, full of goodness and radiant in glory, righteous, upright, opposed to evil, but protective of the vulnerable, loving and faithful, merciful and compassionate, powerful, purposeful, the source of life, joy, and hope. Many psalms show special attention to the monarchy in Jerusalem, and express messianic hopes and interests. The psalms reflect the experience of both individual believers and the whole community of faith, and provide a great description of the life of faith, its blessings, its struggles, its prospects. Consequently the Book of Psalms preserves rather than reveals the truths of God. It is more a collection of confession and worship material than a manual of instruction. Its many psalms give variety of expression to worshipful and prayerful dependence on Israel's covenant God, and together constitute a comprehensive "calling on the name of the LORD".

To "call on the LORD" is actually mentioned explicitly in different psalms found across the whole collection, and occurs some twenty six times. These occurrences help to characterise the Book as a whole, and to reinforce Israel's image as a people who "call on the LORD" in terms of their covenant relationship with God. Add to this other terms which are found throughout the psalms, such as "praying", "asking", "crying out", and similar expressions, and we gain the strong impression that the Book of Psalms is a formalised version of "calling on the LORD". It illustrates the practice of calling on the LORD, and provides devotional aids to stimulate and assist God's people to do so.

About half the "calling" references are occasions when the psalmist calls on the LORD in time of distress, with confidence that the LORD will hear him and save him. The first occurrence of the phrase is a good example of this, in Psalm 4.

"Answer me when I call to you, O my righteous God. Give me relief from my distress: be merciful to me and hear my prayer" (v. 1).

"Know that the LORD has set apart the godly for himself: the LORD will hear when I call to him" (v. 3).

Other occurrences commend the activity of calling upon the LORD, and appeal for listeners to do so. God himself makes that appeal in Psalm 50:15 (see also 91:15):

"… *call upon me in the day of trouble; I will deliver you, and you will honour me*".

Several psalms condemn evil-doers who do not call on the name of the LORD (14:4, 53:4, 79:6).

Psalm 116 stands out especially, because the psalmist repeats the phrase *"call on the name of the LORD"* four times (verses 2, 4, 13, 17). It is a psalm of personal gratitude for deliverance from death, and readily suits both individual and congregational use.

- The psalmist begins with his declaration of love for the LORD who heard and answered his cry for mercy, and of his intention to *"call on him"* as long as he lives (v 1-2).
- He tells about his life-threatening ordeal and how he *"called on the name of the LORD"* to be rescued (v 3-4).
- Then he testifies to God's qualities of character (*gracious, righteous, full of compassion, protects the simple-hearted*), by which he identifies explicit attributes represented by his *"name"*, and which the psalmist personally experienced (v 5-6).
- He urges himself to be at rest (v 7) and acknowledges his deliverance directly to the LORD (v 8-11).
- He asks how he might repay the LORD for his goodness, and provides his own threefold answer (v 12-14). He will *"lift up the cup of salvation"*, which may refer to a drink offering presented to God, or more likely refers figuratively to accepting the outcome of what God's salvation achieved. He will also *"call on the name of the LORD"*, meaning that he will be prayerfully devoted to, and dependent on, the LORD. He will also publicly *"fulfil my vows to the LORD"*, carrying through on promises he made probably at the time of his ordeal.
- Because he recognises that in God's eyes the death of his people is costly (*"precious"*), having been rescued from death, he gratefully declares that he is the LORD's servant (v 15-16).
- He repeats his intention to perform his threefold expression of devotion, including, for the fourth time, that he would *"call on the name of the LORD"* (v 17-19).

The psalm clearly demonstrates the familiarity of this phrase as a description of prayerful dependence on the LORD by those who genuinely seek him.

The same impression is given by the final occurrence of the phrase in the Book of Psalms, in Psalm 145:18,

"The LORD is near to all who call on him, to all who call on him in truth".

The use of the phrase vividly recalls its first occurrence applied to the days of Enosh, condenses the lengthy history of its use in the Books of the Law and Books of the Prophets, and binds together all the contents of the Book of Psalms to characterise them as a composite literary expression of *"calling on the name of the LORD"*.

In addition to the use of the phrase to *"call on the name of the LORD"*, the psalms also contain numerous occurrences of the term *"prayer"*. The first appearance of the term is Psalm 4:1, already cited above as the first occasion of the term for *"calling"* on God. There are more than thirty occurrences of *"prayer"* throughout the Book of Psalms, and five of these (Psalms

17, 86, 90, 102, 142) are titles of psalms. Many other psalms, of course, are prayers even if the actual term is not used. Psalm 72:20 uses the term in a general sense as an equivalent for "psalms" when referring to the collection of the psalms of David.

The use of the term "prayer" is mostly a cry for help or for mercy. It is mainly offered when the psalmist feels endangered, or under attack by enemies, or at a distance from God. Often prayer and praise are associated together, but prayer especially expresses dependence on God, as the ultimate and surest resort. The appearance of the term throughout the psalms adds weight to the impression that the whole Book is virtually a Book of Prayer and that prayer is the meaningful and responsible activity of the LORD's covenant people.

The Book of Proverbs

Surprisingly, there is no mention of *"calling on the name of the LORD"* anywhere in the Book of Proverbs, and only three mentions of "prayer" (15:8, 29, 28:9). Prayer is viewed as a practice performed by the righteous, and is pleasing to the LORD.

The Way of Wisdom (1-9)
    Prologue (1:1-7): *Purpose (v 1-6); Perspective (v 7)*
    Appeals (1:8-31): *Receive, and do not reject, Wisdom*
    Benefits of Wisdom (2-4)
    Dangers of Folly (5-7)
    Appeals (8-9): *Wisdom (8-9:12); Folly (9:13-18)*
Proverbs of Solomon (10-22:16)
Sayings of the Wise (22:17-24:34)
More Proverbs of Solomon (25-29)
Sayings of Agur & King Lemuel (30-31:9)
Epilogue: The Noble Wife (31:10-31)

The Book of Proverbs concentrates on everyday life, and is a book about wisdom and its application to right human living. "Wisdom" refers broadly to the skill of expertise, intelligence, or knowledge which someone possesses which equips them to understand themselves and their world, and cope successfully with life. It is a gift of God. A key statement in the Book's opening introduction sets out its basic perspective: *"The fear of the Lord is the beginning of knowledge"* (1:7).

In the context of the wide-spread "Wisdom Movement" in the ancient world, Israel's wisdom writers followed the methods of the movement, but from a unique perspective. While they also, like the surrounding nations, derived their insights from observation of life, society, and nature, and through subjective reflection, they started from a fixed conviction.

"Fear of the LORD" was their world-view which set the LORD at the centre of all existence. For them, wisdom depended on an understanding of God's purposes in creation revealed in God's providential government of the world, discerned by observation and reflection. Not only did Israel's wisdom writers differ from their contemporaries in neighbouring nations, but their approach differed from their own prophets who reflected on the law and God's salvation history in his special relationship with Israel. The wisdom writers relied on natural discernment, while the prophets received special revelation. Because their respective insights were based on the same foundational conviction, their views were not contradictory, but complementary.

Perhaps this explains why prayer receives less attention in the Book of Proverbs. The Book's focus is on other matters such as the character and conduct of God's people, rather than on God's purpose of salvation. Does this suggest that the purpose of prayer especially relates to God's salvation plans and his covenant relationships with Israel and its king, as we have already identified? The few references to prayer that are found in the Book may indicate that. It is the prayers of the *"righteous"* (those who are in a right covenant relationship) and those who heed the Law (which sets out the requirements of the covenant) which are pleasing to the LORD (who established the covenant).

The Book of Job

The Book of Job also belongs to the genre of wisdom literature. It raises a troubling question frequently pondered by those who seek to be wise and godly.

The Heavenly Council (1-2)	*God permits Satan to test Job*
Job's Lament (3)	*Job screams out in his misery for the peace of death*
First Round of Speeches (4-14)	*Job's friends say he is suffering for his sins*
Second Round of Speeches (5-21)	*The friends speak more bluntly*
Third Round of Speeches (22-26)	*Two friends speak even more harshly*
Job's Declaration (27)	*Job reasserts his innocence and submits himself to God*
The Wisdom Poem (28)	*True wisdom is found in the fear of the Lord*

Job's Final Appeal (29-31)	*Job's former state (29), lament at loss (30), appeal (31)*
Speeches by Elihu (32-37)	*Job's self-justification and friends' inability criticized*
God's Response (38-42:6)	*Two speeches expose Job's ignorance of God's ways*
Epilogue (42:7-17)	*God's verdict and Job's restoration*

The book shows Job and his friends having a heated argument about God's justice in the world in relation to the experience of human suffering. It is not a theoretical argument, but deeply personal, because Job is suffering terribly. He is defending his integrity against his friends' painful accusation that God must be punishing him for his wickedness and godless disposition. He hotly denies their allegations, and claims that God is misjudging him. He screams out to God for the opportunity of a fair hearing before him, so that he might vindicate himself and end his miscarriage of justice. Job correctly claims that he does not deserve what has happened to him, but is wrong in his interpretation of what his experience is all about. The reader is privy to the larger picture of higher factors involved, but Job is in the dark. After the debate goes on and on for several rounds, God ends it by exposing Job's ignorance about the management of the universe in general. The unstated implication is that Job is therefore not in a position to be critical of God's current treatment of him. No explanation is given to Job about his misfortunes, but he repents of his inappropriate outbursts. Nevertheless, God approves Job for his integrity, and restores his health and personal world to even more favourable conditions than before his ordeal. However he angrily rebukes Job's tormenting friends. They had had much to say about God, sometimes even correctly, but they showed no compassion for Job, and at no point had they enquired of God himself. Their "wisdom" was a matter of intellectual opinions about God, but without actual relationship to him.

It is difficult to classify the design of the book. It contains features of an epic story; of lament and wisdom poems; of religious drama full of interacting characters, passionate speech, and highly charged emotion, yet without action; and of a symposium in which the problem of suffering is debated within the context of the prevailing theological views of the time. It is unique and magnificent, in style and message.

The opening prologue (chapters 1-2) and concluding epilogue (42:7-17) are in story form, while the bulk of its contents is composed in poetical style consisting of speeches and dialogue.

The subject of the book is theodicy, the justice of God in the light of human suffering and evil within the world. It is examined by the presentation of a controversy between God and Satan in heaven played out on earth between Job and his "friends". Job is allowed to be put to the test to show that he will maintain the integrity of his trust in God. He passes the test, because of the reality of his faith, not because of his orthodoxy of belief. Wisdom is the "fear of the LORD"

(28:28), not theories about him. Job yearns for friendship with God, which he feels has been broken because of some misunderstanding on God's part, but which he believes will eventually be restored. His friends are convinced that Job has brought disaster on himself because he is guilty of wickedness and is being punished by God. He therefore needs to repent in order to be restored. For them, God is aloof, the just ruler of the world, to be feared and pacified. Job also sees God as the just ruler of the world, but approachable, to be feared in the sense of being revered, to be honoured and trusted. The question of God's justice in a world marred by evil and suffering is not resolved. However, Job demonstrates the wise way to deal with it. He desires God himself more than life, turns to him for answers, and trusts him when there aren't any.

The format of the book is crafted skillfully in a very carefully designed structure. The book does not solve the problem of human suffering. But it demonstrates the intimate connection between God and his world and his careful, detailed supervision of it. It also dispels mechanical views of God and highlights his sovereignty. God gives life, and withdraws it. Meaning in life cannot be understood within its human limitations, but only within the framework of a vision of God which looks for justification of the present puzzles of human existence in a life which is yet to come.

The human characters in the story are not Israelites, and so they are not members of God's covenant people. Yet they are God-fearing men, and within the prologue and epilogue God is identified by his covenant name "LORD". The book is intended for God's people.

It is therefore interesting, and probably significant, that the main term used when alluding to prayer is *"call"*, the characteristic term of God's covenant people (5:1, 9:16, 12:4, 14:15, 27:10). Although it is only referring to prayer in a general sense, the language would certainly prompt readers to remember their privileged relationship to the LORD, and imply that others outside the covenant could also enjoy intimate prayerful dependence on God. Several other terms for prayer also occur (21:15, "intercede"; 33:26, "make supplication").

The book, however, reveals more about prayer than just terms used. It shows Job addressing God personally and directly, and his bold (almost brazen) attitude is illuminating. In the course of his intense debate with his friends, Job's speeches reveal his deep consciousness of God's silent awareness of his predicament. He is confident that God is near, and watching, but unresponsive, and the silence adds to Job's grief. Job's speeches are directed at his friends, either in reply to what they have said or sometimes to what he senses is their attitude. Sometimes he appears to speak to himself as his mind reacts to his crushing experience. Then there are times when his speech bursts out in direct utterance to God himself (7:7, 12-21, 9:28-31, all of chapter 10, 13:20-27, 14:13-22, 16:7-8, 17:3-5). He seems to be so aware of God that, when speaking about God, often his thoughts are lifted towards God. In this, Job shows that prayer is relational, person to person, and natural. Job is at ease with God, and not intimidated, but he is limited because he is a finite, dependent human. God is greater, though not visible, and not always communicative. Job is not demanding in his attitude towards God, but he forcefully expresses his desires and frustrations. He can complain about his lot, and he can appeal for God to treat him differently. His manner is similar to that of a child speaking frankly to its parent.

At the end of the drama God is angry with Job's friends, and they are in need of Job to intercede for them (42:8-10), a role not unlike that of Abraham and the prophets. The picture that the Book of Job paints concerning prayer reinforces its role as a meaningful, intimate, and responsible activity of dependence on God, the Creator and Ruler of the universe.

The Book of Daniel

The book of Daniel represents a new style of literature which developed after the exile. It is not prophetic but apocalyptic. Through symbolism and carefully chosen language, revelation of profound insights is disclosed. The accounts must not be taken at mere face value, but read with discerning eyes. The purpose of this type of literature was to provide assurance and insight into God's faithfulness in times of affliction. The style was used to present divine disclosures of the cosmic forces at work in history's events and encouragement for the future towards which history was moving.

Inspirational Stories (1-6)
    1 Daniel and his friends in Babylon: *Holiness rewarded*
    2 Nebuchadnezzar's Dream: *God's kingdom overrules and outlasts all others*
    3 Nebuchadnezzar's Golden Image and Fiery Furnace: *God saves loyal servants*
    4 Nebuchadnezzar's temporary Insanity: *God is sovereign over earthly kings*
    5 Belshazzar's Writing on the Wall: *God's glory is not mocked*
    6 Daniel in the Lions' Den: *God saves his praying people*

Inspirational Visions (7-12)
    7 Daniel's Dream of Four Beasts: *Destiny of the world revealed*
    8 Daniel's Vision of a Ram and a Goat: *God destroys wicked forces*
    9 Daniel's Prayer: *Confession of national sin and plea for God's favour*
    10-12 Daniel's Vision of the End Times: *Despite wars God will deliver his people*

The primary message of the book of Daniel is the supremacy of God's kingship over the kingdoms of the world. Though God's people live in exile under the oppression of foreign idolatrous powers, God himself remains unrestrained in his authority and power. He is the *"Most High God"*, the *"King of Heaven"*, who is *"sovereign over the kingdoms of men"*. A major shift of interest is evident by the new focus on the wider world instead of the nation of Israel. Following the collapse of God's covenant nation, the progress of God's purposes for history entered a new period, the "times of the Gentiles", which would continue until God's Kingdom became established on earth. Concern has now moved from Israel among the nations to the righteous among the ungodly. While not belonging to the sequence of books tracing out the history of God's covenant purposes and relationship with Israel, the perspective of the book of Daniel nevertheless presupposes that background.

The Book of Daniel consists of 2 halves, the first being a collection of inspirational stories concerning Daniel and his Hebrew associates in exile, and the second containing visions which Daniel had about the future. The stories are related in the third person, and are intended to inspire faithfulness and courage. The visions are presented in the first person, and are described in typical apocalyptic imagery. The book gives the impression of having been written during the exile (sixth century BCE) even though it actually came later (second century BCE), as the visions' focus of interest on the second century makes obvious. The visions provide precise apparent "prediction" of the future until the second century, becoming more specific in details as the second century draws closer, sometimes expressed in explicit details, sometimes by symbolic numbers. Symbolic numbers then trace the vague course of history beyond that period until the time of the End. The purpose of "prediction" is actually not to reveal the future in advance, but to reveal the character of known history in relation to God.

Several significant features shape how the book is written. In the first place, the book is written in 2 languages, Aramaic and Hebrew, with the Aramaic spanning chapters 2 to 7. This means that chapter 1 (in Hebrew) acts as an introduction. Chapters 2-7 (in Aramaic) appear to have a pattern which connects 2 & 7, 3 & 6, 4 & 5. Chapters 8-12 (in Hebrew) flow out from 7. Secondly, there are strong overtones in the terminology and ideas expressed in the book which show the influence of the book of Genesis. "Babylonia" (1:2) is actually "Shinar", taken from Genesis 10:10, 11:2, where the character of that land is vividly depicted. The only other biblical reference to Shinar is in the apocalyptic writings of Zechariah (5:11) where the character of Babylon is also being indicated. Another prominent similarity between the two books of Genesis and Daniel is the similarity of character and role between Joseph and Daniel. Both remained pure and loyal in integrity, rose to high office in the kingdoms of their captivity, and possessed great skill in interpreting dreams. Thirdly, elements within the contents reflect influence from both the prophetic movement and the wisdom movement.

The Book of Daniel is highly sophisticated in its composition, and must be interpreted with careful appreciation for its original intention. It is apocalyptic, not prophetic. It provides a revelation for God's people who were confused by their virtually extended exile beyond their return to their homeland and their ongoing hostile oppression from foreign powers. It gives inspirational examples of loyal and brave trust in God, whose rule and power are greater than that of human monarchs, and who rescues his people. It also exposes the true character of the forces at work in history, and reassures God's people of their eventual triumph by the intervention of God at the end time, establishing his Kingdom.

The book does not provide a detailed programme about the progress of history until the end of time. Rather, it gives an apocalyptic description (symbolic revelation) of the character of the nations until the end of time. They are aggressive "beasts", typified by the oppressive godless empires of the ancient world. In the end they will be accountable to the *"Ancient of Days"* (7:9-12). However, a mysterious *"Son of Man"* will enter the presence of the *"Ancient of Days"* and be given everlasting dominion (7:13-14). He represents the *"saints, the people of the Most High"* (7:27). This revelation is intended to inspire perseverance and trusting loyalty for God's faithful people.

Within that framework the role of prayer is highly esteemed. The final inspirational story concerning Daniel in the first half of the book is all about his brave and loyal devotion to God in prayer (chapter 6). He is miraculously rescued from intended execution for disobeying a royal decree which deliberately targeted his prayer habits. Daniel's enemies recognized that prayer was his vulnerable point. By prayer Daniel acknowledged God as supreme King and maintained a trusting relationship with him. His enemies knew this, and plotted to bring him undone by forcing him to choose between Darius and God. Despite the consequences Daniel publicly showed where his first allegiance lay by continuing his regular prayer routine, maintaining the former temple daily hours of prayer. The story highlights the significance of prayer. It is not merely a religious ritual, but a meaningful dependence on the reality that God is the true and ultimate Ruler over the world and history. Despite being in exile under foreign idolatrous earthly rule, Daniel still revered God as the greater Ruler.

We are not told what Daniel prayed in his daily devotional routines, but in Daniel 9 we may get some idea. Here is recorded a special occasion when Daniel prayed. The prayer itself may have been special, or it may have been typical of his usual approach. What makes the occasion special is that he receives a divine response brought personally by a celestial messenger.

Daniel's prayer was prompted and shaped by the scriptures written by Jeremiah the prophet. Jeremiah had foretold that the exile under Babylon would last seventy years (Jeremiah 25:12, 29:10), and that God would graciously restore his people to their land when Babylon was overthrown by the Medes (Jeremiah 51:28). That time had now arrived, and Daniel indicates

"So I turned to the LORD God and pleaded with him in prayer and petition, in fasting, and in sackcloth and ashes" (Daniel 9:3).

Daniel's words reveal his attitude of mind. He trusted in the personal reality of the LORD and turned to him relationally in self-abasement as to a monarch whose illustrious majesty had been spurned. His outward actions and appearance demonstrated visibly his inner remorse and mourning. His prayer, which is reported in detail, is an appropriate confession for those living in the exile, and Daniel prays in solidarity with his contemporaries who share his circumstances. His prayer shows that he has a clear appreciation for what God is like, that he has knowledge of the writings of "The Law" and

"The Prophets", and has a deep awareness of his nation's faithlessness to God's covenant which had brought them into exile.

> The LORD is *"the great and awesome God, who keeps his covenant of love with all who love him and obey his commands"* (v 4). He is *"righteous"* (v 7). He is *"merciful and forgiving"* (v 9). He is the *"LORD our God, who brought your people out of Egypt with a mighty hand and who made for yourself a name that endures to this day"* (v 15).

Recalling God's name and nature as Israel's covenant God inspires his confidence, but also his deep sense of shame and sorrow because of his peoples' sinfulness as the covenant nation.

His prayer is primarily a lament of confession, before concluding with a heartfelt plea for God's forgiveness and favour.

- He confesses his nation's rebellion in disobeying the Law and disregarding the prophets (v 4-6)
- He confesses that the whole nation has rebelled, from Judah and Jerusalem, all Israel, kings, princes, fathers, near and far (v 7-11)
- He confesses that the judgements written in the Law and spoken against them have been poured out by the LORD upon them and their rulers in incomparable disaster (v 11-14)
- He pleads to the LORD, in keeping with his righteous acts, to turn away his anger from Jerusalem (v 15-16)
- He implores God to hear his prayers and petitions to look with favour on the city's desolation, and because of his mercy, not their righteousness, to act without delay with forgiveness (v 17-19)

Most likely the prayer is presented in full not only to indicate how Daniel prayed, but as a model for readers still living in "exile". Although the terms are not expressly used, it is a prayer which aptly fits the attitude of "calling on the name of the LORD".

The appearance of Gabriel in response to Daniel's prayer (9:20-21) provides important insights concerning prayer. It shows in a visible revelation that prayer is heard and answered. It also shows that answers, while in principle may accord with scriptural assurances, may also be affected by other humanly unknown factors. Daniel correctly prayed according to the word of Jeremiah relating to the seventy years for the period of the exile (Jeremiah 25:12, 29:10). But he did not take into account the principle from the Law of sevenfold punishment (Leviticus 26:27-28). The combined word of the Law and the Prophets meant that the exile was longer than expected, and explained why the prayers of those in the exile were not, as yet, being fully answered. Gabriel explains to Daniel that

"Seventy sevens are decreed for your people and for your holy city to finish transgression, to put an end to sin, to atone for wickedness, to bring in everlasting righteousness, to seal up vision and prophecy and to anoint the most holy" (9:24).

Packed into that statement, and into Gabriel's additional explanation (v 25-27), are allusions to historical details paralleled in Daniel's visions in chapter 8 and chapters 10-12 respectively showing the extension of Jerusalem's exile down to the second century BCE. The "seventy sevens" are symbolic numbers and not to be pressed into exact time calculations. They are expressing principles not chronology. At the same time Gabriel's answer as a whole has an allusive character about it that suggests a deeper revelation of divine purposes which transcend the events of a particular time period. The apocalyptic symbolism has a prophetic significance, whose fulfillment can only be recognized by the advantage of a fuller perspective, as will emerge in the New Testament with the gospel of Jesus Christ. But for Daniel, Gabriel's answer resolved his perplexity and distress in explaining the prolonged exile, although left him with hints of other tantalising questions. That is often the nature of prayer.

The book's final vision (chapters 10-12), which occurs in an experience of mourning and fasting similar to the occasion of Daniel's prayer, although not actually mentioning prayer, reveals to Daniel realities beyond the earthly sphere. These have a bearing on his devotional intercourse with God (10:4-19), and in some way are behind the kingdom players of history (v 13, 20), with heavenly powers key factors in earthly conflicts. Daniel receives the assuring message that ultimately God's true people will survive End-time distress. This apocalyptic vision appears to imply that there is much more to prayer than simply the human elements of dialogue, and that it has a meaningful role in the higher complexities of history.

The Five Scrolls

As we have already indicated, the five scrolls are independent writings, unrelated to one another. They are linked together in the Hebrew Bible for convenience, and because of their acquired association with Israel's festivals. There may also be the thought behind bunching them together that five scrolls are a reminder of the five "Books of the Law". Be that as it may, the five scrolls are very different from one another, and written at very different periods of time, yet are valuable "windows" into life and thought in covenant Israel. Three of the scrolls especially (Ruth, Esther, and Lamentations) shine inspirational light into the midst of dark periods of national history.

Ruth (Pentecost)

The position of the Book of Ruth in English Bibles between Judges and Samuel was no doubt decided because of its content, although it does not actually belong to that series of prophetic historical narrative. The book was probably written during the early days of the monarchy, and presents a simple message. It shows how the hand of God guides the faithful in the details of everyday life, as also in the events through which the purposes of God are advanced.

Introduction (1:1-5):	*Naomi loses her husband and sons in Moab*
Naomi Returns from Moab (1:6-22):	*Ruth accompanies Naomi to Bethlehem*
Ruth Meets Boaz (2):	*Ruth works in the fields of Boaz who treats her kindly*
Naomi Advises Ruth (3):	*Naomi sends Ruth to Boaz who pledges to redeem her*
Boaz Redeems Ruth (4:1-12):	*Boaz buys Naomi's land and becomes Ruth's redeemer*
Conclusion (4:13-17):	*Naomi gains an heir from Ruth, who is ancestor to King David*
Appendix (4:18-22):	*Ancestry of David*

The book is a skillfully told Hebrew short story. The story tells the fortunes of the family of Elimelech of Bethlehem, who migrated to Moab under stress of famine and died there with his two sons. Then his widow Naomi returned to her homeland with Ruth her widowed daughter-in-law who devotedly insisted on accompanying her. There, in their distress, they discovered Boaz, a near kinsman, who willingly assumed the full responsibilities of a "*goel*" (next of kin) by marrying Ruth, thus raising and preserving a family for the dead son of Naomi. Of this union was born Obed the forefather of David.

Essentially the story is about Naomi being brought from emptiness to fullness, from bitterness to happiness, by the covenant loyalty of God, expressed through the loyal kindness of Ruth and Boaz. Although Ruth is a Moabitess, her actions, which stand in contrast to those of Orpah, show that she is a true daughter of God's covenant people. Boaz also shows by his actions, in contrast to those of the unnamed relative, that he is a true son of the covenant. Redemption is the central theme of the story, and the key terms are "*hesed*" (loyal covenant love) and "*goel*" (kinsman redeemer). Significantly, both these terms occur in 2:20, which is the mid-point of the story, and the turning point for Naomi's hopes.

In contrast to the picture of the period in Judges, we see the active piety of true believers, obedience to covenant obligation resulting in blessing, and God's covenantal steadfast love ("hesed") as the background to the later rise of David. Although prayer does not figure overtly in the story, it is nevertheless an underlying covenant disposition. It is expressed in terms of hopeful mood of reliance on the LORD rather than explicit request (1:8-9, 2:4, 12, 13, 20, 4:11).

Song of Songs (Passover)

The legitimate presence of the Song of Songs in the Old Testament has always been disputed, and interpretations are wide-ranging, from literalistic to allegorical. Although there is no mention of God, frequently interpretation allegorically applies the lyrics to either God's relationship to Israel, or Christ's relationship to the Church or to the individual believer. Traditionally the Song of Songs has been associated with Israel's Passover celebration, although the origin of that tradition is unknown.

Perhaps the best approach is to see the book as a collection of love songs which depict the freshness and uninhibited enjoyment of natural human passion. The songs are filled with frank descriptions and evocative allusions and imagery. They could very well be the product of the wisdom movement which reflected on God's purposes in creation, and be presenting an idealised picture of human marriage. This might also represent a miniature of Israel's covenant with the LORD (since the prophets could use similar graphic imagery when speaking of the nation's "harlotry" or devotion). The basic message in the book is given statement in 8:6-7 ("*love is strong as death*") and declares the preeminence of love and of its intensity and perhaps ultimate agony.

The book consists of a title (1:1) and seven songs : 1:2-2:7, 2:8-3:5, 3:6-5:1, 5:2-6:3, 6:4-8:4, 8:5-7, 8:8-14.

The structure and language of the songs are complex and not always easy to decipher. The poetry is ancient, middle-eastern, and rural in expression. It appeals to comprehension more by emotional and experiential understanding than rational persuasion. The songs evoke response on a sensual level. Much of the descriptive imagery and language is not intended to be visualized literally, but to be appreciated for its sensual quality. For example, the lover's description of his beloved in 4:1-7 does not mean that her beauty looked like the imagery he uses, but that her beauty had a similar emotional effect upon him as that imagery did. He was describing how he felt not what he saw.

The songs are illusory in nature. Although the songs seem to present a drama revolving around two lovers, the plot is not clear. Similarly, the garden imagery and some of the expressions (e.g. 7:10) recollect the Garden of Eden, but not obviously so. The focus is on the beauty and pleasure of natural, spontaneous love. Perhaps the songs are intended to approve natural human love and intimacy as what was intended at creation, and when experienced reflect what human relations were like in Eden. Yet outside of Eden it is illusory and an endangered quest.

Perhaps we might be inspired by the songs to value intimacy and passion in prayer, which other writings of the Old Testament would certainly approve, but we cannot claim that the songs have any intention that way. The songs simply make no definite contribution to the matter of prayer, nor to any other religious activity.

Ecclesiastes (Tabernacles)

An unknown editor has evaluated and given qualified approach to the work of a *"Teacher"* (Hebrew, *"Qohelet"*). The words of the Teacher are introduced in 1:1. His theme is stated in 1:2, and expounded in 1:3-12:8. The Teacher's thesis is that the totality of human experience is *"meaningless"*. He reports on his empirical investigation of life and shows how that such an evaluation of life is unprofitable. His painstaking confrontation with life's experiences led him to dead ends. In the search for human significance people must come to terms with their human limitations, and make the most of life. Because they are creatures, and creation is the sphere of life, people must find life's meaning in regard to God as Creator, considered by the Teacher as transcendent and sovereign. The editor's conclusion is summed up in 12:9-14, giving reserved commendation to the Teacher's message. The Teacher has challenged traditional wisdom and recognized that it is the fear of God which leads to life. The editor applauds his findings, and urges readers therefore to *"fear God and keep his commandments"*. The book makes no mention of prayer, so, although its message would applaud the worthwhileness of prayer, we cannot derive any views about prayer from it.

Lamentations (Fall of Jerusalem)

The Book of Lamentations is composed of 5 Songs of Weeping, or Laments of Mourning. They are not connected, except in thought and style, though all prompted by the same occasion (The devastating downfall of Jerusalem), composed by the same author, and expressing similar sentiment. The first 2 songs each have 22 verses of three lines based on an acrostic of the Hebrew alphabet. The third song seems to be a climax since it has 3 verses for each letter and 66 verses in all. The fourth song is also an acrostic but has only 2 verses per line, while the fifth song has 22 verses but no acrostic pattern (perhaps implying discord?). These Laments are expressions of the heart and mind. They sorrow for the tragedy which has struck, but seek to come to terms with the reason, and acknowledge covenant failure and guilt. At the same time there is movement from sadness to hope, as the faithfulness of God is gratefully acknowledged.

Jerusalem's Desolation and Torment (1):	*Zion suffers because of her sin against God*
The LORD's Anger Against Jerusalem (2):	*The LORD has struck down Zion in fierce anger*
A Suffering Citizen's Complaint and Plea (3):	*A cry of sorrow and a cry for help*
Zion's Past and Present (4):	*Former glory has become crushing misery*
Appeal for God's Restoration (5):	*A plea for God to see their disgrace and restore them*

There are two references to prayer, both in the same lament, the third and longest, and written in the most personal terms as if by a typical suffering citizen of devastated Jerusalem. Both references express the same complaint, that the LORD is refusing to receive his prayer.

"He shuts out my prayer" (3:8).

"You have covered yourself with a cloud so that no prayer can get through" (3:44)

Both approaches to prayer indicate desperate anguish motivating them. The first is in classical covenant language, and appeals for personal deliverance from the afflictions and hardship of being besieged by God.

"Even when I call out or cry for help…" (3:8)

The second follows an appeal to contemporaries to join him in returning to the LORD, along with a confession of sin, yet finding God unresponsive and angry (3:40-43).

It is possible that the author of this lament was the prophet Jeremiah. It certainly sounds like him! And it relates to the times and concerns of Jeremiah's prophecies. Whether or not this is Jeremiah, the shut door to prayer is in keeping with what we have already seen concerning him, that he was instructed by the LORD not to pray because his nation's sins had taken it beyond the point of no return (Jeremiah 7:16, 11:4, 16:11).

At the same time the oppressed and embittered pray-er grasps hold of hope based on the LORD's unfailing love.

"Because of the LORD's great love we are not consumed, for his compassions never fail. They are new every morning; great is your faithfulness. I say to myself, 'The LORD is my portion; therefore I will wait for him'. The LORD is good to those whose hope is in him, to the one who seeks him; it is good to wait quietly for the salvation of the LORD." (3:22-26)

Though his prayers are not yet being answered, his covenant perspective concerning God's love and purposes enables him to persist in optimistic expectation that the LORD will not reject him forever. This is what prompts him to make his appeal to return to the LORD. His outlook is in agreement with Jeremiah's revelation that beyond Jerusalem's downfall the LORD had future plans for his people's restoration under a new, inner covenant (Jeremiah 29-33).

Towards the end of his lament, the author recalls a time when he was in dire straits and *"I called on your name, O LORD"*, and the LORD redeemed his life (3:55-58). The language, the action, and the outcome depict the classic covenant dynamics of Israel's prayer relationship with the LORD, and as the lamenting pray-er clarifies his perspective he is stirred to end his lament with a bold plea for the LORD to take revenge against his oppressive enemies.

The fifth and final lament is effectively a prayer, even though terms for prayer are not actually mentioned. It is a lament intended to be uttered by God's covenant people. They appeal to the LORD to remember what has happened to them, and to look and see their disgrace (5:1). They proceed to point out that their inheritance (the land) has been taken over by foreigners and to indicate the tragic state of affairs suffered by the nation's population (5:2-18). Then they acknowledge that the LORD reigns forever, and question why he forgets them, and forsakes them for so long (5:19-20). They conclude by appealing to him to restore them to himself and to renew their days as of old (5:21-22).

This is a significant lament, because it is basically a cry of distress, asking the LORD to rescue them. It is typical of the action of Israel so often over the course of its history. What is helpful is that its contents reveal important details contained in such a cry. They call on the name of the LORD. They appeal on the basis of their covenant relationship. They acknowledge that they are being punished because they have sinned. And they base their appeal for his restoration and renewal on their assurance that the LORD reigns. The lament displays all the hallmarks of the covenant nature of prayer for ancient Israel.

Esther (Purim)

The Book of Esther is a gripping popular story. It relates the experiences of the Jews in the Persian period, and is read every year to mark the celebration of the Feast of Purim (lots) which commemorates the events of the story. The book is entertaining and inspirational, and very cleverly revealing. It contains many skillful literary features as points of interest, and revolves around several feasts, because its purpose is to promote the feast of Purim.

Feasts of King Xerxes (1-2:18):   *Queen Vashti deposed; Esther appointed queen*
Feasts of Queen Esther (2:18-7): *Plots exposed, by Mordecai (Xerxes), by Esther (Jews)*
Feasts of Purim (8-10):   *Jews protected and Mordecai promoted*

Esther was a young Jewish maid who was taken into the harem of Xerxes the Persian king and used to protect her people against national annihilation.

When Vashti refused to appear before King Xerxes' drunken guests at a feast, he deposed her as queen. Esther was subsequently chosen to replace her, and a banquet was held in her honour. Esther's cousin and guardian Mordecai exposed a plot to assassinate Xerxes, yet also offended a high ranking official called Haman. Haman retaliated by plotting to exterminate all Jews. He persuaded Xerxes to make an edict which ordered a pogrom to be carried out against all Jews throughout the empire on the thirteenth day of the last month of the year. Mordecai and the Jewish population reacted in a public display of mourning, by putting on sackcloth and ashes, fasting, and loudly weeping and wailing. Esther was able to expose Haman's evil character to the king, who ordered Haman's execution. Ironically Haman was hung on his own gallows which he had intended for Mordecai. The edict against the Jews was countermanded by the king who made a second edict which permitted Jews to defend themselves by taking up arms on the same day as the decreed massacre. The story ends with Mordecai promoted to high office, second in rank after the king.

The fascinating story reads like a novel. It is faction, not fiction, history in the form of a story. Esther and Mordecai are inspiring characters, motivated by high principles, who behave courageously. The story contains intriguing omissions: no mention of God, prayer, praise, religion. Yet the point of the story is that God can be discerned in his providential actions and in the fortunes of his people. Though hidden he can be "seen" and trusted.

There are many "coincidences" in the story, which need to be read as divine providences. For example, Mordecai happens to overhear a couple of soldiers planning to assassinate King Xerxes, and he is able to foil their plot by informing the King through Esther. His action is recorded in official chronicles. Several years later, at a crucial point in the major drama of the book, the King happens to read these particular chronicles during a restless night when he is unable to sleep, and comes across this record. It proves to be a significant turning point in the overall story. The main villain Haman also happens to have an ancestry (3:1) which links him with the Amalekites who figured significantly with Israel's past history. Similarly Mordecai and Esther happen to have an ancestry which links them with Israel's first king, Saul, (2:5-7) who had unhappy dealings with an Amalekite which brought about the undoing of his kingship (1 Samuel 15). Discerning Jewish readers would easily recognize deeper dimensions to the story of Esther. In fact even to this day the Jewish people identify national enemies which seek their destruction as "Amalek". As far as Jews who experienced the Nazi "holocaust" during World War 2 are concerned, Adolf Hitler was another "Haman".

There is significant irony in the fact that Haman began to arrange for the annihilation of the Jewish population in the month of Nissan (3:7). Jewish readers would instantly realize, without it being stated (although it may actually be alluded to, 3:8), that it was the same month when Israel commemorated Passover, which was their festival to mark Israel's original release and exodus from Egypt. Mordecai's reaction to the royal decree which sentenced the Israelite population to violent extermination, along with the reactions by all Jews throughout every province (4:1-3), may very well have been motivated not only by the crisis confronting them, but also by the past historic events which they were recollecting at that very time. The story is subtle.

The date appointed by the decree for annihilation of the Jews was chosen by lots, or "purim". This was why the commemorating festival of these events is known as the Feast of Purim. What is not stated, but would be recognized by discerning Jewish readers, is that the casting of the "pur" (lot) was a religious superstitious practice for finding an auspicious date pleasing to the gods. This means that the pogrom represented a confrontation not only between the Jews and their neighbouring enemies across the Persian empire, but between God and the gods of the nations. It is what is not said in this story which is the actual drama being presented. The story is a revelation of truth which must be discerned.

The absence of references to prayer, therefore, must be carefully and discerningly pondered. This draws our attention to the public display of mourning by Mordecai and the Jews. It is strategic. It is more than just a cultural expression of distress. It is reminiscent of the enslaved Israelites who groaned and cried out in their affliction prior to the exodus, and were heard by the LORD who sent Moses to their rescue. It is an action which implicitly conjures up the typical picture of calling on the name of the LORD, a practice which punctuates the story of Israel throughout its history. When we discern this, the impact of the story powerfully reinforces this fundamental activity at the heart of Israel's national covenant which constitutes its identity. The apparent absence of prayer in the story of Esther actually highlights its fundamental presence. Its role in the real drama that the story represents is crucially important and powerfully effective.

The continuing celebration of the Feast of Purim ought to be a constant reminder that God's covenant people will only survive in a hostile world by prayerful dependence on him, because their very identity is that they are the people who call upon the name of the LORD.

Ezra-Nehemiah

The books of Ezra and Nehemiah belong together, and Nehemiah was a younger contemporary of Ezra. In turn they came back to Jerusalem to work with the population which had returned from exile. The book of Ezra firstly reports the original return of the exiles (in 538 BCE) and the rebuilding of the temple which was completed in 516 BCE (Ezra 1-6). Then the second half of the book describes Ezra's own return almost 60 years later in 458 BCE and his reforms (Ezra 7-10). Nehemiah arrived in 445 BCE and stayed until he was recalled to Persia in 432 BCE (see Nehemiah 13:6), and then later obtained permission to return to Jerusalem a second time.

Ezra 1-2	Exiled Jews Return to Jerusalem: *Cyrus's Proclamation; Returning Exiles*
Ezra 3-6	Rebuilding the Temple: *Work started; opposition; completed in 4 years*
Ezra 7-8	Ezra's Return to Jerusalem: *Permission to go; dangers; God gives success*
Ezra 9-10	Problem of Intermarriage: *Ezra confesses nation's guilt; identifies offenders*
Nehemiah 1-2	Nehemiah's Return to Jerusalem: *Permission to go; inspects walls*
Nehemiah 3-6	Building the Walls: *Community effort; opposition fails; poor assisted*
Nehemiah 7	List of Returned Exiles: *As in Ezra 2*
Nehemiah 8	Ezra Reads the Law: *Ezra reads, Levites explain; Nehemiah leads feast*
Nehemiah 9-10	Confession and Covenant Renewal: *People respond to the Law*
Nehemiah 11-12	Residents of Jerusalem; Dedication of Walls: *Population; procession*
Nehemiah 13	Final Reforms: *Back to Persia, & return; corrects new abuses*

Ezra was a scribe, and after receiving permission from the Persian authorities he returned with a caravan of exiles to Jerusalem. Their most important piece of baggage was the "Book of the Law", but they also brought valuable temple utensils and money. Upon arrival Ezra took both prayerful (Ezra 9) and practical action to deal with the spiritual state of the community. His mission was to get the people of Jerusalem to accept the Law, and his first instructions were to dissolve the marriages between Jewish men and foreign women. It was probable that these mixed marriages were formed after the men had previously divorced their Jewish wives (cf. Malachi 2:10-16). The prominent message of Ezra relates to the importance of the temple and the Law for the restored nation of Israel, and being a true and faithful covenant community.

While Ezra was working away in Jerusalem, quietly trying to persuade the people to accept the Law, news kept coming to the exiles in Susa, capital of Persia, that conditions in Jerusalem still remained desperate. The city was in ruins, its gates burned, and its walls laid waste. Nehemiah felt the call of God to go there and do something. He obtained permission from the emperor (Artaxerxes I), travelled to Jerusalem, and wasted no time in initiating the rebuilding of the walls. Although he was only an appointed governor, Nehemiah shows similar attitudes to those of a prophet and king. His skill, leadership and courage overcame the obstacles of discouragement and opposition, and he completed the task in less than 8 weeks. After that Nehemiah took further measures to consolidate the position of the people in Jerusalem. He took lists of the population according to their families, joined with Ezra in the ceremonial reading and interpreting of the Law, and in the observance of the Feast of Booths. It was owing to the joint efforts of Ezra and Nehemiah that Jewish society for the next 400 years was shaped around a religion of the Law. Both Ezra and Nehemiah faced their respective challenges in Jerusalem by prayer and practical action.

Ezra had to deal with the problem of intermarriage which corrupted the religious purity of the returned covenant community. He reacted to the situation in prayerful confession (chapter 9) and by publicly identifying the offenders who were required to dissolve their illegitimate families (chapter 10). Ezra's prayer of confession was accompanied by a dramatic display of grief, and acknowledged the seriousness of the offense which was a blatant breach of an explicit covenant prohibition. He confesses that the nation has only survived as a remnant following its recent destruction and exile as a consequence of former disobedience because of God's grace and kindness. This latest offense deservedly exposed them to the threat of total and final destruction.

Nehemiah impresses us as a man of prayer and action, in that order. When news reached him from Judah about conditions there, he promptly responded in grief and prayer, basing his petition on God's own covenant promises made through Moses (chapter 1). Then, putting his own life at risk, and silently praying as he went, he gained audience with the king and sought his authority to return to Jerusalem to rectify the situation (2:1-10). Upon his arrival at Jerusalem he immediately undertook personal inspection of the need, and organized the whole community to set about renovations. Hostile opposition was faced with prayer and practical strategy (4:9). He followed a policy of assisting the poor and correcting the actions of the oppressive rich, and despite efforts to remove him by persuasion, blackmail, and intimidation, the wall was completed in less than 8 weeks. He cooperated with Ezra in having the community listen to the reading of the Book of the Law and an explanation of its meaning, and in celebrating the Feast of Booths. He then led the people in a renewal of the covenant by leading them in prayerful confession and having the leaders seal a renewed covenant agreement. His prayerful confession confessed both God's past faithfulness and compassion and Israel's sinful failures (chapter 9). He traces God's persistence and grace from creation to the choice of Abraham, to Israel's exodus from Egypt, to the covenant formation at Sinai, through the desert wanderings, to the conquest of Canaan, and Israel's disobedient history in the land. Here we see yet again God's character and covenant purposes inspiring and shaping prayer. It is the consistent pattern throughout the whole Old Testament.

1 & 2 Chronicles

Although 2 Chronicles ends with the decree of Cyrus, and Ezra begins with it, most likely the books of 1 & 2 Chronicles were written later than Ezra-Nehemiah (and are placed last in the Hebrew Bible). The author was writing history which led up to their period in such a way as to highlight important principles which reinforced their work and provided the restored community with an optimistic vision for the future. In the post-exilic era there was no monarchy in Israel, and the community existed under the earthly rule of foreign powers. The books of Chronicles show that God's people were a theocracy (rule by God) located in the temple, and that they always had been, even during the days of the monarchy. Using selected material drawn from many sources, including books contained in the Old Testament, but also others, the author presents a filtered view of Israel's history. In particular he highlights the importance of the temple, law, and prophets to demonstrate how God's kingship was expressed. He also emphasizes God's sovereign choice of the tribe of Levi, David as king, Solomon as his successor, of Jerusalem, and of the temple as the place for the presence of God's name, to highlight the special nature of God's covenant bond with the nation, which is consistently referred to as "all Israel". Chronicles shows that the restored community is the legitimate continuation of God's covenant community, despite its loss of monarchy and political identity.

Genealogies (1:1-9):	*Creation to Restoration*
Reign of David (1:10-29):	*Preparation for building the temple*
Reign of Solomon (2:1-9):	*Building the temple & Solomon's splendour*
Kings of Judah (2:10-36):	*Covenant loyalty and disloyalty until the exile*

In 1 Chronicles 1-9 selected genealogies trace God's purposes from Adam to the returning exiles, showing that those purposes are being worked out through Israel. The main emphasis is upon the tribes of Judah (which gave the nation its king) and Levi (which provided the priests) because of their special roles (in connection with the temple).

Tucked away in the middle of these genealogical lists is an intriguing little snippet of information about a man called Jabez (4:9-10). Jabez is described as *"more honourable than his brothers"* because he overcame painful disabilities from birth by prayer. Actually the term "prayer" is not mentioned. We are told that Jabez *"cried out* (literally, *"called") to the God of Israel"*, and asked for God to bless him and enlarge his territory, and to keep him from harm and pain. It is not fully clear what his problem was, because the details given are so scarce. But the content of his prayer is significant. This request echoes God's promises to Abraham (Genesis 12:2-3, 7), and was successful. This record of his experience highlights the importance of prayer with regards to God's intentions to restore his blessing in the world.

The rest of 1 Chronicles, chapters 10-29, presents an idealized picture of King David focused on his role relating to the ark of the covenant and preparations for the building of the temple. At that time the Tabernacle and altar of sacrifice were located at Gibeon, and the ark of the covenant was at Kiriath Jearim outside Jerusalem. David wanted to relocate the ark of the covenant inside Jerusalem, and eventually construct a temple for it. He was permitted to bring the ark into the city, but when, after building a palace for himself, he attempted to next build a temple, he was denied the privilege. Nevertheless he did all he could to prepare for its construction by his son who would succeed him.

When David installed the ark of the covenant in the special tent he pitched for it inside the city, and appointed Levites to serve before it, he presented a thanksgiving psalm to the chief minister Asaph and his associates (16:7-36). The psalm is a combination of extracts from Psalms 105, 96, and 106. It becomes a psalm which urges worshipers to *"Give thanks to the LORD, call on his name; make known among the nations what he has done"* (16:8), to recall his wonderful acts and his covenant with Abraham, Isaac, and Jacob, and to declare his glory among the nations, urging them to acknowledge the LORD and his holy reign. It is a psalm which brings into focus the purpose of God, the theme of the Old Testament's witness to God's actions, covenant, and character, and the role of the ark of the covenant (God's "throne") as a place to call on the name of the LORD. Prayer, in this context, is central and strategic to the progress of God's purpose. David understood this. Hence the psalm.

This understanding of David is highlighted by the only occurrence of the term "prayer" in the whole of 1 Chronicles (17:25), appearing in the context of a recorded prayer by David (17:16-27). David prayed in response to God's message to him through Nathan the prophet that he was not to construct a temple for God as he planned to do, but that God would build a house (kingly dynasty) for him. This occasion of prayer actually marked the next significant stage in the advance of God's outworking strategy in the world! God was promising that David's throne would continue forever, occupied by one of David's descendants.

David also *"called on the LORD"*, at another significant development with regard to the construction of the temple (21:26). He had made a grave error when he ordered a military census, probably indicating his boastful reliance on military might rather than trusting in the LORD. God was displeased, and imposed a severe punishment on the nation in the form of a plague. To stop the plague David was ordered through the prophet Gad to erect an altar on the threshing floor of a non-Israelite called Araunah. David purchased the threshing floor, erected the altar, and sacrificed burnt offerings and fellowship offerings upon it. When he called on the LORD, he was answered with fire. David became convinced that this was to be the location for the future temple. It is apparent from the account that the act of "calling on the LORD" has particular meaning with regard to God's kingly purposes being accomplished through his covenant relationship with Israel, and especially in connection with the place where God chose to locate his name.

2 Chronicles 1-9 presents an idealized picture of King Solomon and focuses on his role as builder of the temple. Chapter 6 contains a record of Solomon's prayer of dedication, which in the main is a reproduction of what is recorded in 1 Kings 8. Like there, its prominence here in the overall account shows its importance. In addition the term "prayer" occurs as many as eight times (6:19, 24, 26, 32, 34, 38, 40, 7:1), as Solomon asked that God would hear the prayers offered in this place, and especially indicated various distressing situations which might prompt such prayers. The conclusion to the prayer here is markedly different from the 1 Kings account which recalls Israel's deliverance and exodus from Egypt, and is a modified version of Psalm 132:8-10 which is about bringing the ark to the temple. Each ending suits the emphasis of each respective account.

When Solomon's construction of the temple and his own palace was completed, the LORD appeared to him in the night and responded to his prayer, as we have already seen in the account of 1 Kings 9. He declared that he had personally chosen and consecrated the temple, but required obedience from those who sat on Solomon's throne. However, inserted between the two verses containing God's declaration about the temple, the chronicler includes additional comments not found in the 1 Kings' account about prayer offered at the temple.

"When I shut up the heavens so that there is no rain, or command locusts to devour the land or send a plague among my people, if my people who are called by my name, will humble themselves and pray and seek my face and turn from their wicked ways, then will I hear from heaven and will forgive their sin and will heal their land. Now my eyes will be open and my ears attentive to the prayers offered in this place." (7:13-15)

What immediately strikes you as you read these comments is the way God identifies his people: *"my people who are called by my* name" (literally, "*My people upon whom my name is* called"). It is as if the characteristic action of "calling upon the name of the LORD" has given rise to a form of expression which suitably identifies their unique covenant relationship.

The comments tap into a theme throughout 1 & 2 Chronicles stressing the LORD's interaction with his people, swift punishment for disobedience or benevolent favour for obedience, which includes repentance. David's earlier advice to his son Solomon expresses the same principle,

"If you seek him, he will be found by you; but if you forsake him, he will reject you forever."
(1 Chronicles 28:9b)

What is also demonstrated by the extra inclusion in the LORD's reply to Solomon's prayer of dedication is the crucial value and role of prayer for the people of God in relating to him, as well as the accompanying disposition which ensures its genuineness. That disposition is expressed in other terms by David's preface to his advice to Solomon that we have just mentioned.

> *"And you, my son Solomon, acknowledge the God of your father, and serve him with wholehearted devotion* (literally, *"a heart of* shalom") *and with a willing mind, for the LORD searches every heart and understands every motive behind the thoughts."* (1 Chronicles 28:9a)

The Chronicler's desire is to promote a strong covenant relationship between the LORD and his people, marked by the LORD's goodness and covenant love and his peoples' responsive heartfelt devotion. Calling upon the name of the LORD in prayer before the Ark of the Covenant in the temple gave outward deliberate expression to that relationship.

Two examples of this type of prayer are reported later in 2 Chronicles, offered by King Hezekiah and King Manasseh. The rest of this book (chapters 10-36) traces the history of the monarchy after Solomon, focusing on the throne in Jerusalem, and effectively ignoring the northern kingdom of Israel. It highlights those kings who acted favourably towards the temple, Law, and prophets, and the book ends with the fall of Jerusalem, exile, and Cyrus' restoration decree.

King Hezekiah (whose reign commenced in 715 BCE) is shown in favourable light by the chronicler because he ruled over the surviving kingdom of Judah after the northern kingdom of Israel had been destroyed by the Assyrians (in 722 BCE), and his kingship was similar in character to that of Solomon. In particular he celebrated the Passover, to which he invited the remaining members of Israel's devastated population to join with Judah, recognising the original united nation. Some ridiculed the invitation, but many accepted and attended. This was the first time in two hundred years since Solomon that the combined nation observed Passover together. Hezekiah made two significant concessions contrary to the covenant stipulations for Passover. Firstly he delayed the celebration until the second month instead of holding it on the prescribed fourteenth day of the first month (Exodus 12:2, 6, Deuteronomy 16:1-8). This was to allow adequate time for the priests to consecrate themselves and for the people to assemble at Jerusalem (30:2-3). It would also be an encouraging gesture to the northern Israelites, in his pursuit of unifying God's people, because at the time of Israel's breakaway into independence from Judah they had altered their own calendar of religious festivals by a month (1 Kings 12:32). Secondly, he waived the requirement of cleanliness rituals for some who attended. Preparation for Passover involved strict ceremonial preparations, but many arrived without having undergone proper consecration, especially from northern Israel. So Hezekiah *"prayed"* for them, and the LORD heard him and healed them (30:18-20). The chronicler's report of this incident obviously uses language which echoes the LORD's earlier response to Solomon's prayer of dedication (7:14). He wants Hezekiah's prayer to illustrate and to confirm the LORD's word to Solomon, and for Hezekiah to be seen as rightly ruling in the tradition of Solomon.

Following that Passover they celebrated the Feast of Booths for seven days, and then extended for another seven days. The festival was a highly joyful occasion, and at the conclusion the priests blessed the people. The account states that *"God heard them, for their prayer reached heaven, his holy dwelling place"* (30:27).

Several observations are prompted by this statement. In the first place, the priests' blessing is described as "prayer", implying that the priests did not bestow the blessing, but requested God to do so. Secondly, heaven, not the earthly temple, is referred to as God's holy place, showing a recognition that God was not confined to a building, even though he had chosen it as a place for his name. Thirdly, to say that *"God heard them"* could only be humanly known by subsequent evidence. Two matters are reported as having followed the festival: the people smashed all articles of idolatry throughout the land before returning to their homes, and they gave generous contributions to the upkeep and services of the temple in response to Hezekiah's order (chapter 31). The first matter was reported in 2 Kings 18:4, but only the chronicler reports the second event. He does so at length, and notes in particular the high priest acknowledging that it was *"because the LORD has blessed his people"* (31:10). This is an example of the prayerful interaction of the covenant people with the LORD, resulting in favourable experience. Through prayer they are entering into God's covenant intention to bless his people.

Manasseh (chapter 33) is a surprise example. He followed his father Hezekiah to the throne, and ruled for fifty five years, but in the way of evil. He restored idolatry and detestable practices throughout the land, and desecrated the temple in Jerusalem. He and the nation ignored God's word to them through seers (33:10, 18), so they suffered invasion by Assyrian forces and Manasseh was taken prisoner to Babylon. His experience illustrates the principle of swift punishment for disobedience. But Manasseh also illustrates the principle of repentance bringing favour. In his captivity he humbled himself before God, and he was restored to his kingdom. The record of his experience is worth noting.

> *"In his distress he sought the favour of the LORD his God and humbled himself greatly before the God of his fathers. And when he prayed to him, the LORD was moved by his entreaty and listened to his plea; so he brought him back to Jerusalem and to his kingdom. Then Manasseh knew that the LORD is God."* (33:12-33)

After his reinstatement, Manasseh repaired Jerusalem's defences, removed all traces of idolatry, and restored true worship at the temple. In summarising his reign the chronicler draws special attention to his prayer which marked the profound turning point in his life.

"The other events of Manasseh's reign, including his prayer to his God and the words the seers spoke to him in the name of the LORD, the God of Israel, are written in the annals of the kings of Israel. His prayer and how God was moved by his entreaty, as well as his sins and unfaithfulness, and the sites where he built high places and set up Asherah poles and idols before he humbled himself – all are written in the records of the seers" (33:18-19).

CHAPTER 7

THE SON'S INHERITANCE

A Covenant Context for Prayer

Before our guided tour leaves the Old Testament for the New, I would like you to focus your attention on Psalm 2. It takes us to the heart of the Bible's message. The psalm condenses the central concern of the Old Testament to a single celebratory song, which the New Testament sees pointing to the gospel about Jesus. It gives us crucial insights about how God's Kingdom will triumph in the world, and strategic to God's victory is the action of prayer.

Both Psalm 1 and Psalm 2 have no titles, and together they are placed at the head of the Book of Psalms and provide an introductory role to the rest of that Book. The two psalms complement one another by declaring the conditions for happiness, which is the subjective experience of blessedness, shown by God's work of creation and God's promise to Abraham to be his purpose for mankind. Psalm 1 has an individual perspective, while the perspective of Psalm 2 is universal. Psalm 1 contrasts the two ways of life which characterise the godly and ungodly respectively, in terms of their conduct and destiny. Psalm 2 declares confidently that through his Anointed King God will conquer his enemies and rule over them, and that therefore it is wise (and blessed) to seek refuge with God. These two themes concerning godly living and God's kingship appear in numerous psalms, and so Psalms 1 and 2 are appropriate introductions to the whole collection.

In particular, almost half of the psalms in the Book are identified as psalms of David, which seem to form the original nucleus of the collection, to which other psalms were subsequently added. The first book of psalms, after the introductory Psalms 1 and 2 (that is, Psalms 3-41) are all psalms of David. This means they were either written by David, or about him, or were included in a collection under his name. They are "royal" psalms, concerned about God's anointed king over his covenant people, Israel. There are other psalms of David scattered through the rest of the Book. And this means that Psalm 2, although it has no title, yet also being a "royal" psalm, is positioned so appropriately at the head of the first book of psalms. Although the psalm itself gives no indication about its author, the New Testament attributes it to David (Acts 4:25).

What is striking is that the psalm does not reflect any particular circumstances during David's reign. It is not about God's rule over his national kingdom Israel, but about his rule over the world and all nations. Certainly there were occasions when rebellion broke out in David's kingdom which might prompt him to compose the psalm, but his experience lifted his perspective to take in the universal sweep of all mankind. David knew that in God's plan his covenant kingship over Israel was destined to be everlasting (2 Samuel 7:16) and universal (2 Samuel 22:44). The psalm is not history but prophecy.

This setting provides a perspective for appreciating its meaning. Psalm 2 is a song of triumph for God's Anointed King facing rebellion amongst the peoples of the world. The Anointed King is God's "Son", because he rules on behalf of God over God's kingdom. Originally the Psalm may have been inspired by a situation during the reign of King David. Or perhaps, as some have suggested, it was composed for coronation ceremonies for successive rulers in David's dynasty. We do not know. But what we can know is that the Psalm reflects the unique status enjoyed by King David and his descendants who ruled in Jerusalem over the nation of Israel, established by God's special covenant with David (2 Samuel 7). God's promise to David gave rise to the expectation of a "Messiah" ("Anointed King"), and Psalm 2 is definitely messianic in outlook. When the Davidic monarchy was removed in 586 BCE, the prophetic outlook gained greater prominence, and nourished the messianic hope. By the time the Book of Psalms was compiled there would have been strong motivation to ensure that the message of Psalm 2 sounded a leading note for the worshipping experience of God's covenant people who called on the name of their LORD.

The fact that Psalm 2 appears without any accompanying details about its origins, indicating whether it was prompted by particular circumstances or composed for a special occasion, allows it to have a wider and more general application. It very concisely depicts the essential message of the whole Old Testament, indeed the whole Bible. Consequently, as the second psalm in the Book of Psalms, it serves as a reminder of the crucial truths witnessed to by the scriptures which are foundational to the life and faith of God's covenant people Israel.

So what is Psalm 2 all about? It is a song, consisting of a series of four vivid word pictures, each three verses long, which proclaims the eventual and certain triumph of God's "Messiah" in the world.

Rebellious Nations on Earth, v 1-3.

Why do the nations conspire and the peoples plot in vain? The kings of the earth take their stand and the rulers gather together against the LORD and against his Anointed One.
"Let us break their chains", they say, "and throw off their fetters."

The first stanza depicts restless subject nations and their rulers rising up in mutiny against God's rule. Perhaps the Psalm was prompted by an occasion of rebellion throughout David's extensive empire, but the language is suggestive of a wider meaning. Such a specific situation of rebellion in God's chosen kingdom of Israel was a reflection of the rebellion against God's kingship throughout the whole world. The picture represents the world's condition before God as a result of the rebellion which took place in Eden.

An abrupt rhetorical question (v 1) and a blunt simple statement (v 2) sketch a bare but clear picture of a kingdom in turmoil. The full force is somewhat lost in translation. The descriptive terms used paint the scene of rage, riot, and rebellious defiance and collaboration. The term *"conspire"* actually means "rage", conjuring up the image of turbulent agitation, like a boisterous rolling sea. The phrase *"in vain"* indicates the meaninglessness and futility of the seething rebellious mob. The scene shows earthly kings and rulers banded together in war-like stance in opposition to the LORD and his *"Anointed One"*. The testimony of the Old Testament reveals that God's kingship has always had to reckon with the problem of rampant evil, and here that reality is depicted dramatically as a rebellion against his authority. The *"Anointed One"* refers to God's appointed earthly king who, like Kings Saul, David, Solomon, and successive kings in Jerusalem, was recognized by symbolic anointing. The phrase means *"Messiah"*, which became a popular title for the future descendant of David who would be the expected king and deliverer of God's people. Here he shares close intimacy with the LORD in world-wide sovereignty, and in the face of the restless revolt against their authority. The question expresses the sense of astonishment at the audacity of such behaviour, and the bald statement suggests a tone of disgust and indignation.

The summary speech (v 3), which gives voice to the common attitude, demonstrates the lawless spirit which breaks out in insurrection. God's ruling judgements are viewed contemptuously as *"chains"* and *"fetters"*, and his authority is resented as constrictive.

The stanza shows graphically the blatant, determined collusion of earthly rulers and people arrayed in opposition to God, rising up in futile rebellion against his anointed King. It is not difficult to identify these symptoms in every generation of the human race since mankind first appeared on the earth. This picture is the story of the Old Testament condensed to a vivid visual scene. It portrays the spiritual and moral state of the human race. All people are enemies of God and strive to break away from his sovereignty.

The Early Church interpreted Psalm 2 as reaching its culmination with the crucifixion and resurrection of Jesus, and identified these lawless rebels specifically with Herod and Pilate and the Jews and Gentiles who had collaborated against, and rejected, Jesus (Acts 4:24-28, 13:32-33). From the perspective of the New Testament the crucifixion of Jesus was the ultimate hour of Mankind's universal rebellion against God's kingship. The New Testament declares that Jesus was the long-expected Messiah promised in the Old Testament. It contradicts the popular opinion of the day that the Messiah would be a political ruler and military leader who would liberate Israel from oppressive Gentile conquerors and reinstate the kingdom of David in Jerusalem. Instead Jesus came to conquer sin and death and to restore God's kingship in the world. All the actions of God in the Old Testament were moving progressively towards this goal, a mission to be accomplished by God's Messiah. In the light of the person and experience of Jesus, and with the benefit of insight from the Holy Spirit given at Pentecost, the Old Testament's preparation and anticipation were more clearly discerned.

The gospel (or, "Good News Announcement") about Jesus is referred to in the New Testament as the gospel of God's Kingdom. Jesus announced the arrival of the Kingdom by his preaching, and inaugurated it by his death and resurrection. The four books in the New Testament called "Gospels" are written proclamations (not biographies or histories) about Jesus. They are written by different authors for different audiences, with different emphases because they have different purposes, and so have variations in their presentations. Yet they all have the same focus. They present Jesus as the Messiah, and culminate in his crucifixion and resurrection. The Gospels demonstrate that Jesus is the "Son of God", which is a messianic title indicating his earthly identity (not his divine status), and report Jesus' self-designation as "Son of Man", which is another messianic title indicating his mission.

The title "Son of God" was a familiar expression which referred to all Israelites, because they belonged to the nation which descended from Abraham and was God's collective "Son" redeemed from slavery in Egypt. The title was also used in a special sense to refer to the kings of Israel who descended from King David (2 Samuel 7:14) because they represented the nation on the one hand, and God himself as ruler over the nation on the other hand, in terms of God's special covenant with David. It became a title for the long-anticipated Messiah. The "Son of God" was God's dependent earthly partner. The Gospels identify Jesus as the messianic "Son of God" by presenting him as a son of Abraham and son of David, who was anointed, not by mere symbolic oil, but the Spirit of God. He announced the arrival of the kingdom of God, and demonstrated its presence by his unique authority, teachings, and signs and wonders, especially healings which were considered acts of God (Exodus 15:26, Psalm 103:3). Although Jesus' identity as "Son of God" referred to his earthly role as God's kingly representative in the world, the Gospels and other New Testament writings reveal that Jesus had a divine pre-existence, and had entered the world as a human being in order to fulfill the divine promises and will.

Jesus actually avoided calling himself "Son of God", and instead referred to himself consistently as the "Son of Man". This was an ambiguous description because it could simply be understood as an impersonal way of mentioning himself, like saying "One does" rather than "I do". Or it could merely mean anyone, any human being. It emphasised their finite human nature, as in Psalm 8:4. Ezekiel was described as "son of man" some 86 times! However, it emerges from Jesus' use of the expression that he meant much more than that. He always referred to himself as "The Son of Man", in a definite sense, implying that he was so uniquely.

He was probably indicating subtly that he represented all mankind. He especially used it to indicate his messianic mission of establishing God's kingdom through crucifixion and resurrection, and was probably drawing on the apocalyptic imagery of the "Son of Man" in the book of Daniel, as his response to the High Priest highly suggests (Matthew 26:64). In keeping with this self-description, the Gospels also show that Jesus carried out his ministry, not as a military warrior in accord with popular messianic expectation, but as a humble suffering servant resembling the mysterious anointed servant of God in the prophecy of Isaiah (Isaiah 42:1-4, 49:1-6, 50:4-9, 52:13-53:12). Because it was not customary to identify the messianic Son of David with the Servant of Isaiah, Jesus was a confusing enigma to all who wondered about his identity. But the Gospels proclaim that Jesus must be recognized as indeed the Messiah, truly fulfilling Old Testament prophecy, yet in a way which went far beyond mere national and political hopes. He was really the King of Heaven, who had come to be the Saviour of the world by becoming a sin-offering to atone for the world's sinful rebellion, and so graciously provide forgiveness and restoration for all who were willing to receive his pardon and submit to his kingship.

The person of Jesus is a phenomenon which confronts the human race. More literature has been generated about his public activities and experiences which occurred during a brief period of only several years than about any other topic in history. He was an event in history which has made a profound impact on every generation since. Following his execution by crucifixion, at the judgement of official authorities, though unjust according to all evidence, his name was soon being proclaimed far and wide as the name to be revered above all names, and his small band of followers erupted into a movement of countless numbers of bold and devoted converts. Astonishingly, Jews identified him as their promised Messiah and worshiped him as divine, while yet maintaining their monotheistic convictions. They did not treat Jesus as a second god, but as the confirmation that their God was true and had sent his unique kingly "Son" into the world to be its Saviour. On the other hand Gentiles also acknowledged Jesus as Saviour of the world and the divine and supreme Lord over all other authorities. Under the name of Jesus an extraordinary social wonder appeared. Jews and Gentiles, who were previously prejudiced and hostile towards one another, spontaneously bonded together in fellowship groups which were conspicuous for their brotherly love. The driving power of this movement, fired by the proclamation of the gospel about Jesus, was the conviction that Jesus had been resurrected from the dead, and the consciousness of his living presence within and among his followers by means of the Holy Spirit.

At the same time there was an angry and even hostile reaction from many against the name of Jesus, directed at his followers. Jews were incensed at the idea of identifying Jesus as Messiah and divine, at the threat to their religious views and traditions, and at the prospect of welcoming Gentiles as equal sharers in God's promises and covenant privileges originally assured to Israel. Their reaction was violent. Gentiles also saw Jesus as a threat to their idolatrous religious customs and social stability. The claims about Jesus completely undermined the entrenched pagan view of many gods and all the associated religious traditions of rituals, festivals, and social habits. Social structures, moral values, and attitudes towards family life, women, slaves, racism, sexuality, interpersonal relationships, and personal integrity and spirituality were confronted by radically transformed views. Gentile reactions were just as hostile towards followers of Jesus as those of antagonistic Jews.

The primary reason for both Jesus' acceptance by his followers and his rejection by his enemies is the claim that he was God's promised Messiah. The crucifixion of Jesus is interpreted by the New Testament both as God's judgement for the sin of the world and the means for its salvation, and as the pinnacle of human rebellion against God and his messianic King. That is why the followers of Jesus who proclaimed his gospel, when they experienced irrational and unjustifiable opposition, discerningly identified the violent extermination of Jesus with the vivid opening picture of Psalm 2.

The Enthroned LORD in Heaven, v 4-6.

The One enthroned in heaven laughs; the LORD scoffs at them. Then he rebukes them in his anger and terrifies them in his wrath, saying,
   "I have installed my King on Zion, my holy hill."

The second stanza switches the scene to heaven, where God is enthroned as absolute monarch over all existence. His simply described settled posture is in marked contrast to the restive frenzy of those on earth who are seeking to unseat him. His dignity and authority remain undisturbed. His reaction to mankind's wild uproar on earth expresses deep, composed feeling in human-like language. With scoffing laughter he derides their puny attempts at rebellion (v 4) and his furious anger terrifies and rebukes the offenders (v 5). The change of scenes eloquently displays the difference between human anger and divine anger. Human anger stems from irrational rebellion and behaves riotously. Divine anger is the indignant and justifiable reaction to unruly rebellion. Throughout the Old Testament God's fierce anger against all forms of evil is a persistent reality, a threat to human experience as a consequence to human disobedience which began in Eden. This second scene identifies the major peril confronting the human race.

God's summary speech (v 6) insists ("*I have installed…*" is emphatic) that his appointed king on earth will not be overthrown. "*Zion*" was the name of a mount in Jerusalem near the temple and the king's palace, and became a term for the place where God ruled and was worshipped. It was God's "*holy hill*". His anointed king was his appointed king, whose rule represented, and intimately shared, God's rule. God and his king were partners, united by an indissoluble covenant, and their reigns were identical. Whatever men might do, God's established kingship was unaltered.

The essential theme of the whole Bible is that God's sovereignty over his creation remains unaltered, despite the rebellion of the world's human population, and is patiently and powerfully working to quell the rebellion, and restore harmony to his kingdom. God is taking his time, and is following an intentional strategy motivated by love, grace, and mercy along a course designed to save the world.

The world needs saving because human rebellion has set the world on a path which will inevitably lead to destruction. It is a path of self-destruction, yet even more than that it is a path which leads to a final day of reckoning with God the kingly Judge, who will have as it were the last laugh.

A final day of judgement for the wicked is a consistent expectation throughout the Bible. Wickedness in the world is the result and evidence of human rebellion against God's sovereignty. Though the wicked often seem to thrive in life, and succeed in their evil and oppressive ways without accountability, God's messengers insist that they will face divine retribution ultimately. Psalm 37 is a typical example. This psalm appeals to the righteous, those who honour God as their covenant King and live according to his will, not to fret because the wicked flourish in their sinful, ruthless activities. Instead, they are to trust in the LORD and to live meekly and blamelessly before him. In the long run they will be saved, blessed, and will inherit the land. Of course these outcomes are in keeping with God's covenant promise to Abraham. In language which has close similarity to Psalm 2, the righteous are assured that the wicked face inevitable consequences for their oppressive, evil ways.

"*The wicked plot against the righteous and gnash their teeth at them; but the LORD laughs at the wicked, for he knows their day is coming*" (v 12-13).

The imagery of God laughing in mockery at his rebellious enemies is a colourful picture to highlight the ridiculous futility of human effort to overthrow God's rule, and assert wilful self-sufficiency. It is similar to the probably not so subtle hint of God mocking the builders of the tower of Babel (Genesis 11:1-9). They aimed to build a tower which "*reaches the heavens*" as they tried to make a name for themselves and to avoid being scattered across the face of the earth. Their actions were a blatant, arrogant, independent attempt to usurp the sovereignty and purpose of God. God's reaction is described almost in humorous vein.

"*But the LORD came down to see the city and the tower that the men were building*" (v 5).

Their efforts fell far short of reaching heaven, and God descended to their level and took action to thwart their plans and to accomplish his own intentions. Psalm 2 asserts the same message.

God's series of harsh "blows" against Egypt to force the hand of Pharaoh to release the Israelites from bondage followed a clear pattern which demonstrated God's superior power (Egypt's magicians called it the "*finger of God*" [Exodus 8:19],) and demonstrated a clear distinction between the Israelites and the Egyptians. Pharaoh was not only defeated, but humiliated.

In Elijah's showdown with the prophets of Baal in the name of the LORD, he taunted them with mocking sarcasm (1 Kings 18:27).

God's mocking attitude also shows out through his prophets who reprimand his faithless people who turned away from him to embrace idolatry. The prophetic denouncements of idols are scathing and dripping with sarcasm. Some of the comments in the Book of Isaiah with regard to the worthlessness of idols in contrast to the reality, omnipotence, and sovereignty of the LORD are typical illustrations.

"As for an idol, a craftsman casts it, and a goldsmith overlays it with gold and fashions silver chains for it. A man too poor to present such an offering selects wood that will not rot. He looks for a skilled craftsman to set up an idol that will not topple" (40:19-20).

"'Present your case', says the LORD. 'Set forth your arguments', says Jacob's King.' Bring in your idols to tell us what is going to happen. Tell us what the former things were, so that we may consider them and know their final outcome. Or declare to us the things to come, tell us what the future holds, so that we may know that you are gods. Do something, whether good or bad, so that we will be dismayed and filled with fear. But you are less than nothing and your works are utterly worthless; he who chooses you is detestable'" (41:21-24).

"The carpenter measures with a line and makes an outline with a marker; he roughs it out with chisels and marks it with compasses. He shapes it in the form of man, of man in all his glory, that it may dwell in a shrine. He cut down cedars, or perhaps took a cypress or oak. He let it grow among the trees of the forest, or planted a pine, and the rain made it grow. It is a man's fuel for burning; some of it he takes and warms himself, he kindles a fire and bakes bread. But he also fashions an idol and worships it; he makes an idol and bows down to it. Half of the wood he burns in the fire; over it he prepares his meal, he roasts his meat and eats his fill. He also warms himself and says, 'Ah! I am warm; I see the fire.' From the rest he makes a god, his idol; he bows down to it and worships. He prays to it and says, 'Save me; you are my god.' They know nothing, they understand nothing; their eyes are plastered over so they cannot see, and their minds closed so they cannot understand" (44:13-18).

Jesus in the New Testament also resorted to humorous scorn when he condemned the hypocritical attitudes of the Pharisees. He said they announced their alms-giving with trumpets, showed off their praying in synagogues and on street corners, and disfigured their faces to show they were fasting (Matthew 6:2, 5, 16). Their religious scruples caused them to strain out a gnat but swallow a camel, and to be like whitewashed tombs which looked beautiful on the outside but on the inside were full of dead men's bones and everything unclean (Matthew 23:22, 27)

On the other hand Jesus himself became the brunt of mockery during his trial and execution. In fact the gruesome details of the crucifixion itself were passed over in the Gospel accounts (no doubt they were only too well known by the original readers), and emphasis was placed on Jesus' experience of mockery. Of course the trial itself was a mockery, since the Sanhedrin broke its own rules of just court procedures. But once the verdict of execution was determined, councillors gathered round him to spit in his face, punch and slap him, and taunt him to prophesy as Messiah by identifying who hit him (Matthew 26:67).

Similarly Pilate's soldiers mocked Jesus after they had flogged him, and before crucifying him, by stripping him and putting a scarlet robe on him, setting a twisted crown of thorns on his head, placing a staff in his right hand, mockingly kneeling before him, and greeting him as "king of the Jews". They spat on him and repeatedly struck him around the head with the staff (Matthew 27:27-31)

Likewise, while hanging on the cross, the charge set above his head identifying that "This is Jesus, the King of the Jews" was probably meant in mockery, passers-by hurled insults at him, the religious leaders mocked him, and even the robbers crucified with him heaped insults on him (Matthew 27:37-44).

Yet of course Matthew deliberately highlighted this pattern of un-orchestrated mockery because he recognized the irony that unwittingly Jesus' enemies were declaring a profound truth. Jesus really was the Messiah, and crucifixion was the pathway of his mission to save the world from sin. Their mockery was rebounding on themselves. It is also significant that Jesus' cry of his sense of abandonment by God, only quoted in Matthew's Gospel (27:46), was an echo of Psalm 22:1 which would be well known to Matthew's Jewish readers. That psalm made much of the suffering psalmist's experience of mocking scorn (Psalm 22:6-7). There is deep pathos in recognizing that God's highest moment of displaying his mocking anger and judgement against his rebellious enemies was when he willingly suffered the scornful abuse and rejection of his world on its behalf through the crucifixion of his Messiah. God's chosen pathway was an appalling action of awe-inspiring grace.

God's mockery of his rebellious enemies was supremely capped off by Jesus' resurrection from the dead. Human rejection of God's kingship was utterly thwarted and forever quashed. The cross of Jesus was both the judgement of the world through its proxy, God's appointed Messiah, and the sacrificial offering of God's Messiah for the forgiveness of the world. His resurrection from the dead was the Messiah's triumph over death, which was God's judgement for sin, the guarantee of reconciliation with God for all who converted to return humbly to God through trust in Jesus, and the beginning of a new era and higher order for God's kingdom. Mankind's puny attempt to unseat the divine Monarch of heaven was absolutely blown away. It seems to me that Matthew wants to make a special point when he describes the event of the resurrection, and notes that an angel of the Lord rolled back the stone and *"sat on it"* (Matthew 28:2). God was having the last laugh!

The apostle Paul taps into this same theme when he comments about the message of the Gospel proclamation and its converts. The message is about a *"crucified messiah"* which is a stumbling block to Jews and foolishness to Gentiles (1 Corinthians 1:23).

"For the foolishness of God is wiser than man's wisdom, and the weakness of God is stronger than man's strength" (v 25).

Converts to Jesus are not particularly impressive according to human standards.

"But God chose the foolish things of the world to shame the wise; God chose the weak things of the world to shame the strong. He chose the lowly things of the world and the despised things – and the things that are not – to nullify the things that are, so that no one may boast before him" (v27-29).

The gospel of Jesus the Messiah about restoration of the kingdom of God confirms the bold optimism of Psalm 2, in an astonishingly unexpected way.

The Divine Decree, v 7-9.

I will proclaim the decree of the LORD:
He said to me, "You are my Son; today I have become your Father. Ask of me, and I will make the nations your inheritance, the ends of the earth your possession. You will rule them with an iron sceptre; you will dash them to pieces like pottery."

The third stanza is all speech. It reports the response of the LORD's Anointed One to the unruly revolt within his kingdom. He is undaunted by the threat of rebellion, and confidently repeats the divine decree regarding his appointment as king. On the day he was anointed, he was chosen and adopted as God's "Son" (v 7). This had been clearly guaranteed in a pledge to King David (see 2 Samuel 7:14). The family terms "Father" and "Son" were typical of ancient covenant relationships between a Great King (or Suzerain) and his representative ruler over a local territory (or vassal). This was the pattern adopted by the LORD for his covenants with both Israel and Israel's earthly king. Both the nation and the king were referred to as "Sons" of the "Father" (Exodus 4:22, Psalm 89:26-27). The "Son" on earth was the "Father's" partner carrying out his will. As God's "Son" on earth, each had an intimate, dependent relationship with God in heaven who acted as "Father", caring, providing, protecting, guiding, and nurturing. In this psalm the stanza is a reminder of the special intimate bond with the LORD which each of David's successors to the throne had in the face of all opposition.

However, the New Testament sees that its primary significance and true fulfilment applies to Jesus and his resurrection (see Acts 13:32-33, Romans 1:3-4). The gospel declares that Jesus is the long-awaited Jewish Messiah, the ultimate Son of David. His resurrection was his crowning moment of inauguration. This event accomplished the promised triumph of God. It marked the declaration of Jesus as the Son of God and the restoration of God's Kingdom. By his resurrection, Christ was enthroned as King, to rule in peoples' lives by resurrection power through his Spirit (see Acts 2:30-36). He has a name above every name, all authority in heaven and on earth, and has sat down at the right hand of God until his enemies are put under his feet (see Philippians 2:9-11, Matthew 28:18-20, 1 Corinthians 15:24-26). The Kingdom of God is not a national or political kingdom, as Jewish hopes had anticipated, but the dynamic reign of God in the hearts of men and women who surrender to the kingship of the risen Christ. The Kingdom of God came in the person of Christ, is a present reality now in the hearts of his people, and will come in the fullness of power and glory when Christ returns. This is the "Good News" which the New Testament announces and expounds, and which it sees was anticipated in the covenant decree of Psalm 2:7.

Jesus' relationship to God as presented in the New Testament is strikingly unique. He is consistently and predominantly identified as "Son" of the "Father". Although this reflects his identity as Messiah there is also an exciting new aspect being expressed. Jesus' relationship demonstrates a unique intimacy and familiarity. The Gospels report Jesus referring to God as "Father", and even "My Father", and in his prayers as addressing God by the homely term "Abba". Such outrageous familiarity was previously unknown.

The fatherhood of God was an idea sometimes expressed in ancient pagan religions and philosophies to indicate mythical views of a deity originally begetting the natural cosmos and human race. The Old Testament however is distinctly different. In contrast to such mythical and biological ideas, God is depicted as a sovereign Creator who simply commanded the universe into existence. The Old Testament only describes God as Father in relation to the nation Israel and to its earthly monarch. This is because God's fatherhood is understood in covenantal terms. The figurative imagery of Father reflects the role of a natural father who is head of his family, having both authority, which must be fully respected, and responsibility for the full welfare of his home. However Jesus' attitude towards God as his Father is distinctly, and uniquely, different again.

Not only does Jesus never refer to God as Father of the universe or of all mankind. Neither does he even call God the Father of Israel. He speaks only of God as his own Father, and to his disciples (because of their relationship to him) as "your Father". This was because Jesus saw himself as "true Israel" and "true Messiah", the "true Son", and his disciples incorporated within himself (which is why he chose twelve disciples, to represent Israel's twelve tribes). He claimed to have a unique status and relationship with God which granted him a uniquely privileged revelation and an authority to disclose to whomever he chose (Matthew 11:25-27).

His disciples could then address God as "our Father", not in common with Jesus, whose intimacy and familiarity with the Father were unique, but through his mediating relationship.

The disclosure of Jesus' unique relationship to God as Son to Father unveiled a further extraordinary revelation. The man Jesus had prior existence, and a prior relationship to the Father, sharing his glory (John 17:5). Throughout the whole New Testament it is consistently clear that Jesus was considered to have been absolutely equal with God eternally. Jesus was God who had become man. There is only one God, and his self-revelation through Jesus the "Son" revealed that in essence God is the ultimate "Father", who has absolute authority deserving reverence and obedience, and who acts in compassionate love and mercy, goodness, and abundant care. We can only contemplate God in terms of human imagery and analogy. So through Jesus becoming the "Son" we learn that God is "Father".

In order to accomplish his divine plan to reconcile the world and restore his kingship, the Father had sent his "Son" into the world to become the promised earthly Messiah of David's line. His mission was to reveal the Father and to rescue the world. This was in order for God to accomplish his original intention for his created world, and to fulfil his covenant promises to Abraham and to David. Through the incarnation of his "Son", God personally became human and took full responsibility for his mission. In the person and mission of Jesus, the "Son" revealed the reality, nature, and purpose of God. Jesus informed his disciples that anyone who had seen him had seen the Father, and that the Father was living in him doing his work (John 14:9-10).

The divine decree in Psalm 2 also declared how the Son was to receive his inheritance (v 8): ***"Ask of me"***. As God's adopted Son and Heir, the king had only to rely prayerfully on his Father in Heaven to inherit dominion over the nations. God himself, who was ultimate Sovereign, guaranteed to give his Son possession of the whole earth. God also promised his Son, using vivid imagery of a powerful monarch rigorously enforcing his rule, that he would reign victoriously (v 9). An "*iron sceptre*" symbolizes the strength of his rule. To "*dash them to pieces like pottery*" graphically depicts their fragile forces of rebellious opposition being smashed and rendered useless. The messianic Son's defeat of hostile enemy nations will be devastating.

The idea of inheritance is an important theme throughout the Old Testament saga. The term can refer to a possession received by lot, or by promise, or by family legacy, or by covenant decree. The theme begins in the Old Testament with God's promise of blessing and a land to Abraham, which then became a legacy for his son Isaac and for subsequent generations. When Israel conquered and settled the promised land of Canaan each tribe and family received a share in the inheritance by lot. Both the nation of Israel and the kingly descendants of David were considered to be God's inheritance, while God himself was Israel's inheritance. Essentially the inheritance was God's Kingdom, the domain where God's blessing and rest were experienced, and his righteous rule was wholeheartedly obeyed.

God's plan to restore his Kingdom in the world, which had rebelled against him, promised his earthly partner, his covenant people, this marvellous prospect as their inheritance. As the plan unfolded God revealed that it would eventually be accomplished by his Messiah, his unique partner. And the means by which the Messiah would receive his inheritance was simply by asking the Father.

This decree explains the primary purpose of prayer and the covenant significance for calling on the name of the LORD. Trusting prayer was the decreed basis of the partnership between the Son-King and his Father-God, the expression of their intimate relationship, and the means by which the disobedient nations of the earth were to be vanquished and restored to their rightful place in God's Kingdom.

This also reveals why prayerfulness was such a prominent feature of Jesus' life and ministry. He was the Messiah of Psalm 2 who carried out his mission in prayerful dependence on his Father in heaven, and in obedience to his will. Both his life and death were virtual offerings of trusting prayer, which is a truth highlighted by the author of the Book of Hebrews who discerningly links Psalm 2:7 to Jesus' reputation for prayerfulness (Hebrews 5:5, 7).

The Gospel about Jesus in the New Testament not only proclaims Jesus' victory over sin and death by means of his crucifixion and resurrection, and the restoration of God's Kingdom. It also declares that his inheritance is shared by his trusting followers. The Book of Revelation also identifies Jesus as the Messiah of Psalm 2, especially indicating his invincible rule in the intimidating imagery of 2:9 (Revelation 12:5, 19:15), and includes Jesus' obedient followers as sharers of his authority and that same invincible rule (Revelation 2:26-27).

Because as Messiah Jesus represented them, God views them as incorporated within him in all that he accomplished. Believers in Jesus are accepted as God's adopted children, and as co-rulers and co-heirs with Christ (see Romans 8:17, Ephesians 1:4-5, 2:6, Revelation 2:27). As co-partners in Christ, they participate in the mission of restoring God's Kingdom by proclaiming the Gospel to the world. This is the reason for the emphasis in the New Testament on reaching the nations and the ends of the earth with the gospel (see Matthew 28:18-20, Acts 1:8). Their role in subduing the nations for Christ does not involve the enforcement tactics of the world (see 2 Corinthians 10:3-5), but requires them to pray and to make known the gospel.

The decree of Psalm 2 shows how strategic prayer is to God's purposes and anticipates the gospel as the meaningful framework for prayer.

Warning to the Nations, v 10-12.

Therefore, you kings, be wise; be warned, you rulers of the earth. Serve the LORD with fear and rejoice with trembling. Kiss the Son, lest he be angry and you be destroyed in your way, for his wrath can flare up in a moment. Blessed are all who take refuge in him.

In the fourth stanza the psalmist speaks like a prophet. He warns the rebellious rulers to submit to this divinely established King. Their actions of service and attitudes of joy must be balanced with appropriate reverence and trembling (v 11). They must pay homage to (*kiss*) the Son to prevent him from flaring up in anger – not that he is touchy, but that he reacts righteously against wickedness and lawless behaviour (v 12). The only place of security and happiness, where God's blessing is experienced (which was God's original intention at creation and the goal of his rescue plan for the world), is to *take refuge in him* (v 12b). This warning to submit to the King and find safety with him is the same as the command of the gospel to repent and believe in the Lord Jesus Christ (Mark 1:15, Acts 16:31, etc.).

Psalm 2 then is a powerful reminder of the fundamental problem with the human race. It is in rebellion against God. Yet God is not thwarted. His righteous rule will prevail. His Kingdom is firmly established, and his anointed Son is on the throne. The Son's prayerful dependence on his Father is the guaranteed means by which he will gain his inheritance. So we must take to heart the warning to fear God, the invitation to return to him for safety from his holy anger and judgement, and the challenge to join Christ in asking for the inheritance of his Kingdom.

CHAPTER 8

ENTREATING THE FATHER

PRAYER IN THE NEW TESTAMENT

Like a plant which bursts into blossom the Old Testament comes into full flower in the New Testament. The story of Israel culminates with the gospel of Jesus Christ, and the focus moves from the nation of God's children to the person of his unique Son. Our tour of discovery now transports us into a new sphere of exploration, which has familiar strains with what we have already examined, yet having undergone radical change.

The advent of Jesus Christ was an explosive event of history. It shattered time and unveiled eternity. It established the reality and authority of God's Kingdom on earth in power and glory.

To the natural human eye that is not obvious. Certainly Jesus is recognized as a renowned figure of history. He made a profound impact on the lives of people in his own time, and throughout the centuries and across the world since. But generally he is acknowledged merely as a famous and successful founder of a religious movement. He is aligned with other prominent and influential people who have left their mark on history.

However, from the point of view of the New Testament Jesus is the unique person of history. He is more than just an outstanding, admirable, influential, religious figure. He is utterly, radically, and uniquely different from all other human beings, both before him and since. His life, death, and resurrection, followed by the dynamic presence of the Holy Spirit of God in the world, proclaimed by the gospel and witnessed to by the New Testament, radically transformed human existence.

To most people such a statement probably seems like hype. Unfortunately, because we are so familiar with the New Testament, its radical proclamation has lost its impact. We fail to recognize that what happened to Jesus historically was an event which had cosmic significance. It was an explosive event with consequences for time and eternity. However, if we thoughtfully consider the events concerning Jesus declared by the gospel, we will recognize several wonderful revelations.

Significance of Jesus

In the first place these events revealed Jesus' true identity. They showed that he was actually pre-existent and divine. He was the eternal "Word" (or "expressed thought") of God, who became human. As God's earthly "Son", he was the veiled manifestation of the eternal living God, Creator King of the universe, and he revealed God to be the heavenly "Father". When he entered history and became a man, his actions and experiences disclosed that he was essentially God. Converts worshipped him, giving evidence of a revolution in their hearts, both Jews who reverenced only one God, and pagan Gentiles who renounced their former many gods.

God, in terms of his "Self-revelation", became a man in order to be God's appointed Messiah. Jesus was anointed by the Holy Spirit, and by his life, death, and resurrection fulfilled the mission of providing salvation for the world which faced divine judgement because of its rebellion against God's kingship. After his final post-resurrection appearance Jesus was recognized as the risen and enthroned King of God's Kingdom, who bestowed the Holy Spirit upon the whole world to immerse it in his overpowering, enlightening, renewing, transforming presence. Wherever the gospel about Jesus and God's Kingdom was proclaimed listeners were converted as they submitted to him in trust, repentance, and joy. To the natural eye of unbelievers Jesus remains nothing more than a conspicuous person of history. But to the Spirit-enlightened eye of believers he is the exalted Lord of glory.

In the second place the advent of Jesus marked a pivotal point of history. By his death, which represented God's judgement upon the world, its true Creator King being destroyed in its place, the end of time arrived. In him the world corrupted by evil and rebellion was punished and removed. By his resurrection a new creation, eternal and evil-free, commenced. In him the old order was resurrected to a new state of existence and metamorphosed by the Spirit into a radically greater reality which transcends the original creation.

Of course, things do not appear that way. History seems to have continued on since the advent of Jesus much the same as it was beforehand. This is because we live in a transition period where two ages overlap. The old age does continue as before. Yet at the same time the new age has begun, not in its fullness, but partially. The reality of the new eternal age is present and evident by means of the presence of the Holy Spirit, although not visible in natural terms. The current era since the advent of Jesus is called in the Bible the "last days". This is the messianic era in which the gospel of the Messiah is being proclaimed by his followers, who are empowered by his Spirit. The gospel announces that God's judgement against his rebellious enemies has taken place in the person of his Messiah at the Cross. It warns the world about God's righteous displeasure and offers salvation and blessing for those who seek refuge in him (as in Psalm 2). Those who reject the warnings of the gospel and continue in their attitude of rebellion choose their own destiny, which has already been determined by Jesus' crucifixion. Converts, on the other hand, who humble themselves before Jesus as King and gratefully trust him for forgiveness, acceptance and reconciliation, become members of the Family which knows, and belongs to, and loves the Father. Although still living within this natural present world, they actually belong already to the new creation of the future which is coming into existence because of Jesus' resurrection. Their eventual destiny will be fullness of life in the fullness of the eternal age.

At this point of time in history God's eternal Kingdom has not yet arrived. Nevertheless, it is also true to say that it has. It came in the person of Jesus its King. It is coming in the current presence of God's Spirit, who through the gospel establishes God's kingship in the hearts of believing converts. According to the gospel we are living in the culminating stage of human history in the current order of creation. The Kingdom will eventually come in its fullness when the task of proclaiming the gospel to the world is complete. According to the gospel the climactic moment will be precipitated by the return of Jesus in glory, the resurrection of the dead, the destruction of the present order, and the inauguration of the new eternal order in its fullness. These are not merely religious ideas but profound realities which God has accomplished within human history.

In the third place the advent of Jesus created a new social phenomenon within the world. The Church came into existence. This is a significant reality not to be misunderstood. From one point of view, two millennia later, the Church is a deeply entrenched, world-wide religious movement consisting of various institutional brands. Christianity is looked upon as one of the major religions of the world, and has a history shaped by cultural, political, theological, and circumstantial factors. It has a dominating presence within the world. That in itself is a remarkable development. But what we see is only the earth-bound institutional shell, the product of natural human religious activity. The true Church of God is even more impressive. It is the fellowship of believers in Christ whose hearts have been changed by God's Spirit. They confess Jesus as Lord and follow him as his devoted disciples and servants. They are the new people of God, whose roots are found in the "old covenant" nation of Israel, but whose fullness through the "new covenant" established by Jesus includes members from all nationalities. The "living", Spirit-indwelt, Church, whose constituent members are not prohibited by differences of age, gender, nationality, culture, social status, or any other discrimination, belongs to the in-coming future age and manifests itself now by its qualities of Christ-likeness and its witness to the gospel. They are the Family of men and women who live to honour the Father, to please him and do his will.

God's Identity

In the fourth place the advent of Jesus revealed magnificent truths about what God is like. The gospel is the culmination of God's plan and purpose for the world, and of his self-revelation. Throughout the Old Testament God's many successive actions in regard to his covenant with Israel progressively disclosed more and more about his identity and nature. The events of the gospel completed the disclosure. They gave a fuller and clearer presentation of what was already revealed, and unveiled yet further insights about his likeness. In particular they revealed that God is uniquely and superlatively personal in nature. This is shown in the way the New Testament highlights God's loving disposition, and identifies him as the "Father".

God's loving disposition is demonstrated conspicuously in the life of Jesus, and declared rapturously by his Apostles. Jesus showed himself to be the Man of Compassion, welcoming all-comers and reaching out to the poor and needy, the downtrodden, diseased and disobedient. He taught his disciples to serve one another, to forgive those who offended them, and to love even their enemies. He offered himself up in self-giving love as a sacrifice for sin to provide mercy and forgiveness for all mankind. The Apostles proclaimed the gospel boldly and enthusiastically, declaring that through Jesus there was forgiveness of sins for all people, without favouritism. They ascribed all that God had done through Jesus, and what they had experienced personally, to God's "grace". The Apostle Paul was especially ecstatic in his gratitude for God's grace and mercy, both in his own salvation and in his service of the gospel. John sums it all up when he asserts that *"God is love"* (1 John 4:8, 16).

We have already noted how Jesus referred to God as Father. This was how he viewed God in terms of his own relationship with him, and how he encouraged his disciples to relate to him. Following Jesus' crucifixion and resurrection, and the arrival of the Spirit, the Apostles knew God distinctively as Father. In particular he was known as the "*God and Father of our Lord Jesus Christ*" (Ephesians 1:3), and, because of their experience of God's Spirit in their hearts, as "*Abba, Father*" (Galatians 4:6). Actions attributed to the Holy Spirit (such as being grieved, being lied to, crying, washing, sealing, and so on) imply his personal nature, and at times grammatical correctness (in the original Greek) is deliberately abandoned in order to emphasise it (John 14-16). God had become revealed and intimately known as the absolute divine Sovereign who was intrinsically personal, gracious and caring by nature.

In the days of the New Testament there was exuberant conviction about one true and living God. He was God the Father. He had made himself known, and accomplished his eternal purpose, through his kingly Son and Holy Spirit. This was why God's identity (his "name") became known as "*the Father and the Son and the Holy Spirit*" (Matthew 28:19). This was not a static name, but a dynamic expression which indicated that his identity was revealed by his divine mission. The Father in heaven initiated his plan of redemption. His messianic Son on earth accomplished redemption through his death and resurrection. God's overpowering Spirit is restoring his redeemed world to fellowship with God, freedom from sin, and fulness of life. Experience of the divine mission's triune operation brought exhilaration from the revelation of what God was like, and joy and gratitude from knowing God personally. God was quintessentially personal, knowable, and near.

Written Witness

There are two confirming witnesses to the truth of the gospel and to the reality of God's Kingdom which is being restored in the world. The first witness is the testimony of the Old Testament. The advent of Jesus culminates and confirms the remarkable revelation of God and of his intentions, acts, and attitudes, recorded in its documents. The second witness is the testimony of Jesus' Apostles presented in various written documents in the New Testament. Their testimony was inspired by divine impulse from the Holy Spirit whose reality is experienced by his enlightening, convincing, transforming, and empowering influence within the world and within individual hearts.

It is important that we clearly understand what the New Testament is declaring in these matters. The gospel proclaims the identity of Jesus and the presence and victory of God's Kingdom in the world. God's original intention to bless his created world, his plan to restore and reconcile his rebellious world, and his promises to Abraham and to King David to restore his blessing and righteous rule in the world, have been accomplished. God has enacted his judgement against evil through the crucifixion of Jesus his Messiah, and at the same time provided forgiveness and salvation for all who humbly trust in Jesus and submit to him as Lord. By raising Jesus from the dead God has created a new realm for his Kingdom and has enthroned Jesus as its King. Through the preaching of his gospel, and by the power of his Holy Spirit whom he has sent into the world, Jesus is calling into existence a new people for his eternal Kingdom. When we recognize these stupendous truths we gain a perspective for living in our present world and a hope for our eternal future.

Prayer

These Gospel realities also provide an exciting framework for prayer. That is why prayer features prominently in the New Testament.

The most frequently used term for prayer in the New Testament was the normal religious term for addressing God. It is a general comprehensive word which indicates offering devotion or making entreaty to God who is the absolute and unique King. Prayer is the act of addressing the Divine Monarch of the universe. Very often the New Testament writers use other common terms for "asking" or "requesting" although obviously in the sense of prayer. On occasions terms for "crying" represent prayer, and this is especially significant when calling God in familiar intimate language as "*Abba, Father*" (Romans 8:15, Galatians 4:6). Overall, the New Testament attitude towards prayer is that of entreating God who is highest Ruler over all things.

The exciting new dimensions to prayer which the gospel brings are intimacy and familiarity with God, knowing God as Father, and understanding the place and purpose for prayer in God's will for his Kingdom, sharing in partnership with God as intercessors. Prayer can be offered to God concerning any matter, but the primary perspectives for prayer are knowing

God, and drawing near to him in devoted partnership. These are revealed by Jesus' personal practice of prayer, his instructions concerning prayer, and the framework of his mission to restore God's Kingdom in the world. The role of prayer in regard to the gospel identifies its meaning and purpose and ensures confidence in its effectiveness. Prayer in the New Testament addresses God, who is the exalted King, as Father, and makes entreaty concerning his kingdom. When we explore the New Testament for its teaching about prayer we discover a treasure of insights. These can enrich our own personal experience of prayer, and transform it from religious performance to realistic and meaningful engagement with the living God who is Father of the Lord Jesus Christ.

New Testament

The New Testament consists of four Gospels, a collection of letters by various authors applying gospel insights to various situations, and several other documents commending truths of the gospel. The literature is not arranged in chronological order. The Gospels appear first because they describe the events concerning the life, death and resurrection of Jesus which constitute the gospel, even though they were written later than most of the other books. A Gospel is not a biography or life of Jesus. It is a written proclamation of the gospel about Jesus, and generally follows the traditional pattern of oral proclamations. Examples of these appear in the Book of Acts. Variations in the four Gospels reflect the fact that they were written by different authors for different situations.

The Book of Acts is located next, after the four Gospels, because it was written by Luke as a sequel to his Gospel, and traces the spread of the gospel after Jesus' resurrection.

A collection of thirteen letters written by the Apostle Paul, some to churches and some to individuals, forms the next section. All these were actually written prior to the four Gospels and the Book of Acts, as well as almost all the other New Testament documents.

The remaining books which complete the New Testament arrangement include a written exhortation (the Book of Hebrews), another collection of letters (one by Jesus' brother James, two by the Apostle Peter, three by the Apostle John, and one by Jesus' other brother Jude), and finally the Book of The Revelation (which describes an apocalyptic vision received by the Apostle John).

It is important to understand the content of each piece of literature in order to interpret what it teaches about prayer in context. This will also deepen and clarify our understanding of the gospel which is the essential framework for true and purposeful prayer.

CHAPTER 9

"SAVIOUR OF THE WORLD"

PRAYER IN LUKE'S GOSPEL AND ACTS

Like the incoming tide of the ocean, a wave of joy sweeps across the pages of Luke's Gospel and Book of Acts. His glowing story about Jesus ripples with a spirit of delight wherever news of his accomplishments spreads. People and angels celebrate his birth with songs and praises. Rumours of his power to heal draw crowds of those who are sick and disabled, and spectators are filled with amazement and praise to God when his word and touch cure them. Jesus himself is full of joy through the Holy Spirit, and his teachings about coming blessing and a future day of joy are heard with rapt attention. He tells parables of people rejoicing when they find their lost sheep, or coin, or son, and of angels rejoicing when sinners repent. His triumphant resurrection from the dead following his brutal crucifixion banishes his followers' fear and disillusionment, warms their hearts with comprehension, and fills them with worship, joy, and praise.

Then, only weeks later at Pentecost, his outpoured gift of the Holy Spirit from his exalted position in heaven immerses them into a bold, vibrant community of joyous enthusiastic worshipers and witnesses.

The new era sees a healed cripple leaping around the temple courts bursting with praise for God. Peter and John publicly declare that his healing was due to Jesus, whom God raised from the dead, and who was God's appointed Messiah. They stare down the threats of the Jewish Sanhedrin, and in prayerful appeal to God continue to speak God's word boldly. When Philip proclaimed Christ in a city in Samaria, and performed miraculous signs there, there was "*great joy in that city*". When the Gentiles at Pisidian Antioch heard Paul and Barnabas preach the gospel, "*they were glad and honoured the word of the Lord*". The word spread throughout that whole region, prompting Jewish led persecution to expel Paul and Barnabas from their city, but the new disciples were "*filled with joy and the Holy Spirit*". At Philippi Paul and Silas were publicly humiliated, flogged, and cast into the innermost dungeon of the prison, yet they are found praying and singing hymns to God in the middle of the night! The wave of rapture keeps rolling on. As the angel announced to the shepherds at his birth, the message about Jesus was "*Good news of great joy*" for all people. The note of joy is a characteristic feature of Luke's presentation of Jesus. His two-book publication is a thrilling read, and is marked by many stimulating recurring features. These distinctive characteristics support Luke's aim of showing the meaning of the gospel concerning Jesus, and his astonishing impact on the Roman world.

Luke's Gospel/Acts

Luke's account of the coming of Jesus, his teachings, execution by Jewish and Roman authorities, astounding resurrection, and the subsequent explosive disturbance caused by the rapidly spreading proclamation about him, is masterly. The skilful outline of his two books, the characteristics and scholarly features of his style, his historical accuracy and thorough detail, vivid description, and literary excellence, combine to bear credible and thought-provoking witness to the momentous phenomenon of Jesus.

Although other documents in the New Testament were written earlier than the Gospels, it is appropriate for us to begin with the Gospels because they present what came first, the life and experiences of Jesus. It is also appropriate to commence with the Gospel of Luke and his Book of Acts, because most likely his preceded the other three Gospels (in my opinion), and Acts provides a historical backdrop for many of the other New Testament writings.

We have already indicated that a written Gospel is not a biography or life history of Jesus. It is a proclamation of the "good news" concerning him. It assumes Jesus' historicity, and reports historical events relating to him, arranged according to a careful pattern which presents the message about him, but not necessarily in chronological order. It is not possible to work out from the Gospel documents an accurate timeline of Jesus' life, but they clearly proclaim what the events of Jesus' life mean. We have to be discerning about the type of language used, too. It is not always to be taken literally as read. Sometimes the language is figurative, or uses Old Testament phrases, or even apocalyptic images (symbols to express hidden or higher realities). The written Gospels were a new and unique style of literature, presenting the person, experiences, and message of Jesus in a compelling and effective way to help disciples understand clearly who Jesus was and what was involved in following him.

At first blink the Gospels of Matthew, Mark, and Luke appear to follow the same pattern. But closer examination reveals huge differences. All four Gospels (including John) basically follow a general standard pattern established by the Apostles' preaching. They developed an oral tradition (and perhaps even partial written versions), which was flexible so that it could be adapted to different situations, but which ensured that the central truths of the gospel were kept in focus. There is evidence of this traditional pattern in the preaching of both Peter and Paul in the Book of Acts, as well as reference to such gospel tradition from the Apostles in the language of several letters in the New Testament.

Both Luke's Gospel and Acts were written to a person called "*Theophilus*" (Luke 1:3, Acts 1:1). He is referred to as "*most excellent*", which was a term to describe a person of distinguished Roman nobility. Since "*Theophilus*" means "lover of God", perhaps this was a colourful way of addressing a Christian convert, who is identified by language used of someone of noble birth and position. More likely, however, the description indicates that Theophilus was a person of high Roman rank, addressed in similar fashion as Roman governors (see Acts 23:26, 24:3). It was customary to dedicate a literary work to an official, or patron, or to a respected representative of a broader group of readers. The opening preface of the Gospel (1:1-4) follows the literary form of ancient Greek scholars. Luke seems to be intentionally making a presentation of the gospel which would appeal to readers of high intelligence and culture.

His purpose was that Theophilus might "*know the certainty of the things you have been taught*". The word "*taught*" usually refers to formal instruction (Acts 18:25, 1 Corinthians 14:19, Galatians 6:6), and the contents and style of Luke/Acts certainly suit that purpose. They present Jesus clearly, fully, and persuasively as God's messianic Son, who was the Saviour of the world and Ruler of the Kingdom of God. Luke's Gospel depicts Jesus proclaiming the good news of the "*kingdom of God*" until his crucifixion, and reveals him to be the "*Son of Man*" who obtains the kingly power and glory of God's kingdom by his resurrection. Acts shows the spread of the good news of the "*kingdom of God*" from Jerusalem to Rome.

Luke/Acts is designed to appeal to a reader who is educated, a Gentile and most likely Roman, and someone who has an interest in the gospel. Luke acknowledges his dependence on other written accounts and handed down tradition, and on his own thorough investigation. His presentation of his Gospel/Acts is very carefully constructed. The two books were deliberately composed in a scholarly format, with the purpose of bearing witness to the reality of Jesus' resurrection, which resulted in his recognition as Lord and Saviour of the world.

A suggestion that Luke's Gospel/Acts was prepared as a defence brief for Paul's trial at Rome is attractive but unverifiable. However, the suggestion recognises the basic character of the books. They include records of several defences made to both Jews and Gentiles, and their overall format is carefully designed to bear witness to Jesus and the reality of God's kingdom. Jesus' own words, "*For the Son of Man came to seek and to save what was lost*" (Luke 19:10), expresses the theme of the Gospel concisely. Peter's words of defence before the Sanhedrin, "*Salvation is found in no one else, for there is no other name under heaven given to men by which we must be saved*" (Acts 4:12), sums up the testimony of Spirit-empowered witnesses who spread the word across the Roman empire.

Influences

Luke's presentation was affected by two conspicuous influences. On the one hand there was a strong Jewish element, for three reasons. The Old Testament, which was the product of

Israelite experience and writers, was the foundation of the gospel, and Jesus was proclaimed as the fulfilment of its divine agenda of salvation and expectations. Then, secondly, Jesus was himself Jewish, and his life and mission took place in Israel, involving the Jewish population and authorities. In the third place, Jewish affairs were sensitive in Roman outlook, affecting political, military, and cultural attitudes. There was rising hostility towards Jews across the empire. Emperor Claudius evicted all Jews from Rome in 49 CE, and in general Gentiles viewed Jews with contempt. They demeaned them as descendants of slaves, mocked their strange customs, and reviled their religion. Luke was a Gentile, although his attitude towards Jews was more moderate. His Gospel/Acts respects Jewish scriptures and the Jewish nation's special purpose as the means of God's salvation for the world, but disparages the generally hostile Jewish response to Jesus and the gospel. The opening section of his Gospel concerning Jesus' infancy and childhood is especially marked by Jewish colouring, probably reflecting his source (Mary?), and deliberately imitating the style of Old Testament writings which were recognized for their scholarly quality. Yet there is also a strong Jewish background throughout the whole book. Acts begins at Jerusalem, and tracks the spread of the Gospel around the Roman world until it arrives at Rome itself. Yet right until the end the Jewish presence is prominent. The apostles' preaching policy was to the Jew first, and then to the Gentiles.

On the other hand, Roman interests are also dominant. Both the birth of Jesus, and his commencement of ministry, are connected to contemporary Roman rulers (Luke 2:1-3, Luke 3:1). These references were not to give precise dating (which is elusive), but to relate the events to a Roman framework. For Luke's cultured Roman readers, these details were relevant. Of course, Jesus' death was at the hands of Roman authorities and by the Roman method of execution. However, throughout Gospel/Acts Roman authority is presented favourably. Both Pilate and Herod were in agreement that there was no basis to the charges against Jesus (and they became reconciled to one another after dealing with Jesus!), even though the Jewish leaders accused Jesus of inciting political rebellion against Caesar (Luke 23:13-16). Pilate allowed Jesus to be crucified, against his own judgement, to appease the Jewish temple authorities. Frequently, Jewish antagonists tried to make out that the apostles were promoting Jesus as a rival king to Caesar, but Roman authorities were unpersuaded. The proconsul in Cypress was receptive to the Gospel (Acts 13:7, 12). The magistrates at Philippi, which was a Roman colony and leading regional city, apologised for unlawfully mistreating Paul and Silas (16:38-39). The proconsul at Corinth dismissed charges against Paul, because they were Jewish matters, not breach of Roman law (18:12-15). The city clerk at Ephesus defended Paul when worshipers of Artemis rioted in reaction to the gospel (19:35-41). The procurators in Israel, Felix and his successor Festus, together with King Agrippa (who was appointed by Rome) and his sister Bernice, agreed that Paul was undeserving of death when the Sanhedrin laid charges against him (chapters 24-26). Acts concludes with Paul permitted by his guards to teach about God's kingdom at Rome.

The ending of Acts sets a minimum date for the finished composition of the two-volume presentation. Paul had been under house arrest at Rome for two years, and the outcome of his trial was still undetermined, although appearing favourable. This period would be about 61-62 CE. There is good reason to conclude that the books were completed soon after the end point of Acts, since there is no mention of the anti-Christian persecution which broke out in 64 CE under emperor Nero. This would make Luke the first Gospel written.

The Remarkable "Journey"

The story which Luke tells is exhilarating. His presentation follows a carefully designed format which highlights important themes and emphases. We need to stand back to take in the big picture. What we see in our mind's eye as we read Luke's Gospel is Jesus on a "journey" to Jerusalem. The person of Jesus impresses us as the presence of abundant, liberating life. Wherever he is, his words and actions display life-giving authority. The "journey" pattern shows that Jesus came to fulfil a mission, which was accomplished in Jerusalem. His mission was to set the world free from evil oppressions and to provide the way into the kingdom of God. God's kingdom was not a political kingdom, but the reign of God over the realm of life. As God's Messiah, representing the world which he came to save, he voluntarily suffered crucifixion in order to enter into glory through resurrection. His "journey" to Jerusalem was his pathway to the cross, and is the pathway for those who follow him.

Acts also follows a "journey" pattern. It tells the story of the spread of the good news about the kingdom of God from Jerusalem to Rome. The pattern also represents the pathway of Jesus' followers whose responsibility was to be his witnesses "*in Jerusalem, and in all Judea and Samaria, and to the end of the earth*" (Acts 1:8).

Luke's Gospel/Acts presentation proclaims a thrilling message which could be appropriately expressed in the words of Isaac Watts the hymn writer, "*Joy to the world! The Lord is come! Let earth receive her King!*"

Prayer in Luke's Gospel

Although we cannot undertake a full commentary of Luke's Gospel, it is worth our while to draw up a condensed version so that we can appreciate Luke's presentation of Jesus, and have a framework for understanding what he reveals about prayer.

Luke's Introduction (1:1-4). Following the typical literary format of scholars in his day, Luke explained his purpose to provide a reliable and orderly account of matters already taught to Theophilus.

The Coming of Jesus: *His Infancy, Baptism, Temptation* **(1:5-4:13).** The births of both John the Baptist and Jesus were miraculous, and deliberately linked by interweaving their narratives. Told in Old Testament language and style, the pervading atmosphere indicates that God was undertaking special activity within human affairs.

Luke's story of Jesus' coming begins in an atmosphere vibrant with the presence of God, marked by various features such as divine activity, angels, Old Testament allusions, songs of praise, prophecy, and including the conspicuous feature of prayer, which is strategic, not merely incidental (1:5-25). A significant event occurred at the temple in Jerusalem when Herod was king of Judea. Herod is mentioned because he was the politically appointed king of the Jews, accountable to the Romans, not a descendant of King David as the promised Messiah would be. The temple was considered to be God's palace on earth, where he lived and reigned among his people. The story commences with the introduction of a priest called Zechariah and his wife, Elizabeth. They were diligent in their devotion to God, but childless, and elderly. One day Zechariah was on temple duty, burning incense before God. That means he was in the Holy Place at the altar of incense in front of the curtain which veiled off the inner Most Holy Place where God's presence was represented. Zechariah had been chosen to serve by lot according to traditional custom. This was considered not simply to be a random choice, but the will of God. Consequently, Luke was beginning his Gospel with a focus on the initiative of God. Not every priest would have the privilege of being selected, and a priest could only be selected once. Therefore, this was Zechariah's once in a lifetime experience, the highlight of his life as a priest. The burning of incense symbolised the offering of prayer, and simultaneously the serving priest prayed before the altar, while the worshipers prayed outside. This practice, morning, noon, and evening, was central to the life of Israel, enabling the nation, and individuals, to draw near to God with praise and petition.

On this occasion, an *"angel of the Lord"* appeared to Zechariah, understandably filling him with fear. The angel was a messenger from God in a visionary experience (v 22). His appearance recalls numerous occasions in Old Testament times when an angel of the Lord performed special tasks for God, especially in connection with Abraham, Moses, and Elijah. This angel identified himself as Gabriel, who was also the heavenly messenger who appeared in the apocalyptic book of Daniel, revealing insights about the time of the end (Daniel 8:16, 9:21). The mere mention of the angel conjured up a backdrop of past abnormal divine intervention in relation to God's agenda of salvation for the world. His appearance to Zechariah presaged similar divine action. Gabriel allayed Zechariah's fears, and informed him that his prayer had been heard. It is unlikely, considering Zechariah's and Elizabeth's advanced ages, and Zechariah's reaction to the angel's message, that his prayer was a personal request for a child. The context, language, and tradition most probably indicate his priestly prayer at that moment, which would have included supplication for the redemption of Israel. Both the prayer and the angel focus the spotlight on God's promised salvation for his people. The surprising answer to the prayer, brought by Gabriel, indicated that Zechariah and Elizabeth were going to be personally involved in God's fulfilment. They would have much personal joy in becoming parents of a son, who would also bring joy to many people because of his special mission. He would be great in the eyes of the Lord, marked in his dedication by his abstinence from drinking wine, and be filled with the Holy Spirit from birth. His task, in true prophetic spirit, was to prepare the hearts of the people for the arrival of the Lord. Although the astounding news was delivered by such an unfamiliar messenger, Zechariah did not believe what the angel told him, because he was so old. Consequently, as a sign to convince him, he was left unable to speak until the child was born. After returning home from his temple commitment, his wife Elizabeth became pregnant.

Although the situations, and their descriptions, are very different, there is nevertheless a similarity in pattern between this event and the period in the days of Enosh when "men began to call on the name of the LORD". In both settings, God took the initiative, the people prayed, and God responded with his plan of salvation. It was a recurring pattern across the ages as the plan progressed. That plan included the appointment of various saviours along the way, and now was about to be culminated in the final Saviour. Prayer was a critical element in the process.

As Luke's story continues, the same angel, Gabriel, who appeared to Zechariah, also went to a virgin, Mary, who was a close relative of Elizabeth, and informed her that she was to have a son who was to be called Jesus (1:26-45). He would be known as the "*Son of the Most High*", and the Lord would give him the throne of David where he would reign forever. Despite being a virgin, Mary would be enabled to conceive by the power of the Holy Spirit. Both she, and Elizabeth in her old age, would have children, because "*nothing is impossible with God*". The experiences of both women, and the births of their respective sons, were the consequence of God's long term plan and the prayers of his people. Mary composed an Old Testament style song to express her joyful praise for God's saving mercy (1:46-56). After John was born to Elizabeth, his father Zechariah also composed a prophetic song under the inspiration of the Holy Spirit, praising the Lord for providing salvation through the house of David (1:57-80). John would be a prophet preparing the way for the Lord, by giving his people knowledge of salvation through the forgiveness of their sins. Luke's account is full of suspense which anticipates a momentous act by God.

Luke is the only biblical writer who gives an account of the actual birth of Jesus, and it was brief (2:1-20). Most of his focus was on surrounding circumstances. It was related to a Roman census decreed by Caesar Augustus, implying that the world's most powerful ruler at the time was serving the purposes of God's true world ruler. Though born in Bethlehem, the town of David, and belonging to the house of David, the baby was placed in a manger because there was no room elsewhere. Joseph and Mary were probably house guests of relatives, since both came from the area ("inn" should actually be translated "guestroom", as at 22:11). Luke mentioned the detail of the manger to convey the impression of Jesus' humble and obscure beginnings, an inhospitable welcome to the world's Saviour King. Angels announced and celebrated his birth, and shepherds were the first witnesses and worshipers of the newborn King. The angel's proclamation to the shepherds identified him precisely. He was a *"Saviour"*, who was *"Christ the Lord"*.

On the day of his circumcision he was named Jesus, and about a month later he was presented to the Lord at the temple in Jerusalem (2:21-40). Two elderly worshipers at the temple, Simeon and Anna, were moved by the Spirit to confirm his identity, thus meeting the Law's requirement of two witnesses. Simeon took the baby in his arms and offered praise to God, and made prophecies concerning the child's destiny. In particular, he spoke of Jesus as God's *"salvation"*, a *"light for revelation to the Gentiles and for glory to your people Israel"*. Anna spent every day fasting and praying, and, when she met the child, she gave thanks to God, and spoke about him to all who were looking forward to the *"redemption of Israel"*. Luke's account was obviously emphasising the action of God, the theme of salvation/redemption, and the background of prayerfulness. God's promise to save was the motive for prayer, and the guarantee for its effectiveness.

Though Jesus was born in obscurity from an earthly perspective, Luke's account bears witness to evidence which affirms that his birth was an act of heaven breaking into human affairs. The Saviour of the world had come!

At the conclusion of his childhood years, an incident in the Temple at Jerusalem showed Jesus' spiritual interests and insights, and, in his first words in Luke's Gospel (2:49), revealed his awareness of God as his *"Father"*. Although he showed respectful submission to his earthly parents, there was an overriding obligation and desire for fellowship with his heavenly Father in worship and learning at God's house.

Just as John's birth preceded Jesus' birth, so John's ministry prepared for Jesus' coming (3:1-20). Preaching a baptism of repentance, he declared that a more powerful successor would baptise, not with water, but with the Holy Spirit and fire. Jesus was baptised by John along with all the rest of the people, thereby aligning himself with the sinners he came to save (3:21-22). Emphasis is placed on his extraordinary experience which accompanied the occasion, rather than on the actual baptism itself. Two events occurred while Jesus was praying. This is the first time Luke makes any mention of Jesus praying, and it is not clear whether it was during his baptism or soon afterwards. The way Luke mentions it, the focus is on what happened as a result, rather than Jesus' activity of prayer. Yet Luke is the only Gospel writer who indicates that Jesus was praying on this occasion, so obviously the activity was important from his perspective. Jesus was commencing his ministry with prayer. He would have been offering praise to his Father, and dedicating himself to his Father's will.

While he was praying, *"heaven opened"* and the Holy Spirit descended on him, accompanied by a voice from heaven. The opening of heaven was not a literal description of something visible in the sky, but a figurative way of indicating the drawing back of the "curtain", so to speak, to expose the hidden realm of heaven. God was revealing his response to Jesus' praying. The Holy Spirit descended on Jesus in bodily form like a dove. This was a vivid picture of Jesus being anointed by God's Spirit, in accord with prophetic expectation (Isaiah 11:2, 42:1). The Holy Spirit was God's own powerful personal presence. The imagery of a *"dove"* was not meant to be a symbol for the Spirit. There was no known Old Testament or contemporary example of a dove being used symbolically, nor did it have any meaning as a fresh symbol. The imagery related to the Spirit's action of descending upon him, which resembled the recognisable movement of a dove alighting upon an object. It was a gentle, directed motion. Jesus was conscious of God's Holy Spirit coming upon him, to anoint him, and to empower him for his mission for God. It was similar to Samuel's anointing of David with oil, resulting in the Spirit of the LORD coming upon him in power (1 Samuel 16:13). Jesus was anointed directly from heaven, and the Spirit's descent in *"bodily form like a dove"* emphasised the reality and substantial nature of the experience.

There was also an accompanying voice from heaven, addressing Jesus in shades of language which recalled significant passages in the Old Testament. *"You are my Son"* echoes God's word to his Messiah in Psalm 2:7; *"whom I love"* is reminiscent of God's word to Abraham about his only son Isaac, whom he asked to offer up in sacrifice, in Genesis 22:2; *"with you I am well pleased"* repeats God's word to his chosen suffering Servant in Isaiah 42:1. This combination of words and sentiments at the commencement of Jesus' ministry confirmed his unique identity and mission. It was Jesus' praying which enabled him to receive this profound revelation.

The genealogy of Jesus (3:23-37) had a theological purpose: to show that Jesus, who was commencing the new messianic era, belonged to the original human race which traced its line back to the first man Adam, and to God himself, the Creator.

The account of Jesus' temptation in the desert (4:1-13) showed how the Spirit of God was guiding and empowering him in his messianic mission, and how, as Son of God, he was obedient and therefore able to fulfill his task. At the outset of his ministry Jesus overcame the Evil One who opposes God's Kingdom.

The whole account of Jesus' advent reverberates with a sense of divine intrusion into the course of history.

The Ministry of Jesus: *His Activities in Galilee* (4:14-9:50).

Luke builds up a composite picture of Jesus in the form of several travelling ministry tours throughout Galilee. An opening summary of Jesus' return to Galilee *"in the power of the Spirit"* (4:14-15) sets a background for two momentous Sabbaths. Firstly, Jesus was rejected at Nazareth (4:16-30). Then, on another Sabbath, after relocating to Capernaum, Jesus stirred up popular, though superficial, attraction, by his authoritative preaching and teaching, supported by mighty works of power (4:31-41). The next day he withdrew to a solitary place, and then resisted the crowds which came searching for him and left for wider spheres (4:42-44).

It is helpful to recognise the contexts of Luke's references to prayer in terms of the pattern of his book. In this section concerning his ministry activities in Galilee (4:14-9:50), prayer is not mentioned frequently, but it does occur sufficiently to show its importance in Jesus' own practice. Behind his public actions and significant decisions was a background of dependent prayer.

The first hint of this background, although not specifically stated, occurred after the accounts of Jesus' memorable Sabbaths in his hometown and at Capernaum. Luke merely reports, "*At daybreak Jesus went out to a solitary place*" (4:42). The term "*solitary*" is actually "*desert*", and recalls Jesus' initial experience after his baptism of being led by the Spirit in the desert when he was tempted by the devil (4:1-2). Jesus' ministry in Galilee also began when he returned "*in the power of the Spirit*" (4:14). The association of terms suggests that Jesus was still being led by the Spirit when he went out to a "*solitary place*". Luke does not explain what Jesus did in that place, only that the people came to prevent him from leaving them. However, Jesus' response was to announce that it was necessary for him to preach "*the good news of the kingdom of God*" to other towns, which he moved on to do. It is obvious that Jesus' experience in the "*solitary place*" was persuasive in his decision to go elsewhere to preach. Luke's description gives the clear impression that Jesus was being led by the Spirit. Mark's Gospel also mentions this incident, and indicates that Jesus went to this "*solitary place*" in order to pray (Mark 1:35). In fact, this was Mark's first reference to prayer in his Gospel. At this point, Luke did not mention prayer in regard to this action of Jesus. Yet a little later, after reporting on several ministry activities, he records a brief summary comment about Jesus' impact, and then adds, "*But Jesus often withdrew to lonely places and prayed*" (5:16). The expression "*lonely places*" is "*desert places*" (!), the same terms as "*solitary place*". Luke's repeated description indicates Jesus' frequent pattern of withdrawal, and this reference reveals that his purpose was to pray. This would mean he was seeking fellowship with his heavenly Father to offer worship and make requests concerning God's will. His praying kept him aware of the Spirit's leading, and guided his decisions and effectiveness concerning his ministry activities.

We should note important details in Luke's description of what Jesus did after his experience of withdrawal. Jesus said, "*I must preach the good news of the kingdom of God to the other towns also, because that is why I was sent*". This was a statement of his mission's purpose. It was the first mention in Luke of the "*kingdom of God*". The phrase occurs more than thirty times in the Gospel, and other expressions also refer to the kingdom. Jesus was sent to preach "*the good news of the kingdom of God*". His mission was firstly to announce, and then finally to bring in, the "*kingdom*". Luke emphasised the task of announcing the kingdom more fully when he concluded with the statement, "*And he kept on preaching in the synagogues of Judea*". This appears to contradict Luke's pattern which presents Jesus' preaching ministry as taking place in Galilee. Every incident included in this section (4:14-9:50) occurred in Galilee. However, his statement referring to "*Judea*" was not meant to be geographical, but theological. Judea was the territory of the kingdom of the Jews. Luke was distinguishing the "*kingdom of God*" from the political national kingdom. Jesus was preaching the good news of God's kingdom in the synagogues where Jews gathered to hear God's word. His prior withdrawal to a desert place (in order to pray) ensured that he kept his mission as his primary focus.

Luke illustrated Jesus' teaching itinerary by relating a series of incidents which demonstrated his effect on various listeners. Jesus called some fishermen to follow him after a miraculous catch of fish (5:1-11). Six incidents roused popular interest in Jesus, but also led to criticism from the Pharisees (5:12-6:11). He healed a leper (5:12-16), forgave the sins of a paralytic and healed him (5:17-26), and called a tax collector to follow him (5:27-32). He explained the celebratory nature of his ministry by his attitude to fasting (5:33-39), and identified his authority and his intention to do good by his attitude towards the Sabbath (6:1-11). Jesus was the source of blessing for the afflicted, the source of grace for sinners, the source of joy, newness and freedom in life.

The tax collector (5:27-32) was called Levi, whom Matthew's Gospel identifies as Matthew himself (Matthew 9:9-13). When Levi responded to Jesus' invitation to follow him, he held a banquet for Jesus and his fellow tax collectors and associates. The Pharisees complained about Jesus' willingness to dine with such sinful company, prompting a revealing rebuff from Jesus. "*It is not the healthy who need a doctor, but the sick. I have not come to call the righteous, but sinners to repentance.*" Jesus' reply pinpointed the aim of his mission. He came to call sinners to repentance. The Pharisees, however, were offended by what they considered was Jesus' lack of appropriate religious decorum. Jesus was too jovial and sociable for their liking.

They went on to criticise him for not practising the ritualistic customs of fasting and praying like the disciples of John and themselves (5:33-39). Yet the only fast prescribed by the Law was on the Day of Atonement. The Jews had developed many additional voluntary fasts which had become religiously obligatory. John's custom of fasting was in keeping with his lifestyle of voluntary abstinence as an expression of dedication to his special ministry. Jesus responded to their criticism about fasting, but notice that he made no comment about prayer. With regard to fasting, he likened his present activities to the festivities of a wedding. It was a time for joy. However, he acknowledged that a time for fasting would come when the "bridegroom" was taken away from them. He illustrated further with a parable. No one cuts a patch from a new garment to mend an old garment, nor pours new wine into old wineskins, because both the old and the new would be destroyed. Jesus' implication was that he brought a profoundly new reality, which was incompatible with the old Jewish religion, and must not have old customs like fasting imposed upon it. He added a final comment, pointedly against his critics, that no one who was content with the old wanted to try the new. Jesus was using the criticism to emphasise that his message, ministry, and mission were something radically new.

On the other hand, with regard to prayer, Jesus' lack of comment was significant. He might not encourage his disciples to observe the ritualistic fixed hours of prayer like the Pharisees, but his own habits of withdrawal for prayer had already shown how meaningful and purposeful prayer was in his personal experience. At a later occasion he will give instructions to his disciples concerning prayer which will enable their outlook on prayer to become new and meaningful also, in contrast to the customary recited rituals (see 11:1-13).

Meanwhile we come to another reference to prayer. Jesus spent a night on a mountainside praying to God (6:12). Obviously prayer was purposeful and pre-eminent for him. Jesus was God's kingly "Son", his earthly "Partner" in their shared mission of redemption for the world, and he was about to make a crucial decision. So he prayed. He prayed in dependence on his Father, to ensure that he was in accord with his Father's will. On the following morning he called his disciples to him and selected twelve to be *"apostles"* (6:13-16). Luke records their names. The whole occasion was described succinctly, but represented a highly important development. The number twelve reflected the number of tribes in Israel, rooting the concept of God's kingdom in God's past association with Israel, yet not equating the kingdom with the nation. The apostles would become the new foundation for the kingdom. As *"apostles"* they were associated with Jesus and his mission, being sent by him as he was by God. Their task was to expand his ministry of preaching the good news of the kingdom of God. The term *"apostles"* was a widely used expression, but Luke applies it exclusively to the Twelve in order to emphasise their special role. He reinforces their uniqueness as a group by naming each of the Twelve. None of them was especially qualified for the role. They acquired their qualifications from their exclusive relationship with Jesus. For his part, Jesus' association with them was a major responsibility, and trial, in his task of establishing God's kingdom.

The last-named apostle was *"Judas Iscariot, who became a traitor"*. He is a surprise. He was chosen after a night of prayer. As with the rest of the Twelve, he was chosen to be given privileged opportunity to know Jesus, and his message and mission. Yet then he chose to betray Jesus. It was not that he was predetermined to be the traitor, so that he was incapable of acting otherwise. It was a course of action which he freely chose, hard-heartedly rejecting all loving appeals to his loyalty. However, his act of betrayal accomplished God's predetermined purpose. It led to the cross, and to God's salvation for the world. Judas was pivotal to God's plan of grace, and therefore his selection as an apostle was necessary. Jesus' gracious choice of Judas, and Judas' treacherous rejection of Jesus became the catalyst which produced God's salvation. The relationship between Jesus and Judas was actually a deeply personalised reflection of the relationship between God and the world. Yet Jesus' choice of Judas after a night of prayer reveals that prayer is not a simplistic transaction. It is a profound expression of a relationship. There is an element of mystery about it. There are unknown, subtle, and complex factors in the outworking process of prayer. For Jesus, prayer was an action of trust in his relationship with God as his dependent "Partner" on earth.

Jesus then took the Twelve to a particular location, and instructed them, together with a wider audience (6:17-20). This segment of teaching is the longest in this section dealing with Jesus' ministry activities. It is often called Jesus' "Sermon on the Plain" (because of its setting), and compared with his "Sermon on the Mount" in Matthew's Gospel (5-7), which has much in common, but is longer and has a different focus.

The "Sermon" here can be analysed into progressive phases. Jesus began with pronouncements of blessings and woes with regard to two categories of people, those who were deprived in this world for the sake of discipleship but who were ultimately blessed, and those who were prosperous in this world but who were ultimately cursed (6:21-26). Then he expressed his essential message, by appealing to those who would heed him to be characterised by love and non-retaliatory attitudes towards their persecutors, to give freely to all in need as they would want others to treat them, having as their reward the character of sons of the Most high (6:27-35). What an extraordinary, life-changing challenge! To become radically transformed, so as to have a disposition of God-like love. This is the description given to Mary of what her child Jesus would be called (1:32). We must especially notice that he urged them to *"pray"* for those who mistreated them! He went on to command them to be merciful as their Father was merciful, not judging others, but forgiving and freely giving, and consequently receiving the same for themselves (6:36-38). He used an illustration (*"parable"*) to stress the foolishness of disciples judging fellow disciples (6:39-42). Just as a blind man cannot lead another blind man, or they will both fall into a pit, so a student cannot be more capable than his teacher. Therefore, why hypocritically try to remove a splinter from a brother's eye while not paying attention to the plank in your own? Jesus then stated the general principle that, like plants which produce good or bad fruit according to their good or bad condition, people speak and do good or bad out of the condition of their hearts (6:43-45). This was the basic thrust of his message, to expose the condition of the human heart. He concluded his "Sermon" with a challenging application, returning to his opening theme about two categories of people (6:46-49). Why fervently call me Lord, and not do what I say? The obedient person is like the man who built his house on a firm foundation on rock, and the disobedient is like the man who built without foundation on the ground. When the flood came, the former was secure, but the latter collapsed.

The "Sermon" was a confronting challenge, concerned about the condition of human nature. It was Jesus' mission to change the human heart, so that it might be responsive (obedient) to the kingdom of God. His message appealed for submission to his lordship, because it would be his death and resurrection which would become the way into the kingdom. As true Son of the Most High, he would enable his disciples to become sons of the Most High. In his appeal to his disciples to behave in loving ways like God, Jesus especially called them to pray for those who mistreated them (v 28). This was not a trivial comment to be rushed past. To pray for your persecutor means to pray for him/her to experience God's forgiveness and salvation. It is in accord with the will of God, and therefore the kingdom of God. It is an action which manifests God's love and mercy, and is evidence of having a sonship relation with the Father. That is why it is significant that Luke (and only Luke) records Jesus' poignant request for his Father to forgive his executors at the moment of his crucifixion (23:34). He was *The* Son of God praying for the forgiveness of his tormentors. At a later time, Luke reports that Stephen, the first follower of Jesus to be martyred, prayed in a similar way for those who were stoning him to death (Acts 7:60). For Jesus, prayer was not a mere religious ritual, and was more than a helpful, meaningful experience. It was a fundamental expression of being in a son's relationship with the Father.

Luke's continued account of Jesus' ministry activities shone more light on him and on the presence of God's kingdom. Jesus displayed a gracious attitude towards the needy and socially avoided, and performed divinely authoritative actions (7:1-50). He healed a Gentile centurion's servant and raised a helpless widow's dead son back to life. He reassured imprisoned John the Baptist by telling two of John's disciples to report back what they saw and heard about Jesus' healing miracles. He confirmed John's special role as a prophet who prepared the way for him. He denounced critics of John and himself, who failed to discern their connection and quibbled over their differing temperate and liberal attitudes, as being childishly perverse. He forgave the sins of a renowned sinful woman who displayed extravagant devotion towards him in contrast to a discourteous Pharisee. These incidents pointed towards Jesus' unique identity, and displayed his compassion, power, and authority.

Another ministry tour was introduced with a brief summary of those who accompanied him, followed by a series of parables and miracles, linked by a short anecdote about Jesus' family (8:1-56). Those who accompanied Jesus were the Twelve and several prominent women. One of Luke's characteristics was Jesus' favourable attitude towards women, and especially the role of prominent resourceful and influential women. Parables stressed the importance of hearing and obeying the word of God. The parable of the Sower and the Soils illustrated that hearing God's word must lead to a fruitful response. The parable of the lamp had the twofold application that what is received must be revealed to all, and those who receive will be given further illumination. An incident concerning Jesus' earthly family became an occasion for emphasising that those who hear and do God's Word were Jesus' true family. Four miracles by Jesus showed his power over natural elements, supernatural demons, disease and death, and at the same time revealed his compassion and willingness to save.

A final tour phase consists of incidents which involved Jesus and the Twelve (9:1-50). The incidents are linked by the themes of Jesus' mission of power and love, and the path of suffering. Jesus sent out the Twelve to preach the kingdom of God, and demonstrate its presence by healing the sick. Herod's perplexity over reports of this campaign highlight that Jesus' power was more than human, prompting the question of who was he. The later miraculous feeding of the crowd shows the inability and attitude of the Twelve in contrast to Jesus. The question of Jesus' identity now comes into central focus and is answered in the account of Peter's confession and Jesus' transfiguration. The theme of Jesus' suffering is also introduced in these incidents, and continues in the account of the exorcising of the demon-possessed boy. This stage of Luke's Gospel concludes by showing the disciples still acting from earthly motives, both amongst themselves, and towards others.

There are two more occasions when Luke records Jesus praying, and both were crucial moments. In fact, the major events in Jesus' ministry which highlight his mission are all preceded by periods of prayer. We saw that Jesus prayed at his baptism (3:21-22), resulting in his being anointed by the Holy Spirit, and then led by the Spirit to face temptation in the desert before returning to commence his ministry in Galilee. We also saw that Jesus prayed in regard to his preaching tours (4:42, 5:16) and before choosing his twelve apostles (6:12). Most likely, judging from the terms Luke used (9:10, 12), it was Jesus' intention to pray when he withdrew to Bethsaida. Instead, he preached about the *"kingdom of God"* to the crowds which followed him, healed those who were sick, and then late in the day performed the astonishing miracle of feeding everyone (5000 men plus) from a mere five loaves of bread and two fish. But now two climactic events occurred, a week apart, when Peter confessed Jesus to be the Messiah (9:18-27), and Jesus was transfigured in front of Peter, James, and John on a mountain (9:28-36). Prior to both events, Jesus was engaged in praying (9:18, 28-29).

Luke does not give many details about the location of Peter's confession, or of the conversation which it provoked, as found in Mark and Matthew. So it is significant that he alone indicates that Jesus was praying privately with his disciples. He was showing Jesus' devoted relationship with the Father, and his complete dependence on God for all his actions and decisions. As a result of his praying, Jesus took the initiative to raise the question of his identity with his disciples. He asked them what the crowds were saying about who he was, and received answers which had been expressed as a result of their preaching campaign (cf. 9:1-9, 19). Then, with deliberate emphasis, he asked them who they thought he was. When Peter answered, *"The Christ of God"*, he warned them not to tell anyone, and informed them that the *"Son of Man"* had to suffer many things, be rejected, killed, and on the third day raised to life. The reason Jesus did not want his identity as Messiah made public was because of popular misunderstanding. The Jews expected the Messiah to be a military, political deliverer who would rescue them from Gentile bondage. They likely expected the apocalyptic figure of the *"Son of Man"* in the book of Daniel to be given power from God to rule over the world on behalf of the Jewish nation. Jesus, however, knew that as Messiah he came to deliver his people from their sins, and that his pathway to glory was via the cross. He went on to add, in figurative imagery, that anyone who came after him must deny himself and take up his cross daily and follow him. Becoming a disciple of Jesus involved being condemned to death on a daily basis as far as life in this present world was concerned. This was the first mention of the cross in Luke's Gospel, and pointed forward to the time when Jesus would literally be crucified as the Messiah on behalf of his followers. Jesus explained that whoever wanted to save his life (in this world), would actually lose it. What good was it to gain the whole world, yet lose yourself? He warned that if anyone was ashamed of him and his words, the "*Son of Man*" would be ashamed of him when he came in his glory and the glory of the Father and his angels. This would be when God's triumphant rule over the rebellious world would be restored. Jesus concludes with an assertive pronouncement that some who were standing there would not "*taste death*" (experience death's bitterness, perhaps as martyrs) before they saw "*the kingdom of God*". This would have been a puzzling and disturbing statement at the time, because of the expectation of a victorious earthly kingdom. Jesus, however, was referring to the future reign of the risen Messiah, who would "rule" by means of the Spirit through the preaching of the Gospel.

The experience of Jesus' transfiguration occurred about a week later, and was meant to provide a preview of the future glory which Jesus had just referred to. It happened while Jesus was praying on a mountain. The mountain was unnamed, allowing the situation to be somewhat reminiscent of Moses on Mount Sinai. The experience which took place revealed something of the true nature of prayer. Jesus on earth was conversing with his Father in heaven. Like Moses, Jesus was in the presence of God. The experience caused his facial appearance to change, as with Moses, and his clothes became as bright as a flash of lightning. Two men, Moses and Elijah, appeared in glory with him, talking about his impending "*departure*" at Jerusalem. The word "*departure*" is literally "*exodus*", likening Jesus' death and departure from this world for the liberation of his people from their sin to Israel's exodus from slavery in Egypt. Moses and Elijah represented the Law and the Prophets of the Old Testament, which revealed God's unfolding plan of redemption until Jesus. This was not just an awesome religious prayer experience. The glory displayed in the experience was a manifestation of God's kingly glory related to his mission of salvation for the world. The three disciples, Peter, James, and John, who were with Jesus, awoke from their drowsiness and saw the epiphany of Jesus' glory. When they saw Moses and Elijah starting to leave, Peter offered to erect three shelters, one each for Jesus, Moses, and Elijah, in order to maintain the exhilarating experience. Peter did not know what he was saying, and presumably thought that the final day of glory had arrived. He had not comprehended Jesus' statement about the Son of Man having to die and rise again. While he was still speaking, a cloud, representing the presence of God, enveloped them, apparently blotting the scene of glory from view. They were filled with fear, and a voice came from out of the cloud. It was the Father speaking, and he declared, "*This is my Son, whom I have chosen; listen to him*". Just as God had spoken to Jesus at his baptism when he was beginning his ministry, now he was speaking to the disciples as Jesus was about to head towards Jerusalem and the cross. He told them to listen to Jesus, that is, concerning his necessity to suffer and die, and rise again. That was the path to glory, which the present experience had prefigured. When the voice finished speaking, the disciples found Jesus alone. The vision was only temporary, and they kept it to themselves. The event revealed the heart of Jesus' prayer. In fellowshipping with his Father, he was taken up with God's kingdom and agenda of salvation, and his own mission in regard to them.

Luke's travelogue depicts Jesus as an impressive figure. He is larger than life, exuding vitality, self-confidence, and independence. A man of purpose, power, and authority. He is totally devoted to honouring and serving God, and undeterred by any human influence. He speaks wisdom, and without favour. He is gentle, protective, yet can be frankly confrontational. He is a commanding presence. He is deeply concerned for the poor and needy, the afflicted and oppressed. He attracts popularity, loyalty, and hostility. In a word, he behaves for all the world like the kingly Son of God! He is a man with a mission, and a clear plan for accomplishing it. In every step he took, as he performed his ministry and proclaimed the kingdom of God, he was led by the Spirit, and consistently consulted his Father in prayer.

The Teachings of Jesus: Moving towards Jerusalem (9:51-19:27)

Luke's literary structure is ingenious. His narrative turned from Jesus' action in Galilee to his teaching on the road to Jerusalem. Jesus' teaching makes up the major section of Luke's Gospel, and is therefore highly important. The journey to Jerusalem occupies almost 10 chapters (9:51-19:27). By way of comparison, Mark takes only a single chapter (Mark 10), and Matthew only 2 (Matthew 19-20). Actually, the journey itself was barely mentioned by Luke, and was simply the framework for presenting the bulk of Jesus' teaching. This is quite conspicuous in modern translations which print Jesus' words in red. Almost the whole section consists of Jesus' teaching, and details of the journey are skimpy. In fact these details are confusing, because they present an inconsistent travel route. There were three major routes from Galilee in the north to the south of the country. The coastal route, known as the "Via Maris" ("Way of the Sea"), was part of the trade route from Syria to Egypt via the Sea of Galilee. This was an inconvenient way to Jerusalem, and there is no record of Jesus travelling that way. The central route passed through the hill country and the territory of Samaria. This was the shortest route, though usually avoided by Jews in order not to encounter Samaritans. At first impression this seems to be the path Jesus travelled (9:51-56). However, incidents mentioned throughout this section regarding his journey provide a very indistinct picture. Along the way he went to the village of Mary and Martha (10:38-42), yet this was Bethany on the Mount of Olives near Jerusalem (John 12:1), which he did not reach until the end of his journey (19:28-29). Also along the way he encountered Pharisees (11:37, 13:31, 14:1, 15:2, 16:14), who would more than likely avoid this route. At one point Jesus travelled along the border between Samaria and Galilee (17:11), which would have been the more popular third route near the Jordan river. This was the route which would take him through Jericho (18:35, 19:1). It is apparent that Jesus' "journey" to Jerusalem was actually a compilation of incidents from several journeys. When he was a child, Jesus' earthly family kept the custom of visiting Jerusalem each year for the Feast of Passover (2:41). It is reasonable to assume he continued the practice as an adult. His single "journey", then, in Luke's Gospel is not chronological, but theological in nature. Multiple journeys are merged into one to represent Jesus' overall mission of going to Jerusalem. It is meant to be seen as a feature of the gospel presentation of Jesus, highlighting the nature of his mission, and his resolve to go to Jerusalem in order to complete it (9:51). It also depicts the path of discipleship for his followers (9:23-27). Discipleship involves accepting Jesus as a crucified Messiah, and accepting his teachings which he gave along the way.

What is surprising is the absence of references to Jesus praying throughout this section of Luke's Gospel. It is the longest segment of the Gospel, and there is no mention of any occasion when Jesus practised his habit of withdrawal for prayer.

On the other hand, prayer is a conspicuous feature of this journey to Jerusalem. It is a prominent topic in Jesus' teaching. There is also one important public occasion when Jesus prayed, which we will consider in due course. Again, it is helpful to have a condensed summary of this segment in order to have a framework for our study of prayer.

At the beginning of the segment various incidents are strung together relating to Jesus' disciples who accompany him on his journey (9:51-11:13). Messengers sent ahead of him encountered hostility from a Samaritan village, a foretaste of Jesus' final rejection, but he refused to retaliate, demonstrating the spirit in which disciples must learn to face inevitable resistance (9:51-56). As he travelled, Jesus interacted with would-be disciples and indicated the cost of discipleship (9:57-62). Then he sent ahead seventy (two) disciples on an advance mission to towns he intended to visit, urging them to pray for additional workers, warning about inevitable dangers, insisting on travelling light with an attitude of urgency, and advising them how to relate appropriately to a house or town, with dire warnings for those who rejected them (10:1-12). He dramatically pronounced judgement on towns in Galilee which had rejected his ministry, and then declared that how people responded to the disciples was effectively their response to him (10:13-16). Eventually (although no time period is indicated) the Seventy (Two) returned, in joy, and Jesus acknowledged Satan's downfall and his disciples' authority, but stressed the greater importance of their certainty of salvation (10:17-20). At that time, Jesus was filled with joy by the Holy Spirit, prompting him to praise the Father publicly for giving him revelation of himself, and to declare privately that his disciples were blessed for their privilege to see what they were seeing (10:21-24). Three stories then provided understanding of three different aspects of the life of discipleship (10:25-11:13). The first emphasised obedience to the two main Commandments, with the story of the Good Samaritan especially stressing the second command to love one's neighbour. The second story about Mary and Martha emphasised the importance of God's word through Jesus, probably intended to show how to obey the first commandment to love God. The third story was about how to pray, with a pattern prayer, a parable about God's willingness to hear, and assurances about God's certainty to answer.

Already prayer has cropped up three times. The first reference was in connection with the mission of the seventy (two) disciples sent ahead in pairs to towns where he intended to go (10:1-16). Their task was to proclaim that the kingdom of God was near (v 9, 11). This was a second, and larger, campaign, following the earlier mission of the Twelve in Galilee (9:1-6). It perhaps explains why Jesus' multiple trips to Jerusalem could be presented as one, because they were part of a single mission. Jesus visited many towns between Galilee and Jerusalem, as, like John the Baptist, his disciples prepared the way for his coming. It is uncertain whether there were 70 or 72 disciples sent out, and whether the number was symbolic. To specify such a number seems to suggest some significance. The figures of 70 (72) may have represented the number of elders in Israel, or the number of members of the Sanhedrin, or the number of scholars who translated the Septuagint (the Greek version of the Old Testament), or perhaps the number of recognised nations of the world at that time. If the Twelve represented the tribes of Israel, the Seventy (Two) could very well represent the nations of the world. In that case they were also a hint of the church's future mission after Jesus' resurrection, when he came into all the world in power. Jesus spoke of a plentiful harvest requiring additional workers, and urged his disciples to ask the Lord of the harvest to send out workers into his harvest field (v 2). The term *"Ask"* is *"Implore"*, and can be translated as *"Pray"*. The Lord of the harvest is God, and Jesus was referring to the final gathering of God's people into his kingdom. This was a large task, to be accomplished through the mission of Jesus' disciples, and therefore required many workers. Prayer was the means for recruiting them. Jesus was showing again that prayer was a priority with regard to the affairs of the kingdom. It was a meaningful and purposeful activity, an expression of complete dependency on God. Jesus was now encouraging his disciples to engage in prayer, similar to his own practice.

The second instance of prayer was Jesus' public exclamation of praise to his Father, inspired with joy from the Holy Spirit (10:21). It was introduced by a time note linking it to the success of his disciples' mission which had demonstrated God's power in the exorcism of demons.

Jesus' prayer was spontaneous and natural. He addressed God directly, and in self-assured familiarity. He called God *"Father"* and *"Lord of heaven and earth"*, demonstrating his intimate personal relationship to God, and his respect for God's absolute supremacy. He was very conscious of his Father in heaven and of himself as Son on earth. Prayer was central to his relationship with God, and to every step of his mission's progress. He offered praise to God for hiding *"these things"* from the wise and learned, and revealing them to little children. In the context, *"these things"* referred to the downfall of Satan evidenced by the submission of demons to the authority of Jesus, which his disciples had exercised on his behalf. The disciples had been privileged to experience the revelation of God's kingly power first hand. Jesus did not mean that God was excluding the wise and learned from this revelation in favour of little children. He was speaking figuratively, indicating the nature of God's revelation. God was not revealing "*these things*" to those who relied on self-sufficient human intellectual competence, but to "*little children*", those (of any age) who recognised their dependence and inadequacy. He stressed his agreement with this conviction by acknowledging that this was the Father's good pleasure. By prayer Jesus was remaining focussed on pleasing his Father, and discerning his will.

The prayer was dramatic and exuberant. It was a prelude to a public announcement. Jesus declared that his Father had committed "*all things*" to him. He meant matters concerning the restoration of God's kingdom which were to be revealed. This revelation was about knowledge of the Son (with regard to his mission in the world), which only the Father knew, and knowledge of the Father (with regard to his motivating love and purpose), which only the Son knew, and those to whom the Son chose to reveal him. The language was cryptic, to express the "hiddenness" of this knowledge to natural human understanding.

Later in private Jesus told his disciples that they were blessed to see what they were seeing. Many prophets and kings had wanted to see and hear what they were experiencing, but unsuccessfully. Jesus was referring to those of the past who shared in the progress of God's plan of salvation, and implying that with him the era of salvation had arrived.

The third reference to prayer was a longer passage (11:1-13), and provided substantial instruction about its practice. The passage was the third of three incidents presented after the occasion of the mission of the Seventy (Two) and Jesus' public prayer, which seem to have been arranged topically rather than chronologically. The trio of incidents was not directly connected with the mission of the Seventy, but more generally with people's relationship with God. The first incident involved a Law expert testing Jesus with a question about what to "*do*" to inherit eternal life, which eventually led to Jesus telling the parable of the Good Samaritan (10:25-37). The question was expecting a legalistic answer, particular laws to be "*done*". Jesus however put the question back to his questioner, asking what answer was given by the Law. When he received the response that the Law required love for God with your whole being, and love for your neighbour as you loved yourself, Jesus agreed, and told the man to go and "*do*" it in order to live. Jesus was not proposing a set of rules, but commending a way of life, a way of relating to God and to others in love. The lawyer did not grasp this implication, and was still wanting specific laws to keep. Wanting to justify himself, he took up the second command and asked the further question, "*Who is my neighbour?*" In response, Jesus cleverly altered the question, and told the parable of the Good Samaritan to illustrate what was meant by being neighbourly.

A second incident is a story taken out of chronological sequence and out of geographical order to illustrate the first command (10:38-42). Luke vaguely says that while Jesus and his disciples were "*on their way*", he came to "*a village*" where Martha opened her home to him. He omitted to name the village, which was Bethany near Jerusalem, and which was at the end of his journey. The story recalls an occasion when Jesus commended Martha's sister Mary for choosing to listen to him, while Martha, the hostess, was too distracted from listening by her meal preparations. She was overly distressed by her efforts to cater for Jesus' needs, but failed to realise the more important task of listening to his word. Jesus was not commending the life of contemplation above the life of action, as often interpreted, nor preferring Mary and her lifestyle above Martha and her lifestyle. This was a particular incident which had to do with Jesus and his message. He was proclaiming the kingdom of God and impending life-changing events which affected peoples' relationship with God. This was the time to be listening, not fussing about elaborate domestic chores. By placing this incident at this point in his narrative, Luke was drawing attention to the connection of Jesus and his message to the Law's primary command to love God.

These two incidents were followed by Jesus' discussion about prayer, prompted by a third incident (11:1-13). Luke's format links the three incidents together, making prayer a primary activity. It was that way with Jesus, and it was one of his occasions of praying which prompted the opportunity for his teaching about it. After he had ceased praying, his disciples asked him to teach them to pray. That was an unusual request since prayer was a familiar activity in Israel. Their history and culture placed strong emphasis upon the regular practice of prayer. The disciples' request probably implies that Jesus' manner of praying was different from the norm. They mentioned that John had taught his disciples to pray, which probably implied that John's approach to prayer had its own characteristics. They were wanting Jesus to teach them a manner of praying which would be characteristic of his community. He responded by setting out a form of prayer for them to use. In Matthew's Gospel (6:9-13), in a different situation, Jesus gave a very similar, though somewhat expanded version of the prayer. This was a characteristic, yet fluid, form of prayer to be used as a basic guide for his disciples.

The prayer was concise and simple (v 2-4). It addressed God, and then presented two sets of petitions. The first set consisted of two parallel requests about God's purposes. The second set contained three requests about the disciples' needs. The prayer was expressed in plural language, making it suitable for both personal and collective use.

Jesus began by addressing God directly and intimately as "*Father*". This was his own practice (see 10:21), and was a radically new posture before God, expressing a close and confident relationship. Jews were familiar with the thought of God as Father, but in a more remote and formal sense. Jesus used the homely terms of a child speaking to his parent.

Jesus was not promoting a trivial attitude towards God, as his first petition demonstrated. He prayed that God's name might be hallowed. God's name represented his identity and character. The prayer appealed for God to act in such a way that people would honour and revere his name as holy. It might be meant in a general sense, so that God's behaviour at all times might evoke respect and praise. However, it might be intended in a specific meaning, praying for God to take special action which would result in him being glorified. This is implied in the second petition, "*your kingdom come*". This petition prayed for God's purpose, and Jesus' mission, to be accomplished. This is how the name of the Father would be hallowed. Jesus was teaching his disciples that the distinctive, and primary, characteristic of their praying was for God's kingdom to be established. For his disciples then that meant praying for his destiny at Jerusalem to be fulfilled. For disciples since then, it means praying for God's kingdom to be established through the preaching of the gospel.

The second set of three petitions were concerned about the welfare of the disciples, from a kingdom perspective. Each petition expressed dependence on God, in respect of personal needs, failures, and trials. The first requested God to "*Give us each day our daily bread*". The term "*daily*" is an unusual and rare word which is difficult to interpret. It seems to have the sense of "*adequate provision for the day*". If we recall the experience of Israel being provided with manna in the desert, sufficient for each day, we have a helpful insight into the intention of this petition. The request for "*bread*" in the prayer should probably be understood broadly as "provisions to sustain life", including both material and spiritual. The purpose of manna is helpful in this regard as well. Moses said that God gave manna to the Israelites in order to teach them that "*man does not live on bread alone but on every word that comes from the mouth of the LORD*" (Deuteronomy 8:3). The prayer, therefore, looked to God to provide for daily needs. However, this was more than just generally petitioning God for personal welfare. Since the disciples were following Jesus to establish the kingdom of God in the world, this task was their primary concern, so this petition looked to God to provide fully for their daily needs. It ensured that the disciples' mindset was focussed steadfastly on the coming kingdom, entrusting their wellbeing to their Father's care. The prayer has the same purpose for disciples today, so that the work of the kingdom has priority in the affairs of life.

The second petition asked God for forgiveness of sins. Forgiveness of sins was integrally related to the coming of the kingdom. The coming of the kingdom was essentially God restoring fellowship and his rule of love with sinners. This was highlighted on two occasions during Jesus' ministry in Galilee when he controversially forgave sins, claiming that the Son of Man had authority to do so (5:20-24, 7:48). Obviously, there are personal benefits experienced by a person who is forgiven, such as peace of mind and heart. However, more importantly forgiveness brings reconciliation with God. Sin is not only a matter of doing wrong. It is any offence towards God, which severs relationship with him. God's forgiveness restores the relationship. King David's psalm of confession after his adulterous affair with Bathsheba recognised this: "*Against you, you only, have I sinned*" (Psalm 51:4). Jesus' added explanatory clause in the petition brings this out, "*for we also forgive everyone who sins against* (literally, *is indebted to*) *us*". To sin against anyone is to become obliged to them and owe them restitution. This added clause is not setting down a condition for forgiveness, as sometimes interpreted, but setting out an illustration. Just as we forgive those who offend us in order to restore friendship, so we pray that God will forgive us in order to restore our relationship with him. For the disciples, or us, to pray this petition was to ask to be included as beneficiaries of God's restored kingdom.

The final petition implored God not to lead into temptation. The word means a testing trial, whether from inward enticement or outward hardship. The petition does not seek to avoid temptation, but to be protected from yielding to it. Jesus himself was led by the Spirit into the desert where he was tested, yet without failing (4:1-2). Jesus' disciples were headed towards experiences of great tribulation which would severely test their faith, loyalty, and courage, so this was a relevant prayer. When the trial arrived, they did not cope with the test very well, although after Jesus' resurrection prayer became a much greater and more intentional priority. Tribulation is inevitable for all who follow Jesus in serving God's kingdom.

When we contemplate this prayer in the context of the coming of the kingdom, it takes on a distinctive relevance, and provides much insight into the character of Jesus' own praying.

Jesus followed up the prayer with a humorous little story and two sets of comments to encourage the disciples in their praying (v 5-13). The story was intended to stimulate persistence in prayer and confidence in God's readiness to answer, while the comments make those points explicit.

Jesus caught the attention of the disciples by involving them in a hypothetical story. He described one of them going to a friend at midnight to get three loaves of bread for a visitor who had arrived late while travelling on a journey. The request for bread was a link to the petition for "*daily bread*" in Jesus' prayer, and three loaves would be sufficient for one man's daily need. Arriving at midnight was not unrealistic, since travel was often carried out in the evening to avoid the heat of the day. The disciples would probably appreciate the situation quite readily, since they themselves were journeying towards Jerusalem, and could perhaps relate to the visitor who caused the inconvenience. In the story, the friend did not want to be bothered, because he and his family had already gone to bed, and the door was locked. Such a response was understandable, but went against the customs of hospitality. It would bring a wry smile to the faces of listeners. Yet the man at the door was persistent, and so more bothersome. Therefore the friend got up and gave him what he wanted, not because he was his friend, but to stop his persistent bothering. Jesus said it was the man's "*boldness*", meaning "shameless insistence", which achieved the desired result, realistically describing a typical situation, and adding to the humour. The point of the story is that prayer needs to be persistent too, not because God is reluctant to answer and has to be pressured. Quite the opposite, he is wanting to be asked and ready to give, generously, "*as much as he needs*". It is the person praying who can be reluctant, because they lack sufficient desire or are uncertain about God's response.

Jesus drew out his conclusion in his first set of comments. In three parallel statements he urged his disciples to "*ask ..., seek, ... and knock*", with assurance that they will "*be given ... find... and be opened*". The statements have the appearance of a compact saying which could almost be proverbial. Jesus repeated them in exactly the same wording in his "Sermon on the Mount" with a different application (Matthew 7:7-8). Here they applied readily to the story Jesus told, but were also relevant to the activity of prayer. Together they gave a threefold emphasis upon the need to persist, with assurance of success. Jesus then stressed that assurance by repeating the three activities and asserting their effectiveness. The comments were intended to encourage the disciples to persist confidently in their praying for matters of the kingdom, because they could be certain that God would ensure that they received what they asked for, find what they sought, and have the door opened to them.

A second set of comments also seems like a standard, though flexible, saying of Jesus. It also appears in the "Sermon on the Mount", in conjunction with the previous comments (indicating that they belonged together), yet with significant variations, and in a different context. Jesus asked the fathers among his disciples (who were on earth) which of them would give "*evil*" ("*harmful*") gifts to their children when they asked for a fish or an egg. Even though they themselves were "*evil*", they would naturally give good gifts. How much more then their Father *in heaven*, who was perfectly good, could be trusted to give good gifts. This comment was not only re-emphasising God's willingness to respond to prayer, but insisting on the goodness of his gifts. In Matthew's situation, Jesus said that the Father gives "*good gifts*", but here in Luke's setting, relating to prayer, Jesus said he will give the "*Holy Spirit*" to those who ask him. The gift of the Holy Spirit was to be the outcome of the coming of God's kingdom, as the Old Testament and John the Baptist (3:16) predicted. The prayer which Jesus taught his disciples asked for God's kingdom to come, so the Father's answer would be the gift of his Spirit.

These instructions by Jesus concerning prayer, both in their content, and in Luke's context, highlighted the primary purpose and crucial role of prayer in regard to the coming of God's kingdom. They inspired a fresh perspective of contemplating God intimately as Father, and of approaching him confidently, relationally, strategically, and persistently. The original disciples had a specific task to fulfill, and, as with Jesus, prayer was at its heart. The same outlook, however, still applies to Jesus' later disciples.

As we move on to the next reference to prayer, again the context is relevant. It occurs further along in the segment containing Jesus' teaching, and the section immediately beforehand is especially notable. It is important to get our bearings of the surrounding presentation in order to grasp what Jesus said about prayer.

On his "journey" to Jerusalem, Jesus encountered criticism and controversy (11:14-54). His act of casting out a demon produced reactions of amazement, and accusation of being in league with the prince of demons. Jesus replied that he was acting by the power (literally, "*finger*", therefore the same as that displayed by Moses, Exodus 8:19) of God as a demonstration of his Kingdom, and that true blessedness is found through hearing and obeying God's Word. In response to a request for a sign from heaven, he declared that the Son of Man will be the sign to this generation like Jonah was to Nineveh. Jonah had come back from the dead, and the Ninevites had repented at his preaching. A cryptic comment about light being put where it can be seen by good eyes, but not by bad eyes, illustrated the point that he was God's "light". Seeing him brought inner illumination, but their asking for a sign implied that they were blind. The controversy climaxed with Jesus attacking the religion and hypocrisy of the Pharisees who criticized him for not observing their rules of ritual cleanliness.

Various teachings were linked by the idea of a coming period of crisis (12:1 - 13:21). Jesus warned about judgement coming upon hypocrites, against amassing earthly wealth which can result in spiritual poverty on judgement day, against worry over earthly possessions. He urged preparation and watchfulness for the coming of the Son of Man. He revealed his own distress to have his "baptism" completed, and that he would bring division within intimate relationships. He urged discernment of their present times. Report of a disaster in Jerusalem caused Jesus to deny that the victims were especially deserving of judgement, and to assert that his hearers were equally in danger of God's condemnation. The healing of a crippled woman on a Sabbath exposed the hypocritical attitudes of the religious leaders and demonstrated the power of God to rescue his people from Satan's bondage. Two parables illustrated how the Kingdom of God was destined from its tiny beginnings to become great, suggesting that Jesus was that small beginning.

Various settings prompted teaching about the way of the kingdom (13:22-14:35). As Jesus travelled through towns and villages on his way to Jerusalem, teaching as he went, he was asked whether only a few would be saved. He replied that the door (of the Kingdom) was narrow and excluded many who complacently expected to be admitted, yet surprisingly accepted many who were unexpected. A warning about danger from Herod caused him to declare his knowledge about his own demanding destiny at Jerusalem and to offer a lament over the city. Scenes around the table in the home of a Pharisee allowed Jesus to criticise religious attitudes of the Pharisees, and to tell a parable which showed who were welcome in the Kingdom. He instructed the accompanying crowds about the cost of being his disciple.

Three parables illustrated God's joy when sinners repent, and exposed the attitudes of Jesus' critics (15:1-32). The first two were about people seeking their lost possessions, a sheep and a coin, but the applications were about lost sinners returning of their own accord. The third parable was about a son who became "lost" and then returned of his own accord but was declared to be "found". It also illustrated in the attitude of the elder brother the attitude of Jesus' critics, and so identified Jesus as the One who seeks the lost.

His teaching included several parables about wealth (16:1-31). A story about a dishonest servant does not condone dishonesty but applauds shrewdness. Worldly wealth must be used wisely for heavenly value. Jesus confronted sneering Pharisees with the fact that although they justified themselves before men, God detested them. He asserted that while the good news of God's Kingdom had now replaced the period of the Law and the Prophets, the requirements of the Law still stood, and he gave an example. The story of Lazarus and the rich man illustrated the danger of trying to serve both God and money.

The final phase of the "journey" contained a variety of instructions and unconnected teachings linked by the recurring thought of the coming of the Son of Man (17:1 - 19:27). It was within this setting that Jesus told two parables about prayer (18:1-14). The first parable, about persisting in prayer, illustrated that, although the coming of the Son of Man was delayed, it was inevitable. The second illustrated who was qualified before God, tax collectors who relied on God's mercy rather than self-righteous Pharisees. The parables were followed by a series of incidents until the "journey" reached Jericho, which was the final point prior to the ascension to Jerusalem. Mothers bringing their children to Jesus prompted the insight that a child-like attitude marks those who receive God's Kingship. Encounter with a rich ruler demonstrated that riches made it hard to enter the Kingdom of heaven, but God could make it possible. Jesus predicted that suffering awaited him in Jerusalem, and drew attention to the true meaning of the coming of the Son of Man. The healing of a blind beggar near Jericho highlighted Jesus' approaching destiny, his identity as the Son of David and his concern for the poor and needy, and the need for faith. The story of Zacchaeus brought Luke's Gospel presentation to a climax, showing who could be saved, what salvation involved, and why the Son of man came. A final parable about a king and his servants implied the rejection of Jesus as King and the need for his disciples to be occupied in profitable service until he returned.

In brief, Jesus' teaching warned against the inadequacy of self-righteous religion and the emptiness of earthly riches, and offered salvation by entering God's kingdom which the coming of the Son of Man would bring. This meant repenting and becoming a disciple of Jesus.

It was this broad framework which gave meaning to the two parables which Jesus told about prayer. The first parable is usually called "The Reluctant Judge", though sometimes "The Persistent Widow", because both characters illustrate important truths about prayer. Luke introduced the parable by indicating that Jesus told it to his disciples "*to show them that they should always pray and not faint*". The parable was short and simple, but contained a profound message. Because God could be trusted to answer prayer, the disciples could persist in their praying. In the parable, a reluctant, self-centred judge, who neither feared God nor cared for people, eventually granted justice in response to a widow's persistent pleading. It was only for his own convenience, because her persistence was an annoying bother. God, however, was not like that, but a sharp contrast. Jesus explained that God would act quickly to the continual prayers for justice by his "*chosen ones*". For God to act quickly did not necessarily mean immediately, which was why those praying had to persevere. The purpose of the parable was to show that the disciples should not give up praying, but persist with confidence that God would certainly and quickly grant justice when it was the right time.

The parable has a relevant meaning for prayer in general. All of life should be faced in prayerful dependence on God, and we should not lose heart when answers are slow in coming. Yet in its context the parable has a specific meaning. Jesus was teaching his disciples about the "coming of the Son of Man", when the kingdom of God would be established (17:20-37). The purpose of the coming of the Son of man was to bring justice, God's justice. So this was what God's *"chosen ones"* would pray for, concerning the world and concerning themselves. The parable ended with the question whether the Son of Man would find faith on earth when he came. This means would he find people who were looking to God in faith when they prayed for justice (for God's will to be done on earth as in heaven!).

The Son of Man was a continual theme in Luke's Gospel. Jesus had earlier predicted that the Son of Man had to suffer many things, be rejected by the religious authorities, be killed, and be raised to life on the third day (9:22). His sacrificial death for sin was the means by which God would establish his justice. In his teaching immediately prior to the parable, Jesus explained that the kingdom of God, and the days of the Son of Man, were not naturally obvious (17:20-23). Yet, on the other hand, they would be like lightning flashing across the sky (17:24)!! Firstly, however, he must suffer many things, and be rejected by that generation (17:25). Jesus meant that the "coming of the Son of Man" was his resurrection from the dead! That would be the day when he was revealed (17:30). He later indicated a similar thing to the Jewish council which condemned him (22:69). After his resurrection, the angels at his tomb reminded the women of Jesus' prior prediction (24:7), and the risen Jesus himself confirmed it to two disciples at Emmaus (24:26). Jesus' resurrection vindicated his death for sin and enthroned him as ruler in God's kingdom. Prayer for justice was answered!

Note: It is popular to assume that the "coming of the Son of Man" referred to Jesus' second coming. This is true in a derived sense, but only because the initial meaning, in the context of Luke's Gospel, referred to Jesus' resurrection. Yet his resurrection was not a single event, but an extended process (as Luke's Book of Acts will show), beginning with the resurrection of Jesus (the first fruits of God's harvest) and concluding with the resurrection of God's "chosen ones" (the fulness of harvest), whose eventual resurrection has been guaranteed by that of Jesus. The risen Messiah, reigning on high, is now baptising God's "chosen ones" with the Holy Spirit in preparation for the resurrection finale at the end of time. The Son of Man "came" when he rose from death. He is now "coming" through the spread of the gospel of the kingdom empowered by the Spirit. At the end of time he "will come" when he returns in glory.

The second parable about prayer, involving a Pharisee and a tax collector, follows straight after the parable about the reluctant judge and persistent widow. The two parables are linked by the mention of prayer. Whereas the first parable referred to God's "chosen ones" praying for justice in connection with the coming kingdom of God, the following parable showed someone actually engaged in such prayer. That person is a bit of a surprise. In particular, the parable illustrated the kind of faith which Jesus meant, which the Son of Man would want to find when he came.

Luke did not say when Jesus told this parable, only who he told it to. They were people who were confident about their own righteousness, and scornfully looked down on others whom they considered unacceptable. The pharisee in the story was typical of them. The tax collector, who was the other character, was typical of those whom they scorned. Both men went to the temple to pray, but their attitudes in prayer were vastly different. Both were praying for acceptance (or justice) with God. The pharisee sought to be justified on the basis of his merits, the tax collector on the basis of God's mercy. Jesus' concluding verdict, speaking with heavenly authority, was that the tax collector, rather than the Pharisee, went home justified (justly acquitted) before God. Jesus pronounced an explanatory principle for the outcome: "*Everyone who exalts himself will be humbled, and he who humbles himself will be exalted*". Remember that the wider context was about the coming of the Son of man and the kingdom of God. Luke's purpose for the parable was to illustrate who was acceptable to the kingdom, and to anticipate Jesus' task in making that possible. With regard to prayer, two important truths are revealed. Firstly, prayer is the means for appealing to God for acceptance (justice, salvation). Prayer acknowledges the reality, supremacy, and authority of God, and addresses him as a living Person. In the second place, prayer requires an attitude of humility before God, confidence to draw near on the basis of his mercy, but no place for boasting.

Opposition to Jesus: *Experiences in Jerusalem* (Chap. 19:28-21:38)

Jesus' arrival at Jerusalem was depicted as the arrival of the King, marked by a series of crucial encounters. The scene where these encounters took place was the temple, which represented God's earthly palace, symbolising his residence and rule in the midst of his people.

Jesus rode a colt into Jerusalem from the east to the acclamation of a crowd of disciples (19:28-44). The Pharisees tried to persuade him to restrain his followers' enthusiasm, and Jesus responded with a prophetic lament over the city. These features fulfilled significant Old Testament prophecies concerning the coming of the Messiah and God's Kingdom.

Jesus entered the Temple, and in typical prophetic confrontation cleared the area of traders, and charged them for turning God's "*house of prayer*" into "*a den of robbers*" (19:45-46). We should recall that Luke had previously reported Jesus saying as a boy at the temple that he had to be in his Father's house (2:49). Jesus had deep reverence for this holy place. Remember, too, that during his temptation in the desert Jesus had refused to show himself to be God's Son by spectacularly throwing himself off the temple in order for God to rescue him by means of his angels (4:9-12). Yet what Jesus was now doing was a sensational and provocative action in the precincts of the temple. Clearing the traders (from the Court of the Gentiles) would have caused much commotion and upheaval, and stirred up widespread curiosity, and official hostility. Luke made no comment about the impact of Jesus' actions, yet they began a process which would end with a divine rescue more extraordinary than Satan's proposed stunt. Resurrection from the dead! Luke's description was kept minimal. He simply recorded the event, without elaborating on details, or drawing out any significance.

Instead, his focus was on what Jesus said at the time. Jesus combined two prominent expressions taken from the prophets Isaiah and Jeremiah. The first quoted expression about God's "*house of prayer*" had been made about the new temple to be built after the restoration of the Jewish exiles from Babylon (Isaiah 56:7). The second expression had been made by Jeremiah about the old temple before it was destroyed and the nation taken into exile (Jeremiah 7:11). Jesus was using these memorable expressions to imply that the current practices at the temple were failing to fulfil its intended purpose, and therefore the temple was in the same condition as the former temple which had resulted in its destruction. He will soon have something to say about that to his disciples (21:5-6).

The purpose of the temple was to be a "*house of prayer*". This was Luke's next occurrence of the word "prayer". Luke began his Gospel with instances of prayer associated with the temple (Zechariah, 1:8-10, 13; Simeon, 2:28-32; and Anna, 2:36-37). His most recent reference to prayer was the parable of the Pharisee and tax collector who came to the temple to pray (18:9-14). To now identify the temple as primarily a "*house of prayer*" made the status of prayer conspicuous. Prayer was the means of his people having audience with their divine King in order to bring their praises and petitions. It was a meaningful and essential activity not to be obliterated by other practices. Luke's brief record of Jesus' stunning performance, overlooking the shocking disturbance he caused, pinpointed what disturbed him: lack of prayerfulness.

Luke proceeded to tell how Jesus maintained a daily teaching role, in the temple, while opposition mounted (19:47-48). Jesus' provocative message brought official deputations from the temple leaders questioning his source of authority, which he refused to declare directly, but implied in a revealing parable about a vineyard owner's son and heir who was killed by the tenants (20:1-19). Representatives from different opponents tried to trap him with cunning questions, but his answers exposed their own condition (20:20-44). To his disciples, he denounced the false piety of the religious teachers (20:45-47), and pointed out an example of true piety in a poor widow (21:1-4). What we should note about the false piety of the religious teachers is that it was all show and no substance. Apart from their ostentatious public attention-seeking, Jesus levelled two particular criticisms against them. They abused their positions (probably as lawyers administering the estates of deceased men) to "*devour*" widows' houses, and made lengthy prayers for show. In effect, they failed to love their neighbour and God, breaking the Law, while pretending to be pious. Jesus' criticism of their prayers was not over a mere trivial matter. It went to the heart of their relationship with God. In stark contrast, the poor widow who contributed her two copper coins to the temple treasury showed genuine love for God. She gave all that she had to live on, and, what was not stated but to be understood, she had come to the temple to pray!

The segment concludes with a final condemnation of the temple (21:5 – 36). When some of his disciples expressed admiration for the beautiful adornment of the temple, Jesus pronounced its total destruction (v 5-7). His disciples asked when this would happen, and what prior sign there would be. Jesus first of all warned them not to be misled by deceivers or unsettling news of wars and revolutions (v 8-9). He was referring to the popular Jewish expectation for a military Messiah, which often led to uprisings by insurrectionists. Jesus agreed that these things must happen first, but the end would not happen immediately. He outlined several kinds of events which would occur in the future (v 10-11). There would be wars, earthly calamities, and heavenly convulsions. These implied an extended period of time. Before these happened, however, there would be persecution for Jesus' disciples, who, with Jesus' help, would bear witness before their oppressors, and, despite even death, would experience no ultimate harm (v 12-19). Then Jesus answered the disciples' first question, about the destruction of the temple. When they saw Jerusalem surrounded by armies, they would know that its desolation was near (v 20). It would be time to flee, because Jerusalem's predicted judgement would have arrived, with distress and downfall, and the city would then remain under Gentile occupation until the time of the Gentiles was complete (v 21-24). For Jews, the temple's destruction would seem to be the end of the age. However, Jesus also foresaw a lengthy, though limited, period beyond.

Then he answered their second question, about a preceding sign. He said the signs would be heavenly and earthly upheaval causing great fear, while the Son of Man would be seen coming in power and glory (v 25-28). This calls for careful interpretation. Jesus was not primarily describing his second coming, as many writers assume. He was using apocalyptic imagery to describe spiritual upheaval. Luke indicates the meaning of the apocalyptic language with a quotation from Joel to explain the coming of the Spirit at Pentecost (Acts 2:17-21). The imagery is not meant to be literal, but symbolic. It indicates cosmic upheaval caused by God's intrusion into the world. Jesus was describing in apocalyptic imagery the divine consequences of his resurrection. There would be a radical overthrow of creation's current condition. To see the Son of Man coming in a cloud with power and great glory means to have spiritual recognition of Jesus as God's triumphant king. We need to understand Luke's message that the resurrection of Jesus would usher in the kingdom of God. This would be a new era in which Jesus, as the risen Messiah, the Saviour King, would rule over the world by the gift of the Holy Spirit and the proclamation of the gospel of the kingdom through his witnessing disciples. Luke's second volume, the Book of Acts, describes the initial phase of that period. Jesus said that when these events began, it would be time to stand erect with head held high, because their redemption would be at hand. Jesus was saying that the culmination of his mission in his resurrection and the giving of the Spirit would be the signal for Jerusalem's judgement and the temple's destruction. As sure as sprouting leaves indicated the approach of summer, these events would indicate the approach of God's Kingdom, which would arrive before their generation ended (v 29-33). Jesus' prediction concerning the temple came true in 70 CE.

Jesus ended his discussion by insisting that the disciples must be prayerfully alert so as not to be ashamed before the Son of Man (34-36). What should they pray as they kept watch for the impending crisis? Jesus had already taught them! He had set an example of devotion to prayer, and had instructed them in what to pray with regard to the coming kingdom (11:1-4). Why might they be ashamed before the Son of Man? He had taught them to persist in prayer, so that when the Son of man came he might find faith on the earth (18:1-8). Luke's presentation is consistent in its references to prayer, and shows that Jesus had a specific concern for prayer. He was concerned about prayer for God's coming kingdom!

Luke's focus on the temple, God's "house of prayer", was highlighted by his concluding comment in this section of his account (v 37-38). Jesus taught every day in the temple, with the people enthusiastically coming early in the morning to listen to him.

The Triumph of Jesus: *Suffering and Resurrection* (22:1-24:53)

Jesus' Last Supper (22:1-38). While the Temple leaders plotted Jesus' death with Judas, Jesus made arrangements for celebrating the Passover. His words at the Last Supper emphasised the sacrificial nature of his death. He announced his betrayal, and told his disciples not to act like Gentile kings, but like him, as one who serves, since they were to be "rulers" like him in his coming kingdom. He assured Peter of restoration after his fall, and warned the disciples that their situation was more needy and dangerous than their earlier mission.

In particular, we should notice Jesus' revelation to Peter concerning Peter's trial of faith (v 31-32). Satan made petition ("*asked*") to sift the disciples ("*you*" is plural), and Jesus made intercession ("*prayed*") for Simon ("*you*" is singular) that his faith would not fail. It was a battle of prayer, brought on by the crisis caused by the coming of the kingdom. This means that God is supreme, and controls all things. Satan has to ask for permission, and can only accomplish what God allows. Similarly, Jesus, too, must depend on God's authority in order to save Peter. Jesus did not ask for Peter to be spared from the trial, but to be protected from being overcome by it. The disciples were being sifted, separating wheat from chaff, and Jesus was confident that Peter would survive because of his prayer for him. Knowing that Peter would stumble, yet rise again, Jesus advised him that when he had returned (to faith), he should strengthen his brothers. The whole episode revealed the nature of the spiritual struggle precipitated by the restoration of God's kingdom. God was King. Satan aimed to put faith to the test. Jesus saved by interceding. Prayer had a crucial role in restoring God's kingdom, because it expressed dependence on God's supremacy and purpose.

Jesus' Arrest and Trial (22:39 - 23:35). Jesus spent his final hours of freedom in a strategic vigil of prayer on the Mount of Olives. Luke's account is quite condensed, yet full of meaningful expression. The whole occasion was an experience of deep trial which mirrored in anticipation Jesus' ordeal of crucifixion. Jesus went *"as usual"* to the Mount of Olives, and reached *"the place"* (v 40). Gethsemane is not named, but it is clear that Jesus was following his normal habit of going to a particular spot where it was his custom to stay overnight with his disciples. When they arrived, he urged them to pray so that they would not fall into temptation. He was repeating the last part of the prayer he had taught them (11:4). It was the same as the advice he had given them in his discussion about the destruction of the temple (21:36). At the end of his prayer vigil, he reiterated the advice, and this was the final time before his arrest (v 46). Jesus was pressing upon his followers the imperative of specific prayer in the face of threatening temptation, and he was practising what he was urging them to do. Luke's description of Jesus' experience showed that he, too, was enduring intense trial and praying so as not to fall. Luke made no mention of Jesus' conversation with his three selected disciples as found in the longer versions of Matthew and Mark. Instead, he simply told how Jesus withdrew even from his disciples a short distance in order to pray alone (v 41). Prayer for Jesus was a deep intimate experience with his Father. Luke summarised his prayer concisely (v 42). *"Father, if you are willing, take this cup from me; yet not my will, but yours be done"*. Jesus naturally recoiled from the prospect of drinking the cup of God's judgement for sin, yet deliberately submitted to his Father's will. His prayer revealed the painful experience of temptation, and his dependence on His Father to succeed. In response to his prayer, an angel from heaven appeared to him and strengthened him (v 43). This means that Jesus was conscious of divine help. On the human level, he suffered great anguish and prayed more earnestly, so that his sweat was falling like drops of blood (v 44). It was not the nature of his sweat, but the nature of its falling, which was like drops of blood, and the imagery foreshadowed his subsequent suffering and death. Similarly, when he *"rose"* from prayer was perhaps suggestive of his subsequent resurrection (v 45). Jesus' experience of praying in order not to fall into temptation mirrored his impending experience of crucifixion, and ensured his strength to triumph over the ordeal. It resulted in the coming of God's kingdom! Jesus' prayer vigil set in motion the extraordinary chain of events which followed, on that night, and over the subsequent days, weeks, and years as God's kingdom came and penetrated world affairs, as Luke's two volume account demonstrated. Jesus' praying was unique, as was his mission. Yet his disciples shared in his mission, by likewise praying as he had taught them, and by proclaiming the gospel of the kingdom.

While Jesus was still speaking to his disciples, Judas led an arrest party to the place where Jesus prayed, and betrayed him with a kiss. Jesus calmed his resisting disciples, healed a wounded servant in the arresting group, and rebuked the temple leaders for treating him like a rebel. Later, at the house of the High Priest, Peter denied Jesus three times, and during the night Jesus was subjected to mockery and ill-treatment. At daybreak the Sanhedrin examined and condemned him for his claim to being the Son of God, but took him to Governor Pilate with charges of political subversion. Pilate and Herod became official witnesses to Jesus' innocence. Despite attempts to free Jesus, Pilate yielded to the crowd's preference for the release of Barabbas.

Jesus' Crucifixion (23:26-49). The details in Luke's version of the crucifixion shape the theme he wanted to emphasise. Simon of Cyrene who helped carry the cross behind Jesus illustrated the ideal disciple. The mourning of the women of Jerusalem for a victim on the way to execution was the occasion for a final prophecy from Jesus regarding the fate of Jerusalem. Eventually Jesus was crucified with two others, who in contrast to himself, were really criminals. While Jesus prayed for his executioners, they selfishly cast lots for his clothes. While the crowd and the soldiers mocked his claims to be Christ and King, the inscription over his cross nevertheless declared him to be the King of the Jews. The two executed criminals also formed a contrast with one another, one hurling insults at Jesus while the other was promised salvation in Paradise that same day. Ominous signs in the sky and the Temple formed the backdrop for Jesus' final loud shout of prayerful trust to God before dying peacefully. The centurion gave final witness to Jesus' innocence, and the crowd lamented his death, while his friends watched from the distance.

Several sub-themes were reflected in Luke's carefully crafted presentation. Jesus remained calm, dominant, and resolute throughout all the proceedings. The roles of Judas, Peter, the guards, the Jewish council, Pilate and Herod, and the two crucified criminals were all displayed in brief revealing cameos. Luke's narrative described successive scenes succinctly and vividly to give a clear account of what transpired, using language which often hinted at fuller meaning (such as Simon from Cyrene symbolising discipleship). Of particular interest was his inclusion of two prayers offered by Jesus at the time of his crucifixion. One was at the beginning when Jesus was being crucified (23:34), and the other was at the end when he died (23:46). They are like two bookends to the sombre period of his experience on the cross. Only Luke of the Gospel writers recorded these two utterances by Jesus, and the pattern of his presentation showed the meaning of Jesus' crucifixion.

Jesus' first prayer was uttered against a grim background, at a place called the *"Skull"* (possibly a gruesome nickname for the site of Roman executions), as he was being crucified along with two criminals, while his executioners callously cast lots for his clothes. *"Father, forgive them, for they do not know what they are doing"*. At that moment Jesus was deeply conscious of his Father. Relationship with his Father was his foremost relationship. He was fulfilling his Father's will and purpose. Requesting forgiveness for those who were participants in the ghastly activities was the reason he was there. He had been consistently praying that prayer for a long time, right up to this point. Its inclusion in the prayer he taught his disciples implied as much. Of course, Jesus was not only praying for his immediate executioners, but for all who were responsible for his death. He was including the Jewish and Roman authorities who decided the verdict for his execution, and ultimately the whole world which rebelliously rejected God's kingship.

From a textual point of view, there is a measure of uncertainty about the genuineness of this prayer. The text does not have strong manuscript support. Some important, reliable manuscripts contain it. Other, equally important, manuscripts do not. Was the prayer part of the original script, and then, for some [intentional or accidental] reason left out by a copyist? Or, was it inserted into the original text by a copyist at a later date? It is not possible on a textual basis to be sure. However, when we recognise that the prayer reflects the purpose of Jesus' crucifixion, and is the only detail in Luke's description of Jesus' experience which did, there are grounds for accepting it as part of the original text. Prayer for forgiveness was also typical of Jesus' revealed character and interests. It was typical of his own habits in prayer, and his instructions for his disciples' praying. The inclusion of the prayer was consistent with Luke's interests as well, as shown by his presentation of Jesus until this point. What is especially striking, and surely not merely coincidence, is Luke's record of Stephen's prayer when he died (Acts 7:59-60). He merged Jesus' two prayers on the cross into a single prayer. Most likely Stephen was taking inspiration from Jesus' example, and Luke was deliberately highlighting the fact. In doing so, he was showing that the two prayers of Jesus were effectively one. In fact, the whole experience of Jesus' crucifixion was not merely begun and ended with prayers, but was an experience of continuous prayer. From Jesus' perspective his crucifixion was effectively prayer. Just as his prayer vigil on the Mount of Olives was an experience which mirrored his crucifixion in advance, his actual crucifixion was itself an experience of prayer.

The second prayer brings that out. While Jesus was hanging on the cross, a period of darkness came over the land from the sixth hour until the ninth hour (noon until 3pm). These were the Jewish hours of prayer! Luke gave no other details about this period, except only to explain the cause of the darkness. The sun stopped shining. This was not an eclipse, since there was a new moon at Passover. Probably, the sky simply became overcast. However, Luke gave the impression of something ominous happening. His brief description suggested apocalyptic imagery, and a sense of divine displeasure. This impression was reinforced by a dramatic event which occurred. The curtain in the temple was torn in two. That could not be known at the crucifixion site, and would only be observed by a priest on duty in the temple, at the hour of prayer(!). It was also the hour of the evening sacrifice. Luke was making a theological statement about the significance of the crucifixion. The sacrifice of Jesus was displacing the need for further animal sacrifices, because the way was now open for direct access to God. Luke left this implication unstated, because he was pressing another point. God was beginning his judgement upon the temple. Not only was Jesus' crucifixion the means of obtaining forgiveness for a sinful world, but it was also destruction for God's house of prayer whose purpose was being abused. Jesus had implied judgement for the temple when he had earlier expelled traders from its courts (19:45-46). Although the temple would not be destroyed until 70 CE, Luke was indicating that Jesus' crucifixion began its judgement. Jesus had previously told his disciples this in apocalyptic language (21:25-27). Luke was not describing Jesus' crucifixion experience. He was presenting an explanation of its meaning.

At the end of the three hour period, at the hour of evening prayer, Jesus called out in a loud voice. This was remarkable for someone nearly dead, and suggested a note of triumph. He said, *"Father, into your hands I commit my* spirit". Then he breathed his last, a sudden and composed end. This second prayer of Jesus on the cross was actually a quotation from Psalm 31:5. That psalm was a prayer of David expressing trust in God when opposed by enemy plots and afflictions, and abandoned by friends. Jesus was mindful of his Father, and facing his ordeal in prayerful dependence, fortified by relevant, faith-stirring scriptures.

Jesus' crucifixion historically was a cruel, callous miscarriage of justice. Theologically, it was the culmination of God's plan of grace to save the world, providing undeserved forgiveness for the lost, and imposing judgement upon the wicked. For Jesus personally, it was an intense experience of prayerful intercession before his Father as he fulfilled his mission in trust and obedience.

Jesus' Burial (23:50 – 56). Jesus was buried by a godly member of the Council, observed by Galilean women from among his followers. Their preparations make it clear that Jesus was truly dead.

Jesus' Resurrection (24:1 – 53). The women were first to learn of Jesus' resurrection when they found his tomb empty. The entrance stone was rolled back, the body not there, and two angels declared he had risen as Jesus had told them. The other disciples did not believe their report, and only Peter went to the tomb to confirm their story. Later in the day the risen Jesus accompanied a couple returning to their home in Emmaus. They did not recognise him by his appearance but eventually by the way he broke bread at the table and explained Old Testament Scripture. When they returned to Jerusalem they learned that others had seen him also. Jesus then appeared amongst all his disciples and demonstrated the physical reality of his resurrection. He reminded them of his predictions during his earthly ministry, opened their understanding to Scripture, and gave them the task of preaching repentance and forgiveness to the nations as his divinely empowered witnesses. The Gospel concludes with Jesus' disappearance into heaven, and the disciples remaining in Jerusalem in joyful worship at the temple, God's house of prayer. Luke's Gospel began and ended at the temple.

Prayer in Acts

Following his resurrection, Jesus commissioned his disciples to be witnesses in the mission of taking the Good News "to all nations, beginning from Jerusalem" (Luke 24:47-48, cf. Matthew 28:19-20). The Book of Acts is the account of how the gospel spread beyond the physical and religious boundaries of Judaism to the Gentile world. Its focus is on the ministries of Peter and Paul, reporting virtually nothing about the activities of the other apostles. There are similar emphases as in Luke's Gospel, and the narrative traces the triumph of God's word as it advances to successive new frontiers.

The Book of Acts relates the journey of the spread of the gospel of the kingdom from Jerusalem to Rome. It is helpful to get a bird's eye view of the book's outline to see how carefully Luke composed his account. The narrative focuses primarily on Peter (chapters 1-12) and Paul (chapters 13-28), although is based on a pattern set out by the words of Jesus concerning the role of the Holy Spirit (1:8).

Section	New Frontier	Summary	Key Person	Key Sermon
1:1-5:42	Jerusalem - Jews	5:42	Peter	Ch.2
6:1-7	Transition to new phase	6:7		
6:8-9:31	Judea/Samaria	9:31	Stephen, Philip	Ch.7
9:32-12:24	Antioch	12:24	Peter	Ch.10
12:25-16:5	Asia Minor	15:35,41, 16:5	Paul	Ch.13
16:6-19:20	Europe	19:20	Paul	Ch.17
19:21-28:31	Jerusalem & Rome	28:30-31	Paul	Ch.20,22, 23,24,26

In order to appreciate what Luke reveals about prayer, we need to set his references in context. This is not the place for a full commentary on Acts, but a brief summary provides a framework.

Chapters 1-2 The Good News Explosion

1:1-2 Introduction Luke's Gospel is linked to its sequel Acts. The Gospel was "all that Jesus began to do and to teach", implying that Acts was his continuing activity, by the Holy Spirit in the life of the Church.

1:3-8 Post-Resurrection Ministry For a period of forty days (shades of Israel's Exodus!) the risen Jesus provided his followers with convincing proofs of the resurrection. He taught them about the *"kingdom of God"*. On a significant occasion Jesus told his disciples not to leave Jerusalem, but to wait, because within a few days they would receive the promised baptism of the Holy Spirit. This was the expected mark of the new age. His disciples asked whether this was the time he would be restoring the kingdom to Israel. They still had ideas of a political kingdom, in which they would have positions of authority. Jesus dismissed their curiosity about dates, and told them that they would receive power to become his witnesses. By the Spirit they would bear witness in Jerusalem, Judea and Samaria, and to the ends of the earth. This agenda of the Holy Spirit covered the territory of the ancient kingdoms of Judah and Israel, and beyond. God's kingdom was spiritual, not political and national. The agenda forms the framework of the Book of Acts.

1:9-11 Ascension Description of Jesus' ascension was meant to relate not only the manner of Jesus' final disappearance, but also the theological significance of his ascension to the right hand of God, the place of supreme lordship (cf. 2:32-33). The promise of his return did not indicate the manner of his reappearance, but the fact that at a future point of time and place he would again break out of eternity into time.

1:12-26 The Waiting Community Following the ascension, the waiting disciples engaged in prayer and selected a replacement for Judas to complete the Twelve. When Jesus had prayed on the Mount of Olives prior to his arrest, the disciples had slept because they were exhausted from sorrow (Luke 22:45). After Jesus' ascension, which also took place on the Mount of Olives, the disciples returned to Jerusalem and gathered in an upstairs room where they were staying, and now prayer became their constant shared activity. Since they were waiting for the Holy Spirit, their united prayer was probably requesting the Father to send what he had promised. Jesus had taught them that their Father in heaven would give the Holy Spirit to those who asked him (Luke 11:13). They also prayed for the *"Lord"* to show them who should replace Judas. This was prayer to the risen and ascended Jesus! Jesus had chosen the original apostles (v 2), and now was choosing Judas' replacement (v 24). Jesus was continuing to *"do and to teach"*. It was necessary to complete the Twelve, because they represented the nucleus of God's 'true Israel'.

2:1-13 Baptism of the Spirit Description of the coming of the Holy Spirit highlights the effects on those who experienced and witnessed his presence. There were sight and sound sensations, manifestations of phenomena traditionally associated with the presence of God (fire and wind). There was an atmosphere of holy excitement, and a miracle of communication. The phenomenon of speaking in other tongues was a familiar religious experience of inspired ecstasy known as glossolalia. What was unique on this occasion was its suddenness and unexpectedness, the accompanying manifestations, the spontaneous outburst by the whole company, and the declarations (ejaculations?) of God's wonders in recognisable languages. The gathered community had been enveloped by an unseen dynamic presence. The event fulfilled the promise of John the Baptist (Luke 3:16, etc.), and was described by Luke with the intention of paralleling the births of the Spirit-filled Jesus in the Gospel and the Spirit-filled Church in Acts. It probably also compared with the giving of the Law at Sinai (Exodus 19), and was a reversal of the Tower of Babel experiment (Genesis 11:1-9). By the miracle of communication which manifested the coming of the Spirit, the gospel was proclaimed to the whole Jewish world and beyond.

2:14-36 Peter's Sermon Peter's explanation declared that the prophecy of Joel (Joel 2:28-32) was now fulfilled. The era of the Spirit had arrived. Peter went on to tell of Jesus' life, death and resurrection, and supported his claims of resurrection by appealing to the Psalms and apostolic witness. The resurrection was the grounds for recognising Jesus' ascension, sovereignty, and identity as Messiah. This was the first of the key addresses which Luke records throughout Acts marking each stage of his story.

The last sentence in Joel's prophecy is worth our attention. "*And everyone who calls on the name of the Lord will be saved*" (v 21). Joel was taking up the familiar Old Testament expression of those who call on the name of the LORD to identify those who would experience the salvation which would come in the last days. That familiar expression now took on a specific focus. Peter was proclaiming that the last days had arrived. Those who were convicted by his preaching asked what they should do. Peter replied, "*Repent and be baptised, every one of you* **in the name of Jesus Christ** *for the forgiveness of your sins. And you will receive the gift of the Holy Spirit. The promise is for you and your children and for all who are far off –* **for all whom the Lord our God will call**". The familiar "calling on the name of the Lord" has undergone subtle variations. Those who will be saved are those who, by repentance and baptism, have called Jesus "*Lord*". This is because the Lord has called them. The title "*Lord*" is applied to both Jesus (v 36) and God (v 39). The LORD in the Old Testament became identified with Jesus! The "*call*" for salvation is a two way appeal, made to God (v 21) and by God (v 39). Calling on the name of Jesus in recognition of him as Lord will become a defining expression of Jesus' followers.

2:37-47 The Church is Born Peter's listeners were struck with conviction, and urged to repent and be baptised in the name of Jesus to receive forgiveness and the Holy Spirit. Three thousand did (v 37-41). The new community founded on the resurrection of Jesus as an extension of the Apostolic band, entered by repentance, confession and baptism, was characterised by a devoted willingness to learn from the teachings of the Apostles and to share in communal fellowship. This new fellowship of the Spirit was the nucleus of a renewed Israel, marked by generosity and joy within, and respect from without (vs.42-47).

Two features of the community's fellowship especially mentioned were "*the breaking of bread*" and "*the prayers*" (v 42). "*The breaking of bread*" indicated shared meals, but probably especially implied commemoration of the Lord's Supper as they maintained a sense of the living Lord in their midst. "*The prayers*" seem to indicate formal sessions. These would include the hours of prayer at the temple (3:1), and perhaps regular gatherings of the new community. The prayer Jesus taught his disciples (11:1-4) would be a natural basis for their prayers, supplemented by psalms and scriptures as they followed the example of Jesus.

Chapters 3-5 The Good News in Jerusalem

3:1-26 Healing of the Cripple A healing miracle in the name of Jesus gave Peter opportunity to witness to the resurrection of Jesus and explain its implications for the Jews. He spoke with courage, confidence, and clarity. The miracle identified the new movement with God who was held to be the healer, and showed Jesus to be still active. The occasion was an example of the impact of the new-born church in Jerusalem. Notably this miracle occurred when Peter and John were making their way to the temple at the evening hour of prayer, 3pm. That was the hour when Jesus had died! Jesus' death and resurrection were having a powerful effect on the apostles' devotion to prayer and their boldness in witnessing.

4:1-31 Trial and Release Many of the population believed, but Peter and John were arrested. This provided them with another opportunity to bear witness, this time before the authorities (v 1-22). After their release, the church community became further united and inspired to speak God's word boldly (v 23-31). A major influence on their outlook was collective prayer. Luke's account highlighted its importance, and plainly revealed their outlook.

After their release, Peter and John returned to their new community and reported on their experience before the Sanhedrin. The community turned to God in prayer. In typical terms from the scriptures, they addressed him as "*Sovereign Lord*", the creator of everything. They confessed that God had spoken by the Holy Spirit through the words of David, which they quoted from the opening verses of Psalm 2. The verses depicted the nations and rulers of the earth rebelliously raging against the Lord and his Anointed One. Words from v 7 in this psalm were spoken by the voice from heaven at Jesus' baptism, calling him "*my Son*", and therefore identifying him as the Anointed One. The apostles' community now applied the verses directly to the conspiracy which rejected Jesus. They identified Herod and Pontius Pilate together with the Gentiles and Jews as the fulfilment of the conspirators in the psalm, doing what God's power and will had previously decided. Then they appealed to the Lord to consider the Sanhedrin's threats against them, and to enable them to speak boldly. They did not ask for divine protection to keep them safe, but for courage to proclaim God's word, and for divine approval of their witness with healings, signs, and wonders. Their prayer was practical and specific, based on scripture and the reality of their experience of the death and resurrection of Jesus. They were only concerned for the advance of God's kingdom. After they prayed, their meeting place was shaken, either literally, or figuratively in terms of their consciousness. Once more (as at Pentecost, 2:4) they were all filled with the Holy Spirit, evidenced by them speaking God's word boldly.

4:32-5:11 Unity & Disunity in the Church The developing Church continued to be marked by unity and its practical expression in the sharing of material goods. Community solidarity was a key to the power in which the Apostles gave witness to the resurrection of Jesus. The two stories of Barnabas (v 36-37) and Ananias and Saphira (5:1-11) show the working of the Holy Spirit inspiring self-sacrifice and mutual dependence, and the activity of the spirit of evil which could infect members of the church and turn even a good impulse into an opportunity for self-glorification and deception. The story of Ananias and Saphira shows the supernatural power which was working in the church, and the first fall from the ideal of love and sincerity in the new community. It parallels Adam's fall in the beginning of creation (Genesis 3), and Achan's greed at the beginning of Israel's entering the Promised Land (Joshua 7).

5:12-42 Further Persecution Another summary segment (v 12-16) highlighted the impact and respect which the new community was having. Then there was further persecution from outside (v 17ff). The Sanhedrin was no doubt becoming alarmed at the growing number of followers of Jesus, meeting as they were in the very precincts of the Temple. So the Apostles were arrested, miraculously released by an "angel of the Lord", arrested again, but then released after a flogging, only to continue their teaching. Nothing could stop the spread of the "good news"! When again arrested they boldly declared their loyalty to God rather than men, and bore testimony to Jesus' resurrection. They found a surprising ally on the Council in Gamaliel, who did not support them or their views, but who cautioned his fellow councillors against the possibility of opposing the work of God. The flogging which the Apostles received did not deter them, but rather gave them a sense of privilege to be so identified with Jesus (cf. Luke 9:21-27, 14:27).

Chapters 6:1-9:31 The Good News Scatters Through Judea & Samaria

6:1-8:1 The Hellenists
Transition, 6:1-7. Division over food distribution between Hebrew and Hellenistic widows threatened to disturb the fellowship's unity and distract the Twelve from their primary task of prayer and preaching. Appointment of the Seven resolved the situation, and ensured the harmonious inclusion of the Hellenistic wing of the Church. As it had been with Jesus, prayer was a priority for the Twelve. Like him, they were maintaining fellowship with the Father and awareness of the Spirit's leading. Prayer was associated with their responsibility for preaching the gospel of the kingdom, and, as it had with Jesus, took precedence in that task. Prayer was ensuring their complete dependence on God's pre-eminence, purpose, and power. When the Seven were selected, the apostles prayed for them and laid their hands on

them. The laying of hands on them associated them publicly with the Twelve, as delegates extending their ministry. We must not overlook Luke's consistent stress on the role of prayer in the coming of the kingdom. It is the earthly counterpart to the heavenly gift of the Holy Spirit, which is the essence of the presence of the kingdom.

Stephen, 6:8-8:1. One of the Seven was Stephen, who proved to be an able debater for the gospel. He preached in the Hellenistic synagogues, and was condemned for speaking against the Law and the Temple. His views and activities drove a wedge between Judaism and the New Way, and paved the way for the later ministry of Paul (who was perhaps a member of the Cilician synagogue [cf. v 9]). Stephen defended his convictions before the authorities, exposing the tendency of Israel to resist God's ways, and accused them of doing the same by killing Jesus. The Council members were furious, but then a final statement by Stephen tipped them over the edge.

While full of the Holy Spirit, Stephen saw the glory of God with Jesus standing at his right hand. He told his opponents, "*I see heaven open and the Son of Man standing at the right hand of God*". This was reminiscent of similar claims by Jesus when he stood on trial before this same tribunal (Luke 22:69). It was the final catalyst which sealed their verdict against him. What was striking about Stephen's statement was that he was the only person other than Jesus himself to refer to Jesus as the Son of Man. The expression was not so much a title, as Jesus' own self-designation as representative of the human race. The Council reacted violently to Stephen's declaration, and stoned him to death, while a young man Saul looked on.

We have already discussed the similarities of Stephen's prayer at the time of his death to that of Jesus upon the cross. Like Jesus, there were two aspects to his prayer. He prayed for his spirit to be received, and for the sin of his executioners not to be held against them (7:60). However, there were several major differences. The order of the two aspects was reversed. Before Stephen reached the point of death, while his executioners were still stoning him, he prayed, "*Lord Jesus, receive my spirit*". He was expressing his willingness to die, without despair. His prayer was addressed to the Lord Jesus rather than the Father, demonstrating his conviction that Jesus lived and guaranteed access to God's presence. It was the second aspect of his prayer which he uttered loudly before his final breath. As the stones pummelled him, he fell on his knees and cried out, "*Lord, do not hold this sin against them*". Still speaking to the risen Jesus, with prayer for forgiveness for his enemies on his lips, he fell asleep. This euphemistic expression indicated a peaceful (despite the violence extinguishing his life) and temporary (because of resurrection hope) death. He entered eternal life in prayer.

8:1-4 The Scattered Church The outbreak of persecution against the Church in Jerusalem was the Holy Spirit's catalyst for the outworking of his agenda to spread the word to Judea and Samaria (cf. 1:8).

8:5-40 Philip's Ministry Philip, one of the Seven, evangelised in Samaria with fruitful response, and then travelled to the south west of Judea (directed by an "angel of the Lord") where he was used in the conversion of an Ethiopian official. Samaria was the territory of the former northern kingdom of Israel. Judea was the territory of the former southern kingdom of Israel. Together they formed the territory ruled over by King David. Philip represented the believers who scattered from Jerusalem and preached the word wherever they went. His mission to Samaria represented not only geographical advance, but a crossing of racial, religious, and cultural boundaries. Simon the Sorcerer's initial belief and baptism seem to be superficial, and Peter's rebuke led to a better response. The contrast between Simon the sorcerer and Simon Peter contrasts mere magic with the reality of God's power.

When the apostles in Jerusalem heard about the response in Samaria, they sent Peter and John to lay hands on them (touch them!) and pray for them so that they might receive the Holy Spirit. As representatives of the apostles, they were making clear that the whole Church participated in this outreach. In particular, Peter was involved. He had a key role at each stage of the gospel's advance across cultural boundaries. He had taken the lead at Pentecost when the Spirit came upon Jews from both the homeland and abroad at Jerusalem. Now he was prominent in the transition to the Samaritans. He will also be the first apostle to participate in the Holy Spirit coming upon Gentiles (chapter 10). Although Luke did not record Jesus' words at the time of Peter's confession of Jesus as Messiah that he would give Peter the keys of the kingdom of heaven, as Matthew (16:19) did, he certainly made it clear that Peter was a "key" figure in the kingdom's coming. The coming of the Holy Spirit was the evidence of the presence of God's kingdom. Luke did not describe any manifestations of the Spirit among the Samaritans, as appeared among the Jews at Pentecost. Yet he made it obvious that something observable occurred (v 18). When the Spirit first came upon the Gentiles, there was again observable manifestation, just like that at Pentecost (10:46). Outward manifestations of the Spirit marked each stage of the Spirit's agenda reached (see 1:8). Luke also made it obvious that prayer was associated with the coming of the Spirit, as Jesus had taught his disciples originally. The effectiveness of prayer was further highlighted by Simon's panic-stricken request for Peter to pray that he might not experience dire consequences for his sin.

The Ethiopian was excluded from full privileges under Judaism, not only because of racial difference, but because he was a eunuch (cf. Deuteronomy 23:1). The early Church saw in the passage he was reading (Isaiah 53) the sufferings of Jesus, which Philip explained to him. The story is an excellent example of evangelism: preaching Jesus as the fulfillment of scripture, majoring on his sufferings, and calling for faith and repentance shown in baptism.

9:1-31 The Conversion of Saul Saul was a Hellenistic Jew, from Tarsus in Cilicia, a Pharisee, who had trained under Gamaliel in Jerusalem, and was antagonistic towards the church and to the idea of the Messiah welcoming people on the fringe of the Law. He persecuted the church at Jerusalem (8:3), and elsewhere (9:2). His conversion was one of the most significant events in the whole history of the Apostolic age. It was an amazing example of the gospel's power and acceptance. The outstanding enemy of the Church was himself arrested by the direct action of the risen Lord, to become an outstanding ambassador of the Church.

In his rage against the followers of Jesus, Saul obtained letters of authority from the high priest to arrest anyone belonging to "The Way" whom he found in Damascus. This name now identified the movement of those who followed Jesus as Lord, indicating their way of life (or way of salvation, or way of God). As he drew near to Damascus, a blazing light from heaven suddenly flashed around him, causing him to fall to the ground. He later said that it was about noon (an hour of prayer), that the light was brighter than the sun, that his companions saw it, and also fell to the ground (22:6-9, 26:12-14). He heard the voice of Jesus speaking to him by name, asking why he was persecuting him. To persecute Jesus' followers (his "body") was to persecute Jesus (the "head"). Jesus told him to enter the city where he would be told what he must do. Blinded by the light he had to be led by hand. For three days he was blind, and neither ate nor drank anything. In Damascus there was a man named Ananias. The Lord called to him in a vision, and gave him directions to go to where Saul was in order to restore his sight. Jesus indicated that Saul was praying, and while doing so had seen Ananias come to him to restore his sight. Understandably, Ananias, who knew about Saul's reputation, and intention for coming to Damascus, was very wary. However, the Lord overcame Ananias' reluctance by informing him that Saul had been chosen for a special task. He was to bear the name of Jesus before Gentiles and their kings, and before the Jews, and would suffer much on behalf of Jesus' name. Ananias went, and laid his hands on Saul so that he might see again and be filled with the Holy Spirit. Saul's sight was restored immediately, he was baptised, then he took food to regain his strength.

Saul's experience was dramatic and abnormal. Any conversion to faith in Jesus as Messiah and Lord is a supernatural experience. It requires a radical change of heart and mind to be brought about by the Holy Spirit. Divine revelation brings inner enlightenment. Saul's experience included the typical elements of conversion, however on a dramatic scale. His experience of brilliant light, blindness, regained sight, and visionary knowledge was a heightened and much more sensational version of what occurs for anyone coming to faith. In fact, his experience illustrated the conversion phenomenon. However, his extreme, abnormal experience was necessary, for several reasons. It was necessary because of his extreme antagonism towards Jesus and his followers. It was needed to convince him unshakeably of the truth of Jesus. It was especially needed to prepare him for his apostolic mission. Not only had he not had the privilege of the Twelve to have been discipled by Jesus, but his mission was to be the apostle to the Gentiles. He was to take the gospel to Jews and Gentiles, and spearhead the union of Jews and Gentiles in the new community of the Spirit. Saul was well chosen for his task. He was a Jew who was well versed in the Law, and he was brought up as a Roman citizen in a Gentile environment and education. He was a suitable envoy for his appointed role. However, his conversion encounter with the living Christ was the essential qualification to equip him for his task. Furthermore, his special calling involved much suffering, so his privileged experience of God's grace which chose him kept him going. The reality of his strange experience was evidenced by the reality of his conversion, and by his zealous devotion to his mission, for his lifetime.

It is the role of prayer in his conversion which is important. It was his spontaneous and characteristic response to his encounter with the risen Lord on the road (v 11). Luke does not indicate the content of his prayer. He simply indicates that in his three days state of blindness and fasting as he waited for further instructions after his earth-shattering event, he engaged in prayer. Inevitably his mind would be full of his experience of Jesus, his previous views of Jesus and hearsay comments about him, and his scriptures and knowledge of the Law. During his prayerful pondering he received a revelation, presumably from the Lord himself who reported it to Ananias. The details were clear. He saw a man, named Ananias, come and place his hands on him to restore his sight. Saul's praying was a two-way experience. He received revelation as well as expressed himself. Saul's situation was unique. Some of the revelation for him was given to Ananias in a vision, probably at a time when he was at prayer. What Luke has highlighted is the key role of prayer. Prayer is an important ingredient in the mix of matters such as conversion, the coming of God's kingdom, receiving the Spirit, and the mission of God's salvation for the world.

Chapters 9:32-12:25 The Good News Spreads to Syria

9:32-11:18 Peter's Ministry Transition from the mission of Peter to the mission of Paul focused on strategic experiences of Peter.

Two Miracles, 9:32-43. Peter's travels to Lydda and Joppa on the coast were part of the movement throughout Judea and Samaria, and the miracles he performed revealed the accompanying power of the Holy Spirit. They were remarkably reminiscent of miracles performed by Jesus in Peter's hometown Capernaum (cf. Luke 5:17-26, 8:40-56), and were evidence of the presence of the risen Lord.

Conversion of Cornelius, 10:1-48. The spreading gospel now crossed another cultural boundary. It crossed the major divide between Jews and Gentiles, and extended God's kingdom beyond the people of Israel. This giant step was taken in the city of Caesarea, which was mainly Gentile in population, and was virtually the Roman capital in Israel. The length of Luke's account indicated the importance of the event. Peter was the apostle involved, although the outreach to Gentiles was initiated by God. A conspicuous feature in the new development was prayer. While a God-fearing centurion called Cornelius was praying at the Jewish evening hour of prayer (3pm, the hour when Jesus died) he had a vision (v 1-8). In the vision he saw an angel of God who told him to send for Peter from Joppa. God-fearing Gentiles adopted the Jewish practices of praying and giving alms (v 2). They were showing their love for God and for their neighbour. The angel told Cornelius that his prayers and gifts had been accepted as a memorial offering before God, a virtual sacrifice. The following day, Peter also had a vision while he was praying at noon, just as Cornelius' servants were approaching the city (v 9-20). Prayer at noon was not a requirement, but very devout Jews liked to pray three times a day - morning (9am), noon, and evening (3pm). Peter's devotion had become heightened since Jesus' resurrection and ascension. He was hungry at the time, waiting for his meal, and he fell into a trance. He had a vision of a sheet being let down from heaven to earth, containing a range of ritually unclean creatures. He heard a voice commanding him to kill and eat, which confronted his religious scruples and prejudices. He replied to the speaker, calling him "Lord", and expressed his reluctance. The speaker told him not to call anything impure which God had made clean. The vision occurred three times. When the visitors from Cornelius arrived, the Spirit informed him of their presence, and told him to go with them. The angel seen in Cornelius' vision, the voice heard in Peter's vision, and Peter's consciousness of the Spirit's prompting were special communications to demonstrate the kingly oversight of the risen Christ, and to convince Peter (and the church) to take this radical new step. Peter's experience persuaded him to respond to Cornelius' invitation. He went and entered the house of Cornelius and proclaimed Christ to him (v 21-43). Peter began by publicly stating that God had shown him that he should not call anyone impure, despite Jewish Law forbidding association with Gentiles. Cornelius explained his own experience which prompted him to invite Peter. Then he declared that they were now gathered in the presence of God to listen to what the Lord commanded Peter to tell them. Consciousness of God's reality and presence was marked. Peter firstly acknowledged his own new conviction. God shows no favouritism, but accepts from every nation people who fear him and behave righteously. Secondly, he affirmed the message of good news of peace through Jesus Christ whom God had anointed (had made Messiah) with the Holy Spirit and power, which he presumed they knew. While he was speaking, the Holy Spirit fell on Peter's listeners (v 44-46). Jewish disciples who were present heard them "speaking in tongues" and praising God just as Jews did at Pentecost. Likewise, as at Pentecost Peter had instructed Jewish believers to be baptised in the name of Jesus, so now he commanded the Gentile believers to do the same (v 47-48). Luke's account thus showed that Peter, as well as Paul, engaged in reaching Gentiles.

Confirmation by the Church, 11:1-18. The circumcision party challenged Peter about eating with Gentiles. Baptism of the Gentiles was not questioned, since proselyte baptism was common. But the circumcision party required Gentile converts to submit to the full demands of Jewish Law. Peter defended his actions by telling about his experience. He told about his unusual vision while he was praying, and what happened when he went to Caesarea and preached. He was accompanied by six brothers, who could vouch for his story as witnesses. The Church recognised God's initiative, and his granting repentance unto life to Gentiles.

The whole remarkable episode launched the church into a broadening of its mission. The gospel of Jesus Christ was for the world. God's dramatic action at Caesarea swept away centuries-long racial prejudice. And his dealings with the central characters in the event took place in the environment of prayer!

11:19-30 The Church at Antioch Meantime, the preaching efforts of the scattered church throughout Palestine reached as far as Phoenicia, Cyprus, and Antioch (in Syria), including Gentiles in Antioch. Barnabas and Saul became involved in the work at Antioch, where disciples were first called "Christians". Prophecy about an impending famine prompted the believers at Antioch to establish a relief fund for the Jewish church, and this was to become a major feature for liaison between Gentile and Jewish communities of the church.

12:1-24 Further Persecution at Jerusalem King Herod's efforts to destroy the church at Jerusalem by executing James and arresting Peter were thwarted by Peter's miraculous release (by an "angel of the Lord") in answer to prayer. This was Herod Agrippa I, nephew of the Herod before whom Jesus had appeared (Luke 23:7-12). He would have been well known to Luke's Roman aristocratic readers. His ostentatious behaviour and miserable death were confirmed in the writings of pro-Roman Jewish historian Josephus. The occasion was Passover, and the whole story was suggestive of similarities with the sufferings and resurrection of Jesus. The incident highlighted the strategic effect of prayer, and quietly removed Peter from the centre of Luke's narrative.

Peter's miraculous rescue was attributed to divine intervention in response to the church's praying. Herod had already had James the brother of John put to death (with the sword, the Roman method of execution). He arrested Peter with the intention of bringing him to trial after Passover. He made sure of his custody by assigning four squads of four soldiers to guard him. Two guards were attached to him by chains, and sentries stood at entrances along the way into his cell. The church at large, however, prayed fervently for him. The night before his trial Peter was awakened by an "angel of the Lord" and a bright light in his cell. This was language to indicate divine intervention. The "angel" guided Peter to freedom outside the prison. Inexplicably his handcuffs fell off his wrists without disturbing his guards, he walked past two sentries unhindered, and the main prison gate opened automatically. Peter thought he was seeing a vision until he found himself alone in the street. His experience was like receiving an inner revelation of divine intervention, which resulted in being outwardly real. He went to the house of Mary, the mother of John Mark, where people were gathered to pray for him. A humorous scene depicted his reception, emphasising the unexpectedness of his escape. Excited Rhoda forgot to open the door to him, and others did not believe that it was really him. They thought it was his "angel" (a vision of a protective messenger from God). Although they were praying for Peter, probably it was for his release at trial, not escape from prison. Luke's account made it quite clear that Peter's release was unexpected and unnatural, yet prayer was a contributing factor. Prayer did not accomplish his escape. God answered their prayer with a powerful reminder of his triumph over death at a previous Passover. His answer was a demonstration of his kingly authority over earthly affairs and rulers, by a divinely enabled escape from death. He had not prevented the martyrdom of James. Neither would he stamp out hostile persecution against his church. However, Peter's undeniable and inexplicable escape was proof of God's kingdom's presence and power. In the morning the soldiers were perplexed at Peter's disappearance. A thorough search and an interrogation of the guards failed to provide an explanation. Herod had the guards executed. Some time later, Herod Agrippa appeared in royal regalia at an official function in Caesarea and was acclaimed as a god. He did not resist the praise, and failed to give honour to God. Suddenly he suffered severe pains, which led quickly to his death. Luke gave his interpretation of the incident. *"An angel of the Lord struck him down, and he was eaten by worms and died"*. He meant that Agrippa experienced divine judgement, and deserved an unpleasant end. By connecting the stories of Agrippa's death and Peter's escape, Luke was implying that both events demonstrated the presence of God's kingdom, and the outcome of dependant prayer.

"The word of God continued to increase and spread" (v 24).

Chapters 12:25-16:5 The Good News in Asia Minor

12:25-13:3 The Church at Antioch When Barnabas and Saul completed their relief mission to Jerusalem, they returned to Antioch, with John Mark accompanying them. Luke's account shifted focus now from Peter to Paul, who was originally known by his Hebrew name Saul. There were several prophets and teachers in the church at Antioch. In addition to Barnabas and Saul, three others are mentioned, Simeon, Lucius, and Manaen. Of interest to Luke's Roman aristocratic readers was Manaen, who was brought up with Herod the tetrarch. Under the inspiration of the Holy Spirit, in an ethos of worship and fasting, Barnabas and Saul were directed by the Holy Spirit, probably through a prophetic message, to be set apart to a new special work. After fasting and prayer, and the laying on of hands, they were sent off. The purpose of prayer would have been to request God's will to be accomplished in their mission. There are not many references to prayer in the remainder of the book, although its practice and priority should be taken for granted.

13:4-12 Mission to Cyprus Cyprus was the first natural port of call from Seleucia, and was the homeland of Barnabas (4:36). They preached to Jews in Salamis, following the policy of preaching the gospel to the Jews first. Then they made their way to Paphos, the centre of Roman government, where Saul took the initiative to deal with a sorcerer called Bar Jesus, and from this point on Saul acted as leader, and became known as Paul (his Roman name).

13:13-52 Pisidian Antioch Paul's party crossed over to Asia Minor and, after an apparently short stay at Perga, went up to Pisidian Antioch, although John Mark returned to Jerusalem. Paul spoke in the synagogue, and proclaimed Jesus as the fulfillment of Israel's history and scriptures. Initially the Jews showed interest, but a week later jealousy of Paul's popularity precipitated a change of mood. So Paul announced that he would take the word to the Gentiles, citing Isaiah 49:6 to support his action. The Gentiles were delighted and responsive, but the Jews incited persecution and expelled them from the region.

14:1-28 Ministry in Asia Minor From then on the mission moved through various cities of Asia Minor, and saw a movement towards focusing mainly upon Gentiles. At *Iconium* (v 1-5) there was response among Jews and Gentiles and they enjoyed a lengthy period of ministry, until unbelieving Jews plotted with Gentiles to stir up hostility. They moved on to *Lystra* and *Derbe* (v 6-20), where at Lystra the crowd firstly thought they were gods when they healed a cripple, then stoned Paul when Jewish antagonists from Antioch and Iconium incited them. He managed to survive and left for Derbe, where he won many disciples. Paul and Barnabas then returned to Antioch (in Syria) through the cities where they had been, consolidating the disciples as they went (v 21-28). In particular they appointed elders in each church, and committed them to the Lord with *"prayer and fasting"*. The purpose of such prayer would be to request God's enabling for the elders, and God's will to be done through them.

15:1-41 Conference at Jerusalem A sharp dispute at Antioch prompted a conference with the Apostles over the issue. Former Pharisees insisted that Gentile converts needed to be circumcised and obey the Jewish Law (v 1-5). As the Apostles and elders discussed this demand, Peter, Barnabas and Paul reported what they had witnessed concerning the gospel among Gentiles (v 6-11). Eventually James (brother of Jesus and apparent leader at Jerusalem) expressed the conviction that circumcision of Gentiles was not required, only rejection of idolatrous practices (v 12-21). This conclusion effectively severed the Church from Judaism, and opened the door widely to the Gentiles. A letter explaining the resolution of the Conference to the church at Antioch was dispatched through Paul and Barnabas (v 22-35). Later Paul and Barnabas planned a return visit to the churches they had established, but parted company over John Mark, who had deserted on the first trip. Barnabas and Mark returned to Cyprus, and Paul took Silas to the churches of Asia Minor (v 36-41).

16:1-5 Timothy Joins Paul and Silas Paul returned to Derbe and Lystra where he had founded a church on his first trip. Timothy, the son of a believing Jewish mother and a Greek father, was a young convert who was well regarded by believers at Lystra and nearby Iconium. Paul invited him to join him as another travelling companion. He arranged for Timothy to be circumcised for the sake of local Jews. Paul was not being inconsistent with the policy about circumcision not being a requirement for Gentile believers, but pragmatic for the purpose of evangelising unbelieving Jews. As they travelled from town to town, they delivered the decisions of the Jerusalem Conference. Luke concluded this phase of his account with a typical progress report that the churches were strengthened in the faith and daily grew numerically.

Chapters 16:6-19:20 The Good News Crosses to Europe

16:1-10 The Call to Macedonia Paul and his party travelled into new territory in the regions of Phrygia, Galatia, Mysia, Bithynia, and Asia guided by the Holy Spirit. The unusual phrase *Spirit of Jesus* (v 7) emphasised that Jesus himself by his Spirit was guiding the progress of the gospel. A vision given to Paul at Troas of *a man from Macedonia* begging for their help convinced him that God was calling them into Europe.

16:11-40 Philippi Paul and his companions made their way to Philippi where Lydia of Thyatira, a proselyte to Jewish beliefs, was the first to respond to the Gospel (v 11-15). Significantly, this occurred at a *"place of prayer"*, emphasised by Luke who mentioned it twice (v 13, 16). Because Paul exorcised a *spirit of divination* from a slave girl, he and Silas were charged before the authorities for causing a public disturbance, and were stripped, flogged, and imprisoned (v 16-24). However, God intervened with an earthquake, and eventually the gaoler and his household members were baptised (v 25-34). Paul insisted that the authorities escort them from the city because they had treated him unjustly, and without respecting his Roman citizenship (v 35-40). This was a fruitful start for the gospel in its first endeavour in Macedonia, after crossing into Europe. But notice this. The earthquake occurred at midnight when, astonishingly, considering their appalling and unjust ordeal, Paul and Silas were *"praying and singing hymns to God"* (v 25)! This was Luke's third reference to prayer in regard to the first gospel campaign in Europe. He was making a strong point of highlighting the role of prayer in the gospel's progress.

17:1-15 Thessalonica and Berea Paul went to Thessalonica where he successfully won converts among both Jews and Gentile God-fearers, including a significant number of leading women (v 1-4). Trouble arose from Jewish sources which resulted in Paul's host Jason and some other brothers being charged with treason and having to pay a bond to keep the peace (v 5-9). Paul and Silas escaped to Berea and campaigned fruitfully in the synagogue, reaching Jews and both Greek women and men, until Jews from Thessalonica came and stirred up trouble, causing Paul to travel on to Athens (v 10-15).

17:16-34 Athens When Paul reached Athens, he addressed the council on the Areopagus, and preached about *Jesus and the Resurrection*. His speech shows how he presented the Gospel to cultured pagans, referring to their own philosophical ideas to gain their attention. Some listeners scorned him, others responded more positively, wanting to learn more, and some actually believed.

18:1-28 Corinth Paul's ministry at Corinth was productive and lengthy, working with Aquila and Priscilla out of a home base. They initially focused on the synagogue, and, after some opposition, the ruler of the synagogue, with his family and others, became believers and were baptized. In a vision the Lord assured Paul of personal protection and of successful ministry. He eventually left Corinth and set out for his home Church in Syria, accompanied by Priscilla and Aquila, whom he left at Ephesus. He travelled to Antioch via Caesarea and the Church at Jerusalem. Later he set off again to consolidate his young churches in Galatia and Phrygia. Meanwhile Apollos arrived in Ephesus, was instructed privately by Priscilla and Aquila, and then went to [Corinth in] Achaia where he exercised a very valuable pastoral and public debating ministry.

19:1-20 Ephesus Ephesus was the main city of the Roman province of Asia, renowned for its famous temple of the goddess Artemis. When Paul arrived there he informed a group of disciples, who only knew of John's baptism, about the coming of Jesus. They were then baptised in the name of the Lord Jesus and received the Holy Spirit, shown in the manifestation of tongues and prophecy. The incident parallels the experiences at Jerusalem (chapter 2) and at Caesarea (chapter 10), signifying the formation of the nucleus of the Church at Ephesus which would be a base for Gentile mission. Paul's fruitful teaching ministry and displays of divine power had a profound impact throughout the city.

Chapters 19:21-23:35 The Good News Faces Antagonists

19:21-20:12 Setting Out for Rome After reaching this highpoint of success, Paul set his sights on a new goal. He decided to return via Macedonia and Achaia to Jerusalem, and then travel to Rome. He was temporally delayed by a riot sparked by the gospel's threat to the lucrative industry surrounding the worship of Artemis. He preached extensively throughout Macedonia and then spent three months in Greece. Thwarted by a Jewish plot from sailing directly to Syria, he returned through Macedonia and then Troas, where he restored a young man called Eutychus to life.

20:13-38 Farewell to Ephesus Paul was in a hurry to reach Jerusalem before Pentecost, but at Miletus he sent for the Ephesian elders in order to say farewell to them, perhaps for the last time. He made a moving speech to them, which was distinctive in Acts. It was his only address to Christians. He recalled his service and sorrows in the face of Jewish hostility, and stated that he was off to Jerusalem under the Spirit's compulsion, despite warnings about prison and hardship ahead. He set no value on his own life, but was compelled to complete his ministry of testifying to the Gospel. He had proclaimed to them God's whole saving plan and purpose. They must now guard themselves and the Church against harmful false teachers, relying on God and his Word to build them up and ensure their inheritance. Like him they should not take financial benefit from anyone, but support themselves and others, especially the weak, remembering Jesus' words, "*It is more blessed to give than to receive*". The speech was highly important. It represented the conclusion of his ministry in Asia as he prepared to move in another direction. He was passing over responsibility for the future to his converts. Then he knelt down with all of them and prayed. His posture and action expressed humble dependence on God for the future progress of the kingdom, both with the elders in Asia and with his own uncertain prospects. As he parted ways with them, they gave him an affectionate and tearful farewell.

21:1-26 Arrival at Jerusalem Paul's party sailed quickly to Tyre, by-passing Cyprus. Paul's haste, in the face of warnings, showed that, like his Master (Luke 9:51), he had set his face to go to Jerusalem to fulfil a God-given destiny, fully aware of the cost. At Caesarea they stayed in the home of Philip, then, despite prophetic warnings and appeals from friends, pressed on to Jerusalem. They were warmly received, and their report on their mission amongst Gentiles gladly heard. Paul sponsored four men taking vows to show that he upheld Jewish customs for Jews, and joined them for purification (after having travelled through Gentile lands).

21:27-22:21 Under Arrest Some Asian Jews saw Paul in the temple, and stirred up the crowd against him. They made accusation that he had violated their temple by bringing Greeks into forbidden areas. Roman troops rushed to quell the riot, and they had to carry Paul out. He was granted permission to address the crowd, and told the story of his conversion on the road to Damascus and his commission to go to the Gentiles.

22:22-23:11 Before the Sanhedrin The crowd erupted in rage at mention of Gentiles. The commander withdrew and prepared to flog Paul, until Paul revealed that he was a Roman citizen, and so legally protected. When brought before the Sanhedrin, Paul announced that he was a Pharisee on trial for his beliefs in the resurrection, sparking a violent dispute between Pharisees and Sadducees. Troops had to forcibly remove him. The Lord assured Paul by night that he would bear witness at Rome just as he had in Jerusalem.

23:12-35 Transfer to Caesarea Paul's nephew exposed a plot by Jewish zealots to kill Paul, so a military guard escorted him to Governor Felix at Caesarea. Felix agreed to give a hearing when Paul's accusers arrived.

Acts 24-28 The Good News Reaches Rome

24 Trial Before Felix The Sanhedrin's lawyer presented three charges, accusing Paul of stirring up strife amongst the Jews, of being a ringleader of the Nazarenes, and of trying to desecrate the Temple. Paul refuted the charges in turn. Firstly, he had only been in Jerusalem for twelve days and had not been involved in any controversy. Secondly, he worshipped the God of the Jews as a follower of the Way, believed the Law and the Prophets, and in the hope of the resurrection. Finally, he had come to Jerusalem to bring gifts for the poor and to present offerings to God. In the temple he had been ceremonially clean and not involved in any disturbance. It should be the Asian Jews, or the Jews who were present, bringing charges if they had any. His only offence was to shout that he was on trial concerning the resurrection. Felix adjourned the hearing until he received a military report, hoping also for a bribe. Paul was kept in custody, with a measure of freedom, for two years.

25:1-22 Trial Before Festus Felix was succeeded as Governor by Porcius Festus, who brought Paul to court. Paul's defense was simply to deny that he had done anything wrong, whether against the Law, the temple, or Caesar. When Festus suggested that Paul stand trial in Jerusalem, he appealed to Caesar. A few days later King Agrippa and his sister Bernice came to pay their respects to the new Governor, and Agrippa expressed an interest in hearing Paul for himself.

25:23-26:32 Defence before Agrippa Paul's speech of defence told how the risen Jesus had confronted him on the way to Damascus and appointed him to be his servant and witness in terms of the Servant of the Lord in Isaiah 42:1-7. Paul was not disobedient to this heavenly vision and it was for this reason that the temple Jews tried to kill him. Therefore, by God's help, he continued to bear witness, saying nothing beyond what the Law and the Prophets taught, that the Messiah would suffer, be the first to rise from the dead, and proclaim light to both Jews and Gentiles. Festus exclaimed that Paul was mad, but Paul appealed to the king's knowledge of these matters. When the audience retired, they acknowledged that Paul deserved neither death nor imprisonment, and Agrippa observed that he could have been freed if he had not appealed to Caesar.

27:1-26 Storm at Sea Paul and some other prisoners, in the custody of a centurion called Julius, set off for Italy. They travelled slowly, first by Asian ship until they rounded Cyprus. Then they transferred to an Alexandrian ship which negotiated adverse winds until they came to Fair Havens along the coast of Crete. Paul warned of the risks of continuing, but they tried to reach a more suitable harbour at Phoenix to spend the winter. A violent north-easterly gale (the "Euraquilo") struck them from the land and they were driven off course towards North Africa. They jettisoned cargo, threw out tackle, and after many days gave up hope of survival. However, Paul announced that he had been assured by an angel that he would yet stand before Caesar to give testimony, and there would be no loss of any life, although they would be cast up on an island.

27:27-28:10 The Shipwreck On the fourteenth night they neared land, and Paul warned everyone to stay on board and to eat. As an encouraging example of his confidence in God and his gospel purpose, Paul took bread, gave thanks to God for it, and ate it (v 35). The ship ran aground on a sandbar so that the stern began breaking up under the pounding surf. However, all reached land safely. It was the island of Malta, and the locals treated them kindly. When a viper bit Paul's hand the locals were superstitiously convinced he was a murderer, who may have escaped the sea but had been caught by divine Justice. However, when he suffered no harm, they concluded that he must be a god himself. The chief man of the island, Publius, generously entertained them for three days. Paul healed his father from fever and dysentery by prayer and placing his hands on him. Far from being a god, Paul showed that he depended on the one true God, who was able to heal. This was Luke's final reference to prayer. When Publius' father was healed, other sick folk on the island came and were also cured. The scene was reminiscent of Jesus' former healing ministry, subtle evidence that he was still at work. The people honoured Paul's company, and provided for their needs when it was time to sail.

28:11-31 Rome at Last After three months they sailed via Syracuse (in Sicily), then Rhegium (in the toe of Italy), to Puteoli (in the Bay of Naples), and then overland along the Appian Way to Rome, meeting with believers en route. At Rome Paul lived under house arrest, and met with local Roman Jews to tell them how he became a prisoner. He insisted that he had done nothing against Jewish customs or Roman law. Because the Jerusalem Jews had objected to his release, he had appealed to Caesar. The reason for his custody was the *hope of Israel* (meaning the coming of the Messiah and the resurrection). The Roman Jews had received no instructions from Jerusalem concerning Paul (so would not be pursuing his prosecution). Nevertheless, they were interested in hearing his views. On an arranged day Paul expounded the *Kingdom of God* to a larger group of them, speaking persuasively about Jesus from the Law and the Prophets. Some were convinced, others disbelieved. The meeting broke up with the Jews disagreeing among themselves. Paul's final word declared the truth of a quotation from Isaiah (6:9-10) which predicted Jewish rejection of God's message. Therefore, God's salvation had been sent to the more responsive Gentiles. For two years Paul remained at Rome, living at his own expense, receiving all comers, and proclaiming the Kingdom of God and teaching about the Lord Jesus Christ boldly and without hindrance.

Luke's story of the spreading word, fanning out from Jerusalem into Palestine, Asia, and Europe as far as Rome, is vividly told. It is the story of God's triumph through the good news of Jesus. The messengers who carried this good news were Jesus' appointed apostles and the rapidly expanding body of converts. They were the risen Jesus' collective "body", God's "partner" on earth, establishing his kingdom among the nations. Indispensable to their task, and to their experience of God, was prayer.

CHAPTER 10

"THE SON ON EARTH"

Prayer in Mark's Gospel

In the year 64 CE Rome was swept by a disastrous fire. Widespread rumour accused Emperor Nero of being responsible. To counteract suspicion Nero blamed the Christians. The consequent outburst of persecution was a fearful crisis for the Church. We cannot be completely certain, but probably this situation (and the martyrdom of Peter [and Paul] at that time) prompted Mark to write his Gospel. Since the prediction of Jerusalem's destruction (Mark 13) is not shown to be fulfilled, the Gospel was probably written prior to 70 CE. It was intended to be a message of "good news" for the afflicted followers of Christ.

Mark's Gospel appears to present an account of the gospel received from the Apostle Peter. Later Church tradition claimed this to be so, and it is possible to detect the presence of Peter as an eyewitness in virtually every incident described in the account. It is also possible to detect from the account what prompted Mark to write. He was writing to followers of Jesus at Rome who were being persecuted for their faith. He wrote to reassure their confidence in the "good news" about Jesus, and to stimulate their devotion to him in the face of hostility, by clarifying the essential meaning of what took place at the "*beginning*".

Mark entitled his book, "*The beginning of the gospel of Jesus Christ, the Son of God*" (1:1). He was indicating how the gospel commenced. "Gospel" was a royal term referring to the birth, coming of age, or accession to the throne of the Emperor's son, or to victory in battle. The Old Testament prophets used the term in connection with the in-breaking of God's kingly rule. Mark's use of the term had special significance for his readers at Rome facing the hostility of a nasty earthly emperor. He was pointing them toward the victorious accomplishments on earth of God's kingly Son who now ruled on high. In particular Mark portrayed Jesus as the conqueror of evil, hostility, and death.

Jesus is identified by two titles which are similar in meaning, both indicating his role as King. The term "Christ" is the Greek form for "Messiah", or "Anointed One", indicating that he has been anointed to be the king who will save God's people. He acts for the people.

"Son of God" means God's chosen representative King on earth, and emphasises his close relationship with God. He acts for God.

Mark immediately opened with a description of John the Baptist's public pronouncements about the impending arrival of someone greater than himself who would *"baptize with the Holy Spirit"*. Then he described Jesus' significant experience of baptism and his temptation (or trial) in the wilderness. Mark's account of Jesus' temptation was brief compared with Matthew and Luke, yet only he mentioned the *"wild animals"* (v 13). This was a significant detail for persecuted readers at Rome who were facing a life-threatening trial, which for some might literally include exposure to ferocious beasts. So much of what Mark included in his Gospel takes on added force when the shadow of Nero's persecution is discerned hovering in the background.

The "good news" was that, in the person of Jesus, God's kingdom had arrived (1:15). That reality was a powerful perspective to counter the ruthless cruelty of a maniacal human tyrant (and Nero has not been the only one to darken history's record). Mark's Gospel is a presentation of Jesus showing that he was the Messiah, God's Son on earth, who, by his preaching, actions of divine authority, death and resurrection, was fulfilling the mission of ushering God's Kingdom into the world. Mark reveals that a primary key to the establishment of the Kingdom was prayer. We find in Jesus a revelation of prayer's significance and purpose, and an inspiring model for prayer.

Messiah With A Mission

In order to appreciate the significance of Jesus, and the place and purpose of prayer, in Mark's Gospel, it is important for us to recognize Mark's message and how he presents it. He begins his account of the Gospel with Jesus' baptism and ends with his death and resurrection. But he does not simply follow the chronological course of Jesus' life. He arranges material about Jesus in units which follow different themes. The book is a Presentation of Jesus, intended to demonstrate Jesus' identity and mission, and inspire faith in him. The overall plan of the book has two phases:

1. Jesus' Ministry in Galilee (1:1-8:26) leading to Peter's confession of Jesus as the Messiah (8:27-30);
2. Jesus' Destiny at Jerusalem (8:31-15:47), climaxing in Jesus' Resurrection (16:1-8; [vs.9-20 seem to have been added at a later date]).

The first 8 chapters present Jesus in a fast-paced story style so that we see and hear him in action. It is like a kaleidoscope of verbal pictures, a slide-show. As we view it, we are prompted to ask the question, "Who is Jesus?" In Chapter 8 Peter confesses that Jesus is the Messiah. Before we understand the mission of Jesus, we must firstly know who he is.

The second half of the book focuses on the crucifixion of Jesus, which Mark shows was Jesus' God-given mission for him. By this means God's reign was breaking into world affairs and re-establishing its heavenly authority. All earthly authorities and the powers of evil and death were destroyed. This presentation demonstrates that Jesus was the all-powerful King in God's triumphant kingdom, more to be revered than a terrifying earthly emperor who was assailing Mark's original readers. Yet his Gospel transcends the immediate crisis which prompted it, because it is "good news" for the whole world for all time.

Mark's fast-paced style skilfully depicts his message about Jesus. However, the details of his narrative (his "brushstrokes") contain insights which add depth to his overall picture. We need to ponder the story discerningly to pick up their full meaning. Similarly, our discovery tour can only be presented in a succinct summary form, which requires thoughtful reading. Try to take in the "travelogue" as we go in order to grasp fully Mark's "good news".

Dependent Petitioner

Throughout Mark's Gospel Jesus is an awesome figure of authority. At the same time he is a humbly submissive dependent petitioner. He fulfils his mission by consistently relying on his Father in prayer at every stage. Mark mentions the term *"prayer"* on nine occasions, which may not seem too remarkable at first glance. Yet the pattern of their frequency is worth noting, and the context for each reference shows their significance. Mark makes it clear that prayer was a crucial factor for Jesus' messianic task.

Note first of all the pattern in which the term *"prayer"* appears in Mark's account. To appreciate the significance of that pattern it is helpful to recognise the structure of his book.

    1:1   Title: *"The beginning of the gospel about Jesus Christ, the Son of God"*. *That is, "The commencement of the royal announcement about Messiah Jesus, God's Kingly Son".*

    1:2-15   **Introduction:** *Jesus' public inauguration and his proclamation about the arrival of God's kingdom.*

    1:16-3:6 Jesus' Commanding Presence: *Jesus speaks and acts with authority in many varied situations, filling everyone with awe.*

    3:7-35   **Jesus Chooses His People:** *Despite popularity, hostility, and family pressure Jesus identifies those who belong to God's kingdom as those who do God's will.*

4:1-34   **Jesus Teaches by Parables:** *Jesus reveals truths about God's kingdom through a series of four parables.*

4:35-5:43   **Jesus' Awesome Power:** *Jesus displays his power over nature, demons, disease, and death.*

6:1-8:30   **Jesus Reveals His Identity:** *A series of incidents provide revealing insights about Jesus' divine nature and purpose, leading to Peter's confession of Jesus as Messiah.*

8:31-10:52   **Jesus Shows the Path of Discipleship:** *Jesus sets out on the way to Jerusalem, foretelling his approaching death and indicating the cost of following him.*

11:1-13:37   **Jesus Approaches His Hour of Destiny:** *Jesus enters Jerusalem in peaceful triumph but provokes conflict from the authorities. He announces the coming glory of the Son of Man.*

14:1-16:8   **Jesus Accomplishes His Mission:** *Jesus shares Passover with his disciples, faithfully endures his ordained ordeal of rejection, suffering and crucifixion, and demonstrates his victory by rising from the dead.*

Mark's first reference to prayer is early in the book, at 1:35. The second is five chapters later at 6:46. These are the only two references in the first half of the book, which has the aim of revealing Jesus' identity. The third reference occurs at 9:29, but no reference in chapter 10 (although 10:16 states that Jesus *"blessed"* the children). These two chapters cover activities of Jesus as he travelled towards his destination at Jerusalem. However upon his arrival at Jerusalem, where he was to accomplish his mission, the frequency of the term *"prayer"* increases in the chapters which describe Jesus' activities up until his capture in Gethsemane. Three occur in chapter 11 (v 17, 24, 25), one each in chapters 12 (v 40) and 13 (v 18), and the final reference is the longest occasion of prayer in the book (14:32-42), which was Jesus' final action as a free man. Mark shows by this pattern that prayer was strategic for Jesus' mission. Three of the occasions (1:35, 6:46, 14:32-42) describe Jesus at prayer, and the remainder are comments by Jesus about prayer. The voice which spoke at his baptism began with an echo of Psalm 2:7 (1:11) and, as in that psalm, Jesus is portrayed by Mark as the Messiah, the kingly Son on earth, who relies prayerfully on the Father.

It is not my intention to give an in-depth commentary on Mark's Gospel. Yet it is necessary to have a sufficient overview of the book to appreciate its message about prayer in context. It also reveals a thrilling image of Jesus.

The Father's Fellowship

In Mark's presentation of Jesus, prayer was the essential activity at the heart of his life. It was the spiritual spring from which flowed all his decisions and actions. For Jesus, prayer was an activity of communing with his Father in heaven and entreating him for his will to be done on earth. It is not actually stated that way, but that is how it is depicted. Not a lot is actually said about the Father in heaven, but a strong emphasis is focused on the Son on earth, beginning with the opening title (1:1), and concluding with the confession of the centurion at the cross (15:39).

Mark's introduction (1:2-15), following the book's title (1:1), sets the scene for the succeeding narrative. It announces the public arrival of Jesus the Messiah. Mark cleverly focuses attention on Jesus' significance by several conspicuous emphases. Three times he repeats the term *"gospel"*, firstly in his title (v 1) and then twice at the conclusion of his introduction (v 14, 15). He is emphasising the royal news of the Divine Emperor in contrast to the authority of the earthly emperor. Twice Mark quotes from the scriptures, the first to identify John the Baptist as the prophetic forerunner to the Messiah (v 2-3) and the second to identify Jesus as the Messiah himself (v 11). Four times Mark mentions the "desert" (v 3, 4, 12, 13), recalling an important tradition of God's dealings with his people Israel in previous history. Through this new experience of desert, a new beginning for God's people was emerging. Three times the term *"Spirit"* occurs, highlighting the commencement of the new era in God's purposes, in accord with the Old Testament's prophetic promise. These four features of Gospel, scripture, desert, and Spirit represent a convincing divine witness to Jesus' identity and superiority. Jesus was God's Spirit-anointed Son sent to restore heaven's kingdom on earth.

It is worth noting what Mark indicates about the gospel. He calls it the *"gospel about Jesus Christ"* (v 1), the *gospel of God* (v 14), and the gospel about the nearness of the *"kingdom of God"* (v 15). This opening introduction is a fanfare for God's royal good news about Jesus his Messiah and God's kingdom. The rest of the book proclaims that Jesus restored God's kingdom by his extraordinary mission of crucifixion and resurrection.

John the Baptist prepared the way for Jesus' coming in fine prophetic style (v 4-8). He preached in the wilderness, was like a second Elijah in appearance, and proclaimed a message about the impending arrival of One who would baptise with the Holy Spirit. His significance was summed up by a composite quote from Moses (Exodus 23:20), Malachi (3:1), and Isaiah (40:3), effectively condensing the whole of the Old Testament to a single thought (v 2-3). As the forerunner to the Messiah, John represented all that the Old Testament had revealed in preparation for the Messiah's coming. He publicly called his listeners to repent in advance by submitting to water baptism. He was giving novel expression to Israel's traditional practices of ritual cleansing in order to highlight their true meaning. John's prophetic mission was a very public preparation for the arrival of the Messiah.

Then Jesus arrived from Nazareth and was baptised by John in the Jordan River (v 9-11). His experience was profoundly meaningful, as he became overwhelmed by his awareness of heaven. Mark described the experience figuratively in terms of what Jesus saw and heard. As he emerged from the water Jesus saw *"heaven"* ripped open and the Spirit descending upon him like a dove, and he heard a voice *"coming from heaven"* declaring, *"You are my Son, whom I love; with you I am well pleased"*. The concise description sizzles with the impression of a welcoming encounter with a delighted, endorsing God. The tearing open of heaven indicated that God was violently breaking through the barrier between God and man in his enthusiastic zeal to draw near to Jesus. The same word will describe the splitting of the temple curtain at the moment when Jesus died (15:38), similarly indicating the removal of the barrier preventing access to God. Since the Spirit is God's essential Self, as it were his very "breath" (as "Spirit" can be translated), his descent upon Jesus meant that God's own personal overpowering presence was coming upon Jesus. He was showing his approval of Jesus, and his solidarity with him in his mission. The sight of the Spirit descending upon him was for Jesus' benefit, and was as real as a dove alighting upon him. For Jesus it represented a visible or discernible aspect of his experience, along with the audible voice, to assure him of the reality of the divine presence. The words which Jesus heard link former statements from Psalm 2:7 and Isaiah 42:1 to identify him as both God's triumphant Messiah and his humble Servant. Hearing the voice calling him "Son", indicated that the Father was speaking. God had come upon Jesus in a unique bond of Father-Son relationship. At this moment, Jesus experienced profound intimacy with God, conscious of fellowship with him as his heavenly Father, and divine anointing for his messianic mission.

Jesus was then led by the Spirit (meaning, by conscious fellowship with the Father's overpowering presence) into the desert to endure a forty days trial of temptation by Satan at the outset of his mission. The repeated reference to *"desert"* was important for Mark's readers. It gave them a perspective for seeing their own circumstances. The term recollected Israel's period in the desert after the exodus from Egypt before entering the Promised Land. The desert was a harsh and hostile environment. That Jesus was led into the desert by the Spirit, and of course eventually to the cross, meant that there was purpose in the ordeal. It was the pathway which led to the kingdom. This was how the readers should view their own circumstances as they followed their King, who understood what they were enduring, and who was sustained by angels (messengers of God) throughout it. He triumphed ultimately by resurrection. They too can be sure of divine support and eventual victory.

Mark's portrayal of Jesus' arrival throbs with a sense of dramatic moment. The atmosphere tingles with the majestic, triumphant, and intimate presence of God. God's personal presence as the Spirit had come upon Jesus ensuring fellowship with the Father. The Spirit was now leading Jesus, who would in turn baptise others in the Spirit, that is, into the same intimate reality of fellowship with the Father. The Spirit is only mentioned on three other occasions throughout the rest of Mark's Gospel (3:29, 12:36, 13:11). However, the presence of the Spirit, and what it represented, conscious fellowship with the Father, are implied by Jesus' personal practice of prayer.

Finally, when John the forerunner was in custody, Jesus began his mission. He went into Galilee proclaiming the good news of God,

"The time has come. The kingdom of God is near. Repent and believe the good news".

Prayer Was The Source Of Jesus' Authority

Mark launches into a fast moving series of incidents concerning Jesus in action in Galilee (1:16-3:6). The incidents cover a range of various situations which are linked together by a common thread. They demonstrate his commanding presence and authority. He calls men to follow him and they instantly obey. He teaches with authority, casts out demons with authority, heals the sick, forgives sinners, ignores human traditions, and claims to be even Lord of the Sabbath. Each incident is impressive in itself, but their cumulative effect is powerful. They present the striking image of a person who acts with awesome divine authority. Mark's original readers would not only realise that this identified Jesus as God's Messiah, but that he possessed greater authority than their oppressor emperor Nero.

In the midst of this sequence of stories which illustrate Jesus' kingly authority, Mark's **first reference to prayer appears (1:35).** It almost seems incidental. Yet it has great significance. It actually reveals that Jesus' prayerful dependence on God is the source of his authority. Mark records,

"Very early in the morning, while it was still dark, Jesus got up, left the house and went off to a solitary place, where he prayed".

The previous day and evening had been highly eventful (1:21-34). Jesus had taught in the synagogue, cast out a demon from an afflicted attender, healed Simon's mother-in-law from fever, and when the Sabbath was over at sunset had been engaged in an extensive work of healing and exorcising. Despite his busyness and pressing demands, and perhaps even because of them, Jesus realized the importance of spending time in prayer. It was the act of seeking audience with God in order to fellowship with the Father and to petition him concerning the kingdom. So before people could absorb his attention again, he made sure that he took the opportunity to pray by rising early and going off to an isolated place alone. In the midst of rapidly changing scenes of public displays of astonishing authority, this glimpse into Jesus' private world of prayer is significant. It shows the practical human side of his fellowship with the Father, and the secret to his authority.

Mark does not give details about what Jesus prayed, but he makes the point that when he prayed it was *dark* and in a *solitary* (literally, *desert*) *place*. The reference maintains the impression of Jesus' intimacy with God as he travels the way to the kingdom, and that God's presence (Spirit) continues to lead him. Through prayer Jesus was led in his decisions and actions. When he was eventually found, he resolved to move on to preach in other towns, despite the successful work he was doing at Capernaum and the widespread popular demand for his services which he had generated. Through prayer Jesus kept his focus steady on the priorities of his mission. Announcing the Kingdom so that people could be rescued from their separation from God was more important than relieving the afflictions which were the symptoms of that separation.

Throughout this phase of the story, Jesus twice identified himself as "Son of Man". He had authority to forgive sins (2:10), and authority over the Sabbath (2:28). Such authority belongs only to God. Similarly in all the incidents mentioned Jesus was exercising divine authority. Although "Son of Man" was an ambiguous title which allowed Jesus to remain anonymous, and emphasized his human status, it also alluded to the apocalyptic figure in Daniel 7:13-14. There a "son of man" approached the "Ancient of Days" and was led into his presence where he was given authority, glory and sovereign power. By this allusion Jesus was subtly declaring exalted claims about himself. Mark's account skillfully draws the picture connecting Jesus' prayer, authority, and identity. Jesus was the "Son of Man" who received heavenly authority by approaching God in prayer. This title "Son of Man" only occurs on these two occasions in the first half of Mark's Gospel, in this phase which highlights his astonishing authority. Yet it will appear later, with more frequency, in the second half of the Gospel which focuses on Jesus' mission.

It is important to recognize that Jesus' title "Son of God" identified him as God's chosen representative on earth, whereas the description "Son of Man" identified him as Man's representative in heaven. Jesus preferred to speak of himself as "Son of Man", because it more readily indicated the mission he was pursuing, and avoided popular misunderstandings about the role of the "Son of God".

Prayer Was Crucial For Jesus' Mission

Mark's **second reference to prayer (6:46)** does not appear until well into his narrative. Yet it demonstrates the high importance Jesus placed on prayer, and reveals further insights into its purpose. Before he gets to that point, however, Mark presents many more stories and details about Jesus' activities to show his identity as the Messiah. It is important to have the fuller picture in mind in order to appreciate the significance of the reference to prayer.

After showing Jesus' authority, and the rise of hostile opposition (1:16-3:6), a new theme emerges in Mark's story. He reveals the true nature of God's People (3:7-35). Jesus was soon followed by large crowds, and became the focus of attention for the whole nation because people were attracted to him as a miracle worker. However, Jesus chose twelve disciples to be the beginning of his new community because it was not the crowd but the chosen who belonged to the Kingdom. The number 12 linked them with the former people of God, Israel. Jesus' earthly family considered him to be out of his mind, and a delegation of specialists in Jewish law from Jerusalem concluded that he was possessed by a prince of demons. Jesus exposed the fallacy of their criticism, and used the opportunity of his family's concern to explain that his true family was made up of those who do God's will.

Mark then includes a segment on Jesus' teaching, by grouping together a selection of parables to throw light on his message concerning the Kingdom of God (4:1-34). Three parables about sowing seed illustrate harvest principles which can be applied to the growth of God's Kingdom. Another about a lamp illustrates that light is intended to be seen, implying that similarly the currently hidden glory of the Kingdom in the person of Jesus would eventually be made public. Parables were not used to make the message simple and plain, but to present the message in a concealed form which needed to be explained. God's truth is only understood by revelation, not by natural ability.

Four spectacular miracles demonstrate the presence of heavenly power (4:35-5:43). They reveal Jesus' awesome power as he subdues natural forces (calming the stormy sea and wind) and supernatural forces (exorcising demons), and vanquishes disease (healing a woman's haemorrhage) and death (restoring a girl to life). These are common forces which are hostile to all mankind. Mankind's other common hostile foe, human forces which persecute, is missing from this particular set, because that is a major concern of the whole book. Each of these stories is intended to stimulate faith in Jesus as a Kingly Conqueror in the face of fear when hostile circumstances and powers are threatening to engulf (see 4:40; 5:33-34,36).

Mark's next section (6:1-8:30) concludes with Peter's confession of Jesus as the Messiah. This is a climactic moment in the book, and Mark's second reference to prayer occurs within this section. That reference needs to be seen within the context of the surrounding matters which are included.

In his home town (6:1-6) the ministry of Jesus prompted amazement, but also offence, because people could not discern his true identity beyond the superficial human level. Consequently, it was inappropriate (not impossible) for Jesus to perform miracles there, and he was amazed at their lack of faith (this is the only occurrence in Mark of Jesus' amazement, indicating the degree of resistance).

Jesus' mission was extended through the Twelve, who were sent out in pairs, having been instructed about the urgency of the task and to expect a measure of rejection (6:7-13). They preached for repentance as they demonstrated the power and the presence of the Kingdom through exorcisms and healings.

The effectiveness of the Twelve was of the order of resurrection power (6:14-30). This was testified to by the [Roman appointed] King Herod, who attributed their ministry to the rising of John the Baptist from the dead. John's beheading, which had already occurred previously, is described in detail by Mark at this point. It is intended to parallel the crucifixion of Jesus, which is at the climax of the book. This conveys to readers the understanding that God's prophetic mission meets resistance, and even the execution of its messengers (whether Forerunner, the Messiah himself, or, by implication, followers). Yet the mission is accomplished in resurrection power.

Mark's narrative now develops a distinctive theme, which can only be recognised by having knowledge of the Old Testament. The sequence and manner of what Mark described is intended to recall Israel's Exodus from Egypt, and to depict Jesus as the Deliverer through a new and greater Exodus. Jesus invited his disciples to join him for rest in a "*quiet*" (literally, "*desert*") place (6:31). After crossing the lake and seeing the crowd, Jesus had compassion because "*they were like sheep without a shepherd*" (6:32-34). This was an allusion to Numbers 27:17 and Ezekiel 34:5, both of which have a wilderness theme. In Numbers Moses prayed for a leader to take his place, and significantly the man appointed was called Joshua (the Hebrew form of Jesus). In Ezekiel God promised the coming of a faithful shepherd, David, whose covenant of peace would cause God's people to dwell securely in the desert (Ezekiel 34:23, 25).

The lengthy story of the feeding of the crowd with five loaves and two fish (6:35-44) shows that the story was highly significant. Later references back to the occasion (see 6:52, 8:17-21) emphasised that significance. It is a reminder both of the manna in the wilderness after the Exodus, and of the figurative expected future "fellowship meal" which will be celebrated with the Messiah.

It is at this point that Mark makes his second reference to prayer.

"*After leaving them, he went up on a mountainside to pray*" (6:46).

Although it almost appears to be a passing casual comment, the reference is strategic. The occasion followed the miracle of feeding more than 5000 people, an event not only significant for its display of power, but for identifying Jesus as the "compassionate Shepherd", and therefore as the promised Messiah. At the end of the day Jesus sent his disciples on ahead of himself by boat while he dispersed the crowd. He then ascended a mountainside to pray. We must note that he and his disciples had already been busy and tired before the day began (v 31), that it was a *solitary* (*desert*) place (v 32), and that he prayed alone, at night (v 47). He prayed from evening until the fourth watch (v 48). That is about three o'clock in the morning! He was engaged in prayer for about eight or nine hours. Jesus' praying was an astonishing commitment. Although this is only Mark's second reference concerning prayer, the picture is emerging that prayer did not occupy second place for Jesus. Fellowship with his Father and presenting kingdom requests were the heart of his life, the secret of his authority and power. Prayer was paramount to all his activities, and the source of his energy, vision, and passion. His public actions flowed from his private praying.

Following his prayer Jesus walked on water in the midst of a turbulent storm and rescued his terrified and helpless disciples who were in perilous danger in a boat (v 47-52)! His primary purpose was to be an epiphany (appearance) of the LORD to encourage them. Jesus words, "*It is I*" (v 50) are literally, "*I am*", the name by which God revealed himself at the Exodus. The followers of Jesus saw much significance in this event. It was a reminder of God's rescue of his chosen people Israel through the Red Sea at the time of the Exodus, and a foreshadowing of Jesus' greater Exodus through the Cross and Resurrection. It was also a reminder of the Creator who subdues the sea and the hostile forces of both nature and the demonic world. For Mark's original readers it was an inspiring reminder that their Lord could come to them in their storm of persecution. Jesus' prayer was a crucial factor in his spiritual engagement with the realm of darkness, with the pivotal task of his self-revelation, and with the fulfillment of his rescue mission as the Saviour-King who had come.

The healings at Gennesaret and elsewhere straight afterwards (v 53-56) represented another epiphany, this time of the Lord who is the healer, the name by which God revealed himself after Israel crossed the Red Sea (see Exodus 15:20). The presence of Jesus was the presence of the God who was with Israel during the Exodus and wilderness.

These stories were intended to reveal Jesus to be a divine Deliverer, greater than Moses. Underlying them all, although only glimpsed once or twice, is an awareness of a profound relationship of prayer.

A lengthy segment next describes a clash between Jesus and the Pharisees over ceremonial washing, prompting him to give extensive remarks to the crowds and his disciples (7:1-23). It highlights Jesus' concern for heart condition rather than external customs, as he criticises Jewish traditions which replace God's commands. He exposes the difference between traditional and real defilement.

Then two miracles performed amongst Gentiles immediately follow the segment about Jewish defilement (7:24-37). The Gentiles show by their faith that their hearts are right, and Jesus' actions show that they are not disqualified for being "unclean" because they are not Jews. He continues to perform other actions among the Gentiles which parallel what he had done among the Jews. He miraculously feeds a crowd of four thousand (8:1-9; cf. 6:31-44). He crosses the sea (8:10; cf. 6:45-56). He engages in conflict with the Pharisees (8:11-13; cf. 7:1-23). He becomes involved in a discussion about "bread" (8:14-21; cf. 7:24-30). He performs a miracle of healing (8:22-26; cf. 7:31-37). There are two reasons for this segment of events. Firstly, it shows the inclusion of Gentiles in the new community of the kingdom. In the second place it highlights the disciples' lack of understanding about the Messiah and the kingdom (see 7:14-18, 8:17-21).

This lack of understanding was especially stressed by the healing of the blind man in two stages (8:22-26). Jesus performed the miracle by making prophetic (symbolic) gestures. He led the man outside the village to avoid mere curious onlookers. He spat on the man's eyes, showing prophetically that true healing and seeing will come through personal association with his own revolting experiences of suffering (Jesus was also spat on and taunted to prophesy, 14:65). The blind man was healed in two stages, giving firstly partial vision, and then full vision, to highlight two truths that had to be "seen" concerning Jesus. These truths are revealed in the next event presented by Mark, which brings his book to its half-way point.

The first half of the book concludes with Peter's confession of Jesus as the Christ (8:27-30). After many questions and misunderstandings about Jesus thus far, Jesus focuses the issue concerning his identity by asking his disciples what peoples' opinions were. Then he asks them directly for their own opinion. It is significant (for readers at Rome) that Peter is the disciple to confess Jesus as Christ, and at the Romanised town of Caesarea Philippi. With this confession Mark brings the narrative to a powerful challenge at the midway point.

Mark's skilful presentation of Jesus in the first half of his book leads to a climactic revelation of Jesus' identity as Messiah. He is recognised by observing the "good news" of his exploits, discerned against the background of God's former actions in the Old Testament scriptures, as Jesus is led through the "desert" by his intimate private relationship of prayer.

Prayer Gave Jesus Power Over Darkness

However, although Peter has "seen" who Jesus is correctly, he has only "seen" partially, with blurred vision. He has not yet understood the true mission of the Messiah. He probably held the typical view that the Messiah would be a military leader who would overthrow Israel's enemies, the Romans who occupied and oppressed their nation. This is why Jesus issues a stern command to his disciples not to tell anyone concerning his identity (8:30), and then proceeds to explain his mission in the next segment. This is the only occasion where Mark explains why Jesus insisted on his identity not being disclosed, and it explains his previous insistence on silence (see 1:34, 44, 3:12, 5:43, 7:24, 36, 8:26). It is not sufficient just to recognise who Jesus is, but to recognise also the necessity of the Cross in obedience to the will of God. Therefore, he would not be revealed until after he had accomplished his mission through death and resurrection.

The second half of Mark's Gospel begins with Jesus revealing that the Messiah would be rejected and killed before his kingdom came in power, and that his disciples must be willing to lose their lives for his sake (8:31-9:1). Not only must Jesus' immediate disciples have to learn this necessity, so too must Mark's Roman readers, and all Jesus' followers.

Significantly, Jesus refers to himself as the "Son of Man", a description which we have earlier indicated means Man's representative in heaven. Following immediately after Peter's confession of Jesus as Messiah, it is obvious that Jesus understands "Son of Man" to be a messianic title. Because the title was ambiguous it allowed him to remain anonymous while actually identifying himself with Daniel's End-time apocalyptic figure. Similarly, the crucifixion was also ambiguous, appearing to be a humiliating, tragic conclusion for Jesus, while actually being the intended pathway to glory and culmination of God's long pursued plan for his people. Jesus was revealing that Daniel's "Son of Man" would receive his sovereign power and dominion by suffering and death. Throughout the second half of Mark's Gospel the title "Son of Man" occurs twelve times (compared with only twice in the first half), consistently in connection with Jesus' impending crucifixion. The title is effectively an alternative for "Crucified Messiah". Since use of the title for Jesus during the first half of the Gospel related to him as the Messiah who received his authority through dependent prayer, there is evidently a close relationship between Jesus' devotion to prayer and his mission at the cross.

Jesus' prediction of his death sparked a sharp interaction between himself and his disciples. In particular, Peter privately rebuked him. His "blurred vision" prevented him from "seeing" the true mission of the Messiah. Jesus discerned in Peter's rebuke the tactics of Satan himself to dissuade him from his mission. His subsequent comments to the crowd not only spell out the cost of discipleship for them, but were probably intended by Mark to fulfil a pastoral purpose to his readers also. The language especially applied to a legal courtroom setting and to Roman execution, which would be very repulsive to the Jewish audience even though meant figuratively with regard to more general life situations. For Mark's readers, Jesus' call to commitment was very relevant and realistic. That some of Jesus' listeners would see God's kingdom come in power before their own death (9:1), points to an imminent future. It would come as the result of the Cross.

The second part of the book portrays Jesus first of all "travelling" towards Jerusalem, the destiny of his mission (chapters 9-10), and then confronting the religious and political authorities (chapters 11-12) who would execute him by crucifixion (chapters 13-16). This literary format for the Gospel, presenting Jesus' ministry in Galilee (first half of the book), followed by a "journey" to Jerusalem where he is crucified and then resurrected (second half), depicts the nature of his mission. This is the Good News, that Jesus is God's illustrious King who rescues God's people by conquering evil and death. Two incidents at the start of his "journey" provided Jesus' disciples with a preliminary insight into his glory and power (9:2-29).

The "journey" began with Jesus leading Peter, James, and John privately up a mountain where he was transfigured before them (9:2-13). This episode of Jesus' transfiguration can only be understood against the background of the Old Testament and God's purpose for his chosen people Israel. The event was a dramatic display of the hidden quality of Jesus' life shining forth in brilliant radiance. It was for the benefit of the disciples. The location on a "*high mountain*" and the presence of Elijah and Moses were reminders of God's former revelations at Mount Sinai in the Old Testament. This event was a revelation of Jesus' glory as God's unique Son, the ideal Israel, who came to fulfil the role which Israel failed to accomplish.

Peter's impulsive suggestion of erecting shelters for Jesus, Moses, and Elijah (v 5-6) indicated that he thought the revelation was permanent and that God's purposes were now fulfilled. He still did not grasp the necessity for Jesus to suffer (see 8:32), failing to realise that the event was only a temporary glimpse of what would not be permanently manifested until after the resurrection. God's response to Peter's proposal, in cloud and word as at Mount Sinai (v 7), identified who Jesus was and urged the disciples to listen to him. They must especially listen to his message that "*the Son of Man must suffer*" (see 8:31).

As the disciples descended the mountain, their confusion remained. They were puzzled about the idea of the Son of Man rising from the dead (v 10), because it was not part of their expectations. Having just seen Elijah in the revelation on the mountain, they recalled what they had learned from the teachers of the law concerning him (v 11). They expected Elijah to restore God's kingdom in Israel (in a political sense) prior to the arrival of Messiah. If Jesus was the Messiah, and Elijah had arrived, why was there further delay? Jesus' reply confirmed that Elijah must come to restore all things, but questioned their expectations about what that meant (v 12). Since the kingdom of God was the rule of God in the hearts of his people, it was necessary for their representative, the Son of Man, to suffer on their behalf and be rejected. In fact, Elijah had already come (meaning John the Baptist who called for a heart restoration), and had likewise experienced rejection (v 13). Twice in this conversation Jesus has mentioned the Son of Man, and with regard to the necessity of his sufferings and resurrection (v 9, 12). Using again the title of Daniel's triumphant figure of glory, Jesus reiterates that the road to glory was the pathway of suffering.

Returning from his experience of transfiguration and the voice from heaven, Jesus encountered a confrontation with the demonic world (v 14-29). These episodes parallel, at the commencement of the book's second half, Jesus' earlier experience of baptism, voice from heaven, and temptation by Satan in the desert at the start of the first half (see 1:9-13). Both Jesus' earlier temptation and now his encounter with a demon-possessed child revealed that his mission as Messiah involved overcoming Satan and his evil forces of darkness.

Jesus found his disciples in a dilemma because they had been unable to cast out a demon from a young boy who had been brought to them in his absence. The situation exposed the powerlessness of the disciples. Jesus' cry of exasperation (v 19) was his reaction to their failure to understand the true nature of their task. Their unbelief caused them to lose sight of their relationship to him and his mission, so that they were acting independently in their efforts to drive out the demon. When Jesus arrived on the scene, he banished the demon instantly. This perplexed the disciples, not only because Jesus had an authority which they did not, but because they had lost the authority they had previously exercised (see 6:7-13). In deep consternation they asked Jesus privately why they were unable to cast the demon out. Mark's **third reference to prayer (v 29)** occurs at this point, and is a statement by Jesus in response to his disciples' question. Jesus declared,

"This kind can come out only by prayer."

The statement confirmed Jesus' personal consistent practice of prayer, and revealed insight into its purpose. Its purpose was in relation to Jesus' coming as King to overthrow evil and restore God's authority on earth. The whole incident highlighted the spiritual conflict which was Jesus' primary mission. Healing the demon-possessed boy demonstrated that Jesus was to enter his glory through conflict with the forces of Satan. His victory in that conflict would be achieved through prayerful dependence on his Father, and ultimately through the Cross. This third reference to prayer strengthens the impression Mark has already presented concerning the crucial role of prayer for Jesus' messianic mission.

The lesson for the disciples was that authority over demons depended on prayer, and that through prayer faith can overcome. This would be pastoral encouragement for the believers at Rome who probably felt themselves powerless and defeated in the absence of their Lord at a critical time. Their trial against the powers of darkness could be faced in prayer and faith.

Jesus' words dramatically conclude the description of this significant incident, and are left hanging. A new stage in the "journey" is marked by a second prediction about Jesus' destiny, again using the title "Son of Man" and referring to his betrayal, death, and resurrection (9:30-32). This naturally recalls the previous prediction (8:31), and the need to "see" fully the nature of the Messiah's mission, and the need for persistent prayerful dependence. No further explicit mention of prayer is made throughout the course of the "journey", but Jesus' words at the beginning continue to hang over all that follows. As Jesus' "journey" progressed, various inter-actions along the way highlighted the cost of being his disciples and the true values of God's kingdom (9:30-10:52).

They came to Capernaum, where a series of instructions by Jesus to his disciples, linked by various catch words (*"in my name"*, *"one of these little"*), taught about values in the Kingdom (9:33-50). An argument along the way led to instruction and a practical illustration involving a child which taught that true greatness lies not in positions of rank but actions of service in Jesus' name (v 33-37). John declared that he had tried to prevent someone from acting in Jesus' name in casting out a demon, but Jesus rebuked him. It was not only the Twelve who had authority to act for Jesus, but anyone who trusted and followed him. In fact, how people treated those who belong to Christ was an indication of how they themselves will be ultimately treated (v 38-42). After warning against causing someone else to sin (v 42), Jesus called for drastic action to guard against sinning oneself, and suffering the ultimate consequence of being cast into hell. The advice to sever offending outward members of the body vividly exposed the reality that it was the inward condition of the body which was the problem (v 43-48). Mention of the fire of hell (v 48) prompted a remark about the fire of sacrifice. Just as Old Testament sacrifices were accompanied by salt, so disciples who offer themselves to God will possess salt-like quality cultivated through fiery trials of hostility. Mark's readers at Rome would appreciate Jesus' word. His final comment about valuing salt and maintaining peace had particular relevance for the disciples who were squabbling about rank and status. Saltiness, not greatness, was to be their distinctive qualification (v 49-50)!

Jesus left Galilee and entered Judea, where a series of incidents seemingly in the vicinity of Jericho provided insight into Jesus' attitude towards the Law and about entering God's kingdom (10:1-52).

The first incident involved discussions about marriage and divorce (v 1-12). In itself Jesus' attitude to marriage and divorce is interesting, yet at first sight the topic at this point could seem irrelevant to Mark's purpose. However, it is meant to show Jesus' attitude to the Law. Jesus was in the region where John the Baptist had been arrested and executed for condemning King Herod for marrying the wife of his brother Philip (v 1). The Pharisees tried to *test* Jesus (exposing him to the threat of Herod) by asking for his opinion about the lawfulness of divorce (v 2). He replied by asking what Moses *commanded* (v 3). They told him what Moses *permitted* (v 4). Rabbis at that time were divided in their interpretation of Moses' law (see Deuteronomy 24), either allowing a man to divorce his wife for any reason, or only on the grounds of her moral infidelity. Jesus declared, however, that Moses' law was only required because of men's hardness of heart (to protect wives who were cast aside by uncaring husbands), since God's intention at creation was that a man should be permanently united with his wife, and should not separate from her (v 5-9). Thus, for Jesus the purpose of the law was not to provide a way of legal acceptance with God (as the Pharisees taught), but to expose the true need of human hearts to be restored.

In private later on, Jesus had more to say to his disciples, asserting that anyone who divorces and remarries is guilty of adultery (v 10-12). Jesus was making three important points. Firstly, his statement, "*...and remarries*", means *in order to remarry*. The law clearly permitted remarriage for a woman who had been divorced. But divorce had come to be used by men as a legal cover-up for immoral intention. Secondly, he declared that a man who did this was committing adultery *against his wife*. This was giving status, dignity and equality to women, since society at that time considered that a man committed adultery only against another man, when he seduced that man's wife. Thirdly, Jesus' comment about the wife divorcing her husband (v 12) was significant, since wives in Jewish society had no rights to divorce. When Herodias deserted her husband Philip, she had sent him a Roman certificate of divorce. Jesus' comment held wives (and especially Herodias) also to be morally accountable. In all this, Jesus' main concern was to deny the view that the law was merely a means of finding *legal* acceptance with God, and to declare that its purpose was to curb and expose the moral nature of the human condition.

In contrast, the brief incident concerning children illustrated how actually to enter the kingdom (v 13-16). The disciples tried to prevent little children from being brought to Jesus in much the same manner as they had tried to stop a man from driving out demons in his name (see 9:38). They still did not understand the way of God's kingdom. The kingdom of God belonged to little children and others who were like them, those who are apparently unimportant, but are humble and trusting. Solemnly Jesus pronounced that anyone without the childlike disposition of being able to receive the kingdom as a gift would never enter it. Then his indignation towards the disciples switched to tenderness and acceptance as he took the children in his arms and blessed them. Entrance into God's kingdom is a blessing bestowed as a gift on anyone who acknowledges their helplessness in relation to it.

Two themes come together in the story of the Rich Young Man, where the absolute demands of the Law are linked with what is involved in entering the kingdom (v 17-27). The man who came to Jesus showed by his actions and words that he had high regard for Jesus, noble concerns, but an expectation that he could achieve eternal life by actions of merit (v 17). Jesus responded by directing his attention to God, and by reminding him of the commandments of the law (v 18-19). Jesus challenged the man's zealous but superficial self-confidence with loving but probing confrontation (v 20-21). Jesus exposed the man's vulnerable heart condition by demanding a radical change of priorities, calling him to abandon his wealth and to follow Jesus. The call to dispose of his riches to the poor was not a general requirement for everyone, but an appropriate demand for this particular man, stripping his self-sufficiency and leaving him helpless and impoverished. It proved to be too great a demand for the man, and prompted Jesus to remark on the difficulty for the rich to enter God's kingdom (v 22-23). To his disciples Jesus added that it was difficult, and even impossible, for anybody to enter the kingdom, but what was impossible for man was possible with God (v 24-27). Salvation is received from God alone.

Peter could identify with Jesus' call to forsake everything to follow him, although his words seem self-applauding (v 28-31). Nevertheless Jesus explained that what was lost in terms of natural family ties and earthly possessions will be more than compensated for by belonging to God's new family, despite persecution, and by the gift of eternal life in the age to come. A concluding gentle warning about the first being last, and the last first, is a caution against becoming too self-satisfied.

Another stage in the "journey" was reached with a third prediction about Jesus' death in Jerusalem (v 32-34). Once more Jesus uses the title "Son of Man" to draw attention to his mission of acquiring his kingly authority through death and resurrection. The details of his future sufferings are more extensive than former predictions, and were taken from descriptions of God's righteous servant in the Old Testament (Psalm 22:6-8, Isaiah 50:6). This third prediction punctuating the account of the "journey" inevitably ensures that the Messiah's mission remains clearly "seen", and is a reminder of the opposing forces of darkness which must be faced by prayerful dependence on the Father. Although prayer is not explicitly mentioned, it is again implicitly understood.

Just as the disciples showed inappropriate responses after the two previous predictions, so they did again following the third (v 35-45). An unworthy ambitious request by James and John led Jesus to reveal that discipleship included a "baptismal" experience like his own (v 35-40). When the other ten disciples showed their own self-interest by their indignant reaction, Jesus explained that their role was not to be "*lord over*", but "*servant among*" (v 41-44). To clarify, he explained his own role, using again the "Son of Man" title (v 45),

"*For even the Son of Man did not come to be served, but to serve, and to give his life as a ransom for many.*"

The final incident before Jesus' arrival in Jerusalem contains the essential elements of Mark's message about following Jesus (v 46-52). Bartimaeus recognised Jesus as Son of David and appealed to him for mercy. He maintained persistent faith even when resisted by the crowd. Though he was blind Jesus gave him sight, immediate and complete, and he followed Jesus to Jerusalem.

Prayer Was A Kingdom Priority For Jesus

The building up of anticipation throughout Jesus' "journey" reached a peak with his triumphant entry into Jerusalem and the temple, marked by noisy acclamation and prophetic expectation, only to evaporate with an apparent sudden anti-climax (11:1-11). Mark's lengthy account emphasised that Jesus' entry to Jerusalem on the back of the colt was deliberately intended, self-initiated, and highly significant. The event may actually have only been a brief moment of enthusiasm, probably causing little stir, since there was no Roman reaction. It was a veiled action, yet deliberately prophetic, recalling such Old Testament prophecies as Genesis 49:8-12, Zechariah 9:9, Malachi 3:1. Only the eye of faith looking back on the event can discern that Jesus' entry to Jerusalem was the arrival of God's promised Messiah and the coming of the prophesied LORD to his temple. At the time, the significance was completely lost on everyone. The climactic moment of reaching the temple seemed to become a non-event. Jesus simply looked around at everything and returned to Bethany. What was Jesus hoping to see at the temple?

His symbolic actions the next day revealed what it was (v 12-19). The cursing of the fruitless fig tree (v 12-14) was not a petulant reaction but a prophetic action, paralleling Jesus' subsequent action at the temple (v 15-16). Because Jesus failed to find spiritual fruit on his first visit, he had then returned and cleansed the temple in prophetic zeal. This was a crucial moment in Jesus' mission. The King had come to his temple, fulfilling the ancient word of prophecy (Malachi 3:1). His people were not ready for his coming, so he dealt with them in judgement. He referred to a prophecy of Isaiah, and condemned them in the same words by which Jeremiah had condemned his generation when the nation's spiritual failure had resulted in exile in Babylon (v 17, Isaiah 56:4-7, Jeremiah 7:11). Jesus' quotation from Isaiah contains Mark's **fourth reference to prayer**.

> *"Is it not written: 'My house will be called a house of prayer for all nations'? But you have made it a den of robbers".*

Jesus' utterance, along with his actions of rejection, denounced them for failing to live according to God's revealed intentions for his restored kingdom as declared by the prophets. This showed that central to and characteristic of the blessings of God's restored kingdom was the privilege for all nations to draw near to God. Prayer is the expression of right worship, the true meaning of the temple's function. When we understand worship as submission to God's majesty and sovereignty, and of fellowship with him, we understand the true purpose of prayer. Prayer is not simply asking God for the pleasing things we desire, but an earnest yearning for God's will to be done on earth as a pleasing offering to God. Jesus was condemning the nation for failing to be God's "kingdom of priests", because its religious system was preventing the nations from enjoying true access to God, and was stifling the reality and priority of prayer.

Jesus' aggressive and provocative assault on the temple's practices prompted an intensely hostile reaction from the religious authorities (v 18-19). Now they were on the lookout for ways to kill him.

Prayer Had Essential Requirements For Jesus

The drastic withering of the fig tree following Jesus' curse gave opportunity for the only explicit teaching on prayer in Mark's Gospel (v 20-25; v 26 seems to have been imported from Matthew 6:15). On the morning following Jesus' sensational actions at the temple, the tree was already completely withered. Peter remembered Jesus' curse, and commented on it out loud. In reply, Jesus spoke to them all, and encouraged them to have faith in God. To emphasise his point, he made a remarkable statement, and then added further succinct instructions about prayer in the form of a couplet (v 24-25). This couplet contains Mark's **fifth and sixth references to** prayer, thereby drawing attention to them, and they occur at a significantly high point in Mark's narrative.

> "'Have faith in God', Jesus answered. 'I tell you the truth, if anyone says to this mountain, "Go, throw yourself into the sea", and does not doubt in his heart but believes that what he says will happen, it will be done for him. Therefore I tell you, whatever you ask for in prayer, believe that you have received it, and it will be yours. And when you stand praying, if you hold anything against anyone, forgive him, so that your Father in heaven may forgive you your sins'."

Two basic attitudes, faith in God and forgiveness towards people, are necessary for effectiveness in prayer. Both requirements are relational in nature, highlighting the relational (as distinct from mere ritual) nature of prayer.

"*Have faith in* God" is an exhortation to have an attitude of confident trust in God, to rely on him in conscious dependence. Alternatively, the statement may be *"You have the faithfulness of God"*, urging the disciples to be assured of God's trustworthiness. Either way, Jesus was encouraging them to have a conscious outlook of confidence in God's ability and reliability. Since this statement was Jesus' answer to Peter's exclamation about the cursed fig tree, it implies that this outlook was the explanation for what had happened. The fig tree had withered at Jesus' word because he had faith in God, or because he relied on God's faithfulness. This incident (at the end of Jesus' "journey") parallels the earlier incident (at the start of the "journey") when the disciples expressed perplexity at being unable to cast out an evil spirit, and Jesus had explained that it was only possible by prayer (9:14-29). Having faith in God is much the same as praying. The attitude and the action go together, and they both represent the source of Jesus' authority. Fellowship with his Father, who was absolute King who rewarded his requesting trust, was the empowering factor to everything Jesus did.

His follow up comment was intended to reinforce his instruction. He begins the comment with a positive affirmation (*"I tell you the truth"*). Then he makes a startling assertion that if anyone, who believes without any doubts, commands *"this mountain"* to throw itself into the sea, it will happen. The way Jesus makes this assertion is meant to shock his disciples, so they will think about it. At that time they were standing on the Mount of Olives, from which it was possible to see the Dead Sea in the distance. Jesus was not proposing that his disciples might consider performing a spectacular feat, nor was he promoting the power of human ability to rise above doubt in order to be able to do it. Rather, he was encouraging trust in God's faithfulness to accomplish his intended purposes. His startling comment was alluding to a written prophecy about the Mount of Olives splitting in two on the Day when the LORD restored his kingship (Zechariah 14:4). The prophecy figuratively uses dramatic physical language of cataclysmic land upheaval to describe the convulsive effect of God's kingship being restored. Jesus' remark about *"this mountain"* is a colourful variation on that familiar prophetic imagery, and the command to the mountain to throw itself into the sea is virtually a bold prayer of faith for God to establish his rule on earth. Jesus was not making a wild assertion to be taken openly and randomly. He was conscious of the momentous reality that the Messiah's time had arrived, and was affirming that God could be trusted to respond to prayer to fulfil his declared purposes.

Jesus was also preparing his disciples for the devastating impending events of his own death and resurrection to which this prophecy pointed. The world was about to experience a cosmic cataclysm of greater significance than what prophetic physical imagery could depict. The restoration of God's kingdom involved the destruction of evil and death, the vindication of God, and the victory of life. Not only was the visible physical universe to be affected, but also the hidden realms beyond human detection. So certain was the triumph of God's kingdom, his disciples could confidently command these convulsive events to occur.

His comment naturally leads on to Jesus drawing a conclusion with regard to prayer (v 24). **This is Mark's fifth reference to prayer.** Jesus tells his disciples,

"Therefore I tell you, whatever you ask for in prayer, believe that you have received it, and it will be yours. "

The word "ask" is a relational term, making prayer an activity which is real rather than ritual or formal. It indicates that prayer involves the idea of petition. Jesus was not making a blanket promise that anyone could ask God for whatever they wanted. He was speaking from the perspective of the messianic era. His general statement revealed that prayer was a relationship of dependent trust, and that any situation, whether difficult or even seemingly impossible, could be resolved by God. To have faith in God means to trust him in regard to his sovereignty, his ability, his will and purposes, his goodness and faithfulness. This requires trusting God and having a heart desire that is aligned with God's desire. Jesus was encouraging his disciples to pray for whatever was pleasing to God, especially concerning his kingdom's restoration, and to believe in the certainty that it would be received.

Jesus suddenly switched his discussion from faith to forgiveness (v 25). His thoughts were still focused on prayer, and he made further comment,

"And when you stand praying, if you hold anything against anyone, forgive him, so that your Father in heaven may forgive you your sins".

This is Mark's **sixth reference to prayer.** Jesus was describing a normal posture for prayer in the temple, typical of a petitioner before a great king. In the context of Jesus' thoughts, his disciples would most likely be praying for God's kingdom to come. Jesus instructed them that petitioners for God's kingdom must be prepared to forgive so that they could be sure that they themselves would be forgiven. This was because to be restored to God's kingdom was a matter of being forgiven and reconciled to God. It was not a matter of forgiving others in order to earn God's forgiveness. Yet a heart that truly desires forgiveness is willing to forgive.

This second requirement for prayer is also relational. Faith relates to God, and forgiveness to others. They are at the heart of the two commands which sum up the Law, to love God with all your heart, and to love your neighbour as yourself. These are the requirements of righteousness, of being true to God and living under his kingship. Therefore they are essential requirements for prayer.

These instructions not only guide the disciples about requirements for prayer, but explain Jesus' dramatic actions in clearing the temple. True prayerfulness was absent when Jesus inspected the temple on his first visit, apparently because these requirements were not present. There was much religious ritual, but no reality of prayer, because no right relationship in prayer. Yet prayer was intended to be the temple's true purpose, for both Jews and all nations, being the central expression of a true relationship with God. So Jesus taught his disciples that to be true and effective, prayer required faith towards God and love towards others.

Mark's Gentile readers in Rome, decades later, had no temple to centralise their approach to God (in fact the temple in Jerusalem was about to be destroyed), but would have recognised that prayerful relationship with God was now through Christ who was the "true temple".

Prayer Is The Epitome Of True Devotion

A **seventh reference to prayer** is found at 12:40. It is made at the end of a lengthy section which reports Jesus' conflict with the Jewish religious authorities while he was still at the temple (11:27-12:44).

The temple rulers came to Jesus while he was walking in the temple (probably the Men's Court), and questioned the authority of his actions (11:27-28). His provocative reply, requesting them to declare their verdict about the origin of John the Baptist's baptism, implied that he came in the authority of heaven (11:29-33).

Having reached his destined place and time, Jesus now confronted his enemies face to face. He took the initiative himself in the conflict, deliberately provoking the authorities. Jesus told a parable which was clearly directed at the rulers, and prompted their hostility (12:1-12). The story was based on familiar customs of the time in renting out border farm estates in Israel to foreign tenants, and to similar parables by rabbis. But the description of the vineyard reflected the prophecy of Isaiah 5:1-7 which referred to the nation of Israel, and the rejection of the servants parallels the history of Israel's reaction to God's servants, his prophets. Obviously Jesus was the son and heir who would be violently rejected as the last of God's messengers. Probably Jesus' listeners did not realise that he literally meant that he would be killed. But they understood clearly that he was predicting divine judgement upon them and the transfer of God's inheritance to others. The quotation from Psalm 118:22-23 (v 10) served as a biblical warning that God overturns human judgement, and therefore would ultimately vindicate him. His enemies well understood his meaning, and would have arrested him on the spot, but were too afraid of a backlash from the crowd.

Sometime later the various parties amongst Jesus' opponents joined forces to trap him in his statements (12:13-34). The first test came from some *Pharisees* and *Herodians* (v 13), a most unlikely combination since the Pharisees hated the presence and dominance of the Romans in their country, whereas the Herodians supported them. The test was political in nature and typical of the concerns of the Herodians (v 14-17). The trap was clever. They posed the question whether or not they should pay taxes to Caesar. If Jesus answered in favour of paying taxes to Rome he would lose favour with the people, but if he denounced taxes he would be accountable to the Roman authorities. However, Jesus' response snared the Herodians in their own trap over the matter of showing priority to God. "*Give to Caesar what is Caesar's and to God what is God's*".

In the second test, the *Sadducees* posed a difficult question by telling a story of a woman who was the childless widow of seven successive husbands, and asking which would be her husband in the resurrection (v 18-23). The Sadducees held strongly to the laws of Moses, but doubted supernatural reality and denied the resurrection. Their trap tried to ridicule belief in the resurrection, by showing that it clashed with the laws given by Moses about earthly relationships (see Deuteronomy 25:5-10). Jesus' reply exposed their ignorance about the Scriptures and the power of God (v 24). In the first place, the popular view that earthly relationships continued beyond earthly life was false, and in the second place, the Sadducees' disbelief in resurrection meant that they doubted the reality of the living God (v 25-27).

Impressed by Jesus' replies to his critics, a teacher of the law asked him which was the most important commandment (v 28). Distinguishing between small and great commandments was a frequent cause for debate. Jesus' response went beyond the normal debate and gave an answer which expressed the purpose of the law. Quoting Deuteronomy 6:4-5 and Leviticus 19:18, he declared the true requirements of God (v 29-31). They must love God with all their heart, and love their neighbour as themselves. The teacher spoke approvingly of Jesus' response, prompting Jesus to acknowledge that the man was "*not far from the kingdom of God*" (v 32-34). Loving God and your neighbour is the response of a heart where God rules.

Jesus' final public teaching in Mark's Gospel warned the crowd against the false veneer of teachers of the law (12:35-40). The critics silenced, Jesus then raised his own questions to stimulate his listeners' thinking (v 35-37). He focused on the nature of the relationship between David and the Messiah, since popular hopes of God's restored kingdom were based on the view, taught (correctly and biblically) by the teachers of the law, that the Messiah was David's son. But how was this to be harmonised with David's own statement (in Psalm 110:1), influenced by the Holy Spirit, that the Messiah was David's lord. The question, left unanswered, undermined the popular idea of a political messiah, and pointed to an exalted Messiah at the right hand of God. The question would not be answered until Jesus' crucifixion and resurrection.

Finally Jesus warned against the hypocritical, pompous parade of piety by the teachers of the law (12:38-40). Instead of taking the law to heart, they sought only public prestige from their role. Jesus criticised them harshly with sharp accusations.

"*They devour widows' houses and for a show make lengthy prayers. Such men will be punished most severely.*" (v.40)

Instead of showing compassion for the needy, they take advantage of their hospitality (*devour*), and their **prayers** to God were only for show. **This is Mark's seventh reference to prayer.** In the context of Jesus' conflict with the earthly Jewish authorities, this passing mention of prayer may seem at first to be merely a minor detail. Yet it comes at the culminating point of Jesus' public activity, and as his final word of condemnation of the religious teachers. He was actually echoing his previous concern expressed in the temple (11:17). His criticism condemned their failure concerning the very requirements of the kingdom which he had explained at that time to his disciples, their lack of true love and prayerful faith (11:24-25). Far from being an incidental detail, the showy long prayers of the teachers of the law were the final reason for Jesus condemning them to severe punishment. This is because their prayers were the ultimate act of religious pretence and hypocrisy, and of offence to God. Prayer for Jesus was absolutely critical. It was the ultimate priority of human experience. True prayer was the vital reality of fellowship with God, and the conscious action of the heart expressing its trusting submission to his sovereignty. The prayers of the religious teachers, however, were only a sham.

A final incident in the Women's Court in front of the Treasury concluded Jesus' public ministry with an example of one such widow whose attitude stood in striking contrast to that of the teachers. Jesus showed his disciples a poor widow who sacrificially gave her last coins, of greater worth than large donations from those who had plenty. Her actions illustrated the true heart devotion of faith and love which God approves (12:41-44).

Prayer Keeps Watch For The Son Of Man

In the format of Mark's Gospel, Jesus' public ministry reached its climax when he came via the Mount of Olives to Jerusalem and visited the temple. The Gospel's lengthy focus on Jesus' experiences there shows its importance for his mission. He is the Messiah who had come to his temple (where God lives among, and rules, his people) to inherit his kingdom. Instead he finds fruitless religious activities which give the false impression of much promise, and a hostile reception from its custodians. So he publicly condemns the activities by physical protest and the religious leaders by provocative denunciation. And then leaves the temple and returns via the Mount of Olives. As he sits with his disciples on the Mount he gives them a lengthy explanation about events which are to come (Chapter 13).

Jesus' discourse on the Mount of Olives is the longest uninterrupted course of private instruction in Mark's Gospel. It provides a bridge between Jesus' public ministry and the culmination of his mission at the Cross. It is important to see this connection when interpreting its message. Because the discourse contains cryptic and apocalyptic imagery, its message must be discerned carefully.

When one of the disciples expressed his wonder at the magnificence of the temple while they were leaving, Jesus replied that it was going to be completely demolished (v 1-2). Later, as they sat on the Mount of Olives, the two pairs of brothers who were Jesus' first disciples, Peter, James, John, and Andrew, asked him two private questions:

"When will these things happen?" "What will be the sign?" (v 3-4).

Before answering their questions, Jesus firstly warned them against being deceived (v 5). He knew that the disciples' future was going to be confusing and dangerous, so it was important for them to have a clear understanding of God's plan. There would be deceivers acting in Jesus' name, wars amongst nations, earthquakes and famines, but these were only the beginning of the pains connected with the birth of the end (v 6-8). The disciples must keep guard, because they would be persecuted as witnesses for Jesus, and the gospel would be preached to all nations (v 9-10). They had no need to worry about speaking when brought to trial, because the Holy Spirit would empower them (v 11). They would face division and betrayal in family relationships, and public hostility for the sake of Jesus, but those loyal to the end would be saved (v 12-13).

Jesus then began to answer the disciples, starting with their second question about the sign that things were about to be fulfilled. He told them of *"the abomination that causes desolation"* (v 14). This expression was taken from the apocalyptic book of Daniel (9:27, 11:31, 12:11) and referred to something so repugnant and horrible that it would cause the service of the temple to cease and leave God's people desolate. Jews interpreted Daniel's "prediction" as referring to the appalling actions of Antioches IV Epiphanes in 168 BCE when he sacrificed a pig to Zeus on an altar in the temple at Jerusalem. Jesus' comment, however, shows that there was a fulfilment which was yet to come. Interpretations of what Jesus meant vary. One popular view is that Jesus was predicting the destruction of the temple in 70 CE, since that was what he had mentioned in v 2. A second view links the sign with Jesus' final return, and suggests that the temple will be rebuilt sometime in the future and then be destroyed once more. A more likely view, however, sees it as an appalling sign which preceded the destruction of the temple in 70 CE, and was critical to the theme of Mark's Gospel (v 14: *"let the reader understand"*). This view interprets Jesus' meaning as the crucifixion of the Messiah, in line with Mark's earlier theme (see 8:31, 9:12, 31, 10:33-34) and with his description of that event as the finale of his Gospel. The sacrificial death of the Messiah was the most abominable and desolating event which could ever happen! This "abomination" was to be a signal to flee.

To highlight the severity of the crisis, Jesus emphasised the urgency for flight (v 15-16), the hardships to be faced (v 17-20), and complacency-causing deception (v 21-22). His warning was to prepare the disciples for the crisis before it came (v 23).

Following the distress caused by the "*abomination*", a cataclysmic event will take place (v 24-25). Jesus' language describes cosmic upheaval, using figurative imagery from the prophets in the Old Testament concerning the Day of the Lord (see Isaiah 13:10, 34:4, Ezekiel 32:7-8, Amos 8:9, Joel 2:10, 3:15). It indicated **the intervention of God in history** to accomplish his divine purposes of judgement and salvation. As we have noted earlier, Joel used the same form of language to predict the pouring out of God's Spirit upon the world (Joel 2:28-32), which came to pass on the Day of Pentecost after Jesus' resurrection (Acts 2:16-21).

Jesus explained that this cataclysmic upheaval was the **coming of the glorified Son of Man** (v 26-27). The popular interpretation of what Jesus meant, without considering the broad context of Mark's message, takes the event as the return of Jesus at the end of history when the natural universe will disintegrate and Jesus' glory will be fully revealed. In the context of Mark's earlier theme (see 8:38-9:1, 9:9, 31, 10:33-34), however, the coming of the glorified Son of Man refers to the resurrection of Jesus after his sufferings and death and the gathering of his chosen ones through the preaching of the gospel. The cosmic disturbance refers to the convulsions of spiritual and supernatural upheaval, as well as natural and historical turbulence, occurring within the natural course of world affairs. The apocalyptic language highlights the true significance of the events, and Jesus' glory is "seen" by faith. The cataclysmic "event", then, is actually a process of divine invasion into human history, beginning with Jesus' resurrection and the arrival of the Spirit, and continuing until the end of time.

Jesus then proceeded to answer the disciples' first question about "*when will these things happen*" (v 4), referring to the demolition of the temple (v 28-31). He used the fig tree as an illustration. The Mount of Olives was famous for its fig trees, which shed their leaves in winter. When they began to sprout shoots and leaves, it was a clear indication that summer was near (see 11:13). In the same way, the sign of the "*abomination*" was an indication that the destruction of the temple was near. Notice Jesus' words, "*when you see…*", linking verses 14 and 29. To answer the disciples' question (in v 4) plainly, Jesus then declared absolutely (in v 30-31) that all "*these things will happen*" within their generation (see 9:1).

Jesus concluded his discourse with a warning (v 32-37). Since absolutely no one but the Father knew when his intervention would occur, it was imperative to maintain constant watchfulness. It was like servants left in charge of their absent master's affairs needing to be prepared for his sudden arrival.

The logical meaning of Jesus' discourse is that he was referring to his own sacrificial death as a desolating abomination which would precipitate the cataclysmic intrusion of God into the world causing supernatural convulsions in the natural order. These cosmic upheavals refer to his resurrection and the subsequent spread of the gospel and its spiritual effects in the lives of converts. Such events would eventually precipitate the destruction of the temple in Jerusalem.

Mark's **eighth reference to prayer** occurs within the context of this discourse, at the place where Jesus was discussing the distressful period which was coming.

"Pray that this will not take place in winter, because those will be days of distress unequalled from the beginning, when God created the world, until now – never to be equalled again." (vs.18-19)

Significantly, Jesus advises his disciples to face the impending crisis in prayer. Apart from fleeing, the only action Jesus advises is prayer. At first glance, prayer might be taken as little more than religious colouring to emphasise the gravity of the picture of distress. Yet the truth of the matter is that Jesus intends the picture of distress to highlight the need for his disciples to pray (as Mark likewise intends for his readers who are experiencing distress). Prayer, as Jesus has already shown by his actions and teachings, is the highest act of dependence on God and obedience to his will. For Jesus to urge his disciples to pray as they face the culmination of his messianic mission and the divine overthrow of the world demonstrates its importance. By prayer they must remain watchfully alert for the coming of the Son of Man. At the same time, to pray that it would not take place in winter was to pray for some alleviation to the circumstances, but implies that the coming distress was inevitable. Jesus explains that the reason for prayer is that the imminent catastrophe is without precedent in the history of creation. His words (v 19) subtly recall utterances of the Old Testament prophets, and especially echo Daniel 12:1. Prayer is their only recourse.

Prayer Pleads For The Father's Will

Mark's final **reference to prayer (14:32-42)** is the most significant. It is Jesus' vigil in Gethsemane where he prepared for the Cross. The Cross was the final battle in the cosmic spiritual conflict for the mastery of the world. It was the hour when God's Anointed King engaged the Enemy and overcame him to establish the Kingdom of God in triumph. Jesus faced that ordeal in prayer. Before confronting the world he firstly interceded with his Father. His prayer vigil was his final action as a free man.

Mark's Gospel account describes pertinent events which took place beforehand (14:1-31). Mark began his account of the climax of Jesus' mission by enclosing the story of an unknown woman's act of devotion in pouring expensive perfume over his head (v 3-9) between the starkly contrasting intentions of hostility displayed by religious leaders plotting his death (v 1-2) and treachery by Judas in arranging to betray him (v 10-11). The Passover and Feast of Unleavened Bread were a week-long festival which celebrated God's redemption of his people, recalling Israel's liberation from Egypt and journey through the wilderness under

Moses' leadership. Now at this time of remembrance, events were unfolding to accomplish God's ultimate redemption through Jesus, whose body was prepared for burial by a beautiful gesture of love, which would always be a memorial.

As Mark wrote about Jesus' last Passover meal (v 12-26), he highlighted three main matters. Firstly, cautious pre-arrangements showed Jesus' firm intentions to eat the meal with his disciples (v 12-16). The two disciples sent to make preparations would have been less conspicuous than Jesus. A man carrying a water jar was an easy sight to follow (women usually carried jars), and avoided public contact which might be noticed by spying eyes. A room had already been engaged. Secondly, Jesus announced his betrayal (v 17-21). This shattering news was highlighted against an emphasis upon the intimacy of the relationship between the Twelve and the intimacy of sharing the meal. The betrayal was in keeping with Scripture's revealed destiny for the Son of Man, but Jesus expressed deep grief for the tragic traitor. Thirdly, Jesus gave new meaning to the meal for his disciples (v 22-26). The distributed bread represented himself, his presence among them. The cup signified his blood shed sacrificially to establish God's covenant relationship with his people. Jesus indicated his submission to his destiny by solemnly vowing to abstain from further festive drinking until "*that day*" (God's day of glory) when he would drink with a new sense of meaning within God's restored kingdom. At the conclusion of the meal they went directly to the Mount of Olives, which was to be the site of God's triumph (Zechariah 14:4).

The conversation following the Passover meal took on a deeply distressing note (v 27-31). Jesus showed his heightened awareness that he was following Scripture's path of prophecy, by pronouncing that his disciples would all fall away in accord with Zechariah 13:7 (v 27). Yet their desertion was not the end, because after his resurrection he would be reunited with them in Galilee (v 28). Peter, more affected by the prospect of Jesus' death than his resurrection, and offended at the suggestion of his own desertion, protested his loyalty (v 29). Jesus emphatically asserted with precise details that Peter would deny him three times that very night (v 30). Still Peter, and the other disciples, protested that they would die for Jesus (v 31).

That brought Jesus to Gethsemane, the place where he engaged in his most momentous act of prayer (v 32-42). The importance of Jesus' prayer is shown by Mark's descriptive details.

> "*They went to a place called Gethsemane, and Jesus told his disciples, 'Sit here while I pray.' He took Peter, James and John along with him, and he began to be deeply distressed and troubled. 'My soul is overwhelmed with sorrow to the point of death,' he said to them. 'Stay here and keep watch.'*

> "*Going a little farther, he fell to the ground and prayed that if possible the hour might pass from him. 'Abba, Father,' he said, 'everything is possible for you. Take this cup from me. Yet not what I will, but what you will.'*

"Then he returned to his disciples and found them sleeping. 'Simon,' he said to Peter, 'are you asleep? Could you not keep watch for one hour? Watch and pray so that you will not fall into temptation. The spirit is willing, but the body is weak.'

"Once more he went away and prayed the same thing. When he came back, he again found them sleeping, because their eyes were heavy. They did not know what to say to him.

"Returning the third time, he said to them, 'Are you still sleeping and resting? Enough! The hour has come. Look, the Son of Man is betrayed into the hands of sinners. Rise! Let us go! Here comes my betrayer!'"

The significance of Jesus' prayer in Gethsemane on the slopes of the Mount of Olives is that it was the decisive act which sealed his death. In prayer he consciously engaged with God in order to deliberately surrender to his will. Mark makes no explanations. He simply relates what happened and leaves it to his readers to discern the significance. Jesus purposefully went to Gethsemane, where he told his disciples to sit while he prayed. He drew their attention to what he was doing, and Mark provides extensive details of what occurred, more than about any other mention of prayer in his book. This occasion was especially crucial. All previous references to prayer have provided a subtle build-up of anticipation which now comes into sharp focus. Usually when Jesus prayed in private, dramatic things happened in public. This time, his prayer precipitated an appalling chain of events. The subsequent decisions of religious leaders and political rulers had only a secondary bearing on the awful process which swiftly swept up Jesus to his unjust execution. His prior intense period of intercession unleashed the traumatic and the triumphant events which came to constitute the core of the gospel concerning Jesus.

Jesus' experience in Gethsemane was an agonising ordeal for his total being as he shared deeply in intimate intercourse with God. The intensity of the struggle was overwhelming. He took Peter, James and John with him as he moved aside from his other disciples to pray. These three could serve as witnesses to his desolation of spirit in the valley, just as previously they had witnessed his display of glory on the mountain (9:2-4). Jesus openly acknowledged to them his sorrow, which overwhelmed him to the point of death. He was being confronted with the reality that his life, in all its dimensions, was about to be cut off. It was not only the prospect of enduring horrifying torture. Jesus was confronted with the burden of submitting to his Father's will to bear the judgement of the world. It was not that he was lacking courage in the face of death, but that he realised clearly the true nature of his death. As Messiah he was laying down his life for the world. He was the Son of Man, rejected by the world and by God. The "abominable" sacrifice. The LORD's Suffering Servant (Isaiah 53). Jesus' words to his three disciples seem to echo Psalm 42:6, suggesting that his mind was especially conscious of being cut off from God's presence.

He was also aware of his need of supporting human fellowship, and, as he moves ahead a little further from his three chosen friends, he urges them to stay behind and remain watchful. Asking his disciples to keep watch, he went aside alone to plead that God's *cup (of wrath)* might pass him by. The instruction to watch is the same warning that he had given them only recently on this same Mount of Olives when he had predicted an impending crisis which would be unequalled in the history of the world (13:32-37). The intensity of his anguish is made visible when he falls to the ground, his whole being collapsing under the heaviness of his sorrow. Jesus' horror and distress during this ordeal contrast with his calm composure throughout his later arrest, trial and crucifixion.

The focus of Jesus' prayer concerned his relationship with God and his mission. He enjoyed a relational intimacy with God as his Father, and addressed him in the everyday homely language of family ties by calling him "*Abba*", which is the Aramaic word for father. This was highly unusual and striking. It was not childish or sentimental. It was respectful, and an adult expression of affection and relational attachment, but a very familiar way of speaking to God. So Mark highlights it by retaining the term as he reports Jesus' words of prayer (probably reflecting Peter's vivid recollection), and adds its meaning "*Father*" for the benefit of non-Jewish readers. It shows Jesus' intimate, trusting, obedient relationship to God as his Father.

Jesus was very conscious of his intimate fellowship with his Father, and grief-stricken at the prospect of separation. He prayed that it might be possible to avoid the "*hour*" and "*cup*" set before him, referring to his time of destiny and the appalling judgement he must "drink". The imagery of the cup representing judgement has its background in the Old Testament prophets (Isaiah 51:17-23, Jeremiah 25:15-29). Although Jesus shrank from the horror of alienation from his Father and of his judgement, he nevertheless submitted to his sovereign will. His plea was conditioned by surrender to his Father. When he prayed that if possible the hour might pass from him (v 35), he was not wanting to avoid his Father's will, but was trusting that everything was possible to his Father (v 36). He asked for the cup to be removed, not in a spirit of rebellion or demand, but as an entreaty in cooperation and accord with his Father's will. Jesus' unconditional surrender is declared by his firm resolution "*Yet not what I will, but what you will*". Jesus' prayer in Gethsemane was his complete surrender to his divinely appointed mission in fellowship with his Father and resolute obedience to his will. We see in Jesus' Gethsemane prayer that prayer is an act of submission to God's sovereign authority. It is the means by which the Son receives his kingly authority.

Jesus' triumph through this struggle was highlighted by the tragic failure of his disciples (v 37-42). It is astonishing that in the midst of his own agony Jesus repeatedly returned to check on his disciples. It was not that he sought their companionship and prayer support for himself, because he knew that only he could walk his appointed path of suffering. Rather, he urged them to pray for themselves because they faced trials and failures which would overwhelm them. They were also being caught up in the ordeal of ultimate spiritual conflict, and watchful prayer was necessary to survive when their loyalty to Jesus was about to be put to the test. Because *the spirit was willing, but the body was weak*, prayer was necessary to submit to God's keeping power. Prayer was the means by which the followers of Jesus (not only those in Gethsemane, but everywhere, including Mark's readers!) could join him in surrendering in faith to the Father's authority and care.

Though Jesus urged his friends to remain watchful and to pray, and three times returned to them, they succumbed to sleep, until it was too late, and Jesus' betrayer arrived.

Jesus' Triumph

Arrest (14:43-52): Judas came with the arrest party from the Jewish authorities (v 43). Mark emphasised the tragedy of Judas' action by identifying him as "*one of the Twelve*". Similarly, Judas' greeting ("Rabbi") and kiss, supposedly gestures of respect and affection, were acts of contempt and betrayal (v 44-45). Jesus was seized roughly, prompting one disciple to attempt impulsive and feeble resistance, and causing Jesus to protest the unnecessary use of force (v 6-49). He objected to being treated like a robber (or insurrectionist) having to be captured at night by armed guards when every day he had been with them teaching at the temple. But while he exposed the Jews' heavy handedness, he again recognised the need for Scripture to be fulfilled. Then all the disciples fled, including an unidentified young man who avoided capture by slipping out of his garment and escaping naked (v 50-52). Probably this young man was Mark himself (the description suits what is known of him), anonymously verifying what happened as an eyewitness.

Jewish Trial (14:53-72): Jesus was taken before the Jewish Sanhedrin at the home of the High Priest, while Peter followed and mingled with the guards in the courtyard (v 53-54). The Council followed correct legal proceedings for hearing witnesses, yet with the intention not of reaching a just verdict, but a conviction and the death penalty (v 55-56). Charges of capital offences required agreement between at least two witnesses, but the many who testified against Jesus disagreed with one another. Further testimony charged Jesus with threatening to destroy the temple and rebuilding another, a false representation of Jesus' actual claim that it would be destroyed by God's judgement, but again the witnesses disagreed (v 57-59). Finally, the High Priest, frustrated by the Council's failure to gain a verdict and Jesus' refusal to answer the accusations, even when he was requested to do so, asked directly if Jesus was the Messiah (v 60-61). Jesus then admitted plainly that he was, and declared that they would be witnesses themselves when they saw his enthronement and coming, which he described in the words of Psalm 110:1 about the King of Zion, and Daniel 7:13 about the Son of

Man (v 62). Jesus' answer showed yet again his awareness of Scripture unfolding and how he understood the meaning of these Old Testament prophecies. The High Priest symbolically tore his garments as a gesture of holy indignation and called for a verdict of condemnation, which was given unanimously without the need for further witnesses (v 63-64). Council members then fiercely set upon him to demonstrate their disgust and rejection of his claims, and taunted him to prove his claims by prophesying while blindfolded (v 65).

At the same time that Jesus was enduring his ordeal before the Council, Peter was in the courtyard below facing his own interrogators, and denying Jesus as was predicted. Firstly, a servant girl scornfully accused him of being with *"that Nazarene, Jesus"* (v 66-68). Secondly, the same girl later declared to others there that he was *"one of them"* (v 69-70). Finally, the others recognised that he was Galilean and also asserted that he was one of them, provoking Peter to deny it hotly with cursing (v 71). Immediately he heard a crock crow and he recalled Jesus' prediction (v 72).

Roman Trial (15:1-15): Since blasphemy was not a capital crime for the Romans, Jesus was handed over to the government authorities on the political charge that he claimed to be the *"King of the Jews"*. This was the political title of the "Messiah", and would suggest to Romans that he was leader of a Jewish resistance movement. It was ironic that Jesus was accused on these terms since it was because he had refused that role that he was being rejected. When questioned by Pilate, Jesus admitted to the title, but without any attempt to explain the role as he saw it. Neither did he defend himself against any of the other charges which the chief priests brought against him.

Pilate allowed the crowd to make a choice between Jesus and another prisoner, called Barabbas, who was a known resistance leader and murderer, to be released according to an established custom. Mark did not give full details, but it is apparent that Pilate tried to thwart the efforts of the chief priests, and he tried to influence the crowd to select Jesus. Pilate would not have been motivated by compassion or a sense of justice for Jesus, but by his hatred and hostile feelings for the Jewish leaders. The priests however persuaded the crowd to choose Barabbas. When asked what he should do with Jesus they demanded he be crucified. Pilate saw the need to please the crowd, so he agreed to their wishes and sentenced Jesus to the torturous punishment of flogging, and then handed him over to be crucified. Mark's readers at Rome would recoil at the mental image of what Jesus endured, but realise that he would understand the terror which they faced.

The trial of the Sanhedrin had asked, "Are you the Christ?" and convicted Jesus of blasphemy. The trial before Pilate asked, "Are you the King of the Jews?" and convicted him on a political charge. Mark's story of the Crucifixion highlighted the recurring theme that Jesus was executed as the King of the Jews.

Execution: Mockery (15:16-20): The harsh brutality of the Roman soldiers found callous amusement in the pathetic sight of a scourged despised Jew who claimed to be king of his people. They called the whole company together to make perverted sport in mock homage. In imitation of royal garments they draped his naked, shredded torso with an old purple cloak, and pressed on his head a plaited wreath of thorny bramble. While saluting him as king on the one hand, they also buffeted him about the head with a staff. Instead of the kiss of homage, they spat at him, and fell on their knees in mock pretence of bending the knee in respect for his majesty. When their fun was over, they stripped him again, and led him off to be crucified. Although they did not realise it, the soldiers' spontaneous behaviour exposed their tragic blindness to the true identity of Jesus, and at the same time contributed to the unfolding drama which identified him as the King of the Jews.

Crucifixion: (15:21-32): Mark's readers needed no description of the cruel process of crucifixion, so what Mark mentioned had special significance for his readers and the theme of his Gospel. A certain Simon of Cyrene, the father of two men whose names seem to be known to the readers, was compelled to carry Jesus' cross (v 21). The readers would quickly recall Jesus' earlier word about discipleship (see 8:34). The site where Jesus was crucified was identified as "*Golgotha*", which is Aramaic for "*Place of the Skull*" (= "*Calvary*" in Latin). It possibly derived its name from being a location for Roman executions, which were usually carried out by beheadings and crucifixions. This would be a relevant detail for persecuted followers of Jesus at Rome. Jesus' refusal to accept pain-numbing drink, as well as the lottery for his clothes, were noted (v 22-24). These were reminiscent of the first part of Psalm 69:21 and of Psalm 22:18, reflecting a scriptural backdrop which confirmed divine purpose in the dreadful event. The brief details showed Jesus tasting this most cruel of deaths at its vilest bitterness (remember 10:38-40).

Mark highlighted the significance of Jesus' crucifixion. It was the supreme "abomination" (see 13:14). The political charge inscribed over the cross ironically also effectively identified him as the Messiah (v 25-26)! The heaven-sent Messiah was ingloriously crucified! He was executed between two "*robbers*" (insurrectionists) because he had taken the place of one of them (v 27). Verbal abuse hurled insults which contemptuously taunted and mocked, yet for Mark's readers recalled profound truths (v 29-32). Ironically, the temple's destruction was linked to Jesus' death, as would soon be made clear (see v 38), and it was Jesus himself (God's true temple) who would rise within three days. The remark that he "*saved others*" referred to his work of healing, but Mark's readers would be reminded that he also "saved" in the ultimate sense. They also knew that belief in Jesus as the Christ was not inspired by his coming down from the cross, but by understanding why he went to the cross.

Death (15:33-41): Unnatural darkness descended upon the whole land for three hours during the middle of the day, from the sixth hour until the ninth hour (v 33). This is the only description given for this period of Jesus' ordeal on the cross. Mark was dramatically depicting the divine reaction to Jesus' crucifixion, using the language of physical phenomenon in an apocalyptic sense. He was not indicating visible darkness (there is no mention of any reaction from anyone to the unnatural phenomenon), but was using apocalyptic imagery for moral and spiritual darkness. This was the meaning of this term "darkness" throughout the rest of the New Testament, and he was recalling Jesus' recent prediction (13:24). Jesus' crucifixion caused cosmic convulsions. The world was rejecting God's kingly representative, the Son of God, and heaven was rejecting its earthly representative, the Son of Man. The "darkness" was a figurative feature indicating God's withdrawal. It was like the final plague in Egypt which preceded the death of the first-born sons of Egypt (Exodus 10:21-29). Back then Israel was not affected by the darkness, nor by the death of first-born sons, who were redeemed by the blood of a lamb smeared on the door frames of their houses. But now "darkness" covered the land of Israel (and perhaps the whole earth, since the term "land" is the same for "earth"). Mark intends the darkness to be understood as a portend for the imminent death of Jesus, who as Messiah was THE first-born. His blood was being shed as a sacrifice for the redemption of God's people. This darkness in the middle of the day was also reminiscent of Amos' apocalyptic forecast for the Day of the Lord (Amos 8:9). What was intended by the description is brought out in what followed.

At the ninth hour Jesus uttered a loud cry. Jesus' actual words are quoted, spoken in a mixture of Hebrew and Aramaic, and then translated into Greek, as they appeared in the Greek version of Psalm 22:1. This is the only utterance of Jesus while on the cross recalled by Mark. It expresses Jesus' experience, his sense of being forsaken by God, and revealed the depth of his horror of alienation from his Father. Yet by citing scripture, he showed that he continued to trust God intimately ("*My God*") in his darkest hour, and was continuously aware of his path traced out in Scripture. Jesus' cry of abandonment explains the significance of the darkness which came over the land. This was the situation from his perspective. His cry of desolation also called attention to the fact that his situation was the "*abomination which causes desolation*" which he earlier foretold (13:14). Nearby listeners misunderstood Jesus' cry, thinking that he was calling for Elijah, so someone ran and offered him a sip of wine vinegar to sustain him, with the sceptical hope that Elijah might come to his aid (v 35-36). The incident both recalled Jesus' comments at an earlier time concerning Elijah (9:12-13), and also showed that Jesus was kept conscious until the end. The gesture of offering a little relief unwittingly completed the quotation from Psalm 69:21. The drinks offered at the beginning (v 23) and end (v 36) of Jesus' crucifixion ordeal, recalling this quotation, together with the two allusions to Psalm 22 at the beginning (v 24) and end (v 34), mark the crucifixion as scriptural fulfilment. From start to finish, Mark's description intends to highlight the scriptural character of what happened, and this aim shapes his presentation.

Finally, Jesus again cried out loudly, and gave up his spirit (v 37). His life was not taken, nor did it ebb away. He gave it away, of his own will. His death came suddenly, consciously, and deliberately, differing from the normal experience of prolonged exhaustion, coma, and slow demise.

The spontaneous rending of the temple curtain (v 38) signified the connection between Jesus' death and the end of the temple, confirming Jesus' prediction of its impending destruction in 70 CE (13:2) and refuting his enemies (14:58, 15:29). Obviously the splitting of the curtain could not be known at the scene of the crucifixion. It could only be known by the priest who was leading the prayers at the temple. Mark was indicating the significance of Jesus' death by using physical imagery to depict spiritual reality. The splitting of the temple curtain implied the removal of the barrier to access into God's presence (Hebrews 6:19-20, 10:19-20). The historical incident represented an eschatological (End Time) event which resulted from the event of the crucifixion of the Messiah. As Jesus had predicted (in chapter 13), his death was a cataclysmic event which marked the end of world history and the beginning of the kingdom of heaven, the collapse of present creation and the coming of the Son of Man in power and glory. Mark was making the point that the death of Jesus marked the coming of the kingdom of heaven!

The confession of the Roman centurion who witnessed Jesus' moment of death was most significant (v 39). It expressed a greater truth than he probably realised, but confirmed Mark's theme about God's Son on earth, and, having been uttered by a Roman, was important for Mark's Roman readers. The confessions of Peter at the mid-point of the Gospel (8:29), and of the centurion at the end, summarise the two stages of the Gospel, and its overall theme (see 1:1). The rending of the temple curtain (from the top!), together with the centurion's confession, complete the story of Jesus, which began with the rending of the heavens and the divine confession at his baptism (see 1:10-11). A group of women, who had travelled with Jesus and served his needs, were eye-witnesses of what happened (v 40-41).

Burial (15:42-47): Although Jesus was executed for high treason against the Roman government, he was nevertheless granted an honourable burial, contrary to normal policy. Joseph of Arimathea was not a relative, who would usually be responsible, and in fact was a member of the Council which had arranged Jesus' death. That he "*went boldly*" to Pilate to request the body was indeed a daring action. Mark indicated that Joseph was "*waiting for the kingdom of God*", a remark which suggested this was his motivation and which emphasised for readers the meaning of Jesus' mission. Pilate was surprised to learn that Jesus had died so rapidly (normally death by crucifixion took several days), and confirmed with his centurion that it was so. Obviously the death of Jesus was abnormal, yet was also confirmed at the highest official level as certain. Furthermore, two of the women who witnessed Jesus' death also witnessed his burial.

Resurrection (16:1-8): Mark's original conclusion was brief, with a startling ending. [V 9-20 were added later by early Christians to compensate for the brevity] The focus was on the small group of women who had been eye-witnesses at the cross and the tomb. Early in the morning after the Sabbath had ended, they returned to the tomb, preoccupied with the task of treating Jesus' dead body and concerned about how to remove the stone from the entrance. When they arrived they were confronted with a startling revelation: "He is risen!" The announcement was made by "*a young man dressed in a white robe*", seen only by the women. The testimony of women was not legally acceptable, so no one would invent such a story to support news so fantastic if it was not factual. The news rested solely upon the statement of the young man, who must be recognised as a messenger from heaven with a divine revelation. Belief in the resurrection is based on revelation and testimony, not human reasoning and physical evidence, even though these are not completely lacking. The young man calmed their fears concerning his own presence, and declared the news that Jesus was risen, indicating where the now absent body had been. He informed them that they would see Jesus himself in Galilee, confirming Jesus' promise made several nights earlier (14:28). Peter was singled out for special mention, the first time his name had occurred since his denial of Jesus, which Jesus had predicted at the same time as his promise to meet in Galilee (14:30). The young man's words would have been reassuring for Peter at the time, and for Mark's readers at Rome.

The narrative ended unexpectedly and abruptly with the women in a state of shocked, panic-ridden terror. Mark's recurring note of amazement and fear towards Jesus throughout his Gospel reached a climax with this awe-struck quaking at the sheer wonder of resurrection. For his readers the message was clear. Far more terrifying than hostile persecution was the Son who conquered death!!

Confirmation (16:9-20): The added ending to Mark's Gospel drew together a series of details taken mainly from the writings of Luke in his Gospel and the Book of Acts. These details confirm Jesus' resurrection and ascension, and his commission to his disciples to preach the Gospel everywhere.

We see in Mark's references to prayer a consistent meaning. The task of prayer is to submit trustingly to God, as the Son to the Father, in order to overcome the forces of darkness, save the world from peril, and restore God's authority on earth. It is a crucial task which we must not neglect.

CHAPTER 11

"THE FATHER IN HEAVEN"

Prayer in Matthew's Gospel

It is fairly obvious that Matthew's Gospel uses Mark's Gospel as its base and adds other material of its own to suit its own purpose. It contains almost all of Mark's narrative, more or less following the same order, with more than half reproduced in Mark's exact words. However, Matthew includes other matters within the narrative to bring about a different emphasis. Whereas Mark has mainly oppressed followers of Jesus at Rome in mind, Matthew is concerned for Jewish readers who were disillusioned about their nation's future at a devastating period in their history, and who were trying to come to grips with the claim that Jesus was their expected Messiah. Matthew also has additional material which consists mainly of teaching by Jesus in block segments inserted at intervals within the course of the narrative, as well as a birth narrative at the start, and an extended post-resurrection ending. The finished product is a considerably different presentation, yet fully consistent with the gospel concerning Jesus.

Matthew presents Jesus as Messiah and Teacher. He is very concerned to portray Jesus as the promised Son of David, who fulfilled Messianic prophecies, and who came to bring the Kingdom of God. He also highlights Jesus' teaching role, and contrasts him to the Jewish teachers of the Law.

An important aspect of Matthew is that his Gospel is clearly aimed at Jews. Its every appeal concerning Jesus is based on the witness of the Old Testament. At every point in the ministry of Jesus, Matthew finds the Old Testament text which throws light on the event or which finds its spiritual fulfilment in the life of Jesus.

A conspicuous feature of Matthew's Gospel is his use of the expression "kingdom of heaven" to replace Mark's phrase "kingdom of God". The usual explanation for this is that Matthew was being sensitive to Jewish sentiments, and their reluctance to refer directly to God. They preferred to substitute alternative terms. However, Matthew frequently refers directly to God in other settings, and only alters the phrase "kingdom of God", and always by calling it the "kingdom of heaven". The more likely explanation is twofold. Firstly, Matthew wants to avoid the idea that God's Kingdom is an earthly political kingdom to be identified with the nation Israel and Judaism. It is a heavenly kingdom, consisting of all who are righteous before God by receiving the Messiah and obeying his teachings. Secondly, God's kingdom does not spring up from within the world, but comes from the realm of heaven and breaks into the world. This explanation taps into the Old Testament view that God reigns from heaven, and is opposed to earthly kingdoms which are in rebellion against him. Through his Messiah on earth he will re-establish his heavenly rule in the world (Psalm 2, Daniel 2:44-45). Matthew portrays Jesus as the true fulfilment of Israel's expected Messiah, who saves his people, not from oppressive foreign powers by leading them in insurrection, but from their sins by laying down his life on their behalf. In the person of Jesus, God was invading the world, not merely restoring Israel as a national, and dominant, kingdom. Israel was as much in rebellion against God's reign as other nations. Prior to his death Jesus sends his disciples to announce the kingdom of heaven firstly to the "lost sheep of Israel" (10:5-7). Tragically, however, his story climaxes with Jesus rejected by the people of his own nation and crucified as the "King of the Jews" (a title for the Messiah). But then Jesus was raised to life again, and given all authority in heaven and on earth. Consequently the mandate given to the disciples was now to make disciples of all nations, teaching them to observe his commands (28:18-20). The kingdom of heaven consists of all who obey God's rule, regardless of national identity.

The date of Matthew's Gospel is worth noting. Such passages as 27:8, 28:15 ("to this day") argue for an interval of some length after the resurrection of Jesus. For Mark's Gospel to be an underlying source, Matthew would have been composed later. Yet, since there is no hint that Jerusalem was already in ruins (as might be expected in Chapter 24), the date does not seem to be later than 70 CE. That narrows down the date to about 68-70 CE. At that time Roman armies were putting down a Jewish uprising, and Jerusalem was under siege. It was a time of great distress, disillusionment, and confusion of faith for the Jewish nation, and Matthew's presentation of Jesus was timely and apt.

There is a clear arrangement for Jesus' teaching. It is presented in the form of five blocks of instruction given in various settings, perhaps imitating the five books of the Torah. The famous "Sermon on the Mount" (Chapters 5-7) teaches about true righteous living (discipleship) in God's kingdom. The second block of teaching (Chapter 10) deals with the theme of the kingdom's mission (apostleship) when the Twelve were sent out to preach and heal. The third section (Chapter 13) contains parables of the kingdom, marking both a characteristic method of Jesus' teaching and a process of moving away from the synagogue into informal settings, and illustrating the unexpected nature of the kingdom. The fourth segment (Chapter 18) is about service in the kingdom, and the fifth (Chapters 24-25) is Jesus' great apocalyptic discourse about the coming of the kingdom and the end of the world (reproducing Mark 13 and adding several unique parables). These blocks of teaching are interspersed within a narrative of Jesus' actions and experiences. The effect is to introduce the reader to the words and deeds of Jesus.

Matthew's Gospel, then, is an effective presentation demonstrating crucial truths for Jews who were facing a devastating crisis of faith. Jesus truly was Israel's Messiah. Faith in Jesus involved no repudiation of the Old Testament, but was actually the very goal toward which Old Testament revelation pointed. God's Kingdom was not an earthly political/religious state, but the heavenly reign of God breaking into peoples' lives. It was not restricted only to Jews, but open to all nations. The design of Matthew's Gospel was ideally suited for the discipling of Jewish converts.

> **Title:** *"Book of the Origin of Jesus Christ, the Son of David, Son of Abraham"* (1:1)
> **Beginnings:** *Arrival of the King: Genealogy, Birth, Baptism, Temptation, Ministry* (1:2-4:22)
> **First Teaching:** *Message of the King (Sermon on the Mount)* (4:23-7:29)
> **Mighty Miracles:** (8:1-9:35)
> **Second Teaching:** *Mission of the King* (9:36-11:1)
> **Messianic Criteria:** (11:2-12:50)
> **Third Teaching:** *Parables of the Kingdom* (13:1-52)
> **Messianic Signs:** (13:53-17:27)
> **Fourth Teaching:** *Sayings about the Kingdom* (18:1-35)
> **Journey to Jerusalem:** (19:1-23:39)
> **Fifth Teaching:** *Arrival of the King* (24:1-25:46)
> **Crucifixion and Resurrection** (26:1-28:20)

The outline of the book shows the creative and easy to remember method Matthew has chosen for his presentation of Jesus. Although he basically follows Mark, even using Mark's exact words most of the time, his different purpose often prompts him to vary his version. The expression *"kingdom of heaven"*, and the inclusion of birth stories, teaching blocks, and resurrection stories, are conspicuous and sizeable differences. Yet there are also minor alterations, both additions and omissions, which reveal Matthew's different emphases. Sometimes he uses different terms. Sometimes he leaves out an incident, or modifies one. Remarkably, the overall effect does not alter the portrait of Jesus, nor the message of the gospel, but shapes the presentation to be relevant for his intended readers. Consequently, Matthew confirms the reliability of the gospel about Jesus, and provides a fuller revelation of his astonishing advent. In Matthew's presentation, Jesus is God's Heavenly King. A close study of Matthew's Gospel is richly rewarding.

For our purposes, however, we will confine ourselves to his references to prayer, although it is necessary to understand them in their literary context.

The first thing to notice is that he does not follow Mark's pattern with regard to prayer. He omits many of Mark's references, and only includes four. He reproduces Mark's account of Jesus praying before walking on the water (14:23). He gives his own abbreviated version of Jesus' instruction at the incident of the withered tree on the Mount of Olives: *"If you believe, you will receive whatever you ask for in prayer"* (21:22). He has an extended version of Jesus' remark about prayer in his explanation to his disciples on the Mount of Olives about the End Time: *"Pray that your flight will not take place in winter or on the Sabbath"* (24:20). His account of Jesus' experience in Gethsemane depends heavily on Mark, yet includes his own occasional freehand touches (26:36-46). Matthew's obvious alteration of Mark's prayer references has the effect of actually confirming Mark's pattern, and therefore of Mark's intention to highlight prayer's importance and value. At the same time, Matthew was not downplaying prayer's importance by dropping many of Mark's prayer references. He had his own input concerning prayer, and different readers in mind. Mark was revealing to Roman readers the strategic importance of prayer with regard to the Messiah's mission. Matthew demonstrates the Messiah's message concerning prayer for Jewish readers. His first teaching block, the "Sermon on the Mount", presents challenging and illuminating instruction which highlights the vitality and priority of prayer.

Matthew makes no mention of prayer until the "Sermon on the Mount", and then he includes extensive treatment. An overview of the "Sermon" shows its basic theme.

Opening Pronouncements (5:3-10): A series of startling one-liners, arranged in a systematic pattern for combined effect, describes who the kingdom belongs to (*"theirs is the kingdom of heaven"*, v 3, 10). They are recognised by distinctive inner characteristics (*"poor in spirit, mourn [over sin], meek, hunger and thirst for righteousness, merciful, pure in heart, peacemakers"*, v 3-9) and consequent outward experiences (*"persecuted because of righteousness"*, v 10).

Encouraging Affirmations (5:11-16): Jesus turns from general pronouncements to directly affirm his disciples. He urges them to rejoice when persecuted for his sake, because of their heavenly reward and their alignment with the prophets. They are the *"salt of the earth"* and the *"light of the world"*. He exhorts them to let their light shine before men in order to bring praise to their Father in heaven. This is the first mention of God as *"Father"*, an unfamiliar practice for Jews, but characteristic of Jesus. It is also characteristic of Matthew's Gospel. Throughout it, God is called *"Father"* 44 times, and frequently as *"Father in heaven"*. To describe God as *"Father"* expressed respect for him, but also familiarity, and implied his caring, providing, protecting nature. It presupposed an intimate relationship with God, which was a startling and provocative notion. It implied that the righteous demands of God's holy law had been met, and there was no fear or doubt before God. Relationship with God had become close and personal, affectionate and respectful. To indicate that he was "in heaven", meant that his existence was not earth-bound, but a higher, holy, divine order of self-existence. Although Matthew's Gospel is about Jesus' mission on earth, this is shown to be the outworking of divine intrusion from heaven, beginning with Jesus' conception (1:20), and culminating in the supernatural results (temple curtain split from the top, earthquake, and resurrections) of his crucifixion (27:51-53). The mission and teachings of Jesus revealed the reality of heaven as a higher realm, in keeping with Israel's unique revelatory experiences testified to by the Old Testament.

Authoritative Assertions (5:17-20): Jesus strongly declares his allegiance to the law. He has not come to abolish it, but to fulfil it. Every element of it must be accomplished. A person's position in the kingdom depends on his compliance with the law. Therefore the righteousness of the disciples must exceed that of the Pharisees and teachers of the law (who were renowned for their scrupulous, though legalistic, observance of the law) in order to enter the kingdom. This startling announcement reveals the "Sermon's" basic concern (and Jesus' role, who, as Messiah, intended to fulfil the law on behalf of his people).

Comparative Illustrations (5:21-6:34): The bulk of the "Sermon" consists of a series of examples of true righteousness in contrast to traditional custom. Jesus interprets the law in terms of a person's inner conformity to its spirit and intention in contrast to mere outward legalistic practice (which actually avoided its true demands). His examples include moral and relational matters such as murder, adultery, divorce, swearing of oaths, seeking revenge, loving one's neighbour (5:21-48), religious practices of alms-giving, prayer, and fasting (6:1-18), and material issues such as pursuit of wealth and living concerns (6:19-34).

Explanation (7:1-12): With a forceful warning against judgementalism (v 1-5), and a blunt appeal for discernment (v 6), Jesus explains clearly how to enter the kingdom (v 7-11). Simply "*Ask …seek …knock*". Essentially, trust "*your Father in heaven*" for entrance. Jesus concludes ("*So*") with a succinct summary of his teaching about what was required by the law and the prophets, "*do to others what you would have them do to you*" (v 12). In other words, Jesus' message comes down to trusting the Father for acceptable righteousness (which Jesus would accomplish) to enter the kingdom (not trying to measure up by self-righteousness), and treating others similarly (accepting them as they are). The thrust of Jesus' "Sermon" was that belonging to God's kingdom was not a matter of national religious conformity but the reality of a right relationship with the Father, based on trusting him, and shown by being like him.

Ultimate Choices (7:13-27): The final section of Jesus' "Sermon" sets out two options. He urges his listeners to enter (the kingdom) through the "*narrow gate*", which he contrasts with the "*wide gate*". He was contrasting his own narrow view of meeting the law's absolute demanding requirements (which only his righteousness would achieve) by asking the Father, with the popular traditional view of legalistic self-righteousness. He warns them against false prophets (the traditional religious teachers), who outwardly appeared harmless, but who were inwardly "*ferocious wolves*". Their true nature could be discerned by the product of their teaching and actions, just as good and bad trees showed their health condition by the fruit they produced. He also warns those who were replacing traditional legalistic attitudes to the law with popular attachment to him, not to rely on their fervent profession of his lordship and impressive performance of ministry in his name. It was obeying the will of the Father (in his law) which mattered. The alternative choices are powerfully illustrated by the wise and foolish men who respectively built their homes on foundations of rock and sand.

Jesus' Impact (7:28-29): Matthew's conclusion to Jesus' "Sermon" contains a series of words which recur at the end of each of Jesus' teaching segments (see 7:28, 11:1, 13:53, 19:1, 26:1), drawing attention to his role as teacher. Although the "Sermon" was taught primarily to Jesus' disciples (5:1), Matthew highlights the reaction of the crowd. They were "amazed". He also contrasts Jesus with the traditional teachers, because he taught with "authority". Unlike them, he was not quoting the respected opinions of recognised rabbis, but declaring his message as King.

Jesus' Teaching about Prayer

It is necessary to clarify the context of the "Sermon" within the framework of Matthew's Gospel, and its content, in order to rightly appreciate his treatment of prayer. After appearing to avoid the subject in the early stages of his Gospel, he then spotlights it more effectively. His first mention of prayer (5:44-45) seems to be only a passing remark, and can easily be overlooked. Yet it is a stark confrontation. It occurs amongst the series of examples of true righteousness, which is a matter of inner disposition rather than outward conformity. When he refers to the Law's requirement to "Love your neighbour", Jesus contrasted his own interpretation with traditional custom. The Law commanded Israelites to "love your neighbour as yourself", but in practice Israelites developed a popular perversion of the command. They narrowed the interpretation of "neighbour" to mean "fellow Israelite", omitted the qualification "as yourself", and added "and hate your enemy". The result was a complete distortion of the Law's intention. Jesus sharply opposed the customary view.

> *"But I tell you: Love your enemies and pray for those who persecute you, that you may be sons of your Father in heaven".*

Jesus' words were stunning in several respects. They starkly contrasted with the prevailing view, not only of the Israelites at that time, but also of the whole world, both then and now. This was a kingly requirement which was unique in history. It even went beyond anything previously taught in the Law. It did not contradict the Law, but took the Law to an absolute level, to which the Law pointed. To love an enemy requires the heart to be free from all enmity and full of benevolent kindness, which is not a natural human condition. To pray for persecutors is probably the greatest expression of love, and is the act of pleading for their forgiveness and salvation. Jesus explained that such an attitude was evidence of being "sons of your Father in heaven". This means that God loves in this manner, revealing what he is like as "Father". Jesus' words not only challenged the prevailing distortion of the Law, but also presented a startling new view of God. As Jesus goes on to illustrate, God shows no discrimination, but causes the sun to rise on the evil and good, and sends rain on the righteous and unrighteous. His love is a heavenly love, divine love, reflecting who he is. It is not determined by the merits of the recipient. If disciples only love in response to the love of others, there is no rewarding benefit. It is a worldly love, and no different than what tax collectors and pagans do. A disciple's heavenly reward is not worldly in nature, based on merit. It is the reward of participation in God's kingdom of grace and peace, and of glorifying the Father (see 5:12, 16). Jesus concluded, *"Be perfect, therefore, as your heavenly Father is perfect"*. To love your enemies and pray for your persecutors is heavenly perfection, expressing heavenly Father-like love. Jesus' view of prayer was astonishing.

Yet there is more. With regard to Jesus' discussion of religious practices (chapter 6), he first of all stated a general warning (v 1). Then he applied it to three examples. Giving to the needy (v 2-4) was religious service to others. Prayer (v 5-15) was religious service to God. Fasting (v 16-18) was religious service relating to self.

Our interest is with what Jesus had to say about prayer.

5 "And when you pray, do not be like the hypocrites, for they love to pray standing in the synagogues and on the street corners to be seen by men. I tell you the truth, they have received their reward in full. 6 But when you pray, go into your room, close the door and pray to your Father, who is unseen. Then your Father, who sees what is done in secret, will reward you.

7 "And when you pray, do not keep on babbling like pagans, for they think they will be heard because of their many words. 8 Do not be like them, for your Father knows what you need before you ask him.

9 "This, then, is how you should pray:
"'Our Father in heaven, hallowed be your name, 10 your kingdom come, your will be done on earth as it is in heaven. 11 Give us today our daily bread. 12 Forgive us our debts, as we also have forgiven our debtors. 13 And lead us not into temptation, but deliver us from the evil one.'

14 "For if you forgive men when they sin against you, your heavenly Father will also forgive you. 15 But if you do not forgive men their sins, your Father will not forgive your sins."

As with his other illustrations, Jesus warned his listeners to avoid parading their practice of prayer in public places like religious hypocrites (v 5). He was not denouncing public prayer, only the attitude which engaged in the performance of prayer (as if addressing God), while actually seeking applause for self. Instead, he counselled them to pray in the privacy of a closed room (v 6). Normal homes in those days rarely had inner rooms where privacy might be enjoyed. Jesus was most likely referring to a storeroom attached to the house outside the living area. Anyone seen entering a storeroom would not be presumed to be going there to pray! There is a sense of humour in Jesus' suggestion, just as there was in his picture of almsgivers trumpeting their actions to draw attention to themselves (v 2). Jesus' words were not to be taken literally, but humorously, as he very effectively made his point. The almsgiver wanted attention; the person praying must avoid seeking attention. What Jesus meant was that true prayer is private, in the heart, as if in a closed, unlikely room, not for public display. Jesus was speaking about personal prayer. He emphasised the need for absolute privacy by advising that the door of the room be closed. Only the Father, in the secret place, must be aware that the person is praying. Personal prayer is meant to be an intimate communion with the Father, not a public performance of religious ritual. The Father would ensure that their hidden efforts of prayer would be rewarded (literally, "repaid"), and that their communion with him was meaningful and real.

At this point Jesus diverges from the theme of his "Sermon" to extend his teaching about prayer. Although he has broken the pattern followed in connection with almsgiving and fasting, which is short and concise, his additional remarks with regard to prayer are still in keeping with the essential message of the "Sermon". His extended treatment of prayer significantly highlights its importance.

The topic of prayer prompts Jesus not only to contrast hypocritical Jews, but also babbling pagans (v 7). This is especially relevant to Matthew's Gospel, which aims to persuade that believing Gentiles are included in the true messianic community, not only Jews. Jesus' comments reveal his interest in Gentiles. His term "babble" was a rare term, coined by him, and literally meant "stammer-speak". He was ridiculing Gentile praying (probably having their glossolalia in mind) as no more than long-winded meaningless prattle, or repetitious twaddle. They thought that prayer effectiveness depended on lengthy gabble. Jesus advises his listeners not to be like them, since their Father already knows their needs (v 8).

To guide his disciples in sincere and intelligible praying, Jesus sets out a basic pattern for prayer (v 9-13). His previous comments forbid it from being merely parroted unthinkingly, or from treating it as a fixed written prayer. It is a guide, a very revealing and meaningful guide. This so-called "Lord's Prayer" was for those who belong to God's kingdom. Here Matthew gives us Jesus' succinct instruction about prayer, which we can unpack.

"Our Father in heaven": God is addressed in the language of family relationship ("our"), intimate respect and tender affection ("Father"), and awareness of his awesome majesty and holiness ("in heaven"). Our approach to God in prayer must consciously recognise who he is.

"Hallowed be your name": the first concern of prayer must be the heart-felt desire that God's name, his identity in terms of the revelation of his character and glory, should be set apart in absolute reverence.

"Your kingdom come, your will be done on earth as it is in heaven": the primary purpose of prayer is to intercede for the restoration of God's kingdom, which is his rule throughout all creation. God's "will" is his plan of salvation through Jesus Christ, already decreed "in heaven", and intended to be "done on earth".

"Give us today our daily bread": After praying for the person of God and his kingdom, request then concerns the personal needs of the children of the kingdom. In the first place, prayer is made for the provision of material needs, an expression of ultimate dependence on the Father for all things.

"Forgive us our debts as we also have forgiven our debtors": Secondly, prayer is made for forgiveness and restoration of broken relationships, the crucial need of the fallen human race. The genuineness and condition of the request is evident by personal willingness to forgive.

"And lead us not into temptation, but deliver us from the evil one": Finally, prayer is made for divine protection from spiritual dangers because of the conflict which rages between God's kingdom and the dominion of darkness.

Jesus added an explanation concerning the importance of forgiveness (v 14-15). Forgiveness is not an optional or conditional matter. It is essential and central to the kingdom, and to relationship to the Father.

This instruction about prayer in Jesus' "Sermon" shows that it is meaningful and purposeful. Prayer expresses dependence upon God as Father, and is concerned about the reality of his heavenly kingdom within the earthly affairs of the world. The prayer is expressed in plural language ("our"), and is addressed to the disciples collectively ("you", plural, v 9), as were his earlier remarks (v 5, 7-8). Yet Jesus' comments about personal privacy were addressed on an individual basis ("you", singular, v 6). Probably, then, Jesus' pattern prayer is meant to be a guide for both private and collective use. This means that even when praying collectively, everyone is personally engaged. The pattern provides a guide for disciples about how to relate to God in a simple, homely, trusting, and personal manner.

Matthew's extended treatment of the subject, relevant to both Jews and Gentiles, and forming a crucial component in Jesus' teaching about the good news of the kingdom, highlights Matthew's intention that this instruction be recognised as a definitive explanation of the nature of prayer in the kingdom of heaven.

The "Sermon" probably has more light to shine upon the nature of prayer, because there is a further segment which is usually assumed as referring to prayer. Matthew 7:7-11:

7 "Ask and it will be given to you; seek and you will find; knock and the door will be opened to you. 8 For everyone who asks receives; he who seeks finds; and to him who knocks, the door will be opened.

9 "Which of you, if his son asks for bread, will give him a stone? 10 Or if he asks for a fish, will give him a snake? 11 If you, then, though you are evil, know how to give good gifts to your children, how much more will your Father in heaven give good gifts to those who ask him!

In the context of the "Sermon", this is Jesus' explanation about how to enter the kingdom. The theme of the "Sermon" has pressed home the point that entry into the kingdom requires a righteousness which surpasses that of the Pharisees and Jewish teachers of the law (5:20). It is a righteousness which is from a person's inner being, not a religious external performance. But how do you get it?

You simply ask the Father, and it will be given to you! You seek [for God's kingdom and righteousness (6:33)], and you will find! You knock, and the door [into the kingdom] will be opened! Your Father in heaven will give good gifts to those who ask him!

This explanation is the climactic moment of the "Sermon". Jesus tells his disciples how to enter the kingdom of heaven. This is his good news of the kingdom. Entry is a gift.

Jesus' requirement for internal righteousness is a crushing message if a person is left to his own resources. But his announcement that entry (and therefore the required righteousness) is a gift for the asking, is a surprising and thrilling relief. Jesus had already prepared his listeners for this surprise by his opening unexpected and unusual pronouncements of blessing on the unlikely (5:3-12). He had also declared that he had come to fulfil the Law and the Prophets (5:17), which revealed God's unfolding plan of salvation for his people to be accomplished by his promised Messiah. The good news was that the Messiah would provide the required inner righteousness for his people, who could then gain entry into the kingdom by asking the Father.

Jesus' explanation is worth looking at closely. His words are so simple, yet his meaning is profound. He speaks of God as "Father", which in that ancient world expressed respect for dignity and authority, while also indicating relational intimacy and approachability. This was a fresh way of thinking about God. To address God in this way implied having a warm and personal closeness to him, and comfortable trust in him.

To "ask", "seek", and "knock" has a similar implication because they suggest an ease and boldness and directness of approach. It was a far cry from standing at a distance from an awesome, austere God and offering ritual sacrifices before daring to draw near him in consciousness of guilt and unworthiness.

Jesus' explanation is basically the familiar approach of "calling on the name of the LORD". But he has introduced a more intimate and personal dimension by identifying the name of the LORD as "Father", and indicating a more informal attitude of approach. Crying out to God from a relationally remote distance is replaced by intimate entreaty. Jesus is depicting the nature of prayer, and showing its crucial earthly role in regard to the kingdom of heaven. Not saying prayers, but having a prayerful relationship with the Father, is the essence of living as a family member of God's heavenly kingdom.

Jesus' Call for Prayer

Jesus' second block of teaching in Matthew concerned the intrusion of God's kingdom into human affairs (9:35-10:42). A brief summary of Jesus' ministry of teaching and healing set the scene (9:35-38). Then Jesus called twelve disciples and gave them authority to drive out evil spirits and to heal every disease and sickness (10:1-4). Then he sent them out with instructions for their task (10:5-42). Initially they were sent to the *"lost sheep of Israel"*, although their instructions also anticipated later periods of mission and hostile trials. The Gospel finally concludes with instructions from the resurrected Jesus to these same disciples to go into all the world and disciple the nations (28:18-20). The intrusion of God's kingdom was by means of announcing and demonstrating that the *"kingdom of heaven is near"*. The twelve were acting in the authority of the king.

The preliminary introduction to the section indicates Jesus' ministry of preaching the good news of the kingdom and healing. In particular, he had *"compassion"* on the crowds because they were *"harassed and helpless, like sheep without a shepherd"*. *"Compassion"* was a conspicuous characteristic of Jesus, highlighted by Matthew, Mark, and Luke, each in their own way. This was a distinguishing characteristic of God in the Old Testament. The expression, *"sheep without a shepherd"*, echoed the concerns of Moses and the prophets at previous times, which Jewish readers would instantly recall. Matthew was portraying Jesus as motivated by the same driving attitude behind God's saving agenda for Israel in the past.

It was this motivation and mission which prompted Jesus' message to his disciples,

"The harvest is plentiful but the workers are few. Ask the Lord of the harvest, therefore, to send out workers into his harvest field".

Although the term *"prayer"* is not explicitly used, the word *"ask"* is the term which Jesus used earlier in his "Sermon" for approaching God in prayer. It is more relational than formal in manner. Jesus was clearly showing that with regard to the kingdom of heaven, whether entering it, praying for its coming, or requesting workers for its harvest, prayer was crucial, and was in terms of personal relationship, not ritual. It is notable that after calling his disciples to ask for harvesters, Jesus then sent them out!

Jesus' Personal Practice of Prayer

Matthew provides a special glimpse of Jesus praying which is not found in Mark (11:25-26). He does not use the term "prayer", or indicate any details about the situation which prompted it. He merely reports what Jesus said, and that was obviously prayer. Apart from a later occasion where Jesus is described in the posture of prayer ("*looking up to heaven*") to give thanks before feeding the crowd of five thousand (14:19, a detail not found in Mark's version), this is the only occasion in Matthew's Gospel where Jesus is depicted praying publicly. Mathew's surrounding context reveals the significance of the prayer, and that context needs to be considered carefully in order to fully appreciate its vital message.

Between Jesus' second segment of teaching, containing instruction for his disciples' mission (chapter 10), and third segment, consisting of parables about the kingdom (chapter 13), Matthew's narrative includes a section about Jesus interacting with confused friends and critical enemies (chapters 11-12). It is a skilful weaving together of separate components to present revealing insights about Jesus' identity and mission. Remember that Matthew wrote for Jewish readers, who were deeply familiar with the writings of the Old Testament.

Although Mathew follows Mark's narrative, he adds material of his own. He presents a series of eight separate components, only three of which come from Mark. These are introduced by general time terms ("*At that time*", "*Then*", "*While*"), which was a literary technique to link them together, and to give an accumulative impression, although they follow a logical, not chronological, sequence. The whole section builds a picture of Jesus. It begins with John the Baptist's uncertainty, and ends with Jesus' mother and brothers wanting to speak with him. Throughout the section there is mounting hostility towards him by the religious authorities, while the crowds benefit from his healing ministry. Most of Jesus' teaching throughout this section was given in response to those who approached him.

Look closely at the first incident (11:2-6). John the Baptist was apparently uncertain about whether Jesus was indeed the one they should expect. This was because of what he heard Jesus was doing. He was not doing what John had said he would do, which was to bring judgement (3:7-12). In response, Jesus told John's disciples to tell him what they saw and heard. On the surface of things, that does not seem to be very helpful, because it only restated what was troubling John. However, Jesus used language which recalled prophetic predictions about God's Day of Salvation, which included both judgement for God's enemies and restoration for his people (Isaiah 35:5-6, 61:1). Jesus was urging John to *discern* what was happening, and to recognise that the Day had arrived, just as both of them had been preaching (3:2, 4:17). As John considered what Jesus was doing, in the light of prophecy, he would discern that Jesus was the one to expect. Jesus did not say so plainly (especially in public) because it was a conviction to be discerned, and because God's coming judgement would take place in a surprising (and shocking) manner, by Jesus' crucifixion.

To the crowd, when John's disciples had departed, Jesus confirmed that John was a prophetic messenger who, like Malachi's predicted Elijah, was sent to prepare the way for him (11:7-15). Jesus was linking John and himself, in fulfilment of prophecy, as inaugurating the arrival of the Day of the LORD, and he appealed for discerning ears to hear what he was saying. However, he criticised his current generation for their childish inconsistency, because they dismissed John for his ascetic habits as having a demon, and himself for being too sociable (11:16-19). They were failing to discern the momentous significance of John's and Jesus' roles.

In a separate second incident Jesus denounced cities which witnessed his miracles but did not repent (11:20-24). He was acting like the Messiah of judgement whom John had expected.

The third incident is the one depicting Jesus praying. It has no background details, which makes it all the more striking. It is simply a three-part public utterance by Jesus, without any specific setting (11:25-30). We will look more closely at this incident in a moment.

A fourth incident describes Jesus' response to criticism for plucking grain on the sabbath, and his subsequent healing a man's shrivelled hand in the synagogue (12:1-14). When his words and actions provoked hostility against him by the Pharisees, he withdrew from public, and warned those he healed not to disclose who he was (12:15-16).

Matthew explained that Jesus did this to fulfil the role of Isaiah's "chosen servant" (12:17-21).

After healing a demon-possessed man of blindness and dumbness, Jesus was accused of acting in the power of Beelzebub. He replied by pointing out the absurdity of their argument, and the unforgivable implication that they were rejecting the work of God's Spirit (12:22-37).

When a delegation of Pharisees and lawyers wanted Jesus to perform a miraculous sign, he called them a *"wicked and adulterous generation"*. He told them that the only sign they would be given was the *"sign of the prophet Jonah"*, and that they would be condemned at the judgement by the men of Nineveh who had repented at Jonah's preaching, and by the Queen of the south who had listened to Solomon's wisdom (12:38-45).

The final incident involved Jesus' mother and brothers who came to speak to him, and his response that his mother, brother, and sister was *"whoever does the will of my Father in heaven"* (12:46-50).

Notice that four of these incidents contain statements by Jesus about the *"Son of Man"*, the title by which he speaks about himself. He was not an ascetic like John the Baptist (11:19). He was Lord of the Sabbath (12:8). Anyone speaking a word against him will not be forgiven (12:32). Like the sign of Jonah, he will be three days and nights in the heart of the earth (12:40).

Jesus was an enigma, doing astonishing acts, yet not conforming to customs and expectations. The emerging picture of Jesus was a mixture of divinely anointed ruler, Daniel's apocalyptic Son of Man, and Isaiah's "Servant of the LORD". This combination of three

Old Testament figures in one person was a totally different concept of the Messiah from traditional Jewish opinion. The series of incidents also shows that the coming of the kingdom was invasive, causing upheaval and violence as it clashed with the powers of evil, both demonic and human. Matthew's presentation reveals Jesus not as a political or military messiah, but as the Messiah from heaven restoring God's kingship on earth. He is the fulfilment of amalgamated Old Testament hopes, concerned not for national fortunes but for the greater issue of the world's relationship with the Father.

Look again now at the brief prayer which Jesus uttered. It is within the broad context of this series of incidents which presents Jesus in the role of mixed Old Testament identities, needing to be discerned. The prayer itself is part of a threefold public utterance, and its significance is highlighted by the full speech given in Jesus' own words. It makes a bigger impact if heard rather than read. Jesus offers a prayer of praise, makes a claim of unique privilege, and issues a sweeping invitation. In its context, it publicly expresses Jesus' essential perspective. Only Matthew contains the full version, although it is partially included by Luke (Luke 10:21-22).

Jesus' prayer is spontaneous and natural. He addresses God directly, and in self-assured familiarity. He calls God "*Father*" and "*Lord of heaven and earth*", demonstrating his intimate personal relationship to God, and his respect for God's absolute supremacy. He is very conscious of his Father in heaven and of himself as Son on earth, partners in restoring the kingdom of heaven. He offers praise to God for hiding "*these things*" from the wise and learned, and revealing them to little children. The meaning of "*these things*" is not explained, but is naturally understood as the matters revealed through the collection of the incidents, which disclose his true identity and the realities of the kingdom which he was teaching and demonstrating. Jesus did not mean that God was excluding the wise and learned in favour of little children. He was speaking figuratively, indicating the nature of God's revelation. God was not revealing "*these things*" to those who relied on self-sufficient human intellectual competence, but to "*little children*", those (of any age) who recognised their dependence and inadequacy. He stresses that this is his conviction by asserting that it was the Father's good pleasure.

The prayer is a prelude to a public announcement. Jesus declares that his Father has committed "*all things*" (which are to be revealed, referring to the restoration of the kingdom of heaven) to him. This revelation concerns knowledge of the Son (with regard to his mission in the world), which only the Father knows, and knowledge of the Father (with regard to his motivating love and purpose), which only the Son knows, and those to whom the Son chooses to reveal him. The language is cryptic, to express the "hiddenness" of this knowledge to natural human understanding. Jesus concludes with an open invitation to the "*weary and burdened*" (inwardly overwhelmed by life's distresses) to come to him to find rest, and to become his servant and disciple. His yoke of service is not burdensome, but pleasant.

Although the term is not used, Jesus' invitation is in keeping with his compassion for the "harassed and helpless".

The prayer demonstrates Jesus' relationship to the Father. The announcement claims intimate mutual knowledge between the Father and the Son, and the Son's exclusive privilege to reveal the Father to whomever he chooses. The invitation chooses everyone, offered to all who are "burdened". The whole public speech identifies Jesus, in his own words, as the Mediator between the Father and the troubled world. Prayer was the foundation for his mission.

Jesus' two other occasions in Matthew of engaging in prayer confirm this conclusion. Matthew closely follows Mark, although he uses his own words and adds minor variations. After his notable feat of feeding a large crowd in a remote area, Jesus sent his disciples ahead of him by boat while he ascended a mountain to pray (14:22-23). Matthew adds the phrase "*by himself*", perhaps to show that Jesus was practising what he taught about praying to his Father in secret (cf. 6:6). At the fourth watch of the night, when the disciples were struggling in their boat against the wind, Jesus walked to them across the surface of the lake (14:24-27). Matthew follows Mark's account, with the same purpose of identifying Jesus in comparison with Israel's exodus and crossing of the Red Sea. The event demonstrates that prayer was foundational to Jesus' mission. Yet Matthew adds two further details. He describes how Peter requested and attempted to walk on the water to Jesus, until he lost confidence when he saw the wind, and began to sink, needing to be rescued by Jesus. Jesus questioned Peter, "*Why did you doubt?*" Whereas Mark follows Peter's eye-witness account with regard to Jesus, Matthew is also interested in Peter's own experiences, since he became the prominent Apostle to the Jews. Matthew probably included this incident for the benefit of his Jewish readers, who might be affected by the adverse winds of opposition to turn their eyes away from looking at Jesus. Matthew's second addition is his different ending. Where Mark concludes that the disciples were "*completely amazed*", Matthew says that they "*worshiped*" Jesus, and identified him as the "*Son of God*". They were not ascribing the popular political messianic title to him, but recognising Jesus' special relationship with God. Matthew's words were intentional. Compare them with the end of his Gospel, when the disciples met Jesus after his resurrection. "*When they saw him, they worshiped him; but some doubted*" (28:17).

When we recognise how carefully Matthew has composed his Gospel, we can appreciate that Jesus' lengthy period of prayer on the mountain (until the fourth watch of the night!), prior to his walking across the lake, was strategic. It was the prelude to a demonstration of his mission. Discerning this provides perspective for Jesus' next, and final, lengthy period of prayer, immediately prior to completing his messianic mission of crucifixion and resurrection (26:36-46). This was his prayer in Gethsemane. Matthew's description of the disciples' reaction after the resurrection highlights the pattern of his account: Jesus prayed; Jesus performed his mission; the disciples reacted in mixed worship and doubt (hesitation).

Matthew's version of Jesus' ordeal in Gethsemane basically repeated Mark's narrative, slightly modified by his own words (26:36-46). The event was pivotal to Jesus' mission. He demonstrated his conscious awareness of the imminence of his end, and made his final choice of commitment to his unique assignment. It was also there that his disciples showed their lack of understanding and empathy with regard to what Jesus was facing, and the hollowness of their recent declarations of loyalty. The experience for Jesus was one of overwhelming sorrow and horror, shared intimately and privately with his Father in prayer. He struggled within his spirit with the prospect of drinking the cup of God's wrath. The gist of his praying is condensed to two brief summaries as he contemplated whether it was possible for him to be spared from drinking the cup, that is, from suffering the judgement for the sin of the world (v 39, 42). Throughout, Jesus consistently maintained the desire to do only his Father's will. His isolation in his role was highlighted by the sleepy indifference of his closest, chosen, companions, who were unmoved by his deep distress, and failed his request to keep watch with him. They probably did not understand what he prayed, or its significance, until it was explained later, even though they were close at hand at the time. Jesus gained courage and strength for the task ahead from his Father, not from his friends. Jesus' statement to them that the "*spirit is willing, but the body is weak*" expressed a profound insight, which applied not only to their failure at that point of time, but to their behaviour, and that of the other disciples, in general. They had all said they would not fall away and disown Jesus (v 33, 35), yet they were soon to desert him. Their weakness magnified the display of Jesus' strength. There is much pathos in his final words to his sleeping friends for them to see the nearness of the hour, in that the Son of Man was being betrayed into the hands of sinners, and that his betrayer (another friend) was coming. Because of his prayer at this time, Jesus saw clearly the way forward, and resolutely entrusted his destiny to the Father. He endured ignominious arrest, trial, and death with purpose and serenity. His heavenly reward was resurrection and exaltation to the "*right hand of the Mighty One*" (26:64).

God's Right Hand Man

Matthew's Gospel ends with a triumphant announcement by the risen Jesus. He claimed that he had been given absolute sovereignty, "*all authority in heaven and on earth*". He was now ruler over all realms of existence. All rebellion and wickedness, and every opposing force to God and his purposes, were defeated. As God's messianic Son on earth, he had successfully accomplished his mission, and was now at his Father's right hand in heaven. The kingdom of heaven had arrived! He therefore commissioned his disciples to go and "*make disciples of all nations*" in order to extend the kingdom throughout the world. Converts were to be baptised into a personal relationship with God, whose name (his revealed identity) was a summary of the threefold features of Jesus' accomplishments in restoring the heavenly kingdom. God was now known as the "*Father*", the identity revealed by his messianic "*Son*", who, by his victorious crucifixion and resurrection, abolished the barriers to access into the intimate eternal realm of the "*Holy Spirit*". (In later practice, these convictions were included in the condensed expression of baptising converts simply into the name of Jesus Christ, or the Lord Jesus [Acts 2:38, 8:16]. God was identified as the "God and Father of our Lord Jesus Christ" [Ephesians 1:3]). The risen Jesus assured them of his own continuing presence. The kingdom of heaven was not a Jewish kingdom, but a world-wide kingdom of redeemed sinners from all nations. Strategic to the kingdom's intrusion into the world is prayer on earth asking the Father to let his kingdom come.

CHAPTER 12

"IN MY NAME"

Prayer in John's Gospel

John's Gospel is different. It has a different format than Matthew, Mark, or Luke, and a different style of language and thought. It is the only Gospel of the four which has an opening prologue. In fact, it copies the only other book in the whole Bible, Genesis, which begins in this fashion, apart from 1 John which was written at a similar time, and adopts the same approach. The prologue is a declaration, expressing deep theological convictions about the historical Jesus.

The Gospel was written to convince readers that the Messiah was Jesus (20:30-31). The original readers were Jews who lived more than half a century after the resurrection of Jesus, and about 100 years after Jesus was born. They also lived after the Jewish war with Rome in 66-72 CE. The Jewish uprising against Roman occupation in Israel had been brutally crushed, and the nation left in tatters. Jerusalem had fallen, the temple destroyed, and the nation's priestly leadership terminated. The population in Israel was decimated. Thousands had been killed. Thousands had fled from the country to other lands. Jews, both in the homeland and in the dispersion, were disillusioned about their faith in God and their hopes of a Messiah. Throughout the empire Jews were despised and oppressed. John wrote his Gospel to persuade them to have faith in Jesus. He reveals wonderful truths about Jesus' messiahship in a manner which stimulates the mind and heart.

Traditionally, the author of the Fourth Gospel has been held to be John the son of Zebedee. The book claims to be the testimony of an eyewitness (1:14, 21:24,25), who seems to be the one referred to as the *"disciple whom Jesus loved"* (13:23, 19:26-27, 20:2, 21:20-24). Internal evidence points strongly to the identification of this disciple with John the Apostle. For example, John the Baptist is simply referred to as John, and is the only John named throughout the Gospel. The name of John the Apostle, the son of Zebedee, is never mentioned. The narrative shows evidence of the author's familiarity with Israel. His knowledge of Jewish customs, feasts, and topography is unquestionable. At the time of writing, the Apostle John would have been elderly, probably the last of the Twelve. He wrote about Jesus with deep insight and conviction.

Four places have been proposed for the writing of John's Gospel. Alexandria is suggested because of apparent affinities of language and thought with the writings of Philo, a Jewish philosopher from that city. Close comparison, however, shows vast differences of outlook. Nevertheless, the superficial likeness indicates something about the contemplative nature of much of the book. Antioch is argued because of similarities with other works from Syria, which was an early hub of Christian activity. Palestine is thought to be a possibility because of the close familiarity with cultural and topographical details. However, the traditional location is Ephesus where John was believed to have spent his final years. What we should recognise is that the style and content of the book imply that the readers had Jewish, Hellenistic, and Christian background. They seem to be facing hostility and a crisis of faith. The most likely situation was that experienced by both Jews of the Dispersion and Christians during the reign of the emperor Domitian (81-96 CE). A date around 90 CE for John's Gospel would make it the last of the four Gospels in the New Testament to be written. The crisis of faith was eschatological (concerned about End Times), sacramental (concerned about rituals for drawing near to God), and mystical (concerned about experience of higher realities) in nature. The Gospel is both evangelistic and instructive in its aim.

> The purpose of the book is stated in John 20:30-31: *"Jesus did many other miraculous signs in the presence of his disciples, which are not recorded in this book. But these are written that you may believe that Jesus is the Christ, the Son of God, and that by believing you may have life in his name"*.

From a strict grammatical point of view, the wording of the main statement should be reversed. The translation should read, "*...that the Christ, the Son of God, is Jesus ...*". The aim was to convince Jews who were disillusioned about failed military "messiahs" that the true Messiah was Jesus. This was so that they could "*enter into life*" through faith in him. This was life in terms of its fulness and ultimate sense. It was a radically different Messiah's mission than the popular expectation of political liberation from Roman control.

John sought to achieve his aim by the emphases, structure, and style of his presentation of Jesus. He strongly emphasised historical reality and familiar incidents. He assumed that the incidents were well known, and told them in a manner to draw out an intended interpretation. For example, only John tells the story of turning water into wine, but careful examination recognises that he does so in a way which presupposes familiarity, in order to highlight its "sign" nature (2:11). Certain terms and ideas throughout the book are either included repetitively (life, truth, love, etc.) or completely avoided (prayer, Lord's Supper) to meet the faith crisis being experienced. For example, activities which could become "sacramental" or "mystical" are presented so as to stress their "real" and "relational" meaning, and to avoid misunderstanding. For instance, he writes "ask" rather than "pray" (14:13-14, etc.). He omits mention of the institution of the Lord's Supper, yet includes a discussion in another setting (6:53-58), which gives profound insight into the Supper's true meaning. History has shown the tendency for both these practices to be treated as religious and mystical rituals, even though John deliberately avoided them being represented in that light. Frequently his language is figurative and cryptic. He expresses ideas which require thoughtful contemplation to grasp his latent meaning. This is because he is using earthly terms to indicate "heavenly" truths.

Jesus' identity was demonstrated in his deeds and explained in his words. Both his deeds and words were *"signs"*. What he did and what he said signified realities of a "heavenly" nature. To eyes enabled by knowledge of the Old Testament to discern, they signified that he was indeed the promised Messiah. Only a few incidents from the life of Jesus were actually included in the Gospel, but they were told at considerable length. John's approach assumes that the reader was already familiar with the stories. The way he tells them, including what he omits and what he adds, was designed to suit his overall aim. They are usually accompanied by a lengthy discourse or dialogue. The "sign" incidents bear resemblance to "sign" actions of God in the Old Testament, especially those at the Exodus. Each incident occurs against the backdrop of the Passover or Sabbath, which were themselves given to Israel as "signs". Essentially John shows Jesus to be the Messiah in a "heavenly" sense, revealing the truth of God and restoring eternal life to the world. He is greater than Moses. He came from heaven to earth to achieve a greater exodus than Moses, by his crucifixion and resurrection. His "exodus" was the way to eternal life. Eternal life is a transformed and transcendent life through the reality of knowing God. God is known through knowing the Messiah Jesus, who was sent to reveal God, and to relate God, to all who trust him.

John's Gospel is composed in simple language yet presents profound and far reaching theological and spiritual insights. It is intended to be read and re-read reflectively. It relates significant historical incidents against a skilfully constructed reminder of Israel's past Exodus experience, in a way which reflected the readers' current circumstances. The work/mission (note John's terms *"work"*, *"sent"*) of Jesus is the dominant theme, resulting in the life which comes from the Spirit, who is given by the Father at the request of the Son. The Spirit is received by disciples who receive Christ in obedient trust (the noun "faith" never occurs, only the verb "believe", or even "obey" - not mere assent in the mind, "belief", but active commitment, "trust"). The life of the Spirit is expressed in the obedience of love and witness.

Jesus' farewell discourse to his disciples and final prayer (chapters 13-17) are unique to John's Gospel. They provide an insider's insight into the meaning of "eternal life". That life is the relational reality of knowing the Father through the Son by the Spirit, and of belonging to the community characterised by loving unity and dependent prayerfulness, being joyfully fruitful and bearing witness to truth in a hostile world.

That is why it is so striking that John never uses the term "*prayer*"!! Translations which insert the word where it does not actually occur, miss John's point and confuse the issue. For example, it is surprising that John does not refer to Jesus' ordeal in prayer in Gethsemane, even though he describes Jesus' arrest there (18:1; the phrase translated "*finished praying*" is literally, "*having said these things*"). By omitting Jesus' prayer in Gethsemane, John has actually highlighted it for those who are familiar with what happened. Similarly, by avoiding the term "*prayer*", John was able to highlight the matter of prayer by other means. This is because John wants to challenge his readers to the exciting and meaningful nature of prayer, rather than let them think of it as a mere ritual.

John's presentation of Jesus is sometimes called the "spiritual" Gospel, because of its reflective character. It emphasises Jesus' heavenly origin and heavenly messianic role to contrast with earthly political quests. It reveals the reality and nature of eternal life to distinguish faith in Jesus from the religious views and trappings of Judaism. It is the product of John's own personal eyewitness experience of having known Jesus, and his developed comprehension under the influence of the Holy Spirit. John's Gospel bears witness to exhilarating and liberating truth.

1:1-18 The Declaration: The Word Became Flesh

John commences his Gospel with a magnificent declaration about the unique "*Word*" ("*Logos*") of God becoming the historical Jesus to reveal the Father's glory and grace. He obviously follows the opening format of Genesis, since both books begin with the words "In the beginning". John's statement is steeped in Hebrew language and concepts. His declaration has two parts. V 1-13 concern the presence of the Word, in eternity before time (v 1-5), then in history (v 6-13); V 14-18 concern the glory of the Word.

John's use of the term "Word" ("*Logos*") was relevant and creative, because he was tapping into a widespread range of contemporary ideas which were based on the term - among Jews, Greeks, Christians, and heretics. The simple term "*word*" basically referred to inner thought and outward speech. It was the means by which peopled "expressed" themselves. The term could be used in many ways, from the mere term ("word"), to an idea, to profound arguments or messages, to powerful and lofty concepts. The Greek philosopher Plato used the term "*Logos*" for the principle of reason which he claimed governed everything in existence. The Jewish philosopher Philo, influenced by Plato, applied it to an impersonal, ideal concept between the infinite God and the finite creation. John, however, writing to Jews, uses the term to refer to the familiar idea by which God always operates. The "*Word*" was the means by which God always expressed himself in order to make himself known and to accomplish his purposes. The Jewish scriptures (the Old Testament) were essentially a collection of God's "*Word*", a record of all that God had spoken to reveal and fulfil his intentions for his world.

By his "*Word*", God commanded creation into existence (Genesis 1), proclaimed his name to Moses (Exodus 33-34), and declared his will for redeeming the world through promises (to Abraham and David), Law, and prophetic messages. God's "*Word*" was the expression of his divine will, and his agency for achieving it.

John's meaning for the "*Word*" could be adequately understood by the eloquent prophecy of Isaiah 55:8-11, which is worth quoting.

> "*My thoughts are not your thoughts, neither are your ways my ways, declares the LORD. As the heavens are higher than the earth, so are my ways higher than your ways and my thoughts than your thoughts. As the rain and snow come down from heaven, and do not return to it without watering the earth and making it bud and flourish so that it yields seed for the sower and bread for the eater, so is my word which goes out from my mouth: it will not return to me empty, but will accomplish what I desire and achieve the purpose for which I sent it*".

John's use of the term "*Word*" means God's "self-expression", or "expression of his mind and heart and will", his "Self-revelation" which is the ultimate cause and controlling influence behind the outworking of his divine rule. It is a living, active, and supernaturally powerful reality. In the opening prelude to his Gospel about Jesus, John makes preliminary declarations about the presence of the "*Word*", and the glory of the "*Word*".

Echoing the language of Genesis, John starts at the beginning of all things He opens with a declaration about the pre-existent divine "*Logos*", depicted as God's agent in creation and the source of life and light (v 1-5). What he says about the "*Logos*" is succinctly and meaningfully stated. Twice he indicates that the Word was "*in the beginning*", emphasising that it was always there, before anything else existed. Then he adds that the "*Logos*" was "*with God*". He uses a phrase which indicates an intimate association with God, similar to saying "face to face with God". The "*Logos*" was not separate or independent from God. In fact, he says "*The Logos was God*". He means that there was no distinction between the "*Logos*" and God himself, since the "*Logos*" was simply the means of God's own activity and influence. Strikingly, he personifies the "*Logos*", by saying "*He was in the beginning with God*". It is as if the "*Logos*" was an agent of God. He was not indicating another person apart from God, but personifying God's "*Word*", or "*Self-Expression*". This was a typical Hebrew literary tactic. Qualities or characteristics of God were treated as if they were persons in their own right, who acted on God's behalf. For example, the "Wisdom" of God, like "*Logos*", was also personified as an agent of God in bringing creation into existence (Proverbs 8:22-36). John treats the "*Logos*" like a person, and declares that "*he*" was there, in intimate association with God, at the beginning. The "*Logos*" was not someone other than God, nor a mere abstract characteristic of God, or impersonal, independent entity. The "*Logos*" was the expression of

God himself. John was not referring to the entity of God, his being, but to his activity, his doing. God's identity is revealed, and named, in terms of what he does, not in terms of his metaphysical essence. The reason John wrote about the "*Logos*" of God in this personified way was to prepare for God's incarnation in Jesus.

For emphasis John repeats that the "*Logos*" was with God in the beginning. He was always there! The outward expression of God's inner being was responsible for absolutely everything which was created. John states that both positively and negatively. He means that all creation came into existence as God expressed himself. With regard to this, John further states that in the "*Logos*" was life, and that life was the light of men. The imagery of both "life" and "light" are prominent themes throughout John's Gospel presentation of Jesus. Here in his prologue, John introduces the images to give some indication of their meaning, although their full meaning only emerges as the book proceeds. Life, says John, exists within the "*Logos*", within the "Self-expression" of God's intrinsic disposition. He means the eternal self-existing life of God. Not merely his existence, but the fulness of his essential nature. That life of God was the light of the human race. It illuminated the meaning of human existence by revealing the excellence of God's attributes, actions, and intentions.

John's firm declaration that "*The light shines in the darkness, but the darkness has not understood it*" is cleverly ambiguous. The term translated "*understood*" means to seize with the mind. However, the underlying term can also mean to seize with power, and therefore be translated as "*overcome*". John's declaration was probably referring to several ideas. Since he was writing about creation, he could have been alluding to the Genesis account where it was stated "*darkness was over the surface of the deep*", and God said, "*Let there be light*" (Genesis 1:2-3). God's "*Word*" displaced darkness with light. In this sense, John was merely making a statement about creation, and not implying anything hostile about darkness. However, John was also likely to be thinking of the harsh reality of human rebellion. When original mankind disobeyed the Creator King, it was banished from God's presence. Life, and its light, were in danger of being extinguished as darkness descended over creation. The human race was overshadowed by moral and spiritual darkness, and death, and was headed for oblivion. Yet the light of life still shines! Darkness cannot eclipse it!! Human history continues, because God's purpose of grace remains!!! A third possible idea in John's mind appears within the prologue. The Baptist came as a witness to the light which was coming into the world, but the world did not recognise him, i.e. did not *understand* him (1:8-10). These possible meanings are subtle, but the primary purpose of the statement is to prepare the way for John's presentation of Jesus. Throughout the rest of John's Gospel there is sharp conflict between light and darkness. Jesus is portrayed as the "*light of the world*" who shines in the darkness, which is not able to overcome him. John's imagery was linking God's creation and salvation, just as was his reference about the "*Logos*".

John jumps from this absolute starting point at the beginning of creation to the traditional starting point of the Gospel message, the ministry of John the Baptist (v 6-9). John the Baptist was sent from God. He was sent as a witness to the light which illuminates all people, and which was coming into the world. God's pre-existent "Logos", his active, creative "*Word*", which is the source of light and life, was coming into the world. He is alluding to the coming of Jesus, although at this point Jesus is not named. The focus is upon the Baptist. Yet the extraordinary event of the light entering the world is recognised. The Baptist was not the light. He was a witness concerning the "true light" so that through his testimony all might believe.

Presence of the light prompted two opposite reactions (v 10-13). Most people rejected him, although some who were *born of God* received him and he granted them the right to become children of God. John especially makes a poignant comment when he mentions those who rejected the light, whom he speaks about as a person. He was not recognised by the world which he made. He was not received by his own people. They did not discern that he was the light of God. John was presenting Jesus as Saviour of the world, but he was writing with the Jewish people at the forefront of his thinking. Neither the world at large, nor the Jews in particular, accepted him. The right to become children of God was not based on natural human descent (Jewish ancestry), but on being born of God, which was to receive the one who came into the world, and believe on his name.

John then shifts focus to the second part of his proclamation (v 14-18), and makes an astonishing assertion. The "*Word*", God's "Self-expression" by which he accomplished his purposes, became human "flesh". God's dynamic self-revelation entered the human race! John simply states the fact, without explaining any details of the process. To underscore the reality of the "*Word's*" incarnation, and to counteract sceptical, heretical notions which circulated at that time, John declares that the "*Word*" became "*flesh*". This was a rather inelegant, almost crude term to boldly make the claim unambiguous that the "*Word*" took up residence in a human body.

John confirms his claim with the testimony of two witnesses, the followers of Jesus (v 14) and John the forerunner to Jesus (v 15). The followers of Jesus ("we") testify to having personally seen God's qualities of "*grace and truth*" displayed within him (v 14). John's language clearly links God's incarnate glory, belonging to the Father's *One and Only* (his unique messianic Son on earth), with the presence of his glory in the time of Moses. When Moses asked to see God's glory, the LORD told him he would cause all his goodness to pass in front of him and proclaim his name in his presence. He proclaimed, "*The LORD, the LORD, the compassionate and gracious God, slow to anger, abounding in love and faithfulness, maintaining love to thousands, and forgiving wickedness, rebellion and sin. Yet he does not leave the guilty unpunished; he punishes the children and their children for the sin of the fathers to the third and fourth generation*" (Exodus 33:18-19, 34:6-7). This revelation, proclaimed by God's "*Word*", became the essential view of God's character and nature throughout the Old Testament. God's glory is the glory of his loving disposition which seeks reconciliation with sinners. The phrase *"grace and truth"*, alluding to *"love and faithfulness"* within God's proclamation, basically summarises that description. Jesus' glory showed that he was the LORD (Israel's covenant God) in human flesh! God is now known as the *"Father"*, because the incarnate "Word", as the *"One and Only"*, came from him, thereby revealing his fuller identity.

John the Baptist also testifies to him (v 15). Though he was long since dead, his cry of witness continued. He testified that the *"Word"* which came after him surpassed him because he was before him. The *"Word"* had been in action long before John came on the scene, commanding creation into existence, declaring the Ten Commandments and Israel's covenant laws to Moses, making promises to Abraham and to David, and revealing God's will to his prophets. As the final witness in God's long line of preparation by the *"Word"*, John recognised and confirmed that the *"One and Only from the Father"* was indeed the incarnate *"Word"*.

The Gospel's opening proclamation ends with a couple of conclusions. From the fullness of grace in the Son greater blessing is received than in the past (v 16-18). The law given through Moses has been surpassed by grace through Jesus Christ, who is now named for the first time. Whereas no one has ever seen God, *"God the One and Only"* has now made him known. What a startling statement! The *"Logos"* and Jesus are explicitly identified as the unique God. Furthermore, just as the *"Logos"* was said to be intimately *"near God"* (v 1), so here *"God the One and Only"* is stated as being *"at the Father's side"* (v 18). The vivid imagery depicts intimacy, rest, security, satisfaction. It was not implying another God together with the Father. It was depicting the inseparable closeness of the unseen Father and the person of Jesus who was the incarnate "Self-expression" of God. His continuing intimate closeness with the Father qualified Jesus to be able to make him known. The "Self-revelation" of God was on display in the world in the person of Jesus!

From this profound introduction, John launches into his presentation of Jesus in narrative style. A concise overview will help us place his revelation about prayer in context.

1:19-51 Forerunner and Followers

The Gospel begins its focus on the person of Jesus of history by recording the witness of John the Baptist, his forerunner, and then the witness of several who became his followers. These were the confirming witnesses in the opening proclamation. These witnesses all urge to *"look"* and *"see"* Jesus, thus providing a two-fold witness from both before (John) and after (followers). The occasion of John's testimony was his response to an official deputation from the Jewish authorities, in which he denied that he himself was the Christ, or Elijah, or another prophet, and claimed that he baptized (ritually cleansed) people to prepare for the One who was coming after him (v 19-28). The next day John drew attention to Jesus, *"the lamb of God who takes away the sin of the world"*, and testified that he was the *"Son of God"* (v 29-34). These identifications indicated that Jesus was to be a sacrifice provided by God for the atonement of the world's sin, and the messianic Son chosen by God to rule over the world. The following day two of John's disciples followed Jesus, one being Andrew who then fetched his brother Simon (v 35-42). The day after that Jesus called Philip to follow him, and he in turn persuaded Nathanael, who, after meeting Jesus, declared him to be *"King of the Jews"* (v 43-51). *"Son of God"* and *"King of the Jews"* were titles of the Messiah.

Chapters 2-12 Public Ministry of "Signs"

Jesus' "signs" were actions which resembled those performed by God in the Old Testament relating to Israel at the time of the Exodus and in the Wilderness. Often they were done against the backdrop of the Sabbath or Passover, which were also "signs" to Israel.

- **"Signs" of Glory.** John's narrative sets out the appearance of a sequence of "signs", beginning and ending at Cana (chapters 2-4). The pattern is reminiscent of the "sign" plagues on Egypt performed at the time of Moses. Jesus' signs (of grace) contrast in character with those (of judgement) by Moses, in keeping with their contrasting ministries: law through Moses; grace and truth through Jesus (1:18). Jesus' first "sign" was turning water into wine at Cana in Galilee, revealing his *"glory"* (2:1-11). Moses' first sign was turning water to blood (Exodus 7:20). John then describes Jesus' visit to Jerusalem at the time of Passover where he cleansed the temple (2:12-22). He highlights Jesus' deliberate preparation for his action (*"he made a whip"*). It was not a spur of the moment act, but an intentional prophetic gesture. This event was out of chronological sequence, because it actually happened at the end of Jesus' period of ministry, as the other Gospels report. However, it was included here to fit John's sequence of Jesus' "signs". Notice that Jesus' action at the temple prompted the Jewish authorities to ask him for a "sign". There was another purpose as well for inserting this event at this point in the narrative, out of chronological sequence. It focused attention on Jesus' prediction of the destroyed temple being replaced by his resurrected body (2:19). At that moment of writing, the temple lay in ruins, and the proclamation of Jesus' resurrection was spreading throughout the world. Jesus was not only in contrast with Moses, but also with the temple. They were precursors of what he was the reality. While in Jerusalem at the Passover, Jesus performed "signs" which prompted many people to believe in him (2:12-25). Nicodemus from the ruling Council came to him because of his "signs", and engaged in dialogue with him about the need for spiritual birth to enter God's Kingdom (3:1-21). As Jesus' ministry began to surpass that of John the Baptist, the Baptist testified that this was appropriate, since he was only the forerunner to Jesus, the friend of the bridegroom (3:22-30). He also, being from the earth, was a precursor, bearing witness to the one from above (3:31-36). While travelling through Samaria, Jesus engaged in dialogue with a Samaritan woman about true worship being "in Spirit and in truth", and was welcomed by her village as the Saviour of the world (4:1-42). The sequence concludes with Jesus performing a second "sign" at Cana in Galilee by healing the son of an official from Capernaum at a distance (4:43-54). Emphasis is placed on Jesus' words, *"Your son will live"* (v 50, 53). Moses' final plague in Egypt was the passing over of the angel of death, when God's son, Israel, lived! Jesus' "signs" revealed his glory (of *"grace and truth"*) and pointed to his resurrection.

- **The Healer.** Jesus next healed a man who had been an invalid for 38 years at the Pool of Bethesda on a Sabbath, sparking Jewish hostility and an audacious response from Jesus (chapter 5). 38 years was the period of Israel's judgement in the wilderness for failing to enter the Promised Land (Deuteronomy 2:14). Jesus' action of healing compared him with God's first act in the wilderness after Israel's exodus from Egypt and crossing the Red Sea, thereby identifying him as the "Lord who heals" (Exodus 15:26). In his response to the Jews, Jesus claims to have received authority from his Father to grant eternal life, indicated by the human testimony of John, and confirmed by the two-fold divine witness of the Father in his works through Jesus and his word in scripture.

- **The Bread of Life.** Jesus' feeding of the 5000 followed by walking on the water caused discussion about "signs" and God's provision of manna in the wilderness. Jesus spoke about the "bread of life" and about eating his flesh and drinking his blood (chapter 6). Moses gave manna, which was earthly bread, but the Father gave Jesus, who was heavenly bread which gives life to the world. Jesus' *"I am"* announcements (v 20, 35, 41, 48, 51) identify him with God who called Moses at the burning bush (Exodus 3:14), and his "signs" of feeding the crowd and walking on water confirm him as God who led Israel across the Red Sea and through the wilderness. His comments about consuming his flesh and blood refer to him becoming a sacrifice. Jesus' comments about his flesh and blood offended many of those following him so that they ceased being his disciples (v 60, 66). This is an occasion when Peter confessed faith in Jesus' identity (v 69), and was an alternative confession to the familiar one at Caesarea Philippi in the other Gospels.

- **Giver of the Spirit.** While Jesus was in Jerusalem for a Feast of Tabernacles, half way through the Feast he began to teach in the temple courts. On the last day of the Feast he made a dramatic appeal for people to come to him to receive the living water of God's Spirit, provoking the Jewish authorities (chapter 7). This Feast celebrated harvest and God's care of Israel during the wilderness period. Jesus' teaching and actions further identified him with God's dealings with Israel in the wilderness.

- **Teacher of the Law.** [An independent story from an unknown document has been inserted within John's Gospel (7:53-8:11). A woman caught in adultery is brought by

Pharisees to Jesus for his judgement in an effort to entrap him. Jesus skilfully avoided their trap by doodling on the ground and pronouncing that those without sin should stone her. No one stepped forward to condemn her, and he declared that neither did he condemn her.]

- **The Light of the World.** In a public statement in the temple Jesus made another "*I am*" claim as the "*light of the world*", which led to a hostile clash with the Pharisees (8:12-59). When they claimed to be children of Abraham, Jesus accused them of being children of the devil. They accused him of being demon-possessed, but he claimed to be "*I am*" even prior to Abraham.
- **The Giver of Sight.** Jesus healed a man born blind by making mud and putting it on his eyes, and sending him to wash in the Pool of Siloam (chapter 9). His actions provoked the Pharisees because he had worked on a Sabbath. The former blind man came to "see" who Jesus was, while the Pharisees were exposed for their spiritual blindness.
- **The Good Shepherd.** Having accused the Pharisees of being guilty of spiritual blindness, Jesus figuratively compares a true shepherd with thieves and robbers, and then explains that he is the good shepherd who lays down his life for his sheep (10:1-21). His imagery is taken from the Old Testament, and he identifies his own position and mission in relation to the Father.
- **The Son of God.** While walking in Solomon's Colonnade at the time of the Feast of Dedication, Jesus was confronted to state plainly whether he was Christ, and he antagonized the Jewish authorities by claiming that he was at one with the Father (10:22-42). He declared that his "*works*" in his Father's name spoke for him, but only his "*sheep*" followed his voice. To them he gave eternal life. Those who accused him of blasphemy should recognize his oneness with the Father because he was doing the same works as his Father was doing.
- **The Resurrection and the Life.** When told that his friend Lazarus was seriously ill, Jesus waited until he died before going to visit. Then he raised him back to life (chapter 11). He told Martha that he was the "*resurrection and the life*", and that whoever believed in him would live even if he died. Outside the tomb Jesus wept and groaned, an action to be compared with enslaved Israel in Egypt (Exodus 2:23-24). Lazarus' resuscitation ("Come out!") parallels Israel's exodus (coming out) from Egypt, and anticipates Jesus' own resurrection (a new exodus for the new covenant). The Jewish authorities now plotted Jesus' death for political reasons, with Caiaphas unwittingly prophesying that Jesus would die for the Jewish nation and the "scattered children of God".
- **The Hour of Glory.** Several significant incidents indicated that the time for Jesus' death had arrived (chapter 12). Mary anointed Jesus' feet with perfume which he interpreted as preparation for his burial (v 1-11). The crowds acclaimed him as he rode on a donkey into Jerusalem (v 12-19). Greeks came looking for him at the Passover Feast and Jesus

recognized that the hour had come for the "Son of Man to be glorified" (v 20-36). He declared this publicly and asked his Father to glorify his name. An audible reply from heaven prompted him to announce the judgement of the world and that he would be lifted up in death. Despite his "signs" the people refused to believe in him. Jesus cried out that he was a light so that believers might not remain in darkness (v 37-50).

Chapters 13-17 Private Discourses

Jesus' final night with his disciples is a memorable occasion of farewell gestures and discussions, concluded by his farewell prayer for them. He prepares them for his departure and the traumatic events which will soon occur. He explains that when he goes he will be replaced by the presence of the Holy Spirit, and that a new era will begin because of the triumph of his mission. He instructs them about what it means to live in a true and intimate relationship with God.

- Jesus washes his disciples' feet in an astonishing display of self-humiliation, to demonstrate his love, symbolize the cleansing of salvation, and provide an example for his followers. He then predicts Judas' betrayal and Peter's denial, while at the same time commanding his disciples to *"love one another"* (13:1-38).
- Jesus comforts his disciples with promising reassurance. He will prepare a place for them with his Father (14:1-4). He himself is the "way" to the Father (14:5-11). He will bring the Father glory (14:12-14). He promises the Holy Spirit to be within them, to make real their relationship with the Father and himself, and to take his place as their teacher (14:15-31).
- Jesus depicts his relationship with his disciples in imagery of the vine and its branches, and urges them to remain in his love by obeying his commands to love each other (15:1-17). He forewarns his disciples that the world will hate them because he exposed its sin (15:18-25). Both the Spirit and they will bear him witness (15:26-16:4).
- The Spirit will convict the world of its *sin, righteousness,* and *judgement,* and guide the disciples into all the truth about Jesus (16:5-16). After a short period of mourning while the world rejoices, there will be a new era of joy when they will see him again (16:17-24). They will no longer be confused, because they will be able to ask the Father directly in his name, since he will have completed his mission (16:25-28). The disciples will desert him (although the Father will remain), but when restored they will have *peace* in him (16:29-33).
- In his farewell prayer (chapter 17), Jesus firstly asked to be restored to the glory he shared with his Father before the world began (v 1-5). Secondly, he prayed for his immediate disciples that they would be protected and sanctified in terms of the truth they had

been given about God (v 6-19). Note: The truth was revealed in Christ (v 6), [would be explained by the Spirit (16:13)], and would be revealed through the disciples to the world (v 18). Thirdly, he prayed for those who would believe the apostles' message, for their oneness, shared with the Father and the Son, which will show the world that Jesus was sent from God (v 20-26).

Chapters 18-20 Passion Narrative

The familiar account of Jesus' arrest, trial, and crucifixion is told by John in a manner which highlights particular emphases, and includes little details not found in the Synoptic Gospels. It is an eye-witness account. Jesus' words to the arresting officers, "I am", are noted (18:5). Before Pilate, Jesus admits that he is a king, though not of this world, and that he came into the world to testify to the truth. He was crucified as King of the Jews. The reality of his death, as well as the prophetic significance of various details, are stressed.

John records three statements by Jesus while he was hanging upon the cross. The first was a word to his mother and his "*disciple whom he loved*" (19:26-27). He passed over the care of his mother to the disciple, thus severing ties with all his earthly responsibilities. The second statement was towards the end of his ordeal, when he said, "*I thirst*" (19:28). He was aware that his task was completed, so his utterance showed that he was consciously fulfilling scripture. After he took the drink which was offered, he uttered his final statement, "*It is finished*" (19:30). Then he bowed his head and gave up his spirit. Jesus' life was not taken from him, but voluntarily given. The three statements demonstrate Jesus' conscious and controlled completion of the work given to him by the Father. That completion is also plainly stated in Jesus' farewell prayer (17:4), his awareness while hanging on the cross (19:28), and his final utterance (19:30). John's Gospel intends to make it clear that Jesus' crucifixion was his God-given mission as Messiah.

Similarly, the reality and significance of his appearances after his resurrection are stressed. Peter and the "*disciple whom he loved*" saw evidence of the resurrection at the tomb. Mary Magdalene met the risen, but not yet ascended, Lord outside the tomb. Jesus appeared to the disciples inside a locked room on that same first day of the week. A week later Jesus showed himself to Thomas, who was not present the previous week, and convinced him of the reality of his resurrection. Thomas' response captured the significance of it all by his confession, "*My Lord and my God!*"

The message of John's Gospel is definite. Jesus' death and resurrection are his greatest "sign", confirming him as Messiah, revealing God's glory, and guaranteeing eternal life.

Chapter 21 Restoration

A post resurrection appearance by Jesus to a group of disciples at the Sea of Tiberias (a late name for the Sea of Galilee, confirming the late date for John's Gospel) stirred memories of earlier experiences. These prompted convictions about Jesus' resurrection, led to restored relationships, and stimulated commitment to the mission which the "truth" revealed in Jesus produces.

Regarding Prayer

There is sufficient evidence both from within John's Gospel and from the period in which he wrote to show that Jews looked upon activities like prayer as religious rituals. John makes it clear that for Jesus prayer was a special relationship. He totally avoids even using a religious term like "prayer". Instead, he uses terms like "says", "asks", or "desires". John emphasises Jesus' intimate association with his Father (e.g. 1:18, 5:19-23, 10:30, 14:6-7, etc.), and shows that whatever Jesus does or says springs out of the perfect oneness of their relationship.

There are two special moments in John's Gospel, as events move towards their culmination at the Cross, where Jesus' intimate communion with his Father was observed publicly. Critical circumstances prompted Jesus to slip spontaneously into natural conversation with his Father. He simply looked skywards and spoke. The first occasion was at the tomb of Lazarus (11:41-42). After ordering the entrance stone to be removed, he then thanked his Father for hearing him. He had not yet actually spoken, nor had God yet replied. He was simply expressing his gratitude for what he knew would happen, and he did so only that others around would recognise the source of his authority. It is as if he does not need to make a request because he always stands, as it were, as the asker and receiver. This is the nature of their relationship. Jesus was sent by the Father in heaven, and as the obedient and dependent Son on earth he received from the Father whatever was necessary for him to accomplish his Father's mission. On this occasion he ordered Lazarus to come back from the dead!

The second occurrence was a time of deep anguish for Jesus (12:27-28). The arrival of Greeks (v 20) triggered in Jesus' mind the recognition that his appointed hour had come (v 23). Because that hour involved the Cross, he was deeply troubled, and his inner conflict was voiced audibly. Jesus displayed publicly the same distress which other Gospels reported he showed privately in Gethsemane. On the one hand, the horror of what was before him caused him to ask the Father to save him from the hour. But on the other hand, he denied his own request because his obedient commitment was resolved not to avoid the hour. The motivating passion of his life, overriding all other considerations, was to glorify his Father. So that is what he prayed for. In response, there was an audible voice from heaven, intended to be a sign of confirmation to the crowd that Jesus was heard.

These two incidents show that prayer for Jesus was natural conversation with his Father as he himself on earth pursued the mission he was sent to fulfill. His conversation, whether spoken or assumed, was a continual request for his Father to be glorified through his own life of obedience to his task.

John's Gospel contains an extended report on aspects of Jesus final night before his crucifixion (chapters 13-17). In particular, it records Jesus' farewell instructions to his disciples about their future role in the day that was coming. He taught that they would act *"in his name"*. This means that they would act on his behalf. That role would especially be one of "prayer". He does not actually use the term "prayer", but *"ask"*.

In the first mention of this role, Jesus informed his disciples that they would do *"even greater things"* than he had done, and guaranteed that he would do whatever they asked him (14:12-14). Jesus' teaching must be understood in its context, and in the light of the whole book. The *"greater things"* are the higher matters of salvation and judgement, as Jesus had made clear on a previous occasion (John 5:19-30, see v 23). The disciples' role was to take Jesus' place on earth to complete his mission of salvation and judgement for the world. This would involve testifying about Jesus, together with the Spirit (15:26-27). The promise to give whatever they ask is not unlimited in its extent, but according to what they ask *"in his name"*. This does not mean adding a formula phrase to their prayer request ("in Jesus' name", amen). It means requesting, "on his behalf", what he would want. The disciples' future relationship with him will be as his is with his Father, one of intimacy, obedience, and continual dependent asking and receiving. This is an astonishing privilege and responsibility.

Since Jesus was about to leave his disciples, he informed them that his place would be taken by *"another Counsellor"*, the *"Spirit of Truth"* (14:16-17). The Spirit would be present with them (*"in"* them) in a different manner than Jesus' physical presence, and would maintain their relationship with Jesus and with the Father (v 18-20). Jesus was referring to the day beyond his coming resurrection, indicating the spiritual relationship believers would have with the Father through the Son by the Spirit. God's Spirit within them would enable them to act in Jesus' name, God's collective partner on earth. The point to note is that Jesus said, *"I will ask"*. The coming of the Spirit would be the result of Jesus praying. It was a prayer that he had not yet made, as the future sense *"will"* suggests. The term *"ask"* in this statement is different from the term Jesus used in v 13-14, deliberately distinguishing between himself and his disciples, while indicating that their function was the same.

The imagery of the Vine and its branches (15:1-8) illustrated very clearly what Jesus had already taught about his disciples' future role and relationship in regard to himself. They would be incorporated in him like branches in a vine, and would act on his behalf. The point of the analogy was to warn the disciples to remain in relationship with him to ensure their fruitfulness, because to lose that relationship would result in their destruction in judgement. A branch which does not produce is dead, and is discarded. A fruitful branch produces more branches. Jesus expanded on the nature of the relationship, and guaranteed their fruitful role (v 7-8). The relationship was a matter of continuing in accordance with Jesus' sayings (about his own identity and mission). They were to remain true to him and to the task of making disciples. When they did so, their role of asking was guaranteed to be successful. This was because such fruitfulness achieved the Father's glory and showed that they were his disciples.

To prevent his disciples' self-confidence and self-sufficiency, and at the same time to bolster their faith in their mission, Jesus pronounced an important truth (15:16). He declared that it was not their choice of him, but his choice and appointment of them which was the reason for their privileged relationship and role. He assured them that the Father would give them whatever they asked in his name.

Towards the end of his farewell speech, Jesus pointed out that in the day which was coming they would no longer be asking their puzzled questions, but asking his requests for the success of his mission (16:23-24). Two different terms play on the idea of "asking". They will no longer be making enquiries because of confusion, since, in the light of the crucifixion, resurrection, and arrival of the Holy Spirit, God's purposes would be clear. Instead, as restored, believing, Spirit-indwelt followers they would be acting in the name of Jesus, requesting God's purposes of salvation to be accomplished. This would bring them into a dimension of relationship and prayer they had never yet experienced.

Jesus' Final Prayer (chapter 17) reveals what Jesus himself asked. It provides insight about how Jesus related to his Father, and is a model for his followers who must ask in his name. It is the prayer Jesus said he would make when he promised to ask for *"another Counsellor"*. The same term *"ask"* used then, in the future tense (14:16), recurs consistently throughout his prayer in the present tense (17:9, 15, 20). The Holy Spirit is the One who fulfills what Jesus requests. Jesus' prayer flows out through three phases. At the beginning he requests his own glorification, which means the fulfilment of his mission to the cross to provide eternal life for the world (v 1-5). Then he asks for his disciples who have been given to him, that they will be protected and sanctified (v 6-19). Next, he asks for those who will believe in him through his disciples' message, that they might all be one (v 20-23). He concludes by asking that all who are given to him might see the glory he had with the Father before creation began (v 24-26).

Jesus' Farewell Prayer (Chapter 17)

Jesus' farewell prayer in John's Gospel is his most extensive prayer in the New Testament. It is profound. Although his words are very simple, his thoughts are quite complex. The language is cryptic, and the meaning at times almost vague. Yet the prayer expresses deep truth. It is worth a more in-depth examination.

To understand the prayer correctly, we must pay close attention to what is said, and think carefully about Jesus' meaning. The reason Jesus spoke in this apparently complicated way was to cause his Jewish listeners to rethink their religious and nationalistic expectations. Jesus' messianic mission was not political and earthly, but about spiritual salvation and heavenly consequences. All that Jesus had done and taught until this moment comes to focus in his prayer. Much of what he prays resonates with his farewell discussion. Its truth is exhilarating.

Jesus Prays Concerning Himself (v 1-5)

The time for Jesus, as the messianic Son, to be glorified (see 11:4, 12:23, 31-32) had arrived (v 1). So he prays to the Father for it to happen. This means bringing on his death, resurrection, and exaltation. His request is not for his own benefit, but that *"your Son may glorify you"*. The Father's glory would be manifested in the Son's glory, which ironically would be gained through the shame of the cross. The shared glory of the Father and the Son was the divine authority (as King of heaven) given to Jesus to confer eternal life (v 2). This means that by completing his mission of crucifixion and resurrection, Jesus the Messiah would be exalted to be the mediator of God's rule of life. His authority would be over *"all people"*, not only Jews (a significant message for Jewish readers), and the gift of eternal life was granted to *"all those you have given him"* (who are those who believed in him), not just everyone.

The essence of eternal life is defined as knowing *"you, the only true God, and Jesus Christ, whom you have sent"* (v 3). Eternal life is not merely eternal existence, but the reality of knowing the eternal God. He is the only true God, who has revealed himself through Jesus the Messiah whom he sent to accomplish his mission of salvation. The only way to fully know God is to know also Jesus the Messiah. Jesus refers to himself in the third person, to emphasise how important his identity and mission as Messiah are for identifying the Father as the true God. The gospel proclaims the true God as the Father-who-sent-Jesus-the-Messiah. Jesus states that he has glorified his Father on earth, by completing the work (his assigned mission) he was given to do (v 4). He now requests his Father to glorify him in his presence (in heaven) with the glory they shared before the world began (v 5). That was the glory of *"grace and truth"* which saves sinners. This is a clear claim of his pre-existence as the "Word", and shows that his mission is about to come full circle as he returns to the Father who sent him.

Jesus Prays Concerning His Disciples (v 6-19)

After praying for himself to be glorified, so that as ruler of heaven he might give eternal life to those the Father has given him, he next prays for them. He firstly identifies them, in words which have to be unraveled (v 6-8). Jesus says that he has revealed the Father (literally, *"your name"*) to them. God's *"name"* includes all that he is as a person, all his identity and nature, the "Father-who-sent-Jesus-the-Messiah". Jesus as "Son" revealed (through his own person, his words and works, and his victorious sacrificial death) that *"name"*, which he appropriately represents by the name *"Father"*. The Father has given the disciples to Jesus out of the world. They belonged to him (from a heavenly point of view), who gave them to Jesus; and they obeyed the Father's word (from an earthly point of view). They now knew that everything about Jesus was from the Father. This is because Jesus had given them the words (message) given to him by the Father, which they had received. They knew that Jesus came from the Father, and was sent by him.

Secondly, Jesus prays ("asks") that the Father will keep them (v 9-12). He prays for them, but not for the world. This is because they belong to the Father, who has given them to him. All that belongs to the Father, belongs to the Son, and vice versa. Such is their oneness of purpose and partnership. Glory has come to Jesus through them (because they have believed in him and his message of truth about the Father). Since Jesus has prayed that he might be glorified (v 1), and since his glory comes through them (v 10), this is the reason he prays for them. It is also because he is leaving the world to come to the Father, while they are still in the world (v 11). He means that for him to be glorified in them, he must return (via the cross) to the Father. So, addressing God as *"Holy Father"*, he prays that God will keep them. (The translation, *"protect them by the power of your name"*, v 11, can be misleading. Jesus actually says *"keep them in your name"*. This means *"keep them true in respect to the Father's revealed nature and purpose"*). The name *"Holy Father"* is only found here in the whole Bible, and was revealed uniquely to Jesus, the messianic Son. The name combines the revelation of God as the "Holy One" of the Old Testament and the revelation of God as "Father" by Jesus. The purpose of keeping them is so that *"they may be one as we are one"*. This means sharing in the oneness of purpose and partnership between God the Father and Jesus in their joint mission of saving the world. During his ministry while with his disciples Jesus had kept and guarded them in the *"name"* (revelation of God) given to him, and, except for Judas, had lost none of them.

Thirdly, Jesus prays that they will be sanctified by God's truth (v 13-19). He indicates that while he is still in the world, he prays for his disciples so that they might experience the fulness of his joy (see 15:11), which is the spiritual thrill of knowing the Father's love and serving him obediently. He has passed on the Father's word (the revelation of his truth) to them, and they are now hated by the world, because, like him, they are no longer of the world. He does not ask his Father to take them out of the world, but to keep them from the evil one (who is the prince of the world, 12:30). *"Sanctify them by the truth; your word is truth"*.

To sanctify means to make holy, to consecrate, or to set apart from common use for divine purpose. God is the *"Holy Father"* (v 11), Jesus was *set apart* by the Father and sent into the world (10:36), the other Counsellor yet to be sent is the *Holy Spirit* (14:26), and now Jesus prays that his disciples *will be made holy* because he has also sent them. Just as

Jesus had been sanctified and sent into the world to accomplish his Father's purpose, so the disciples will be sanctified and sent to share in that mission. The *"word"* which sanctifies is the truth embodied in Jesus which revealed his Father. His means of revelation includes his own crucifixion and resurrection. The revelation is essentially the gospel. So Jesus sanctifies himself to complete his mission. He is voluntarily consecrating himself to the sacrificial role of going to the cross so that his followers might be qualified to be also sent into the world, in order to make the gospel known. The sending of the Holy Spirit to impart the benefits of Jesus' sacrifice to his disciples will be the answer to his prayer.

Jesus Prays Concerning Future Believers (v 20-26)

Since Jesus consecrated himself to go to the cross as a sacrifice on behalf of the world, so that his disciples could be consecrated to God and his service by the truth about God and Jesus' death and resurrection, it is natural for Jesus to pray next for the outcome of their service. He prays (*"asks"*) for those who will believe in him through their message (v 20). He prays that all of them may be one (v 21). This is not institutional unity, and is more than even loving relational unity. It is gospel unity, the spiritual unity of sharing in the oneness of purpose and partnership with the Father, Jesus, and the disciples, in terms of God's mission of salvation for the world. In simple terms, it means being united with God, by means of, and in the work of, the gospel. The reason Jesus prays for future believers and their spiritual oneness in God's salvation is so that the world might believe that God sent Jesus. This is picking up on Jesus' earlier comment that the Spirit of truth and Jesus' disciples would bear witness to him before the world (15:26-27).

Jesus has given these future believers the glory given to him (v 22-23). This is the glory of *"grace and truth"*, experienced by sharing in oneness with the Father and Jesus, conquering sin and death, and participating in eternal life. As that oneness is brought to completion (in both quality and quantity), the world will know that the Father sent Jesus, and loves believers as he loves Jesus.

Jesus says he wants (literally, *"wills"*) his disciples to be with him where he is (v 24). He means in intimate union with the Father, sharing the glory of his purposes of salvation. This was where he was going (14:3). He was no longer of the world (v 11). The disciples are *"those you have given me"*, described from God's perspective; they are those who believe the truth, from a human perspective. Jesus wants them to see his glory which God gave him because he loved him before the creation of the world. God's glory is *"grace and truth"*, the outshining of his divine love, to reconcile sinners with himself! Even before God created the human race, which sinned against him in disobedience, God loved the one who would redeem the human race! When we link v 2, 5, 24 we see that the glory of God's love was already expressing itself before time began, was displayed in Jesus' mission in the world and supremely at his crucifixion and resurrection, and was authorizing the gift of eternal life.

This was expressed in more straight forward terms earlier in the Gospel. "*For God so loved the world that he gave his One and Only Son, that whoever believes in him shall not perish but have eternal life*" (3:16).

Jesus concludes his prayer with several personal assertions (v 25-26). He calls God "*righteous Father*", another name found only here in the Bible. Jesus uses this expression to indicate his confidence in God's absolute trustworthiness. The Father is "*righteous*" in all that he is and in all that he does. Jesus also asserts that the world does not know the Father, but he does, and his disciples know that the Father sent him. Jesus has made the Father known to them, and will continue to do so (by the Spirit of Truth). This is so that the Father's love for Jesus will live "*in them*" (personally and collectively), as Jesus will himself.

Jesus' farewell prayer reveals his intimate fellowship with his Father in heaven. It expresses the inner beat of his heart and joyful, triumphant passion to complete his heavenly mission. He does not recoil in horror from the prospect of shame and suffering. Rather, he enthusiastically anticipates the opportunity to glorify his Father by displaying his Father's eternal love and bestowing eternal life upon his believing followers. It is a prayer of self-consecration. It is a unique prayer, which only Jesus could offer. It is not a model prayer for others to repeat. However, it does inform and inspire those who receive his eternal life how to pray in his name. They, as his representatives on earth, can now pray for what he wants, as his completed work achieves its purpose. As they bear witness to Jesus and his finished work, in partnership with the Holy Spirit, so also they can ask on his behalf for whatever will bring glory to the Father. Jesus himself, now with the Father, will do it.

***

The four Gospels of Matthew, Mark, Luke, and John are presentations of Jesus from different perspectives. Like spotlights focused on a single actor on a theatre stage, they illuminate him from different angles. Their characterisations of Jesus are consistent and convincing. They declare Jesus to be the Messiah, the Son of God and Son of Man. He revealed God to be his Father in heaven, and obediently fulfilled his Father's will. He undertook the mission of saving the world from the consequences of its sinful rebellion by his crucifixion, resurrection, and ascension to the Father on its behalf. As God's partner in the world, he successfully accomplished his mission by maintaining fellowship with his Father and intercession for the world in prayer. His disciples on earth now act in his name by proclaiming the good news about his victorious salvation throughout the world and praying for God's kingdom to come.

CHAPTER 13

"IN ACCORD WITH GOD'S WILL"

Prayer in Paul's Letters

The Apostle Paul was a man with a mission. He had met the risen Christ who completely turned his life around. He was conscious of being loved by God who forgave his sins and crushed his self-righteous arrogance. He was overwhelmed by the revelation of God's grace. That grace was in action before the beginning of time. It formulated God's agenda of salvation. It was manifested in Jesus Christ, the Saviour of the world, who destroyed sin and death, and brought about eternal life. It freely offered salvation to all who would receive it.

Not only was Paul saved by God's grace, but he was also called by grace to be a messenger of the gospel. God sent him to the Gentiles, and he went willingly, thankfully, and zealously. He was fully devoted to Jesus as Messiah and Lord. He proclaimed Jesus' crucifixion and resurrection as the demonstration of God's love, the basis of salvation for the world, the pivotal point of human history, and the guarantee of eternal life. Salvation was God's gift of grace, to be received in faith. It ensured forgiveness of sin, and reconciliation with God.

Paul's faith and life were governed by the Holy Spirit. The Spirit made the presence of God real, convinced him of the truth of Christ, and enlightened his heart and mind to the knowledge of God's purposes, power, and life.

Wherever Paul went, God's will was his overruling principle. It determined his decisions and actions. God's will was God's sovereign plan for the world. It was God's eternal purpose, determined before creation, pursued through history, accomplished in Christ, and to come to fulfilment at the end of the ages. It was God's plan of salvation, his purpose to restore his Kingdom, his intention to create a restored and reconciled humanity in Christ through resurrection. This was the *"mystery"* of God, unveiled in Christ. Paul became possessed by the will of God, and obsessed to make it known. It was the message he preached. It was the driving force in his prayers.

Paul knew that his task was a divine work. It needed divine power to overcome the spiritual blindness and hardness of human hearts, the resistant structures of human traditions and systems, and the strategies and power of demonic forces. But he trusted in a living Lord who had already conquered these obstacles and was reigning supreme above all other authorities. Therefore, to ensure that he always relied on divine power and always pursued God's will, he made prayer a foremost activity.

The New Testament contains 13 letters composed by Paul at various times during the course of his ministry. Six were written prior to a period of imprisonment. Four were written during that imprisonment. Three were written (most probably) after his release. The account of Paul in the book of Acts provides a framework for helping to date his letters. The contents of the letters deepen our understanding of the gospel and its application to personal and church life, and set the context for understanding Paul's occasional references to prayer. Not every letter mentions prayer, but a brief summary of each letter fills out our knowledge of Paul's outlook.

Letters Written to Troubled Churches

Galatians was a red hot tract, like a flaming missile, which sizzled with heat. It was a fierce attack against exponents of Jewish religious legalism who rejected the gospel of grace. They were Jews who accepted Jesus as their long-awaited Messiah. They even accepted Gentiles as members of God's people, provided they were willing to become Jews. However, they saw the gospel as an extension of Judaism, and insisted on Gentile converts being circumcised and adopting traditional Jewish customs. Paul recognised their error and threat. He insisted on salvation by grace alone through faith alone.

It is a toss up whether Galatians or 1 Thessalonians was written first. It is possible Galatians was written about 49 CE, which would make it one of the earliest documents in the New Testament (together perhaps with the book of James). It certainly would not have been more than a few years later. The letter played a key role in the battle for freedom which wracked the early church as Gentiles responded to the gospel which spread across Asia and into Europe. Paul's first missionary journey took him to Galatia where from town to town he planted churches of new Gentile converts. Following his return, conflict broke out when zealous Jews campaigned for Gentiles to submit to their Judaistic rules. A major church conference was held in Jerusalem to debate the matter (described in Acts 15), concluding that Gentiles were acceptable just as they were, on the basis of faith in Jesus alone. This was a watershed moment for the church, and effectively separated the gospel movement from Judaism. Galatians makes no mention of the verdict of the Jerusalem conference, which would authoritatively clinch Paul's argument. The early date for Galatians would explain the absence of any mention of the conference.

Paul makes no mention of prayer in Galatians. However, from the outset he sets his focus on the will of God. His letter is virtually an exposition of God's will, which was his gracious plan for mankind. Paul begins by introducing himself, stressing his authority as an apostle (1:1). He was not sent by men, but by Jesus Christ and God the Father, a striking association. He adds that God raised Jesus from the dead. This was the foundational reality of the gospel, not religious customs. It was also relevant for his authority as an apostle, because an essential qualification was to be an eyewitness of Jesus' resurrection (Acts 1:22). Paul was not one of the Twelve, but he had met the risen Jesus in a unique encounter (Acts 9:5). Paul's greetings to the churches in Galatia emphasised basic elements of the gospel, *"grace and peace"* (1:3), the motivation and outcome of the gospel. This was a creative modified version of typical greetings to Gentiles and Jews, "cheers and shalom". What is notable is the linking of *"God our Father and the Lord Jesus Christ"*, on this occasion qualifying Jesus in terms of his offering himself for sin. Paul has referred to this relationship twice in his opening remarks. Each time, he qualified Jesus in terms of his gospel credentials, being resurrected and offering himself for sin respectively. God and Jesus are distinguished from each other, yet are united in partnership as equals. Although Jesus was a man, he is titled *"Lord"*, a title reserved for God. The risen Messiah had been exalted to the status of God. Paul was not implying that Jesus was a second God, but indicating that, in terms of his person and mission, he was an inseparable extension of God himself. God was now known as *"Father"* who shared an inseparable partnership with Jesus, his crucified, resurrected, and exalted Messiah. God had revealed himself - expressed himself - through the whole advent of Jesus, his incarnation, crucifixion, resurrection, and ascension. Make sure you grasp this concept. God's fuller identity was displayed through the astonishing gospel events concerning Jesus, and is depicted in terms of the partnership of *"God our Father and the Lord Jesus Christ"*. This description recurs repeatedly throughout the writings of the New Testament. It is apparent from this early letter of Paul's that this radical fresh identification of God was already a recognised conviction of the gospel movement. Paul was highlighting this description because it was crucial to the arguments he was about to make. He wanted his readers to cling to the truth of God's manifested identity, and his will that salvation from the present evil age was through his Messiah's self-sacrifice for sin, not through keeping the Law as promoted by his antagonists.

Without pausing for niceties, Paul went abruptly to the issue which troubled him (1:6-9). He blurted out his astonishment that already his readers were deserting God and the gospel for a false alternative. He damns those who were causing confusion and perverting the gospel. He protests that he was not seeking human popularity by making religion easy, but preaching what he received by direct revelation from Jesus Christ (1:10-12). He defends his claim of divine authority by relating his early life, conversion, and commission as an apostle (1:13-17), and then his first visit to the apostles at Jerusalem (1:18-24).

Having declared his independence from the Jerusalem apostles, he then related how they endorsed both his message and his mission (2:1-10). In sharp contrast to the private discussion and hand of fellowship between Peter and Paul at Jerusalem (v 9), when Peter visited Antioch Paul publicly rebuked him (2:11-16). Initially, Peter had been willing to share in the fellowship meal with Gentiles, but when certain Jews arrived from Jerusalem he withdrew, prompting other Jews, including Barnabas, to follow suit. Paul told Peter that they, being Jews and not Gentile "sinners" by birth, both knew that a person was not justified by the Law, but by faith in Christ.

That prompted the crucial question which troubled his opponents, leading Paul to make an explanation about the revolutionary new way of living (2:17-21). He asked, *"If, while we (Jews) seek to be justified in Christ, it becomes evident that we ourselves are "sinners" (like Gentiles), does that mean that Christ promotes sin?"* Behind the question was concern about dispensing with the Law. If salvation is by grace through faith, and the Law is not necessary to ensure righteousness, does that mean there is freedom to sin? *"Absolutely not!"* says Paul. He explained that to promote living by Law was to rebuild what the gospel demolished. That would show him to be a lawbreaker (therefore condemning him, not saving him). Instead, through the Law he had died to the Law so that he might live for God. He means that he fulfilled the demands of the Law, in Christ (God's messianic proxy for sinners), who died on his behalf, so that he was now dead to the Law, and free to live [acceptably] for God. Paul described his perspective inspiringly. *"I have been crucified with Christ and I no longer live, but Christ lives in me. The life I live in the body, I live by faith in the Son of God, who loved me and gave himself for me"* (2:20).

After relating his own past experiences to confirm his message and authority (chapters 1-2), Paul then turned to the past experiences of the Galatians before the Judaists arrived on the scene (3:1-5). Six rhetorical questions, in a sharp and uncomplimentary tone, recalled their original response to the gospel. Jesus Christ had been portrayed before their eyes (in the message of the gospel) as having been crucified. They had received the Spirit, with accompanying supernatural confirmation, not by observing the Law, but by hearing the message. Why were they now shifting their position and relying on their own human efforts?

To refute the Judaists, Paul argued from scripture that the gospel was announced beforehand to Abraham (3:6-14). Abraham believed God and was credited as righteous. Those who have faith are Abraham's children, and are blessed along with him. The Law does not justify, but rather imposes a curse. However, Christ has redeemed us from the curse by his crucifixion, so that God's blessing might come to the Gentiles, and that the promise of the Spirit might be received by faith.

Paul then argued further from reasoning, using the illustration of a covenant (3:15-18). Just as a human covenant cannot be set aside once it has been properly established, neither can God's promise to Abraham be superseded by the Law which came later. He digresses for a moment with a bit of Jewish reasoning to insist that the promise specified *"seed"*, not *"seeds"*, referring explicitly to Christ. His arguments raise the question of the purpose of the

Law, which he declared was to expose mankind's sinful condition, and was temporary until the promised "*seed*" had come (3:19-24). The Law was given through mediators (whereas God gave his promise to Abraham directly), and was not opposed to the promise. The Law held men prisoners, locked up until the time when faith would be revealed. With the arrival of faith, we are no longer under the supervision of the Law, but are sons of God in union with Christ through faith (3:25-29). We have been baptised into Christ, clothed with Christ, where there are no human distinctions of race, rank, and gender. If you belong to Christ, you are Abraham's descendant, and therefore heirs of the promise.

In the light of this, Paul expressed his concern that they wanted to return to their former slavery (4:1-11). He uses a legal illustration to indicate that before Christ came they were no better off than slaves. However, in the "*fulness of time*" God sent two divine agents. He sent his Son to redeem them so that they might have full rights as sons. He also sent the Spirit of his Son into their hearts to give them the inner assurance of being sons. Since formerly they did not know God, but now they did, why did they want to turn back to the "*weak and miserable*" principles which had enslaved them? With tender affection because of their former warm and joyful relationship, he makes a personal plea to them (4:12-20). He warns them against the Judaists' selfish motives, and expresses his deep longing to be with them to resolve his anguish.

Using a familiar rabbinic style argument, Paul directed his remarks specifically to the Judaists, to refute them on their own terms (4:21-31). He takes the example of Abraham's two sons, one from a slave woman, and the other from a free woman, and interprets them in an allegorical sense to contrast the religious slavery of the legalists and freedom in Christ. He then defends freedom in Christ on two levels (5:1-12). Firstly, he warns against the disastrous consequences of falling back into legalistic bondage, in contrast to the hope of righteousness which comes by faith through the Spirit. Secondly, he criticises and condemns the troublemakers who were diverting them from the true gospel. Then, having dealt with the danger of freedom in Christ being perverted by legalism, he immediately swings to face the opposite threat of abusing freedom by permissive self-indulgence (5:13-15). Both problems were emerging in the young churches of Galatia, causing in-fighting. Paul's message was "liberty, not bondage; liberty, not licence"! He told them to "*serve one another* (literally, be a slave to one another) *in love*". To both groups he said, "*The entire Law is summed up in a single command: 'Love your neighbour as yourself'*".

To correct both errors, Paul urged his readers to "*live by the Spirit*" (5:16-26). The life of a believer in Christ is actually the life of Christ in the believer (see 2:20). This is by means of God's indwelling Spirit. The source of the believer's life is not an external Law, but an internal presence. The life of freedom is the life of the Spirit. The Spirit replaces the Law as the controlling authority in life, and is the enabling power to overcome sinful self-indulgence. The contrasting lifestyles of the sinful human nature and the fruit of the Spirit are obvious.

The Law is not opposed to the Spirit's harvest of graces. Neither is it needed when sinful nature and its passions have been crucified with Christ.

Paul concluded his letter by applying his message to his Galatian converts with practical exhortations (6:1-18). He gave practical advice about acting in love towards other believers. He pointed out the certainty of harvesting either *"works"* of sinful nature or *"fruit"* of the Spirit, depending on their response to their matters of tension. He ended with a final swipe at the motives and views of the Judaists.

Galatians was a passionate explanation of the gospel and God's will, and a demonstration of Paul's zeal.

1 and 2 Thessalonians reveal helpful insights into Paul's ready recourse to prayer. Prayerfulness was obviously a consistent characteristic of his life and ministry.

These two letters were written within a few months of each other, and had a similar purpose. Paul wrote the letters while he was in Corinth, in the year 51 CE, not long after he had established a group of converts in Thessalonica. Because he had to leave that city hastily, owing to a public riot stirred up by opponents to his message (Acts 17:1-9), he was concerned that his work with the new believers was incomplete. They faced a hostile environment, and they were confused about aspects of their new faith. In particular, they had misunderstandings about the risen Christ's coming again, and about how they should live in the meantime.

Paul began the **first letter** on a note of prayer (1:1-3). His opening greetings addressed the church of the Thessalonians *"in God the Father and the Lord Jesus Christ"*, stressing the essential relationship which identified God, and united their newly formed community. These former pagans now acknowledged God as the true and living God, and called him Father. They recognised Jesus who had been crucified and resurrected as Messiah, and revered him as Lord. Paul then indicated that he mentioned the Thessalonians in his prayers before *"our God and Father"*, continually giving thanks for them, and remembering their progress. Here he revealed his attitude towards prayer. He gives the impression that prayer was his habitual practice. He was conscious of his relationship to God, as he came to pray to their mutual Father. He prayed for his converts, entrusting them to God's care. He gave thanks for them, recognising that God had called them to faith. He prayed about their progress, expressed in terms of a triad of qualities, their work generated by *faith,* their labour prompted by *love,* their endurance inspired by *hope*. Progress was clearly not easy, but was achieved by the *faith, love, and hope* derived from their relationship *"in our Lord Jesus* Christ". This triad of qualities was a characteristic mark of Christian disciples.

The response of the Thessalonians to the gospel was genuine and inspiring (1:4-10). They were not simply influenced by Paul's words, but convinced by the power of the Holy Spirit. They became like Paul and the Lord in their way of life, and an example to all believers throughout Greece. Their witness became known in Macedonia (northern Greece) and Achaia (southern Greece, where Paul was currently). They had turned to God from idols to serve the living and true God, and to wait for his Son from heaven. This was Jesus whom God raised from the dead, and who rescues from the coming wrath. Teaching about Jesus' second coming was apparently part of Paul's original message to the Thessalonians, and it is evident that anticipation of that happening soon was high. This was the first of many references to the subject in these early letters, and the first in the writings of the New Testament.

Paul appealed to his readers to remember his behaviour while he was with them as proof that he had not tried to exploit them in any way (2:1-16). His sudden departure from them probably brought criticism from opponents. Jealous Jews had stirred up civic unrest against the new converts, causing him and Silas to move on quickly. There were many travelling pedlars of religious and philosophic views in those days, who took advantage of gullible listeners for their own personal gain. Paul was not like that. He had not sought to impress or please anyone. As apostles of Christ sharing God's good news, he and his companions had behaved like loving nurturing parents towards them, working night and day to support themselves independently. Their conduct had been holy, righteous and blameless, and they had urged their converts to live lives worthy of God who had called them into his kingdom. The converts had accepted the gospel as the word of God, not men. Their response in the face of hostility from their fellow countrymen was like the churches in Judea which had suffered from the Jews. Those Jews had killed the Lord Jesus and the prophets. They had also driven out Paul and his associates, and were trying to prevent them from speaking to Gentiles so that they might be saved. God's wrath was upon them.

Following his abrupt departure from Thessalonica, Paul's several attempts to return were frustrated, and he only obtained relief for his concern for them when Timothy brought him good news of their on-going progress (2:17-3:10). He considered that it was Satan who thwarted his efforts to return. He intensely yearned to see his converts, because they would be the crowning source of his joy and glory in the presence of their Lord Jesus at his coming. Therefore, he sent Timothy in his place, to strengthen and encourage them in the face of the inevitable persecution which he had forewarned would come, so that they would not be tested by the tempter. Timothy's report of their faith and love, and their fond memories of Paul, brought him relief and joyful gratitude. It prompted him to pray earnestly night and day for the opportunity to see them again, and add to their developing faith. He indicated the nature of his prayer in revealing details (3:11-13). He looked to *"our God and Father himself and our Lord Jesus"* to clear the way for him to come to them. This revealed how believers viewed both God and Christ, and their inseparable union. Paul showed here his reliance on prayer with regard to the affairs of his ministry. In addition, he prayed for the Lord to increase their love, revealing its great importance as a characteristic in relationships. It had been exemplified by Paul and his associates. He also prayed for the Lord to strengthen their hearts so that they would be blameless and holy in the presence of *"our God and Father when our Lord Jesus*" comes. This emphasised the importance of personal behaviour. Love and holiness were inseparable qualities in Christian living, the outflow of the inseparable union of the Father and Messiah. The second coming of Jesus was an incentive for believers to live and serve in a worthy manner. Paul's repeated mention of "*our God and Father and our Lord Jesus*", relating to present praying and future prospect, stressed the inseparable Father/Messiah union as his basic personal outlook.

Paul concluded his remarks on these matters by appealing to the Thessalonians to live according to his previous instructions (4:1-12). He appealed firstly for sexual purity, declaring that it was God's *will* to be sanctified (holy). Then he commended them for showing brotherly love, and urged them to do so even more. He encouraged them to have a quiet and diligent life in order to win the respect of outsiders.

To ease the anxiety of the Thessalonians, Paul provided explanation about matters concerning the return of the Lord (4:13-5:11). In those early days of the spreading gospel, the Lord's return was expected imminently. That prospect gave urgency to Paul's evangelistic work, and affected the daily outlook of believers. Apparently there was uncertainty among the Thessalonians about whether believers who died before Jesus came back would participate in the event. In stirring imagery, Paul assured them that they would. He metaphorically described believers who died as having fallen "*asleep*", implying that death was not permanent. Because they believed that Jesus died and rose again, they could believe that God would bring with Jesus those who had "*fallen asleep in him*". At his return, they would be raised first, before those who were still living were caught up to be together with them. In other words, in their death they were sharing in the death of Jesus, in order to share in his resurrection. The "*loud command, voice of the archangel, and trumpet call of God*" was verbal imagery to emphasise the divine authority which would guarantee it happened. The "*clouds*" symbolised God's presence where all believers, those who had died, and those still living, would be with the Lord forever. With regard to time, the day of the Lord would come unexpectedly like a thief, and bring sudden destruction on those confidently declaring "*peace and safety*". However, believers, who were "sons of the light", did not belong to the night, but to the day, and would not be taken by surprise. They wore the triad of faith, love, and hope as their armour, because they were appointed to receive salvation through our Lord Jesus Christ. He died, so that whether we are "*awake or asleep*", we may live together with him.

The letter ended with some final exhortations about living together responsibly, a concluding prayer, and farewell greetings (5:12-28). Amongst the exhortations was a trio of noteworthy encouragements. "*Be joyful always; pray continually; give thanks in all circumstances, for this is God's will for you in Christ Jesus*". Paul was urging a characteristic positive disposition to be maintained, motivated by the perspective of being "in Christ". God's plan of salvation, his will, was accomplished by Christ. All who were "in Christ" were beneficiaries. They belonged to God, and were destined for eternal salvation. Their current earthly circumstances were under God's control, and were purposeful, whether good or bad. Therefore, they could be joyful, prayerful, and thankful as they faced them. For Paul, all of life came under God's will, and prayer was offered according to God's will. Prayer was not for seeking personal desires, but God's.

His concluding prayer expressed the wish that God would thoroughly sanctify them. He desired that their "*whole spirit, soul and body*" might be kept blameless at the coming of the Lord Jesus Christ. He was emphasising the whole person, to stress thoroughness of holiness, not indicating that a person consists of segregated parts. He referred to God as the "*God of peace*, which was a typical practice of his. It expressed the outcome of Christ's salvation, peace between mankind and God, and peace between Jew and Gentile. His reference again to the return of Christ kept that perspective as the incentive for holy living. He assured them that the one who "*calls*" is faithful and will do it. God's call was an invitation to be restored to intimate fellowship with him. Yet that required them to be holy. Only God could make and keep them holy, and he was faithful and would do it. Hence Paul's prayer. At the same time, they were responsible to submit to God's will as willing participants. Paul's prayer was relevant to the situation at Thessalonica. It was shaped and motivated by the gospel, providing rich insight into his practice of prayer.

Paul's farewell firstly requested their prayer for him, revealing the high value he placed upon the effectiveness and priority of prayer. He greeted them affectionately, yet issued a solemn injunction for his letter to be read to all the fellowship. He wanted everyone, idlers and those anxious included, to receive his explanations and advice. His final benediction was typical, expressing the beat of his heart.

The **second letter** to the Thessalonians was prompted by fresh news from there indicating continued problems of misunderstanding and misbehaviour. There was also an unsettling influence from some form of message supposedly from Paul. An unhealthy excitement had been roused about the day of the Lord, that it was imminent or had already arrived. Paul set about correcting their confusion.

He began, after his opening greetings, with thanksgiving and prayer (chapter 1). He expressed his sense of obligation to be grateful to God for their growing faith and love in the face of persecution and trials. He even boasted about their perseverance amongst other churches. Their endurance was evidence that God's judgement was right. They would be counted worthy of God's kingdom. Their enemies would be paid back for the troubles they caused. When Jesus Christ was revealed from heaven "*in blazing fire with his powerful angels*" (an awesome symbolic picture of God's holy presence coming to punish wickedness), he would bring them relief, and punish with everlasting destruction those who do not know God or obey the gospel. They would be shut out from the presence of the Lord and from the majesty of his power. On that day, however, the Lord would be glorified in his holy people, including the believers at Thessalonica. This prospect motivated Paul's constant prayer for them. He prayed that God would count them worthy of his calling, and that by his power he would fulfil their every good purpose and act of faith. This was so that the name of the Lord Jesus might be glorified in them, and they in him, according to the grace of *"our God and the Lord Jesus Christ"*. Again we see Paul's praying was governed by the immediate situation at Thessalonica and the gospel of the Father/Messiah union. He prayed that God's will through the gospel would be accomplished in the lives of the believers. His praying was inspired by his deep conviction and understanding of God and his revealed achievements and intentions.

To correct their misunderstanding and misapprehension about the day of the Lord, Paul explained particular events which must precede its coming (2:1-12). There will be a breakout of full-blown rebellion and the coming of a *"man of lawlessness"*. This person is doomed to destruction. He will oppose, and exalt himself over, everything which is called God or is worshiped. He will set himself up in God's temple and proclaim himself to be God. At present there is a constraint holding him back, so that he will be revealed at the proper time. The secret power of lawlessness was already active, but held back until the constraint was removed. Then he will be revealed, but overthrown and destroyed by the coming of the Lord Jesus. The coming of this lawless one will be in accord with the work of Satan displayed in counterfeit miracles, signs and wonders, and every form of deceptive evil. These will deceive those who are perishing because they refuse to believe the truth and be saved. God will send them (allow them to be taken in by) a powerful delusion so that they will believe the lie (that the lawless one is God). All who have not believed the truth (of the gospel), but have delighted in wickedness, will be condemned. Paul did not identify the constraint, which would eventually be removed. It could be one of many suggestions, including political power, the gospel, or the Holy Spirit. Perhaps Paul had the Roman empire in mind, and was reluctant to be specific about it being taken away, because of charges against him at Thessalonica that his activities were a disruption to Roman society (Acts 17:6-7). Paul had experienced both lawless opposition, and protection by civil law enforcement, while he was at Thessalonica. It is likely that his description of the lawless one's claim to be God, and setting himself up in God's temple, was influenced by just such an action ten years earlier. Emperor Gaius had tried to have his statue erected in the temple at Jerusalem, but was restrained by established powers of law and order. At the time of writing, the temple at Jerusalem was still standing, so a literal fulfilment in the foreseeable future was a high possibility. However, Paul was probably using the imagery to illustrate the principle of dethroning God and usurping his honour and authority. With the temple now destroyed, the exact manner of fulfilment is difficult to predict precisely. At the same time, history has frequently witnessed the unruly spirit of lawlessness on display, and the rise of numerous examples of powerful personalities who have aspired to self-deification.

Although those who are deceived by the lawless one will perish, it will be a different outcome for the brothers at Thessalonica. They were a cause for gratitude and support in prayer (2:13-17). They were loved by the Lord, because from the beginning God chose to save them through the sanctifying work of the Spirit and belief in the truth. He had called them through the gospel so that they might share in the glory of the Lord Jesus Christ. Paul was indicating that God's chosen people were those who responded in faith to the call of the gospel. The brothers had no reason to be alarmed about the destruction which the coming of the Lord would bring. The Lord loved them and would save them, provided they stood firm and held on to Paul's *"teachings"* (literally, *"traditions"*, meaning the gospel truths delivered by Christ to his apostles, and passed on by them to their converts). Therefore Paul prayed for their encouragement and continued progress (v 16-17). His prayer was revealing and relevant. He looked to the *"Lord Jesus Christ and God our Father"* to take care of them, revealing his conviction of their inseparable bond of oneness in purpose and performance. His heart's outlook was governed by the Father's love, and by the Father's grace which gave eternal encouragement and good hope. He prayed for encouragement for their hearts, and strength for their deeds and words.

In turn, he asked them to pray for him and his fellow workers (3:1-5). In particular, he wanted them to pray for the spread and acceptance of their gospel message, and for protection from evil opponents. He acknowledged that not everyone had faith, but asserted that the Lord was faithful. He assured them that the Lord would protect them from the evil one, and expressed his confidence in the Lord that they would continue in obedience. Paul's remarks were urging his readers to rely prayerfully and trustingly in the Lord as they coped with their hostile circumstances. He then expressed the further prayer that the Lord would direct their hearts into God's love and Christ's perseverance. In this he was reflecting his deep personal confidence of the reality and power of the risen Lord, and reminding the Thessalonians of the Father/Messiah partnership which was the foundation of their faith.

On the other hand, he issued a stern warning against the idlers in their community (3:6-15). They were ignoring the gospel "tradition" and the example of the apostles. Their expectation of Christ's soon return was probably causing them to think there was no need to work for a living. Instead of being busy, they were busybodies! Paul instructed the rest of the community to order them to earn their living, and to shun and shame any who refused. Nevertheless, they were not to be regarded as enemies, but brothers to be warned.

Paul concluded his second letter to the Thessalonians with a prayer to the *"Lord of peace"* to give them peace at all times and in every way, signing off by his own hand, and with a final word for the grace of the Lord Jesus Christ to be with them all (3:16-18).

A prayerful tone permeated both letters, demonstrating the vibrant reality of dependence on God and Christ which now characterised the new movement of believers in Jesus.

1 and 2 Corinthians are longer letters, packed with practical instructions for resolving a range of problems, relationships, and views affecting church life at Corinth. Not much is said explicitly about prayer per se. However, Paul's teachings provide an in-depth look into the community life of the church, which was the vibrant environment where prayer was offered. A brief overview of the letters presents a backdrop for its activity.

The city of Corinth was a wealthy seaport in southern Greece in a strategic location for trade and commerce. Dominating city life were three powerful religions. The worship of Aphrodite, the goddess of love, was dedicated to the glorification of sex, and promoted prostitution as a sacred ritual. The worship of Melicertes, the patron god of sea travel, sprang from the same origins as the religion of Baal which disastrously penetrated Israel during the days of Ahab and Jezebel (1 Kings 17ff). The worship of Apollo, god of music and poetry, especially promoted male nudity and homosexual practices. Consequently, society was obsessed with sex. The population was a hotchpotch of many races, religions, cultures, languages, classes, trades, and vices. Corinth was a popular destination, but a harsh place to live in.

Paul founded the church at Corinth, after arriving there from Thessalonica and Athens. He spent eighteen months consolidating the new fellowship, which included both Jews and Gentiles. After his departure, he maintained close interest because he had strong affection for the church. Sadly, relationships between Paul and the church severely deteriorated, owing to the influence of some arrogant leaders and a serious distortion of understanding about the gospel. Paul kept in touch by correspondence, visitors from Corinth, a personal visit to Corinth, and a visit by Paul's colleague Titus. The whole experience was very painful for Paul. Eventually, however, the confusions were sorted out, and there was a joyful reconciliation.

1 Corinthians was one of Paul's letters to Corinth during the early stages of the growing tensions between him and the church. It was written, in about 55 CE at Ephesus, to correct a number of reported serious problems in the church, and to answer questions about matters which were puzzling and causing conflict within the community. Underlying the mixed up views and practices which were disturbing the Corinthian members was a distorted understanding of the gospel. Basically, the Corinthians had a distorted view of spirituality, and this affected their outlook on everything else. Influenced by their cultural background, spirituality for the Corinthians appears to have been a matter of having already entered a new and higher level of existence, a "resurrection" existence which made them like angels. Life in their present existence involved living out their experience of the Spirit, which was the energising power of their higher existence. Apparently life in the Spirit was especially manifested in impressive expressions of ideas (wisdom) and speech, typical Greek interests, and with disregard for the material world and normal human interactions. The Corinthians' confused views of spirituality inspired elitist attitudes of arrogance and fervent interest in boastful performance. It all gave rise to a mixed bag of problems. In the course of his letter, Paul addressed issues of party factions (chapters 1-4), sexual immorality and litigation actions (chapters 5-6), marital matters (chapter 7), social choices, personal rights and freedoms (chapters 8-10), gender differences and the Lord's Supper (chapter 11), spirituality and charismatic gifts (chapters 12-14), and the future bodily resurrection of the dead (chapter

15). Distorted views about all these matters sprang from the Corinthians' cultural background and their "super spirituality". Paul sought to correct the problems by explaining and applying the gospel. Throughout the whole letter, Paul's central and dominant focus was the lordship of Jesus Christ. True spirituality was found, not in exalted experiences, but in knowing Jesus as Messiah and Master. He was a crucified Messiah, who turned earthly wisdom on its head. All God's people in fellowship with him were fully spiritually enriched, lacking nothing. Their identity, resources, and destiny were all found in relationship to him, guaranteed by God's faithfulness. For the Corinthians, spirituality focused on individual experience and expression. For Paul, it was all about relationships, with God, and with others.

The notable emphasis in Paul's opening greeting was on the idea of *call* (1:1-3). Paul was "*called*" to be an apostle. The church was "*called*" to be holy (set apart for God). So too were all who "*call*" on the name of the Lord Jesus Christ. The term "*church*" is, literally, "*those who are called out*". The focus on God's "*call*" is repeatedly emphasised (v 9, 24, 26). God's call was central and significant to the experience of belonging to God. Those who hear God's call respond by calling on the name of the Lord! Paul wanted to emphasise that God's call was fundamental to his relationship with the Corinthians. He was an apostle called to issue God's call, and they were those called out to be God's holy people. True spirituality was the relationship of being in right fellowship with God the Father, as a member of the holy community of believers in Jesus Christ, by being immersed into one body by the Holy Spirit, on the basis of God's gracious call.

Prayer was mentioned only incidentally in the letter. It was only referred to in regard to three matters, and these assumed the value and importance of prayer.

Apparently there was a view at Corinth which promoted sexual abstinence, even within marriage, as a higher level of spirituality (7:1-7). Paul's counsel encouraged normal marital sexual relations to avoid Satan's temptations. However, he permitted temporary abstinence, by mutual consent between a husband and wife, to allow them to devote themselves to prayer (v 5). Spirituality was not a matter of ascetic behaviour (disciplining the body for the sake of freeing the spirit), whether celibacy or marital sexual abstinence. It was sharing fellowship with God, and therefore expressed in prayer.

Paul's notoriously difficult discussion about the public participation of women in the assembled community concerned the manner in which they prayed and prophesied (11:1-16). His arguments included cultural customs, theological ideas, and appeals to nature. The problem seems to have been another example of the "super spirituality" being expressed in unleashed individualism, by which women ignored natural decorum, social conventions, and interdependent male/female relationships. They literally "let their hair down", in frenzied performance. Paul's counsel, somewhat obscure in parts, urged a recognition of basic relationships with Christ and with one another, and dignified public behaviour. In particular, he encouraged respectful interdependent relationships between men and women, rather than individual performance. Spirituality for Paul was not in performance, but in relationships centred in Christ. This was especially relevant for prayer and prophecy, which were forms of two-way communication between God and his people, not exalted experiences as ends in themselves. Prayer was an activity of meaningful engagement with God. The gospel fully permitted men and women to participate equally in the church's public gatherings.

Prayer and prophecy also come to the fore in discussion about spiritual matters and gifts (chapters 12-14). The distorted spirituality of the Corinthians was ignoring the "body life" of the church and the true purpose of charismatic gifts. "Speaking in tongues" was a highly prized gift, and seems to have been considered speaking the language of angels. The assembled community expressed their spirituality in inspirational enthusiasm. Paul's counsel insisted on the priority of love as the true manifestation of spirituality. Paul's eloquent exposition on love in chapter 13 emphasised that true spirituality was not the performance of charismatic gifts and ministry activities, but a matter of character and motives. When someone is full of the Spirit, they show it by living in love. Paul applied this principle to the conduct of the assembly where prayer and prophecy were prominent features. He urged the Corinthians to follow the way of love and eagerly desire spiritual gifts. Prophecy was desirable because it strengthened and encouraged the listeners. Prayer was a different matter, because the Corinthians placed an overemphasis on "speaking in tongues" (glossolalia) when they prayed. Glossolalia was the outward expression of a person's inner spirit in inspired uncontrolled utterance. It had been a prominent feature of the Corinthians' former pagan religion. With regard to their new faith in Christ, they still understood spirituality in terms of inspired speech, rather than sharing in meaningful, understandable, and edifying relationships with God and with one another. Paul's discussion of "tongues" in the assembly promoted the governing principle of intelligibility and edification. Paul did not forbid glossolalia, but he downplayed it, because it was unintelligible both to the speaker and the listener. It needed to be interpreted, since the speaker was uttering mysteries to God, and was only edifying himself. This was not the way of love. It was not glossolalia's fascinating, exotic nature which had merit. It was its contribution of encouragement and insight to edify the church when interpreted which gave it worth. Paul admitted that when he prayed in a "tongue", his spirit prayed, but his mind was unfruitful. Speaking in tongues gave expression to Spirit inspired ecstasy, manifesting personal enthusiasm. It was the human spirit under the inspiration of the Holy Spirit expressing itself. It may have been expressing praise and thanks to God, or uttering profound truths, but no one actually knew, not even the speaker. Tongues were not relational in nature, nor meaningful to the mind. This was not a form of intimacy with God, nor a form of fellowship with others, or service to them. It was a solo experience which only benefitted the speaker. Therefore, Paul said he would pray, and sing, with his spirit and also with his mind. He was grateful for his own ability to "speak in tongues", but in the church he would only speak what was intelligible, in order to instruct others. His counsel shows that prayer was not merely a religious activity, but meant to be a vital expression of a meaningful relationship with God.

Before moving on, we might pause to contemplate the significant statement Paul made in 8:6. In contrast to pagan idols, Paul declares that *"for us there is but one God, the Father, from whom all things came and for whom we live; and there is but one Lord, Jesus Christ, through whom all things came and through whom we live"*. God and Christ share a unique, intimate, and inseparable relationship in the activities of both creation and redemption. God the Father accomplished his work through his Messiah, who performed divine work and existed prior to creation. God's identity as *"Father"* was revealed through his incarnate earthly "Son".

2 Corinthians reflects the same attitude to prayer. There are few references to prayer, yet these reveal Paul's strong prayerful dependency. His letter begins and ends with his open acknowledgement that he was handling his responsibilities prayerfully.

This letter is probably the most personally revealing of all Paul's letters. He refers to two dramatic experiences which had a deep impact on his life, escape from expected death, and a vision of entering heaven. He discloses an astonishing record of traumatic sufferings and hardships he has faced. He is openly frank about his pain and distress over the breakdown in his relationship with the Corinthians, and his joyful relief when matters were reconciled. He reveals inspiring insights into his views and attitudes towards his ministry as an apostle. It is a source of great encouragement and motivation, and a rich background for appreciating the value of prayer.

As in his first letter to the Corinthians (1:1), so in his second (1:1), Paul identifies himself as an apostle of Christ Jesus *"by the will of God"*. God's will was his sovereign purpose accomplished through Jesus his Messiah. This was God's gracious plan of salvation for the world, achieved through the death and resurrection of his Messiah. For Paul, it was God's real and radical intrusion into world affairs to redeem the world and reconcile it to himself. Paul was a chosen messenger privileged to proclaim the good news abroad. God's *"will"* was the framework for his outlook and mission, and therefore of all his activities, including prayer.

Paul begins his letter with an outburst of praise to God, who is identified (in terms of the revelation of the gospel) as the *"the God and Father of our Lord Jesus Christ, the Father of compassion and the God of all comfort"* (1:3-7). God comforts those who share in Christ's sufferings, so that they can comfort others who share in those sufferings. This theme of comfort permeates chapters 1-9. Paul's glowing appreciation for God was due to a recent virtual "resurrection" experience because God had delivered him from a perilous situation which he had thought was a sentence of death (1:8-11). He does not describe the situation, and nothing is known about it from other sources. Paul was convinced that God was the living sovereign God who engaged in human affairs, motivated by his compassion. For this reason, Paul had confidence in prayer. Because he had set his hope on God, he was sure that God would continue to deliver him. The Corinthians would help by their prayers! Prayer was appealing to God to rescue his gospel messengers from the dangers of opposition. It was trusting God, desiring God's will to advance, requesting the protection of God's servants. Quite clearly, prayer was a vital and effective activity for Paul and the community of believers in Christ. It was a purposeful feature of their relationship to God.

Now that Paul's strained relations with the Corinthians were reconciled, he proceeded to write an extensive explanation about his misunderstood behaviour and his attitude towards gospel ministry as an apostle. His changes of plans about visiting them were not because of apparent indecision, but out of deep love for them, and the desire not to cause them pain (1:12-2:5). He encouraged them to forgive the person who had caused the grief, and had been severely punished (2:5-11). At some length, he expounded his privileged role as an apostle (despite its humiliations and sufferings), the glorious nature of the gospel message, and his ministry as an ambassador of Christ announcing reconciliation for the world (2:12-6:13). He issued a brief warning against pagan associations (6:14-7:1). Then he expressed his joyful relief and comfort when he received Titus' news that his severe letter to the church had had the desired effect, even though he was sorry he had sent it (7:2-16). He urged the Corinthians to participate in the collection being gathered from his churches to be taken to the church at Jerusalem (chapters 8-9).

The end of the letter takes a sudden, sharper tone, as Paul defends his apostolic authority (chapters 10-13). No explanation is given for the changed mood, although it is evident that he was reacting against critics who were masquerading as false "super" apostles. Possibly a new development had occurred, or perhaps these chapters were part of Paul's earlier severe letter which became attached to this letter, as some scholars suggest. Whatever prompted this section, it reveals eye-opening details about Paul's experiences, including a litany of sufferings and a visionary experience of being caught up into the third heaven (beyond earth's atmosphere and outer space, into God's own presence). Paul reluctantly, and sarcastically, allowed himself to "*boast*" about his apostleship because of his concern that the Corinthians might be adversely influenced by his critics. Then he apologises for his foolish boasting, and warns that he is about to make a third visit to them. Instead of demanding proof that Christ was speaking through him, they should examine themselves for evidence that Christ was living in them. He did not want them to fail the test, and he wanted them to know that he had not failed the test. Consequently, he prays that they will do no wrong. Not that they will see that he has stood the test, but that they will do what is right even if he seems to have failed. He is praying for their perfection. This concluding note to his letter indicates Paul's concern for the Corinthians' spiritual development above all else, even his own status in their eyes, and his reliance on prayer for that to be accomplished. The prayerful benediction which ends the letter succinctly states his gospel perspective.

"May the grace of the Lord Jesus Christ, and the love of God, and the fellowship of the Holy Spirit be with you all".

God's magnificent salvation is the result of God's trinitarian action. Paul was not making a statement about God's being, but about his doing. In the first place, God's eternal love motivated his mission of salvation from beginning to end. Secondly, God's Messiah Jesus gave himself in sacrifice as a gift of grace to accomplish salvation, by destroying sin and death through his crucifixion and resurrection, and by becoming glorified as absolute Lord. Thirdly, God's Holy Spirit culminated salvation by immersing all believers in Christ into an eternal, spiritual community, to become Christ's collective "Body", and, in Christ, into intimate fellowship with God and with one another. Paul's benediction expresses his prayerful desire that his readers might experience the reality of God in terms of his threefold operation.

Romans is spiritual dynamite! Its message has had explosive effect several times in the course of history, triggering a dynamic tsunami which has swept across numerous lands, revolutionising church life, society, theology, culture, politics, and personal experience. Wherever and whenever Romans has been taken to heart, there has been a radical mindshift and reorientation of life.

Romans was written in about 57 CE to pave the way for Paul's travel plans, and to give a detailed explanation of the Gospel he preached. He especially dealt with issues concerning the relationship of Jews and Gentiles in God's plan of salvation. Jew/Gentile relationships were causing troublesome tensions both within the wider world and within the Church. Paul prepared to undertake a three stage journey. He intended to visit Jerusalem to bring a collection from his Gentile churches as a gift to the Jewish mother church. This was an expression of love and fellowship to strengthen ties between Jewish and Gentile believers.

Then he hoped to go to Rome to help strengthen the church there. Jews had previously been evicted from Rome by the emperor. Gentile suspicion towards Jews, and Jewish reluctance to accept Gentiles as welcome to God, generated tensions even amongst believers. Paul's mission to Gentiles, and his compromise of entrenched Jewish traditions, placed him and his message under suspicion in Jewish eyes. He wrote Romans to explain carefully and thoroughly the Gospel which he preached.

Paul's third stage was a plan to reach out in a new campaign to Spain, using Rome as a base of operations and support.

Paul's letter to the believers in Rome had a bearing on all these intentions. It was a statement about the gospel, in terms of its Jewish origins and Gentile outreach. The goal of the gospel was to create a single people for God consisting of redeemed Jews and Gentiles together. The goal of the letter was indicated by Paul's concluding prayer and appeal in 15:5-9.

> "*May the God who gives endurance and encouragement give you [Jews and Gentiles] the same attitude of mind toward each other that Christ Jesus had, ⁶ so that with one mind and one voice you may glorify the God and Father of our Lord Jesus Christ. ⁷ Accept one another, then, just as Christ accepted you, in order to bring praise to God. ⁸ For I tell you that Christ has become a servant of the Jews on behalf of God's truth, so that the promises made to the patriarchs might be confirmed ⁹ and, moreover, that the Gentiles might glorify God for his mercy. As it is written: "Therefore I will praise you among the Gentiles; I will sing the praises of your name."*

Paul's basic argument throughout the letter is that God's true covenant people, composed of Jews and Gentiles alike through faith in Jesus Christ, are made righteous by the crucifixion and resurrection of Christ and the gift of the Holy Spirit. Righteousness is the requirement for being in a right covenant relationship with God. Paul makes the startling claim that the Jewish Law (Torah) failed to produce righteousness in anyone (a bombshell for Jews!), and so should be discarded as a means for trying to attain it. Instead, righteousness was God's gift, credited to anyone, Jew or Gentile, who put their trust in Jesus Christ. The life of righteousness is not lived by keeping the Law, but by being led by the Spirit.

The letter is a lengthy discussion about many central aspects of the gospel, and is a Christian "manifesto" for mission. It provides profound insight about the gospel and its implications for faith, personal living, church and community life, and God's great plan for human history and the nations.

In the course of his letter, Paul reveals significant insights about his attitude to prayer. Although he only mentions prayer several times, these are very revealing. The first occasion is at the start of his letter, after his opening introduction and greetings. There he identifies both himself and his readers in terms of their "*calling*" by God, and makes a brief statement about the gospel which culminates God's plan of salvation begun with Israel (1:1-7).

Then Paul opens his heart to reveal his prayer (1:8-10), his plans (1:11-13), and his passion for the gospel (1:14-15). Concerning his prayer, he writes,

> "*First, I thank my God through Jesus Christ for all of you, because your faith is being reported all over the world. God, whom I serve with my whole heart in preaching the gospel of his Son, is my witness how constantly I remember you in my prayers at all times; and I pray that now at last by God's will the way may be opened for me to come to you*".

What Paul says illuminates his attitude concerning prayer. In the first place, he gave thanks to God for the widely renowned faith of the church at Rome. He had nothing to do with planting the church at Rome, but as God's messenger of the gospel he had a deep interest in the development of God's kingdom in the capital of the empire. He was pleased and grateful that there were already believers there who had embraced the gospel. More than that, he recognised that the faith of the Romans was evidence of the power of God at work (v 16). Paul's prayer of gratitude demonstrated his personal conviction about God as the living, active, saving divine ruler of the world, revealed through the gospel concerning Jesus Christ. Typically, he had extended his greetings to the saints at Rome, "*Grace and peace to you from God our Father and from the Lord Jesus Christ*", identifying God in terms of his unique partnership with Jesus the exalted Messiah (v 7). Paul appeals to God as his witness that in his regular prayers he constantly remembered the believers at Rome. Praying was his habit, representing his devotional and dependent relationship with God. Perhaps Paul maintained the Jewish practice of praying three times a day, and followed Jesus' example of praying for lengthy periods. Paul uses terms for prayer which indicate his intensity ("beg"). His praying was a purposeful and strategic activity. Through prayer Paul was sharing a partnership with God in spreading the gospel about God's kingdom throughout the world, beyond the reach of his own preaching efforts. In particular, he prayed that by God's will he might have opportunity to go to Rome in order to have some ministry there. His commission and passion to proclaim the gospel, especially to Gentiles, drove him to consider going to Rome itself. But it had to be according to God's will. God was his Master, and he determined how, when, and where the gospel was to spread. Although Paul formulated his own plans, they were always subject to God's overruling sovereignty. Paul prayed that his own travel plans were **in accord with God's sovereign plans for the spread of the Gospel.**

As it transpired, Paul did eventually reach Rome several years later. However, he did not go as a free traveller. He was arrested in Jerusalem by the Roman authorities, and kept in custody at Caesarea for more than two years. Then he was transported under guard to Rome, surviving a stormy voyage and shipwreck at sea, and several months with castaways on the island of Malta on the way. At Rome he was kept under house arrest for at least another two years. Paul's prayers were answered, but not as he had anticipated. God's will intended Paul to go to Rome, yet included other factors which were unknown to Paul.

There are some deep thoughts in Romans, which take serious effort to grasp. But the spiritual rewards are worth it. The underlying theme, *God's covenant relationship*, is not a familiar concept to many Christians, yet is a major key to understanding the Bible and knowing God. Which just proves that Romans is a book worth knowing!

God has devised and accomplished a magnificent plan of salvation for the world. The Bible bears witness to that plan, and reveals its processes and principles. The plan is all about covenant relationship with God. The gospel is the announcement that God's plan has been achieved.

Paul's exposition of the gospel in Romans has a Jew/Gentile audience in mind, and this affects his style and themes. He is also stimulated by his passion for the gospel, and so his tone reflects that enthusiasm. His thoughts and lines of argument are sometimes complicated, forcing us to have to work hard to understand his meaning. But the insights gained are worth the effort. In fact it is this very difficulty which shows that the gospel is not a simplistic matter, to be taken lightly. It is profound, affecting our knowledge of God, the processes of history, our spiritual struggles, and our eternal destiny. To become the people God intends us to be calls for whole-hearted effort. In particular we must strengthen our grasp of God's word, because this is the means by which God makes himself known to us, and by which we become spiritually mature and alive.

The gospel is about God's Son, his 'righteous servant' and 'covenant partner'. Adam was *created* to be God's righteous, covenant son, but disobeyed God. Israel was *chosen* to be God's righteous, covenant son, but also disobeyed. Jesus obeyed, and by his resurrection was declared to be God's true Son. The title "Son of God" does not refer to his divine status, but to his earthly covenant identity. Through faith in him, we are credited with being God's righteous sons, restored to covenant relationship with God.

The letter begins by showing that all have sinned (Jews and Gentiles), and are only justified and reconciled to God by grace, through faith in Christ (chapters 1-5). God's promises to Abraham to establish a people in covenant relationship with God through whom the world would be blessed are fulfilled. The plan included Israel as God's chosen nation to bring salvation to the world, and Jesus as God's promised Messiah to provide redemption. Jesus was God's sin offering on behalf of the world, the means by which God dealt with unrighteous rebellion. As a gift of grace God accepts everyone who believes in Christ, crediting them as righteous, and reconciling them with himself. They are restored to covenant relationship and lavished with God's love. God created and completed his covenant.

This is the gospel, and the implications are liberating (chapters 6-8). Having explained God's actions of grace to grant us our righteous standing, Paul proceeds to work through some of the critical implications for personal life and faith. He especially has Jewish/Gentile concerns in mind, and the issues of our moral responsibility, our practical struggles with sinful nature and human weaknesses, and our experience of God's Spirit. He reveals God's astounding purpose of love.

God's gospel of grace means that individuals are freed from the tyranny of sin, the condemnation of the law, and the sentence of death. The resurrection life of Christ is a powerful reality in the experience of believers who are "in Christ", as also is the Holy Spirit. The Spirit provides a new mindset of assurance of being freed from condemnation, an inner power to deal with sin, and the intimate awareness of belonging to God as one of his children. Believers have a hope which faces earthly sufferings, and know that nothing can separate them from God's covenant love.

At this point in his letter Paul makes a profound statement about the role of the Holy Spirit in prayer, as he comments on the hope of creation (8:18-27). Paul realised that there were human limits to understanding God's will in life's circumstances, but that as he prayed

God's Spirit interceded on his behalf **in accord with God's intended purposes.** Responding to his previous statement (v 17) about needing to suffer with Christ in order to share his glory, Paul enthusiastically declares his personal conviction ("*I consider*") that present sufferings are not worth comparing with future glory. He has already explained that our present sufferings lead to that glory (5:1-5). Now he assures that it will be "*revealed*" in us. To a degree now because we already belong to the coming age, but in complete fulness when it arrives, ultimate glory will be revealed in our transformed lives. Expanding his horizon, Paul declares that the whole creation waits for that time. Personalising creation, he depicts it waiting "*in eager expectation*" for God's sons to be revealed. Creation's own destiny is wrapped up with God's glorious inheritance for his sons. The inheritance of God's people is more than merely the land promised to Abraham and Israel. It includes the whole world (4:13). The reason for creation's eager longing is that it has been "*subjected to frustration*", sharing in the consequences of human rebellion, not by its own choosing, but imposed by God. Man was appointed to have dominion over creation, so his perversion has had consequences for his realm. However, there is also hope of freedom, sharing in the benefits of salvation. Creation will be liberated from its "*bondage to decay*" to experience the freedom of the "*glory of the children of God*". Final salvation will be freedom from all current sin, death, and corruption in the world.

The vision of creation longing to achieve its freedom was not new. "*We know*", writes Paul, of all creation "*groaning*" and writhing in "*childbirth*". This was familiar Old Testament imagery, and popularly known in Jewish circles as the "birth pangs of the Messiah". Convulsions in nature and history were viewed as the beginnings of the end of time, when there would be total cosmic upheaval and the creation of new heavens and earth. These pains have been going on "*right up to the present time*".

But not only creation. "*We ourselves*" also groan inwardly in eager expectation. Those who belong to Christ share the same discomfort and frustration as creation, waiting for the great moment of full birth. Our struggles with sin and suffering cause deep inner cries of distress and longing. We already have the "*firstfruits of the Spirit*", a colourful reminder that the gift of the Spirit at conversion is the beginning of the "harvest" which will take place at resurrection. That will be our "*adoption as sons, the redemption of our bodies*". Although we have received redemption through Christ (3:24), and the Spirit of adoption (8:15), the full reality will not be complete until we share in the harvest time when God's children and all creation enter into the freedom of God's glory. This is the hope by which we are saved. It keeps us persevering through present struggles, knowing that salvation is a future certainty. Some believers were overly excited about their experience of the Spirit, as if that was the full measure of salvation, and dismissed the need for personal renewal and bodily resurrection (see 2 Timothy 2:18). So Paul counteracted such false ideas by declaring that hope which is seen or possessed is not really hope. If we wait for a hope not yet possessed, we will wait eagerly and patiently.

These thoughts prompted an explanation about prayer. Not only does our future hope keep us pressing on, but the Spirit helps by interceding for us. He helps us in our *"weaknesses"*. We find it difficult to cope with earthly afflictions and moral struggles, and we do not know what we ought to pray for. So the Spirit helps out by interceding for us *"with groans which words cannot express"*. Repetition of the term *"groans"* (v 22, 23, 26) indicates that the Spirit joins us and all creation in yearning for the day of redemption, and implies that prayer is meant to be directed towards that goal. Prayer is not primarily for matters of self-interest in the present world, but for the progress of God's purposes for the end of time. When God searches our hearts as we pray, he knows what is in line with the mindset of the Spirit (see also 8:6), who intercedes according to God's will.

Through all the uncertainties of our world, and our own inconsistencies as we struggle with moral and spiritual responsibilities, we can be assured that God will accomplish his purpose. *"We know"* that in all things God works *"for the good"* of those who *"love him"* (v 28).

But what about Israel? Has God abandoned the nation which he chose to bring salvation to the world? This is the question which Paul takes up in chapters 9-11. The letter was written to explain the gospel to Gentile and Jewish believers, and the implications for fellowship between them and for their shared mission to the world. With his explanation of the gospel as the background, Paul then raises important questions about the place of Israel in God's plan, because in the main Jews had rejected Jesus as the Messiah. As Paul discusses this problem, he reveals thrilling insights about God and his purposes. In brief, he reveals that the "Israel of God" is not national Israel, but the fellowship of believers in Christ, which included both Jews and Gentiles. He reveals the character by which God's purposes are accomplished. He handles the issues of God's sovereignty and human responsibility. He announces a special revelation concerning God's plan for Israel. Above all he reveals awe-inspiring truths about the nature of God. What he says is heady stuff, which requires thoughtful consideration, but is beyond our present investigation. How he says it reveals his deep feelings about the issue. He is full of sorrow and anguish (9:1-3), strong desire (10:1) and personal consciousness (11:1), and passionate wonder for God's extraordinary riches and wisdom in devising such a marvellous salvation (11:33-36). With respect to our interest, he makes reference to his praying on the matter.

"Brothers, my heart's desire and prayer to God for the Israelites is that they may be saved" (10:1).

What would give great pleasure to Paul's heart, and what he prayed for, was the salvation of his countrymen. Paul knew that the gospel of salvation was for the Jew first, as well as the

Gentile (1:16). Since God had a special part for Israel in his plan of salvation for the world, Paul prayed for his people accordingly. He had confidence that his prayers on behalf of his fellow Jews were in accord with God's own intentions. His recourse to prayer shows the depth of his desire, and the confidence he had in prayer's efficacy. He was not praying for God to alter his plans, but to fulfil them by including Jews in the "True Israel". He could point out that God had not rejected the Jews, since he himself was one who had experienced God's grace (11:1-2). For Paul, prayer was a strategic priority. He prayed about his travel plans. He prayed about earthly struggles and life's perplexities as he journeyed towards the final day of redemption and resurrection. He prayed for his converts and the new churches he planted. He prayed for the salvation of the Jewish people. In all his prayers, he was governed by the will of God.

Having redrawn the boundaries of what it means to be in covenant relationship with God, the final chapters of Romans (12-16) explain some practical implications for living, and include personal information and greetings to prepare for Paul's visit to Rome. On the basis of all that he had explained about God's mercy in providing salvation for both Jews and Gentiles through presenting Christ as a sacrifice of atonement (3:22-25), Paul urged his readers to offer their bodies as "*living sacrifices, holy and pleasing to God*" (12:1-2). This was their logical response of worship. Since Christ was sacrificed for them, they should sacrifice themselves (the rest of their earthly lives) for him. Paul replaces the image of dead animal sacrifices with living human bodies. Apart from the colourful comparison, he was also referring back to earlier remarks (6:1-14). The death of Christ put to death sinful human nature so that mortal bodies could now live new lives in the reality of his resurrection. Paul was urging his readers to devote the rest of their earthly lives freed from sin-bound tendencies to please God by living according to his will.

By way of practical application, Paul firstly emphasised the interrelationships of the new covenant community (12:3-13). All believers, both Jews and Gentiles, are members of one "*body in Christ*" (v 3-5). It is a "charismatic" community in which members function according to their various "grace gifts" (v 6-8). The distinctive quality of life in God's community is "*love*" (v 9-13). Paul expounds on love with a staccato series of instructions to motivate his readers. Although at first glance these all seem randomly selected and unrelated, closer attention reveals echoes of Paul's earlier discussion of the gospel. Amongst them we should notice a particular trio. "*Be joyful in hope, patient in affliction, faithful in prayer*" (v 12). These were expressions of life in the Spirit identified in 8:18-27. The life of love in the covenant community springs directly from life in the Spirit, which is the life of faith, the life of Christ in his collective body. Prayer is a crucial ingredient. It is the means of communion with God, actual, vital, meaningful fellowship with him, who is the essential source of the community's life. The term translated "*faithful*" has the sense of perseverance and intensity. In a world of adversity and antagonism to the ways of God, it is necessary to persist fervently in engaging with God in prayer to rely on his resources and to pursue his purposes.

Paul finished his letter, apart from final extensive greetings, by laying out his intended future ministry plans, and appealing for his readers' prayer support (15:23-33). His apostolic role in the east had concluded and he was now shifting his vision towards the west. He wanted to fulfil a long-held desire to visit the believers at Rome, while passing through to Spain. He wanted to benefit from being with them, and to be assisted by them in his next ministry venture. In the meantime, he intended to visit Jerusalem, to bring a generous gift from his Gentile churches to the church at Jerusalem. This was to ensure strong solidarity between them. The Gentiles were spiritually indebted to the believers at Jerusalem for the gospel, and saw that they had an obligation to serve them in return with material support. When that task was completed, Paul would travel via Rome to Spain. The reason for explaining his intended visit to Jerusalem was to seek their prayer support. Addressing them as "*brothers*", he appealed to them in terms of their common covenant relationship, "*by our Lord Jesus Christ and by the love of the Spirit*". Jesus was Lord of God's new community, and its life generated by God's Spirit was the experience of love which transcended racial, social, and worldly distinctions. Paul urged them to join him in his struggle by praying for him. He knew from first hand experience that service for God in spreading the gospel was a battle, so he sought their prayerful support in obtaining God's help. Specifically, he wanted prayer for his safety from hostile unbelieving Jews, and prayer for his service of bringing the Gentiles' collection to be accepted. He knew that his work amongst Gentiles was not popular with Jews, both outside the church and within. Therefore his visit to Jerusalem was fraught with danger. This was the reason for his request for prayer, and for writing such a full treatment of the gospel. Because this was God's will, he was confident that God would answer their prayers, and enable him to join them eventually, and be refreshed from the ordeal. Appropriately, he concluded with the prayerful wish that the "*God of peace*" be with them all (Jew and Gentile).

Paul's explanation of the gospel in Romans is profound and rich. It pulsates with the thrilling comprehension of God's identity, nature, and will revealed by Jesus the Messiah who accomplished redemption for all mankind. It reveals the joyful reality of experiencing God's Spirit in overcoming sinful nature to live righteously, and in establishing peaceful and loving relations with God and between members of his redeemed community. It declares a glorious eternal destiny for the universe and for God's resurrected, united, and redeemed family. Within the framework of God's intrusion into human affairs to fulfil his gospel purposes, prayer is a strategic, effective, and cooperative activity. Paul's prayers were motivated by God's self-revelation as the God of mercy and grace, and his consciousness of personal dependence on God, intimate relationship with him, and privileged partnership as his messenger.

Letters Written from Prison

Ephesians is one of the most inspirational books of the Bible. Its exciting message reveals God's ultimate intention for his creation. At the heart of his purpose is the person and mission of the Lord Jesus Christ, who by his life, death, resurrection, and enthronement fulfilled God's eternal plan of grace. Everything is governed by grace, which expresses the essential character of God.

Ephesians is the only book in the New Testament not prompted by particular circumstances which needed attention. Instead, it was written, in about 60 CE, out of Paul's own circumstances of being held in custody by the Romans, awaiting trial before Caesar. He wrote to believers at Ephesus and other centres in the region of Asia (Turkey today), which was emerging as the heartland of the growing Christian church, to clarify and deepen their understanding of God's magnificent plan of grace, and to appeal to its readers to walk worthy of God's calling. It contains several thrilling revelations about Jesus and the church, and God's blessings for believers in Christ. Through Jesus Christ, God has brought forgiveness, risen life, and reconciliation to all believers. In Christ they have been made alive and "*seated*" in heavenly realms (2:6). Therefore, on earth they must "*walk*" in a renewed way (4:1), and "*stand*" firm against evil powers (6:13, 14). God's special revelation is that Jews and Gentiles share equally in God's will, which is to unite all things in a new creation in Christ. Ephesians also presents revolutionary instructions about how to live as God's people in a world which is spiritually dead. The book is carefully written in two parts, firstly providing explanation about what God has done through Christ (chapters 1-3), and then application about what God's people do as a result (chapters 4-6). Although still living in the world, God's people are his heavenly family, belonging to heaven, and united as a newly created family which replaces former Jew and Gentile identities. The book is presented in the framework of a letter, yet its contents take the form of a homily or discourse. Most of the first half of the discourse consists essentially of prayers. Paul shows in his letter that prayer is the key for grasping the amazing message about the thrilling realities being disclosed, and has a significant part to play in the fulfilment of God's will. Let us take a closer look.

1:1-2 The Apostle's "Hello". Paul begins his letter in the typical pattern of ancient letter writing, but not as a mere formality. He deliberately uses Christian language and ideas. He identifies himself as an apostle of Christ Jesus according to the will (or plan) of God to stress his own special role as a messenger of the gospel. He addresses his readers in terms of their earthly ("*in Ephesus*") and heavenly ("*in Christ Jesus*") settings, calling them "*saints*" and "*the faithful*" because they share in Christ's holiness and faithfulness. The phrase "*in Christ Jesus*" (or similar phrases, "*in him*", "*in the beloved*", etc.) is at the heart of the message of Ephesians, and of the gospel itself. It basically means that believers are included as sharers with Christ in all his achievements and benefits. He acted on their behalf, so they are credited as being "in him" when he did so. His greetings of "*grace and peace*" express two rich benefits of the gospel, and introduce two themes of his discourse. These blessings come from "*God our Father and the Lord Jesus Christ*", the unique partnership which portrays God's true and rich identity. Paul makes a clear distinction between God (who is divine) and Christ (who is human), yet emphasises their shared role as source of the blessings. God is "*Father*", because he is the loving originator of salvation and "*Father*" of his earthly Messiah. He is "*our*" Father, because his salvation is granted to both Jews and Gentiles. Jesus is the Messiah, who, like Israel and King David, was God's chosen earthly Son. Yet he was unique, perfectly representing his heavenly Father in accomplishing his blessings of salvation. By fulfilling his Father's will, Jesus was designated "*Lord*", a title which was used as an equivalent for God's name Yahweh. As God's "Son", Jesus shared the prerogatives of divine sovereignty with his heavenly Father, fulfilling God's promise to King David (2 Samuel 7:14, Psalm 2:7, 89:26). Paul's threefold mention of Christ Jesus emphasises Christ's central role in God's salvation plan.

1:3-3:21 The Apostle's Exhilaration. The first part of Paul's discourse is a mixture of various kinds of prayers and explanations. The prayers are part of the explanation, and the explanation is included in the prayer. Paul's mood is full of exhilaration and optimism, which is especially remarkable considering his circumstances of prolonged imprisonment and hostile opposition. He is bursting with enthusiasm over the revelation of God's gracious plan for mankind. In particular, he highlights the privileged experience of his readers as beneficiaries of God's purposes, and his own privilege as messenger of God's saving grace. It is helpful to follow his presentation in its successive stages.

God's Gracious Plan, 1:3-14. Paul opens with jubilant praise for God's eternal will for his creation. His language shimmers with excitement and adoration as he sketches the drama of God's activity from before time began, then through history, and ultimately into eternity beyond time. God's plan is trinitarian in nature. The Father in heaven administers the whole process, choosing before time began, as an act of grace, to bless those who are in Christ. Jesus the Messiah fulfils his special mission on earth, by redeeming those in him through his sacrificial blood, providing forgiveness for their sins. God's Holy Spirit qualifies believers as participants in the benefits of God's salvation, by sealing them with the stamp of God's ownership. God's plan of grace will reach its consummation in Christ at the end of time. Paul is enraptured at God's grace which initiated and accomplished his eternal will to redeem the world and unite all mankind through Jesus Christ and by his Holy Spirit. God's grace is the essence of his glory (v 6, 12, 14).

It is important to recognise the form of Paul's presentation. It is a prayer of blessing in response to God's blessings, typical in style to familiar Jewish "berakahs" (Hebrew for "blessings"). Only God blesses, but the berakah "blessed" God as a joyful response of praise and gratitude for his benefits. This passage is a single sentence in the original Greek, probably spoken aloud by Paul, and follows a hymn-like pattern with three "stanzas" separated by a recurring refrain, like a psalm. With an outburst of praise and celebration, Paul extols the glory of God and his blessings.

V 3-6 The Father Choosing. Paul "*blesses*" God for "*blessing*" believers with every spiritual "*blessing*". His repetition of the theme of "*blessing*" picks up on God's promise to Abraham long ago (Genesis 12:2-3), which was the foundation of Israel's faith. Paul was showing that the promise was fulfilled in Christ, and was a richer fulfilment than popular Jewish expectation of national prominence. Paul addresses God as "*the God and Father of our Lord Jesus Christ*", expressing an advanced view of God beyond the usual Jewish perspective of him as creator and ruler of the universe and the Holy One of Israel, which was itself a unique outlook among the nations. As God of Jesus the Messiah, God revealed himself to be his Father by bestowing on him the blessings of salvation for the benefit of all mankind. It was not Abraham the father of Isaac, but God the Father of the Messiah who was the source of blessing. As mediator of God's salvation, Jesus is recognised as supreme "*Lord*", not only for Jews but for all mankind. The blessings received in Christ are "*spiritual*". This is not to contrast them with material blessings, since God is the giver of all good things, whether material or immaterial. The blessings are "*spiritual*" to distinguish them from natural outcomes. They are not the result of natural processes of history, but of the supernatural activity of the Holy Spirit, God's personal active presence. The blessings are "*in the heavenly realms*", which is the sphere where God is present, beyond the reach of natural senses. They are not historical earthly benefits. These blessings began in the limitless past prior to creation when God predetermined his purpose for believers within Christ. Using pictures from Jewish and Gentile customs, Paul says that God chose them to be "*holy and blameless in his sight*" (the necessary condition for a Jewish sacrifice to be acceptable), and predestined them "*in love*" to be "*adopted as his sons*" (referring to the Gentile procedure for legally adopting a son). Both Jews and Gentiles were in God's mind from the outset. Although in history God's chronological process began with Jews before turning to Gentiles, in eternity beforehand his plan included both, all humanity. This prompts a refrain of praise for the glory of God's grace, "*which he has freely given us in the one he loves*". It was Christ who was loved, but on the basis of sheer grace believers "within Christ", Jews and Gentiles, are seen by God as acceptable to him and are adopted into his family. Paul's language in speaking of Christ as the "*one he loves*" probably intends to point to Abraham's willingness to give up Isaac whom he loved as an analogy (see Genesis 22).

V 7-12 Christ Redeeming. Paul's thoughts move from before creation into history, to focus on the redeeming work of Christ. Redemption from slavery was a familiar practice in the ancient world by which a slave obtained freedom from his master's control by payment for his release. Christ redeemed us "*through his blood*", a familiar expression in temple courts where animals were violently slaughtered as sacrifices for sin. Here it means Christ's sacrificial death as the price for our freedom, the forgiveness of sins. This astounding blessing is "*in *accordance with*" (not just "*out of the resources of*") God's grace which he lavished on us with all wisdom and understanding. Redemption and forgiveness by God's extravagant grace display a profound wisdom which baffles worldly reason. The "*mystery*" (a term from the mysterious secrets of ancient religions) "*of his will*" refers to God's hidden plan for the universe. God has made it known to "*us*" (believers). This plan was according to God's "*good pleasure*", which he "*purposed*" (decided before time) to be "*put into effect*" (managed) "*when the times will have reached their fulfilment*" (at the end of time). Paul's words present a picture of God's management of the whole creation (both the natural realm and the supernatural in heaven) being brought together under one "*head*" (Christ) at the end of history. The natural and supernatural spheres of existence were separated when mankind was banished from God's presence because of original disobedience. The idea of "head" meant source of life and benefits for whatever was dependent on it. It was God's predetermined plan to make his Messiah the source of life for restoring the created universe at the end of time. Then, having revealed the cosmic nature of God's salvation, Paul narrows his focus to humanity's participation. Firstly, the Jews. Predestined by God's plan, and being the first to hope in Christ, Jews ("*we*") were chosen within Christ, to be for the praise of God's glory.

V 13-14 The Spirit Sealing. Paul quickly adds that "*you*" (Gentiles) were also included in Christ. Jews came first in the historical process of God's plan, but Gentiles were also included when they heard "*the word of truth, the gospel of salvation*". They believed what they heard, and their response of faith was evidence that they were "*sealed in Christ by the Holy Spirit*". The seal in ancient times was a mark of ownership, like a brand or logo. The traditional Jewish mark of belonging to God's people was circumcision. Now the mark of God's ownership was the "*promised Holy Spirit*". The Spirit had been promised by the prophets and by Jesus for the age of the Messiah. The Spirit came at Pentecost following Jesus' crucifixion and resurrection, inaugurating the new people of God. Gentiles were not becoming part of the Old Covenant Jewish people, but both Jews and Gentiles were entering the New Covenant people of God in Christ by being stamped with the Holy Spirit. The Holy Spirit is also a "*deposit*" (down payment) guaranteeing full payment of "*our inheritance*", which is the "*redemption of those who are God's possession*". God's people have already been purchased from slavery, and belong to him, but still await their full and final release. Paul concludes his berakah by yet again repeating his refrain of praise for God's glory.

What a prayer!! Paul's cascading thoughts and swirling images pour from his heart in an outflow of passionate praise. They are not random, disjointed, spontaneous thoughts. They flow freely, but they are the outpouring of deeply pondered, carefully composed articulations, channelling profound convictions in a eulogy of heartfelt gratitude. It is obviously the product of lengthy reflection and deep devotion.

God's Life-Giving Power, 1:15-2:10. After his ecstatic opening of praise for God's magnificent plan of grace, Paul then reveals his prayer for his readers. He wants them to have a clear understanding of their new position as Christians. He highlights God's incomparable power which gave Christ ultimate victory, and supreme authority in all the universe. Then he explains how Christ's achievement benefits believers, those who are "in Christ". God's incomparable grace has saved them from a state of spiritual death because of sinful disobedience to share in the heavenly life of Christ.

V 15-23 The Apostle's Prayer

Giving Thanks (V 15-16). After praising God for his gracious plan fulfilled in Christ ("*for this reason*"), he now gives thanks for his readers because of what he has heard about them, and remembers them in prayer. They showed evidence of "*faith in the Lord Jesus*" and "*love for all the saints*". They had responded in faith to the message of God's accomplished plan of grace, submitting to Jesus as Lord, and relating to fellow believers in loving fellowship. These are basic marks of being a Christian. God's fulfilled gracious will and his readers' conversion were the motivations for Paul's praying. Notice that he does not compliment or congratulate them for their attitudes of faith and love, but rather gives thanks to God. It was the outworking of God's salvation in their lives which inspired Paul's gratitude, and it was their faith and love which assured him of its effectiveness.

Making Request (V 17-19). From praise for God's salvation plan, and gratitude for his readers' conversion, Paul's prayer turns to intercession for them. In addressing God, he describes him in terms of his relationship to Christ ("*the God of our Lord Jesus Christ*") and the revelation of his nature ("*the Father of glory*"). God revealed himself through the person and mission of Jesus Christ. Jesus was the Messiah who accomplished God's gracious eternal will of redemption and reconciliation. His resurrection from the dead installed him as Lord over all creation. By his achievement, Jesus showed what God is like. He is the Father whose glory is grace!

Paul prays that God will give his readers spiritual insight ("the *Spirit of wisdom and revelation*"). In accord with God's trinitarian plan, God's Spirit enables us to be wise in discerning God's revealed truth. This is in order to know God better, both in understanding what he is like, and in relating to him. Paul wants his readers to know God truly and fully. The process involves having "*the eyes of your heart*" enlightened in order to know (understand) certain matters. We come to know God more fully when inwardly we understand three wonderful truths. Firstly, "*the hope of his calling*", which can mean either the certainty and confidence which God's calling inspires, or the goal to which he calls us. Or both. God has called us to be his people, to live holy lives and serve him, and to receive a destiny with him in eternity. We can be certain of it, because it has been guaranteed by Christ, Secondly, "*the riches of his glorious inheritance in the saints*" may mean the glory of grace displayed in the saints who make up God's own inheritance in the saints. More likely, however, it refers to the abundant riches of the shared destiny in glory which God's own (holy) people will inherit (see the parallel statement in Colossians 1:12). Thirdly, *"his incomparably great power for us who believe"* is the power which will keep them to the end. It acts according to the *"working of his mighty strength"*, which is absolutely enormous, as Paul then goes on to show.

Extoling God's Power (V 20-23). To demonstrate the nature and reality of God's power, Paul indicates two actions of God where it was exerted — in raising Christ from the dead, and in seating him at his right hand in the heavenly realms. These mean victory over mankind's greatest mortal enemy in the earthly realm (death), and supreme authority and honour in the heavenly realm. His authority is absolute, *"far above all rule and authority, power and dominion, and every title that can be given, not only in the present age but also in the one to come"*. Christ has been given supremacy over every political, social, and supernatural authority in existence, both now and forever. Paul goes on to state the implications of Christ's twofold triumph of resurrection and enthronement by God's power, in reverse order. Firstly, by being enthroned above all other ruling authorities, *"God placed all things under his feet"*. This was God's doing, and *"all things"* refers to all creation. Paul is quoting from Psalm 8:6, showing that Christ is now in the position of authority originally intended for mankind before the Fall into sin. Secondly, by Christ's resurrection, God appointed *"him to be head over everything for the church, which is his body, the fullness of him who fills everything in every way"*. The translation is awkward, but basically means that Christ is the life-giving head of the church and also of the whole universe. In ancient times the human body was thought to be filled with life and personality from its head, just as a river's fulness flowed from its head, and likewise a mountain's fulness was derived from its head. As the risen supreme Lord, Christ is source of restored life for a redeemed humanity and for all creation. No wonder that Paul prayed for his readers to be given insight concerning their calling and inheritance in Christ, and the astounding power which is at work in believers!!

The Apostle's Explanation (2:1-10). After enlightening his readers about the supremacy of the risen Christ, Paul moves on to explain how the benefits graciously apply to the salvation of sinners in Christ. Not only could God's surpassing greatness of power be seen in the resurrection and enthronement of Christ, but also in the resurrection and enthronement of those "in Christ". Once Paul's readers were *"dead"*, having no living relationship with God, who is the source of true life (see 4:18). Their former sinful lifestyle was dominated by three forces: the world's ungodly culture, the ruler over evil forces who incites disobedience, and the desires of corrupt human nature. Consequently, they were *"objects of wrath"* (under God's condemnation).

However, in striking contrast, Paul abruptly says, *"But ...God..."*. Motivated by *"his great love for us"*, because by nature he is *"rich in mercy"*, God performed three actions to reverse mankind's position. He *"made us alive with Christ even when we were dead in transgressions"* (so we are now spiritually alert and conscious of God). He *"raised us up with Christ"* (setting us free from dominating tyrant forces so that we can respond to God and develop a new way of living). He "*seated us with him in the heavenly realms in Christ Jesus*" (replacing condemnation with enthronement, sharing with Christ in the sphere of God's presence and purpose. For Christ this is already a full reality; for believers it is a spiritual consciousness at present, to become full reality in eternity). There is now a resurrected, living, corporate person seated on the throne of the universe! This is the tremendous perspective which Paul prays for his readers to know. Jesus Christ is the Monarch of heaven, together with all believers who are incorporated within him. God's purpose for his actions was to show "*in the coming ages*" (throughout eternity) "*the incomparable riches of his grace, expressed in his kindness to us in Christ Jesus*". Just as the resurrection and enthronement of Christ demonstrated the incomparable power of God's greatness (1:19), so the resurrection and enthronement of believers in Christ demonstrated the incomparable riches of his grace.

God's grace is the sole grounds of salvation, which is experienced through faith alone. Salvation is the gift of God, not achieved by any human effort. What God has done in Christ is a new work of creation. In Christ, and through his death and resurrection, God has recreated the universe, and re-peopled it with a new human race. Those who are in Christ were brought back to life, raised, and re-appointed to the place of dominion in order to do God's preordained good works. It is for his readers to have this perspective which is the aim of Paul's prayers.

God's Reconciled People, 2:11-22. Jesus is God's "peace plan" for the world! Paul's explanation about the resurrection of Christ and the benefits of grace for those "in Christ" (v 1-10) now shifts to an explanation about the benefits of peace for those "in Christ" (v 11-22). A radical change has come about in the world, and a new transcendent social reality has burst into existence. Those who are "in Christ", both Jews and Gentiles, not only have been redeemed from the bondage and penalty of sin, and been reconciled to God, but they have also been reconciled to one another. In fact, collectively they constitute a newly created community, a new human race. This is God's remedy for a polarised world.

God's Revealed Purpose, 3:1-21. God's purpose for the world and history gives meaning to life's experiences, and a framework for serving and trusting God. After explaining the big picture of God's grand scheme ("*for this reason*"), Paul began to make a further statement, but broke off to make comment about himself (v 1-6). He was exhilarated by the revelation of God's purpose graciously granted to him personally, and the privileged role he had to play in its outworking (v 1-6). The "mystery" about God's will (1:9-10) and the Messiah (3:4), had now been revealed by the Spirit through the gospel. Jews and Gentiles in Christ were "*fellow heirs*", "*fellow members*" of the same body, and "*fellow sharers*" of the same promise.

Not only did Paul receive revelation of the "*mystery*" by God's grace, but also a ministry to make it known (v 7-13). He became a "*servant of the gospel*" through the working of

God's power. His mission was twofold, to preach to Gentiles so that they could be saved, and to make known to everyone (Jews and Gentiles) the administration of the mystery so that they could be united. He calls his message *"the unsearchable riches of Christ"*, meaning truths of inestimable value beyond fully exploring. The administration of the mystery is the development of the new Jew/Gentile community which was hidden in ages past but always in the mind of God the Creator. Paul adds an unexpected reason for his mission. God's intention was that through the phenomenon of the church (God's new heavenly family) the *"manifold* (many coloured) *wisdom of God"* should be made known to the *"rulers and authorities in the heavenly realms"*, the same (evil) powers which had been made subservient to the risen Christ (1:21). This was according to his eternal purpose accomplished in Christ Jesus our Lord. This accomplishment allows free and unrestricted access to God for both Jews and Gentiles, in union with Christ, through faith in him. Therefore, Paul's readers must not be discouraged because of his sufferings for their sake, since his sufferings were actually a reason for their glory.

After his brief comment, Paul returns to the statement he had previously intended (*"for this reason"*, v 14-19). He turns again to prayer, to intercession. He kneels before the "Father" to pray for God's "Family", which derives its name from him, and which stretches into the heavenly realm as well as being on earth. He prays that God will give them inner power for a twofold purpose. Firstly, he prays that, out of his *"glorious riches"*, God will give them power through his Spirit in their inner being so that Christ might dwell within their hearts through faith (v 16-17a). The Spirit enables understanding of the truth about Christ (1:17), evoking inner faith and assurance in him. Indwelling power from the Holy Spirit ensures inner confidence in Christ. Relating to Christ inwardly on a heart level enables him to live effectively within the inner life, and to transform the outer life to be like him. When the mind is convinced by the Spirit, the heart becomes the home where Christ lives!

The second petition was for power to grasp the limitless outflowing love of Christ (v 17b–19). Appreciation for the greatness of Christ's love is also motivated by the power of understanding granted by spiritual revelation. Because they are *"rooted and established"* in love (drawing on the imagery of gardening and building), which is God's love expressed in Christ, Paul prays that they will comprehend the full outflowing dimensions of it. The love of Christ is expressed not only in personal salvation, but also in Family relationships where human barriers are transcended. The dimensions (*"wide and long and high and deep"*) flow out in all directions from a central point, picturing the all-encompassing measure of God's love. Paul wants them to *"know"* (experientially, not merely with the mind) this love of Christ, which actually surpasses knowledge. Its reality can be truly experienced, but not fully exhausted. Entering into this love, personally and collectively, is to become *"filled to the measure of all the fullness of God"*.

Paul concludes both his prayer and his explanation with an appropriate doxology, ascribing glory to God (v 20-21). He refers to God in terms of his power, which has been his recurring emphasis. In his earlier prayer he had explained God's *"incomparably great power"* exerted in the resurrection and enthronement of Christ (1:19-21). Here he has just prayed for indwelling power for Christ to live within their hearts and for the love of Christ to fill them. Now he attributes God with *"immeasurably more"* ability than all we ask or imagine, according to that power at work within us. There are no limits to what God can do! In particular, Paul ascribes glory to God in the *"church"* (the *Body*, the community of peace) and in *"Christ Jesus"* (the Head, the Peacemaker) throughout all generations (history), for ever and ever (eternity). Amen!!

4:1-6:20 The Apostle's Exhortation. The second half of Paul's discourse exhorts his readers to manifest this glory in a practical commitment to harmony and love. Having explained their new perspective of being *"seated"* with Christ on the throne of the universe, he appeals to them to *"walk"* worthy of their calling (4:1-6:9) and to *"stand"* firm against the devil's schemes (6:10-20). A brief sketch of his revolutionary instruction will provide a backdrop for his concluding call for his readers to engage in serious prayer.

Paul had previously prayed that his readers might understand their calling (1:18), which he explained was belonging to God's newly created mankind in Christ (2:15). They were now citizens of God's people and members of God's family (2:19, 3:15), a Spirit-filled community which was God's temple (2:22). Paul visualises them (Jewish and Gentile believers together) as a "Collective Christ". Now he urges them to *"walk"* worthy of their calling. He means the way they should live. He sees them as a "Collective Man" *"walking"* through life. He repeats the term several times to stress the point.

God's Mature Family, 4:1-16. His first focus is on their community life. They must maintain unity (v 1-6), and attain maturity (v 7-16). The essential unity of God's family is in accord with God's trinitarian actions: one body, one Spirit, and one hope; one Lord, one faith, one baptism; one God and Father of all. Maturity is expressed by every member living out God's love in works of service, as the "Body" is built up by various ministries of God's word, until the community reaches the full likeness of Christ.

God's New Lifestyle, 4:17-32. Paul insists on the need to live according to a new mindset. They must no longer *"walk"* according to their former pagan lifestyle, which results from empty thinking, darkened understanding, and being separated from the life of God. This condition of their minds stemmed from the hardening of their hearts, and plunged them into sensuality and impure, lustful indulgence. Paul was describing their inner condition of mind, heart, and emotions. In sharp contrast he describes the process which brings about radical change. It is learning the *"truth that is in Jesus"*. Using the language of creation and the imagery of changing clothes, Paul urges them to put off their old humanity, to be renewed in the attitude of their minds, and to put on the *"new self"* which has been created to be like God "*in true righteousness and holiness*". Practical examples, all having to do with relationships, are added to show the change from old to new.

God's Characteristics for Living, 5:1-21. The term "*walk*" is repeated three more times to identify distinctive guidelines to follow on "life's journey". They are to "*walk in love*" as "*imitators of God*" (v 1-2). The example and standard are Christ, who loved in self-sacrificial love, and whose sacrifice for others was a fragrant offering to God. They should "*walk as children of light*" shunning and exposing the moral and social darkness of the pagan world. For two reasons. Those who live immoral lives face the certainty of judgement. Believers were once in darkness by nature, but now are "*light in the Lord*". Therefore (in order to live like God in love, and to break with the practices of darkness to live in light), they should "*walk – not as unwise, but as wise*". They must understand the "*Lord's will* (plan)", which Paul had expounded in the first half of his discourse, in order to live accordingly. Instead of living in drunken debauchery (like their pagan neighbours), they must be filled with the Spirit. This means being filled with the message of Christ (see the parallel passage in Colossians 3:16). Four practical applications illustrate: edifying fellowship (v 19a), joyful worship (v 19b), thankful prayer (v 20), submissive relationships (v 21). These practices relate to the whole community, because the renewed lifestyle is both a personal and community affair. The first and last practices concern interaction between members, and the second and third concern actions towards God. Belonging to God's family calls for devotion to God and to one another.

Spirit-Filled Relationships, 5:22-6:9. Paul illustrates the general principle of mutual submission (v 21) within the established patterns of households in his day. He was not confirming these patterns, nor establishing permanent structures for family life. He was not defining social positions and roles for husbands, wives, and children, any more than he was entrenching the position of slaves. He was concerned about relationships of members of God's new Spirit-filled community, within the framework of cultural structures which tended to be authoritarian and hierarchical.

His instructions were revolutionary! He blatantly broke with contemporary cultural conventions. In the first place he addressed wives, children, and slaves as persons in their own right, appealing to them as people who were responsible for their own behaviour. This just was not normal for that society. Secondly, he addressed these socially subservient groups before he addressed the man of the household to whom they were relating. Normally that would be offensive and disrespectful, but Paul does it in each case, deliberately. In the third place, his remarks were intended to be read out in a public gathering. The listeners would have been astonished. In a single action Paul totally blasted the fixed social order of his day based on structures of authority and power, and replaced it with a new social policy of treating all people equally with dignity and respect, and relating to one another in an attitude of humble submission.

Paul's choice of examples was extremely relevant. He illustrated his principle in the area of family relationships, which were at the heart of the ancient social system. Furthermore, God's new community was being portrayed in the imagery of family. God's heavenly Family, consisting of all believers in the Lord Jesus Christ, filled with God's Spirit, and characterised by relationships of loving mutual submission, was displacing and transcending both the ordinary family household, and the whole social system.

The idea of submission must be clearly grasped. Paul was not advocating positions and structures of superiority and subordination. He was calling on all members to have **attitudes** of submissiveness to one another. This does not mean being under obligation to carry out the demands and wishes of others, but being willing to be humble and considerate with regards to the worth, needs, and welfare of others. The point to be noted is that there is only one Master, Christ, and all members are equal under him—regardless of racial or social standing. In each of his examples Paul points out that it is Christ who is Lord (5:22, 6:1, 8, 9), and all family members are to relate submissively to one another with that perspective. Christians are to submit to one another on earth because they have a common Master in heaven.

Another significant change which Paul introduces is to replace the traditional idea of master and subservient relationship with the concept of "head" and dependent ("body") relationship. It is similar to the relationship between Christ and the church, not in the sense of Christ being Lord, but "Saviour" (v 23). Just as Christ rescues and protects the church, and as head is its source of life and growth, so the husband is the source of security, freedom, worth, and development for his wife and dependants in that society where they were socially disadvantaged.

Ready for Battle, 6:10-17. Paul's final encouragement to his readers is a call to arms (v 10-13). "*Be strong in the Lord and in the power of his might*". Paul is aware of the difficulties and harsh realities which oppose them. To encourage their vigilance he uses the graphic imagery of preparing for war. Inspired by the familiar Roman battle dress, Paul urges them to put on the full armour of God in readiness for battle, and to take their "*stand*". He is not visualising solo believers engaging in hand-to-hand combat alone, but a Roman army in regimental order standing shield to shield, each doing his part, but together forming a wall of resistance to the enemy. The opposition is in the heavenly sphere, and the enemy is the devil and his dark spiritual forces which rule over a fallen world. Yet they have already been conquered by the mighty resurrection power of the Lord!

The armour (v 14-17) is patterned after a typical Roman soldier's battle dress, although Paul is also influenced by the picture of God as a warrior (Isaiah 59:7). The six pieces of uniform and equipment are listed in the order in which they were put on, and each item represents an effect of the Gospel in the believer's life. Everything is defensive, except perhaps the sword, although this is the short sword used for close encounter, and therefore is also defensive. Since the offensive action of rescue has already been accomplished by Christ, the church only has to maintain a holding position of defence.

The Call to Prayer, 6:18-20. As God's family takes its stand against the onslaught of the enemy, protected by the armour of the achievements of Christ, combat is engaged in prayer. Coming at the culmination of Paul's discourse, it is obvious that prayer is strategic! To pray is to depend on the Father as his family in Christ. To pray *"in the Spirit"* is to pray with the insights which the Spirit gives concerning God's purposes (1:17). Prayer is all encompassing (on *"all occasions"*, with *"all kinds of prayers and requests"*, being *"alert and always keeping on"*, for *"all the saints"*). The readers are urged not only to pray for all the saints, but also for Paul himself, not for the prison doors to be opened for his release, but for his mouth to be opened to fearlessly proclaim the gospel. Paul's mission was always at the forefront of his mind, so that he saw himself as an *"ambassador in chains"*. His task was dangerous, and his circumstances daunting, so his repeated request was for *"fearlessness"*, or *"boldness"*.

6:21-24 The Apostle's Farewell Paul winds up his letter with a personal word and final greeting. Tychicus, from Asia and perhaps the vicinity of Ephesus (Acts 20:4), would hand deliver Paul's letter, and bring a verbal report on Paul's circumstances (repeated twice) for their encouragement. Paul was not only praying for his readers, and writing to them, but keeping in touch in as personal a way as possible, maintaining strong ties of fellowship. His farewell greeting is virtually a final prayer, and an appropriate summary of the key terms and ideas of his discourse. The farewell is an expansion of the opening greeting (1:2), and sums up the message of the letter, and of the Gospel. By *"grace"* through *"faith"* we have *"peace"* which is shown in *"love"*.

Colossians was written at about the same time as Ephesians, about 60 CE, while Paul was in custody waiting to appear before Caesar. Many thoughts and statements in Ephesians are repeated in Colossians, showing a close link between the two documents. Colossians, however, is a letter specifically written to counteract a grave threat which was disturbing the group of believers at Colossae.

The city of Colossae was situated on the Lycus River on the great trade route which travelled westwards from Ephesus on the Aegean Sea to the Euphrates River. It had once been a major centre in its region, but was becoming overshadowed by the nearby developing cities of Hierapolis and Laodicea. The gospel was taken to these cities by Epaphras (1:7-8, 4:13), who had probably been converted during Paul's three-years ministry at Ephesus (Acts 19:10). Paul himself had not been to these cities, but he was deeply concerned for believers there (2:1).

Epaphras was a fellow-prisoner with Paul (Philemon 23), and had informed Paul of the troubling threat which had arisen. An attractive, but deadly, false teaching was being promoted which mixed popular, deep-seated pagan ideas, together with Jewish rites and practices, with the message of the gospel. The result was a curious and bizarre religious hotch-potch.

Without going into much detail here, Paul had one main answer to the erroneous teaching. The gospel of the person and work of Jesus Christ. He set forth Jesus Christ as pre-eminent in every sphere, and as all-sufficient for the believer's need. The believer was complete "in Christ". Christ is Lord, and the believer's life is one of trusting loyalty to him, not a matter of religious experiences, rituals, or rules.

After his opening greeting, thanksgiving, and prayer (1:1-14), Paul begins with a declaration about the **supremacy of Christ** (1:15-20). He is pre-eminent over all things, the source and sovereign of all existence – of original creation (v 15-17) and reconciled creation (v 18) – because of who he is (v 19) and what he has done (v 20). In his person, Christ reveals God to mankind. In his mission, he reconciles mankind to God. In view of this exalted gospel statement about Christ, Paul then reminds his readers of the effect Christ has had on them (1:21-23). He had radically changed their relationship with God and their lifestyle – provided they continued to trust the gospel.

Paul described himself as a servant of the gospel, and explained his personal involvement in the task of spreading the message about Jesus (1:24-2:7). His present sufferings and imprisonment were an inevitable part of his ministry, because they were his share of the affliction which the indwelling Christ was experiencing through his "Body", as it made the gospel known to the world. Paul's task was simply to "*proclaim*" Christ, warning against what was false, and teaching what was true. His goal was to "*present everyone perfect (complete) in Christ*". To that end he worked hard, relying on divine resources of strength. He wanted his readers to know how strenuously he was exerting himself on their behalf so that they would not be misled by false ideas. He appealed to them to continue to live in Christ, in the same way as they had received him as Lord.

Paul went on to warn the Colossians not to be highjacked by deceptive ideas which had their source in human and superstitious origins, but to look to the **sufficiency of Christ** (2:8-19). In Christ, the fullness of God lived in a human body. Because they were "in Christ", they were given fullness themselves, having been "*circumcised*" (crucified), buried, and raised in him. Therefore, they could not be criticised over matters of religious rules, customs, and experiences. To encourage the Colossians to enter into the new life in Christ, Paul explained the implications of Christ's death and resurrection (2:20-3:4), and then their application (3:5-17). He illustrated living under the lordship of Christ in the typical family relationships of households of his day, very similar to what he had written in Ephesians (3:18-4:1).

Although Colossians is short and deals with a pressing, tense situation, Paul concludes with a large personal segment (4:2-18). It includes a final exhortation about prayer and witnessing (v 2-6), information about his own personal affairs and companions (v 7-14), and farewell greetings (v 15-18). What is conspicuous in this brief letter, is the prominent focus on prayer, which we will take time to appreciate.

After his opening greetings, where he identifies himself as an apostle of Christ Jesus "*by the will of God*", Paul begins his letter by informing the Colossians of his prayer for them, consisting of thanksgiving (1:3-8) and intercession (1:9-14). Thankfulness is a conspicuous characteristic of believers in Christ, and is emphasised throughout this letter (1:3, 12, 2:7, 3:15,17, 4:2). Paul was grateful to "*God*", whom he deliberately identifies as "*the Father of our Lord Jesus Christ*". This was how believers viewed God as a result of the gospel. It also emphasised Jesus' relationship to God in his unique position as Lord and Saviour, a conviction which cut right across the views of the false teachers at Colossae. Paul was grateful for the triad of distinguishing Christian qualities, "*faith*", "*love*", and "*hope*". He had heard of their commitment of faith in Jesus Christ and the evidence of its reality in their love towards all other believers. Considering their various backgrounds this would be a remarkable topic. These attitudes sprang from the hope (the certain destiny) which was "*stored up*" (securely guaranteed) in heaven for them. They had come to learn about it through the message of God's grace in all its truth, the gospel, which was spreading throughout the world with fruitful effectiveness. Paul was deliberately reminding his readers of their own experience, to distinguish the gospel from the ideas of the false teachers, who advocated ritualism, intellectualism, and legalism. They had learned the gospel from Epaphras, whom Paul refers to with deep appreciation as a person who is loved and is a faithful fellow servant ("*bondslave*"). It was from Epaphras himself that Paul had received report of their "*love in the Spirit*". Paul's prayers for the Colossians were the overflow of a grateful heart inspired by his relationship with God the Father, the thrilling message of the gospel, and the delight of hearing reports of clusters of believers experiencing God's transforming grace and power.

The evident spiritual vitality at Colossae not only prompted Paul's thankfulness in prayer, but also his intercession for their on-going progress. From the day he had learned of their spiritual fruitfulness, he had been praying constantly and specifically for them. Since he had never met them, Paul's remark is highly revealing about his priorities in ministry, and especially regarding prayer. Clearly, there was both spontaneity and intentional regularity about Paul's praying. He gave time and effort to maintaining purposeful prayer as an essential feature of his apostolic work. In particular, Paul specifically prayed that God would fill the Colossian believers with the knowledge of his will. The Father's will was his plan of grace fulfilled through Jesus Christ. This prayer was the same essential prayer which he had encouraged in his letter to the Ephesians, which was probably a circular letter to the region, including Colossae. It was the kind of prayer inspired by the gospel. Yet it was especially relevant to the situation at Colossae, so Paul reiterates it to them. The heresy of the false teachers at Colossae, which he was writing to refute, majored on the idea of possessing knowledge and intellectual understanding (2:8, 18, 23). However, it was not esoteric knowledge which they needed, but knowledge of "*God's will*". God's will was his plan to overcome sinful rebellion, give resurrection life to believers, and develop loyalty to Christ, quality of personal lifestyle, and unity of fellowship. The rest of Paul's letter explains what this will is.

In order that the Colossian believers might press on in the positive direction which they had so far followed, and not be diverted by heresy, Paul prayed that they might be "*filled*" with the knowledge of God's will "*in all spiritual wisdom and understanding*". These were familiar terms in vogue at that time, referring to philosophical ideas ("*wisdom*") and the ability to apply them ("*understanding*"). Paul, however, wanted them to have a perspective derived from the Holy Spirit ("*spiritual*"). He wanted them to be saturated with a thorough, sound knowledge of who Jesus was and what he had accomplished. He wanted them to have total ("*all*") insight which they could apply to their personal and practical commitments of life.

Knowing God's will had a twofold purpose. It was so that they might "*live a life*" (literally, "*walk*", a metaphor used in the regional letter to the Ephesians, suggesting that there is purpose and direction in the believer's lifestyle) "*worthy of the Lord*" and to "*please him in every way*". Believers are motivated not just by a sense of duty, but out of delight to bring pleasure to Christ.

The lifestyle which pleases and honours Christ is one which shows a healthy growth in spiritual qualities (v 10-12). Paul highlights four characteristics. The lifestyle is spiritually productive ("*bearing fruit*") in all its efforts of good works. It is "*growing in the* [intimate and personal] *knowledge of God*". It is becoming stronger by God's power to have "*great endurance and patience*" (ability to endure life's trials and pressures steadfastly and to be long-suffering towards trying people). It is always "*joyfully giving thanks to the Father*". The grounds for being thankful were not just the simple blessings of daily experience, but the magnificent realities of salvation. For Paul, salvation was real and present. It was not a transaction in some distant heaven, but a personal experience with the living God who produced real changes in people's lives.

Three life-changing aspects of God's gifts to people through Christ are stressed (v 12-14). The Colossian believers had been "**qualified [by the Father]** *to share in the inheritance of the saints in the kingdom of light*". This was the Father's verdict, based on Christ's merits, not theirs. The language reflects the allotment received by the tribes of Israel in the Promised Land conquered under Joshua. Paul, however, replaced "land" with "light", to show the true inheritance God has for his saints, who are God's true Israel. The spiritual victory of Christ brought them into the "light" of God's presence where they have an allotment amongst God's people.

They had been "**rescued [by the Father]** *from the dominion of darkness*". Just as Israel had been rescued from Egypt before entering the Promised Land, all believers (Paul says "*us*" to include himself and others with the Colossians) have been delivered from the "*authority*" of darkness. That is, the rule of Satan and the power of evil, rebellion, and sinful independence.

They had been *"transferred [by the Father] into the kingdom of the Son he loves"*. Just as Israel had been uprooted from Egypt and relocated to the Promised Land, so God has resettled his rescued people in a new realm. They belong to the reign of Christ and a state where God's love is focused. In the Son, they have *"redemption, the forgiveness of sins"*. They have freedom from the control of sin and pardon from the guilt of sin. All of these privileges are present realities.

Paul's praying was motivated by his experience of God's marvellous grace and transcendent kingdom. The passionate yearning of his praying was for others to experience deeply the same life-changing reality for themselves.

The depth of Paul's anguish and concern for the spiritual welfare of his readers becomes very conspicuous at a later point in his letter (2:1-5). After describing his conscientious efforts to proclaim the gospel to everyone, using words which indicated his suffering and strenuous labour (1:24-29), he went on to reveal his exertions on their behalf. He wanted them to know how much he was *"struggling"* for them. His term means to *"strain like an athlete in agony"*. It is the same image he had used to depict his efforts in preaching (1:29), and which he repeats in regard to the praying of Epaphras (4:12). Paul had used the same image in connection with his appeal to the believers at Rome to pray for him (Romans 15:30). The expression conveys the idea of strenuous effort, intense concentration, self-discipline and consistent routine as practised by an athlete in preparation for, or participation in, sporting contest. Since Paul was writing to the Colossians from custody, unable to undertake external activity, his struggles on their behalf, and for those at Laodicea, were his intense efforts through intercessory prayer and indirect means such as letters. Paul certainly took his commitment to the spread of the gospel fully to heart. The burden of his struggle was that they might be *"encouraged in heart and united in love"*, so that they might be settled in their knowledge of Christ, and not misled by false ideas.

The importance of prayer for Paul, and his confidence in its effectiveness, become emphasised by his final exhortation to the Colossians (4:2-4). He urges them to *"devote"* themselves (be aggressively persistent) to prayer. They must be *"watchful"* (alert to distractions, needs, opportunities) and *"thankful"* (for God's goodness in all circumstances). Significantly, while asking for prayer for himself, it is not for his release, but for his opportunity to preach the *"mystery of Christ"* within prison.

The group of companions who gathered around Paul to encourage him in prison was a living example of the power of fellowship under the lordship of Christ (4:7-14). Tychicus, a free man, and Onesimus, a slave, were to be couriers of Paul's letter. The remainder included Aristarchus, a Greek fellow-prisoner; Mark (son of a Roman father) and Jesus called Justus, both Jews; Epaphras, an Asian; Luke, a doctor, and Demas, both Greeks. Ethnic and social distinctions were no barriers because of oneness in Christ and his service. In particular, Epaphras is described as *"one of you"*, having come from Colossae, and having been responsible for taking the gospel to them (1:7). He was always *"wrestling"* (the same term as *"struggling"* in 2:1) in prayer for them. His earnest concern was that they might *"stand firm in all the will of God, mature and fully assured"*.

In addition to his specific letter to Colossae, Paul also urged the Colossians to read a letter from nearby Laodicea (4:16). This may have been a separate letter addressed to the believers there, or was perhaps the general letter to Ephesus and the wider region. Paul was obviously keen to press home his message as thoroughly as he could. There was also another letter carried by Tychicus and Onesimus to Colossae. This was a personal letter to Philemon, who hosted the believers at Colossae in his home, and was the slave-owner of Onesimus. We should take a quick look at that letter while Colossae is in our mind.

The purpose of the letter to **Philemon** was to appeal to him, in a warm, friendly persuasive tone, to be willing to accept Onesimus, his runaway slave, back. Onesimus had stolen from Philemon, and absconded, but had met Paul in Rome, and had become a believer. He was willing to return to his master, and Paul was willing to trust him to accompany Tychicus in hand delivering his mail. In his letter Paul encourages Philemon to welcome Onesimus back, not merely as his possession, but as his brother. Under Roman law, Philemon was legally entitled to have Onesimus put to death. Paul does not defend Onesimus, or campaign against the evils of slavery, or impose demands on Philemon. Instead, he pleads on the basis of love, in terms of his personal bond with Onesimus, and his relationship with Philemon, for Philemon to welcome Onesimus generously as a brother in the Lord. He was not resorting to emotional blackmail, but boldly and persuasively applying a revolutionary gospel perspective. His appeal planted seeds which undermined the whole enterprise of human slavery.

In typical fashion, even though the letter was personal, Paul commenced by declaring his gratitude and prayers to God concerning Philemon (v 4-7). He was thankful for Philemon's faith in the Lord Jesus and love for all the saints, which were the essential characteristics of a genuine Christian outlook. True faith showed itself in love. Paul's prayer, that Philemon's faith would become active, was so that he would have a full understanding of everything good possessed in Christ. Already Paul had gained much joy and encouragement from Philemon's actions of love which *"refreshed the hearts of the saints"*. It was against this background of Philemon's conduct and Paul's prayers that Paul made his pitch on behalf of Onesimus. Prayer for Paul was integral to his gospel approach to all aspects of life and ministry.

This is shown again at the end of his letter (v 22). Paul fully expected to be released from prison, a prospect which he attributed as answer to Philemon's (and others') prayers. Though Paul requested prayer primarily for opportunities to proclaim the gospel (Colossians 4:3-4), he also submitted his circumstances to prayer. His prayer was that God's will might be done, whether or not that would be his release. His comment to Philemon indicates his developing sense that God's will might be the possibility of his acquittal. He indicates a similar hope in his letter to the Philippians.

Philippians was written during Paul's same period of custody in Rome. His prospect of being released seems to be more likely, so his letter is probably a little later, about 61 CE. He was not writing to another Asian church, but to Philippi, the first church he founded in Europe (Acts 16). Paul had gone to Philippi with Silas and Timothy, after splitting with Barnabas and Mark, and after having been prevented by the Spirit from preaching in Phrygia, Bithynia, and Mysia (northern modern Turkey). The city of Philippi was named after King Philip of Macedon, the father of Alexander the Great. It was granted the status of a Roman colony in honour of Emperor Augustus, who had become emperor after winning victory in battle in that region over the forces of those who had assassinated Julius Caesar, his uncle. Retired Roman generals and military personnel were rewarded with properties in Philippi for their services in the army. The city represented Rome in northern Greece, and Roman citizenship was a prized honour.

There was no Jewish synagogue in Philippi, and the first converts to the gospel came from a prayer group which met on the outskirts of the city. Paul and Silas fell foul of influential business owners in the city, and were unjustly flogged and imprisoned by the city authorities. After surviving an earthquake in the middle of the night, which led to the conversion of the head gaoler and his household, Paul and Silas were released and escorted from the city. Because Paul was a Roman citizen, who was illegally punished, he demanded an apology from the authorities, but did not press charges against them. They could have been put to death. In his letter to the Philippians, Paul criticised those whose mind was on earthly things, and emphasised that *"our citizenship is in heaven"* (3:20). Astonishingly, Paul and Silas had been singing hymns and rejoicing in prison at the time the earthquake struck. This was a typical example of Luke's theme of joy throughout his Gospel/Acts. The same note of joy flows throughout Paul's letter to the Philippians. The terms "joy" and "rejoice" occur 16 times. The Philippian converts remained strong supporters of Paul after he moved on to other places. Similarly, Paul held strong affection for the Philippians, and remained deeply interested in their ongoing spiritual welfare. The underlying purpose of his letter to them was to encourage their progress towards maturity in their relationship to Christ.

The letter addresses a variety of matters, relating to the central theme of conscientiously living out salvation in Christ, with the future prospect of his return (1:6, 10, 2:16, 3:20-21, 4:5; 2:9-11). Paul's opening prayer of thanksgiving and intercession reveals his purpose (1:1-11).

His joyful prayer of thanksgiving was prompted by his remembrance of them, by their consistent partnership in his ministry of the gospel, and by his confidence that God would go on completing the good work he had begun in them until the day of Christ. He held them in his heart, because they shared in God's grace with him, whether he was in prison, or engaged in defending and consolidating the gospel. He yearned for them with the compassion of Christ Jesus. Paul's prayer of thankfulness was not motivated by his personal benefits received from the Philippians, but from the evidence of their continued allegiance to Christ and the gospel.

His prayer of intercession (v 9-11) contains a complex mix of ideas, which need to be prised apart. He firstly requests that their love might abound more and more in knowledge and depth of insight. This petition presupposes their love. It presumes that their faith in Jesus Christ as Lord manifests itself in love for one another. A community of conspicuous mutual love is the spontaneous outcome of responding to the gospel about God's love revealed in Jesus Christ. Paul prays that their love may increase. Not merely an increase in love per se. Unqualified love can be superficial and inappropriate. Paul prays that their love will increase *"in knowledge and depth of insight"*. He means knowledge of the gospel and moral discernment. Basically he prays that they will grow in their understanding of gospel truth and behaviour so that their love for one another will become stronger and more mature. It is not a matter of having more knowledge as an end in itself, nor of being more loving in sentimental friendliness, but having true knowledge which produces mature love.

This is so that they *"may be able to discern what is best"*. They will become wise in making the best decisions in life's choices. It is more than simply choosing between right and wrong. It is being able to discern between what is good, better, and best in behaviour and course of life. The pursuit of the best is so that they may be pure and blameless until the day of Christ, filled with the fruit of righteousness which comes through Jesus Christ. To be pure and blameless is the goal of earthly life for believers. Such a condition is the gift of grace, based on the death and resurrection of Jesus. At the end of the day, when the day of Christ arrives, believers will be made perfect. At the present time they are in the process of becoming in condition what they already are in status. Until that day, God is working to complete what he has begun (v 6), and believers pursue it as their life's aim (v 10). When that day comes, they will be filled with the *"fruit of righteousness"* which comes through Jesus Christ. The *"fruit of righteousness"* are the products of being right with God, consisting of qualities of character and conduct.

Paul's prayer, then, requests the personal and communal growth of his readers towards maturity in Christ in terms of their love for one another, their life's priorities and gospel understanding, and the spiritual characteristics of Christlikeness. The chain of ideas and instructions throughout the rest of the letter have these same objectives in mind.

A primary concern is evangelism and the advance of the gospel (1:12-29). Paul is pleased that his imprisonment has resulted in the whole palace guard knowing about Christ, and other believers being emboldened to speak God's word. Some rivals have even been motivated to preach the gospel in order to stir up trouble for Paul, but he is content that Christ is being made known. Knowing Christ is the only way to become right with God, so the task of making him known is a top priority.

Paul also urges his readers to show love and humility towards one another, in order to maintain harmony (2:1-18). Since Christ died to bring reconciliation among people, as well as with God, maintaining harmony is also a crucial priority. As a model to imitate, Paul points to the attitude of Christ Jesus, who did not cling to his divine majesty, but took on the indignity of a slave. Paul describes Jesus' self-humbling with an eloquent tribute, either reciting a familiar hymn, or virtually composing one (v 6-11). He demonstrates Jesus' attitude towards his outward reputation. He did not cling to his divine dignity, but made himself nothing by becoming human and submitting to death by shameful crucifixion. Paul uses terms which express the idea of appearance or reputation. He contrasts Jesus' *"nature"* of God (v 6) and *"nature"* of a servant (literally, slave, v 7) using a word which means *"form"*, referring to *"outward appearance"*. It is only found elsewhere in Mark 16:12, which shows its true meaning. Jesus set aside his appearance as God (his glory) to take on the appearance of a slave (his ignominy). Paul says that Jesus did not consider *"equality with God something to be grasped"*. He means he did not need to cling to the reputation of equality with God. Paul was referring to Jesus' pre-existent dignity, but what he declares implies his pre-existent divine identity. In tracing the process of Jesus' self-humbling, Paul continues to focus on his appearance. He refers to his *"human likeness"*, and *"appearance as a man"*. He was not denying Jesus' real humanity, but stressing his lower status in becoming merely human. Then, as a human, Jesus humbled himself further to become obedient to death, and death on a cross at that, a humiliating end. Jesus' self-humbling was flabbergasting! But then God exalted him to the highest place in heaven and earth, giving him a name honoured by all and confessed as Lord, to the glory of God the Father! This example is extreme to the highest degree. Yet it is more than an example to imitate. It implies that believers who are "in Christ" must share his attitude, since he was representing them. What is also quite startling about this statement is its implication about Christ's divine pre-existence. It is early evidence of belief that the Messiah was God incarnate. In the light of what Christ has done, Paul urges his readers to work out their salvation with fear and trembling, knowing that God was working in them to will and act according to his good purpose.

Paul next indicates his intention to send Timothy to visit them, and their own messenger Epaphroditus back home (2:19-30). He wants to maintain close fellowship ties for mutual encouragement. Finally, as he draws near to the conclusion of his letter, Paul warns the Philippians against Judaists who want to insist on circumcision for Gentile converts, contrasting his own experience of rejecting impressive legalistic achievements in favour of knowing Christ as Lord and finding full contentment in him (3:1-20). He testifies that he wanted to know Christ and the power of his resurrection and the fellowship of sharing in his sufferings, and to press on to the goal of perfection for which Christ had taken hold of him. Although he had not yet reached maturity, he pressed on to win that prize for which God had called him in Christ. He goes on to plead for two ladies, Euodia and Syntyche, to be reconciled over their disagreements, and for all to rejoice in the Lord (4:1-9). Eventually, he concludes by declaring his own joy in the Lord, and expressing appreciation for their material gifts of support (4:10-20). Throughout the whole of his letter, Paul's outlook is the pursuit of the goal of being complete in Christ when the day of Christ arrives.

That outlook governs a special exhortation he makes towards the end of his letter (4:4-9). Following his appeal to the two women Euodia and Syntyche to resolve their differences, Paul urges all his readers to rejoice in the Lord always, and to let their gentleness/forbearance be evident to all. He reminds them that the Lord is near, meaning, in the light of the recurring theme, Christ's return. He encourages them not to be anxious about anything, but to handle everything with prayer. He emphasises this by a range of elements in prayer: "prayer and petition", "thanksgiving", "present your requests". Paul's advice has been aptly expressed: "Be anxious for nothing, pray about everything, be thankful for anything"! As a general policy, Paul's encouraging advice is sound and relevant for any situation. However, in its context, Paul was giving instruction for ensuring harmony in the community and encouraging growth to maturity. Just as he had prayed about such things at the commencement of his letter, now he was urging them to pray likewise. Prayer was a key activity, because it ensured a focus on relationship with God. Prayer took God seriously. Prayer assumed that God was actively working out his salvation in their lives, and willingly cooperated with him by way of intercession. The desirable outcome was the transcendent peace of God which would safeguard their hearts and minds. Such peace would result not only from focusing their thoughts and practices on virtues of excellence, but from his own presence itself.

Everything in Paul's letter to the Philippians is motivated by the conviction and conclusion he expresses in his response concerning their material gifts to him.

"And my God will supply all your needs according to his glorious riches in Christ Jesus.

To our God and Father be glory for ever and ever. Amen."

Letters Written to Associates

After Paul's imprisonment at Rome, apparently he was released and undertook further travels. Luke's Book of Acts and Paul's letters from prison were optimistic about his likely release. Details about where Paul then travelled are few, gleaned from his letters to his two associates Timothy and Titus. There is no record that Paul ever went to Spain, as he had earlier contemplated when he wrote Romans. However, from his letter to Titus we learn that Paul and Titus spent time in Crete where they made converts, and where Titus was left to consolidate them (Titus 1:5). Paul also went to Ephesus, where he left Timothy to resolve serious issues of false teaching, while he travelled on to Macedonia (1 Timothy 1:3-4). In his previous letter to the Philippians, Paul had indicated that he had sent Timothy to them, and expected to be released from custody soon, and would follow (Philippians 2:19-24). Paul's letter 1 Timothy was probably written from Macedonia, because Paul was delayed in returning to Ephesus in person (1 Timothy 3:14). His letter to Titus was probably written at a similar time as he made further travel plans, urging Titus to join him at Nicopolis in Western Greece (Titus 3:12). These movements would have taken place in the period 63-65 CE. Attitudes at Rome towards followers of Jesus drastically changed in 64 CE when Emperor Nero aggressively turned against them. Paul and Peter were caught up in the hostile campaign, and imprisoned. In his earlier imprisonment Paul had been kept under house arrest. This time he was gaoled. 2 Timothy was written shortly before he was executed (about 66-68 CE).

1 Timothy contains instructions to guide his younger colleague in resolving the internal wrangles at Ephesus, and to add his apostolic weight in support of Timothy's authority. Timothy was a well experienced operator in his own right. Paul looked upon him as his own son in the faith (v 2, 18). He was held in high regard by those who knew him, and was endorsed by prophecy. He had accompanied Paul in earlier missionary travels. He had remained with Paul during the previous custody at Rome. He was associated by name in many of Paul's letters to the churches. Paul entrusted the welfare of the strategic church at Ephesus to his oversight. Paul's letter was not prompted by lack of confidence in Timothy, but a recognition that the situation required unquestionable authority. This is why he identifies himself, to his close, intimate associate, by heavy duty credentials, *"an apostle of Christ Jesus by the command of God our Saviour and of Christ Jesus our hope"*. Paul's instructions throughout the letter are like military commands.

The underlying problem at Ephesus was complex and powerful. Paul's letter can only be properly understood against the background of the false teachings and practices unsettling the church community. Without discerning the background, Paul's own instructions lead to serious misunderstandings. The problem included false doctrines (1:3), controversies over Jewish myths, genealogical fantasies, and legalism (1:4-7), hot-headed men (2:8), seductive, domineering women (who probably carried over into the church their former customs of dominance and sexual promiscuity associated with the temple of Artemis, 2:9-15), contentious and ill-behaved overseers and deacons (3:1-13), ascetic practices (4:1-5), abuses amongst leaders and widows (chapter 5), and quarrels, malicious talk, and love of money (6:3-10). It was all very ungodly. Timothy's task was to teach the true faith (4:6), appoint sound leaders (chapter 3), be a true man of God (6:11-16), and pursue the goal of love (1:5). This was an enormous responsibility. However, his first step was to get the church to pray (2:1-7)!

In the face of all the issues troubling the community at Ephesus, Paul urged Timothy to focus first of all on priorities. These were prayerfulness, godliness, and evangelism. With regard to prayer, he lists various forms of praying, such as *"requests, prayers, intercession and thanksgiving*". He was stressing the need to turn to God by all means, to honour and respect him in dependence and submission. The Ephesians were focused on themselves and their own opinions and interests. They needed to reset their focus away from their religious controversies and performances onto God himself. They needed to relate to God.

Their prayers were to be made for "*everyone*". He means everyone without discrimination. The squabbles at Ephesus sprang from the interactions of various cultural groups asserting their own views and values. They were missing the point that the gospel was about God's salvation for sinners, which included everyone, regardless of their ethnic and social backgrounds. Cultural differences were irrelevant, and the various religious ideas and practices which they promoted were distortions of the truth. What counted was seeking the salvation of all by all means of prayer.

Not only were they to pray for everyone, but in particular they were to pray for "*kings and all those in authority*". This was so they could live peaceful, quiet lives in all godliness and holiness. Paul was not seeking a life of ease and comfort, but a world free from disturbances and pressures to allow the pursuit of godly lifestyles. Nero was now emperor, and the mood of the world was changing in its attitude towards the followers of Jesus. Paul's confidence, however, was in God and his will, and in the effectiveness of prayer to overrule human authorities. Prayer is subversive! It can influence the political and cultural forces in the world, and attitudes and relationships in church life. God's salvation rescued sinners so that they might become godly and righteous. The church community at Ephesus was more characterised by unhealthy controversies, rivalry, prestige, and financial gain than holiness. It was a far cry from the glowing picture of the church's calling presented in Paul's letter to the Ephesians only a few years earlier. In light of the church's calling, and in face of potential official threat, Paul urged prayer for external circumstances to be conducive to cultivating internal health.

Paul explains his advice concerning prayer. "*This is good, and pleases God our Saviour, who wants all men to be saved and to come to a knowledge of the truth. For there is one God and one mediator between God and men, the man Christ Jesus, who gave himself as a ransom for all men – the testimony given in its proper time*" (v 3-6). Prayer would refocus attention on the primary task of evangelism, and be effective in enabling the salvation and sanctification of people from all nations and social backgrounds without distinction. Paul reinforces his explanation by strongly asserting his own appointed role as herald, apostle, and teacher of the true faith to the Gentiles (v 7).

Applying his advice to the situation at Ephesus, Paul specifically expresses the desire for the men to "*lift up holy hands*" in prayer, "*without anger or disputing*" (v 8). He was not giving instructions about public worship, and permitting only men to pray, excluding women. Paul's letter was not setting out institutional procedures for church life. He was addressing the problems at Ephesus, which included men behaving badly! His practical solution was to get the men to pray – for the salvation of all people, without discrimination – in a holy and peaceable manner. Prayer, in accord with the gospel, looked to God for the way forward.

The women were also behaving badly. They were dressing and behaving indecently, acting in a domineering manner, and teaching false ideas. Most likely their background was their association with the temple of Artemis, where women dominated as priestesses, and seduced men by sensual appearance and charms, and sexual prostitution. Paul's instruction concerning women was not laying down guidelines for their role in church life generally, but correcting abuses at Ephesus in line with gospel truth. This is a topic which calls for fuller discussion beyond our purpose here. However, what is important, is to keep the gospel perspective clear, and understand the context as fully as possible. Paul does not comment about women praying at this point. This is not because praying was a man's privilege and not a woman's. Later in his letter, in correcting misbehaviour amongst widows, Paul describes the truly needy widow as one who puts her hope in God, and *"continues night and day to pray and ask God for help"* (5:5). Prayer was the mark of her godly outlook, and dependence on God. To pray *"night and day"* is a way of saying prayer was a prominent and primary feature of life. It is similar to the blessed man in Psalm 1 who meditates day and night on God's law. It was a characteristic, life-shaping occupation.

There is another reference to prayer in this letter (4:5), which indirectly reveals its importance. Paul was reacting to ascetic teaching which forbade marriage and promoted abstinence from certain foods. Some foods purchased in the marketplace came from offerings made to pagan idols. False teaching promoted the need to avoid earthly attachments and pagan influences because they were unholy. Paul, however, declared that such teaching came from demons, and affirmed everything created by God as good. Nothing should be rejected if received with thanksgiving. It was consecrated (made holy) by the word of God and prayer. These are the elements of "conversation" with God, God's word in the gospel which pronounces us holy in Christ, and our response to God in prayer. Prayerfulness is the expression of fellowship with God in all aspects of life.

Chronologically, **Titus** was Paul's next letter. In it he gives instructions to his younger associate concerning his task of consolidating the work at Crete. In particular, he has to establish them firmly in sound doctrine which promotes godly behaviour. He has to appoint appropriate elders, whose lifestyle is an example to others, particularly in contrast to influential Judaists. He must teach appropriate behaviour to the various members of a household, and how to behave in relation to earthly authorities and society. In the course of the letter, Paul gives a brief, succinct statement about God's gracious salvation through Jesus Christ (3:4-8). He makes no reference to prayer at all, although his instruction about true doctrine and true godliness provides a suitable foundation that would give rise to prayerful devotion.

Finally, we turn to **2 Timothy**. This is a poignant letter. It was Paul's last preserved letter, and he was aware that he faced inevitable execution (4:6). The day of that event was unknown, and still a little way off. Paul appeals to Timothy to come quickly, preferably before winter, and to bring Mark and Paul's cloak and scrolls with him (4:9, 11, 21). This shows that he expected there might still be some weeks and perhaps months before his end. He was acutely conscious of being alone. Acquaintances in Asia had deserted him (1:15). So too had Demas, who had gone to Thessalonica, and other associates (4:10, 16). Several colleagues were in distant places, and only Luke was with him (4:10-12). Paul especially longed to see Timothy, his *"dear son"*, whom he remembered fondly (1:2, 4). The main purpose of his letter, however, was to embolden Timothy as a servant of the Lord in the cause of the gospel. Since the *"you"* at the very end of the letter is plural, the letter was also intended for the church at Ephesus where Timothy served.

Paul wanted to encourage Timothy to guard the gospel unashamedly (chapter 1). He urged him to share the suffering he himself was experiencing. God's power had saved them. God's grace in Christ had been given to them. Paul had been appointed by God to be a herald of the gospel, and that involved suffering. He commanded Timothy to be strong in the grace which was in Christ, and to endure hardship like a good soldier (2:1-13). He must remember Christ's resurrection from the dead and his descendancy from David. These referred to his victory and identity as Messiah, the core truths of the gospel. He told Timothy to avoid harmful controversies, and to handle the word of truth correctly (2:14-26). His conduct and teaching must be in an exemplary, gentle manner approved by God. Paul warned that the last days would be marked by godlessness, but that Timothy should follow his example and Timothy's own convictions based on the scriptures (chapter 3). He solemnly charged Timothy to preach the word and discharge his duties faithfully, testifying that his own race was finished, and he now looked forward to the victor's crown (4:1-8). He completed the letter with a range of personal remarks (4:9-22).

For our purposes, we need to note the brief comment at the beginning of the letter concerning Paul's prayer habits (1:3). He prayed *"night and day"*. Like the godly widows in 1 Timothy 5:5, Paul's life was characterised by prayerfulness. In his prayers he expressed gratitude to God. Even though he was incarcerated in a dungeon awaiting death, he remained thankful to God. Though he was on death row, soon to be executed as an enemy of the empire, his allegiance remained true to God.

This was because of his convictions about God, and his purpose and grace. When we look ahead in the letter, Paul confesses this clearly to inspire Timothy and the Ephesian readers.

"This grace was given us in Christ Jesus before the beginning of time, but it has now been revealed through the appearing of our Saviour, Christ Jesus, who has destroyed death and has brought life and immortality to light through the gospel. And of this gospel I was appointed a herald and an apostle and a teacher. That is why I am suffering as I am. Yet I

am not ashamed, because I know whom I have believed, and am convinced that he is able to guard what I have entrusted to him for that day" (1:9-12).

Here was the perspective behind Paul's gratitude. It was what inspired his service for God. He writes that like his Jewish forefathers, he had served God with a clear conscience. Paul saw his own role, as a messenger of the gospel, as part of God's strategic plan to save the world. That plan was based on God's grace, predetermined before time began to be accomplished by his Messiah. It was pursued in history through God's promises to Abraham and his dealings with Israel, Paul's forefathers. It was culminated in the victory of the Messiah Jesus over death, establishing eternal life. It had been Paul's privileged calling to proclaim to the nations the good news of Jesus' magnificent triumph and gracious gift of life. He was grateful for God's salvation, grateful for God's grace in his life, and grateful for his privileged task. His gratitude overflowed into prayer, as he offered his thanks to God and interceded for the work of the gospel. It was now Timothy's task to continue the work after Paul was gone. Paul's remarks were intended to encourage his younger colleague not to be daunted by his responsibilities and its dangers.

Remembering Timothy in his prayers brought recollections of Timothy's tears and faith. When the tears occurred is not stated. Probably, it was when they last separated. The two men had a close bond, after many years of travelling and working together. Timothy's tears demonstrated his deep affection for Paul. Recalling them stirred Paul's longings to see him again, which would fill him with joy. Timothy's company, while Paul was in a dark period, would be uplifting. Paul also recollected Timothy's sincere faith, which Paul had first witnessed in Timothy's grandmother, and then mother. Mention of Timothy's tears and faith probably implied that Paul prayed about these matters. He would pray that Timothy might be able to join him, and that his faith might be kept strong.

It was because he recollected Timothy's faith, that Paul reminded him to *"fan into flame the gift of God"* (v 6). Timothy's faith was the gift of grace (*"charisma"*), the gift of the Holy Spirit. At the time he received this gift, it was through the laying on of Paul's own hands. Paul's reminder of his own involvement was intended to fortify Timothy's resolve. This was probably another reason Paul wanted Timothy to visit him, so that he could more directly encourage him to be strong. Timothy seems to have been a gentle man, entrusted with a daunting task, in perilous times. He needed robust buttressing. More than Paul's encouragement, however, he should look to God. Paul went on to declare that God's gift was not a spirit of timidity, but of *"power, of love and of self-discipline"* (v 7). Timothy had already received the resources he needed for his task! He simply had to resist his natural tendency to feel intimidated, and rely on God's enabling. Paul's reminder of these things to Timothy probably reflected what Paul prayed for him. Paul's constant praying was consumed by the mission of the gospel. He prayed about its proclamation. He prayed for its messengers, for its listeners, for its converts, for its opponents, and for all aspects of the spread of the gospel throughout the world. He prayed especially for colleagues he held in high regard and warm affection, and who were to take over the reins after his departure. This whole opening paragraph in Paul's letter is not only a word of encouragement, but probably reflects the gist of Paul's prayers for Timothy. With his own death staring him in the face, Paul's prayers were consumed with his intercession for the cause of the gospel.

We have seen, then, that Paul's letters consistently show that his prayer life was governed by the sovereign will of God as disclosed in the Gospel, and in making the Gospel known.

CHAPTER 14

"DRAW NEAR TO GOD"

Prayer in Other New Testament Books

The other letters of the New Testament reflect the same outlook about prayer as the Gospels and Paul. There are few references, but they challenge and guide us in our praying.

HEBREWS: Jesus Is Our Kingly High Priest

The Book of Hebrews is a written pastoral exhortation. Its inspiring message calls readers to experience the joy and freedom of God's forgiveness and peace through Jesus Christ, and the privilege of belonging to God as a member of his eternal family and relating to him in spiritual reality.

The author is unknown, although seems to be someone like Apollos, the eloquent teacher of the gospel in the early church. The original readers are also unknown, although they seem to be a community of Jewish believers in Jesus, possibly living at Rome. Owing to cultural pressure and social antagonism, they are in danger of losing their spiritual zeal and returning to their ritualistic Jewish religion. Since the temple at Jerusalem was still operating at the time of writing, the date of this exhortation must have been prior to 70 CE when both the city and the temple were destroyed.

The message of Hebrews is an encouragement to Jewish believers to *"draw near to God"* in full and confident possession of the privileges and blessings made available by Christ. Confidence to draw near is based on Jesus' identity as God's royal Son and heir, and on the role of Jesus in eternity as High Priest who offers unceasing intercession for those who follow him in the way of faith. *"Drawing near to God"* is a Jewish expression, derived from Israel's experience at Mount Sinai and the old sacrificial system and priestly functions associated with the Temple. Imagery from Israel's religious culture is used figuratively in Hebrews to describe everyday life now lived in dedicated service. All of life is viewed as constant communion, worship, and prayer. The message can be confusing to readers who are unfamiliar with ancient Jewish sacrifices and religious regulations. However, when the background is understood, everything becomes clear, and the sublime revelation about Jesus stimulates a thrilling new way of living. Israel's old rituals are exposed as ineffective, and acceptance with God is through Jesus because of his sacrificial death. Jesus has become our kingly High Priest, who makes spiritual nearness to God a present reality, as well as our eternal destiny. A substantial feature of the exhortation is a series of five warnings which cautions against the danger of rejecting Christ (2:1-4, 3:7-4:13, 5:11-6:12, 10:26-31, 12:14-29).

The exhortation opens with a bold pronouncement about God's Son, which sets the theme for what follows (1:1-3). The pronouncement declares that God has revealed himself and his purposes in two stages. God "spoke" in the past to Israel's forefathers through his prophets, but in the last days he has "spoken" through his Son (God's kingly representative on earth). God's "word" is the means by which he accomplishes his purposes. With regard to the Son's relation to God's purpose for the ages, two declarations are made. God appointed him to be heir of "*all things*" (God's final estate), having made the whole universe through him (implying his pre-existence). That is, he began it all, before time, and will culminate it all, beyond the end of time. Three statements are made about who the Son is, and two about what he has done. The Son is the radiance of God's glory, the exact representation of his being, and he sustains everything by his powerful word. He provided purification for sins, and afterwards sat down at the right hand of the Majesty of heaven. That is, he reveals God, redeems mankind, and rules over all existence. Although the Son is God's human representative, the exhortation indicates his prior divine identity and his final divine authority. His pre-existent state is not named, because he is actually God's self-expression. The Son's pre-existent identity is the personal "outshining" of God himself (like impersonal sunshine is to the sun), the authentic and authoritative representation of God himself. This is equivalent to John's term the "Word" (John 1:1). The Son's ultimate authority shares the majesty and supremacy which belong to God alone. This is a profound perspective.

The exhortation then proceeds to stress that the Son was superior to angels (1:4-2:18). If the "*message spoken by angels*" (referring to the Law given to Moses at Mount Sinai, believed by Jews to have been communicated through angels) had serious consequences if violated, what escape was there for ignoring the Son's "*great salvation*" (God's message "spoken" personally by his representative's rescue mission)? Jesus was made lower than angels by becoming human. This was so that by his death he might destroy the devil who holds the power of death, and as a merciful and faithful high priest might make atonement for the sins of people. This was salvation from mankind's greatest enemies.

Not only was Jesus superior to angels, but also to Moses, as a faithful son is greater than a faithful servant (3:1-6). Holy brothers who share in the heavenly calling must fix their thoughts on Jesus who will bring them to God's "*Sabbath rest*" (3:7-4:13). God's "*rest*" is the condition of existence which God enjoys since he completed his work of creation. It is the "*rest*" of sharing with God in eternal perfect fellowship. God's new holy family must not become hard-hearted like former Israelites during the time of Moses, and turn away from the living God. They must make every effort to enter that rest.

Jesus is also superior to the high priests of the order of Aaron (4:14-8:13). He is a *"great high priest"* who has triumphantly *"gone through the heavens"* into God's actual presence. They serve in an earthly sanctuary which is only a copy and shadow of what is in heaven. Jesus is God's Son, who is a priest after the order of Melchizedek. Discussion of this order uses complex arguments, but essentially makes the point that this order of priesthood is indestructible. This high priest remains in God's presence forever, and serves on the basis of a new covenant, which renders the old Israelite covenant obsolete. This was an astonishing and liberating revelation for Jewish outlook.

Within the context of this discussion, significant description is given about Jesus. Jesus' earthly life is described as one of *"entreaties and petitions with loud cries and tears"* to emphasise his intercessory priestly role (5:7-10). His intensity vividly recalls his anguish in Gethsemane, which was the pinnacle of his commitment to completing his mission at Calvary. He prayed to God, who alone could save him from death, which was the penalty for sin. The implication is that God did save him, not by preventing his death, but through resurrection. Jesus' whole life was virtually a prayer, characterised by his devotion to the practice of praying. He was heard because of his *"reverent submission"*, choosing to trust and obey his Father even when the cup of suffering was not removed. Although he was Son (preferable to *"a son"*), he learned obedience from what he suffered. Not that he was previously disobedient. He lived to the full extent of obedience by fulfilling the will of God, through suffering. As a result, he was *"made perfect"*, completely qualified to be Saviour (*"source of eternal salvation"*) and High Priest (*"designated by God ... in the order of Melchizedek"*) for his people. Prayerfulness was the characteristic mark of Jesus' intimate, dependent relationship with his Father in heaven as he perfectly obeyed his will as Son on earth.

Because Jesus now lives forever, he has a permanent priesthood (7:24-25). Therefore, he is able to save completely those who come to God through him, *"because he always lives to intercede for them"*. Because of his intercession, we are cleansed, and qualified to join him.

The exhortation adds further that Jesus is superior to the ineffective old religious system (9:1-10:18). The earthly tabernacle and its practices of worship and sacrifice, prescribed by the Holy Spirit, demonstrated an important truth. They showed that the way into the Most Holy Place (representing God's actual presence) was not yet revealed. In contrast, Christ provides the reality of good things which result from unhindered access to God. He went through the *"greater and more perfect tabernacle"*, by means of a more perfect sacrifice (himself), and obtained *"eternal redemption"*. His unblemished sacrifice is able to cleanse our consciences from sins which condemn us (*"acts which lead to death"*), so that we can worship and serve the living God.

The exhortation comes to a climactic conclusion with a fivefold appeal (10:19-25). Jesus' role of unending intercession establishes a new situation and relationship for those who trust him. Therefore, the appeal calls for a threefold general response with respect to faith, hope, and love, and two practical applications.

"Let us draw near to God with a sincere heart in full assurance of faith, having our hearts sprinkled to cleanse us from a guilty conscience and having our bodies washed with pure water". There is no need for ritual cleanliness, nor for anxiety. Just a heart which is true and trusting because of full spiritual cleanliness, both inward and outward.

"Let us hold unswervingly to the hope we profess, for he who promised is faithful". Despite threatening pressures or enticing distractions, hold fast to the hope of the ultimate goal of fellowship with God, because he is faithful to keep what he has promised.

"Let us consider how we may spur one another on toward love and good deeds". As members of the same family, we egg one another on. Love and good deeds are the spiritual expression of our new relationship with God, replacing old ritual traditions. Two practical applications of this third response concern attendance at church meetings, which has special relevance for meeting for fellowship in prayer.

"Let us not give up meeting together, as some are in the habit of doing". Those letting go the habit were perhaps drifting back to former ritual practices, or were fearful of public hostility, or were complacent, or were waning in confidence that the "Day" was approaching.

"Let us encourage one another – and all the more as you see the Day approaching". Don't neglect meeting, and actively encourage one another to meet.

The appeal is followed by a sudden outburst against those who persist in hostile rebellion against the gospel (10:26-39). It is the fourth warning in the book, but seems to be connected with those who were neglecting church meetings. It is a warning against apostates, and pronounces pretty dire consequences for them. Nevertheless, a word of encouragement is given to the continuing community (10:32-39). The whole exhortation concludes with strong encouragement to persevere in faith (chapters 11-12), and some final remarks (chapter 13).

The writer requests prayer for himself, and offers prayer for his readers (13:18-21). His identity and circumstances are unknown, but his attitude is admirable. He states that his conscience is clear, and that he desires to live honourably. Perhaps his actions were attracting criticism or causing complications. When the matter is concluded, he hopes to be reunited with them.

His own prayer for them is sublime. He entreats the "*God of peace*" (salvation and harmony), who brought the Lord Jesus back from the dead (the only mention of the resurrection, because elsewhere the emphasis has been upon his exaltation to God's right hand). God did this by the "*blood of the eternal covenant*", because God accepted Jesus' self-sacrifice and established his new covenant on that foundation. Jesus is the *"great shepherd of the sheep"* (the only place in the Bible where this title is used, but which aptly depicts his role). He asks God to *"equip"* (*"repair"* or *"complete"*, suggesting that God can mend what is broken and provide what is lacking) them with everything good so that they can do his will, and to work in *"us"* (him and them) what is pleasing to him, through Jesus Christ, to whom be glory forever.

JAMES: True Religion

For a writer to introduce himself simply as "James", without other identification except *"a servant of God and of the Lord Jesus Christ"*, implies that he was a prominent Christian figure. The traditional view that he was Jesus' own brother is most likely correct. Although James did not believe in Jesus prior to the crucifixion (John 7:5), he was converted when the risen Jesus later appeared to him (1 Corinthians 15:7). He was leader of the church in Jerusalem (Acts 15), until his death, apparently killed by Jews in the year 62. The letter is a written public address to a mixed Jewish community scattered abroad.

Jewish culture was very religious. All Jews worshiped God exclusively and habitually. Believers in Jesus, however, experienced a vibrant awakening to God's reality, grace, and glory. Their ritual religion became an exhilarating relationship with God who had kept his promise to Abraham by raising up his Messiah to save and rule the world. Judging from the contents of James' message, his readers included both believers in Jesus and non-believers. Among the believers were some who were immature, and others who were slipping back into less virtuous habits. Among the non-believers some appear to have been violent (perhaps Jewish zealots) and others rich, self-indulgent, and oppressively arrogant (4:1-5:6). At first glance, James seems to jump randomly from topic to topic. Yet actually there are careful links between them all. These form a patchwork pattern which displays a religious faith which is acceptable to God and copes with life's experiences. Practical, down to earth guidance gives instruction about how to cope with adversity and temptations, true religion, wealth and poverty, matters of speech and relationships, the prospects of life now and hereafter, suffering and backsliding. James' rhetorical style is partly teaching, and partly preaching. Numerous commands throughout give it an authoritative tone.

A striking absence in the address, especially from the point of view of presenting faith in the Lord Jesus Christ (1:1, 2:1), is any reference to central features of the gospel. There is no mention of Jesus' death and resurrection, the coming of the Holy Spirit, forgiveness of sins, baptism, or the formation of the church. Yet what is said is consistent with faith in Jesus, and is not unlike some of Jesus' own teachings. Neither is there mention of prominent features of Jewish religion, such as the temple, sacrifices, or Sabbath. James was not proclaiming the gospel like Paul. Nor was he denouncing Jewish religion like Stephen. The probable reason for James' approach is that he was being sensitively indirect towards his readers, in consideration for barriers concerning the gospel in the minds of many of them.

It is quite evident that for James prayer was highly valued. He encouraged it at the outset of his address (1:5-8) and at a couple of later stages (4:2-3, 8, 5:13-18).

He had begun his address in a startling manner (1:2-4). He had told his readers to consider it pure joy when facing adversity. That is not a natural reaction. But James went on to explain that the trial was a test of faith, intended to produce perseverance. Perseverance should persist until its work of cultivating maturity was complete, lacking nothing. With a play on the term "lacking", he then wrote that if they lacked wisdom, they should "*ask*" for it (1:5-6). Wisdom means insight and skill for managing the affairs of life. James was counselling his readers to have a focus on God in life's experiences. They should understand his purpose when facing trials, and depend on him for wisdom in how to cope. To inspire their confidence when asking, he described what God was like by nature. "*Who gives generously to all without finding fault*" (literally, "*the giving-to-all-unreservedly-without-reproach*"). Because God naturally gives graciously, generously, ungrudgingly, and unrebukingly, he can be asked for wisdom, and he will give it. Yet the request must be in faith, not doubt (1:7-8). The doubter is like the wave of the ocean driven to and fro by the wind. He is "*double-minded*" (divided in loyalty to God's interests and his own interests) and "*unstable*" (vacillating under the influence of changing circumstances, unsettled in his ways, and hesitant in his decisions and actions). James was contrasting God's nature and the nature of the doubter. Prayer is a vital and realistic expression of depending relationally on God in the affairs of life.

A major problem in Jewish society was relational tension and conflict. Criticism, quarrels, violence, and slander were all too frequent. James confronted these tendencies directly (4:1-12). He diagnosed the problem (v 1-5), prescribed the remedy (v 6-10), and issued a firm prohibition (v 11-12). The source of external relational conflicts was their inner personal warring passions. Using the vivid language of warfare, James speaks of disappointed lust leading to murder, frustrated jealousy precipitating quarrels and battles. He explains that desires are thwarted because they do not ask God. Just as earlier prayerful dependence on God was the way to obtain wisdom, now it is the way to find true satisfaction. James hastened to add that those who may ask, yet not receive, do so because of wrong motives, wanting to indulge their desires for pleasure. Prayer can be either neglected or abused because of self-interested passions.

The solution is found in a scriptural proverb. "*God opposes the proud but gives grace to the humble*". This pinpoints a basic truth. God's grace is the key to fulness of life, from birth to maturity. It is available to all who turn humbly to God. James applies this truth with a staccato of commands. "*Submit to God ... Resist the devil ... Come near to God ... Wash your hands ... purify your hearts ... Grieve, mourn, wail ... Humble yourselves before the Lord ...*". Humble obedience is the appropriate response to abundant grace. These commands are couched in familiar religious Jewish language. At their heart is the imagery of "drawing near to God", which involves devotion to all means by which closeness to God can be expressed. Central to that devotion will be prayer.

A final command from James by way of application forbids slander. The command is designed to prevent conflicts. To get right with God requires also getting right with people. To defame and criticise others is to defame and criticise God's law. It ignores and disobeys the law, and sets itself above the law, and therefore above God who is the only lawgiver.

James ends his address by encouraging confidence in the reality and effectiveness of prayer, and urging care for backsliders (5:13-20). Interpretations of this passage have given rise to different and dubious practices. It was not meant to promote confessions to priests or rituals for faith healing. James was providing pastoral advice for coping with life's varied circumstances. He counsels his readers to face them with prayer and praise, as is appropriate for the situation (v 13). As an example of this principle, he takes up the common complaint of sickness (v 14-15). He advises them to call the elders to pray over the sick person. Having just advised a person who is suffering to pray, why does he now suggest calling the elders to pray? It is because James realises the debilitating effects of sickness, causing anxiety, doubts, and confusion, and even sin. Elders were appointed to provide pastoral care, and ensured the offering of spiritually mature prayer. James was wisely advising the sick person to deal with their sickness prayerfully in fellowship with reliable, spiritually mature leaders. The anointing with oil, which James mentions, is not meant to be a Christian healing ritual, but simply treating with oil for medical purposes, but *"in the name of the Lord"*. Take your appropriate medicine, but put your faith primarily in the Lord! Verse 15 is usually poorly translated, and thus gives confusion. Literally, James said, *"The prayer of faith will save the exhausted person"*. The *"prayer of faith"* is not a special kind of prayer. It is prayer offered in an attitude of faith, as distinct from merely formal ritual. Such trusting prayer will *"save"* (not *"make well"*) the sick person, and the Lord will raise him up. The term *"save"* is ambiguous, allowing both physical and spiritual healing. Similarly, the Lord's raising up might be physical or spiritual restoration. There may be physical healing or there may be spiritual benefits, depending on the purposes of God. The sick (literally, *"exhausted"*) person will be saved in some respect. When the sick person has reached the end of personal resources (physically, mentally, and spiritually), and becomes exhausted, he/she is not in a fit state to pray for themselves. That is why it is wise to call the elders. The elders will pray appropriately, in accord with God's will. Spiritual well-being is the primary concern, as the assurance of forgiveness and the encouragement for confession of sin make clear. In times of sickness, a person may sin, in word, or thought, or deed. Restoration as a result of prayer will bring forgiveness.

James then draws a conclusion ("Therefore", v 16). Close bonds of mutual fellowship and concern for spiritual well-being must be maintained. When people offend one another, they are to confess their sins to one another and pray for one another, so that healing will result.

The picture is ambiguous, and the imagery of healing is present, but the primary concern is for healing of relationships and spiritual condition. James then states plainly the principle he has been advocating. "*The prayer of a righteous man* (a person in close relationship with God who has a working faith!) *is powerful and effective*". James' main point is to assert the importance of prayer in maintaining spiritual health through all of life's fluctuating events. The example of Elijah demonstrates just how powerfully effective prayer is (v 17-18).

James' message ends abruptly (v 19-20). Having expounded his theme of practising true religion by having reality of faith in God through life's circumstances, he suddenly, yet tenderly, concludes with a word about the conversion of backsliders. Religion is not a game, nor a formal veneer. It is a matter of life and death. To turn a sinner from the error of his way will save him from death, and cover over a multitude of sins. James' final word about saving sinful souls reveals the motivating spirit behind his book. It proves that his previous comments about prayer for the sick person were primarily concerned for his spiritual state.

For James, true religion was a lifestyle of trusting God in all circumstances. Prayer was the essential expression and epitome of such a relationship.

1 & 2 PETER: A Living Hope

The gospel assures a glorious future for those who trust Jesus as their Saviour and Lord. The risen Jesus has entered the presence of God in eternity and received supreme authority over all that exists. At an appointed time, which is unknown to humans on earth, Jesus will return to the earth to bring an end to the present state of existence. All evil, suffering, sorrow, and death will be eliminated. The current order will be replaced by a transcendent new order ("*new heavens and earth*") which will last forever. God will reign over a kingdom of love, joy, peace, and righteousness. All who belong to Jesus Christ will experience the fulness of God's blessings. This is the destiny for creation which God determined before time began, and decreed on the basis of grace to be accomplished through his Messiah. By his sacrificial death, resurrection, and ascension to the Father, Jesus triumphantly fulfilled God's plan of grace. This magnificent good news is the hope of the world which is now being proclaimed to people of all generations and cultures living on the earth.

Peter's two letters preserved in the New Testament apply his conviction about future hope to life in the present. 1 Peter was written, probably in the early 60's, to newly baptised converts facing the threat of hostility. 2 Peter was written several years later to deal with the threat of heresy.

1 Peter was addressed to believers living in northern Asia Minor (north Turkey today), who are described in terms which highlight their relationship to God and to the world (1:1-2). They are "*God's elect*", a description originally applied to Israel, meaning those who are selected to share in the fulfilment of God's promises and plans. They are also "*strangers in the*

world, scattered…", a description usually applied to Jews dispersed beyond their homeland. Peter meant that they were "True Israel", having only temporary residence in the world where they did not belong. God is identified by his trinitarian operations in providing their redemption, *"the foreknowledge of God the Father, … the sanctifying work of the Spirit, … obedience to Jesus Christ and sprinkling by his blood"*.

The letter has two parts, which are clearly marked (1:1-4:11, 4:12-5:14). The longer first part instructs the new converts how to live in the present world as they look forward to their coming salvation and the end of all things. Peter begins with praise for the hope, joy, and wonder of their salvation (1:2-12). God has given them *"new birth into a living hope"*. Peter then commands them to live according to their new birth in disciplined holiness, reverence for God, and love for one another (1:13-25). He proceeds to instruct them how to live as members of God's chosen community (2:1-10), in general society (2:11-12), in a spirit of submission to civic authorities, to their masters if slaves, to one another in marriage (2:13-3:7), and in social relationships generally (3:8-12). Peter concludes the first part of his letter with advice for coping with persecution (3:13-4:11). Maintain an outer disposition derived from an inner consciousness of Christ as Lord in the heart, follow Christ's example of suffering unjustly, and be governed by the outlook that the end is near. The second part of Peter's letter returns to the subject of persecution, which his readers were experiencing at that time (4:12-5:14). Painful trials of hostile antagonism are inevitable, because it is sharing in the sufferings of Christ and the beginning of judgement, which will be far worse for those who disobey the gospel. Peter exhorts elders and younger leaders to shepherd God's flock responsibly, and for the whole community to clothe themselves with humility towards one another, as they humble themselves before God in their trying sufferings, casting their cares on him, and staying alert to the devil's hostility.

In the course of the letter, Peter's attitude towards prayer is expressed briefly, but profoundly. He reveals the radically new relationship which Christ brings to marriage (where husbands and wives are viewed as social and spiritual equals), and shows how it expresses itself in shared prayer between a husband and wife (3:7). Effectiveness in such prayer depends on the couples' attitudes within the relationship. Appreciation for the value of prayer is highlighted by Peter in a quotation from Psalm 34:12-16 (3:10-12). He was counselling his readers about their attitudes in social relationships, and especially towards unfriendly and offensive people. They must avoid evil and seek peace, knowing that God is attentive to their prayer. Though prayer is mentioned only incidentally in both these references, they assume the priority of prayer, and the reality of God's attentiveness. Peter also shows the importance of prayer for living Christianly in the crucial period of the "End Times" (4:7). The coming of Christ brought God's final days for history near, and these call for mental and spiritual alertness, keeping God's purposes and actions prayerfully in mind in how we live.

2 Peter was written near the end of Peter's life (1:12-15). He died as a martyr sometime prior to 68, during the reign of Nero. Peter indicates that he had written a previous letter to these same readers (3:1), very likely referring to 1 Peter. This second letter tackles the problem of infiltration by false teachers into his readers' church community. In their heretical teaching, they were scoffing at the prospect of Christ's return (3:3-4). Peter makes no mention of prayer in his letter, because his focus is on rebutting their false ideas. He does this by firstly encouraging them to cultivate virtuous qualities (1:1-11). He asserts that God's divine power is sufficient for living a godly life. Therefore, he urges them to make every effort to add godly virtues to their faith in order to make their calling and election sure. This is so that they will receive a rich welcome into Christ's kingdom. He reminds them that the truth of the kingdom is based on eyewitnesses of Christ's majesty at his transfiguration and on the prophecy of scripture (1:12-21). He then warns them against false teachers, who will bring destruction upon themselves (chapter 2). He concludes by reminding them of the inevitability of evil scoffers and the certainty of Christ's coming, insisting again that they make every effort to be spotless, blameless, and at peace with him when he comes (chapter 3).

1, 2, 3 JOHN: Walking in the Truth

Towards the end of the first century, an insidious heresy emerged which had popular appeal. In following centuries, it developed into a sophisticated system of distinctive beliefs and lifestyle based on the claim of possessing true knowledge ("gnosis" in Greek) of God. The system is generally called Gnosticism. Its early roots were prominent in Asia Minor (Turkey), which was fast becoming the major heartland of the growing churches. Ephesus in particular was the major city, and was where the elderly apostle John spent the last decades of his life. In reaction to the impact of the developing perversion on church life, John wrote a tract to promote the truth of the gospel. It is usually called a letter, although there are no typical features of a letter, such as recipients, greetings, or farewells. It is known as 1 John because two short letters, known as 2 and 3 John, are clustered with it. In both these letters, John uses a phrase *"walking in the truth"*, to mean living according to the gospel, especially in contrast to popular false ideas. 1 John does not use that expression, but that is its essential theme.

Awareness of the confused background helps understand the message of 1 John more clearly. The heretical views were complex, arising from pagan philosophical and religious views of the day. In brief, beliefs were based on imaginative speculations about the universe and the Supreme Being, leading to a mystical knowledge of God. Spirit was considered good, and matter evil. Since the human body was matter, the gospel claim that God became incarnate, and its commands to practise moral purity, were rejected. Consequently, the human mind and philosophy were elevated above divine revelation, and mystical experience was valued rather than faith and right moral behaviour. 1 John counteracts these ideas by presenting the truth of the gospel and what it means to truly "know" God.

The style of 1 John is more like a free-flowing, swirling current, than systematic, carefully arranged arguments. It is rhetorical, appealing to the heart, rather than logical, appealing to the intellect. John simply proclaims the truth about God, and then, in a tenderly, fatherly manner, seeks to persuade his readers to live accordingly.

In presenting his message, John follows a sweeping approach. He begins with a proclamation (similar to his Gospel), testifying to what he has personally seen and heard and touched, with regard to the appearance of the Word of Life (1:1-4). As in John's Gospel (1:1-18), written at a similar time, the incarnation of the Word (God's dynamic "Self-expression" or "Self-revealing" by which he accomplished his purposes) is the source of eternal life, granting fellowship with God, and inspiring fellowship with one another. The rest of his message revolves around two statements about the nature of God. God is light (1:5) and God is love (4:8, 16). His first appeal is for his "children" to walk in the light (1:5-2:14). Then he warns against straying from the truth that Jesus is the Christ (2:15-3:10). His second appeal is for them to love one another (3:11-4:21), including within the appeal a brief warning to discern the Spirit of truth (4:1-6). He concludes by confirming that the person who has faith in Jesus Christ overcomes the world and has eternal life (5:1-21).

What concerns John is the matter of belonging to the truth. We can know that we belong to the truth, if we believe in the truth about Jesus, and live like him in obedience to God's commands, and love like him in caring for one another. In the course of John's second appeal (3:11-4:21), about the need to love one another, he writes a paragraph which explains how his readers can know that they belong to the truth (3:19-24). It begins and ends with the words, "*This is how we know…*". His explanation includes insights into the intimate experience of drawing near to God in prayer.

In the lead up to this explanation, he expounded the truth of the gospel in terms of love (3:1-18). The Father lavished his love upon us, by calling us to be his children (v 1). We know what love is, because Jesus Christ laid down his life for us (v 16). Therefore, we should also lay down our lives for our brothers. We must share our possessions with those in need, and love "in truth", not merely words (v 17-18). It is by loving others "in truth", that we can know that we "belong to the truth". Essentially John's message was that God was known by his self-sacrificial love expressed in Jesus Christ, and those who know God show it by their self-sacrificial love to others.

This knowledge has a profound effect upon our relationship to God. It affects both the negative and positive states of our heart. John is realistic in understanding how our hearts behave, sometimes condemning us, sometimes assuring us. He writes firstly that, when we know that we belong to the truth, we can "*set our hearts at rest in his presence whenever our hearts condemn us*" (v 19-20). Since we are imperfect people, our hearts can make us conscious of our failings when we draw near to God's presence. We feel condemned and unacceptable, like a guilty offender before a strict judge. *"But God is greater than our hearts, and he knows everything"*. God knows all about our sinfulness, and about Christ's atoning sacrifice for sin (2:2). Our acceptance with God does not depend on how our hearts feel, but on the truth about Christ. By belonging to the truth, we can set our hearts at rest in God's presence, like sons coming before our Father. When John writes about being in God's presence, he has in mind coming *"before God"* (his literal words) in intercession. He was implicitly revealing that prayer is the epitome of fellowship with God, the privileged blessing which results from Christ's extinguishing the contamination of sin. Prayer is not merely a religious ritual, but the sublime reality of conversing with God.

John reveals this even more fully in his next comment (v 21-22). *"Dear friends, if our hearts do not condemn us, we have confidence before God and receive from him anything we ask, because we obey his commands and do what pleases him"*. When we come into God's presence in prayer, with a heart which has been set at rest, we experience a two-fold blessing. We have confidence (literally, "boldness") to meet God face to face. And we receive what we request. We enjoy untroubled, intimate, two-way conversation. We ask, and God gives. There is a qualification to this relationship. We obey God's commands and do what pleases him. This is not merit on our part, as John goes on to explain. God's commands are to believe in his Son, Jesus Christ, and to love one another (v 23). That is, to belong to the truth. Or, as John puts it, to live in Christ, and he in us, a relationship which we know to be real by means of his Spirit (v 24). The risen Christ has given his Spirit to convict sinners of their guilt before God; to convince them of the truth about Christ who forgives their sin and reconciles them to God; and to convert them to live according to God's light and love. This is what it means to "know" God. Prayerful fellowship with God, intercession, is its intimate expression. It is not mystical experience, but realistic inter-personal conversation. John's teaching echoes what Jesus taught his disciples on his last night with them before his crucifixion. John himself recorded that teaching in his Gospel which he wrote at about this same time (John 14-17).

John's claim that we receive from God anything we ask, is not a blank cheque. He qualifies this general statement in his concluding remarks at the end of his document (5:13-21). There he explains why he wrote. It was to assure those who believe in the name of the Son of God (everything which identifies him) that they might know that they have eternal life. Earlier John had indicated something similar (2:24-27). Letting the truth which they heard from the beginning remain in them, they would remain in relationship with the Son and the Father, which was eternal life. He said then that he was writing about these things because of those trying to lead them astray. They must remain with the teaching taught by the anointing (with the Holy Spirit) which they had received from God. In other words, eternal life is a personal relationship with the eternal God, entered through faith in Christ, whose truth (reality) is revealed by the Holy Spirit. It begins here and now. In his Gospel, John had quoted Jesus expressing the same truth in his farewell intercessory prayer, that eternal life was knowing the only true God, and Jesus Christ whom he had sent (John 17:3).

This is why John immediately refers to prayer. Prayer is approaching God to engage in intimate fellowship with him. John repeats the two aspects of prayer he indicated previously. Confidence to draw near to God, and answers to requests. The emphasis is upon our role in asking. However, John now qualifies our requests. They are *"anything according to his will"*. Prayer is not seeking our own will, or seeking to modify God's will. It is praying as Jesus taught his disciples, and as he himself prayed. "Let your will be done". It is praying in accord with the truth of the gospel, and God's outworking purposes in the world and in our lives. Intercession!

By way of illustration, John encourages prayer for a brother who is seen committing a sin, in order that God might give him life (v 16-17). He means that God might restore him to the full fellowship of eternal life. This is an example of praying according to God's will. In our own fellowship with God, we share his concern for our brother, so we intercede for him. Praying is being in partnership with God as an intercessor. God's willingness to forgive sin was emphasised at the beginning of John's message (1:5-2:2). However, there is a limit. It only applies to sin which *"does not lead to death"*. God is willing to forgive any wrongdoing, except the sin which leads to death. This is the sin of rejecting Jesus' atoning sacrifice for sins, the sin of antichrist (2:2, 22).

When we turn to 2 and 3 John, there are no references to prayer. Both letters are concerned about providing hospitality to travelling teachers, and the need to discern between genuine teachers of the gospel and false teachers who promoted heresy. 2 John was written to a local church, personified as *"the chosen lady and her children"*, commending its members for *"walking in the truth"*, and warning against deceptive antichrists. 3 John was written to a prominent member of a local church, called Gaius, commending him for providing hospitality for teachers of the truth. However, a self-serving, bombastic person called Diotrephes is rebuked for refusing to welcome them, and Gaius is warned against being influenced by evil from doing good. Another person, Demetrius, possibly the bearer of the letter, is commended as a person of good reputation. Although not contributing anything specific about prayer, these letters add colouring to the background of the message of 1 John.

JUDE: Contending for the Faith

A younger brother of Jesus and James intended to write a general letter about the common salvation shared by those *"called"* to put their trust in Jesus Christ (v 1-4). Instead, he was constrained to write in defence of the *"faith"* (an alternative term for the gospel). This was because godless infiltrators were perverting the truth. They were changing the grace of God into a license to commit immorality, and were denying that Jesus Christ was their only

Sovereign and Lord. Much of what Jude wrote to confront the issue (v 5-16) is similar to 2 Peter 2, which probably adapted Jude's letter for its own purpose.

Jude described three examples of those who had formerly rebelled against God, and who received eternal punishment (v 5-7). He then condemned the disturbers within the Christian community who were immorally polluting their bodies, rejecting authority, and speaking derogatively against heavenly beings (v 8-13). He drew on biblical and apocryphal examples as comparisons. He then went on to quote from an apocryphal prophecy (the Book of Enoch) to declare that their judgement was foretold (v 14-16). Finally, he reminded them that the apostles had predicted the rise of such divisive scoffers (v 17-19).

Jude concluded with a series of short instructions for keeping themselves true, and for relating to anyone who was unsettled by the defectors (v 20-23). *"Build yourselves up in your most holy faith. Pray in the Holy Spirit. Keep yourselves in God's love as you wait for the mercy of our Lord Jesus Christ to bring you to eternal life. Be merciful to those who doubt. Snatch others from the fire and save them, to others show mercy mixed with fear – hating even the clothing stained by corrupted flesh."* They must conscientiously strengthen their understanding and experience of the gospel.

To pray in the Holy Spirit is to intercede in accord with the Spirit's mind and enabling (Romans 8:23, 26-27). The Spirit inspires awareness, and fuller understanding, of God the Father and his purposes (Galatians 4:6, Ephesians 1:17). To pray in the Spirit is to rely on the power of the Lord through prayer in the battle against the forces of evil (Ephesians 6:1, 18).

Jude ends his letter with an appropriate doxology to assure his readers of God's ability to keep them secure.

> *"To him who is able to keep you from falling and to present you before his glorious presence without fault and with great joy – to the only God our Saviour be glory, majesty, power and authority, through Jesus Christ our Lord, before all ages, now and evermore! Amen."*

CHAPTER 15

"FIRE ON THE EARTH"

Prayer in The Book of Revelation

We are reaching the end of our journey. As we complete our tour through the Bible, we turn to the intriguing Book of Revelation which closes the New Testament. It is a fascinating book of symbols and imagery. Its message is intended to inspire God's people to persevere in the face of persecution because of confidence that the crucified Christ is the risen and exalted Lord and the coming Judge, whose Kingdom will be victorious. God's people are victorious over a hostile world. At a significant point in its drama, the book "reveals" the strategic role of prayer.

The Revelation unveils the hidden realm of eternal realities. It is sublimely majestic, mysterious, and fascinating, filled with awe-inspiring, heart-thrilling visions and symbolic imagery. It pulsates with the powerful presence of almighty God and his triumphant Lamb. God's faithful and victorious people overcome grotesque powers of evil and horrendous forces of opposition to enter and enjoy the heavenly blessings of the rewarded conqueror. The book exalts the glory of God, affirms the gospel of Jesus Christ, guarantees the eternal security of the church and its loyal witnesses and servants, and reveals the exciting dimensions of the ultimate life destined for God's people. It aims to inspire God's people to remain loyal and trusting in the face of diabolical opposition.

However, the Book of Revelation is notorious as a happy hunting ground for many fanciful interpretations and schemes for mapping the course of history until the time of the End. It is obviously a complex book. It could easily be relegated to the "too hard" shelf. Yet of all the books of the Bible this is the only one which is a direct revelation from the risen Jesus himself. It must then have an important message. Understanding the book calls for careful exegesis (drawing out the meaning from the text and context), and avoidance of eisegesis (reading into the text preconceived ideas). It is necessary to gain a good understanding, in order to appreciate the strategic role of prayer. Although it is tantalising to want to explore everything in the book, we will have to be satisfied with an explanation of its literary genre and an overview. With an understanding of the literary context, we can grasp the significance of its brief focus on prayer.

Keys for understanding the book are found in the opening verses. It is a "*revelation*" (an "*apocalypse*", 1:1). This term gave its name to a whole class of Jewish religious writings which appeared between about 200 BCE and 200 CE, known as "apocalyptic literature", although characteristics of the genre occurred earlier in the writings of some prophets. Truths (e.g., concerning the spiritual realm, and concerning the coming End of the age) which could not be discovered by normal investigation are unveiled, usually through the agency of angels, in vivid and colourful imagery, and with a wealth of curious symbolism – stars and mountains, monsters and demons, and complex number schemes.

The Revelation is distinctive among the numerous compositions of apocalyptic literature. Although it includes the usual features of apocalyptic style, it also has several marked differences, which are significant. Typically, it uses dreams and visions to communicate its message. Its language is cryptic and symbolic. It is obscure, puzzling, and needing to be decoded. Its meaning is not plain, but disguised, as in a cryptic crossword. It uses symbols and numbers to indicate ideas. However, the book's symbols fall into two types, imagery which is typical, and reasonably comprehensible, whose meaning is derived from the Old Testament (chapters 1-5, 18-22), and imagery in the middle of the book, which is unique, and often bizarre (chapters 6-17). This is intentional. It reflects the purpose of the book. Usually apocalyptic literature depicts history moving toward a cataclysmic End. That End overthrows God's enemies and rescues God's people, who continue into the era of salvation. The Revelation, however, does not anticipate the End, but participates in the End which has already arrived. The apocalyptic style shows that there is consciousness of the End, but two absent apocalyptic features indicate a different attitude towards it. Normally an apocalypse is pseudonymous, written under an assumed name, often of a well-known person from a past era. The Revelation identifies its author John from the start. Apocalypses also include instructions to "seal up" the book until the End, to give the impression of having been written at a much earlier period. The Revelation instructs not to "seal it up" (22:10). This is because the End has already come.

It is important to distinguish between historical and eschatological events. Historical events are the natural events which take place in the course of everyday circumstances as history progresses towards the End. They are described in normal language. Eschatological events are supernatural events which take place when the End intrudes into history. These can be described in normal language, even though they are abnormal in nature, and are recognised from their context. However, they are often described in apocalyptic (symbolic) language.

The Old Testament prophets foretold the coming of the Day of the Lord. They usually used either figurative description of what was familiar, or apocalyptic imagery, to describe the future. The New Testament declares that the Day of the Lord has come. It arrived with the coming of Jesus, who, by his ministry, death, resurrection, ascension, and bestowal of the Holy Spirit, inaugurated the kingdom of God. For example, the prophet Joel predicted the coming Day of the Lord in graphic apocalyptic imagery (Joel 2:28-32). Peter declared that Joel's prophecy was fulfilled by the coming of the Holy Spirit on the day of Pentecost (Acts 2:16-21). The End had come! However, instead of history ceasing at that time, it continued on, overlapped by the End, so that God's purpose of grace could be accomplished.

The "coming of the Son of Man" (apocalyptic language) was fulfilled by the resurrection of Jesus, which includes the resurrection of God's saints. However, instead of these two resurrections occurring simultaneously, they are separated by a lengthy period of history. The End overlaps history. During that overlapping period, the saints are being gathered by the preaching of the gospel, so that there will be saints to be resurrected! The preaching of the gospel is normal activity, but the effect of the gospel in conversion is abnormal, supernatural, intrusion of the End into history. The resurrection of Jesus, the gathering of the elect by God's angels (apocalyptic language for reaching the lost through the proclamation of the gospel), and the resurrection of the saints when the risen Jesus returns, are eschatological events. They belong to the time of the End. The historical period from Christ's resurrection until his return is the Day of the Lord (in terms of the End), or the "last days" of history. During this period there is eschatological activity, not discernible to the natural human eye. The Revelation provides a glimpse beyond the historical realm, into the eschatological realm. It reveals the realm of the End intruding into the realm of history, and uses apocalyptic style and language to do so.

The book is also a *"prophecy"* (1:3, 22:18). While the apocalyptic style indicates that the End has begun, the prophetic nature is concerned with the present from the perspective of ongoing history. It discloses the will of God, primarily by forthtelling, though including elements of foretelling. The Book of Revelation predicts events which must soon take place (1:1). The Revelation was providing a message to fortify believers who were about to experience a harsh persecution campaign unleashed against them (which would last about 200 years). Like many prophecies this is in the form of a *"vision"* (1:11). It is a vision of both present and future realities (1:19). Although the book had the immediate future in mind, its revelation unveiled hidden realities which would continue until the end of time.

It is also in a "letter" format (1:4), a circular to churches in Asia Minor. It was to be read aloud in the hearing of the church fellowship (1:3). Members who were familiar with the apocalyptic style (which appealed to the imagination), who were fresh in their desire to know the scriptures (which were the background to much of the imagery), who were aware of their own historical, political, and religious circumstances, and not yet confused by centuries of conflicting interpretations, and who were used to listening to a good reader who could make the vivid narrative live, would find the message inspiring.

The narrative presents a majestic visionary drama, in which John the author is a spectator and participant. He experiences being "in the Spirit" (1:10). In the opening stage, while still on earth, he sees the awesome, vibrant risen Christ, who commissions him to send prophetic letters to churches on the mainland of Asia (chapters 1-3). Then in the next stage, still "in the Spirit" (4:2), he enters heaven. There he sees God himself, majestically enthroned, with the risen Christ at his right hand, who unveils the heavenly realities which exist behind earthly affairs, and are the reason for them, but are hidden from normal human view (chapters 4-22). The basic message of the book is that followers of Christ are living within a hostile world which persecutes them, yet they are "reigning" with Christ by faithfully bearing witness to him. They will ultimately be triumphantly victorious.

The pattern of The Revelation is generally in sequences of sevens, which is its most frequent symbolic number. Recurring phrases act as transition points, dividing the structure into subsections. If the Latin chapter divisions found in our regular Bibles are ignored, and the original sequences followed, the book becomes more comprehensible. In particular, there is an obvious recurring pattern for the seven seals (chapters 6-7), seven trumpets (chapters 8-12), and seven bowls (chapters 15-16), using a 4-2-1 sequence with a twofold interlude between the sixth and seventh feature. This suggests a relationship of some kind between the three sequences. The number three is also a frequent symbol.

At the time when The Revelation was written, round about 95-100 CE, the Roman Empire, powerful in many respects, exercised one particular power, which became a cause of great trial to early Christians. The growing practice of emperor worship meant that an increasing number of Christians were required publicly to make the fateful choice between Caesar and Christ. Every age has its equivalent test of a Christian's true allegiance, so The Revelation has a relevant message for every generation. For them it meant actual persecution and the threat of martyrdom. The Revelation preceded, and prepared for, an imminent and lengthy firestorm of official persecution against the followers of Christ. This is why the prominent theme of the book is God's *Holy War*. The language and imagery of war permeates everything. God is at war with the powers of a godless world. To appreciate the importance of this theme, it needs to be understood in the context of the whole Bible. God's Holy War began in the Garden of Eden when mankind fell into sin (Genesis 3:15). Throughout the Old Testament the events of the exodus, the military census of Israel, invasion of Canaan, obliteration of the Amorites, Israel's kingship, conflicts with the world super powers, and the language of numerous psalms, reflect the perspective of holy war. The New Testament proclaims God's magnificent victory over all his rebellious enemies. The gospel of Jesus Christ is the good news that by his death and resurrection God's kingdom has come in power and glory. Evil, death, and the world have been conquered. The war has been won, and the gospel is the good news announcing it. However, although the decisive battle has been won, the war continues on a different front. History has entered the "last days", in which human affairs continue as normal, but at the same time the affairs of God's kingdom overlap as God calls the redeemed into his eternal family. God's kingdom is invading the earth to reclaim its territory from rebellious usurpers. The Holy Spirit has been given to empower the preaching of the gospel throughout the world until the End comes. The preaching of the gospel is part of the war, and the kingdoms of the world resist hostilely. God's people, who are his servants who bear witness to the kingdom, become targets for the enemy, and suffer. They experience great tribulation, but only temporally. On the other hand, the rebellious world which generates this tribulation is accountable to God and his judgement. The godless people of the world also suffer, ultimately and finally. Though the battle rages during these last days of history, the victory has already been won at the cross, and the final outcome is guaranteed. At the End, the present universe will be destroyed, along with all evil, to give way to "a new heaven and a new earth" (21:1).

The purpose of the Book of Revelation was to bring encouragement, in true apocalyptic manner, to Christians who were under great pressure, assuring them that their enemies would in the end be destroyed, and God (and they) would be triumphant. It was also to bring challenge, in true prophetic style, to combat, even within themselves, the subtle forces of evil, because Satan must be overcome, and Christ must be given his rightful place here and now in their own spiritual and moral lives.

Blessing is guaranteed to those who take to heart what is written in the book (1:3, 22:7, 14). By carefully examining the details and patterns of the book, and being cautious about dogmatic schemes of interpretation, the thrilling message of the Book of Revelation is waiting to be discovered. Suffering believers in Christ on earth will face their tormentors, and even death, with courage and faith, and experience the blessing of eternal love and life.

A concise outline of the book, instead of a detailed explanation, provides an overview for locating its presentation of prayer.

Outline

1:1-8	The Prologue: Title and Greetings
1:9-20	Revelation of the Living Lord in the Midst of His Churches
2:1-3:22	Seven Prophecies to the Churches
4:1-5:14	Revelation of the Triumphant lamb in the Midst of Creation
6:1-22:19	Seven Visions for the Churches
6:1-8:1	Seven Seals: Horrors of History
8:2-11:18	Seven Trumpets: Woes on the World
11:19-15:4	Seven Scenes: Opponents in the Holy War
15:5-16:21	Seven Bowls: Judgement for the World
17:1-19:10	Seven Sayings: Babylon the Prostitute
19:11-21:8	Seven Sights: The Last Battle
21:9-22:19	Seven Realities: Jerusalem the Bride

22:20-21   The Epilogue: Final Word and Farewell

The opening magnificent vision revealed the risen Christ standing sublimely in the midst of his church on earth (1:9-20). John was asked to write and send seven prophetic messages to the churches to inspire their loyalty and devotion to their Lord (chapters 2-3).

Then a dramatic change takes place as John's vision switches to a new scene (chapters 4-5). He is elevated into heaven where his view takes things in from a vastly different perspective. After seeing things from below, he now is able to see from above, and his gaze is drawn toward the activity of God's kingdom in the world from the context of eternity. Having become aware of the impending crisis on earth, John is now granted the opportunity to look up, as it were, and see into heaven.

Before him was "a throne in heaven" with "someone sitting on it", who appeared in dazzling splendour. The throne represents the awesome power and majesty of God's kingship. Thrones are a dominating feature throughout the book. The aim of its message was to counteract the intimidating threat of Caesar's throne, and the thrones of earthly kings and pagan gods. John's spiritual vision of heaven's throne was a stirring reminder of the absolute authority and sovereignty of God's kingdom. In the scene of awesome glory, God was surrounded by adoring worshippers representing all creation and all God's people.

God held a sealed scroll in his right hand (5:1). It was written on both sides, so contained a lot of material, since it was usual only to write on one side. The scroll was sealed by "seven seals", which probably meant that it was sealed by God. We need to realise that all seven seals would have to be removed before the scroll could be opened. Although the removal of each seal exposed a new scene, these scenes would actually occur simultaneously, not in succession. The opened scroll revealed an overall picture consisting of seven distinctive features. Initially there was a note of deep disappointment because there was no one in the universe who was worthy to take and unseal the scroll. Eventually, however, attention is drawn to One who is the Lion/Lamb. The symbolic imagery is derived from the Old Testament, and vividly identifies the conquering kingly Messiah who gave his life as a sacrifice for sin, a victorious victim. In dramatic, unhesitating, deliberate action he stood in the centre of the throne, bearing the power ("*horns*") and discernment ("*eyes*") of the Spirit, and took the scroll from the hand of the One who occupied the throne. This was an astonishing scene. He was standing in the place of God, interacting with God! No other exalted being, in heaven or history, has ever been so depicted. It is a dramatic apocalyptic portrayal of the intimate, inseparable partnership between God and his Messiah. The Lion/Lamb was an extension of God himself, and the scene celebrates the gospel's revelation of God's true identity. The identity of the scroll is not stated, but subsequent events provide insight about what it represents, God's secret purposes. The triumph of God's purposes and kingdom is determined by the crucified Christ, who is omnipotent and omniscient!

Then John's vision, which had been focused on the throne, swept back to a broader panorama to see all of God's triumphant saints and the whole adoring universe pay homage to the triumphant Christ. The four living creatures and twenty-four elders, who represent God's world and God's people, hold harps and golden bowls of incense (v 8). The harps were to accompany them as they sang their new song, which praised the Lamb's worthiness to open the scroll. The bowls of incense were the prayers of the saints. Nothing further is said about them at this point.

When the seals of the scroll were removed, a sequence of gruesome horrors was unleashed on the world (chapter 6). The sequence is 4-2-1. The first four released seals unveiled similar situations. The "four horsemen of the apocalypse", as they have been called, depict hardships affecting the whole world until the End comes, although especially reflecting the ominous shadow of Rome: military conquest, harsh administration of justice, economic hardship and inequality, tyranny of death. Removal of the fifth seal reveals martyred believers. When the sixth seal was opened, an earthquake and the extraordinary upheaval of the natural order took place. Supernatural overthrow represented divine intervention, striking terror into peoples' hearts. Thus, the released seals reveal insights concerning the nature of future history ("what must take place after this", 4:1) from a heavenly (eschatological) perspective. History will consist of the grim distresses of warfare, violence, injustice, grief, and the persecution of God's people. Yet the preaching of the gospel will strike the nations with great dread, and confront them with God's judgement. All this characterises the coming of the End. These are the insights which stimulate Christian faithfulness when the world's hostility and threats cause doubt and fear.

Nevertheless, during this final era of history, which is a period of tribulation, God's servants are marked for security by God himself (chapter 7).

Then there was a dramatic lull in proceedings (8:1-2). The opening of the seventh seal is intriguing. When it was removed, there was silence in heaven for about half an hour. Yet in heaven there is no time!! What does this mean? When we realise that the previous six unleashed seals revealed the same period of history in terms of six different features, we can assume that the seventh seal also relates to the same period. This suggests that from heaven's point of view, the final era of history, from the cross until the End, is only about "half an hour". It is relatively short, and will eventually end. It also means that while horror and tumult fill the world, heaven is silent. Silence suggests both awe and absence of turbulence. This is great comfort for believers in Christ. Though confronted with horrendous hardships and dangers in the world, their real home is completely undisturbed by these things. Heaven is where, in Christ, they actually are. Their current earthly experience will eventually, in fact soon, in about "half an hour", come to an end.

Before anything else occurs, the prayers of the saints are offered with incense on the altar before the throne (v 3-4). The imagery is taken from the earthly temple which used to be in Jerusalem, where the priest offered incense at the daily hours of prayer. Now the prayers come before the throne in heaven. The scene is a reassuring revelation that the prayers of those who call upon the name of the Lord, who intercede for God's will to be done and for sinners to be saved, and who offer their devotion of praise, adoration, thanksgiving, and petitions, will be heard.

Then the angel who offered them filled the censer with fire and flung it to the earth (v 5). Natural and cosmic convulsions occur. It is a vivid picture of the significance of prayer. Human prayer and divine fire mix together to determine the judgements and purposes of God in earthly affairs.

John's graphic imagery not only depicts the role of prayer, but does so in a stirring and electrifying manner. Prayer is the incense of submissive worship which deeply affects the person of God. It is an ingredient in the mixture of divine rule and judgement which powerfully affects the purpose of God. Prayer is a dynamic activity of those who have been made "*a kingdom and priests to serve God*" and who "*will reign on the earth*".

Graphic scenes continue as seven trumpets herald a sequence of divinely imposed woes upon the earth as warnings to the world of coming judgement. Seven scenes identify the opponents in God's holy war, followed by seven bowls of God's final judgements. Seven sayings expose "Babylon the Prostitute" which represents the godless system of the world, followed by seven sights which depict God's last battle against his evil enemies. The final series of seven describes God's future "new heaven and new earth" in which God's people are represented by the "New Jerusalem". The book presents a fascinating, stimulating *revelation* which inspires faith, courage, and hope for God's people.

At the end of The Revelation, in response to a final declaration by Jesus that he was coming soon, there is a brief, poignant prayer.

"*Amen. Come Lord Jesus*".

AFTERWORD

TWENTY - TWENTY VISION

Unprecedented! Extreme! Apocalyptic! Biblical proportions! Terrifying! Horrific! Overwhelming! Phenomenal!

The repetitious use of sensational terms by commentators to indicate abnormal circumstances during the years 2020 and beyond has become almost slogan-like. It has certainly been an unusual period.

The Covid-19 global pandemic has caused the death of millions, the suffering of hundreds of millions, and has shut down business as usual around the world. The impact has been horrendous. The world is in mourning from the loss of lives. It is devastated by the loss of livelihoods, as economies collapse, businesses close, and unemployment rises. Social gatherings for celebrations, commemorations, hospitality, or companionship have been constrained or even curtailed. National and regional borders have been closed to prevent the spread of the virus. The pandemic has been a grim reaper and havoc wreaker everywhere.

Yet the pandemic has not been the only woe. Earthquakes, tsunamis, sinkholes, tornadoes, volcanoes, and mudslides have wiped out villages and towns. Building and bridge collapses have shocked communities and killed numerous victims. Extreme weather events have caused widespread destruction. Wild storms have battered coastlines, ruined landscapes, and demolished properties. Droughts have dried up rivers and lakes, turned pastures into scorched earth, starved herds and shriveled crops, and brought farmers to their knees. Floods have washed away homes and possessions. Fires have annihilated forests, communities, flora and fauna. Such calamities have fueled anxiety about global warming. The spectre of global climate change is becoming a nightmare in the eyes of many. Panic reactions are beginning to set in, and concern is generating political tensions and activism.

Politics itself is a major vexation. Scenes which occurred during the US presidential elections were disturbing to say the least. Violent protests did not present good images for democracy. The spate of protests were not only about partisan politics either. Activists for other causes, such as Black Lives Matters, women's equality, climate change, gender issues, domestic violence, abortion, euthanasia, democratic rights, resorted to protest rallies and marches as a political strategy, flouting the rules of social distancing in the middle of the

Covid-19 pandemic. The period of pandemic has also witnessed a global political shift, with mounting tensions between national democracies and autocracies.

The big picture shows that serious threats confront the world's security and well-being. Despair and distress, suffering, hopelessness, and chaos are widespread. The years of 2020's have been a conspicuous period of abnormal challenge for the human race. What can we do?

Twenty-Twenty Insight

The Bible presents a unique perspective for facing the current crisis. You may have found our tour through the Bible a bit of a stretch at times as we delved into every book within its collection. Even then, we did not fully explore any of them. So much was glossed over, and there is so much more to investigate. What a vast array of so many literary forms contained within the Bible, and what a variety of subjects and ideas! The reason for our protracted tour was to demonstrate an uncanny truth about the Bible. Its many books make up a single whole. They are bound together by a single purpose. They bear witness to a thrilling revelation. The Bible reveals a divine two-part plan of salvation for a fatally wounded human race. Promise and fulfilment. Preparation and culmination. Old covenant and new covenant. The overall formation of the Bible was not humanly orchestrated, but humanly recognized. It reveals a higher hand at work. The Bible bears witness to the reality and glory of the living God who is the Creator King of all which exists. He has accomplished his plan of grace to save the world and produce his holy family of righteous sons and daughters. His Messiah Jesus has come, and, through his crucifixion, resurrection, and ascension to the place of utmost authority, has provided redemption for the world, reconciliation with God, and restoration of God's rule of love. This good news is being proclaimed throughout the earth. Those who call upon the name of the Lord are being saved. This is not religious jargon, but reality. It presents a perspective for seeing our present world, and looks beneath the surface appearance of events. Through the lens of the Bible's revelation we can discern underlying tendencies which are exposed by our world's current crises.

On the one hand, there have been many noble human reactions. Frontline workers perform their duties heroically. Development of technologies are producing solutions for moving forward. Throughout the world, people have displayed commendable attitudes of patience, cooperation, generosity, and courage.

On the other hand, stressful pressures expose shortcomings. Human nature is on full display. There are many expressions of anger, depression, hubris, grief, fear, and bitterness. Many people look for someone to blame, whether politicians, care-workers, or careless sceptics. There have been examples of people greedily and fraudulently ripping off the support funding provided by governments and charities for disaster victims. Corruption, sensuality, malice, scepticism, rebellion, ugly violence, and self-centred motivation have all been manifested.

Our vision of the world in the 2020's confirms the Bible's witness that human nature bears the likeness of God, yet is dominated by the devil.

A conspicuous absence during this period of global distress is acknowledgement of God or need for God. No world leader has called on his people or the people of the world to turn to God in prayer. Even church leaders seem quiet. The Bible has been ignored. Yet the Bible bears witness that God listens to the cries of the afflicted, and is willing to rescue. 2020 shows that the world urgently needs to reach out to God.

Twenty-Twenty Hindsight

We can often discern things more clearly when we look back. Twenty-twenty hindsight is a great asset. Something we should discern as we look back with the hindsight of 2020 is that all the calamities faced by the world now have happened in the past. It is just that they are now condensed into a briefer period, and on a larger scale. They represent a picture of the world "groaning" for liberation (Romans 8:22). These things should inspire us also to "groan", and, with the help of God's Spirit who also "groans", intercede for God's will to be done.

When we look back from our present day at the history of the Christian Church during the past 2000 years, its course is chequered. The Church's presence and influence have spread around the globe to all lands. Its story has been both noble, and, tragically, many times appallingly disgusting. Human nature has often been exposed in its worst light. That is because we live in a fallen, sinful world, and the Church is not exempt. At the same time, the Church has been the messenger of God's gospel of grace. It has possessed a "treasure in clay jars". Wherever that message has been spread, it has planted seeds of truth, peace, and righteousness. The crop is growing fruitfully, yet within a world of weeds. Harvest time will separate the wheat from the chaff. In the meantime, we must pray for the harvest to be complete, and for harvest time to come. By prayer we partner with God in his plan of redemption for his world.

We can learn much from past history. Let me mention an interesting and conspicuous phenomenon which dominated the institutional church for more than a thousand years from the sixth to the sixteenth century and beyond. Monasticism was a powerful movement which influenced church life, society and culture, and the global spread of Christianity. Unfortunately, it featured many unhelpful, this-world characteristics. Nevertheless, at its core it maintained a focus on God's word and devotion to prayer. The Bible owes its preservation to the diligence of monasteries. Treasure in clay jars! The world of 2020 would do well to rediscover a focus on God's message in the Bible and prayer. The conditions of our time are an urgent reason why we should pray!

In 1727 the Moravian Community of Herrnhut in Saxony commenced a prayer vigil which continued non-stop for over a hundred years. The Community consisted of refugees from persecution residing on the estates of Count Nikolaus Zinzendorf. During the community's first few years it had experienced dissension and squabbling. Then its members entered into a covenant to pray for revival, and they maintained a prayer watch around the clock, for several generations. Relationships were healed and devotion to Christ became fervent. Within 65 years 300 members were sent out in missionary service. Simultaneously, during this same period, numerous other men and women from other countries were similarly motivated to undertake missionary endeavours into foreign regions, upheld by praying supporters at home. Many influential preachers and missionaries, including those like John and Charles Wesley, were directly inspired by the writings and work of the Moravians. This missionary activity coincided with the discovery of new lands from navigational exploration, and the gospel was taken to the Americas, Far East, and South Pacific. The meeting of the Old and New Worlds precipitated a world-wide reshaping of international affairs, including both constructive developments and devastating consequences. Human nature continued to display the same dignity and depravity in the new world order. At the same time, for 200 years missionary promotion of the gospel made a world-wide impact on the nations. An explosion of devotion to Jesus swept across all cultures, characterized by faith in God, enthusiasm for the Bible, and lifestyles of virtue and love. Prayer was viewed as critical to the effective spread of the gospel.

Our current world's great need for God's magnificent message of grace and salvation is an urgent reason why we should pray!

Twenty-Twenty Outlook

The city of Paris has a long and eventful history. It is renowned for its political, cultural, religious, and military prominence over the course of centuries. It has had a significant influence in such historic developments as the Holy Roman Empire, the Papacy, the Reformation, the Enlightenment, the French Revolution, colonial expansion, trade, science, art, academia, medicine, sport, World Wars I and II, and modern nuclear armament. A brief sample list of personalities associated with Paris who have left their mark illustrate the diversity and impact of this remarkable city. Saint Denis; Joan of Arc; Charlemagne; Henry IV; Louis XIV, the "Sun King"; Louis XVI, executed by the Revolution; Robespierre; Marie Antoinette; Voltaire; Rousseau; Napoleon Bonaparte; Pascal; Monet; Madame Curie; Victor Hugo; Pierre de Coubertin; Charles de Gaulle, Brigitte Bardot. Palaces, museums, and monuments remain as reminders of its heady days and achievements. Paris is a cosmopolitan city which can be looked on as a mini version of the world at large.

Let me draw your attention to two conspicuous structures which rise above Paris' skyline. In 1889 the Eiffel Tower was erected to mark the 100-year anniversary of the French Revolution, and to serve as the entrance to the World Fair held that year. Located in Central Paris, and standing at over 300 metres (almost 1000 feet) tall, the Tower was the highest structure in the world at that time, built to demonstrate France's industrial prowess. Today it is one of the most popular tourist attractions in the world. It is a worthy symbol of human ambition and pride, a tower reaching up to the heavens.

In 1914 (only 25 years later) the magnificent Basilica Sacre-Coeur, located at the highest pinnacle overlooking the city, was opened on the summit of Montmartre, considered to be the most rebellious district in Paris. With its top tower at more than 200 metres above sea level, the Basilica is the second highest structure after the Eiffel Tower. Like the Eiffel Tower, it is a highly popular tourist destination, attractive for its beautiful internal and external presentation, and panoramic views. Montmartre means "Mount of Martyrs", because it is the site of many martyrdoms, including Saint Denis, the first bishop of Paris in the third century, and nuns from the previous abbey there, who were guillotined during the French Revolution of 1789. Today the Basilica is an active place of prayer, where local Parisians and tourists from around the world are invited to use its facilities as a quiet venue for prayer. It is an eminent symbol, on the foundation of sacrifice and suffering, which reminds us of the imperative need of prayer in the midst of a rebellious, self-sufficient, and ambitious world.

Twenty-Twenty Upward Look

Our discovery tour through the Bible has revealed why we on earth should pray. God is the living gracious Creator King who has accomplished his plan to redeem the world from its rebellious and chaotic state, and to restore his loving rule over his creation. Jesus is the redeemer of the world, and the Lord over all creation. Integral to God's plan is prayer. By prayer we partner with God in saving the world. We dependently petition God for all our earthly needs, and we intercede on earth to ask God to complete the restoration of his kingship in the hearts and lives of men and women throughout the world. The world in 2020 has highlighted its plight, and the need for intercession to be made to God on its behalf. Prayer acknowledges dependence on God, and seeks his will to be done. The basis of prayer is a personal, intimate relationship with God, and the experience of prayer is to fellowship with God in the outworking of his purposes.

Let me end with a couple of practical tips for taking prayer seriously. Firstly, like Jesus set aside a time and place for frequently rendezvousing with God, drawing near to him in faith.

Secondly, follow a routine of "AWE" in approaching God.

Awareness of God: Instead of being conscious of yourself and your circumstances, focus your mind and heart to be aware of God. We come to the Father, through the Son, by the Holy Spirit. (a) Consciously remember that the Holy Spirit ensures that you are in God's presence. The Spirit stimulates our awareness, enlightens our understanding, empowers our faith, intercedes according to God's will. We pray in the Spirit. (b) Recall who Jesus is, and what he has done. He is the pre-existent "Word" of God who became human in order to be God's Son on earth accomplishing God's gracious plan of redemption for the world. His crucifixion, resurrection, and ascension rescued the world from condemnation, reconciled the world with God in heaven, and restored God's kingdom over creation. Jesus is the risen Saviour and exalted Ruler who guarantees our access to God's presence. (c) The Father is the eternal God, the Creator Ruler of all existence. He has revealed himself as Father of the Lord Jesus Christ, who accomplished his eternal plan of grace. He is the holy and living Father, whom we know as "our Father".

Worship of God: Draw near to God in reverent adoration. Contemplate his attributes, such as holiness, majesty, might, goodness, grace, wisdom, purity, righteousness, and fulness of life. Reflect on his accomplishments, such as creation, providence, salvation, and his work through the gospel and answers to prayer. Express praise and gratitude in simple conversation.

Engage with God: Confess all your personal needs to God. Observe natural, social, political, spiritual trends, and critical events and developments, seeking to discern God's presence and activity. Interact intimately, confidently with God in your heart, and intercede for his will.

Jesus said: "*I will do whatever you ask in my name, so that the Son may bring glory to the Father*".

INDEX

KEY SUBJECTS

Abraham 24, 30, 36, 37, 38, 39, 40, 43, 44, 45, 46, 47, 48, 49, 50, 51, 52, 54, 55, 56, 59, 60, 61, 67, 70, 72, 75, 80, 81, 88, 90, 92, 93, 101, 105, 106, 108, 117, 122, 125, 128, 135, 137, 153, 166, 167, 168, 173, 176, 179, 184, 191, 198, 201, 284, 303, 306, 309, 322, 323, 338, 339, 345, 368, 374

Ark of the Covenant 73, 77, 95, 97, 98, 99, 102, 113, 114, 116, 122, 168, 170

call (cry), on (to) God 17, 24, 25, 35, 37, 39, 40, 41, 45, 46, 47, 48, 50, 51, 54, 55, 60, 61, 63, 67, 69, 90, 91, 111, 112, 115, 116, 120, 125, 126, 134, 135, 136, 137, 138, 140, 143, 145, 146, 147, 148, 149, 156, 162, 164, 168, 174, 185, 199, 230, 291, 331, 391, 393

    by God 25, 73, 327, 331

covenant:

    Abrahamic 24, 38, 39, 42, 43, 44, 45, 47, 50, 51, 59, 60, 70, 79, 81, 168, 179

    Davidic 116, 117, 118, 119, 120, 121, 122, 123, 124, 126, 127, 150, 174, 176, 184

    General 21, 52, 62, 77, 82, 87, 129, 139, 152, 158, 162, 177, 182, 185, 322, 337, 338, 393

    New 22, 23, 117, 136, 162, 178, 189, 273, 309, 336, 341, 346, 372, 374, 393

    Sinaitic 22, 23, 24, 28, 29, 32, 37, 39, 57, 58, 65, 66, 67, 68, 69, 70, 71, 72, 73, 75, 80, 81, 83, 84, 85, 87, 88, 89, 90, 91, 92, 93, 96, 97, 99, 100, 101, 103, 107, 108, 109, 112, 113, 114, 115, 116, 117, 123, 125, 126, 130, 131, 133, 135, 141, 143, 146, 147, 150, 156, 157, 159, 162, 164, 166, 167, 168, 169, 171, 173, 189, 306, 346, 372

creation 23, 24, 31, 32, 33, 34, 40, 54, 69, 88, 133, 147, 150, 159, 160, 166, 173, 179, 186, 188, 189, 222, 232, 261, 272, 280, 290, 302, 303, 304, 305, 306, 314, 317, 319, 333, 338, 339, 340, 343, 344, 345, 346, 347, 348, 349, 351, 355, 371, 377, 389, 396, 397

exile 27, 28, 29, 32, 35, 40, 41, 43, 85, 93, 100, 109, 127, 129, 130, 132, 133, 135, 136, 138, 139, 142, 146, 153, 154, 155, 156, 157, 165, 166, 167, 170, 221, 264

exodus 23, 29, 39, 59, 79, 81, 83, 85, 95, 99, 112, 133, 138, 146, 164, 166, 169, 208,

INDEX

251, 296, 301, 308, 309, 387

God's Agenda, Will, Plan, Purpose 13, 24, 25, 39, 40, 41, 42, 43, 44, 45, 46, 49, 50, 56, 70, 82, 84, 94, 112, 113, 128, 133, 135, 144, 150, 168, 174, 185, 189, 191, 198, 202, 204, 212, 214, 219, 227, 239, 240, 248, 254, 259, 264, 270, 304, 306, 319, 320, 324, 326, 327, 328, 333, 334, 335, 336, 337, 338, 340, 342, 343, 344, 346, 349, 356, 357, 359, 371, 376, 377, 382, 386, 391, 394, 396

God's Names:

    Father 19, 22, 25, 43, 111, 119, 182, 183, 184, 185, 186, 188, 189, 190, 191, 192, 200, 202, 204, 205, 206, 207, 208, 209, 210, 211, 212, 213, 214, 216, 220, 224, 225, 226, 227, 229, 232, 233, 248, 249, 250, 251, 252, 253, 256, 260, 263, 265, 266, 271, 272, 273, 274, 275, 276, 279, 281, 285, 286, 287, 288, 289, 290, 291, 292, 294, 295, 296, 297, 298, 301, 302, 305, 306, 308, 309, 310, 311, 312, 313, 314, 315, 316, 317, 318, 321, 324, 325, 326, 328, 329, 331, 333, 336, 337, 344, 345, 347, 350, 351, 354, 356, 357, 358, 362, 363, 372, 377, 378, 380, 381, 383, 396, 397

    God Almighty (El Shaddai) 42, 43, 51, 54, 56, 61, 62

    God Most High (El Elyon) 41

    I Am 60, 61, 256, 308, 309, 311

    LORD 24, 25, 32, 33, 34, 35, 37, 38, 39, 40, 41, 42, 44, 45, 46, 47, 48, 49, 50, 51, 52, 53, 54, 55, 60, 61, 62, 63, 64, 65, 66, 67, 68, 69, 70, 71, 72, 73, 74, 75, 76, 77, 78, 79, 80, 81, 82, 83, 84, 86, 87, 88, 89, 90, 91, 96, 97, 98, 99, 100, 101, 102, 103, 104, 105, 106, 107, 108, 109, 110, 111, 112, 113, 114, 115, 116, 117, 118, 119, 120, 122, 123, 125, 126, 128, 131, 132, 133, 134, 135, 136, 137, 138, 139, 140, 142, 143, 144, 145, 146, 147, 148, 149, 150, 151, 152, 155, 156, 159, 161, 162, 164, 168, 169, 170, 171, 172, 174, 175, 178, 179, 180, 182, 185, 199, 201, 214, 230, 256, 263, 265, 274, 291, 292, 294, 303, 305, 306

Gospel 22, 42, 139, 157, 173, 176, 177, 178, 181, 182, 183, 185, 186, 187, 188, 189, 190, 191, 192, 193, 194, 195, 196, 197, 198, 200, 202, 203, 205, 207, 208, 209, 210, 213, 214, 218, 219, 221, 222, 224, 225, 227, 228, 230, 232, 233, 234, 235, 236, 238, 239, 240, 241, 242, 244, 246, 247, 248, 249, 250, 252, 253, 257, 258, 264, 268, 269, 270, 271, 272, 274, 278, 280, 281, 282, 283, 284, 285, 287, 289, 292, 293, 296, 297, 299, 300, 301, 302, 303, 304, 305, 306, 308, 311, 312, 313, 314, 315, 317, 318, 319, 320, 321, 322, 323, 324, 325, 326, 327, 328, 329, 330, 331, 332, 333, 334, 335, 336, 337, 338, 340, 341, 342, 343, 346, 349, 353, 354, 355, 356, 358, 359, 360, 361, 365, 366, 367, 368, 369, 370, 373, 374, 375, 377, 378, 379, 380, 381, 382, 383, 384, 386, 387, 388, 389, 390, 394, 395, 397

Holy Spirit 176, 177, 187, 188, 190, 191, 193, 199, 200, 201, 207, 210, 211, 216, 219,

222, 228, 229, 230, 231, 232, 233, 234, 235, 236, 237, 239, 241, 242, 247, 250, 268, 270, 298, 302, 310, 314, 316, 317, 318, 319, 324, 328, 331, 332, 335, 336, 338, 344, 345, 346, 350, 357, 368, 372, 374, 381, 383, 386, 388, 396

Holy War 100, 387, 388

Inheritance 47, 49, 72, 80, 81, 82, 83, 84, 88, 90, 93, 94, 96, 105, 106, 162, 182, 184, 185, 186, 242, 267, 339, 346, 347, 348, 357

Jesus' Mission 48, 176, 177, 181, 184, 185, 192, 201, 202, 203, 204, 205, 206, 207, 208, 210, 211, 212, 214, 223, 224, 227, 235, 236, 248, 249, 251, 252, 253, 254, 257, 258, 259, 260, 262, 264, 269, 270, 272, 275, 280, 285, 295, 296, 297, 310, 313, 314, 315, 317, 318, 321, 335, 350, 355, 372

    Prayer activities 202, 203, 204, 205, 207, 209, 210, 211, 212, 213, 214, 215, 216, 218, 219, 223, 224, 225, 253, 274, 296

Jesus' Titles:

    Messiah 22, 142, 174, 175, 176, 177, 178, 181, 182, 183, 184, 185, 188, 191, 193, 197, 198, 201, 207, 208, 210, 219, 220, 222, 230, 234, 235, 237, 244, 245, 246, 247, 248, 249, 250, 251, 252, 253, 254, 255, 257, 258, 259, 260, 263, 266, 268, 269, 270, 271, 274, 276, 277, 278, 279, 280, 282, 283, 284, 285, 286, 291, 294, 295, 299, 300, 301, 307, 311, 315, 316, 318, 319, 320, 321, 324, 326, 328, 329, 331, 333, 335, 337, 338, 339, 340, 342, 344, 345, 346, 347, 349, 362, 367, 368, 374, 377, 389, 393

    Son of God 22, 119, 176, 183, 201, 206, 209, 225, 246, 247, 248, 253, 279, 296, 300, 306, 307, 309, 318, 322, 338, 381

    Son of Man 155, 176, 177, 195, 207, 208, 214, 217, 218, 219, 220, 222, 223, 233, 249, 253, 258, 259, 260, 262, 263, 271, 272, 273, 274, 276, 279, 280, 294, 297, 310, 318, 386

    Word 188, 302, 305, 306, 371, 397

Kingdom 19, 22, 58, 93, 112, 121, 122, 124, 126, 127, 154, 157, 173, 176, 182, 183, 184, 185, 186, 187, 188, 189, 191, 192, 195, 197, 201, 202, 203, 204, 205, 206, 208, 209, 211, 213, 214, 215, 216, 217, 218, 219, 220, 222, 223, 224, 228, 229, 232, 233, 234, 243, 245, 247, 251, 252, 253, 254, 255, 257, 259, 260, 262, 263, 268, 269, 272, 280, 282, 283, 284, 285, 286, 290, 291, 292, 293, 295, 297, 298, 307, 319, 357, 358, 379, 384, 386, 388

Law 24, 28, 29, 83, 87, 88, 90, 92, 96, 127, 146, 148, 150, 156, 157, 165, 166, 200, 203, 208, 212, 213, 218, 221, 230, 233, 234, 235, 236, 243, 244, 245, 254, 261, 262, 267, 282, 287, 288, 291, 308, 321, 322, 323, 336, 371

Literary Forms:

    Compositional patterns and styles 20, 22, 23, 26, 27, 28, 29, 30, 32, 34, 36, 37, 57, 58, 59, 65, 66, 85, 88, 92, 93, 94, 95, 112, 122, 123, 127, 129, 139, 146,

148, 163, 194, 195, 197, 209, 258, 284, 293, 303, 384, 385, 393
  Apocalyptic 22, 139, 142, 153, 154, 155, 157, 177, 192, 194, 198, 207, 222, 226, 227, 253, 258, 270, 271, 278, 279, 283, 294, 385, 386, 388, 389
  History 30, 57, 58, 59, 65, 66, 85, 88, 92, 93, 95, 99, 108, 109
  Letters 192, 194, 235, 320, 324, 325, 329, 330, 333, 358, 363, 364, 369, 370, 377, 379, 382, 387
  Prophecy 126, 127, 132, 134, 136, 137, 138, 139, 157, 174, 177, 198, 225, 230, 242, 264, 265, 266, 267, 273, 293, 294, 303, 332, 364, 379, 383, 386
  Saga 57, 58, 59, 60, 63, 65, 75, 84, 85, 88, 95, 99
  Sermon 205, 216, 228, 230, 283, 284, 285, 286, 287, 289, 290, 291, 292
  Short Story 158, 163
Moses 28, 29, 57, 59, 60, 61, 62, 63, 64, 65, 66, 67, 68, 69, 70, 71, 72, 73, 74, 75, 76, 77, 78, 79, 80, 81, 82, 83, 84, 85, 86, 87, 88, 89, 90, 92, 93, 95, 96, 98, 99, 101, 102, 103, 104, 105, 106, 107, 108, 109, 111, 114, 123, 125, 131, 164, 166, 198, 208, 214, 217, 250, 255, 256, 259, 261, 268, 273, 292, 301, 303, 305, 306, 307, 308, 371, 372
Prayer Forms:
  Draw Near 66, 74, 77, 123, 198, 220, 251, 264, 291, 370, 373, 381, 382
  Entreaty (supplication) 18, 35, 36, 48, 49, 52, 65, 114, 120, 123, 145, 152, 155, 166, 171, 172, 191, 192, 198, 213, 214, 215, 223, 252, 266, 275, 292, 350, 361, 362, 363, 396
  Intercession 18, 19, 45, 46, 47, 48, 65, 68, 70, 71, 76, 80, 84, 90, 91, 92, 114, 117, 118, 135, 137, 140, 145, 152, 153, 223, 227, 274, 290, 318, 347, 350, 356, 360, 361, 363, 364, 369, 370, 372, 373, 381, 382, 383, 391, 394, 396, 397
  Praise & Thanks 18, 64, 119, 120, 146, 149, 163, 193, 198, 199, 200, 210, 211, 214, 239, 285, 295, 332, 333, 336, 344, 345, 346, 347, 376, 378, 391, 397
Redemption 14, 39, 58, 62, 63, 68, 74, 84, 133, 190, 198, 200, 204, 208, 223, 272, 273, 279, 333, 338, 339, 340, 341, 342, 346, 347, 358, 372, 378, 393, 394, 397
Tabernacle 68, 69, 72, 73, 75, 113, 114, 122, 168
Temple 27, 88, 93, 107, 113, 122, 123, 124, 126, 127, 130, 132, 137, 138, 140, 141, 146, 155, 165, 167, 168, 169, 170, 171, 178, 193, 196, 198, 199, 200, 220, 221, 222, 223, 224, 225, 226, 227, 231, 242, 243, 244, 251, 263, 264, 266, 267, 269, 270, 271, 272, 276, 278, 280, 286, 299, 307, 308, 309, 328, 345, 351, 364, 366, 370, 374, 390

NEW TESTAMENT BOOKS

Matthew 177, 180, 181, 183, 185, 190, 194, 203, 205, 207, 209, 213, 216, 224, 228, 234, 247, 264, 282, 283, 284, 285, 287, 289, 290, 292, 293, 294, 295, 296, 297, 299, 318

Mark 186, 194, 202, 207, 209, 224, 238, 239, 240, 246, 247, 248, 249, 250, 251, 252, 253, 254, 255, 256, 257, 258, 260, 261, 263, 264, 266, 267, 268, 269, 270, 271, 272, 273, 274, 275, 276, 277, 278, 279, 280, 281, 282, 283, 284, 285, 292, 293, 296, 297, 299, 318, 358, 360, 362, 367

Luke 192, 193, 194, 195, 196, 197, 198, 199, 200, 201, 202, 203, 204, 206, 207, 208, 209, 210, 212, 213, 216, 218, 219, 220, 221, 222, 223, 224, 225, 226, 227, 228, 229, 230, 231, 232, 233, 234, 236, 237, 238, 239, 240, 241, 243, 245, 247, 281, 292, 295, 299, 318, 358, 360, 363, 367

John 48, 184, 190, 192, 193, 194, 197, 199, 200, 203, 206, 207, 208, 209, 211, 213, 216, 230, 231, 234, 238, 239, 240, 242, 247, 250, 251, 252, 255, 258, 259, 260, 261, 263, 267, 270, 273, 274, 293, 294, 299, 300, 301, 302, 303, 304, 305, 306, 307, 308, 311, 312, 313, 314, 318, 371, 374, 382, 385, 386, 389, 390, 391, 395

Acts 139, 174, 175, 183, 185, 186, 192, 193, 194, 195, 196, 197, 206, 219, 222, 226, 228, 229, 230, 242, 243, 271, 281, 298, 320, 321, 324, 328, 354, 360, 363, 374, 386

Romans 185

1 Corinthians 182, 183, 195, 330, 331, 332, 333, 374

2 Corinthians 185, 329, 333, 334

Galatians 42, 190, 191, 195, 320, 322, 324, 383

Ephesians 185, 190, 298, 343, 354, 355, 356, 357, 365, 383

Colossians 348, 352, 354, 355, 356, 357, 358, 359

Philippians 183, 359, 360, 361, 362, 363, 364

1 & 2 Thessalonians 320, 324, 325, 326, 327, 329

Philemon 354, 359

1 & 2 Timothy 339, 363, 364, 366, 367, 368, 369

Titus 330, 334, 363, 364, 366

Hebrews 19, 185, 192, 280, 370

James 42, 192, 207, 208, 238, 239, 240, 258, 263, 270, 273, 274, 320, 374, 375, 376, 377, 382

1 & 2 Peter 192, 377, 378, 379, 383

1, 2 & 3 John 190, 299, 379, 380, 382

Jude 192, 382, 383

Revelation 185, 192, 384, 385, 386, 387, 388, 391

OLD TESTAMENT BOOKS

Genesis 23, 24, 28, 30, 31, 33, 35, 36, 37, 39, 46, 48, 49, 52, 54, 55, 56, 60, 61, 63, 73, 75, 80, 81, 85, 88, 92, 99, 105, 108, 117, 133, 135, 137, 154, 167, 179, 201, 230, 232, 263, 299, 302, 303, 304, 345, 387

Exodus 23, 30, 32, 45, 48, 57, 58, 59, 60, 61, 62, 63, 67, 68, 72, 73, 74, 75, 76, 80, 82, 85, 88, 95, 99, 100, 103, 106, 114, 119, 124, 140, 170, 176, 179, 182, 217, 229, 230, 250, 255, 256, 279, 301, 303, 305, 307, 308, 309

Leviticus 23, 30, 57, 65, 72, 73, 74, 78, 85, 88, 95, 114, 156, 268

Numbers 22, 23, 30, 57, 65, 72, 74, 75, 78, 80, 81, 83, 84, 85, 88, 95, 97, 100, 105, 107, 255

Deuteronomy 24, 28, 30, 32, 57, 67, 84, 85, 88, 89, 91, 92, 93, 99, 103, 108, 109, 111, 122, 127, 135, 170, 214, 234, 261, 268, 308

Joshua 28, 58, 85, 88, 92, 93, 94, 95, 96, 97, 98, 99, 100, 101, 102, 103, 104, 105, 107, 108, 112, 232

Judges 28, 85, 93, 94, 109, 110, 111, 112, 113, 120, 158, 159

Ruth 92, 145, 157, 158

1 Samuel 73, 113, 114, 115, 116, 164, 201

2 Samuel 28, 85, 93, 112, 113, 114, 116, 117, 119, 174, 176, 182, 344

1 Kings 121, 122, 124, 125, 127, 169, 170, 180, 330

2 Kings 28, 29, 85, 88, 92, 93, 94, 112, 121, 125, 126, 133, 134, 139, 171

1 & 2 Chronicles 103, 145, 146, 167, 168, 169, 170

Ezra-Nehemiah 145, 146, 165, 166, 167

Esther 145, 157, 162, 163, 164

Job 145, 150, 151, 152, 153

Psalms 119, 140, 146, 147, 148, 149, 169, 173, 174, 175, 176, 178, 179, 181, 182, 183, 184, 185, 186, 188, 201, 214, 227, 231, 249, 251, 262, 267, 268, 275, 276, 278, 279, 283, 344, 348, 366, 378

Proverbs 145, 149, 150, 303

Ecclesiastes 145, 160

Song of Songs 159

Isaiah 29, 92, 126, 129, 131, 132, 133, 134, 135, 139, 177, 180, 201, 221, 234, 240, 244, 245, 250, 251, 262, 264, 267, 271, 274, 275, 293, 294, 303, 353

Jeremiah 28, 129, 130, 132, 135, 136, 137, 139, 155, 156, 161, 162, 221, 264, 275

Lamentations 92, 145, 157, 160

Ezekiel 28, 129, 130, 138, 139, 176, 255, 271

Daniel 92, 145, 153, 154, 155, 156, 157, 177, 198, 207, 253, 258, 259, 270, 272, 276, 283, 294

Hosea 129, 131, 132

Joel 129, 130, 138, 139, 222, 230, 271, 386
Amos 129, 131, 132, 271, 279
Obadiah 129, 130, 139
Jonah 129, 130, 139, 140, 141, 217, 294
Micah 129, 131, 132
Nahum 129, 130, 136
Habakkuk 129, 130, 137, 138
Zephaniah 129, 130, 137
Haggai 129, 130, 141, 142
Zechariah 129, 130, 141, 142, 143, 154, 198, 199, 221, 263, 265, 273
Malachi 92, 129, 130, 141, 143, 144, 165, 250, 263, 264, 294

www.ingramcontent.com/pod-product-compliance
Lightning Source LLC
Chambersburg PA
CBHW060521010526
44107CB00060B/2645